The freedom of religion is one of the oldest and most controversial of the claims that are now recognized as forming part of the corpus of human rights. In this important and fascinating book Malcolm Evans provides a detailed account of the ways in which the freedom of religious belief came to be acknowledged within the international community. He goes on to examine the mechanisms by which this freedom is guaranteed, and a number of problematic cases which have recently been discussed in the Council of Europe. In a concluding section he outlines a number of developments which will influence the direction that the search for the protection of religious liberty under international law may take.

Religious liberty and
international law in Europe

CAMBRIDGE STUDIES IN INTERNATIONAL AND COMPARATIVE LAW

This series (established in 1946 by Professors Gutteridge, Hersch Lauterpacht and McNair) is a forum for studies of high quality in the fields of public and private international law and comparative law. Although these are distinct legal sub-disciplines, developments since 1946 confirm their interrelationship. Comparative law is increasingly used as a tool in the making of law at national, regional and international levels. Private international law is increasingly affected by international conventions, and the issues faced by classical conflicts rules are increasingly dealt with by substantive harmonisation of law under international auspices. Mixed international arbitrations, especially those involving state economic activity, raise mixed questions of public and private international law. In many fields (such as the protection of human rights and democratic standards, investment guarantees, international criminal law) international and national systems interact. National constitutional arrangements relating to 'foreign affairs', and to the implementation of international norms, are a focus of attention.

Professor Sir Robert Jennings edited the series from 1981. Following his retirement as General Editor, an editorial board has been created and Cambridge University Press has recommitted itself to the series, affirming its broad scope.

The Board welcomes works of a theoretical or interdisciplinary character, and those focusing on new approaches to international or comparative law or conflicts of law. Studies of particular institutions or problems are equally welcome, as are translations of the best work published in other languages.

General Editors	James Crawford *Whewell Professor of International Law, University of Cambridge* David Johnston *Regius Professor of Civil Law, University of Cambridge*
Editorial Board	Professor Hilary Charlesworth *University of Adelaide* Mr John Collier *Trinity Hall, Cambridge* Professor Lori Damrosch *Columbia University Law School* Professor John Dugard *Director, Research Centre for International Law, University of Cambridge* Professor Mary-Ann Glendon *Harvard Law School* Professor Christopher Greenwood *London School of Economics* Professor Hein Kötz *Max-Planck-Institut, Hamburg* Dr Vaughan Lowe *Corpus Christi College, Cambridge* Professor D. M. McRae *University of Ottawa* Professor Onuma Yasuaki *University of Tokyo*
Advisory Committee	Professor D. W. Bowett QC Judge Rosalyn Higgins QC Professor Sir Robert Jennings QC Professor J. A. Jolowicz QC Professor Eli Lauterpacht QC Professor Kurt Lipstein Judge Stephen Schwebel

A list of books in the series can be found at the end of this volume

Religious liberty and international law in Europe

Malcolm D. Evans
University of Bristol

CAMBRIDGE
UNIVERSITY PRESS

PUBLISHED BY THE PRESS SYNDICATE OF THE UNIVERSITY OF CAMBRIDGE
The Pitt Building, Trumpington Street, Cambridge CB2 1RP, United Kingdom

CAMBRIDGE UNIVERSITY PRESS
The Edinburgh Building, Cambridge, CB2 2RU, United Kingdom
40 West 20th Street, New York, NY 10011–4211, USA
10 Stamford Road, Oakleigh, Melbourne 3166, Australia

First published 1997

Printed in the United Kingdom at the University Press, Cambridge

Typeset in 9.75/13 pt Swift

A catalogue record for this book is available from the British Library

Library of Congress Cataloguing in Publication data

Evans, Malcolm D.
Religious liberty and international law in Europe / Malcolm D. Evans.
    p.   cm.
Includes bibliographical references and index.
ISBN 0 521 55021 1 (hardcover)
1. Freedom of religion – Europe.   2. International law – Europe   I. Title.
KJC5156.E93   1997
341.4′81 – dc21   96–44609   CIP

ISBN 0 521 55021 1 hardback

CE

Contents

DEC 11

Acknowledgments

This work has been long in the making, and I am deeply indebted to all those who have helped and encouraged me along the way. I should like to acknowledge my particular gratitude to David Feldman, now Barber Professor of Jurisprudence at the University of Birmingham, who persuaded me to proceed beyond the first jottings, and Chris Clarkson, now Professor of Criminal Law at the University of Leicester, who supported me through other testing moments. Lest it be thought that this project has driven away all colleagues to whom I have turned, I should like to thank Julian Rivers and Steven Greer, still of the University of Bristol, for their careful reading and helpful comments on various parts of the text.

I am grateful to members of staff at the Human Rights centre in Geneva and at the Court and Commission of Human Rights in Strasbourg for their help in providing materials and to the staff of the Wills Memorial Library in Bristol for their patience and good humour in coping with some extremely awkward bibliographic requests. In the early stages of the work I was fortunate to profit from the research assistance of Giles Warrington whilst the latter stages were expedited by the help of Heindreen Kaal and Jessica Alexander. The awesome efficiency which Pat Hammond brought to the production of the typescript transcends acknowledgment.

Finally, I should like to express my gratitude to my wife, the Rev. Dr Alison Evans, for her encouragement and support (and for allowing me to plunder her library) and to our children, Olivia and Isobel, whose first years have been lived under the shadow of this book and to whom it is therefore appropriately dedicated.

Chronological table of international treaties

Other principal international instruments

Table of cases

Judgments and Advisory Opinions of the Permanent Court of International Justice and the International Court of Justice

European Court of Human Rights

European Commission of Human Rights

Alphabetical list of cases

Numerical list of cases

Views and Decisions of the Human Rights Committee

Alphabetical list

Abbreviations

AJIL	*American Journal of International Law*
ANET	*Ancient Near Eastern Texts*
BYIL	*British Yearbook of International Law*
CAHMIN	Ad Hoc Committee for the Protection of National Minorities
CD	*Collected Decisions* (of the European Commission of Human Rights)
CETP	Council of Europe, 'Collected Edition of the "*Travaux Préparatoires*" of the European Convention on Human Rights'
CHR	Commission on Human Rights
CSCE	Conference for Security and Cooperation in Europe (replaced by OSCE)
CTS	*Consolidated Treaty Series* (Parry's)
DR	*Decisions and Reports* (of the European Commission of Human Rights)
ECHR	European Convention on Human Rights
ECOSOC	Economic and Social Council
EHRR	*European Human Rights Reports*
EJIL	*European Journal of International Law*
ETS	*European Treaty Series*
FHIG	*Fontes Historiae Iuris Gentium*
GAOR	*General Assembly Official Records*
HPC	*A History of the Peace Conference of Paris* (Temperley)
HR	*Hague Recueil (Recueil des Cours de l'Académie de droit International)*
HRC	Human Rights Committee
HRLJ	*Human Rights Law Journal*
HRQ	*Human Rights Quarterly*
IBP	*De Iure Belli ac Pacis Libri Tres*

ICCPR	International Covenant on Civil and Political Rights
ICJ	International Court of Justice
ICLQ	*International and Comparative Law Quarterly*
IHRR	*International Human Rights Reports*
ILEA	Inner London Education Authority
ILM	*International Legal Materials*
ILO	International Labour Organisation
ILR	*International Law Reports*
Is.LR	*Israeli Law Review*
Is.YHR	*Israeli Yearbook of Human Rights*
IYIL	*Italian Yearbook of International Law*
LNOJ	*League of Nations Official Journal*
LNTS	*League of Nations Treaty Series*
Mich.L.Rev	*Michigan Law Review*
MLR	*Modern Law Review*
NYIL	*Netherlands Yearbook of International Law*
ODIHR	Office for Democratic Institutions and Human Rights
OSCE	Organization for Security and Cooperation in Europe
PCIJ	Permanent Court of International Justice
PL	*Public Law*
PPC	Paris Peace Conference, *Papers Relating to the Foreign Relations of the United States, The Paris Peace Conference, 1919*
RDP	*Revue du droit public*
RGDIP	*Revue général de droit international public*
SD	*Selected Decisions* (of the HRC)
UDHR	Universal Declaration of Human Rights
UNCIO	United Nations Conference on International Organization
UNTS	*United Nations Treaty Series*
YbHRC	*Yearbook of the Human Rights Committee*
YBECHR	*Yearbook of the European Convention on Human Rights*

Introduction

The freedom of religion is one of the oldest and most controversial of the claims that are now recognized as forming part of the corpus of human rights. Individuals may themselves make a claim for religious freedom against their own State. The response by the State to such a claim is, ultimately, a matter of domestic policy and law. States themselves may seek to ensure that their own nationals living in other countries are free to practise their religion. Historically, this has been an aspect of the treatment of aliens but is now increasingly subsumed within the ability of States to seek to ensure that other States allow religious freedoms to all within their jurisdiction, including their own nationals. This is the area now embraced by international law under the language of 'human rights'.

Although not couched in the language of 'human rights', much of the earliest writing from which international law has grown was concerned with the relationship between God and mankind. Whereas the modern focus is upon the freedom of man to act in relation to God as he (man) feels is appropriate, the original focus was upon the capacity of God to limit the range of temporal actions permitted by man. Thus while we today are concerned with the freedom of worship and the manifestation of religious beliefs, earlier writers were concerned with the limits to the power which the secular authorities could legitimately wield with regard to their subjects, or, indeed, their enemies.

Early societies identified themselves with their deity in such a way as to make the concept of freedom of religion an irrelevance. Each people worshipped its own god(s) and those who questioned the existence and power of the titular deity questioned the authority and power of the State. The followers of one god did not generally dispute the existence of the gods of other peoples, but to worship a 'foreign' god was akin to

1

'treason' against the State. Individuals were free to worship those gods 'recognized' and 'adopted' by the State – but not others. It was the Jews who, perversely, adopted a different approach. They believed in a universal God and denied the existence of all others. This approach would have remained a mild eccentricity if it were not for the growth of Christianity as a 'proselytizing' and 'evangelizing' religion which sought to convert all peoples to the same brand of monotheism.

When Christianity was adopted as the official religion of the Roman Empire, religious freedom was replaced by religious oppression as enemies of the Church and enemies of the State became more or less interchangeable. Moreover, since many 'enemies of the State' were also Christian, this resulted in wars which pitted believers against believers. This provided a conundrum from which the writers of the later Middle Ages and Renaissance attempted to extricate themselves by means of the 'just war' concept. The crucial step came with the recognition that not all wars fought against non-Christian powers could automatically be considered legitimate. This marked the beginning of the end of the temporal manifestation of the spiritual claim of Christian universalism since it demonstrated that non-Christians could benefit from the application of 'just war' rules and that the 'law of nations' was not limited to 'Christian' nations. This marched hand in hand with the emergence of the growth of the sovereign State in Western Europe and combined to produce the proposition that each sovereign was entitled, under the law of nations, to regulate religious affairs within its own jurisdiction as it saw fit.

In essence, the last 300 years have seen the international community attempting to resile upon this settlement. States (or individuals) have become increasingly aware and distressed at the restrictions placed by other States upon the freedom of individuals, including the practice of their religion, and a variety of mechanisms have been used to attempt to address this. In particular, several nineteenth century treaties making territorial settlements were conditional upon the State in question respecting the religious freedoms of particular groups. Particularly noticeable in this regard was the Treaty of Berlin (1878) which, *inter alia*, obliged the newly established Romanian State,[1] as a condition of its recognition, to respect the religious liberties of its citizens, and in particular, of the Jews.

There was a direct link between the failure of this treaty and the

---

[1] As a general rule, the spelling of countries, places and people(s) in the text has been regularized to conform to current usage.

creation of the minorities treaty system following the First World War. At the Paris Peace Conference, Jewish lobbyists applied immense pressure to ensure that Jewish minorities were given special protection in the newly created States of Central and Eastern Europe and that these obligations be subject to an international guarantee. Although they expanded to take account of other aspects of minority protection, the original purpose of the minorities treaties was to protect the religious liberties of Jews. It need hardly be said that they proved disastrously inadequate and their failure contributed towards the adoption of an 'individual rights' approach to the protection of human rights following the Second World War. It is not entirely fanciful to observe that it is the failure of the current 'individualistic' approach to the protection of the rights of religious minorities in the Balkans which is, once again, occasioning a reassessment of the merits of the discarded minority treaty approach.

Like it or not (and many will not) it is in Europe that the formative developments have taken place. It is, then, appropriate to consider the European experience in attempting to balance the freedom of each State to regulate its internal affairs with the desire of the wider community to ensure that individuals enjoy religious freedom. Moreover, Europe enjoys a highly developed regional system of human rights protection and a sophisticated jurisprudence has developed. Rightly or wrongly, it is probable that the European experience is likely to be of greater significance to the evolution of other regional or global enforcement mechanisms than the development of these others is to be to the European. In sum, the European experience is unique, both in terms of its historical and contemporary significance, its diversity, its documentation and its development.

It is possible to protect religious liberties in a number of different ways. First, almost all international human rights instruments contain a non-discrimination clause which bars discrimination on the grounds of religion. The 'non-discrimination' question, however, does not address the issue of the substantive rights which must be enjoyed on a non-discriminatory basis. The major division is between direct and indirect guarantees. The 'freedom of religion' is the sum of many different parts, many of which are 'standard' civil and political rights, such as the freedom of assembly, the freedom of movement and the freedom of expression, and it is possible to consider the extent to which religious freedom is in fact protected by these separate heads. Religion is also a 'social' right (religious education); an 'economic' right (from the money changers in the Temple at Jerusalem, via St Paul and the silversmiths at Ephesus, the Jewish bankers at York and Sabbath working, through to the opening of super-markets on a Sunday); a 'cultural' right; a 'collective' right; a 'peoples'' right; an indigenous peoples' right; a right to self-determination . . . In short, it touches upon aspects of almost any individual and collective right possible to imagine. However, no matter what 'indirect' avenues are pursued, some fundamental facet of religious well-being is likely to be outside of its scope. Moreover, the freedom of religion is merely an aspect of the broader right in question and, in consequence, runs the risk of being marginalized within it.

On the other hand, the Universal Declaration of Human Rights, the International Covenant on Civil and Political Rights and the regional human rights conventions all contain a basic provision in substantially similar terms which confers a direct guarantee of religious freedom. It is more rewarding to consider how this direct guarantee has been inter-preted since this reveals more about the nature of religious freedom than does the indirect protection offered by other heads. For example, torture has been used to persuade 'heretics' to conform to 'orthodox' views. Thus outlawing torture might provide an indirect means of enhancing reli-gious freedom. Yet it is clearly an inappropriate vehicle through which to consider the freedom of religion since it tells us nothing about the nature of religious freedom itself. This is true of all such indirect means of protection, and particularly true of the freedom of expression which, because of the nexus between them, is a right which is as likely to come into conflict with the freedom of religion as it is to protect it.

Of course, indirect means are a useful supplement – and may often prove an easier and less controversial form of protection, but that is not to point. The question under consideration concerns how the desire to protect 'religious liberty' has manifested itself under (or in) international law and how it is currently interpreted, particularly under the European Convention on Human Rights. Although this may seem a 'narrow ques-tion' in the contemporary context, that context is itself distorting. This book attempts to place the topic within a much broader historical perspective than that of the past fifty years and which is already showing signs of fraying at the edges.

To this end, chapters 1 and 2 provide an historical overview of develop-ments up to the First World War. Chapter 3 examines the attempts made to place an obligation concerning religious liberty into the Covenant of the League of Nations, whilst chapters 4 and 5 examine the background to, and emergence of, the minorities treaty system. The workings of that system relative to religious liberty are considered in chapter 6. The following three chapters then look at the emergence of international norms relating to the direct protection of religious liberty within the UN system: Article 18 of the Universal Declaration of Human Rights (chapter 7), Article 18 of the International Covenant on Civil and Political Rights, and its subsequent development by the Human Rights Committee (chapter 8), and the 1981 Declaration on the Elimination of All Forms of Intolerance and of Discrimination Based on Religion or Belief and the work of the UN Special Rapporteur on Religious Intolerance (chapter 9). The remaining chapters turn to the work of the Council of Europe, where there has been something of a surge of recent cases raising difficult questions under Article 9 of the European Convention on Human Rights (ECHR). Chapter 10 looks at the background to that Article, whilst chapters 11 and 12 examine the jurisprudence of the European Commission and Court of Human Rights in relation to it and chapter 13 looks at Article 2 of the First Protocol to the ECHR, concerning parental rights over the religious education of their children. Finally, and by way of conclusion, chapter 14 outlines a number of developments which bear upon the direction that the search for the protection of religious liberty under international law might next take.

1 Early antecedents

The Ancient Near East

The idea that a State ought to tolerate the religious beliefs and practices of other communities would have appeared irrational to early civilizations. From earliest times, the institutions of what might be called 'secular' authority were so closely interwoven with religious authority as to be practically indistinguishable.

In Sumerian and Mesopotamian mythology, man was created in order to relieve the gods from the burdensome task of providing for themselves: men were created as the servants of the gods.[1] This was also reflected in the Akkadian and Babylonian myths which have come down to us[2] and which represent a continuation and transformation of the earlier Semitic material. It was also implicit within this understanding of the created order that each deity had its own particular dwelling place; and men living there were its servants. If the servants of one god (that is, the people

---

[1] See S. H. Hooke, *Middle Eastern Mythology*, (Harmondsworth: Penguin, 1963), p. 26 for the myth of Lahar and Ashnan, and also S. N. Kramer, *Sumerian Mythology: a Study of Spiritual and Literary Achievement in the Third Millennium BC*, (Philadelphia: American Philosophical Society, 1944), p. 61.

[2] Hooke, *Middle Eastern Mythology*, pp. 29–30, 45 and see *The Enuma Elish (The Babylonian Creation)*, Part VI, in which the god Marduk says:

> Blood I will mass and cause bones to be.
> I will establish a savage, 'man' shall be his name
> Verily, savage man I will create.
> He shall be charged with the service of the gods
> That they might be at ease!

Trans. in J. B. Pritchard (ed.) *Ancient Near Eastern Texts relating to the Old Testament (ANET)* (Princeton, NJ: Princeton University Press, 1950), p. 68. See also N. K. Sanders (trans.), *Poems of Heaven and Hell from Ancient Mesopotamia*, (Harmondsworth: Penguin, 1971), p. 97.

of one city) fell under the sway of those of another, then this was perceived as having some connection with the relationship between the gods themselves. The physical destruction of a city or temple represented the final humiliation of the god.

The versions of the early creation myths that have come down to us reflect the shifts in political power between the warring powers of the region. The written version of the Babylonian creation myth derives from a period of Babylonian supremacy, so it is Bel-Marduk, the god of Babylon, who is invested with supremacy over the other gods of the region. When Assyrian power rose in the north of Akkad and threatened Babylonian supremacy, local versions of the creation myths were varied and Bel-Marduk replaced with the local titular deity.[3] Religion was to be understood in terms of political events: if Babylon fell, then Bel-Marduk was vanquished; if Bel-Marduk is portrayed as supreme, then Babylon has reasserted her political supremacy. If this was the case as between peoples sharing the same pantheon, it is hardly surprising that there was little room for the idea that the religious practices of those who believed in an entirely different cosmology were entitled to respect or toleration.

The correlation between State and deity went deeper than mythological reconstructions of creation. The relationship between god and man was mirrored in the relationship between the king and the people under his dominion. This was often reflected in the king being portrayed – in literature or art – fulfilling the role assigned by the religious myths to the titular god of the State, or, indeed, to that of a rival, or defeated, State.[4] The ruler sought to be identified with the deity. The interrelationship between the State and its gods was also reflected by the very structure of authority.

In parts of the ancient Middle East, such as Egypt, the ruler was considered divine.[5] In others, the high priest of the god was 'king' by virtue of his special relationship, as priest, with the deity. In time the relationship became inverted and the king assumed the function of high priest.[6] No matter what the order of relationship, however, the resulting

---

[3] Hooke, *Middle Eastern Mythology*, p. 42; Sanders, *Poems*, pp. 34–35.

[4] This practice continues down to more modern eras: the allegorical paintings of the seventeenth and eighteenth centuries were intended to underscore the divine right of the monarch. The monumental statuary of Communism took on a not dissimilar function in the context of an atheistic society.

[5] See, for example, the hymns expressing joy at the accession of various pharaohs to the throne in *ANET*, pp. 378–379.

[6] This was also true of early Roman practice, where the kings also acted as high priests. Whereas the other powers of the king passed to the consuls under the Republic, the

concept of 'priest-king' was very powerful. The obligation to serve the deity in a priestly function could be extremely onerous and so it is not surprising that, over time, the relationship between divinity and ruler was expressed by the anointing of the ruler by the high priest in the context of a liturgical rite. The Babylonian Creation formed a part of the liturgy associated with the annual rite in which the king 'took the hands' of Marduk, inaugurating the new year and renewing the relationship between god and the king; divine ruler and temporal ruler; king and subject.[7]As a part of the ritual:

the urigallu-priest shall leave [the sanctuary] and take away the sceptre, the circle and the sword [from the king]. He shall bring them [before the god Bel] and place them [on] a chair . . . He shall accompany [the king] into the presence of the god Bel . . . he shall drag [him by] the ears and make him bow down on the ground.

After the king has made a petition to the god, the priest reassures the king of the god's favour and restores the symbols of authority to him.[8]

The Bible provides further examples of the manner in which the authority of rulers was derived from the authority of God. For example, Samuel was called by the God of the Israelites to be his prophet and, as such, 'Samuel's word had authority throughout Israel'.[9] As he grew old, the Elders of Israel asked him to appoint a king over them, as other nations had. God instructed Samuel to appoint Saul, and he was duly anointed by him.[10]

Not only were rulers often seen as being either appointed by, or a

religious functions passed to the *Pontifex Maximus* whilst the concept of the 'priest-King' was preserved in the office of the *Rex Sacrorum*. See H. F. Jolowicz and B. Nicholas, *Historical Introduction to the Study of Roman Law*, 3rd edn, (Cambridge University Press, 1972), p. 45.

[7] For the text of the New Year Festival ritual see *ANET*, pp. 331–334.
[8] *Ibid.*, p. 334.   [9] 1 Samuel 3 v. 19–4 v. 1.
[10] 1 Samuel 8–10. It is hardly worth continuing to demonstrate the relationship between kingship and divine investiture. Whilst Napoleon Bonaparte might have seized the imperial crown from the hands of the bishop in order to demonstrate that he considered himself to have achieved his throne by his own efforts and not from the hands of God, the current monarch of the United Kingdom was still invested by her archbishop. Down the ages, the ideas of divine ordination and temporal authority have gone hand in hand, even if this now manifests itself in a ritual the theological significance of which is not universally acknowledged. Even when on Christmas Day AD 800 Charlemagne was crowned Emperor by Pope Leo III in Rome, this was more by way of reward for his help in reasserting the Pope's authority than as a moment of divine investment of temporal authority (graphically recounted by Einhard, *The Life of Charlemagne*, §28 and by Notker the Stammerer, *Charlemagne*, book I, §26 (trans. L. Thorpe, *Two Lives of Charlemagne* (Harmondsworth: Penguin, 1969)). Such acts are better

manifestation of, god, but the rules by which they governed were also seen as being of god. Some of the earliest legal codes were associated with divine revelation, such as the Ten Commandments given to Moses.[11] Others pointed to the divine authority and guidance given to the promulgator.[12] The Greeks also believed that their earliest legal codes were given to them by the gods, as did the Romans. Moreover, the sanctity of law derived from the sanctity of its source. To break the law was to commit an offence against god. Divine punishment would fall upon the law breaker[13] and it was to god that reparation was due.[14] This also took the form of tracing the establishment of some ancient courts of law to a divine origin.[15]

To the extent that the deity was seen as a source of secular authority, the idea of a power tolerating the religious practices of another power within the territories under its direct control[16] would have potentially undermined its authority.[17] All these factors combined to reinforce the

seen as symbolizing a relationship rather than as being invested with actual ritual significance.

[11] Exodus 34 and Deuteronomy 5. See also Leviticus, Numbers and Deuteronomy for further series of commands revealed by God to Moses and Aaron.

[12] E.g. the Law Code of Hammurabi (*circa* 1720 BC), which was inscribed on a stele which depicted Hammurabi receiving a commission to write his code from the god of justice, Shamash. See *ANET*, pp. 163–180. See also the earlier Code of Lipit-Ishtar: 'I, Lipit-Ishtar, . . . [estab]lished [jus]tice in [Su]mer and Akkad in accordance with the word of Enlil' (*ANET*, p. 159).

[13] Thus the Law Codes of both Lipit-Ishtar and Hammurabi conclude with epilogues which call down the wrath of the gods upon any who desecrate the stele on which the laws were written or fail to honour the laws themselves (*ANET*, pp. 161; 177–180). The Mosaic laws also concluded with similar injunctions, promising the blessing of God on those who obey and the wrath of God on those who are disobedient. See Leviticus 26 vv. 3–39; Deuteronomy 28 and 29 vv. 15–20.

[14] See C. Phillipson, *The International Law and Custom of Ancient Greece and Rome*, vol. I (London: MacMillan, 1911), p. 43.

[15] The Court of the Areopagus in Athens, for example, was allegedly founded by Athena in order to try Orestes for the murder of Clytemnestra. See Aeschylus, *The Eumenides*, trans. by P. Vellacott, *The Oresteian Trilogy* (Harmondsworth: Penguin, 1956), p. 170.

[16] This is to be contrasted with the situation of vassal States which were under the sway of neighbouring powers to which they paid tribute. Vassal States tended to retain their religious autonomy. The Assyrians, however, tended to implement a more militant imperialism which sought to bring vassal States (on which even the Assyrians did not impose their religion) within their Empire and subject them to direct control.

[17] 'These are the statutes and laws that you shall be careful to observe in the land which the Lord the God of your fathers is giving you to occupy as long as you live on earth. You shall demolish all the sanctuaries where the nations whose place you are taking worship their gods . . . You shall pull down their altars and break their sacred pillars, burn their sacred poles and hack down the idols of their gods and thus blot out the name of them from that place' (Deuteronomy 12 vv. 1–3). 'When the Lord your God

single most important aspect of religious belief in the ancient world: the correlation between religion and place.[18]

Hence the idea of religious toleration was subsumed within the general policy of the authority. A war between two powers might be couched in the language of a conflict between the rival deities.[19] Certainly, the triumph of one power over another would often be complemented by the destruction of the places of worship of the 'defeated' deity and, perhaps, the physical removal or destruction of the statue or symbol of the god. However, such acts were not aimed at the religious beliefs of the defeated peoples as such. Rather, they served to symbolize – and, indeed, realize – the destruction of the temporal power that was associated with its worship. Destroying the sacred places of a rival power was not so much an act of religious imperialism as an act intended to assert the authority of the conquering power over the defeated peoples by displacing their god – the source of authority – with another.

Nevertheless, the power of place and the religious traditions associated with it often proved overwhelming[20] and a conquest might soon be

exterminates, as you advance, the nations whose country you are entering to occupy, you shall take their place and settle in the land. After they have been destroyed, take care that you are not ensnared in their ways. Do not inquire about their gods and say, "How do these nations worship their gods? I will too do the same"' (Deuteronomy 12 vv. 29–30).

This is graphically illustrated by the laws delivered by Yahweh to Moses: 'When you hear that miscreants have appeared in any of the cities which the Lord your God is giving you to occupy, and have led its inhabitants astray by calling on them to serve other gods . . . you shall put the inhabitants of that city to the sword' (Deuteronomy 13 vv. 12–15).

These laws were to apply to the areas granted by God to the Israelites. Thus when Jehu, who had been anointed King of Israel by one of the prophets of God, succeeded in wresting the Northern Kingdom from the descendants of the house of Ahab (who had forsaken Yahweh and had introduced the worship of Baal) he 'brought out the sacred pole from the Temple of Baal and burnt it: and they pulled down the sacred pillar of the Baal and the temple itself and made a privy of it' (2 Kings 10 vv. 26–28).

[18] See generally N. Bentwich, *The Religious Foundations of Internationalism*, 2nd edn, (London: George Allen & Unwin, 1959), chapters 2 and 3; also D. J. Bederman, 'Religious Sources of International Law in Antiquity', in M. W. Janis (ed.), *The Influence of Religion on the Development of International Law* (Dordrecht: Martinus Nijhoff, 1991), pp. 3, 12–14.

[19] For example, during the revolt of Hezekiah, King of Judah, the Assyrian King Sennacherib taunted the inhabitants of Jerusalem by saying that his God had told him to 'Attack this land and destroy it' and that their God would not save them, for 'Among all the gods of the nations is there one who saved his land from me?' (2 Kings 18 vv. 25 and 35; 2 Chronicles 32 vv. 13–15).

[20] The history of Israel is rich in stories of attempts by prophets of Yahweh to prevent the population from lapsing into the worship of Baal, the local Canaanite deity in whose former lands the tribes of Israel had come to reside.

followed by the adoption by the conquering power of the very practices which it had previously destroyed.[21] As the world of the ancient Near East grew more cosmopolitan the tendency was to recognize correlations between the deities worshipped, and aliens would often worship the gods of one locality as being a manifestation of members of their own pantheon.[22] In like measure, aliens could be permitted to establish the worship of their own gods in other lands when relations between powers were cordial.[23] Hostility was reserved for the gods of one's enemies.

Moreover, attitudes of out and out hostility were double edged. Israel and Judah themselves became vassal States of Assyria and then of Babylon.[24] Following a series of unsuccessful revolts, they passed into their direct control and were subjected to the indignities that the Mosaic laws had prescribed for others. Both the Northern Kingdom of Israel and the Southern Kingdom of Judah became vassal States of Assyria following the campaigns of Tiglath-Pileser III (the latter by invitation).[25] Samaria, the capital of Israel, ultimately fell to Sargon II in 722 BC and its population was carried off into exile two years later by Shalmaneser V. Judah remained in a state of vassalage to its neighbours until Jerusalem was eventually sacked by Nebuchadnezzar of Babylon in 587/6 BC, the temple destroyed and the people taken into captivity.[26] Babylon itself fell to the armies of Cyrus the Great of Persia in 539 BC. It is with the advent

[21] Following the division of the Davidic Kingdom, the Northern Kingdom, Israel, moved towards a policy of accommodation with its Phoenician and Aramaean neighbours which resulted in the re-emergence of the worship of local deities, much to the outrage of the Yahwehistic prophets. The re-establishment or re-emergence of religious practices by a defeated people could, however, be interpreted as a challenge to the secular authority and resisted for that very reason.

[22] By way of example, the Greeks of Cyrene came to associate the local shrine of the Libyan God Ammon at Siwah with that of Zeus. The resulting shrine of Zeus Ammon became an important oracular centre and was visited by Alexander the Great, for whom the shrine symbolized the coming together of the various parts of his Empire, then in the making. It also enabled him to identify with the son-ship of the Egyptian God Amon (himself associated with Ammon) and hence enhance the legitimacy of his newly won position as pharaoh. This incident serves to illustrate the blending and blurring of religions and of religion and authority. See R. Lane Fox, *Alexander the Great* (London: Allen Lane, 1973), pp. 200–218.

[23] A well-known example is the Jewish community established at Elephantine near the first cataract of the Nile in Egypt, established in or around 525 BC. Interestingly, this appears to have been polytheistic. See J. A. Soggin, *A History of Israel: From the Beginning to the Bar Kochba Revolt, AD 135* (London: SCM Press Ltd, 1984), p. 281.

[24] See generally, Soggin, *A History of Israel*, pp. 221–257.

[25] Moreover, the King of Judah, Ahaz, introduced the worship of Assyrian Gods into the Temple at Jerusalem. See 2 Kings 16 vv. 12–18. This seems to have been voluntary.

[26] 2 Kings 25 vv. 1–17; 2 Chronicles 36 vv. 17–20.

of the Persian Empire that it is possible, however, to trace the beginnings of a fundamental shift in outlook.

Cyrus did not seek to assert his supremacy by destroying what he had won.[27] Nor did he seek, as a matter of course, to destroy the temples of his enemies. He adopted a conciliatory attitude, intended to win the support of the local gods – and of the local populace. This policy is celebrated on the Cyrus Cylinder,[28] where Cyrus declared that it was Marduk himself who had called on him to march against Babylon and liberate it from Nabonidus, 'the [Babylonian] king who did not worship him'. Cyrus recounted how 'Marduk, the great lord [induced] the magnanimous inhabitants of Babylon [to love me], and I was daily endeavouring to worship him' and concluded by saying how he:

returned to the sacred cities on the other side of the Tigris, the sanctuaries of which have been ruins for a long time, the images which used to live therein and established for them permanent sanctuaries . . . Furthermore, I resettled upon the command of Marduk, the great lord, all the gods of Sumer and Akkad whom Nabonidus had brought into Babylon to the anger of the lord of the gods, unharmed, in their (former) chapels, the places which make them happy.

Cyrus also exploited the fears of those he defeated. In an age in which the natural consequence of defeat had been death and destruction, the humanity of Cyrus won him extravagant praise and, as was always intended, the gratitude of those he spared. Once again, the policy had less to do with principle than practicality.[29] The vast Persian Empire could not

---

[27] Herodotus gives Croesus, King of Lydia, credit for this policy. After the fall of his capital, Sardis, Herodotus says that Croesus asked Cyrus why the Persian army was sacking the city, since it was Cyrus himself that they were robbing (*The Histories*, trans. A. de Sélincourt, rev. edn (Harmondsworth: Penguin, 1972) book I, §88).

[28] *ANET*, pp. 315–316.

[29] The behaviour of Cambyses, Cyrus's successor, following his conquest of Egypt was particularly brutal. In *The Histories* Herodotus recounts that he ordered the embalmed body of the Pharaoh Amasis to be burnt – in violation of the religious sensibilities of both Egyptians and Persians (book III, §16) – and killed the sacred Apis (bull god) at Memphis by stabbing it in the thigh (book III, §29). Cambyses died from gangrene that set in following an incident in which he pierced his own thigh with his sword when mounting his horse – in the same spot, Herodotus says, as he stabbed the Apis (book III, §64). Herodotus saw these and other incidents of impiety to the gods (book III, §37) as evidence to support his theory of the growing madness of Cambyses. It should perhaps be said that Herodotus was probably drawing on a source hostile to Cambyses and favourable to Darius I. When Babylon took the opportunity of the turmoil caused by his seizing the throne to rebel, Darius I put down the revolt with great cruelty. It was probably in order to provide a countercheck against any further Babylonian rebellion that Darius revived and reinforced the pro-Jewish policy of Cyrus, securing a loyal ally in the region. Nevertheless, the killing of the Apis was sufficiently well remembered to allow Alexander the Great to endear himself to the Egyptians by

be run from the centre and a decentralized system of government was established, based upon pre-existing territorial units. The Persians encouraged continuity, and respect for traditional religions formed an important part of this. It was the application of this policy towards the Jews that was, perhaps, of the greatest long-term significance. Having found them as captives in Babylon, Cyrus permitted them to return to Jerusalem and rebuild the temple.[30]

The significance of Cyrus's attitude towards the Jews has been immense. The Jews considered the Persians to be the agents of Yahweh.[31] They came to understand the fall of Jerusalem and the Babylonian exile as being a punishment from God, rather than as an event that had diminished their God by displaying his impotence at the hands of others.[32] It also marked a shift away from a covenant relationship between God and man in the form of a territorial compact. There was to be a new covenant relationship[33] between God and his people which was to be understood as a direct, personal and individual relationship, unconnected with the temporal order as such.

One consequence of this development was a heightened need for co-existence with other religious practices. Since the sovereignty of God was no longer manifested in political supremacy, it followed that the practice of Judaism would have to exist within a framework premised upon the existence of other religious beliefs. This was not, however, a particularly

paying homage to the god when he captured Memphis from the Persians two centuries later.

[30] For the biblical account of the return, see Ezra 1 and 6, vv. 3–5. For an alternative perspective see A. Toynbee, *Mankind and Mother Earth*, (Oxford University Press, 1976), pp. 188–189, who argues that in permitting the implementation of the extreme nationalist policies (characterized as 'religious and social apartheid') of Ezra and Nehemiah, the Persians were unwittingly reversing their general policy of toleration.

[31] 'I say to Cyrus, "You shall be my shepherd to carry out my purpose so that Jerusalem may be rebuilt and the foundations of my temple laid"' (Isaiah, 44 v. 28. See also *ibid.*, 45 vv. 1–13). This pro-Persian attitude is reflected in 2 Chronicles 36 vv. 20–21, which was most likely written during the middle years of the fourth century BC at a time when Jerusalem formed a part of the Persian Empire: R. J. Coggins, *The Cambridge Bible Commentary: the First and Second Book of Chronicles* (Cambridge University Press, 1976), pp. 4, 6 and 308. The books of Ezra, Nehemiah, Esther and the apocryphal books of Esdras and Esther similarly evidence the generally favourable position of the Jews under Persian rule.

[32] Thus the writers of the closing chapters of 2 Kings and 2 Chronicles laboured the point that the downfall of both the Northern and Southern Kingdoms was a consequence of their rulers having done 'what was wrong in the eyes of the Lord', even though this meant that God's own temple was destroyed by the agents of his punishment. See also Deuteronomy, 28 vv. 36–68 which was also composed at around this time.

[33] See Jeremiah 31 vv. 31–34.

difficult problem for polytheists. Naturally, each believed that their god was greater in power than others, and often held the practices of others in contempt, but the existence – and divinity – of other gods was not questioned. It was, however, a problem for the Jews. They saw their liberation by Cyrus as demonstrating the triumph of their God: he had been able to use the king of another land to achieve his will for his people and henceforward they considered their God to be the only and universal God.[34]

There remained, however, the need to reconcile this belief with his people's lack of temporal authority. This was achieved by their emphasizing their claim to be the 'chosen people' of the universal God. His people did not seek to impose their religion on others, merely to preserve it amongst themselves. There was only one God and he was only concerned with his people. Provided that they were allowed to continue in their own religious practices they would be satisfied. That others around them should worship other 'gods' was a matter of no direct concern[35] and the link with political autonomy was broken.[36]

In essence, this remained the pattern for the years following the death of Alexander the Great and through the period of Hellenization to the Roman era and the Great Revolt which culminated in the capture of Jerusalem and the destruction of the temple in AD 70. For some, of course, nothing short of the re-establishment of a Jewish Kingdom would be adequate. Should Jewish intolerance be coupled with sufficient strength to challenge the authority of the dominant power, then retribution could be expected – and was, down the years, forthcoming. But this was no different from the general temperament of the times. If religious influences provided a focus for dissent, then they would be dealt with, by

[34] Indeed, the Babylonians were also portrayed as agents of Yahweh: 'the anger of the Lord burst out against his people . . . So he brought against them the king of the Chaldeans . . . God gave them all into his power' (2 Chronicles 36 v. 17). In consequence, the sack of the temple was also seen as the work of God (2 Chronicles, vv. 18–19). This would have been unthinkable but for the return and restoration of Jerusalem mediated by God through Cyrus. Thus God is seen as behind both the evil and the good which befell his people.

[35] Cf. the prophet Zachariah who looks forward to the day in which God would 'erase the names of idols from the land'. This is portrayed as an idealistic aspiration, rather than an immediate expectation (Zachariah 13 v. 2).

[36] This was substantially facilitated by the religious toleration of the Persians who, whilst controlling civil governance, were quite prepared to allow the Yahwist priesthood to re-establish the temple in Jerusalem as a centralized place of worship, reviving the traditions of the seventh century BC reformers and reflected in the Deuteronomic writings and the Chronicles, compiled at this time. See Soggin, A History of Israel, p. 278.

violence if necessary.[37] The general attitude is well described by Herodotus who, commenting on the actions of Cambyses in Egypt in an earlier period, wrote:

> I have no doubt whatever that Cambyses was completely out of his mind; it is the only possible explanation of his assault upon, and mockery of, everything which ancient law and custom have made sacred in Egypt. For if anyone, no matter who, were given the opportunity of choosing from amongst all the nations in the world the set of beliefs which he thought best, he would inevitably, after careful consideration of their relative merits, choose that of his own country. Everyone without exception believes his own native customs, and the religion he was brought up in, to be the best; and that being so, it is unlikely that anyone but a madman would mock at such things.[38]

Although it might be wondered whether this reflected cynicism rather than toleration, the result was much the same. Provided that public order was not threatened, individuals could do much as they pleased, and most were pleased to accept the religious traditions of their ancestors. Moreover, respect for the various religious practices came to be expected. The desecration of places of worship or of statues of the gods ceased to be a matter of pride, as it had been in earlier times. Writers considered it necessary to explain away such acts of impiety towards gods of other lands whilst conquerors redoubled their efforts to identify, and be identified with, the religious beliefs of their subjects.[39]

Rome and Christianity

The simple truth which both the Persians and Alexander had grasped was that a large multi-ethnic empire could not be built upon the destruction or belittlement of its members' beliefs, but had to win loyalty by showing respect and tolerance where possible. Above all, dogmatic repression was to be avoided. These trends were built upon by the Romans.

---

[37] However, many of the instances of persecution of the Jews can be ascribed to other factors not concerned with religious tension as such. Rarely was the simple fact of religious dissent alone a reason. For example, the enforced Hellenization of Temple worship under the Seleucid king Antiochus IV (194–167 BC), which is often seen as a classic example of religious intolerance, was probably motivated chiefly by political and economic factors. See Soggin, pp. 293–304.

[38] Herodotus, *The Histories*, book III, §38.

[39] This reached, perhaps, its apogee with Alexander the Great, the Macedonian conqueror of the Persian Empire and beyond. See above, n. 22.

Toleration

The Romans, more than most, tended to adopt and assimilate the gods of other powers, resulting in a cosmopolitan attitude towards religious worship that was remarkably tolerant. As Gibbon wryly concluded:

> The policy of the emperors and the senate, as far as it concerned religion, was happily seconded by the reflections of the enlightened, and by the habits of the superstitious, part of their subjects. The various modes of worship which prevailed in the Roman world were all considered by the people as equally true; by the philosophers as equally false; and by the magistrate as equally useful. And thus toleration produced not only mutual indulgence, but even religious concord.[40]

Tolerance ended, however, when religious rites threatened to disturb the peace or provided a focus for opposition to Roman rule.[41] This again underlines the essence of religious tolerance in the ancient world: it was not born of philosophical conviction but was based upon political expediency.[42] In the highly diverse world of the Roman Empire this meant that freedom of worship became very much a matter of local policy. Judaism might flourish in Jerusalem and Alexandria, whilst being subject to restriction or persecution elsewhere.

From the latter years of the first century onwards, however, all such local patterns of toleration or persecution operated alongside the uniform operation of the cult of Rome and the emperor, which provided a common point of unity and a touchstone of loyalty.[43] Expediency, however, could cause even this point to be stretched and a principal exception to this general rule concerned the rigidly monotheist Jews and Judaism was accepted as a *religio licta*. Although it was generally understood that the Jews were religiously intolerant, this could be accommodated by recalling that this represented the traditional religious practice of the region. Roman toleration of established customary practices within the Empire even extended to tolerating the intolerant provided, of course, that civil order was not threatened.[44]

---

[40] E. Gibbon, *The Decline and Fall of the Roman Empire* (first published 1776), edited by D. Womersley (London: Allen Lane, 1994), chapter 2.

[41] See H. Chadwick, *The Early Church* (Harmondsworth: Penguin, 1967), pp. 24–25.

[42] See H. B. Workman *Persecution in the Early Church* (first published 1906), (Oxford University Press, 1980), pp. 30–32.

[43] Although all the Augustan emperors asserted their divinity to a greater or lesser extent, the cult of emperor worship took on a greater force under the reign of Domitian (AD 81–96) and thereafter.

[44] The Romans were not able fully to comprehend the degree to which the Jews were prepared to carry their monotheism. Some of the incidents that are recorded by

Such was the general pattern at the time when Christianity began to spread outside of its native Palestine. If Judaism was unusually anti-thetical to the religious practices of others, resulting in an extremely strong sense of nationalism and exclusivity, then early Christian thought was equally hostile. Unlike Judaism, however, Christianity ultimately coupled its universality with a strong call to proselytism:[45] Christianity was not to be limited to Jews, but was to be preached to the Gentiles.[46] In the passage of the New Testament which has become known as 'the Great Commission', Christians were enjoined by Christ to: 'Go forth therefore and make all nations my disciples.'[47] Not only did this promise a confrontation with the essentially tolerant polytheism of the Roman world but, unlike Judaism, it was not possible to appeal to traditional practices and custom in order to legitimize the claim of the Christians for their beliefs to be respected.

At first, it is probable that the Roman authorities either did not, or could not, distinguish between Judaism and Christianity, but as bitter hostility developed between Jews and Christians, the position of Chris-tians within the Empire came into focus and the chief point of conflict concerned the Imperial Cult. To the Roman, the Christian's refusal to accept the Imperial Cult was more than a mark of religious intolerance, or, indeed, of disloyalty: it was tantamount to sedition. They were setting up their own God in opposition to Caesar and challenging the bond that bound the Empire together. Hence it is not surprising that persecutions of Christians tended to occur around the time of festivals celebrating the Imperial Cult. For example, Polycarp, Bishop of Smyrna was martyred during festivities associated with the Imperial Cult. On his arrest his

---

writers as deliberate provocations to the religious sensibilities of the Jews can probably be attributed to the failure of the Romans fully to understand the seriousness with which the Jews held to their brand of intolerant monotheism. Naturally this caused tensions and, ultimately, revolts against Roman rule which, predictably, were forcibly repressed. The Revolt of AD 117–138 did, however, result in measures which were deliberately aimed against the practice of Judaism and Jerusalem was made a Roman colony, Aelia Capitolina. The Romans had simply had enough. See generally Soggin, *A History of Israel*, pp. 327–336.

[45] See Chadwick, *The Early Church*, pp. 68–69.

[46] The controversy over the question of whether Christianity was limited to Jews or whether it embraced the Gentiles racked the Church in its early years, with the universalist approach of Paul prevailing over the views of Peter, the leader of the Church in Jerusalem. See generally *ibid.*, pp. 12–23.

[47] Matthew 28 v. 19. This passage probably dates from the resolution of the controversy noted in the previous footnote.

captors urged upon him: 'Where is the harm in just saying "Caesar is Lord" and offering the incense, and so forth, when it will save your life?'[48] When the Asiarch (the head of the confederation of Asian cities, who presided at festivities associated with the Imperial Cult) had it announced that Polycarp had admitted to being a Christian: 'the whole audience, the heathens and the Jewish residents of Smyrna alike, broke into loud yells of ungovernable fury: "That teacher of Asia! That father-figure of the Christians! That destroyer of our gods, who is teaching whole multitudes to abstain from sacrificing to them or worshipping them!"' The seditious overtones are underlined by the postscript added to the written version of the story which recounts: 'The official responsible for [Polycarp's] arrest was Herod; the High Priest was Philip of Tralles; and the proconsul was Statius Quadratus – but the ruling monarch was Jesus Christ, who reigns for ever and ever.'[49] The writer put the name of Christ in the place where, according to all literary conventions of the time, the name of the emperor would have been found. Clearly, Christianity could not be fitted within the framework of the Empire and, ultimately, one would have to yield.[50]

Nevertheless, not all Christian writings set out to antagonize the Roman authorities. Tertullian pointed out that the Scriptures expressly called upon Christians to 'pray for kings, and princes and powers, that there may be peace in the land' for 'when the empire is disturbed then we . . . find ourselves sharing in the calamity'.[51] He scorned those who sought divine aid for the emperor by 'seeking where it is not, in asking it from those who have it not to give, passing by him in whose power it lies' whilst at the same time 'persecuting those who know where to seek it, who, because they know, are also able to obtain it'. He asserted that: 'Without ceasing, for all our emperors we offer prayer. We pray for life prolonged; for security to the empire, for protection to the imperial house; for brave armies, a faithful senate, a virtuous people, the world at rest, whatever as man or Caesar, an emperor would wish.'[52] The problem, put simply, was that the emperor did not see it that way.

The long series of persecutions to which the early Christians were subject were, then, not so much a manifestation of religious intolerance

---

[48] *Martyrdom of Polycarp*, §VIII.   [49] *Ibid.*, §XXI.

[50] It is normally understood that it was Christianity which ultimately triumphed, though it has been argued that this came about only by surrendering its monotheism and subsuming other religious traditions within it, e.g. , by developing the tradition of Mary into the equivalent of a 'mother goddess', akin to Cybele and Isis. See Toynbee, *Mankind and Mother Earth*, chapter 38.

[51] Tertullian, *Apology*, XXXI, quoting 1 Timothy 2 v. 2.   [52] *Ibid.*, XXIX–XXX.

on the part of the authorities against the Christian religion *per se*, but a reaction to the refusal of the Christians to acquiesce in the pluralistic status quo. Indeed, the mere fact that their religion forbade their doing so would not of itself have led to persecution. It was the implications of such a refusal upon the authority of the secular powers that was the principal concern – refusing to acknowledge the divinity of the emperor was perceived as a challenge to the secular authorities and a threat to civil order. Once again, this underlines the essentially pragmatic nature of Roman 'toleration'.

Throughout the second and third centuries AD the official Roman policy veered between toleration and persecution. The crucial turning point came with the Edict of Toleration issued on his deathbed by Galerius in 311 which granted Christians the indulgence of 'allowing Christians the right to exist again and to set up their places of worship; provided always that they do not offend against public order'.[53] This amounted to an acceptance that the great wave of persecutions launched under Diocletian (284–305), and which he had continued, had failed.

This was followed by the accession to the throne of the Western Empire of Constantine following his victory in the battle of the Milvian Bridge, which he ascribed to the intervention of the Christian God. In AD 313 he promulgated the Edict of Milan which provided that:

All who choose [the Christian] religion are to be allowed to continue therein, without let or hindrance and are not in any way to be molested . . . At the same time all others are to be accorded the free and unrestricted practices of their religions; for it accords with the good order of the realm and the peacefulness of our times that each should have the freedom to worship God after his own choice; and we do not intend to detract from the honour due to any religion or its followers.[54]

There would be little point in examining the relations between the Roman authorities and the early Christians if it was not for the ultimate triumph of Christianity in becoming the official religion of the Roman Empire,[55] which was finally achieved under the emperor Theodosius I

---

[53] Lactantius, *De mort. pers.* XLVIII, quoted from H. Bettenson (ed.), *Documents of the Christian Church*, 2nd edn, (Oxford University Press, 1963), p. 15. The Edict also put Christians under a duty to pray for the emperor and Empire.

[54] Bettenson, *Documents*, pp. 15–16. The Edict of Milan was made jointly by Constantine and Licinius, the emperor in the East. Licinius was a pagan and Constantine ultimately used his continued harassment of Christians as an excuse to depose him and assume the position of sole emperor in AD 324.

[55] The nature of Constantine's Christianity is a matter of debate. He probably saw Christianity as representing the most potent manifestation of a universal religion that

(378–395). It would, however, be a mistake to see the influence as working in only one direction: the Roman Empire impacted upon the Church as much as the Church impacted upon the Empire.

One of the reasons why the early Church felt aggrieved by the charges made against it during times of persecution was that not only did it not purport to have any pretensions to temporal political authority, but it tended towards the renunciation of the very means by which such authority might have been achieved, or maintained.[56] Certainly, the Church initially believed that the last days were approaching and the second coming of Christ would establish his kingdom, but this eschatological vision, whilst undoubtedly disconcerting for the authorities if they chose to accept it, had few practical consequences for anyone but the believers themselves. Of greater concern to the authorities was the attitude of the early Christians to participation in the general life of the community. Christians tended to see themselves as being a 'community within a community'. Naturally, the fear of persecution can be advanced as a reason for this, but the issue went far deeper than this and was associated with a belief that the Christian had to maintain purity in all things.

Again, this might not have been of any particular significance, since the perception of aloofness that this engendered was unlikely to cause harm to anyone but themselves, had it not been for the consequences of this as regards the fulfilment of public service and, in particular, military service. There were strong pacifist tendencies in the early Church. The New Testament does not specifically endorse pacifism, but the teachings of Christ, certainly as reflected in the 'Sermon on the Mount', seem to demand that Christians refrain from the private use of violence.[57] Against this, however, runs the teaching concerning respect for the authority of the State.[58] It has often been asserted that the early Christian Church was pacifist[59] but this is too simplistic an assertion. At the very least it must be

---

was revealed in other gods in other places. His conversion facilitated the acceptance of Christianity into the syncretist polytheism of the late Roman world, which it then proceeded to destroy. Indeed, the militant universalism of Christianity was the natural religious counterpart of the Empire.

[56] 'For what wars should we not be fit, not eager, even with unequal forces, we who so willingly yield ourselves to the sword, if in our religion it were not counted better to be slain than to slay?' Tertullian, *Apology*, XXXVII.

[57] Matthew, 5–7, particularly 5 vv. 38–39; 43–45.

[58] Most famously exemplified by Mark 12 v. 17: 'Pay Caesar what is due to Caesar, and pay God what is due to God.' See also Romans 13 vv. 1–6. Although the extent to which this is based in the teachings of Christ as opposed to the writings of Paul is now a matter of some controversy, at the time there was no questioning their authority.

[59] E.g. C. J. Cadoux, *The Early Christian Attitude to War* (London: Headly Bros, 1919);

understood that there was a distinction drawn between the legitimacy of warfare waged by the Empire and the participation in such warfare by individual Christians.

Tertullian and Origen (185–254) both argued that Christians could not serve in the Roman army but whether this was because, as Christians, the use of violence in the public service was forbidden them or whether it was because all soldiers had to take an oath of allegiance to the emperor in terms that were incompatible with Christian belief is a matter of debate.[60] What is evident, however, is that neither claimed war *as such* was wrong. Certainly, the consequences of warfare might be regretted, but the necessity of war was accepted.[61] Christian participation, however, was not.

It was Origen who faced the task of addressing the question, posed by Celsus, of whether the Christian was simply attempting to avoid his public duty in refusing to fight to preserve the Empire that they purported to respect. Like Tertullian before him, Origen claimed that the Christians defended the Empire by prayer and the godly lives that they led. Further, he argued that many religions forbade priests to bear arms, so that they would remain pure and untainted, and he argued that, by analogy, Christians should fight 'as priests and worshippers of God'.[62] The problem, as Celsus had pointed out, would arise if Christians achieved their aim of converting all of the Empire: who would then fight in defence of the Empire? Origen insisted that if *all* men were Christian, then there would be no war at all but, as he realized, that simply avoided the real question, which concerned what would happen to the Roman world if all the Romans became Christian? Origen could only respond by pointing to the power of prayer to protect believers from harm.[63] Until that day arrived there still remained the related problem of when Christians ought to act as 'co-defenders of the State' by means of prayerful intercession. Origen saw this as being done 'on behalf of those who are fighting in a righteous cause, and for a king that reigns righteously'.[64]

S. Windass, *Christianity Versus Violence: a Social and Historical Study of War and Christianity* (London: Steed and Ward, 1964), p. 11.

[60] The former view is taken by Cadoux, and R. H. Bainton, *Classical Attitudes to War and Peace* (London: Hodder & Stoughton, 1961), but is questioned by E. A. Ryan 'The Rejection of Military Service by the Early Christians', *Theological Review*, XIII 1 (1952), p. 1, and J. Helgeland, 'Christians and the Roman Army, AD 173–337', *Church History* 43 (1974), p. 149. See also A. Harnack, *Militia Christi: the Christian Religion and the Military in the First Three Centuries*, (1950), trans. by D. M. Gracie (Philadelphia: Fortress Press, 1981) and the translator's introduction (pp. 9–22), and J. Helgeland, R. J. Daly and J. P. Burns, *Christians and the Military: the Early Experience* (Philadelphia: Fortress Press, 1985).

[61] E.g. Tertullian, *Apology*, XXV.   [62] *Contra Celsum*, VIII, §§73–74.
[63] *Ibid.*, VIII, §§68–70.   [64] *Ibid.*, VIII, §73.

The seeds of a *modus vivendi* can be seen. If the State would respect the teachings of the Church and not expect military service from Christians, then the Church would not condemn out of hand the use of force by State authorities. Of course, non-believers would be urged to abandon their idolatrous practices and accept Christianity, but as long as the practices of the believers were respected, the resort to warfare by the authorities would not be condemned *per se*. Prayerful support, however, was predicated upon the righteousness of the king and the cause. This amounted to little more than a particular manifestation of Origen's general view that the laws of God (which he equated with the laws of nature) must prevail over man-made laws which were impious in the sight of God.[65] He did not, however, examine the instances in which the unrighteousness of the king or cause would result in the withdrawal of the prayerful support. This was left to others – notably Augustine – to address.

In a sense, the Church was a victim of its own success and the pressure for relaxation of its views came from within the Church itself. Even at the time of Tertullian, there were a sizeable number of Christians serving in the army[66] and as Christianity spread numbers increased. Certainly, the issue could not be avoided once, as emperor, Constantine embraced Christianity. How could an officially recognized religion of the Roman Empire seriously maintain an attitude of hostility towards warfare? How could it urge individuals not to engage in warfare when the very fabric of a Christian Empire was at stake? Rather than being merely recognized by the authorities, Christianity was now becoming adopted by them. It became desirable for the Church to respond by accepting that, under certain circumstances, the individual Christian could bear arms on behalf of the Empire. By this time, however, a less ambiguous accommodation between the teachings of the Church and imperial imperatives was emerging. This drew upon the well-established Roman law concept of the 'just war'.

The just war

Eusebius, Bishop of Caesarea, paved the way. He saw the Empire as a manifestation of God's will, a vehicle through which peace and justice would be brought to mankind.[67] Christian believers were to fulfil the

---

[65] *Ibid.*, V, §37.

[66] *Cf.* the story of the 'Thundering Legion', in which the prayers of Christian soldiers in the Twelfth Legion were alleged to have saved Marcus Aurelius from defeat by Germanic tribesmen in AD 173. See Helgeland, Daly and Burns, *Christians and the Military*, chapter 4.

[67] Eusebius considered it no accident that Christ had been born in the early years of the

duties of citizenship – including serving in the army – whilst the clergy remained set aside for the prayerful support of the State. In the writings of Ambrose, Bishop of Milan and confident of Theodosius I, the interests of the Church and of the Empire became virtually indistinguishable; heretics within the Christian Church became enemies of the State,[68] and the barbarian enemies of the Empire became enemies of the Church.[69] It is in this convergence of Church/State interests that the seeds of active intolerance to those of other faiths can be found. That Christians should have been hostile to those within their own religious tradition who they perceived as heretical was understandable (though doubtless regrettable). Christian monotheism and intolerance dictated the necessity of attempting the eradication of all other forms of religious observance within the Empire.

A crucial question was whether it was permissible to use force against those of different religious persuasions who lived and worshipped other gods outside of the Roman world. The militant universalism of the Church would seem to suggest that it would be. In fact, it seems as if it was the restraint of the pre-existing Roman notions of the 'just war', which the earlier Christian writers had used to legitimize their compromise with the State, that provided a framework which ultimately restrained the extremist potential of Christian dogma.

The 'just war' tradition was concerned with identifying the circumstances which legitimated resort to arms with foreign powers. Since it was concerned with external relations, not internal affairs, it presented no restrictions upon the use of force to quash sedition within the Empire – and heresy was tantamount to sedition, just as had been the refusal of the early Christians to adhere to the Imperial Cult. The violent suppression of heresy within the Roman world, therefore, need not have been subject to scrutiny under the 'just war' concept. However, since the Church had used the just war as a means of reconciling itself to the use of force in general, it is hardly surprising that it was also used to justify the use of force against both internal and external enemies of the faith.

The Roman 'just war' tradition originated in the *ius fetiale*. The College

---

Roman Empire and that the unity of the Roman world was a necessary preliminary to the establishment of Christianity (see *Ecclesiastical History*, book I, §2.16, §2.23).

[68] Theodosius presided over the triumph of eastern Catholic orthodoxy and the Nicene Creed over western Arianism and took vigorous action against both pagan believers and 'heretics' within the Church.

[69] See F. H. Russell, *The Just War in the Middle Ages* (Cambridge University Press, 1975), pp. 12–15.

of Fetial Magistrates had sacerdotal, diplomatic and judicial functions. This included the responsibility for determining whether a wrong had been committed against the Roman State sufficient to justify hostilities.[70] Although this originally reflected a belief that the fetials were discerning the will of the gods concerning the matter, in its mature form the process had assumed a more formalistic nature.[71] Cicero, for example, considered that 'no war is just unless it is waged after a formal demand for restoration, or unless it has been formally announced and declared beforehand'.[72] The essence of the doctrine was the commission of a wrong. If a wrong was not put to rights, then war would follow as the legally appropriate sanction. It came to be understood, however, that such formalities could only apply between peoples organized into civilized societies. Thus actions against pirates and other brigands were not subject to the *ius fetiale*.[73]

The significance of this for the purposes of an understanding of religious toleration is twofold. First, the simple fact that a people worshipped other gods could not amount to a wrong so as to justify war against them. Indeed, the fetial procedure often included an appeal to the gods of the enemy, that they might observe the wrongdoing of their people and desert them for the Roman cause.[74] Secondly, although barbarians, and others beyond the scope of the *ius fetiale*, might worship other gods, this fact did not of itself render a people *hostes*. Neither principle survived the adoption and adaption of the tradition by Christian writers in the West.[75]

The Roman just war tradition was adopted by Augustine as a means of reconciling the Christian Church with the Roman State. He followed

---

[70] See Phillipson, *The International Law and Custom of Ancient Greece and Rome*, vol. II, pp. 179–192 for an examination of the evolution of justifications in early Roman history, and pp. 329–342 for a description of the fetial proceedings. Also A. Nussbaum, *A Concise History of the Law of Nations* (rev. edn) (New York: Macmillan, 1954), pp. 10–11.

[71] Phillipson, *The International Law*, vol. II, pp. 343–348. But *cf.* G. H. J. Van der Molen, *Alberico Gentili and the Development of International Law*, 2nd edn, (Leyden: A. W. Sijthoff, 1968), pp. 66–68.

[72] *De Officiis*, book I, §36.

[73] Cicero, *De Respublica*, book I, §25. Phillipson, *The International Law*, vol. II, p. 195.

[74] Phillipson, vol. II, p. 341.

[75] It should be noted that thought within the Eastern Empire did not develop along similar lines. Justinian's *Institutes* do not consider the 'just war' and the Eastern Empire evolved into a despotic autocracy under an absolutist emperor under whom the Patriarch of Constantinople exercised only nominal autonomy. The theoretical supremacy of the Roman Church in the East ended with the excommunication of the Patriarch of Constantinople by Pope Leo XI in 1054. See Nussbaum, *A Concise History of the Law of Nations*, pp. 44–49.

Cicero in saying that 'Just wars are usually defined as those which avenge injuries, when the nation or city against which the warlike action is to be directed has neglected either to punish wrongs committed by its own citizens or to restore what has been unjustly taken by it. Further that kind of war is undoubtedly just which God himself ordains.'[76]

Augustine drew on two different traditions: the 'just war' tradition of Roman law and the 'holy war' tradition of Judaism. Although Augustine's presentation of the just war tradition seems to follow Cicero's formulation closely, there is a crucial difference. Cicero suggested that the very consideration of the justness of a war was premised upon the violation, by the enemy, of a pre-existing legal right of the party resorting to war. Augustine was concerned less with rights than with righteousness;[77] he considered that any violation of the moral order justified a State resorting to war irrespective of whether a right of the State had been infringed. The (Roman) State could, therefore, act as the guardian of the moral order, by which was meant the Christian moral order. All the more so could force be used against heretics, not only because they threatened the continuance of that moral order, but also simply because they infringed it.

The real evil was not so much war itself but the evils in man which prompted resort to war. Thus the aim of war was to be the restoration or maintenance of peace. In addition, war should be sanctioned by those in authority. Since all power came from God, participation in a war on the orders of a temporal power invested in its authority by God would ensure protection from such evils.[78] If the ruler had been wrong to wage war, then the ruler might be guilty of an offence, but the soldier would remain innocent if obeying orders.[79] If this were so when the orders came from the ruler appointed by God, then there could be no doubting the justness of the act when it was ordained directly by God. This raised the question of the 'holy war' as found in the Judaic tradition. A holy war was a war initiated by God for the fulfilment of a religious purpose. The Old Testament wars waged by the Israelites to secure for themselves the 'promised land' of Canaan were holy wars, since they were entered into in

---

[76] *Quaestiones in Heptateuchum*, book VI, §10.
[77] Russell, *The Just War in the Middle Ages*, p. 21.
[78] *Contra Faustum*, book XXII, §75. Augustine believed that all temporal authority was God-given, even if the ruler was himself irreligious.
[79] Indeed, the soldier would be wrong not to do so, since 'not even that which is undertaken from human greed can cause any real harm either to the incorruptible God or to any of his holy ones', *ibid*.

order to realize God's promise to his people.[80] Moreover, God himself was present and engaged in the battle on behalf of his people.[81]

The distinctions between the various categories were not well marked in fourth- and fifth-century Christian writing and, when juxtaposed with the Roman just war theory in the context of a Christian Empire under severe military pressure from non-Christian forces, it was not difficult to conclude that religious considerations were a factor in the evaluation of the justness of a war.[82] Thus it was, strictly speaking, unnecessary to distinguish between the 'holy war' and 'just war' approach since both had much the same impact. The just war, at the hands of Augustine, was a war waged against the forces of unrighteousness. Since earthly authority was given by God, any war against the unrighteous became, in one sense, a 'holy war'. The precise modality of its initiation – by man or by God – was of lesser significance.

During the early Middle Ages wars continued to be waged against 'infidels' at the behest of both the Carolingian emperors and successive popes. The establishment of the Holy Roman Empire by Charlemagne was premised upon the desire to construct an empire which would embrace sovereignty over all Christian States. The Empire and the universal Church were, in reality, two aspects of the same concept of empire, each of which had its own head and was a dually lead theocracy, with 'the Pope as the Vicar of God in matters spiritual and the Emperor as his Vicar in things secular'.[83] Inevitably, this led to conflict as pope and emperor each attempted to assert their supremacy over each other.

Whereas the papacy had, at first, urged the emperor to use his secular authority to wage wars which would receive the Church's blessing, later popes, and in particular Gregory VII and Urban II, faced with increasing dissention within the Empire, took it upon themselves to authorize

---

[80] E.g. Deuteronomy 11 vv. 31–32.

[81] E.g. Deuteronomy 9 vv. 1–5; 20 vv. 3–4. Bainton argued that the holy war was fought with the assistance of God (obtained by means of cultic and ritual practices) and that it was to be differentiated from a 'crusade', which was a war fought by man on God's behalf for a divine, rather than a human, cause. Both were to be contrasted with a war entered into for human purposes, and which were subject to the limitations imposed by the just war tradition: Bainton, *Classical Attitudes to War and Peace*, pp. 44–45. For criticism of this distinction, see D. Little, ' "Holy War" Appeals and Western Christianity. A Reconsideration of Bainton's Approach', in J. K. Kelsay and J. T. Johnson (eds.), *Just War and Jihad: Historical and Theoretical Perspectives on War and Peace in Western and Islamic Traditions* (Westport, CT: Greenwood Press, 1991), pp. 123–135.

[82] See Little, ' "Holy War" ', p. 135.   [83] Van der Molen, *Alberico Gentili*, p. 3.

military action.[84] This tendency reached its logical culmination in the preaching of the Crusades against the Saracens, launched with the intention of reclaiming the Holy Land for Christendom.

Central to the preaching of the first Crusade in 1096 was the argument that it was not a sin to kill in a war waged on the authority of the Church against non-Christian powers.[85] Nevertheless, whilst the Crusades could be understood as justified within the 'holy war' tradition, violence between the Christian kingdoms of Christendom itself could not be convincingly justified on the ground that they had been ordained by God. This ultimately led to a reappraisal of Augustine's legacy, and a renewal of interest in the 'just war' strand of his thinking that had been marginalized by the nature of political society during the intervening years.

The revival of the just war tradition

Around 1140 the monk Gratian, who taught at Bologna, produced a compilation of canon law known as the Decretum. Not only did this provide the framework for subsequent consideration of canon law, but it also breathed new life into the just war concept.[86] Gratian believed that there were two fundamental conditions for a just war. First, it had to be sanctioned by an authoritative edict, emanating from a legitimate authority and, secondly, its purpose had to be either to repel an attack or to avenge an injury.[87] In this context, 'authority' meant secular authority and 'injury' meant the infringement of a legal right.[88] Action to defend the Church against heretics and infidels was the prerogative of the Church itself and its authority to do so derived from the 'holy war' rather than the just war tradition.[89]

This reflected the political developments of the time. The Empire had ceased to be a temporal manifestation of Christ's kingdom and Christendom was plagued by wars between Christian kingdoms. The Church

[84] Russell, *The Just War in the Middle Ages*, pp. 27–37; Windass, *Christianity Versus Violence*, pp. 36–48.
[85] Indeed, in doing so, remission would be earned for sins already committed.
[86] See Russell, *The Just War in the Middle Ages*, pp. 55–85.   [87] *Causa* 23, q. 2. c. 2.
[88] Russell, *The Just War in the Middle Ages*, pp. 65–68.
[89] *Ibid.*, p. 84. *Cf.* J. T. Johnson, *Ideology, Reason and the Limitation of War: Religious and Secular Concepts, 1200–1740* (Princeton University Press, 1975), pp. 35–38, who argued that Gratian did not support the idea that wars could be commanded by God and that he considered 'holy wars' to be wars waged on the authority of the Church to redress wrongs committed against it.

itself aspired to temporal authority[90] and, in this capacity, was competent to declare a 'just war' whilst retaining its residual authority to declare a 'holy war'.[91] When the temporal authority of the papacy waned, this residual authority remained. Although the general trend amongst those who wrote commentaries upon Gratian's Decretum (the Decretists, or Glossators) and of those who studied subsequent compilations of canon law (the Decretalists) was to continue to include reasons of religion as factors which could in themselves generate a just war,[92] they tended to do so in the context of wars waged by the Church against non-Christian powers, rather than in the context of wars waged between Christian powers. Hostiensis, for example, argued that wars within Christendom were not 'wars' at all but were 'civil wars'. These were *bellum judicale*, that is, wars waged by higher authorities against rebellious subjects and therefore to be considered just. War itself, *bellum romanum*, was reserved for unbelievers and, once again, unimpeachable.[93]

It was, however, Thomas Aquinas (1225–1274) who provided the framework within which future developments were to take place. Basing himself upon the writings of Augustine, he concluded that a just war required 'right authority', a 'just cause' and a 'right intent,'[94] and ensured that the subsequent consideration of these concepts would be rooted in the context of Christian moral theology and, indeed, that much of what is now accepted as the subject-matter of international law be considered in order to determine whether it furnished a 'just cause'

[90] The origin of the temporal authority of the papacy dates from the emancipation of central Italy from Byzantine rule in the seventh century AD. See T. F. X. Noble, *The Republic of St Peter: the Birth of the Papal State 680–825* (Philadelphia: University of Pennsylvania Press, 1984).

[91] The papacy ultimately resorted to declaring crusades against its Christian political opponents during the thirteenth and fourteenth centuries. There was, however, no hard and fast division between 'just' and 'holy' wars, and although wrongs against the temporal authority of the State were alleged, these were usually transformed into offences against the Church which would justify a crusade 'in defence of the faith'. See N. Housley, *The Italian Crusades: the Papal–Angevin Alliance and the Crusades against Christian Lay-powers, 1254–1343* (Oxford: Clarendon Press, 1982), chapter 2.

[92] Paradoxically, it was at the very time when the unity of the Empire was dissolving that the idea of its being united under the spiritual authority of the pope and the temporal authority of the emperor was advanced by the Decretalists. See J. D. Tooke, *The Just War in Aquinas and Grotius* (London: SPCK, 1965), p. 15.

[93] See Van der Molen, *Alberico Gentili*, p. 74. This distinction resonates with the distinctions between internal and international armed conflict during the twentieth century. *Cf.* also the condemnation by the Third Lateran Council (1179) of piracy committed against Christians, but not against others (see Nussbaum, *A Concise History of the Law of Nations*, pp. 31–32).

[94] *Summa Theologica*, Part II, q. 40.

for war.[95] Beyond this, his general contribution was relatively unhelpful because it paid little heed to the underlying realities of the political circumstances of the time and did little to elaborate upon the meaning of the various elements he had identified.[96] Nevertheless, in underlining the significance of the source of authority, he foreshadowed, and to an extent facilitated, the emergence of the sovereign competence of the State.

The nature of political society was in reality very different from that which underpinned much Canonist and Scholastic writing.[97] The sovereign authority of the emperor was a pious fiction. Although in theory all rulers derived their authority from the emperor, the reality was that Christendom was composed of a large number of autonomous powers which pursued their own policies. The warring of princes could not be explained in terms of maintaining the peace and seeking redress for wrongs. The marriage between Christianity and the Roman just war tradition had come about because Christianity had to come to terms with the necessity of war in order to preserve the Roman Empire. Once the Empire had ceased to exist as a single political unit, the focus of attention shifted away from the preservation of a Christian State and moved towards assessing the legitimacy of the use of war between Christian powers.

A just war concept derived from Christian moral theology could not accept the possibility that both sides in a conflict were 'just', since the will of God was not divisible. This was of practical significance, since those engaged in a 'just war' were permitted a greater freedom of action, as regarded both the conduct of the war and the 'gains of war'.[98] Although various writers proffered a variety of solutions to these problems, either by arguing in favour of a war being 'just' on both sides, or by allowing justness to be assumed in doubtful cases on the basis of 'probable opinions', the underlying tensions could not be fully dealt with until a juristic concept based upon authority, rather than cause, became accepted as the norm.[99]

---

[95] Nussbaum, *A Concise History of the Law of Nations*, p. 37.

[96] This might, however, have been deliberate. See Tooke, *The Just War in Aquinas and Grotius*, pp. 28 and 170.

[97] J. Von Elbe, 'The Evolution of the Concept of the Just War in International Law', *AJIL* 33 (1939), 665 at p. 670.

[98] See M. H. Keen, *The Laws of War in the Late Middle Ages* (London: Routledge & Kegan Paul, 1965), pp. 137–185.

[99] Even this was not entirely satisfactory. Ayala, for example, who accepted that a war could be just on both sides, argued that the revolt of the Netherlands against Spanish rule was not governed by the laws of war, since it was tantamount to heresy or

Even in the context of wars waged against infidels outside of Christendom, however, distinctions came to be drawn between wars fought
solely on account of unbelief and wars fought against them on the basis
of violence inflicted by them upon the Church or upon believers. Admittedly, the line between the two categories was, at first, barely discernible,
since the very fact of being an unbeliever was considered by some to be so
wicked as to amount to an act of violence against the Church.[100]

Huguccio, a Decretist, considered the Crusades against the Saracens
justified because the Saracens were violating the Church's rights by
occupying the 'Holy Land'. By implication, however, he accepted that there
could be no justification for waging war against unbelievers unless the
Church had a legal claim to title over the territory in question,[101] and this
view was later adopted by the Decretalist Hostiensis and acted upon by
Pope Innocent IV.[102] Although they considered wars of conversion to be
impermissible,[103] they believed that the Church could act against those
who violated its rights. Although these rights included spiritual authority
both within and beyond Christendom, and over Christian and Infidel alike,
the Church tended to rely either on the illegal occupation of its territories
or upon acts of violence committed against Christian pilgrims (over whom
the Church claimed a personal jurisdiction), rather than the advancement
of the faith, as the justification for its crusades against infidels.[104]

Moreover, the Church itself ultimately ceased to provide a focus for
unity. Indeed, with the advent of the Reformation and the establishment
of the Protestant Churches the very unity of the Church was itself
destroyed. The final collapse of imperial authority meant that there no

parricide. See G. I. A. D. Draper, 'Grotius' Place in the Development of Legal Ideas
About War', in H. Bull, B. Kingsbury and A. Roberts (eds.), Hugo Grotius and International
Relations (Oxford: Clarendon Press, 1990), p. 189. This finds a modern parallel in the
debate surrounding the applicability of the Geneva Conventions of 1949 to cases of
civil wars and wars of national liberation, for which see H. A. Wilson, International Law
and the Use of Force by National Liberation Movements (Oxford: Clarendon Press, 1988),
pp. 34–52, 149–180.

[100] See Russell, The Just War in the Middle Ages, pp. 112–113.

[101] Russell concludes that Huguccio 'looked towards a limited toleration of unbelievers
and infidel dominion that pointed toward the equality of sovereign states which
underlies modern international law' (ibid., pp. 122–123).

[102] Ibid., pp. 199–201; J. Muldoon, Popes, Lawyers and Infidels: the Church and the non-Christian
World 1250–1550 (Philadelphia: University of Pennsylvania Press, 1979), chapter 2.

[103] Heresy within Christendom was, of course, another matter, and both considered the
Church competent to declare a crusade against heretics in order to defend the faith.

[104] Johnson, Ideology, Reason and the Limitation of War, p. 51. Christendom was taken to
include the Holy Land which was believed to have been unjustly taken from Christian
control. The crusades against the Moors in Spain were also justifiable on this basis.

longer was a single empire within which the faithful could live and which needed defending from pagan forces: the Reformation meant that there was no common faith to be defended. The concept of a just war being initiated upon the ultimate authority of the pope or emperor on behalf of the faith within Europe was thus finally rendered untenable. Although religious zealots would continue to argue the case for 'holy wars' against the enemies of their faiths,[105] the embryonic law of the emerging State system turned to a secularized just war concept derived from natural law thinking and which expunged religious differences from the catalogue of causes justifying war, and it is in these writings that the origins of modern international law are found.

Writing at the end of the fourteenth century, John de Legnano thought that men were not to be 'compelled to the faith' and 'jurisdiction may be delegated to the infidel over those who are converted to the faith, provided it do not burden them too heavily'. Nevertheless, 'the Pope, as a matter of law, has jurisdiction over infidels, though not as a matter of fact'. The key question was whether the pope had the right to assert his jurisdiction. The Holy Land was 'consecrated by the birth of Christ' and was, in addition, the lawful property of the Roman Empire, having been wrongfully seized by infidels. Thus 'the Pope may recover it by reason of the principality which he holds'. Elsewhere the situation was very different: 'in other lands which are not consecrated, and where neither the Empire nor the Church had jurisdiction, the Pope may in fact command that they do not molest their Christian subjects. Otherwise he may by a judgment deprive them of their jurisdiction.'[106]

The distinction that John de Legnano drew was between spiritual and temporal jurisdiction. Although the pope had, as a matter of (natural) law, a general and universal spiritual jurisdiction, it could only be exercised in those lands which were factually under the territorial jurisdiction of Christian princes (that is, those rulers who accepted the spiritual authority of the Roman Church[107]) or lands over which the pope was entitled to exercise territorial jurisdiction. Spiritual jurisdiction did not give a right to territorial jurisdiction. In addition, however, the pope had a particular 'protective' jurisdiction, which permitted the exercise of a punitive jurisdiction over anyone who interfered with his Christian flock.[108]

---

[105] For a consideration of English 'holy war' thinking in the sixteenth and seventeenth centuries see Johnson, chapter 2.
[106] John de Legnano, *De Bello*, chapter XII (p. 232).   [107] *Ibid.*, chapter XIII (p. 233).
[108] This is a somewhat restrictive reading. Legnano concludes by observing that he has

Later writers pared the jurisdictional capacities of the papacy even further and, at the same time, laid the foundations for the emergence of the sovereign State as the sole agency competent to declare a just war. This process reached its culmination in the writings of Franciscus de Victoria (1492–1546). The Spanish writers were generally hostile to claims of papal supremacy in temporal affairs, and tended to lay stress upon the sovereignty of the State.[109] This desire to restrict the scope of papal authority permeates *De Indis*, his examination of a number of questions that had arisen in the wake of the Spanish conquest of the New World. First, he considered whether the aborigines were true owners of the lands they occupied and, having concluded that they were,[110] proceeded to consider the legitimacy of justifications advanced for the Spanish conquest. Victoria rejected the idea that the emperor was 'Lord of the World', and as such was entitled to take possession of the territories.[111] He also rejected the argument that the pope exercised universal temporal authority and, as such, could grant the New World to Spain. He believed that: 'The Pope has temporal authority only as far as it is in subservience to matters spiritual, that is, as far as is necessary for the administration of spiritual affairs.' Since the pope did not exercise spiritual power over the Indians, there could be no temporal power either.[112]

Victoria considered at some length the question of whether the conquest was justified on the grounds that the Indians had refused to accept the Christian faith when it had been preached to them. He accepted that the Indians were bound to listen to the preaching of the faith, and that they would commit a mortal sin if they refused to accept it, if it were presented 'not once only and perfunctorily, but diligently and zealously', but he did not believe that such a refusal justified making war.[113] Moreover, he asserted that 'Christian Princes cannot, even by the authorization of the Pope, restrain the Indians from sins against the law of nature or punish them because of their sins', for 'it would be a strange

demonstrated the justice of a war declared by the Church against infidels. This has been taken by some to mean that the pope was always able to declare such a war (e.g. Von Elbe, 'The Evolution of the Concept of the Just War', p. 665 at p. 672).
Alternatively, it could mean that the justice of the wars which, at the time, were likely to be waged against infidels (i. e. in the Holy Land or against non-Christian groups within Europe) was proven beyond doubt.
[109] See Von Elbe, *ibid.*, p. 674.   [110] *De Indis*, Section I, §24.
[111] *Ibid.*, Section II §§1–2. Interestingly, Victoria asserts that even those who argued in favour of the emperor's 'Lordship of the World' believed that this invested him with rights of universal jurisdiction, as opposed to a right of ownership.
[112] *Ibid.*, §§5–6.   [113] *Ibid.*, §§7–15.

thing that the Pope, who cannot make law for unbelievers, can yet sit in judgment and visit punishment upon them'.[114] Thus when, in *De Iure Belli*, Victoria considered the causes of a just war, his first proposition was 'Difference of Religion is not a cause of just war'.[115]

Nevertheless, in Section III of *De Indis*, when setting out those titles which he considered to be lawful, Victoria made it clear that he endorsed the view that Christians had a right to preach the Gospel to unbelievers and, in an exercise of his spiritual authority, the pope could vest what might be called 'exclusive preaching rights' to Spaniards over a given area.[116] Should there be resistance, 'the Spaniards ... may preach it despite their unwillingness and devote themselves to the conversion of the people in question, and if need be they may then accept or even make war, until they succeed in obtaining facilities and safety for preaching the gospel'.[117] Furthermore, converts could be protected, by means of war if necessary, from attempts to re-convert them to their previous religion and, should a large number become converted, then the pope might place a Christian ruler over them.[118]

Of particular interest, more for what it symbolizes than for what it says, is his opinion that if the native rulers enforced human sacrifices or indulged in cannibalism then 'without the Pope's authority the Spaniards can stop all such nefarious usage and ritual ... being entitled to rescue innocent people from an unjust death'. He considered that a refusal to stop such practices was 'a good ground for making war on them and ... for changing their rulers and creating a new sovereignty over them ... punishment can be inflicted for sins against nature'.[119] In this passage, Victoria signals a move away from the medieval idea of a theological just war concept and a move towards a secular concept based upon natural law.[120]

---

[114] *Ibid.*, §16.   [115] *De Iure Belli*, §10.
[116] Moreover, this justified the exclusion of other powers from these regions since not only would this course be 'most conducive to spiritual welfare' but 'inasmuch as it was the Sovereigns of Spain who were the first to patronize and pay for the navigation of the intermediate ocean ... it is just that this travel should be forbidden to others and that the Spaniards should enjoy alone the fruits of their discovery' (*De Indis*, Section III, §10. See also Muldoon, *Popes, Lawyers and Infidels*, pp. 133–139.)
[117] *De Indis*, Section III, §§9–12.
[118] *Ibid.*, §§13–14. Given that the pope would have already granted ecclesiastical jurisdiction to a particular State, the 'Christian ruler' appointed would inevitably be that State's sovereign, who would be able to appoint his own representative.
[119] *Ibid.*, §15.
[120] Johnson, *Ideology, Reason and the Limitation of War*, pp. 154–170. *Cf.* the similar position taken by Grotius, see below at n. 141.

The essence of Victoria's teaching was that the law of nations (the *ius gentium*) only recognized violations of natural law as justifying recourse to war. Should the missionary endeavours of the Christian princes be thwarted, the justification for war was not the affront to the faith but the violation of the natural right of all people to travel freely in other lands. So, for example, if local rulers harassed converts, they would be putting obstacles in the way of the Indians 'such as their princes have no right to put there' and therefore, 'in favour of those who are oppressed and suffer wrong, the Spaniards can make war'.[121]

Although the just war concept was subject to much analysis, refinement and development by subsequent writers, the idea that adherence to a different faith qualified as just cause was never again seriously entertained. Balthazar Ayala (1548–1584), for example, confirmed that: 'War may not be declared against infidels merely because they are infidels, not even on the authority of emperor or Pope, for their infidel character does not divest them of those rights of ownership which they have under the law universal, and which are given not to the faithful alone but to every reasonable creature'.[122]

Like Victoria, he denied that the pope had any jurisdiction, spiritual or temporal, over unbelievers, except as far as was necessary for the peace and prosperity of the Christian commonwealth,[123] and, once again in common with Victoria, considered that all kings and princes who were able to declare a just war on the basis of their own authority might also declare a just war for the protection of Christians in pagan lands.[124] John de Legnano had limited that right to the pope.

Heresy, however, raised different issues. Following Thomas Aquinas, Ayala believed that, since those who had accepted the Christian faith accepted the authority of the Church over them, 'a just war may be waged on heretics who have abandoned the Christian faith'.[125] Moreover,

---

[121] *De Indis*, Section III, §12. There is, however, no suggestion that missionaries of other faiths should benefit in a similar fashion when travelling in Christian lands. Missionary work was seen as a Christian prerogative. Christ had commissioned the universal proclamation of the Gospel, he had not sanctioned the preaching of other beliefs to Christians.

[122] Ayala, *De Iure et Officiis Bellicis et Disciplina Militari Libri III*, book I, chapter II, §28.

[123] *Ibid.*, §29.

[124] A just war could be waged if infidels 'are found hindering by their blasphemies and false arguments the Christian faith and also the free preaching of the Gospel rule, this being a wrong to Christians, who are entitled to preach the Gospel over the whole world' (*ibid.*, §31). The source of this right, is, however, not dwelt upon.

[125] *Ibid.*, §30. This seems to place the authority to wage war on heretics in the hands of the Church, rather than the secular authority. However, Ayala took the view that

Ayala stressed the importance of the source of authority, and reduced the legal significance of the cause to almost nothing: 'seeing that the right to make war is the prerogative of princes who have no superiors, discussion of the equity of the cause is inappropriate'.[126] Nevertheless, the causes that justified war continued to attract the attention of writers.

The writings of Alberico Gentili (1552–1608), a devout Protestant who had fled his native Italy in order to escape the attention of the Inquisition,[127] represent a crucial point in the development of international law. Gentili lay the foundations for the view of international law as a world system which derived its authority from natural law, which he saw as itself being a part of the divine legacy. His conception was of a body of law which governed a society of nations and which was not in thrall to the theologians.[128]

Gentili was clear that 'holy wars', that is, wars which are ordered by God himself, are just.[129] He was equally clear that wars waged with religion as their sole motive are unjust. This was because a just war could only be waged as a response to a wrong, and: 'since the laws of religion do not properly exist between man and man, therefore no man's rights are violated by a difference in religion, nor is it lawful to make war because of religion . . . Therefore a man cannot complain of being wronged because others differ from him in religion.'[130]

rebellious subjects committed a crime against their sovereign which permitted a response unregulated by the laws of war. As a Spanish nobleman born in Antwerp, he saw rebellion against the sovereign as a form of heresy. Since religious dissent was a form of rebellion there could be no doubting the legitimacy of the response. There was, then, no need to resort to the concept of the 'just war', particularly because this would place some fetters upon the means of action available to the sovereign such as, for example, the principle of keeping good faith. See Nussbaum, *A Concise History of the Law of Nations*, pp. 92–93.

[126] *Ibid.*, §33.

[127] See Van der Molen, *Alberico Gentili*, pp. 40–42. Both Alberico and his father, Matteo, were sentenced to penal servitude in their absence and had their possessions confiscated.

[128] *Ibid.*, pp. 240–241.

[129] *De Iure Belli*, book I, chapter VIII (p. 36). Gentili quotes Augustine and gives as an example the war waged by the Jews against the Canaanites. This had, however, become something of a standard example and Gentili observed that 'we must go to the root of things and consider whether their religious feeling in these instances is correct' (*ibid.*, p. 37).

[130] *Ibid.*, chapter IX (p. 41). On the other hand, Gentili asserts that this does not apply to 'those who, living rather like beasts than like men, are wholly without religious belief: for I should hold that such men, being the common foe of all mankind, as pirates are, ought to be assailed in war and forced to adopt the usages of humanity'.

If Grotius is accorded the title of 'father of international law', then Gentili deserves the title of 'father of religious toleration under international law' – and, indeed, beyond. As a Protestant and (probably) a Calvinist, Gentili was scathing in his denunciation of the papacy but he was also above the intolerance of many of his own theological persuasion.[131] His understanding of the nature of religious belief was that:

Religion is a matter of the mind and of the will, which is always accompanied by freedom . . . Our minds and whatever belongs to our mind are not affected by any external power or potentate, and the soul has no master save God only, who alone can destroy the soul. Do you understand? Yet hear still one more thing. Religion ought to be free. Religion is a kind of marriage of God with man. And so, as liberty of the flesh is resolutely maintained in the other wedlock, so in this one freedom of the spirit is granted.[132]

It was the logic of this belief that took Gentili beyond the position adopted by earlier writers. He thought that a conqueror ought not to impose his religion on a defeated people in preference to their own,[133] even though a different religion might be a cause, and not merely a pretext, for rebellion: 'Seditions are to be checked by other remedies.'[134] All the more did he reject the claim of a sovereign to use force against his own subjects in order to maintain the practice of religion within a State.[135] In an age in which religious dissent within Europe had already destroyed the theory of the universality of the empire and papacy and was threatening to undermine the stability of the emergent States within Europe, the plea for internal tolerance was of greater significance than the reiteration of the by now near orthodox denial of the legitimacy of waging war on infidels.

Gentili argued that 'if truly the profession of a different form of religious belief by their subjects does not harm princes, we are . . . unjust . . . if we persecute those who profess another religion than our own'[136] and that 'violence should not be employed against subjects who have

---

This, however, is coupled with the belief that 'no nation exists which is wholly destitute of religion', *ibid.*

[131] See Van der Molen, *ibid.*, pp. 245–256.   [132] *De Iure Belli*, book I, chapter IX (p. 39).

[133] *Ibid.*, book III, chapter XI, §§558–560 (pp. 341–342). Should the defeated peoples have no religion, however, the matter would be different and 'the victor . . . may most justly compel to change conduct which is contrary to nature', *ibid.*

[134] *Ibid.*, §562 (p. 343). Gentili was harder on schismatics than on both unbelievers and even sects, because schisms were by their very nature divisive since they separated those sharing the same belief from the common body (*ibid.*, §563, p. 344).

[135] Gentili was writing at the time when the principle of *cuius regio, eius religio* was being asserted following the Peace of Augsburg (1555). See below, p. 46.

[136] *De Iure Belli*, book I, chapter X, §69 (p. 43).

embraced another religion than that of their ruler'[137] – but subject to the qualification 'unless the State suffer some harm in consequence'.[138] On the other side of the coin, he also argued that sovereigns also had the right to change their religion and 'it would not be just for subjects to make war upon the sovereign on that account'.[139]

In short, Gentili not only rejected the claim that differences of religion could justify wars between States, he also called for the toleration of religious differences within States. In the turbulent world of the late Reformation and the wars of religion that it spawned, this was more of a plea than an observation. Nevertheless, this marks the beginning of a shift in perspective. The decay of the concept of empire and papacy as forces uniting Christendom is reflected in the separation of temporal and spiritual power. In doing so, Gentili prefigured the emergence of the secularized society of nations.[140]

Although he does not put it in quite such stark terms, the position taken by Grotius (1583–1645) in his seminal work, De Iure Belli ac Pacis Libri Tres, is very similar. Grotius saw the *ius gentium* as being derived from natural law, which he defined as 'a dictate of right reason, which points out that an act, according as it is or is not in conformity with rational nature, has in it a quality of moral baseness or moral necessity; and that, in consequence, such an act is either forbidden or enjoined by the author of nature, God'.[141]

War represented a method of dispute settlement between States which was justified only if there was a just cause. These were self-defence, the recovery of property wrongly taken and punishment of States that had

[137] Gentili pointed out that Jews and Christians were tolerated under Turkish rule, and Turks, Jews and Greeks worshipped in Rome; that Lutherans were tolerated in the German principalities 'belonging to the Austrian family', whilst 'men do not live under a single religion in the . . . free cities of Germany' (*ibid.*, §72, p. 45). The factual background to these assertions is explored in chapter 2.

[138] *Ibid.*, §71 (p. 44). Alongside this qualification, he also observed that 'whether heretics ought to be punished and what men are heretics is another question' and one which is not directly addressed in De Iure Belli.

[139] *Ibid.*, chapter XI, §78 (p. 49).

[140] Gentili remarked, 'War is not waged on account of religion . . . Let the theologians keep silence about a matter which is outside of their province' (*ibid.*, chapter XII, §92, p. 57).

[141] De Iure Belli ac Pacis Libri Tres (IBP), book I, chapter I, §10 s. 1. For criticism of Grotius's conception of natural law see Tooke, *The Just War in Aquinas and Grotius*, pp. 196–200, 207–217. Grotius's attitude to, and use of, religion is examined by M. W. Janis, 'Religion and the Literature of International Law: Some Standard Texts', in M. W. Janis (ed,) *The Influence of Religion on the Development of International Law* (Dordrecht: Martinus Nijhoff, 1991), pp. 61–66.

committed a wrong.[142] Self-defence included pre-emptive action against imminent threats. For Grotius, the outward form was of greater significance than the inner reality in ascertaining the justness of war. Thus, although he pays lip service to the Augustinian requirement of 'right intent', it is all but forgotten. The traditional requirement of 'authority' is satisfied by a legitimate exercise of power by the sovereign power of a State. Although the 'cause' is central to the determination of 'justness', it is to be based upon objective criteria.[143]

Like others before him, Grotius was clear that war could not justly be waged against those who were of other faiths and whose 'wrong' was their unwillingness to accept Christianity, even if proffered as it ought to be. This was because belief required not only the preaching of the word but the secret aid of God. Since God does not lend his aid as reward for works but for reasons known only to God, a failed attempt to convert an unbeliever was as much the work of God as was a successful missionary endeavour.[144]

Grotius extended a similar latitude towards those who 'erred in interpretation of the Divine Law', whether this related to matters which, on the one hand, lay 'outside the [Divine] law' or which appeared to be ambiguous or, on the other, were more serious errors which 'may be easily refuted before impartial judges by sacred authority'.[145] In either case, their misplaced devotion to a pious belief provided no reason to proceed against them. Grotius closed his consideration of this by quoting Plato's observation that 'the punishment of the erring is: to be taught'.[146]

Both heathen and heretic were protected: neither the belief in other gods nor the errant doctrine of a Christian believer provided a just cause for war. The reason for this was that both of these 'offences' were, ultimately, offences against God. Although Grotius did not agree with those who argued that it was impermissible to punish those who had committed crimes against God, his reason for this was that piety was essential for the effective functioning of human society, whether it be the internal working of a State or the wider international community.[147] Rulers could, therefore,

---

[142] *IBP*, book II, chapter I, §2 s. 2.
[143] See Johnson, *Ideology, Reason and the Limitation of War*, pp. 213–214.
[144] *IBP* book II, chapter XX, §48 s. 1.   [145] *Ibid.*, §50 ss.1–2.   [146] *Ibid.*, §50 s. 5.
[147] *Ibid.*, §46. Indeed, he maintained that: 'Religion is of even greater use in that greater society than in that of a single state. For in the latter the place of religion is taken by the laws and the easy execution of the laws; while on the contrary in that larger community the enforcement of laws is very difficult, seeing that it can only be carried out by armed force, and the laws are very few. Besides, these laws themselves receive their validity chiefly from the fear of divine power; and for this reason those who sin

only seek to punish those individuals or States whose beliefs or actions amounted to 'impiety' and this was a very limited class.

Thus Grotius maintained that those who denied the very existence of a god, Christian or otherwise, violated a law of nature,[148] and 'may be restrained in the name of human society, to which they do violence without a defensible reason'.[149] Also to be classed 'with the impious rather than the erring' were those 'who establish with divine honours the worship of evil spirits, whom they know to be such, or of personified vices, or of men whose lives were filled with crimes'.[150] The essence of these forms of impiety was that their wrongfulness was manifest even to those who adopted them, which served to undermine the very concept of religious piety which stood at the threshold of a just society.

This explains why it is permissible to punish 'those who are irreverent and irreligious towards the gods in whom they believe'.[151] This may also explain the single exception to the general acceptance of other religions:

against the law of nations are everywhere said to transgress divine law (*ibid.*, §46 s. 6).
This tends to equate the 'law of nations' with divine law: but it is a form of divine law that is observable in the practice of all nations and religions, rather than the injunctions of the Christian faith itself. See text below. Nussbaum concluded that Grotius's International law, 'whilst inspired by Christian ideas . . . was secular to all intents and purposes' (*A Concise History of the Law of Nations*, p. 109).

[148] He argued that: 'These ideas, that there is a divinity . . . and that he has a care for the affairs of men, are in the highest degree universal, and are absolutely necessary to the establishment of religion, whether it be true or false' (*IBP*, book II, chapter XX, §46 s. 1). In this, he followed Gentili, who wrote (*De Iure Belli*, book I, chapter IX, §65 (p. 41): 'Religion is a part of the law of nature and therefore that law will not protect those who have no share in it. And yet I will add this: that no nation exists which is wholly destitute of religion . . . Those are not without the pale of this law of nature who are victims of human liability to error and who, although led by the desire to do what is good, adopt a religion that is evil.'

[149] *IBP*, book II, chapter XX, §46 s. 4. There remains the question of when a ruler might take such action against an impious member of the international society. It seems to be enough that such impiety existed. In current terminology, it would appear to be an obligation *erga omnes*: writing in this context, Grotius remarked that 'kings, in addition to the particular care of their own state, are also burdened with a general responsibility for human society' (*ibid.*, §44 s. 1). This is a particular example of a general theme in his writing. He had earlier maintained that 'kings . . . have the right of demanding punishments not only on account of injuries committed against themselves or their subjects but also on account of injuries which do not directly affect them but excessively violate the law of nature or of nations in regards to any persons whatsoever' (*ibid.*, §40). See B. Kingsbury and A. Roberts, 'Introduction: Grotian Thought in International Relations', in Bull, Kingsbury and Roberts (eds.), *Hugo Grotius and International Relations*, pp. 38–42.

[150] *Ibid.*, §47 s. 4.

[151] *Ibid.*, §51 s. 1. This section is headed 'But war may justly be waged against those who show impiety towards the gods they believe in'. 'Impiety' here must mean acting in a

those whose worship of their god involved shedding innocent blood – human sacrifice – were also to be regarded as impious.[152]

At this level,[153] it was, then, the concept rather than the content of religious belief that lay at the heart of Grotius's thinking on this question. However, Grotius also claimed that it was just to wage war on those who treated Christians with cruelty solely on account of their religion. This included the punishment of those that taught or professed their beliefs. This was not because such acts were against divine law, but because they were 'against the dictates of reason itself'.[154] That there was nothing in Christianity which was other than beneficial to society was, according to Grotius, a matter of observable fact, 'and those not of the faith are obliged to recognize them'.[155]

It cannot be assumed that Grotius would have said the same of other beliefs and it may be doubted whether he could have accepted the justness of a war waged by non-Christians against Christians who had acted with similar 'cruelty' towards them.[156] Indeed, he claimed that there was a duty of Christian States to protect themselves against the enemies of Christianity. Whilst it might be true that Grotius advocated

fashion which the believer knows to be wrong, or else the section becomes tautologous.

[152] *Ibid.*, §47 s. 5.

[153] Of course, this only relates to the justness of punishment meted out to wrongdoers. This does not mean that a higher standard of conduct could not be expected of Christian believers than was provided for in the *ius gentium*. For example, when considering the *temperamenta belli*, Grotius distinguished between the *ius gentium* and 'charity', the latter being, essentially, a Christian gloss upon the rather minimalist rules embraced by the *ius gentium* and only applicable between Christian combatants. Whereas natural law formed the basis of the *ius gentium*, divine revelation formed the basis of charity. Such acts might be incumbent upon the true believer, but the failure to 'go the extra mile' was not a violation of the *ius gentium*. Similarly, although captives were not to be enslaved in wars between Christians, enslavement of captives was not contrary to the *ius gentium* – even though a similar rule applied between muslim combatants. These rules were only applicable *inter se* (*IBP*, book III, chapter VII; Kingsbury and Roberts, 'Grotian Thought in International Relations', in Bull, Kingsbury and Roberts, *Hugo Grotius and International Relations*, pp. 47–48).

[154] *IBP*, book II, chapter XX, §49 s. 1.   [155] *Ibid.*

[156] There does seem, therefore, to be a distinction here between the right of non-christian believers to worship their gods and their ability to seek to convey their beliefs to others (or, at least, to Christians). This is difficult to reconcile with the concept of 'piety'. If holding non-Christian beliefs does not threaten the fabric of international society because it nevertheless evidences a respect for religion, piety is preserved, no matter what religion is adhered to. There is, then, no reason to differentiate between religions. However, whilst Grotius believed that evidencing respect for any religion was of value, he does not accept that all religions are of equal value. In short, whilst Christianity is best, some religion is better than none.

'peaceful co-existence'[157] with non-believers, this did not imply equality, or even toleration.[158]

In fact, Grotius, in a chapter entitled 'On undertaking War on Behalf of Others', later advanced the more general proposition that if a ruler 'should inflict upon his subjects such treatment as no one is warranted in inflicting, the exercise of the right vested in human society is not precluded'.[159] This amounts to a form of 'humanitarian intervention' that would easily subsume these particular manifestations of what amounted to an 'obvious wrong'.[160] This both contrasts with and, perhaps, complements, his earlier discussion of the position of the individual who is subject to a tyrannical sovereign. Though not wishing to condemn those who did resist unwarranted impositions, Grotius thought that 'resistance cannot rightly be made to those who hold sovereign power'[161] and even when death is threatened to Christians on account of their religion, the most that is permitted to them is that they might flee.[162]

This, then, begins to present the outlines of a pattern which has since become familiar: that the subject is bound to abide by the laws of his sovereign, but that the sovereign may be subject to limitations which flow from the laws of nature, which are derived from reason and which itself is underpinned by the will of the divine. The enjoyment of the rights which flow from the laws of nature to the individual are mediated through the sovereign and violations of that law are violations of the law of nations, which are to be redressed by the society of nations. Although Grotius adds little to what had already been prefigured in the works of Victoria, Gentili and others concerning attitudes to religion among the nations, it is in his treatment of these issues that the structure of modern international law is most easily recognized.

[157] See M. Suganami, 'Grotius and International Equality', in Bull, Kingsbury and Roberts, *Hugo Grotius and International Relations*, p. 221 at p. 235.
[158] But *cf.* Nussbaum, *A Concise History of the Law of Nations*, p. 110, who overstates the extent of Grotius's toleration and seems to overlook the claims of Gentili in this regard.
[159] *IBP*, book II, chapter XXV, §8.
[160] *Ibid*. The parallel is not exact. The modern conception of humanitarian intervention is of a limited action which falls short of war, whereas for Grotius such acts against common humanity provided a just cause for war. See R. J. Vincent, 'Grotius, Human Rights and Intervention', in Bull, Kingsbury and Roberts, *Hugo Grotius and International Relations*, pp. 241–248.
[161] *IBP*, book I, chapter IV, §7 s. 15.
[162] *Ibid.*, s. 8. Even the right to flee was restricted 'to those, at any rate, whom the necessary discharge of duty does not bind to a particular place.'

2   From Augsburg to Paris

The previous chapter has charted the broad outlines of the path which led towards the emergence of the secularized society of States which has characterized international relations since the mid-seventeenth century. Whereas the influence of the Judaeo-Christian tradition played a dominant role in the shaping of this system, that system, once established, paid less and less heed to its religious origins. It has been seen that the 'just war' concept itself first grew from Christian roots but then grew away from Christianity and became a vehicle of the *ius gentium*. With Victoria, Gentili and Grotius, the freedom of peoples to adhere to religions other than Christianity was recognized, albeit subject to a series of caveats which demonstrate a less than perfect adherence to principles of tolerance and equality.

It has now become a commonplace to fix the date of the Treaties of Westphalia (1648) as a milestone in the evolution of the international system. Whether this be true or not,[1] they are of particular significance in the context of religious freedom since they paralleled these doctrinal

---

[1] For an overview of the extensive literature surrounding this debate see A. Cassese, *International Law in a Divided World* (Oxford: Clarendon Press, 1986),pp. 37–38. Of particular interest in the current context is the argument of R. Ago that the origins of the modern international system date back to the emergence of the three discrete empires of Charlemagne, of Byzantium and of the Islamic world – each following a different religion and interacting with each other (see 'Pluralism and the Origins of the International Community', *IYIL* 3 (1978), 3; see also 'The First International Communities in the Mediterranean World', *BYIL* 53 (1982), 213 for a consideration of earlier forms of international law). For M. Zimmermann, the crucial date is the emergence of a society of Christian States (see 'La Crise de l'organization international à la fin du moyen âge', *HR* 44 (1933–II), 315, 352). Rather than marking a beginning, these are best seen as phases in the evolution of the system, as, indeed, are the Treaties of Westphalia themselves. In any case, the importance of religion in the formation of that system is well evidenced by the debate.

developments by recognizing the Protestant (Lutheran and Calvinist) faiths at an international level and placing the States party to them under an obligation to respect the religious beliefs of those subject to their jurisdiction.[2]

It is Richard Zouche who is credited with having coined the phrase 'ius inter gentes'.[3] This marks the shift that was taking place from the inchoate concept of a society of nations in which all sovereigns derived both rights and duties under the laws of nature to the concept of a society of States in which rights and duties are owed to each other. From here, it is a comparatively small step to the proposition that the source of these rights and duties comes not from the 'law of nature' at all, but from the reciprocity of obligations accepted by the States themselves.

This reflects the influence of the thinkers of the Enlightenment, whose reaction to the chaos caused by the Thirty Years War and the war of the Spanish Succession was to question the theological, moral and above all political presuppositions upon which the late medieval world had been based and which had been dismantled by the struggles induced by the Reformation. Whereas the authority of the sovereign had previously been associated with divine grant, albeit mediated through the pope or emperor, the source of authority became associated with the will of the people. If sovereignty resided within the State, then the only source of obligation that could fetter the State was the State itself.

Thus the concept of legal positivism entered into international law during this formative period,[4] and remains the dominant force within contemporary international practice – if not always in contemporary legal theory. Consequently, the path of subsequent development did not lie in doctrinal writing concerning the nature of the international system and of international law, for which religion and religious issues were no longer seen as having any direct relevance. The focus of attention shifted away from determining the extent to which State authority and activity was justified by religious doctrine and moved towards the degree to which individual religious liberty was to be enjoyed within the State.

---

[2] A. Nussbaum, *A Concise History of the Law of Nations*, rev. edn, (New York: Macmillan, 1954), p. 116. The struggle for the realization of religious liberty within States is, of course, still in progress and it is beyond the scope of this work to chart the degree to which States both did and do respect these obligations.

[3] See R. Zouche, *Iuris et Iudicii Fecialis, sive Iuris inter Gentes, et Quaestionum de Eodem Explicatio* (first published 1650) part I, s. 1(1): 'the law which is observed in common between princes or peoples of different nations . . . I choose to describe as "Ius Inter Gentes" or law between nations'.

[4] See Nussbaum, *A Concise History of the Law of Nations*, pp. 232–236.

Religion no longer provided a fetter upon the State but became a crucible within which to test the limits of the State's respect of individual freedom against the competing demands which the State might legitimately make upon its citizens as a part of the social contract.[5]

One result of this was that the question of individual religious liberty became 'domesticated' and has only become a matter of concern for the international lawyer in recent years when, under the guise of human rights, international law has (re)penetrated into the domestic jurisdiction of States. On the other hand, religious questions have never been entirely excluded from international concern and have loomed large in the treaty practice of States. Indeed, the contemporary international legal concern for human rights can be traced back through the treaty practice of States and this 'transmission' will be examined in the remainder of this and subsequent chapters of this work. The essential point is, however, that this State practice was not in any sense dictated by a belief that religious freedom was required by any imperative other than the religious or political convictions of the States concerned.

Nevertheless, it is the practice of States which must be examined in order to continue the examination of the development of religious freedom under the law of nations and this practice is best considered by an examination of their treaty relations. This in itself raises a problem which greatly concerned the writers of the fifteenth and sixteenth centuries and which assumed a critical importance: was it possible for Christian sovereigns to enter into binding agreements with non-Christian powers? The significance of this question is that, following the Peace of Westphalia, the most significant developments related not to the treaty practice between Christian powers but to the treaties entered into with the Ottoman Empire.

Treaties between Christian and non-Christian powers were hardly novel. In the East, the Byzantine emperors frequently entered into treaty relations with their Muslim neighbours. Even if these treaties were not always honoured, the religious beliefs of those with whom the treaty had been made were not a ground for invalidity. Although early Western writers

---

[5] This, perhaps, is best exemplified in the writings of Vattel, *The Law of Nations or the Principles of Natural Law* (1758), book I, chapter XII (and in particular §§127–131 and 134–135). See also M. W. Janis, 'Religion and the Literature of International Law', in M. W. Janis (ed.), *The Influence of Religion on the Development of International Law* (Dordrecht: Martinus Nijhoff, 1991), pp. 66–69, who observes that: 'It was Vattel, much more than Grotius, who can rightly be said to have provided a secularized form of international law' (p. 67).

had taken a very different view, Grotius had no doubt that, according to the law of nature, 'the right to enter into treaties is so common to all men that it does not admit of a distinction arising from religion'.[6]

Broadly speaking, the treaty practice falls into a number of distinct categories. First of all, there are the treaties concluded between the Christian powers which form the basis of the 'public order of Europe', culminating in the Treaties of Westphalia, the basic principles of which (as regards religious freedom) were reflected in subsequent treaties. Secondly, there are arrangements with non-Christian powers which provide for the protection of Christian believers in the Ottoman Empire. Finally, there are treaties which chronicle the withdrawal of the Ottoman power from the bulk of the European mainland. Although conceptually distinct, these categories are not mutually exclusive. Indeed, the third is in many ways an amalgam of the first and second. Nevertheless it is more convenient to examine these developments under two headings, the first dealing with religious issues between the Christian powers and the second examining the interaction of the European powers and the Ottoman Empire.[7]

European 'public order' treaties

The Religious Peace of Augsburg (1555) marked an important point in the evolution of religious liberty within Europe.[8] The Protestant Reformation had taken hold in many of the German territories and the attempts made by the emperors to eradicate the Lutheran 'heresy' proved ineffective. The Peace of Augsburg provided for a settlement which cannot be understood without a basic understanding of the essentially feudal structure of the Empire at that time.[9] In essence, the Empire was made up of a number of

---

[6] *IBP*, book II, chapter XV, §8. Grotius accepted, however, that whether this was also so as a matter of divine law was a matter of debate but he ultimately concluded that: 'In such alliance, wrongfulness is not inherent or universal, but is subject to judgment according to the circumstances', these chiefly being whether the alliance posed a threat to Christianity by unduly increasing the power of the heathen (*ibid.*, §11).

[7] It should be noted, however, that the religious accommodations embodied in the European 'public order treaties' were themselves influenced by the threat posed to Central Europe by the Ottoman Empire in the early sixteenth century. See generally S. Fischer-Galati, *Ottoman Imperialism and German Protestantism: 1521–1555* (Cambridge, MA: Harvard University Press, 1959).

[8] The way had, however, already been paved by the Peace of Nürnberg (1532) and the Treaty of Passau (1552).

[9] For which see *New Cambridge Modern History*, vol. III (1968), pp. 326–328; G. Pagès, *The Thirty Years War* (London: A & C Black, 1970), pp. 26–28.

different classes of territories. The first of these comprised some eighty territories governed directly by their own princes or rulers. Of these some fifty were ecclesiastic territories and about thirty secular. The authority of emperor was 'mediated' through these princely rulers. The remaining territories comprised either the 'free' imperial cities of the Empire or were the private possession of a large number of lesser knights of the Empire, who held their often quite small possession directly from the emperor, whose authority in both these instances was 'immediate'. The emperor himself was elected by the seven 'electors' of the Empire and would, of course, exercise princely (direct) authority in his own personal territories.[10]

The cornerstone of the Peace of Augsburg lay in its recognizing that the Lutheran princes and rulers should enjoy a status equal to that of the Catholic princes within the Empire and, at the same time, permitting the lay princes of the Empire the right to determine which of these two religions was to be adopted within their territories; the principle *cuius regio, eius religio*.[11] This marked the first step towards the abandonment of

---

[10] The electors comprised the three archbishops of the ecclesiastic territories of Cologne, Trier and Mainz, and four 'princely' rulers, the Count Palatine of the Rhine, the Margrave of Brandenburg, the Duke of Saxony and the King of Bohemia. To make matters a little more complicated, the Habsburg Dukes of Austria acquired the throne of Bohemia in 1526 and so were themselves electors to the imperial throne which was an almost exclusive preserve of the Habsburgs. They also held additional titles some of which fell within the Empire and others, including the Crown of Hungary, which did not.

[11] The Peace provided:

15. In order to bring peace into the Holy Empire of the Germanic Nations between the Roman Imperial Majesty and the Electors, Princes and Estates, let neither His Imperial Majesty nor the Electors, Princes, etc., do any violence or harm to any estate of the Empire on account of the Augsburg [Lutheran] Confession, but let them enjoy their religious belief, liturgy and ceremonies as well as their estates and other rights and privileges in peace: and complete religious peace shall be obtained only by Christian means of amity, or under threat of the punishment of the Imperial ban.

16. Likewise the Estates espousing the Augsburg Confession shall let all the Estates and Princes who cling to the old [Roman Catholic] religion live in absolute peace and in the enjoyment of all their estates, rights and privileges.

This was further buttressed by the obligation that: 'No Estate shall try to persuade the subjects of other Estates to abandon their religion nor protect them against their own magistrates' (Article 23). Text in G. Benecke (ed.), *Germany in the Thirty Years War* (London: Edwin Arnold, 1978), p. 8 and see *New Cambridge Modern History*, vol. II (2nd edn, 1990), pp. 193–197, 523–524; Nussbaum, *A Concise History of the Law of Nations*, p. 61.

the theory of empire based upon a common religion.[12] Moreover, the Peace explicitly recognized the freedom of the Lutheran Church to self-government over matters of internal church order.[13] This surrender of ecclesiastical jurisdiction meant that in the free and imperial cities of the Empire, both religions were allowed to co-exist.

Nevertheless, this was a long way from amounting to an acceptance of religious freedom within the Empire. Not only were the cities and the lay princes limited in their choice to either Roman Catholicism or the Lutheran Confession[14] as the single form of religion within their territories, but there were no equivalent rights in the Peace for the ecclesiastical principalities of the Empire, which were governed by what became known as the 'Ecclesiastical Reservation'.

Due to the influence of the Protestant nobility, a number of ecclesiastic territories had been won over to Lutheranism. The Peace provided that these should return to the Catholic faith and, for the future:

where an archbishop, bishop or prelate or any other priest of our old religion shall abandon the same, his archbishopric, bishopric, prelacy and other benefices together with all their incomes and revenues shall be abandoned by him without further objection or delay. The chapter and such as are entitled to it by common law or the custom of the place shall elect a person espousing the old religion who may enter on the possession and enjoyment of all the rights and incomes of the place without any further hindrance and without prejudging any ultimate amicable transaction of religion.[15]

When coupled with the application of the principle of *cuius regio, eius religio*, this had the practical consequence of requiring the nobles and cities within ecclesiastical principalities that had already adopted Lutheranism to renounce their faith. To meet this, the emperor agreed to make a

---

[12] Although this is clear now, the Peace itself was couched in terms of an interim arrangement, to take effect until some 'ultimate transaction of religion' took place. Thus it was premised upon the universality assumptions that it in fact undermined. See *New Cambridge Modern History*, vol. II, p. 195.

[13] Article 20 provided that: 'The ecclesiastical jurisdiction over the Augsburg Confession, dogma, appointment of ministers, church ordinances, and ministries hitherto practised . . . shall from now cease and the Augsburg Confession shall be left to the free and untrammelled enjoyment of their religion, ceremonies, appointment of ministers . . .'

[14] Article 17 of the Peace provided that 'all such as do not belong to the two above named religions shall not be included in the present peace but be totally excluded from it' (Benecke, *Germany in the Thirty Years War*, p. 8). The exclusion of Calvinism further alienated the Swiss Cantons (which had broken away from the Empire in 1499) and antagonized the Netherlands, by this time a possession of the Spanish Habsburgs.

[15] Article 18.

declaration, the *Declaratio Ferdinandea*, which would permit those living in these territories who were already practising Lutherans to continue in their faith.[16]

The very existence of this limited concession to the beliefs of the subjects of the ecclesiastical rulers underlines the point that the Peace was more of a political and territorial than a religious settlement and did not purport to extend a general freedom of religion to their subjects. The only concession to individual conscience made by the Peace was that it granted Catholic or Lutheran subjects the right to move (the *ius emigrandi*) to a territory where the religion of the prince was more congenial.[17]

The control of the Low Countries by Spain proved to be a flashpoint. In the 1560s Calvinism began to take a hold in the northern provinces and this was combined with mounting dissatisfaction with the increasing impact of Spanish interests in their affairs.[18] A rebellion against Spanish rule was at first dampened down by the Duke of Alva, but in 1572 the provinces of Holland and Zeeland recognized William of Orange as their governor and in practice, though not yet in form, established a separate State. William wished to unite all of the Low Countries in opposition to Spain and therefore sought to bridge the gap between Catholic and Protestant within the provinces. This culminated in an agreement between William and the States-General known as the Pacification of Ghent (1576) in which they agreed to assist each other in expelling foreign troops from the Low Countries and in ensuring the supremacy of the States-General in government. In matters of religious adherence, it was specified that individuals were to enjoy freedom of religion and no one was to be persecuted or questioned concerning their religion. Thus the Catholic

---

[16] See *New Cambridge Modern History*, vol. II, p. 195. There was also a very practical concern to be met. The seven electors were split 4–3 in terms of their religious adhesions, the Catholic majority depending upon the three ecclesiastical electors and King of Bohemia, a Catholic Habsburg from whose family the emperor was usually drawn. Any possible introduction of Lutheranism into the prize electoral ecclesiastical territories would have threatened to disrupt the Habsburg succession to the imperial crown. Similar concerns motivated the Catholic (and Spanish Habsburg) response to the Protestant uprising in Bohemia in 1618. See below at p. 50.

[17] Article 24 provided that: 'In case our subjects whether belonging to the old religion or the Augsburg Confession should intend leaving their homes with their wives and children in order to settle in another place, they shall be hindered neither in the sale of their estates after due payment of local taxes nor injured in their honour.' (Benecke, *Germany in the Thirty Years War*, p. 9, and see *New Cambridge Modern History*, vol. III, p. 491.)

[18] See *New Cambridge Modern History*, vol. III, pp. 264–281.

supremacy in the bulk of the provinces and the Calvinist dominance in Holland and Zeeland was both recognized and accommodated.

In 1579 the seven northern provinces of the Netherlands entered into a Treaty of Union (the Union of Utrecht), which was designed to bind them even more closely together in the face of Spanish attempts to undermine the coalition against them. The seven provinces undertook to render each other assistance if, *inter alia*, the Spaniards attempted to 'restore or introduce the Roman Catholic religion by force of arms'.[19] As between themselves, they recognized the right of each province to introduce, without hindrance:

such regulations as they consider proper for the peace and welfare of the provinces, towns and their particular members and for the preservation of all people, either secular or clerical, their properties and rights, provided that in accordance with the Pacification of Ghent each individual enjoys freedom of religion and no one is persecuted or questioned about his religion.[20]

This culminated two years later in the Declaration of Independence from Spain by the States-General of the United Netherlands provinces in which their inability to achieve 'some degree of liberty, particularly relating to religion (which chiefly concerns God and our own conscience)' was given as a reason.[21]

The struggle between Catholic and Protestant, Lutheran and Calvinist was played out within all the countries of Central and Northern Europe, intermingled with and reflected in the rivalries of the various royal houses. The ambitions of the Spanish and Austrian Habsburgs to dominate Europe were met with opposition from both Catholic France, the Calvinist Netherlands and the predominantly Lutheran Protestant princes of Northern Germany. The tensions within the Empire were accentuated by the creation

---

[19] Treaty of the Union of the Seven Northern Provinces of the Netherlands (Utrecht, 1579), Article II. Text in W. H. Grewe, (ed.), *Fontes Historiae Iuris Gentium (FHIG)*, vol. II (Berlin: Walter de Gruyter, 1988), p. 81.

[20] *Ibid.*, Article XIII.

[21] Edict of the States-General, 26 July 1581. Text in Grewe, *FHIG*, p. 90. The preamble to the edict is a powerful statement of the rights of the citizen and the duties of their ruler towards them: 'a prince is constituted by God to be ruler of a people, to defend them from oppression . . . God did not create the people slaves to their prince, to obey his commands, whether right or wrong . . . And when he . . . oppresses them . . . he is no longer their prince, but a tyrant.' Defence against such tyranny was a 'dictate of the law of nature'. Moreover, 'Most of the Provinces receive their prince upon certain conditions, which he swears to maintain, which, if the prince violates, he is no longer sovereign.' Thus although the religious oppression of its subjects was seen as a justification for revolt against the sovereign authority, both natural law and contractarian theories of sovereignty were used to support the claims of the provinces.

of the Protestant Union in 1608, and, by way of response, the Catholic League in 1609. It was, however, the unexpected Protestant seizure of Bohemia, a possession of the Habsburg crown, in 1618 (and the occasion of the famous 'defenestration' of Prague) that finally precipitated the series of conflicts which have since become known as the Thirty Years War, and which are commonly taken as being the last of the wars of religion.

The ebbs and flow of this most violent and destructive of conflicts, which drew in almost all of the principal European powers, are beyond the scope of this work. The ultimately enfeebled imperial forces finally came to terms with their opponents in the Westphalia Treaties concluded at Münster[22] and Osnabrück,[23] Catholic France taking precedence at the former and Lutheran Sweden at the latter. Although motivated, at least in part, by the underlying religious tensions, the principal effect of the treaties was not so much religious as secular in the sense that they recognized the changed relationship of the imperial crown to the constituent territories of the Empire. First and foremost, the German princes, though remaining a part of the Empire, achieved a form of territorial sovereignty that was, for all practical purposes, independence.[24] This expressly included independence in spiritual as well as temporal matters.[25] To that extent, spiritual supremacy was simply an adjunct of their temporal supremacy. What was significant was that the pretence of an Empire held together by, and reflective of, the universal Catholic faith was finally laid to rest.[26]

The Peace of Westphalia, then, represents a key turning point in the struggle for religious liberty within the Empire.[27] But it was the religious freedom of the State rather than of the individual that predominated.

---

[22] Treaty of Peace between France and the Empire, signed at Münster 14 (24) October 1648 (1 CTS 271).

[23] Treaty of Peace between Sweden and the Empire, signed at Osnabrück 14 (24) October 1648 (1 CTS 119).

[24] The form of territorial competence granted was known as 'Landeshoheit' and was defined in Articles 64 and 65 of the Treaty of Münster. Article 65 of the Treaty also obliged them not to use their powers against the emperor or Empire, but this was of little practical significance. See Pagès, *The Thirty Years War*, p. 230.

[25] Likewise, the treaties finally gave recognition to Swiss independence. See Treaty of Münster, Article 63 and Treaty of Osnabrück, Article VI.

[26] The papacy was not represented at the conferences and, in the bull *Zelo Domus Dei*, Pope Innocent X denounced the religious aspects of the treaties as 'null, void, invalid, inequitable, unjust, condemned, reprobated, frivolous, of no force or effect'. Nevertheless, the treaties were honoured by the parties. See Nussbaum, *A Concise History of the Law of Nations*, p. 116.

[27] The resolution of the conflict between the Netherlands and Spain, also concluded at Münster, did not extend religious liberties to the Catholics of those parts of Flanders,

This is made clear by the religion clauses in the treaties. The Treaty concluded at Münster between the two Catholic powers, the Emperor and France, has comparatively little to say concerning religious issues.[28] Both powers were equally affirming of their common faith and this was not a matter that divided them. Theirs was not a religious conflict as such.[29] Nevertheless, the Treaty of Münster directly affirmed the religious settlement provided for in the Treaty of Osnabrück[30] which, as might be expected, was more expansive as regards religious issues.

The Treaty of Osnabrück confirmed the basic framework for religious governance set out in the Peace of Augsburg but expanded and refined it in several important respects. First, it was provided that:

'the same right or advantage . . . grant[ed] to the Catholic States and Subjects, and to those of the Confession of Augsburg, ought also be granted to those who call themselves Reformed . . . But besides these religions no other shall be received or tolerated in the Sacred Roman Empire.'[31]

Brabant and Limburg which passed to the Netherlands, despite the attempts of Spain. See *New Cambridge Modern History*, vol. IV, pp. 381–382.

[28] Article 28, however, ensured freedom of worship for Lutherans in areas of the Palatine remaining under the control of Catholic barons and provided: 'Those of the Confession of *Ausburg*, and particularly the inhabitants of *Oppenheim*, shall be put in possession again of their Churches, and Ecclesiastical Estates, as they were in the year 1624, as also that all others of the said Confession of *Ausburg*, who shall demand it, shall have the free exercise of their religion, as well in public churches at the appointed Hours, as in private in their own houses or in others chosen for this purpose by their Ministers, or by those of their Neighbours, preaching the Word of God.'

[29] Indeed, the position of the Catholic faith is affirmed. Article 77 of the Treaty of Münster provided that in those territories ceded to France:
> The most Christian King [of France] shall, nevertheless, be obliged to preserve in all and every one of these countries the Catholic Religion, as maintained under the Princes of Austria, and to abolish all innovations crept in during the war.

[30] Treaty of Münster, Article 49 provided:
> And for the great Tranquillity of the Empire, in its general assemblies of Peace, a certain Agreement has been made between the Emperor, Princes and States of the Empire, which has been inserted in the Instruments and Treaty of Peace, concluded with the Plenipotentiaries of the Queen and Crown of *Swedeland*, touching the Differences about Ecclesiastical Lands, and the Liberty of the Exercise of Religion; it has been found expedient to confirm and ratify it by this present Treaty, in the same manner as in the abovesaid agreement has been made with the said Crown of *Swedeland*: also with those who call'd *Reformed*, in the same manner as if the words of the abovesaid Instrument were reported here *verbatim*.

A further endorsement of the Treaty of Osnabrück, and its confirmation of the Peace of Augsburg and the *cuius regio, eius religio* principle, came by way of its recognizing the independence of the German Princes and States in ecclesiastical matters. See Treaty of Münster, Article 64 and Pagès, *The Thirty Years War*, p. 233.

[31] Article VII, §§1–2.

Thus the Reformed (Calvinist) Church was now accepted as a permitted confession alongside the Lutheran and Catholic faiths. Although this hardly qualifies as a recognition of freedom of religion *per se*, it was a significant advance. Moreover, the application of the *cuius regio, eius religio* principle was confirmed and refined. Previously it applied only to the lay principalities but it was now made clear that it applied also to the free and imperial cities.[32] At first sight, this might seem a step back, since these cities had been permitted to enjoy a degree of religious co-existence that went beyond that allowed to the princely territories, both ecclesiastic and lay. However, the general application of the principle was modified by the adoption of the year 1624 as the date against which the ownership of religious property and the enjoyment of religious freedoms was to be assessed throughout all the territories of the Empire, mediate and immediate. In effect, the treaty sought to enforce the religious status quo as of that date,[33] and where religions had co-existed the continuation of both was affirmed.[34]

The Treaty of Osnabrück also offered some modest enhancement to the position of the individual when compared with the Peace of Augsburg. Catholics and Lutherans who were not entitled to the public or private exercise of their religion in 1624 because of their being in the territory of a different religious allegiance (in which it was confirmed by the treaty) were to be 'patiently suffered and tolerated, without any hindrance or impediment' in both public and private worship, and were also to be able to send their children to foreign schools or have private tutors,[35] but only

---

[32] Article V, §24.

[33] The choice of the date was a contentious issue. The Peace of Augsburg had adopted 1552, the date of the Treaty of Passau, as the critical date for determining the ownership of church property. During the course of the Thirty Years War, the emperor had attempted to rigorously enforce this by means of the Edict of Restitution (1629). This was modified by the Peace of Prague (1635) which adopted 1627 as the critical date, and which also granted a forty-year moratorium on the return of property taken between that date and the date of the Peace. Article V, §2 of the Treaty of Osnabrück settled on 1 January 1624 as the 'standard date' from which restitution in ecclesiastical affairs was to be applied, this being more advantageous to the Protestants.

[34] Indeed, the treaty contained detailed clauses requiring a balance of religious adherence amongst the magistrates and other public officials in a number of the Free Cities, including Augsburg and Ravensburg (Article V, §§2–9). Moreover, the treaty provided that:

> Neither of the two parties shall abuse the power of the adherents to their religion to destroy the other. Nor shall they prefer directly or indirectly a greater number of their party to the dignities of presidents and Senators, or other public posts (Article V, §5).

[35] Article V, §28.

for a short period. The lord of the territory was entitled to require a subject of the different faith to move elsewhere after a period of five years.[36]

The greatest potential threat to the religious liberty of the subject, however, lay not in the threat of expelling those of a different religious persuasion but in the possibility of the sovereign changing the entire religious practice of the State by exercising the *ius reformandi*. The treaty is, however, rather ambiguous in this regard. Whilst upholding the general concept, it appears to limit its exercise to the reintroduction of the state of affairs as at the critical date.[37]

Special provisions also applied to the Protestant territories which at the same time seem to both assert and deny the *ius reformandi*. The Treaty provided that:

as the differences in religion which are between protestants [i.e., Lutheran and Calvinist] have not yet been terminated . . . it has therefore been agreed betwixt both parties, touching the right of reformation, that if a prince . . . should afterwards go over to the religion of another party . . . it shall not be lawful to change the exercise of religion . . . or to give any trouble or molestation to the religion of others directly or indirectly . . .[38]

Thus the Protestant prince could enjoy the private exercise of his religion but could not change that of his State. Should a community seek to adopt the Protestantism of their lord, however, the prince could grant it, provided that the rights of the established church and its adherents were not affected.[39] It seems to have been beyond the contemplation of the treaty that rulers might seek to change from Protestantism to Catholicism, or vice versa.[40] Nevertheless, the legitimacy of a form of religious debate and diversity within the Protestant States was acknowledged. There was no such acknowledgment concerning the Catholic States, and particularly as regards the personal possessions of the Habsburgs.[41] Certain limited concessions for nominated Protestant princes in Silesia

---

[36] Article V, §30. Those who changed their religion subsequent to the treaty could be required to leave after a period of three years (*ibid.*). On the other hand, the individual had the right – first recognized by the Peace of Augsburg – to emigrate immediately, and without hindrance, if he wished to do so (Treaty of Osnabrück, Article V, §29).

[37] Article V, §32.   [38] Article VII.   [39] *Ibid.*.

[40] This is indirectly supported by the reiteration of the obligation, first undertaken in the Peace of Augsburg, to refrain from attempting to subvert the religious adherence of a neighbouring territory. See Treaty of Osnabrück, Article V, §25.

[41] The treaty records that 'a greater liberty of the exercise of religion has been several times endeavoured to be agreed during the present Negotiation in the [territories] belonging to . . . the house of Austria, and that nevertheless it could not be obtained because of opposition made by the Imperial plenipotentiaries' (Article V, §31).

were granted, but solely 'in consideration of the Mediation of her Royal Majesty of Swedeland and in favour of the interceding states of the Confession of Augsburg'. The right to future peaceful mediation and intercession on behalf of Protestant groups within the Austrian domain was specifically reserved, prefiguring the notion of treatment of believers as a matter of ongoing international concern at the very dawn of the 'modern' era.[42]

Although the actual terms of the Treaties of Westphalia present little more than a number of incremental developments, the spirit of the treaties is very different. Whilst acknowledging and reaffirming the dominance of the State in religious governance, there is a shift away from restrictions upon the freedom of belief and its private practice. Certainly, the subsequent treaty practice between the European powers is very different. Grandiose interstate settlements of religious differences are replaced by comparatively scanty provisions which seek to preserve existing patterns of religious practice in the face of territorial change and which seem to evidence the comparative irrelevance of religious issues in the face of the territorial and dynastic ambitions of the States concerned.[43]

For example, Sweden and Brandenburg entered into a series of treaties aimed at the seizure of parts of Poland, including the Duchy of Prussia. The Calvinist Elector of Brandenburg was to recognize Swedish overlordship and then be invested as Duke. In the Treaties of Königsberg,[44] Marienburg[45] and Labiau[46] of 1656 Brandenburg promised to respect the freedom of worship for Lutherans in the areas which were to pass to it. Subsequently, Brandenburg deserted Sweden and, by Article 16 of the Treaty of Verlau,[47] agreed to respect the freedom of worship for Catholics in the Duchy which Poland had now agreed to cede to Brandenburg

---

[42] This concern was to be expressed both through the Imperial Diet 'and elsewhere'.

[43] Nevertheless, it laid the foundations for the establishment of a treaty–based system of intervention for the protection of religious minorities. See F. X. De Lima, *Intervention in International Law* (The Hague: Uitgeverij Pax, 1971), pp. 104–105.

[44] Article 17 of the Treaty between Sweden and Brandenburg, signed at Königsberg, 7 (17) January 1656 (4 CTS 31).

[45] Secret Article 4 of the Alliance between Sweden and Brandenburg, concluded at Marienburg, 15 (25) June 1656 (4 CTS 101).

[46] Treaty between Sweden and Brandenburg signed at Labiau, 10 (20) November 1656 (4 CTS 185).

[47] Article 16 of the Treaty between Poland and Brandenburg, signed at Velau, 19 September 1657 (4 CTS 435). This was subject to a reversion should the male line of the house of Brandenburg fail. This reversion was given up by Poland at the time of the first partition by the Polish–Prussian Treaty of Warsaw, 18 September 1773 (45 CTS 253), Article III of which expressly revoked Article 16 of the Treaty of Verlau (*inter alia*) on the grounds that it no longer corresponded to the contemporary circumstances.

directly. In fact, Brandenburg had already promised to respect the freedom of religion of the Catholic population in a treaty with France concluded at the time of the original pact with Sweden.[48] The Treaty of Oliva (1660), by which this round of hostilities was concluded, provided for the continuation of the exercise of both the Catholic and Protestant religions, to the extent that they had been enjoyed before the war, in the towns of Prussia.[49] Liberty of conscience and the 'private use of their own religion and worship at home' was also granted to the Catholic population of Livonia, which was ceded by Poland to Sweden.[50]

There are numerous other examples of treaties which, though ostensibly seeking to protect the religious freedom of a particular group, chiefly served to defuse the ever waning potential for doctrinal differences to upset otherwise useful strategic[51] – or, indeed, commercial[52] – arrangements. Nevertheless, there was a general expectation that when territory was ceded by one sovereign to another, subjects would be allowed to

[48] Article 9 of the Treaty between France and Brandenburg, signed at Königsberg, 24 February 1656 (6 CTS 41). Sweden had itself earlier promised to respect the freedom of conscience of the Polish militia – the Quartians – if they transferred their allegiance from Poland to Sweden (Articles between Sweden and the Polish Militia, signed at Cracow, 6 (16) October 1655 (3 CTS 507)).

[49] Article II, §3 of the Treaty between Poland, the Empire and Brandenburg and Sweden, signed at Oliva, 23 April (3 May) 1660 (6 CTS 9).

[50] *Ibid.*, Article IV, §2.

[51] See, for example, the treaties of alliance concluded between France and Sweden, 22 September 1661, Article XX (6 CTS 447), Mecklenburg, 18 December 1663, Article IV (8 CTS 59) and Brandenburg, 6 March, 1664 Article IX (6 CTS 81). France also acted to secure guarantees for the Reformed Church in areas of Savoy (see the Articles accorded by the Duke of Savoy to the Inhabitants of the Valleys of Piedmont, Pignerol 18 (19) August 1655 (3 CTS 482).

[52] Article XIV of the Peace of Westminster (1654) concluded between England and Portugal observed that:

> forasmuch as the rights of commerce and peace would be null and void, if the people of the Republic of England should be disturbed for conscience sake, while they pass to and from the kingdoms and dominions of the King of Portugal, or reside there for the sake of their wares; that commerce may therefore be free and secure by both land and sea, the King of Portugal shall effectively take care and provide that they be not molested by any person, court or tribunal, for any English bibles or other books which they may have in their custody, or make use of: and it shall be free for the people of this Republic to observe and profess their own religion in private houses, together with their families, within any of the dominions of the said King of Portugal . . . and the same to exercise on board their ships and vessels . . .

(Treaty between England and Portugal, signed at Westminster, 10 (20) July 1654: 3 CTS 281; trans. Grewe, *FHIG*, p. 295). See also Article XV of the Treaty of Peace and Alliance between Portugal and the Netherlands, 6 August 1661 (6 CTS 375).

continue in the private exercise of their religious beliefs or be permitted to move elsewhere and this was reflected in many of the principal peace treaties concluded between European powers in the eighteenth century.[53] In some cases, the rights to be respected went beyond the private exercise of belief, and involved the preservation of the status quo, whether it be Catholic or Protestant,[54] tolerant or intolerant. In all this, the principal motivation was the elimination of possible causes of conflict. There is no sustainable evidence of international practice motivated by the desire to promote religious liberty or tolerance as an end in itself.[55]

[53] For example, by virtue of Treaties of Peace concluded at Utrecht in 1713 (which brought to an end the wars of the Spanish Succession) Great Britain undertook to allow Catholics the free exercise of their religion (as far as the laws of Great Britain permitted) in those areas of Newfoundland ceded to it by France (Article XIV of the Treaty of Peace and Friendship between France and Great Britain, signed at Utrecht, 11 April 1713 (27 CTS 475)) and in Gibraltar, ceded to Great Britain by Spain (Article XIV of the Treaty of Peace and Friendship between Great Britain and Spain, signed at Utrecht, 13 April 1713 (27 CTS 295)). Great Britain undertook similar obligations when acquiring Canada from France and Florida from Spain under Articles IV and XX of the Peace of Paris, 1763 (Definitive Treaty of Peace between France, Great Britain and Spain, signed at Paris, 10 February 1763 (42 CTS 279)).

[54] See, for example, Article X of the Treaty of Nystadt, 1721 concerning the free exercise of the Protestant religion and the maintenance of Protestant schools in areas ceded to Russia by Sweden (Treaty of Peace between Russia and Sweden, signed at Nystadt, 30 August 1721 (31 CTS 339)); Article XIV of the Treaty of Hubertusburg (1763) in which Prussia undertook to maintain Catholicism in Silesia (ceded by Austria), whilst not 'detracting from the complete freedom of conscience of the Protestant religion', (Treaty of Peace between Austria and Prussia, signed at Hubertusburg, 15 February 1763 (42 CTS 347; trans. Grewe, *FHIG*, p. 336)); Article VIII of the Treaty of Warsaw (1773) securing to the Catholic populations of Pomerania and other areas of Greater Poland ceded by Poland to Prussia the exercise of their religion as at September 1772 (Treaty between Poland and Russia, signed at Warsaw, 18 September 1773 (45 CTS 253)); Article VIII of the Treaty of Grodno, 1793 which secured to both the Latin and Uniate Catholic population of Lithuania (ceded by Poland to Russia) full enjoyment of their possessions and rights within the ceded territories and, in addition, the freedom of worship throughout the entire Russian Empire (Treaty of Cession and Limits between Poland and Russia, signed at Grodno, 13 July 1793 (52 CTS 83)).

[55] That is not to say that there were no moves towards religious tolerance. On the contrary, the spirit of the Enlightenment engendered a liberalization of internal regulation of religious affairs throughout Europe. The Napoleonic reordering of the western German States further eroded the doctrinal rigidity of many of the client States. See J. J. Sheehan, *Oxford History of Modern Europe: German History 1770–1866* (Oxford: Clarendon Press, 1989), pp. 268–269. Some, however, have argued that the treaty practice outlined above, from Westphalia onwards, provides evidence of intervention in the affairs of another state on the grounds of religion (see generally A. Rougier, 'La théorie de l'intervention d'humanité', RGDIP 17 (1910), 468 and M. Ganji, *The International Protection of Human Rights* (Geneva: Librairie E. Droz, 1962), pp. 17–18, quoting R. J. Phillimore, *Commentaries Upon International Law*, 3rd edn, vol. I

Treaty practice from Westphalia onwards also reveals another trend. Rather than simply committing themselves to the fulfilment of their own obligations, States also entered into obligations to act as guarantors, either of specific elements of the settlements that were being concluded[56] or, as in the Treaties of Westphalia themselves, of the entire settlement.[57] This trend culminated in the Congress of Vienna of 1815 and in the system of the 'Concert of Europe'. Although not an express treaty obligation,[58] the basic premise underlying the post-Napoleonic territorial settlement was the intervention and interaction of the Great Powers in order to preserve the balance of power, without this necessarily implying the preservation of the status quo. Unlike the Treaties of Westphalia, the treaties concluded at the Congress of Vienna said little relating to the religious liberty of the peoples who were affected by the settlement.[59]

(London: Butterworths, 1879), pp. 621–622). It should be noted that Phillimore was writing at the time of the Bulgarian crisis and when the involvement of the European powers in the dismemberment of the Ottoman Empire was reaching a climax and 'intervention' on behalf of the Christian subjects of the Porte was a very real issue. See below, pp. 69–74. Moreover, this accorded with Phillimore's general belief in the supremacy of divine law and that 'Christian nations deserved a privileged position in International Law'. See J. E. Noyes, 'Christianity and Late Nineteenth Century British Theories of International Law', in M. W. Janis (ed.), *The Influence of Religion on the Development of International Law*, p. 85 at pp. 96–101.

[56] For example, Article IX of the Polish–Prussian Treaty of Warsaw (1773) provided that:
> the King of Prussia . . . shall guarantee all and such constitutions that shall be drawn up . . . in the Diet . . . both upon the structure of the free government . . . and on the pacification and the status of the Uniate religion and of the Protestants, Calvinist and Lutheran.

(45 CTS 253; trans. Grewe, *FHIG*, p. 617). See also Article VI of the Polish–Prussian Treaty of Grodno (1793) (Treaty between Poland and Prussia, signed at Grodno, 25 September 1793 (52 CTS 137)).

[57] The Treaty of Münster, Article 123, provided that all parties 'shall be obliged to defend and protect all and every article in this peace against anyone, without distinction of religion'. Although not novel, this provided a key affirmation of this practice at the dawn of the modern era. See J. Headlam-Morley, *Studies in Diplomatic History* (London: Methuen, 1930), p. 108 (*cf.* chapter 4 below for the involvement of Headlam-Morley in constructing systems of guarantee following the First World War) and L. Gross, 'The Peace of Westphalia', *AJIL*, 42 (1948), 20 at pp. 23–24.

[58] But *cf.* Article VI of the 'Quadruple Alliance' of 20 November 1815, which provided for regular meetings between the Allies.

[59] Act of the Congress of Vienna, signed between Austria, France, Great Britain, Portugal, Prussia, Russia and Sweden, 9 June 1815 (64 CTS 453) and see J. Fouques-Duparc, *La Protection des Minorités de Race, de Langue et de Religion* (Paris: Librairie Dalloz, 1922), pp. 81–89.

There were, however, three exceptions.[60] The first related to Cracow, which was constituted a Free City under the protection of Austria, Prussia and Russia.[61] The second concerned the cession of parts of Savoy from the Kingdom of Sardinia to the Canton of Geneva. The rights of the Catholic population were expressly protected, including the right to have Catholic school teachers in areas where Catholics outnumbered Protestants. Moreover, the Kingdom of Sardinia was granted a right of appeal to the Swiss Diet should these provisions be breached, an early example of an 'implementation mechanism' associated with such an obligation.[62]

The third exception concerned the Low Countries. It had been decided by the Treaty of Paris (1814) that Holland should be constituted as a monarchy and 'receive an increase in territory'.[63] This was brought about on the basis of the 'Eight Articles', the second of which provided: '*Il ne sera rein innové articles de cette Constitution, qui assurent a tous les Cultes une Protection et une favour égales, et garantissent l'admission de tous les Citoyens,*

---

[60] Provision was also made for securing the rights of both Christians and Jews within the newly constituted German Federation. Article XVI of the Act Relative to the Federal Constitution of Germany, signed at Vienna, 8 June 1815 (64 CTS 433) (and annexed to the General Treaty as Act IX) provided that:

> 'La différance des Confessions Chrétiennes dans les Pays et Territoires de la Confédération Allemande, n'en entraînera aucune dans la jouissance des droits civils et politique.
>
> La Dièta prendra en considération les moyens d'opérer, de la manière la plus uniform, l'amélioration de l'état civil de ceux qui professent la Réligion Juive en Allemagne, et s'occupera particulièrement des mesures par lesquelles on pourra leur assurer et leur garantier dans les Etats de la Confédérations, la joissance des droit civil, à condition qu'ils se soumettront àtoutes les obligations des autres Citoyens. En attendant, les droit accordés déjà aux Members de cette Religion par tel ou tel Etat particulier leur seront conservés.'

The other major powers were not a party to this Act and so it was not a matter of international obligation as such.

[61] Article I of the Constitution established Roman Catholicism as the religion of the territory, but Article II provided 'Touts les Cultes Chrétiens sont Libres et n'établissent aucune différence dans les Droit Sociaux'. See Treaty Between Austria, Prussia and Russia respecting Cracow, 21 April (3 May) 1815 and the Annex thereto (64 CTS 165: annexed to the General Treaty as Act III).

[62] See the Territorial Treaty between Austria, France, Great Britain, Prussia, Russia and Sardinia, signed at Vienna, 20 May 1815, Annex to Article VII, Article III (64 CTS 309 at 318; annexed to the General Treaty as Act XIII). It was on this basis that the King of Sardinia intervened in 1821 regarding marriage laws which were in conflict with the Catholic faith: see H. Rosting, 'Protection of Minorities by the League of Nations', *AJIL* 17 (1923) 641, at p. 644.

[63] Definitive Treaty of Peace and Amity between Austria, Great Britain, Portugal, Prussia, Russia and Sweden and France, signed at Paris, 30 May 1814, Article VI (63 CTS 171).

quelques soit leur croyance réligieans, aux Emplois et offices Publics.'[64] This situation persisted until the final separation of Belgium and Holland in 1839, and with it the perceived need for such a provision.[65]

The European powers and the Ottoman Empire

Despite the hesitations of many of the early writers, treaties between the Christian and non-Christian powers were by no means uncommon. The bulk of this practice, however, concerned the Eastern Roman Empire, which was frequently called upon to enter into arrangements with its non-Christian neighbours and, not surprisingly, many of these concerned religious freedom. As far back as AD 532 the Emperor Justinian entered into a treaty with Chosroes I of Persia which guaranteed Christian believers the right to maintain and worship in their churches and exempted them from participation in the official religion, Zoroastrianism. Proselytism, however, was not permitted.[66]

The rise of Islam had profound repercussions for the exercise of religious freedoms. Although, like Christianity, Islam was an aggressively universalist religion, it also displayed far more tolerance to followers of other faiths, and particularly towards Jews and Christians who, like followers of Islam, were considered to be 'peoples of the book'. Jewish and Christian communities were, therefore, permitted a large degree of freedom in both religious and civil affairs through the *millet* system.[67]

---

[64] Protocol of Conference between Austria, Great Britain, Prussia and Russia, signed at Vienna, 21 June 1814 (63 CTS 239); Treaty between Austria, Great Britain, Prussia and Russia and the Netherlands, signed at Vienna, 31 May 1815 (64 CTS 377; annexed to the General Treaty as Act X). H. Nicholson, *The Congress of Vienna: A Study in Allied Unity: 1812–1822* (London: Constable, 1946), p. 208 described this as representing 'the first "Minority Treaty" to figure in diplomatic practice'.

[65] Following the revolution of 1830, the London Conference agreed a separation on the basis of the 'twenty-four Articles'. This was accepted by Belgium, but the Netherlands withheld its consent until 1838. Separation was finally achieved in 1839. See Treaty for the Definitive Separation of Belgium from Holland between Austria, France, Great Britain, Prussia, Russia and Belgium, signed at London, 15 November 1831 (82 CTS 255), Treaty between Austria, France, Great Britain, Prussia and Russia and the Netherlands, signed at London, 19 April 1839 (88 CTS 424) and the Treaty between Belgium and the Netherlands relating to the Separation of their Respective Territories (88 CTS 427). See E. H. Kossmann, *The Low Countries: 1740–1940* (Oxford: Clarendon Press, 1978), pp. 108, 158, 173–175.

[66] See Nussbaum, *A Concise History of the Law of Nations*, p. 48. Zoroastrians were not, however, accorded similar privileges within the Roman Empire.

[67] The legal system of the Empire was based on Muslim religious law, which was

This held out the prospect of arrangements being made under which Christian traders might permanently establish themselves in Muslim countries for mutual benefit. The Muslim rulers ultimately adopted the practice of issuing unilateral grants to westerners, known as Capitulations, which permitted them to establish communities[68] and to exercise a considerable degree of self-government (including the exercise of both criminal and civil jurisdiction over co-nationals). Additionally, the Capitulations always permitted the right of free and public worship.[69]

In 1453 the Byzantine Empire fell to the Ottomans with the taking of Constantinople. In the city that became the Ottoman capital, the religious independence of the Christian believers was preserved.[70] Ottoman power continued to expand westwards, ultimately threatening the very heart of the Holy Roman Empire.[71] Relations with France were, however, very

considered not to apply to disputes between non-Muslims. This affected the entire social structure of the Empire, which was based around the various *millets*, national groups, to which all subjects belonged. Therefore, status and legal capacity in the Empire was conditioned by religious adherence. See S. J. Shaw, *History of the Ottoman Empire and Modern Turkey* (Cambridge University Press, 1976), vol. I, pp. 151–153. This serves to distinguish the Turkish Capitulations from the 'unequal treaties' which China concluded with western powers during the nineteenth century (see below, p. 62, n. 77). Although they granted similar jurisdictional concessions to the western powers, they were imposed, rather than granted.

[68] In 1361 the Byzantine Emperor had permitted the establishment of an autonomous Turkish community within Constantinople. Rather than a mark of tolerance, this was a sign of weakness and a precursor to the catastrophe that was to come. Nussbaum, *A Concise History of the Law of Nations*, p. 52.

[69] See *ibid.*, pp. 54–58. It should not be thought that 'Capitulations' were only granted by Muslim powers. Christian communities in the East (such as the Kingdom of Jerusalem and Christian Armenia) granted similar rights to western traders. To an extent, therefore, they represented a form of local custom concerning the reception of foreign interests into the community which transcended the purely religious (Islamic) dimension.

[70] The Orthodox Patriarch of Constantinople remained (and remains) head of the Greek Orthodox Church which at that time still embraced the Orthodox Christians of Russia (the Patriarch of Moscow becoming the recognized head of the Russian Orthodox Church in 1589). In fact, the Orthodox Church fared quite well under the Ottomans. It became a recognized *millet*, and acquired civil as well as religious jurisdiction over Orthodox believers throughout the expanding Empire. The Orthodox Church supported the Ottomans in many of their struggles with the western Catholic powers, who they saw as a greater threat. See A. Palmer, *The Decline and Fall of the Ottoman Empire* (London: John Murray, 1992), pp. 28–31.

[71] In 1529 Ottoman forces besieged Vienna, but withdrew. Vienna was again besieged in 1683 but this time the withdrawal of the Ottoman forces became the overture for the steady collapse of Ottoman power in East-Central Europe.

warm[72] and in 1535 Suleiman the Magnificent entered into a reciprocal agreement with Francis I of France which conferred upon the French king the power to appoint consuls with authority to determine 'all causes, suits and differences, both civil and criminal, which might arise between merchants and other subjects of the King'.[73] The local *Cadi*[74] was to have no criminal jurisdiction over French subjects, such cases having to be referred directly to the Sublime Porte. As regards religion, it was provided that:

the said merchants their agents and servants, and all other subjects of the King shall never be molested nor tried by the *cadis, sandjak-beys,* or *soubashis* or any person but the Sublime Porte only, and they cannot be made or regarded as Turks (Mohammedans) unless they themselves desire it and profess it openly and without violence. They shall have the right to practise their own religion.[75]

This placed France in a privileged position which non-French Christians capitalized upon by placing themselves under French protection. Although similar privileges were granted to England by virtue of a Capitulation of 1583, the predominance of France was underscored by further Capitulations in their favour, including that of 1604 which vested in them the custody of the Holy Places of Palestine as well as the protection of all Catholic pilgrims.[76] Above all else, however, these early Capitulations legitimized the intrusion of the interests and jurisdiction of Western European States into the Ottoman world. Even so, the extent of these intrusions was a matter of dispute.

These privileges were originally bestowed at a time when the Western States were economically and politically inferior to the Ottomans but, as the balance of power shifted in their favour, they became a potent means of furthering their strength and the enfeebled Empire was unable to

---

[72] At this time France was struggling against the imperial vision of the Habsburgs under Charles V. Suleiman was able to exploit the division between the Catholic powers, which were themselves struggling to resist the spread of Protestantism. See C. A. Frazee, *Catholics and Sultans: the Church and the Ottoman Empire 1453–1923*, (London: Cambridge University Press, 1983), pp. 24–28, 67–69.

[73] First Franco-Turkish Capitulation, Articles III and IV. The local authorities were also to assist in the enforcement of the French Consul's decisions. See Grewe, *FHIG*, p. 71.

[74] The scope of the judicial and administrative functions of the *Cadi* is outlined in Shaw, *History of the Ottoman Empire*, vol. I, pp. 134–138.

[75] First Franco-Turkish Capitulation, Article VI.

[76] See Nussbaum, *A Concise History of the Law of Nations*, p. 65.

resist. Within this framework, the role of the Western European States as protectors of the religious freedom of their subjects within the Ottoman domains easily elided into a claim entitling them to champion the liberties, religious and otherwise, of all Christians in the Empire.[77]

The last of the true Capitulations was granted to France in 1740. Not only did this reaffirm privileges previously granted, but it expanded them even further.[78] By now, however, the Ottomans had been forced into a series of Peace Treaties with Austria and Russia which contained further pledges of religious liberty. As early as 1615, a twenty-year treaty had been concluded between the Habsburgs and the Ottomans which had recognized the Austrian interest in the freedom of Catholics to worship and repair churches.[79] The Treaty of Carlowitz (1699) and the Treaty of Passerowitz (1718) confirmed Roman Catholics (Latin rite) in the enjoyment of 'whatever privileges the preceding ... Emperors of the Ottomans have favourably granted in their realms, either by earlier sacred treaties or by other imperial marks, either by edict or by special

---

[77] During the nineteenth century similar agreements, the 'Unequal Treaties', were forced upon China by the western powers, which had come to appreciate the commercial and political advantages of one-sided arrangements. See Nussbaum, p. 194. Some of these also contained clauses concerning the exercise of religion. See, for example, Article 8 of the Treaty of Peace, Friendship and Commerce between Great Britain and China, signed at Tientsin, 26 June 1858, which provided that:

> The Christian religion, as professed by Protestants or Catholics, inculcates the practice of virtue, and teaches man to do as he would be done by. Persons teaching or professing it, therefore shall alike be entitled to the protection of the Chinese authorities nor shall any such, peaceably pursuing their calling and not offending against the law, be persecuted or interfered with. (119 CTS 163.)

See also Article 29 of the Treaty of Peace, Amity and Commerce between China and the United States, signed at Tientsin, 18 June 1858 (119 CTS 123); Article 8 of the Treaty of Peace, Amity, Commerce and Navigation between China and Russia, signed at Tientsin, 1 (13) June 1858 (119 CTS 113); Article 13 of the Treaty of Amity, Commerce and Navigation between China and France, signed at Tientsin, 27 June 1858 (119 CTS 189).

Anti-Christian sentiment often ran high, exacerbated by the use of 'gunboat' diplomacy by the western powers to support the Christian communities and missionaries, although Chinese religious sects themselves traditionally offered their members protection. The Boxer uprising of 1899 commenced with attacks on Chinese Christian converts. See J. Gray, *Rebellions and Revolutions: China from the 1800s to the 1900s* (Oxford University Press, 1990), pp. 115–116, 137.

[78] Articles 32–37 and 82 (36 CTS 41; Grewe, *FHIG*, p. 361). See also Nussbaum, *A Concise History of the Law of Nations*, p. 122.

[79] See Shaw, *History of the Ottoman Empire*, vol. I, p. 189.

mandate'.[80] The Treaty of Kutschuk-Kainardji, concluded between Russia and Turkey in 1774, took this a stage further by granting similar freedoms to Orthodox Christians.[81]

In addition, all these treaties granted rights of intercession to the European powers, the effect of which was to require the Sublime Porte to pay attention to the arguments advanced on behalf of their subjects within the Ottoman Empire. The Treaties of Carlowitz and Passerowitz had followed the Capitulations in granting the Austrian Emperor the right to intercede on behalf of all Roman Catholics.[82] The Treaty of Kutschuk-Kainardji was, however, more equivocal. It expressly permitted the construction of a new Russian Church in Constantinople and recognized the right of the tsar to intercede on its behalf and on behalf of ministers of the Orthodox faith. Nevertheless, Russia interpreted this as granting it the right to intercede on behalf of all Orthodox believers in the same manner as granted to France and Austria as regards Roman Catholic believers.[83] More importantly, the right of 'intercession' was interpreted as placing believers – Catholic and Orthodox – under the

---

[80] Article XIII of the Treaty of Peace between the Emperor and the Ottomans, signed at Carlowitz, 26 January 1699 (22 CTS 219). This article was repeated verbatim as Article XI of the Treaty of Peace between the Emperor and the Ottomans, signed at Passarowitz, 21 July 1718 (30 CTS 341; trans. Grewe, *FHIG*, p. 355). These articles also permitted Catholics to 'restore and repair their churches' and carry on their customary rituals and provided that 'no one be permitted to establish any kind of vexation or monetary demand on the religious people . . . to hinder the practice of that religion, but rather let the adherents of it flourish and rejoice in the customary imperial sense of duty'. Nevertheless, this did not alter the predominance of the French interest which was, if anything, enhanced: the French were considered to be friends to whom privileges had been granted whereas the Austrians were enemies to whom concessions had to be made. See Frazee, *Catholics and Sultans*, p. 168.

[81] Article 7 of the Treaty of Perpetual Peace and Amity between Russia and Turkey, signed at Kutschuk-Kainardji, 10 (21) July 1774 (45 CTS 349).

[82] Article XI of the Treaty of Passerowitz permitted the Austrian Emperor

> to set forth to the Sublime Porte the matters entrusted to him concerning the religion and the places of Christian pilgrimage in the Holy City, Jerusalem, and in other places where the aforementioned religious people have churches, and to bring his requests to the Imperial [Ottoman] throne.

For the debate surrounding the interpretation of Article XI see R. H. Davison, 'Russian Skill and Turkish Imbecility', *Slavic Studies* 35(3) (1976), 463, reprinted in R. H. Davison, *Essays in Ottoman and Turkish History 1774–1923: The Impact of the West* (London: Saqi, 1990), p. 29.

[83] In fact, the Russians did not build a church in accordance with the provisions of this treaty at all. It has been suggested that this was deliberate, and enabled them to interpret the rights of intercession as being of general application. See Palmer, *The Decline and Fall of the Ottoman Empire*, pp. 46–47.

'protection' of the relevant power,[84] which would later provide a pretext for intervention on their behalf.[85]

It has been suggested that a general distinction can be drawn between the treaties concluded between Christian powers, which tended to provide only for the religious freedoms of particular communities in ceded territories, and those concluded by the Christian powers with the Ottomans, which were of a general application. Various explanations can be offered for this distinction, such as the nature of the religions themselves, the traditional *millet* system of governance within the Empire and its extension by means of the Capitulations and the emergence of a more 'secularized' State system in Europe.[86] Whilst all these factors doubtless played a part, the underlying reason for the nature of the treaty practice with the Ottomans in the eighteenth and nineteenth centuries had more to do with power: the European powers could insist and the Ottomans were unable to resist.[87]

The nineteenth century witnessed the gradual 'assumption of a collective authority on the part of the [European] powers to . . . regulate the disintegration of Turkey' and, alongside this, the emergence of 'a sort of *corpus iuris publici orientalis*, in which the rights of Turkey, of the new states which have been carved out of it, and of the semi-independent provinces which still remain subject to its suzerainty, are declared and defined by

---

[84] See Nussbaum, *A Concise History of the Law of Nations*, p. 122. It is interesting to compare this interpretation of the treaty with the express provisions of its second article by which both Russia and the Ottomans recognized the independence of the Tartars. Whilst accepting that, as Muslims, the Tartars should be free to place themselves under the religious authority of the sultan, this should be 'without compromising the stability of their political and civil liberty' and it was accepted that there should be no interference 'under any pretext whatever . . . in [its] domestic, political, civil and internal affairs'. Although this recognized the sultan as the supreme religious head of the Muslim world, there is no recognition of a right to intercede – or intervene – on behalf of believers before their territorial sovereign. It was, then, a very different form of relationship than that claimed by Russia with the Ottoman Empire in respect of the Orthodox believers.

[85] See Shaw, *History of the Ottoman Empire*, vol. I, pp. 189, 250.

[86] See P. Thornberry, *The International Protection of Minorities* (Oxford: Clarendon Press, 1991), pp. 29–30.

[87] On those occasions when the European powers did cede territory to the Ottomans, clauses akin to those found in the inter-Christian treaties of the seventeenth century are found. For example, when Russia returned Bessarabia, Wallachia and Moldova to the Ottomans, the Sublime Porte undertook 'To obstruct in no manner whatsoever the free exercise of the Christian religion' in those territories (Treaty of Kutschuk-Kainardji, Article XVI (2)).

the authority of the great powers collectively'.[88] The significance of this emergent practice is that it not only provided the conceptual means by which the Western powers dealt with the Eastern Question, but also that it provided precedents which were drawn upon at the last of the great conferences providing for the settlement of European territorial questions, at Paris in 1919.

The first developments related to Greece. Russia and Great Britain agreed in 1826 to propose that Greece should become a tribute-paying dependency of the Ottomans, within which the Greeks would, *inter alia*, enjoy 'a complete liberty of Conscience'.[89] This was followed in 1827 by the Treaty of London,[90] to which France was also a signatory, in which the parties continued to offer their services as mediators in the dispute between the Ottomans and the Greeks and which (under an additional article) established an *ad hoc* conference of the signatories, the Conference of London.

In 1829 the war between Russia and the Ottomans was concluded by the Treaty of Adrianople,[91] Article 10 of which committed the Porte to adhesion to the 1827 Treaty of London and acceptance of the protocol adopted by that Conference in March 1829, which provided for Greece to be governed by a Christian prince under the suzerainty of the Porte.[92] In 1830, however, the Conference produced three new protocols,[93] the first of which provided for an independent Greek State under a Christian prince.[94]

---

[88] T. E. Holland, *The Concert of Europe in the Eastern Question* (Oxford: Clarendon Press, 1885), pp. 1–2. Holland noted that whilst the Eastern Question had been ignored at the Congress of Vienna, the ensuing period of comparative peace in Europe meant that the western powers had 'the leisure . . . to extend their sympathy to the subject races of the Ottoman Empire'. For the relevance of this practice to religious freedom, see Fouques-Duparc, *La Protection des Minorités*, pp. 89–97.

[89] Protocol of St Petersburg, 23 March (4 April) 1826, Article 1 (76 CTS 175).

[90] Treaty between France, Great Britain and Russia for the Pacification of Greece, signed at London, 6 July 1827 (77 CTS 307).

[91] 80 CTS 83. Article 5 of this treaty also provided that the inhabitants of Moldova and Wallachia should 'enjoy the free exercise of religion'.

[92] Protocol of Conference between France, Great Britain and Russia, signed at London, 22 March 1829 (78 CTS 361).

[93] Protocols of the Conference relative to the Independence of Greece between France, Great Britain and Russia, signed at London, 3 (20) February 1830 (80 CTS 327).

[94] Second Protocol (80 CTS 331). This prince was to be appointed by the original signatories of the Treaty of London (thereby excluding the Ottomans who had acceded) and was not to be drawn from their own royal houses. The Second Protocol nominated Prince Leopold of Saxe-Coburg but he declined. The Kingship of Greece was ultimately conferred upon Otto, the second son of the King of Bavaria, in 1832. See Protocol of Conference between France, Great Britain and Russia, signed at London, 13 February 1832 (82 CTS 333).

The third was concerned with religious affairs and by its terms France handed over the rights conferred upon it by the Capitulations[95] within the territory of Greece to the incoming King Otto.[96] Additionally, all subjects, of whatever religion, were to be eligible for all forms of public office and employment 'on the footing of perfect equality, without regard to difference of creed, in all their relations, religious, civil or political'.

This set the pattern for the *'corpus iuris publici orientalis'* as it was to apply to religious issues. The new States which were created by the intervention of the major European powers were required to guarantee the freedom of worship and toleration in the private sphere, whilst at the same time preserving any pre-existing rights of particular faiths or creeds. Otherwise, general principles of non-discrimination were to apply in the public sphere. Similar principles were applied when further territories were added to these States, whether from further inroads into Ottoman possessions or when areas were later redistributed between them. Stipulations in treaties of cession, however, related only to the areas to be transferred.

Thus when in 1863 the European powers decided that the United States of the Ionian Islands should be ceded to Greece,[97] freedom of worship and toleration for Christians in conformity with existing practices was, along with the treaty as a whole, placed under the guarantee of France, Russia

---

[95] It noted that France, a party to the Treaty of London, 'has been entitled to exercise in favour of the Catholics subjected to the Sultan, an especial protection, which [the King of France] deems it to be his duty to deposit at the present moment in the hands of the future sovereign of Greece'. To this end, the Third Protocol (80 CTS 332) records that 'it was decided that the Catholic religion should enjoy in the new state the free and public exercise of its worship . . . which they have enjoyed under the protection of the Kings of France'.

[96] Otto was himself a Catholic. Not unnaturally, this caused resentment among his Orthodox subjects. In 1852 it was agreed that any future prince succeeding in default of heirs of Otto should profess the Orthodox faith (Treaty between Bavaria, France, Great Britain, Germany and Russia, relative to the Succession to the Crown of Greece, signed at London, 20 November 1852 (109 CTS 107)). Following his deposition in 1862, the crown was conferred on Prince William of Denmark, known as King George I of Greece. It was decided that George's legitimate successors must profess the Orthodox faith (Article VII of the Treaty between France, Great Britain, Russia and Denmark relative to the Accession of Prince William of Denmark to the Throne of Greece, signed at London, 13 July 1863 (128 CTS 37)).

[97] Great Britain agreed to surrender its power as protector of the United States of the Ionian Islands, which it had been exercising in accordance with the terms of the Treaty of Paris, 15 November 1815. See Protocol of Conference between Austria, France, Great Britain, Prussia and Russia relative to the Ionian Islands, signed at London, 1 August 1863 (128 CTS 123).

and Great Britain.[98] In a similar vein, when further territories were added to Greece at the expense of the Ottomans under the Treaty of Constantinople (1881) it was provided that 'the lives, property, religion, and customs of those of the inhabitants of the localities ceded to Greece who shall remain under the Hellenic administration will be scrupulously respected'. This general provision was followed by the particular obligation that freedom of religion and public worship be 'secured to Mussulmans in the territories ceded to Greece'.[99]

In the meanwhile, significant developments had occurred. In 1839 the new Sultan, Abdulmecid, ushered in a period of reform and modernization, the *Tanzimat*. The Imperial Rescript, known as the Gulhane Decree, which set out the principles of reform recognized the equality of all subjects before the law, thus implicitly abandoning the Shari'a.[100] These principles were confirmed in a further Reforming Decree of 1856[101] which represented an attempt to reform the *millet* system and secularize the Empire. It promised 'energetic measures to ensure to each sect, whatever the numbers of its adherents, entire freedom in the exercise of religion'

---

[98] Article V of the Treaty between Austria, France, Great Britain, Prussia and Russia relative to the Ionian Islands, signed at London, 14 November 1863 (128 CTS 277). This was repeated verbatim as Article IV of the Treaty between France, Great Britain, Russia and Greece respecting the Union of the Ionian Islands to the Kingdom of Greece, signed at London, 29 March 1864 (129 CTS 97). These articles, whilst acknowledging the dominance of the Orthodox Church, expressly preserved the special rights of not only the Catholic but also the Anglican Church.

[99] Articles III and VIII of the Convention for the Settlement of the Frontier between Greece and Turkey, between Austria-Hungary, France, Germany, Great Britain, Italy, Russia and Turkey, signed at Constantinople, 24 May 1881 (158 CTS 367). These articles further provided that

no interference shall take place with the autonomy or hierarchical organizations of Mussulman religious bodies now existing, or which may hereafter be formed . . . no obstacle shall be placed in the way of the relations of these bodies with their spiritual heads in matters of religion. The local courts of the *Cheri* shall continue to exercise their jurisdiction in matters purely religious.

Article IV also recognized title to property (*vacoufs*) used for the upkeep of Muslim religious and associated foundations.

[100] See S. J. Shaw and E. K. Shaw, *History of the Ottoman Empire and Modern Turkey*, vol. II (Cambridge University Press, 1977), pp. 59–61, who consider the decree to be, in some ways, an Ottoman equivalent of the French Declaration of the Rights of Man and the Citizen of 1789. See also Palmer, *The Decline and Fall of the Ottoman Empire*, p. 126; B. Jelavich, *History of the Balkans*, vol. I (Cambridge University Press, 1983), pp. 284–285.

[101] The *Isahat Fermani* is often referred to as the *Hatti-Humayun*. This, however, simply describes its mode of promulgation ('Imperial Rescript'), and does not distinguish it from other such instruments.

and outlawed discrimination on religious grounds. The free profession of any religion was to be assured and 'no one shall be forced to change his religion'.[102]

The Decree was formed against the background of the Crimean War, which had, in part, been precipitated by the claim of Russia to speak on behalf of all Orthodox subjects of the Porte.[103] The war was settled by the Treaty of Paris (1856).[104] Article IX of the Treaty provided:

His Imperial Majesty the Sultan, having, in his constant solicitude for the welfare of his subjects, issued a Firman which, while ameliorating their conditions without distinction of religion or race, records his generous intentions towards the Christian populations of his Empire, and wishing to give a further proof of his sentiments in that respect, has resolved to communicate to the Contracting Parties the said Firman emanating from his sovereign will.

The Contracting Parties recognize the high value of this communication. It is clearly understood that it cannot, in any case, give to the said powers the right to interfere, either collectively or separately, in the relations of His Majesty the Sultan with his subjects, nor in the internal administration of his Empire.

Although Article IX did not subject the Porte to any additional obligations, it did not, of course, affect the pre-existing rights of the European powers. Article VII did, however, oblige the contracting States to respect the independence and territorial integrity of the Ottoman Empire. This could have been taken to imply the withdrawal of whatever rights of intervention on behalf of religious groups they previously possessed and this would certainly have been a logical consequence of the rearrangement of the Empire's structures that the reform movement was attempting. On the other hand, the contracting States undertook to

---

[102] Shaw and Shaw, *History of the Ottoman Empire and Modern Turkey,* vol. II, pp. 124–128; R. H. Davison, 'Turkish Attitudes Concerning Christian–Muslim Equality in the Nineteenth Century', in Davison, *Essays in Ottoman and Turkish History,* p. 112.

[103] For a detailed examination of this aspect of the background to the Crimean War see B. Jelavich, *Russia's Balkan Entanglements, 1806–1914* (Cambridge University Press, 1991), pp. 120–124. At another level, this was a manifestation of the general competition for influence waged by the European powers in the Ottoman lands. In effect the Empire became an area in which the 'Concert of Europe' was working out its manoeuvres to preserve the balance of power. See Shaw and Shaw, *History of the Ottoman Empire,* vol. II, pp. 136–138; Frazee, *Catholics and Sultans,* pp. 225–226.

[104] General Treaty of the Re-establishment of Peace between Austria, France, Great Britain, Prussia, Sardinia and Turkey and Russia, signed at Paris, 30 March 1856 (114 CTS 409).

guarantee the observance of the treaty and this provided ample opportunity for intervention[105] without having to look to the Firman at all.[106]

Subsequent uprisings against Ottoman rule or overlordship sparked a further series of conflicts and interventions which ultimately resulted in the convening of the Congress of Berlin[107] and culminated in the Treaty of Berlin[108] which laid the foundations for much of the contemporary structure of the Balkans and Eastern Europe. The Treaty of Berlin addressed religious questions in a common formulation that provided:

In ... the difference of religious creeds and confessions shall not be alleged against any person as a ground for exclusion or incapacity in matters relating to the enjoyment of civil and political rights, admission to public employment, functions, and honours, or the exercise of the various professions and industries in any locality whatsoever.

The freedom and outward exercise of all forms of worship shall be assured to all persons belonging to [the territorial unit concerned], as well as to foreigners,

---

[105] For example, the territorial provisions of the Treaty of Paris confirmed Ottoman suzerainty over Wallachia, Moldova (Article XXII) and Serbia (Article XXVIII), subject to a specific undertaking to preserve, *inter alia*, 'full liberty of worship'. Exclusive rights of protection (i.e. Russian) over these territories was forbidden, but a collective interference was implicitly sanctioned. See also Jelavich, *History of the Balkans*, vol. I, p. 284. Moreover, in April 1856 Austria-Hungary, France and Great Britain entered into the Treaty between Austria, France and Great Britain Guaranteeing the Independence and Integrity of the Ottoman Empire, signed at Paris, 14 April 1856 (114 CTS 497). Under the terms of this treaty, any infraction of the Treaty of Paris was to be considered as a *causus belli*.

[106] Possibly the most well-known 'intervention' in the years following the Treaty of Paris was the so-called 'French Intervention' in what is today the Lebanon, 1860–1861, in the wake of anti-Christian violence. This is often cited as an example of 'humanitarian intervention' but, formally speaking, it was authorized by all the parties to the Treaty of Paris (1856), including the Porte, by way of an additional protocol (Protocol of Conference, signed at Paris, 3 August 1860), later converted into a treaty (of 5 September 1860) and extended by a further treaty (of 19 March 1861). See Holland, *The Concert of Europe*, chapter 4; Ganji, *The International Protection of Human Rights*, pp. 24–25; N. Ronzitti, *Rescuing Nationals Abroad through Military Coercion and Intervention on Grounds of Humanity* (Dordrecht: Martinus Nijhoff, 1985), pp. 89–91.

[107] The Russo-Turkish war of 1876–1877 had been concluded by the Preliminary Treaty of Peace between Russia and Turkey, signed at San Stefano, 19 February (3 March) 1878 (152 CTS 395: the Treaty of San Stefano). Austria-Hungary and Great Britain considered its terms – particularly the creation of a large and powerful Bulgaria as an autonomous tributary principality (with a Christian government (Article VI)) – to be so damaging to their interests that they took up positions against Russia. At the Congress of Berlin Russia made substantial concessions which went some way towards restoring the balance of power and influence in the region.

[108] Treaty between Austria-Hungary, France, Germany, Great Britain, Italy, Russia and Turkey for the Settlement of Affairs in the East, signed at Berlin, 13 July 1878 (153 CTS 171).

and no hindrance shall be offered either to the hierarchical organization of the different communions, or to their relations with their spiritual chiefs.

This was inserted in the sections of the treaty which constituted Bulgaria as an autonomous principality under Ottoman suzerainty[109] and which recognized Montenegrin independence.[110] The treaty also recognized the independence of Serbia[111] and of Romania,[112] but in both of these cases recognition was made conditional upon the stipulations concerning religion.[113] Austria-Hungary remained in occupation of Bosnia-Herzegovina and undertook its administration:[114] in 1879 the Porte agreed that this should continue, with the proviso that the Muslim population be permitted the free practice of their faith.[115] On the other hand, Great Britain promised to preserve Muslim religious jurisdiction in Cyprus when that island passed into British control in 1878.[116]

[109] Article V, in which it was said to form 'the basis of the public law'. The area immediately to the south of Bulgaria was constituted as the new province of 'Eastern Roumelia' (Articles XIII–XXII). This remained under the direct political and military control of the sultan, but with administrative autonomy under a Christian governor-general. The sultan undertook 'to enforce there the general laws of the Empire on religious liberty in favour of all forms of worship' (Article XX). This merely confirmed and emphasized the application of Article LXII (for which see below) to this region.

[110] *Ibid.*, Article XXVI. All Contracting States with the exception of the Porte and England had already recognized Montenegro.

[111] *Ibid.*, Article XXXV.   [112] *Ibid.*, Article XLIV.

[113] *Ibid.*, Articles XXXIV and XLIII respectively. In the case of Romania an additional stipulation was that: 'The subjects and citizens of all the Powers, traders or otherwise, shall be treated in Romania, without distinction or creed, on a footing of perfect equality.'

[114] Article XXV.

[115] See the Convention between Austria-Hungary and Turkey, relative to the Occupation of Bosnia-Herzegovina, signed at Constantinople, 21 April 1879 (155 CTS 59). Article II provided that: 'The freedom and outward exercise of all existing religions shall be assured to persons residing or sojourning in Bosnia and the Herzegovina.' See also Shaw and Shaw, *History of the Ottoman Empire*, vol. II, p. 192. This was reaffirmed following the Austro-Hungarian annexation of the territory in 1908. See Protocol between Austria-Hungary and Turkey relating to Bosnia-Herzegovina and the Sanjak of Novi-Bazar, 26 February 1910, Article IV (208 CTS 355).

[116] This had been agreed by the Convention of Defence Alliance between Great Britain and Turkey, signed at Constantinople, 4 June 1878 (153 CTS 67), before the Congress of Berlin was under way. Great Britain undertook to assist the sultan to resist further Russian inroads into Asiatic territories and, in return, Turkey had promised 'to assign the Island of Cyprus to be occupied and administered by England'. The sultan also promised 'to introduce necessary reforms into the Government, for the protection of the Christian and other subjects of the Porte in these [Asiatic] territories' (Article I). The pro-Ottoman policy gave Britain a good deal of leverage and, following the Treaty of Berlin, she was able to exert considerable influence in favour of Christians in the Asiatic areas. The change of British Government in 1880, however, saw a reversal of this policy, and with it a decline in British influence (later capitalized upon by

The Porte also undertook a range of obligations in respect of its remaining territories similar to those required of the newly recognized States. Article LXII of the treaty provided:[117]

The Sublime Porte having expressed the intention to maintain the principle of religious liberty, and give it the widest scope, the Contracting Parties take note of this spontaneous decision.[118]

In no part of the Ottoman Empire shall difference of religion be alleged against any person as a ground for exclusion or incapacity as regards the discharge of civil and political rights, admission to the public employments, functions and honours, or the exercise of the various professions and industries.

All persons shall be admitted, without distinction of religion, to give evidence before the tribunals.

The freedom and outward exercise of all forms of worship are assured to all, and no hindrance shall be offered either to the hierarchical organizations of the various communions or to their relations with their spiritual chiefs.

Ecclesiastics, pilgrims, and monks of all nationalities travelling in Turkey in Europe, or in Turkey in Asia, shall enjoy the same rights, advantages and privileges.

The right of official protection by the Diplomatic and Consular Agents of the Powers in Turkey is recognized both as regards the above-mentioned persons and their religious, charitable, and other establishments in the Holy Places and elsewhere.

The rights possessed by France are expressly reserved, and it is well understood that no alterations can be made to the *status quo* in the Holy Places.

The monks of Mount Athos, of whatever country they may be natives, shall be maintained in their former possessions and advantages, and shall enjoy, without any exception, complete equality of rights and prerogatives.

Despite these extensive provisions, and as the dismemberment of the

---

Germany). Indeed, it is both tragic and ironic that the ultimate adoption of Gladstone's more anti-Ottoman policies (see n. 121 below) worsened rather than improved the position of Christian communities whose situation had, at least in part, prompted it. See G. E. Buckel, *Life of Benjamin Disraeli, Earl of Beaconsfield*, vol. VI (London: J. Murray, 1920), pp. 300–301, 366–367.

[117] The stipulations in Article LXII built upon the provisions of the Treaty of San Stefano, which had provided for the rights of Russian ecclesiastics and monks within the Empire, and granted Russia the right to exercise diplomatic protection on their behalf. The wording was retained in the Treaty of Berlin, but was generalized so as to apply to all nationalities and to representatives of all the powers. A similar alteration took place concerning the rights of monks (in the Treaty of San Stefano, only Russian) on Mount Athos. The clause concerning the giving of evidence was inserted to address the incapacities of, and discrimination against, non-Muslims in this regard, which had been a source of particular concern in Great Britain.

[118] *Cf.* Article IX of the Treaty of Paris (1856). Unlike the earlier treaty, the Treaty of Berlin did not merely note the declaration of intent but went on to incorporate its substance into the treaty, making it a source of international obligation.

Ottoman Empire unfolded,[119] the focus of attention moved away from the rights of the powers to represent the interests of the non-Muslim subjects of the Empire and towards the newly established States, over which they sought influence. Religious factors played a significant role, with Russia continuing to assert itself as the champion of the Orthodox cause (Greece being manifestly unable to exert the same degree of political influence) whilst Austria-Hungary supported the Catholic interest in the west of the Balkans. The most important development, however, was the precedent provided by making Romanian and Serbian recognition conditional upon their according religious equality and freedom of worship to all 'belonging to' the territory. This added a new element to the *corpus iuris publici orientalis*.

The motivation for this lay in the immediate cause of the crisis leading up to the Congress of Berlin. Great Britain in particular had followed a policy of supporting the Ottomans as a check on Russia and as a means of securing the route to India. Domestic revulsion at the massacre of Christians during the suppression of the Bulgarian revolt of 1876 had made this policy politically unpopular[120] and thus the treatment of religious groups was a matter of particular concern. The situation in Romania was particularly volatile since the Romanian Organic Law of 1866 discriminated against non-Christians by rendering them ineligible for citizenship and Romania possessed a large Jewish population which was rapidly expanding due to immigration by Jews seeking to escape from Russian anti-Semitism. Making recognition conditional upon the implementation of these guarantees was intended to ensure that religious tensions would not precipitate further interventions.[121] It is, then, ironic

---

[119] Article LXII did, however, provide the Great Powers with a basis for responding to further allegations concerning the ill-treatment of religious groups within the Empire and, in consequence, a justification for further territorial truncations.

[120] Gladstone precipitated a crisis by publishing in May 1876 his famous pamphlet 'The Bulgarian Horrors and the Question of the East'. See generally R. T. Shannon, *Gladstone and the Bulgarian Agitation 1876* (London: Nelson, 1963).

[121] In fact, they very nearly precipitated the very eventuality they were designed to forestall and the threat of intervention by Britain and France was needed to induce Romania to repeal the discriminatory provisions, following which recognition was granted by all the Contracting States. See G. Castellan, *History of the Balkans from Mohammed the Conqueror to Stalin* (New York: Columbia University Press, 1992; Boulder: East European Monographs), pp. 340–341. The role of Jewish groups in prompting the Great Powers to intervene on behalf of the Jewish population and in fighting for the extension of the religious guarantees to the new States is considered by N. Feinburg, 'The International Protection of Human Rights and the Jewish Question (An Historical Survey)', *Is.LR* 3 (1968), 487, 495–497. The experience of the Romanian Jews following the treaty is examined by Fouques-Duparc, *La Protection des Minorités*, pp. 99–113.

that the practice of the period is often examined in order to see whether it provides evidence supporting a rule of customary international law concerning humanitarian intervention.[122]

The most forthright critic of British policy and of the Treaty of Berlin was Gladstone.[123] Yet he considered the religion clauses of the treaty to be one of only two things that had been 'done well' and noted that: 'In the case of Lord Beaconsfield [Disraeli] it is appropriate to remark that he, who had with a courageous consistency insisted on the emancipation of the Jews at home, was taking a part very appropriate in insisting on this provision in the arrangements abroad.'[124] Irrespective of whether this stance was principled or not, the involvement of the European powers in the Balkans continued in a similar footing right up to the outbreak of the First World War. The territorial ambitions of Greece, Bulgaria[125] and Serbia, as well as the strategic goals of Russia and Austria-Hungary, next became focused on Macedonia[126] but soon became caught up in the consequences of the Young Turk uprising and the Balkan wars of 1912–1913 which saw the final expulsion of the Ottomans from

---

[122] See generally E. C. Stowell, *Intervention in International Law* (Washington DC: John Byrne & Co., 1921); Ganji, *International Protection of Human Rights*, pp. 9–44. I. Brownlie, *International Law and the Use of Force by States* (Oxford: Clarendon Press, 1963), p. 340 concludes that, with the possible exception of the 'French Intervention' of 1860–1861, 'no genuine case of humanitarian intervention' has occurred. Although subsequent developments might call for the modification of this view (see e.g. C. Greenwood, 'New World Order or Old? The Invasion of Kuwait and the Rule of Law', *MLR* 55 (1992), 153) it remains the case that the nineteenth-century practice does not provide compelling evidence for the existence of such a rule.

[123] See generally R. W. Seton-Watson, *Disraeli, Gladstone and the Eastern Question: a Study in Diplomacy and Party Politics* (London: Macmillan, 1935).

[124] Gladstone, *The Berlin Treaty and the Anglo-Turkish Convention* (1878, revised version of a speech in the House of Commons, 30 July 1878). However, he added, with prophetic insight, that: 'It is . . . a little amusing to observe with what edifying zeal all the great states of Europe united to force religious liberty upon those new-fledged bantlings of politics, on their very first light of day; and yet these great States have hardly in any case learned . . . to adopt it at home.' Some forty years later, exactly the same charge was to be levelled at the negotiators at the Paris Peace Conference following the end of the First World War.

[125] Bulgaria declared itself independent and renounced its status as an Ottoman vassal in October 1908, the day before Austria-Hungary annexed Bosnia-Herzegovina.

[126] Once again, allegations of ill-treatment of Christian communities led to a series of demands (the 'Murzsteg Programme') issued by Russia and Austria-Hungary on behalf of the European powers, justified by reference to Article IX of the Treaty of Paris and Articles XXIII and LXII of the Treaty of Berlin. This, however, was not followed by any direct intervention by the major powers. See Ganji, *International Protection of Human Rights*, pp. 29–37.

Europe, with the exception of Istanbul itself and a small area of Eastern Thrace.[127]

The first phase of the war was terminated by the Treaty of London, under which all the continental areas newly conquered by the Balkan Allies were, with the exception of Albania, assigned to them.[128] Disagreements concerning how they should be allocated between them led to a second wave of fighting which was terminated by the Treaty of Bucharest.[129] Neither of these treaties contained any provision regarding the free practice of religion. The Treaty of London vested responsibility for Albania in the major powers who established it as an independent State but, surprisingly, did not insert guarantees of religious freedom into the Organic Statute concluded later that year.[130] Following the Treaty of Bucharest, however, the Balkan States entered into a series of bilateral peace treaties with Turkey, each of which included elaborate provisions dealing with the rights of the Muslim population to the free practice of their religion, the maintenance of religious foundations and the jurisdiction of Muslim religious courts.[131] Indeed, the treaty concluded with Bulgaria went further than any other so far concluded by exempting the Muslim population from any obligation to pay military taxes and to undertake military service.[132]

Religious factors and the post-WWI territorial settlement

The Paris Peace Conference of 1919 was the last of the great gatherings at which combatant States concluded peace treaties that reshaped the map

[127] Shaw and Shaw, *History of the Ottoman Empire*, vol. II, pp. 207–211, 287–298; Castellan, *History of the Balkans*, pp. 368–385.

[128] Treaty of Peace between Bulgaria, Greece, Montenegro, Serbia and Turkey, signed at London, 30 May 1913 (218 CTS 159), Articles II and III. Crete was also assigned to the Balkan Allies (Article IV) whilst all the other Aegean Islands, and Mount Athos, were placed under the control of the major powers (Article V).

[129] Treaty of Peace between Bulgaria, Greece, Montenegro, Romania and Serbia, signed at Bucharest, 10 August 1913 (218 CTS 322).

[130] Organic Statute of Albania agreed between Austria-Hungary, France, Greece, Great Britain, Italy and Romania, signed at London, 29 July 1913 (218 CTS 280).

[131] Treaty of Peace between Bulgaria and Turkey, signed at Constantinople, Articles VII, VIII, XII and Annex 2 (218 CTS 375); Convention between Greece and Turkey for the Consolidation of Peace and Friendship and the Restoration of Normal Relations, signed at Athens, 14 November 1913, Articles XI, XII and Protocol 3 (219 CTS 21); Treaty of Peace between Serbia and Turkey, signed at Constantinople, 14 March 1914, Article 7, 8 and 9 (219 CTS 320). Greece had already undertaken to respect the traditions, customs and religions of the inhabitants of Salonica: Protocol between Greece and Turkey for the surrender of Salonica, 26 October 1912, Annex, Article V (217 CTS 186).

[132] *Ibid.*, Article VII.

of Europe in the Westphalian tradition. As on previous occasions, the religious composition of the territories concerned was a factor to be taken into account but, in line with the practice in Western Europe since the eighteenth century and in Central and Eastern Europe following the withdrawal of Ottoman power, it was accorded very little – if any – weight. Authoritative contemporary studies identified a whole host of factors which influenced the new territorial order, such as self-determination, nationality, equality of nations, justice, rights, freedom and the wishes, natural connections, racial aspirations, security and peace of all people.[133] Moreover, although religious factors and conditions were also listed as principles to be taken into account when deciding whether a particular State should retain, or another acquire, sovereignty over a particular territory, they were not included among the factors relevant for determining whether an area or nationality should acquire statehood in its own right.[134]

Nationality was considered to be the key to the settlement, national self-determination having been the leitmotif of President Wilson's Fourteen Points[135] and a recurrent theme of his speeches prior to the conference.[136] Religious factors were not mentioned in Wilson's speeches

[133] See H. W. V. Temperley (ed.), *A History of the Peace Conference of Paris* (*HPC*), 6 vols. (London: Henry Frowde and Hodder and Stoughton, for the Institute of International Affairs, 1920–1924), vol. II, p. 381. These principles were all ultimately drawn from statements made by the leaders of the Allied powers during the latter years of the war. Much of the analysis and criticism devoted to the peace treaties focused upon the extent to which they gave effect to them. The criteria were, however, so numerous and ephemeral that almost any decision could be both castigated as violating or justified as upholding some of the stated principles. In fact, the settlement was chiefly dictated by political, economic and strategic considerations.

[134] Temperley, *HPC*, vol. II, pp. 411–413. This is of particular significance given the status, and claims, of many members of the Jewish community. At one point, France had argued for the establishment of a number of independent Rhenish States. One of the justifications put forward for this idea was that these areas were chiefly Roman Catholic. The real reason, however, was that France wanted them to be buffer States between France and Germany and felt that a wedge could be driven between them and the rest of Protestant Germany. See D. Lloyd George, *The Truth About the Peace Treaties*, vol. I (London: Victor Gollancz, 1938), pp. 581–582.

[135] See, for example, points 9 (Italy), 11 (Romania, Montenegro and Serbia) and 13 (Poland). On the other hand, there was no mention of nationality in point 8, concerning Alsace-Lorraine: it was axiomatic that this was French territory, rendering principles of nationality and self-determination irrelevant. Text in Temperley, *HPC*, vol. I, pp. 431–435.

[136] E.g. speech of 11 February 1918 ('The Four Principles') in which he said: 'All well-defined national aspirations shall be accorded the utmost satisfaction that can be accorded them without introducing new or perpetuating old elements of discord and antagonism that would be likely in time to breach the peace of Europe, and

as having any particular relevance for the territorial settlement. At best they had a marginal influence, buttressing decisions made chiefly on other grounds or being used as a factor in determining the often difficult question of nationality in parts of Central and Eastern Europe.[137] It has been observed that: 'Religion was taken into account mainly negatively, that is, so far as it threw doubt upon the natural sympathies of people who clearly belonged to a particular nation by race and language, but were of a different religion.'[138] This is illustrated by the following sections which present an overview of the principal elements of the territorial settlement in Europe in which religious factors were of at least potential relevance.

The Treaty of Versailles

Peace was concluded with Germany by the Treaty of Versailles.[139] Religious factors had very little impact upon the territorial provisions of this treaty. They had no discernible effect at all in the west and were ignored in instances where they offered a potential justification.[140] Even in Alsace-Lorraine, where religious factors were known to be an issue, they were marginalized.[141] The sole, and partial exception concerned the Saar basin, where Germany ceded governance to the League of Nations

consequently the world . . . Self-determination is not a mere phrase. It is an imperative principle of action which statesmen will henceforth ignore at their peril.' The emphasis here is on securing self-determination not as an end in itself but as a necessary prerequisite for world peace. As such, it may clearly be subordinated to other means of achieving that overriding goal. Text in Temperley, *HPC*, vol. I, pp. 435–440, and see also the other speeches reproduced *ibid.*, pp. 440–448.

[137] For example, religious censuses were sometimes used in preference to national censuses in gauging the true character of certain areas.

[138] Temperley, *HPC*, vol. VI, p. 242.

[139] Treaty of Peace between the British Empire, France, Italy, Japan and the United States (the Principal Allied and Associated Powers), and Belgium, Bolivia, Brazil, China, Cuba, Czechoslovakia, Ecuador, Greece, Guatemala, Haiti, The Hedjaz, Honduras, Liberia, Nicaragua, Panama, Peru, Poland, Portugal, Romania, The Serb–Croat–Slovene State, Siam and Uruguay and Germany, signed at Versailles, 28 June 1919 (225 CTS 188; LNTS No. 34).

[140] For example, Germany ceded Eupen and Malmedy to Belgium and recognized Belgian sovereignty over Moresnet, which had been under joint Prussian and Belgian administration since 1815. Although the 64,000 people living in these areas were predominantly Roman Catholic, the motivation for the transfers was not religious but economic (Temperley, *HPC*, vol. II, p. 388).

[141] Alsace-Lorraine was ceded to France and, although it was recognized that this would create religious tensions, given the separation of Church and State in France, this was not specifically addressed. Article 53 rather laconically provided that: 'Separate agreements shall be made between France and Germany dealing with the interests of the inhabitants of the territories . . . particularly as regards their civil rights . . .'

and the right to exploit the region's coal mines to France for a fifteen-year period,[142] during which it was expressly provided that 'the inhabitants will retain their local assemblies, their religious liberties, their schools and their language'.[143]

Although the subject of greater consideration, religious factors were of equally little impact in the east, where the cardinal feature of the post-war settlement was the resurrection of the Polish State.[144] This brought about a major dismemberment of Germany's eastern territories. The greater parts of Posnania and West Prussia were ceded and plebiscites were held in the Allenstein and Marienwerder areas.[145] Religious affiliations were of potential significance in the Allenstein plebiscite area where the population was 85 per cent Protestant, despite half of the inhabitants being of Polish origins. Both history and religion connected the area with Germany and the result of the plebiscite, held in July 1920, was an overwhelming vote for union with East Prussia.[146]

Religious factors might also have influenced the outcome of the plebiscite held in Upper Silesia.[147] Although a sizeable majority favoured union with Germany, this was brought about by the overwhelmingly pro-German vote in the North and West divisions where the Polish commu-

[142] This was intended to compensate France for the destruction of her coal mines in the north and to provide an element of war reparations.

[143] Treaty of Versailles, Annex, chapter II, clause 28. At the end of this period the inhabitants were to choose between either French or German sovereignty or the continuation of the League Trusteeship. There was nothing to indicate that France would be bound by a similar obligation if as a result of the plebiscite she acquired full and permanent sovereignty.

[144] The inevitability of this, in the wake of the demise of the Russian Empire, was acknowledged by both Germany and Austria-Hungary who had themselves planned to establish a Polish Kingdom, based chiefly upon the formerly Russian areas, which would, however, be under German domination.

[145] Treaty of Versailles, Articles 94 and 96 respectively. These areas had been a part of the old Polish State and were of economic and strategic importance. They were, however, so predominantly Germanic that it would have been unconscionable to assign them without some form of expression of the wishes of the inhabitants. The final element of the Polish settlement concerned the Baltic port of Danzig (now Gdansk) of whose 324,000 citizens only 16,000 were of Polish origin. Since the pro-German result of any plebiscite could not be doubted, and given that it was considered vital that the new Polish State should have an outlet to the sea, it was decided that Danzig should become a Free City under the protection of the League of Nations (but with Poland responsible for conducting its foreign relations and exercising diplomatic protection on behalf of its citizens). See Treaty of Versailles, Articles 100–108.

[146] In the Allenstein area 363,209 voted for union with Prussia against 7,980 for Poland. In the Marienwerder plebiscite 96,923 voted to remain with East Prussia against 8,018 for Poland. See Temperley, HPC, vol. VI, pp. 248–250 and p. 257.

[147] Treaty of Versailles, Article 88 and Annex thereto.

nities were predominantly Protestant. This threw doubt on their nationalist sympathies and may have substantially contributed to the overall
results not reflecting the national characteristics of the region. Upper
Silesia was finally partitioned in a settlement that bisected the area and
satisfied no one.[148] Since Poland was obliged by the terms of the
Minorities Treaty to grant protection to the German minority in Polish
Upper Silesia, it was considered only equitable to impose a similar set of
obligations upon Germany with regard to the Polish minority in the
German areas. This will be considered further below.[149]

The principal source of religious tension, however, concerned the
substantial number of Jewish communities in the new Poland. This
proved too difficult an issue to address within the Treaty of Versailles and
provided the impetus for the Minorities Treaty concluded between Poland
and the League of Nations which itself provided a model for subsequent
treaties with other Central and Eastern European States. This will be
considered in detail in chapter 4.

This brief sketch of the territorial settlement with Germany in Europe
indicates that religious factors had very little influence. In their reply to
the German Observations on the draft treaty, the Allies said that 'every
settlement of the [draft] Treaty of Peace has been determined upon after
the most careful consideration of all the *religious*, racial and linguistic
factors in each particular country'.[150] Whatever the role given to religious
factors, it was certainly subordinate to racial and linguistic factors and all
of these were subsidiary to wider economic, strategic and political
concerns.

The Treaties of St Germain and Trianon

The circumstances surrounding the territorial settlement in those areas
which had formed parts of the Austro-Hungarian Empire made it a very
different settlement from that concluded with Germany. The defeat of

---

[148] This was brought about by an Award of the League of Nations and approved by the
Conference of Ambassadors of Japan, Italy, the British Empire and France pursuant to
Article 88 of the Treaty of Versailles on 20 October 1921. The United States was not a
party to the Award since it had not ratified the treaty. For the result of the plebiscite
and the League of Nations Award see Temperley, *HPC*, vol. VI, pp. 261–265 and Annex
III, pp. 617–630.

[149] See below, p. 142 and Treaty of Versailles, Article 93 (see below, chapter 4). See also
Article 86, which required the newly created Czechoslovakia to enter into similar
agreements with the Allied powers and which applied, *inter alia*, to the German
minorities in those areas of Silesia ceded to it by Germany (see below, pp. 129–130).

[150] Allied Reply, 16 June 1919 (emphasis added). See Temperley, *HPC*, vol. II, p. 265.

Austria-Hungary brought about the disintegration of an Empire that had been seething with national and racial tensions. Superimposed upon this was a complicated pattern of religious affiliations which were not consistent with either racial, linguistic or geographical factors.[151] Religious affiliations played a part in fostering political tensions within the Empire[152] and, whilst the predominance of Catholicism, until overwhelmed by nationalist pressures, tended to have a unifying influence,[153] it also underscored national divisions between the central and northern areas and those in the south and east.

For example, the religious antipathy between Serbs and Croats did not guarantee Croatian support for the Empire[154] and their sense of rejection overcame ties of religious sentiment and formed the basis for a pan-Slavism that matured into the idea of Yugoslavia during the course of the war.[155] That an embryonic Yugoslavia would contain within it a potent mix of religious tensions – Catholic, Orthodox and Muslim – demonstrated an acceptance that solutions to nationalist problems could not be

[151] Roman Catholicism was the principal religion in Austria and Hungary as well as of the Italian minorities in the Istrian peninsula and the South Tyrol and of the western Slavs (that is, the Poles of Galicia, the Czechs of Bohemia and Moravia and the Slovaks). Of the Southern Slavs, the Slovenes and Croats were predominantly Roman Catholic, whereas the Serbs were Orthodox, as were the Romanians in Transylvania and Bukovina. The Eastern Slavs (Ruthenes) of East Galicia were Uniate (Orthodox following a Latin (Catholic) rite). Some 600,000 of the Serbs and Croats in Bosnia and Herzegovina were Muslim. There were also significant Protestant minorities throughout the Empire, notably of German Lutherans in Transylvania and Slovakia and Calvinists in Hungary. In addition, there was a large number of Jewish communities scattered throughout the Empire as well as a large gypsy population.

[152] For example, when Bosnia-Herzegovina was annexed to the Crown in 1908, Count Burián, responsible for Bosnian affairs at the time, observed that the Catholics were 'to a man' in favour of the union but that the Serbs were, naturally, against, but would not oppose it (S. Burián von Rajecz, *Austria in Dissolution* (London: Ernest Benn, 1925), p. 299).

[153] But priests of the Slovak Catholic Movement pressed for separation from Hungary and, following the national uprising in September 1918, the Czech clergy described 'the realization of an independent Czechoslovakia as an act of God's historic justice' (H. and C. Seton-Watson, *The Making of a New Europe: R. W. Seton-Watson and the Last Years of Austria-Hungary* (London: Methuen, 1981), pp. 45–46, 83 and 303). In Croatia, the Catholic Bishop Strossmayer was an early exponent of Yugoslavism, albeit within the monarchy (see D. Djordjevic (ed.), *The Creation of Yugoslavia 1914–1918* (Santa Barbara, CA: Clio Press, 1980), pp. 6–7).

[154] In order to placate its Italian minority, their demand that Dalmatia be incorporated into Croatia was consistently rejected.

[155] The concept of 'Yugoslavia' as a political ideal had older roots and had manifested itself during the nineteenth century in calls for South Slavic union, either within the Habsburg monarchy (which would have been unacceptable to Russia, as well as to independent Serbia) or outside of it. See Djordjevic, *The Creation of Yugoslavia*, pp. 1–14.

solved by territorial settlements along religious lines and underscored the subsidiary role that such factors were to play throughout the old imperial lands.[156]

Like Germany, Austria-Hungary had sued for peace on the basis of President Wilson's Fourteen Points, which Austria-Hungary thought provided a better negotiating basis than could have been established with France and Britain.[157] Nevertheless, when the end came Wilson abandoned the Fourteen Points, in so far as they referred to Austria-Hungary, precipitating the final disintegration of the crumbling Empire. On 21 October, the German Austrians declared their intention to form a separate State and this was followed by the overthrow of the Hungarian government.

By the time the first German Austrian government took office on 31 October, Czechoslovakia and Yugoslavia had already established separate governments, based on National Councils.[158] On 3 November Austria-Hungary signed an armistice with the Allies and the Emperor Charles renounced his role in the Government of Austria and Hungary on 11 and 13 November respectively. Austria declared itself a Republic on 12 November, as did Hungary on 16 November. It was, therefore, with these republican governments that the Allies concluded the peace treaties. The

---

[156] As the Slavonic expert R. W. Seton-Watson pointed out at the time, 'religious persuasions can no longer be accepted as the basis of state organization in the twentieth century'. H. and C. Seton-Watson, *The Making of a New Europe*, p. 157.

[157] Britain and France were tied by the Treaty of London, 26 April 1915 (221 CTS 56) to assign the southern Tyrol, the Istrian peninsula and significant portions of the Adriatic littoral to Italy. The treaty secured Italian entry into the war on the side of the Allies. Although secret, the gist of its provisions was widely known in diplomatic circles and was seen by Austria-Hungary as a bar to peace. Austria itself had offered to cede to Italy areas of the Tyrol after the war in return for Italian neutrality. See O. Czernin, *In the World War* (London: Cassell & Co., 1919), pp. 190–4 and 275–9 (text); Burián, *Austria in Dissolution*, pp. 51–53; and Temperley, *HPC*, vol. IV, pp. 280–291.

[158] Masaryk, Beneš and Stefanik formed a provisional government in exile on 14 October and published a declaration of independence on 18 October. The National Council had already been recognized by the Allies as representing an embryonic independent State. On 19 October the Czech National Council in Prague proclaimed itself the sole legal representative of the Czechoslovak people, and on 28 October took control of the administration. The first meeting of the new National Assembly of the Republic took place on 14 November.

In Yugoslavia a National Council was formed on 14 October and it finally broke with the Empire on 29 October. In the face of Allied hostility (Italy still had outstanding claims upon 'Yugoslav' territory under the Treaty of London) the National Council united with Serbia on 4 December to form the Kingdom of the Serbs, Croats and Slovenes. Montenegro was also received into the new kingdom on 16 December.

territorial dismemberment foreshadowed by the Fourteen Points had happened of its own accord. The Peace Treaties with Austria and Hungary, were, therefore, concluded under an entirely different set of circumstances than those which influenced the Treaty of Versailles. Moreover, the shadow of Bolshevik revolution hung over the process, and although the Allies would not deal with the regime of Hungarian Communist Bela Kun,[159] they were afraid of the arrival of the Bolsheviks on their doorstep. The prevailing circumstances did not permit a particularly principled approach to the reshaping of Central and Eastern Europe.[160]

Peace was concluded with Austria by the Treaty of St Germain[161] and with Hungary by the Treaty of Trianon,[162] the territorial provisions of which were conditioned by the establishment and recognition of the new States of Czechoslovakia, Yugoslavia and Poland and the enlargement of Romania. The boundaries were largely dictated by events[163] and religious considerations were irrelevant. They were, however, encompassed by Articles 51, 57 and 60 of the Treaty of St Germain and by Articles 44 and 47 of the Treaty of Trianon, which obliged the 'Serb-Croat-Slovene' State, Czechoslovakia and Romania to enter into minorities treaties with the Allied powers,[164] following the model established by Article 93 of the

[159] The government of Bela Kun exercised power from March until November 1920 and the refusal of the Allies to negotiate with it meant that the dismemberment of the Hungarian Kingdom was decided upon without reference to Hungary and the Magyar people.

[160] As Lloyd George later observed, 'The task of the Parisian Treaty-makers was not to decide what in fairness should be given to the liberated nationalities, but what in common honesty should be freed from their clutches when they had overstepped the bounds of self-determination.' Lloyd George, The Truth About the Peace Treaties, p. 91.

[161] Treaty of Peace between the British Empire, France, Italy, Japan and the United States (the Principal Allied and Associated Powers), and Belgium, China, Czechoslovakia, Cuba, Greece, Nicaragua, Panama, Portugal, Romania, the Serb–Croat–Slovene State and Siam, and Austria, signed at St Germain-en-Laye, 10 September 1919 (226 CTS 8; LNTS No. 37). Ratification did not take place until 16 July 1920.

[162] LNTS No.152. The Treaty was signed on 4 June 1920 and ratified on 13 November 1920.

[163] The dominant successor States were able to indulge themselves at the expense of the smaller national groups since the Allies had neither the will nor the ability to intervene effectively to prevent it. For example, the plebiscites in the Duchy of Tschen and in the Zips and Orava districts, over which Poland and Czechoslovakia were in dispute, were abandoned in the face of military intervention. Similarly, the Polish invasion of Eastern Galicia was met with acquiescence and the area was ultimately given to Poland, ending Ruthenian hopes of statehood.

[164] In Articles 43 and 47 of the Treaty of Trianon the Serb–Croat–Slovene State and Romania 'recognized and confirmed' in relation to Hungary the obligations they had undertaken in relation to Austria in Articles 51 and 60 of the Treaty of St Germain. There was no provision equivalent to Article 57 of the Treaty of St Germain since the Czechoslovak minorities treaty had already been concluded.

Treaty of Versailles and itself derived from the example of the Treaty of Berlin (1878). Unlike the Treaty of Versailles, however, both treaties obliged the States with which they were concluded to ensure the rights of racial, religious and linguistic minorities.[165]

The only gap in this otherwise comprehensive picture concerned the areas ceded to Italy[166] which was not required to sign a minorities treaty. Nevertheless, the bond of a common form of religion – Roman Catholicism – between the Italians and the bulk of the peoples of the areas in question made interference or discrimination on religious grounds unlikely, whatever might be the shortcomings of the settlement as regarded racial or linguistic discrimination.[167]

Conclusion

The territorial settlement following the First World War marked the final rejection of religion as a means of determining the physical boundaries of the State. However, by building upon the traditions that had been crystallized by the Treaty of Berlin, the Allies created an entirely new set of conceptual apparatus through which to achieve the peace and stability that had once been associated with the *cuius regio* principle. International concern no longer manifested itself through the simple expedient of regulating the territorial extent of the State or, indeed, by simply providing for the continuance of the religious practices of the inhabitants of transferred areas. Rather, attention switched to exercising effective international oversight of obligations placed upon States under international law. The background to, the development of and the practice under this system will be explored in the following chapters.

[165] Treaty of St Germain, Section V, Articles 62–69; Treaty of Trianon, Section VI, Articles 54–60. See below, pp. 135–136.

[166] See Article 36. These were the Tyrol south of the Brenner Pass, Istria, and parts of Dalmatia, including the town of Zara.

[167] This does not mean that priests were immune from persecution. In the parts of Dalmatia which Italy occupied in pursuance of its claims under the Treaty of London politically active priests, agitating for Slav nationalism, were soon deported or expelled as part of a general policy of repression. See Temperley, *HPC*, vol. IV, p. 305.

3   The League of Nations: drafting the Covenant

The establishment of the League of Nations reflected a move away from Great Power diktat and towards international action mediated through international organizations. The negotiating process that brought the League of Nations into being itself acted as a bridge between the nineteenth century practice, as typified by the Treaty of Berlin (1878), and the contemporary international system. The manner in which the Peace Conference handled concerns now described as human rights issues and considered to be of international concern further reflects this changing outlook.

Of course, these developments were in embryo and did not approach maturity in either the establishment or during the lifetime of the League. Nevertheless, the importance of the Paris Peace Conference is currently underestimated, eclipsed by the establishment of the United Nations at San Francisco in 1945, and the question of which of these conferences best stands comparison with the Treaties of Westphalia as a defining point in the evolution of international affairs is a matter for legitimate debate.

The drafting history of the Covenant of the League reveals that a number of concerted attempts were made to incorporate within the text some reference to guarantees of religious freedom. Although these attempts were ultimately unsuccessful they paved the way for the Minorities Treaties that were to follow. The following sections will look at the evolution of the Covenant, focusing upon the manner in which concerns for religious liberty came to be considered within its framework. The spill-over of this into the minorities treaties and their subsequent development will be looked at in the following chapter.

The first steps

The origins of the Covenant lie in a series of proposals and draft texts prepared before and during the early stages of the Paris Peace Conference.[1] By a process of discussion and compromise, these were moulded into a draft which was formally considered by the Commission established by the Conference to oversee the establishment of the League.[2]

Preliminary sketches

In 1916 Mr Balfour, the UK Foreign Secretary, acting on the advice of Lord Robert Cecil, established a 'Committee on the League of Nations'. This Committee was headed by Lord Phillimore and produced what became known as the 'Phillimore Plan'. Following in the traditions of the Concert of Europe, the Phillimore Plan envisaged a 'Conference of Allied States' which could be summoned by a State in time of crisis (if prior negotiation or arbitration had failed) and which could make recommendations to the parties concerned.[3] The Committee itself said that: 'The primary object of the proposed alliance will be that whatever happens peace shall be preserved between members of the alliance. The secondary object will be the provision of means for disposing of disputes which may arise between the members of the alliance.'[4] The plan therefore included provisions on the 'avoidance of war' and the 'pacific settlement of disputes' but it did not include provisions relating to matters that might cause disputes between members to arise. It was primarily concerned with disposing of disputes, rather than with matters that might give rise to them.

Other preliminary proposals had much the same focus. The French proposal contemplated a more permanent structure – an International Council which would meet yearly and be serviced by a permanent committee and an International Tribunal. The role of the Council would be to 'apply all means for the prevention of international disputes'.

---

[1] See F. P. Walters, *A History of the League of Nations*, 2 vols. (London: Oxford University Press, 1952), vol. I, pp. 20–24 and 27–30; D. H. Miller, *The Drafting of the Covenant*, 2 vols., (New York: G. P. Putnam's Sons, 1928), vol. I, pp. 3–39. All further references to Miller in this chapter are to this two-volume work, unless it is indicated otherwise.

[2] The Conference formally opened on 18 January 1919. The League of Nations Commission was established at the second Plenary on 25 January, this being the first Commission to be set up. See *Papers Relating to the Foreign Relations of the United States, The Paris Peace Conference, 1919 (PPC)* (Washington: US Government Printing Office, 1943–1946), vol. III, pp. 177–201.

[3] Articles 3–12. For text see Doc. 1 in Miller, vol. II, p. 4.

[4] Interim Report in Miller, vol. I, p. 4.

Nevertheless, the intention was to assist dispute settlement by means of the good offices or mediation of the Council. Disputes of a legal nature were to be submitted to the 'Court of International Jurisdiction', the decisions of which would be enforceable by the Council.[5] Although more elaborate mechanisms were proposed, the French approach was, in essence, similar to that of the British.

The commitment of the President of the United States, Woodrow Wilson,[6] to a League of Nations was outlined in the last of his Fourteen Points of 8 January 1918, which stated that: 'A General Association of nations must be formed under specific covenants for the purpose of affording mutual guarantees of political independence and territorial integrity to great and small States alike.' The first concrete American proposals, however, derived from a draft drawn up by Colonel House, at the request of Wilson, in the light of the Phillimore Plan.[7] The Preamble to the House Draft described the formation of a League, 'having for its purpose the maintenance throughout the world of peace, security, progress and orderly government'.[8] The House Draft did, however, go further than the UK or French proposals by recognizing that attempts should be made to address the causes of disputes, rather than merely provide structures for dealing with them once they had arisen. Thus at the head of the draft stood a series of articles emphasizing openness and morality in international relations which were described by House as 'the keystone of the arch'.[9]

[5] Minutes of first meeting of the League of Nations Commission, Annex II (Articles iv (d), vi (i)). See Doc. 19, Miller, vol. II, p. 289.

[6] Wilson's commitment was tinged with an almost more than 'missionary' zeal, which may shed some light on his advocacy on behalf of religious liberty. D. Lloyd George, *The Truth About the Peace Treaties* (London: Victor Gollancz Ltd, 1938), vol. I, p. 225. recounts that: 'His most extraordinary outburst was when he was developing some theme – I think it was connected with the League of Nations – which led him to explain the failure of Christianity to achieve its highest ideals. "Why" he said, "has Jesus Christ so far not succeeded in inducing the World to follow His teachings in these matters? It is because He thought the ideal without devising any practical means of attaining it. That is the reason why I am proposing a practical scheme to carry out His aims."'

[7] Doc. 2, Miller, vol. II, p. 7. House sent this plan to Wilson on 16 July 1918.

[8] *Ibid.* Some elements, however, were not derived from the Phillimore Plan, such as the provisions regarding an International Court and the realization that the 'Conference' would be 'in almost continuous session'. Disputes would also be subject to compulsory arbitration (Miller, vol. I, p. 15).

[9] Articles 1–4. See Miller, vol. I, pp. 12–15. This reflected the then current belief that secret diplomacy had been a factor contributing to the outbreak of the war and that if dealings between States were conducted openly there would be less room for dispute and misunderstanding. The first of Wilson's Fourteen Points called for 'Open Covenants of peace, openly arrived at, after which there shall be no private international

An even more significant example of such thinking was reflected in Article 20 of the draft, which provided that:

The Contracting Powers unite in several guarantees to each other of their territorial integrity and political independence subject, however, to such territorial modifications, if any, as may become necessary in the future by reason of changes in present racial conditions and aspirations, pursuant to the principle of self-determination and as shall also be regarded by $\frac{3}{4}$ of the delegates as necessary and proper for the welfare of the peoples concerned: recognizing also that all territorial changes involve equitable compensation and that the peace of the world is superior in importance and interest to questions of boundary.[10]

Without considering the merits of the provision itself, it did bring together a number of themes that have since been developed, such as self-determination, the threat to peace posed by the existence of minorities and the international interest in the preservation of peace as a counterweight to principles of State sovereignty.[11] Nevertheless, the chief concern was that without this degree of flexibility the League might find itself guaranteeing territorial boundaries, the protection of which was not consonant with the overriding aim of preserving the peace. There was as yet no move towards the recognition and protection of rights themselves as a means of lessening tensions and thereby enhancing the goal of peace.[12]

Early drafts

President Wilson produced four draft texts of a Covenant during the period immediately prior to the deliberations of the League of Nations

understandings of any kind, but diplomacy shall proceed always frankly and in the public view'. The practice of the Paris Conference itself hardly lived up to this ideal.

[10] Miller, vol. II, p. 10.

[11] House commented: 'It is quite conceivable that conditions might so change in the course of time as to make it a serious hardship for certain portions of one nation to continue under the government of that nation' (letter accompanying Draft, Miller, vol. I, p. 14).

[12] Cf. the Italian Draft, Doc. 19, Annex III, Miller, vol. II, pp. 246–255. This contained a list of principles designed to reflect the 'necessary conditions' of 'independent and autonomous development' which included equality before the law, territorial integrity, equal participation in international commerce and traffic, freedom of merchant navigation and adequate distributions of foodstuffs and raw materials. These proposals are of a different nature to the others so far considered in that they sought to achieve that equity and justice in international relations which would ease international tensions. (They also followed the others in submitting disputes not settled by negotiation or arbitration to the Council of the League, which could pass the matter on to the Conference or a Court of International Justice.) These proposals do not, however, seem to have as much significance in the moulding of the Covenant as the American and British proposals. Despite their being included in the minutes of the first meeting of the League of Nations Commission, Miller said they were not tabled and were only included in the minutes as a matter of 'politesse'. (Miller, vol. I, p. 132.)

Commission.[13] The first was drawn up in the light of the House Draft and closely followed its general outline. Article 20 of the House Draft received greater prominence and some elaboration with the result that the League's guarantee would not extend to protecting the territorial integrity of Member States as against each other where racial, social, political or other pressures demanded the redrawing of boundaries.[14]Nevertheless, the relevance of such issues was still restricted to the context of territorial guarantees.

A far broader vision was elaborated by General Smuts in his 'practical suggestion'.[15] He argued that: 'Peace and war are resultants of many complex forces, and those forces will have to be gripped at an earlier stage of their growth if peace is to be effectively maintained . . . it must become part and parcel of the common international life of states.'[16] Drawing upon the twin principles of 'no annexation' and 'self-determination', Smuts outlined a system of mandates which will be looked at further below.[17]

Wilson's second draft reflected elements of the Smuts proposals, not only in the alterations made to its thirteen articles, but also in the addition of six 'supplementary agreements'. The first four of these dealt with the question of mandates and the fifth with fair hours and humane conditions of labour. The Sixth Supplementary Agreement, however, was of a different order and represented the first real attempt to include

[13] First Draft (Washington Draft, drawn up privately by Wilson in the light of the House Draft of 18 July 1918), Doc. 3, Miller, vol. II, p. 12 (for an analysis of other US proposals made during the latter part of 1918 see Miller, vol. I, pp. 18–33); Second Draft (First Paris Draft), 10 January 1919, Doc. 7, Miller, vol. II, p. 65; Third Draft (Second Paris Draft), 20 January 1919, Doc. 9, *ibid.*, p. 98; Fourth Draft (Third Paris Draft), 2 February, Doc. 14, *ibid.*, p. 145. See generally Miller, vol. I, pp. 15–17, 40–50, 72–75.

[14] To changes 'necessitated by racial conditions and aspirations' was added 'or any other change demanded, in the opinion of $\frac{3}{4}$ of Delegates, by the welfare and interests of the peoples concerned', as were territorial adjustments necessitated by 'present social and political relationships'. It should be noted that the agreement of the State from whom such people were to be detached was not necessarily required under this provision.

[15] This was dated 16 December 1918. See Doc. 5, Miller, vol. II, p. 23. General Smuts represented the Union of South Africa within the British Empire delegation at the Paris Conference.

[16] *Ibid.*, pp. 23, 25.

[17] Smuts believed, however, that a system of mandates should not apply to German colonies in the Pacific and Africa 'which are inhabited by barbarians, who not only cannot govern themselves, but to whom it would be impractical to apply any idea of self-determination in the European sense', (*ibid.*, p. 28). This underlines the salutary truth that much of the principled posturing of the Allied powers at Paris was motivated by a barely concealed self-interest. The long history of South African interest and involvement in what was German South West Africa (now Namibia) is well known.

within the framework of the Covenant a requirement that sought to protect the rights of individuals *per se*. It provided that:

The League of Nations shall require all new states to bind themselves as a condition precedent to their recognition as independent or autonomous States, to accord to all racial or national minorities within their jurisdictions exactly the same treatment and security, both in law and in fact, that is accorded the racial or national majority of their people.[18]

The shortcomings of this provision are clear enough. First, it only applied to States to be newly established and was simply following the precedent offered by the Treaty of Berlin. Commenting upon the text, Miller felt that this obligation should also be placed upon some – but not all – existing States, such as Bulgaria.[19] Secondly, Miller also argued that it would be impossible to accord equal rights to all minorities in all matters, for example, the use of minority languages in official records, and felt that this general clause would need elaborating in the light of the particular circumstance pertaining to each of the countries to which it was applied. He did, however, express the view that: 'Doubtless equal religious and cultural privileges should be accorded in all cases . . .',[20] thus suggesting that freedom of religion was encompassed by the supplementary agreement. Nevertheless, any protection was of a very low order. As with any such right, it would exist for the minority group only to the extent that such freedom was extended to the racial or national majority. There was certainly no guarantee of religious freedom *per se*.

In the meanwhile, the UK had submitted further proposals. Lord Cecil presented a draft convention, dated 20 January, which, whilst retaining 'the promotion of peace among the nations of the world' as the primary object of the League, sought to achieve this '*by eliminating, so far as possible, the causes of international disputes*, by providing for the pacific settlement of such disputes as they arise and by encouraging a general system of

---

[18] Miller, vol. II, p. 91.

[19] *Ibid*. He later remarked that stronger provisions for the protection of minorities were found in the Treaty of Berlin (1878) – and sardonically drew attention to Turkish massacres in Macedonia as a witness to their efficacy (Miller, vol. I, p. 47). This is, perhaps, an unfair criticism since international recognition of Ottoman suzerainty over Macedonia was not conditional upon respect for minority rights. On the other hand, Article LXII of the Treaty of Berlin did impose international obligations upon the Porte which were as applicable to Macedonia as to any other part of the Empire, as was the *Hatti Humayoun* of 1856, as recognized by Article IX of the Treaty of Paris (1856). See above, p. 71.

[20] Miller, vol. I, p. 91.

international co-operation for promoting the peaceful purposes of mankind.'[21]

The need to address the causes of conflict was placed above the establishment of means to resolve them. However, the 'causes of international disputes' that were contemplated were still of the restricted nature envisaged by the earlier proposals and the draft was chiefly concerned[22] with regulating the build up of armaments[23] and the need to preserve and guarantee territorial integrity, to the extent that such existing boundaries 'conform to the requirements of the situation'.[24] This proposal, though more open-ended, was not dissimilar from that contained in Article 3 of the second Wilson Draft.[25] Both foresaw that the League ought not to provide a blanket guarantee for territorial boundaries established by the post-war settlement which were likely to give rise to unrest by groups of people suddenly finding themselves living in countries dominated by others.

The drawback of both the Wilson and Cecil proposals was that they sought to meet this problem by providing the League with an 'escape mechanism' which would enable it to retreat from its obligations to the States concerned. They were more interested in protecting the position of the League than with the position of those groups which sought protection by seeking either autonomy or union with a neighbouring State. Miller recognized that this essentially negative attitude would 'simply

---

[21] Doc. 10, Miller, vol. II, p. 106. (emphasis added). This was a revision of an earlier proposal drawn up by Lord Cecil on 14 January. See Doc. 6, *ibid.*, p. 61.

[22] Some concern for broader issues was evidenced by Chapter I, Article 1(vi) which called for studies into economic and social matters, with the League having the power to recommend action where shown to be necessary.

[23] Chapter I, Article 1(vi).

[24] If these boundaries were no longer suitable, the League could recommend 'modification which it may think necessary'. If these recommendations were rejected, the League's obligation to protect the territory would cease (Chapter I, Article 1(ii) and Article 2).

[25] 'The Contracting Powers unite in guaranteeing to each other political independence and territorial integrity; but it is understood between them that such territorial readjustments, if any, as may in the future become necessary by reason of changes in present racial conditions and aspirations or present social and political relationships, pursuant to the principle of self-determination, and also such territorial readjustments as may in the judgment of three-fourths of the Delegates be demanded by the welfare and manifest interest of the peoples concerned, may be effected if agreeable to those peoples; and that territorial changes may in equity involve material compensation. The Contracting Powers accept without reservation the principle that the peace of the world is superior in importance to every question of political jurisdiction or boundary.' See Doc. 7, Miller, vol. II, p. 70.

tend to legalize agitation in Eastern Europe for a future war'[26] and he urged that 'as the drawing of boundaries according to racial or social conditions is in many cases an impossibility, protection of the rights of minorities and acceptance of such protection by the minorities constitutes the only basis of enduring peace'.[27] As has been seen, the force of Miller's criticism is somewhat lessened by the presence in Wilson's second draft of the Supplementary Agreement VI and, indeed, Miller did not press for the removal of Article 3 of the second Wilson Draft,[28] which, along with Supplementary Agreement VI, was carried over into Wilson's third draft of 20 January 1919.

The third draft contained, however, four further Supplementary Agreements and it is the first of these, Supplementary Agreement VII, which for the first time explicitly provided for the protection of religious freedoms within the League framework. It stated:

> Recognizing religious persecution and intolerance as fertile sources of war, the Powers signatory hereto agree, and the League of Nations shall expect from all new states and all states seeking admission to it the promise, that they will make no law prohibiting or interfering with the free exercise of religion, and that they will in no way discriminate, either in law or in fact, against those who practise any particular creed, religion, or belief whose practices are not inconsistent with public order or public morals.[29]

Supplementary Agreement VII marked a radical departure from the previous drafts. These had tentatively felt their way towards the realization that the League must concern itself with the causes of international disputes and wars, rather than merely provide machinery for dealing with the actual disputes themselves. However, their recognition of this had not advanced much beyond preambular rhetoric or statements of general principles regarding non-discrimination by newly created States or States seeking to accede to the League.[30] Supplementary Agreement VII went beyond this and provided for an outright prohibition on interference with the exercise of religion or discrimination against those engaged in religious practices, subject to the caveat regarding public health and morals. Moreover, this was to be a basic standard applicable to all

---

[26] Miller, vol. I, p. 52.   [27] *Ibid.*, p. 53 and see vol. II, p. 67.
[28] Miller, vol. I, p. 53. But he did suggest that there should be a reservation so as to bring it into line with the Monroe Doctrine of non-intervention by extrinsic powers in American affairs.
[29] Miller, vol. II, p. 105.
[30] That is, in accordance with Supplementary Agreement VI of Wilson's second draft. As will be seen below, the system of minorities treaties in fact spread the web of protection beyond the limited scope envisaged by this proposal.

members of the League. This marked it off from Supplementary Agreement VI, under which no obligation would be assumed by the existing powers at all.

It was by no means universally acknowledged that such a provision was needed in the first place, let alone that it should be of general application. Lord Eustace Percy suggested an amalgamation of Wilson's third draft with that of Lord Cecil, commenting that: 'Article VII is to a certain extent covered by a provision in the British Draft Convention regarding Mandataries. In regard to new and independent states, this is a matter of internal government which it is almost impossible for the League of Nations to supervise or enforce. It might therefore be better to omit this Article.'[31] On this view, then, League protection might be desirable for mandataries but where the League had no direct control it ought not to set standards or assume obligations which it could not enforce. The concern, as in the case of territorial boundaries, was to protect the League from undesirable commitments.

Moreover, the comments of Lord Percy emphasized that such matters were of internal rather than international concern. This contradicted the premise of Supplementary Agreement VII, which was that religious persecution and intolerance were matters of international concern because they were 'fertile sources of war'. Percy also suggested that Supplementary Agreement VI, concerning non-discrimination, be omitted. The British felt that these matters were best dealt with in treaties to be drawn up with the individual States affected or created by the peace process and which would be backed by the guarantee of the League. Although, as the UK argued, this would have the advantage of tailoring the provisions to the specific needs of the minorities concerned (as also Miller had suggested), it would also mean that the Covenant of the League would be silent on these issues.[32]

Miller and Cecil met together on 27 January and produced an amalgam of the UK and US proposals known as the Cecil–Miller Draft.[33] Supplementary Agreement VII (religious discrimination) was adopted unchanged but Supplementary Agreement VI (non-discrimination) was reserved for

---

[31] Miller, vol. II, p. 130. Although this does not specifically refer to the signatory States, the clear implication is that such a provision would be of little or no value in relation to them.

[32] *Ibid.*, p. 129. The UK delegation was not opposed in principle to the Covenant touching upon these matters, considering it a useful 'fall-back' position if it proved impossible to address them in the individual treaties.

[33] Doc. 12, *ibid.*, p. 131.

further consideration. These three drafts were then considered by Miller and Hurst, the UK Legal Advisor, on 1 February and the document they produced – the Hurst–Miller Draft – became the standard negotiating text for the remainder of the work.[34] Supplementary Agreement VI was dropped altogether, but Supplementary Agreement VII was retained in a slightly modified form and, as Article 19, provided:

The High Contracting Parties agree that they will make no law prohibiting or interfering with the free exercise of religion, and that they will in no way discriminate, either in law or in fact, against those who practice any particular creed, religion, or belief whose practices are not inconsistent with public order or public needs.[35]

Consideration by the Commission

Once the Conference had decided that a League of Nations should be established 'as an integral part of the general Treaty of Peace', the discussions were brought under its formal umbrella by establishing the Commission on the League of Nations,[36] the previous work having been no more than a series of private negotiations between the Great Powers – and primarily the United States and the British Empire. The Commission was initially composed of fifteen members – two from each of the Great Powers (USA, the British Empire, France, Italy and Japan) and one from each of five of the Associated Powers, those chosen being Belgium, Brazil, China, Portugal and Serbia.[37] It was subsequently enlarged to nineteen members by the addition of Greece, Poland, Romania and Czechoslovakia.[38] The Commission on the League of Nations held fifteen meetings,[39] ten of which were held between 3 and 14 February and led to a draft

---

[34] For text see Minutes of the Commission on the League of Nations; 1st Meeting, Annex I. Miller, *ibid.*, p. 231. President Wilson was unhappy with the Hurst–Miller Draft and put forward a fourth draft of his own on 2 February which retained Supplementary Agreements VI and VII in their original form, but it was the Hurst–Miller Draft which was considered by the Commission of the League of Nations when it began its consideration of the Covenant on 3 February.

[35] Miller, *ibid.*, p. 237.

[36] See resolution of the Plenary Session of the Paris Peace Conference on 25 January. The Commission commenced its work on 3 February 1919.

[37] See *PPC*, vol. III, pp. 176–201.

[38] Clemenceau placed the request of the Associated Powers for greater representation before the Council of ten on 3 February 1919. Although opposed by Wilson, the request was passed on to the Commission which agreed to it. See *PPC*, vol. III, pp. 857–858; Minutes of the Commission, 4th Meeting, Miller, vol. II, p. 263. The enlarged Commission first sat at the fourth meeting, on 6 February.

[39] The Minutes of the Commission are found in Doc. 19, Miller, vol. II, pp. 228–394.

covenant which was presented to the third Plenary Session of the Conference on 14 February.[40] This text did not contain any provision concerning religious liberty. The question had, however, received extensive consideration.

At the sixth meeting of the Commission, on 8 February, Lord Cecil proposed replacing Article 19 of the Hurst–Miller Draft with a new provision which read:

> Recognizing religious persecution and intolerance as fertile sources of war, the High Contracting Parties agree that political unrest arising therefrom is a matter of concern to the League, and authorize the Executive Council, whenever it is of opinion that the peace of the world is threatened by the illiberal action of the Government of any state towards the adherents of any particular creed, religion or belief, to make such representations or take such other steps as will put an end to the evil in question.[41]

This represented both a weakening and an expansion of Article 19. Rather than acknowledging that any restriction upon religious liberty was a matter of concern to the League, as representing a potential threat to peace, the text only addressed situations in which such restrictions had actually led to political unrest. Further, only if political unrest presented an actual threat to peace could the Executive Council take action. Most crucially, there was no longer any prohibition of such 'illiberal action' *per se*. Provided that world peace was not threatened, the international community would not be concerned. As in the earlier British Draft,[42] the regulation of religious affairs was seen primarily as a matter of domestic jurisdiction. Although purporting to recognize 'religious persecution and intolerance as a fertile source of war', the Cecil proposal represented a regression towards the earlier drafts of the Covenant, concerned with the question of how to deal with international disputes, rather than attempting to address their causes.

On the other hand, the proposal sought to authorize the League to make recommendations *or take any other steps necessary* in the face of actions by States. This went beyond the obligation contained in Article 19 of the Hurst–Miller Draft which did not confer any specific right of action upon League members. Perhaps even more significantly, the new proposal did not limit its concern to the 'illiberal' actions of the High Contracting Parties, but sought to extend the – admittedly more limited – powers of the League to 'the action of the Government of *any* state'.

---

[40] See *PPC*, vol. III, p. 208. The text of the Draft Covenant is found in Annex 1 (p. 230) and in the Annex to the 10 Meeting of the Commission (Miller, vol. II, p. 327).

[41] Minutes, 8th Meeting, Annex 5, Miller, vol. II, p. 276.   [42] See above at n. 31.

Although Wilson explained that the motive behind the original article was the desire to prevent religious persecution or wars in the future, others in the Commission apart from Cecil were opposed to it. Views were expressed that such a provision might conflict with the Constitutions of some States, whilst the flexibility inherent in terms such as 'intolerance' or 'persecution' was felt by others to be dangerously open ended, and would draw the League into internal political disputes. It was also pointed out that draft Article 9 of the Covenant gave the League power to consider internal troubles which threatened international peace.[43] Given the extent of these disagreements, Article 19 was referred to a Drafting Sub-Committee, composed of Mr Hymans (Belgium), Mr Bourgeois (France), Lord Cecil (British Empire) and Mr Veniselos (Greece)[44] – all of whom had expressed dissatisfaction with the Hurst–Miller Draft.

The Sub-Committee presented a new text to the seventh meeting which read:

Recognizing religious persecution as a fertile source of war, the High Con-tracting Parties solemnly undertake to extirpate such evils from their terri-tories, and they authorize the Executive Council, whenever it is of opinion that the peace of the world is threatened by the existence in any state of evils of this nature, to make such representations or take such other steps as it may consider that the case requires.[45]

This compromise text preserved an element of obligation regarding the elimination of religious persecution but omitted any reference to reli-gious intolerance.[46] However, it retained the rather expansive provisions conferring upon the League the power to make representations 'or other steps as . . . the case requires'. In some ways, this represents the strongest proposal concerning the protection of religious liberty that is found in the drafting history of the Covenant since it combined a prohibition with partial measures of enforcement. In his role as a Legal Advisor, Miller, who was generally hostile to the inclusion of such a clause,[47] advised

---

[43] *Ibid.*, pp. 273–274. Those expressing doubts included the representatives of Italy, France, Belgium, Greece and Portugal. Thus eight of the eighteen members of the Commission expressed opposition to Article 19, either in principle or as drafted.

[44] Minutes, 5th Meeting, Miller, vol. II, p. 269.

[45] Report of the Drafting Committee, Annex I. Minutes of 7th Meeting, Miller, vol. II, p. 283.

[46] This was presumably to accommodate the views of Mr Hymans (Belgium) who had objected to such a reference when the original draft had been discussed in the full Commission.

[47] Miller later identified the inclusion of this article as one of his two principal criticisms of the draft. See Miller in E. M. House and C. Seymour (eds.) *What Really Happened at*

Wilson that this provision went 'further than any other provision in the Covenant'.[48]

This new version of Article 19 was, however, rejected by the Commission, which adopted yet another new text put forward by Wilson. It is recorded in the French Minutes as reading:[49]

Les Hautes Parties Contractantes décident qu'elles ne permettront pas que leurs citoyens, adherénts d'une foi, religion ou croyance quelconque, qui ne porte pas atteinte à l'ordre ou aux moeurs publiques, soient pour cette raison inequiétés dans leur vie, leur liberté et leur poursuite du bonheur.

By only outlawing discrimination on the grounds of religion or beliefs that affected the life, liberty or pursuit of happiness of citizens, the draft left open the possibility of other forms of discriminatory practices. Further, and most importantly, the draft only extended its protection to the citizens of States Parties, and did not address the position of non-citizens resident within a State,[50] or persons to whom citizenship was denied. This removed from its ambit some of the most vulnerable groups that ought to have been its prime focus.

By this time, the position of the text concerning religious freedoms had fallen into disarray. At the end of the eighth meeting of the Commission the entire Draft Covenant was referred to a Drafting Committee consisting of Lord Cecil (British Empire), Mr Veniselos (Greece), Mr Larnaude (France) and Mr Vesnitch (Serbia).[51] In the resulting proposals, Article 19 became renumbered as Article 21 and read:

The High Contracting Parties agree that they will not prohibit or interfere with the free exercise of any creed, religion or belief whose practices are not inconsistent with public order or public morals and that no person within

Paris (London: Hodder & Stoughton, 1921), chapter XVII, p. 406. See also Miller, vol. I, pp. 191, 196 and 269.

[48] Miller, vol. I, p. 196.

[49] Miller, vol. II, pp. 449–450. The English version of the Minutes (Minutes, 7th Meeting, *ibid.*, p. 282) gives the text as:
> The High Contracting Parties agree that they will make no law prohibiting or interfering with the free exercise of religion, and they resolve that they will not permit the practice of any particular creed, religion, or belief whose practices are not inconsistent with public order or with public morals, to interfere with the life, liberty or pursuit of happiness of their people.

This is clearly a nonsense and, as Miller (vol. I, p. 196) points out, the true intention must surely have been the opposite, as is recorded in the French Minutes of the Meeting.

[50] It must be presumed that the draft presupposed that each State's obligation would be limited to its territorial jurisdiction.

[51] Minutes, 8th Meeting, Miller, vol. II, p. 212.

their respective jurisdictions shall be molested in life, liberty or the pursuit of happiness by reason of his adherence to any such creed, religion or belief.[52]

Apart from expressing in correct English the general tenor of the text found in the French Minutes, the only substantive alteration made was that the scope of the provision was extended from 'citizens' of a country to those 'within their respective jurisdictions'. The Drafting Committee, a majority of which had long been hostile to such a provision at all, recommended that 'in view of the complications of this question, it would be preferable to omit this article altogether'. They put forward the above draft for consideration only 'if ... there is a strong feeling in the Commission that some such provision should be inserted'.[53]

It was President Wilson who had been the champion of a provision on religious freedom. It was he who had originally raised the question by including Supplementary Agreement VII in his third Draft. Yet at the tenth meeting of the Commission, when a proposal to delete the provision was formally made for the first time, Wilson was not present[54] and Lord Cecil chaired the meeting. House stated that Wilson strongly desired the inclusion of the article but this was opposed by Mr Larnaude, the French Legal Advisor, who said that the Drafting Committee had agreed with Cecil that 'in spite of the great advantage that there would be in proclaiming freedom of conscience and worship, the drafting of these reflections was so difficult that it was better to suppress it'.[55] Moreover, he expressed the view that there was no cause for anxiety regarding freedom of worship in the countries which were to be members of the League: 'the anxiety shown is for other countries ... But this is besides the question, since for the moment we are considering especially countries where freedom of worship is accorded to all.'[56]

If this were indeed so, it is difficult to understand why there was any hostility to its inclusion. The Commission had agreed to it in principle and the Drafting Committee had produced a workable text. Moreover, it was strongly supported by Wilson. However, just when it appeared that the text might be adopted because it was considered relatively unimpor-

---

[52] Minutes, 9th Meeting, Annex II, *ibid.*, p. 307.

[53] Report of the Drafting Committee, Annex I, Minutes, 9th Meeting, Miller, *ibid.*, p. 307.

[54] This meeting took place on 13 February. Wilson was due to return to the United States on the following day. In his absence pressure had grown in the US Senate against participation in an international organization that could commit the US to intervene in European affairs and it was to meet this opposition that the President was returning.

[55] Miller, vol. I, p. 267.   [56] Miller, *ibid.*, pp. 267–268.

tant and certainly not worth offending Wilson by removing it,[57] a dramatic intervention by the leader of the Japanese delegation, Baron Makino, totally changed the nature of the debate.

The Japanese 'equality amendment'

Baron Makino proposed to add to Article 21 an additional clause providing that:

The equality of nations being a basic principle of the League of Nations, the High Contracting Parties agree to accord, as soon as possible, to all alien nationals of states members of the League equal and just treatment in every respect, making no distinction, either in law or in fact, on account of their race or nationality.

He explained that:

racial and religious animosities have constituted a fruitful source of trouble and warfare among different peoples ... [Article 21] as it stands attempts to eliminate religious causes of strife from international relationships, and as the race question is also a standing difficulty which may become acute and dangerous at any moment in the future, it is desirable that a provision should be made in this Covenant for the treatment of this subject. It would seem that matters of religion and race could go well together.[58]

At first sight, the proposal appears to be an ambitious attempt to extend the scope of the Covenant to address an additional but related concern which was just as much a source of potential international tension as religious questions. On that basis it was simply an extension of the 'pre-emptive' function of the League, addressing the underlying causes of international disputes rather than waiting for them to erupt. However, it was not well received[59] and was rejected – but in the process precipitated the deletion of draft Article 21 in its entirety.

If the racial equality provision was unacceptable and no satisfactory

---

[57] Lord Cecil, as Chairman, observed (ibid., p. 268) that: 'As President Wilson especially desires the inclusion of this article in the text . . . I think it cannot be very well omitted'. Mr Larnaude also said that 'since President Wilson insists on the insertion of this article, I should be unwilling to demand its abrogation'.

[58] Minutes, 10th Meeting, Miller, vol. II, pp. 323–324. See also R. P. Anand, 'Sovereign Equality of States in International Law', HR 197 (1986–II), 9, at pp. 89–91.

[59] Lord Cecil felt that: 'It was a matter of a highly controversial character, and in spite of the nobility of thought which inspired Baron Makino, he thought that it would be wiser for the moment to postpone its examination.' The Chinese were 'in full sympathy with the spirit of the amendment' but reserved their position pending government instruction while Mr Veniselos, agreeing that race and religion would go together, felt 'it would be better for the moment not to allude to them' (ibid., p. 325).

ground could be presented for distinguishing between racial equality and freedom of religion then both would have to go. In Wilson's absence, none of the Commission were sorry about this and Miller remarked that: 'The [Japanese] proposal, however, served a good purpose at the meeting, for it helped to make impossible any article on religious liberty in any form: any such article in the Covenant would have been most dangerous; and perhaps fatal to the League: the subject was never again considered.'[60] Wilson was informed of this by Colonel House and he agreed that it should be dropped. With his departure for the United States the next day he was in no position to do otherwise.

In fact, the Japanese intervention was not unexpected. The Japanese proposal had first surfaced in Paris on 4 February when Baron Makino and Viscount Chinda sought the advice of Colonel House, who told them to prepare two drafts – one they wanted, and a compromise. House received these the next day and showed them to Wilson. The first was discarded, the latter amended and returned to Chinda who initially thought it satisfactory.[61] The next day, however, he returned to say his advisors had told him it was meaningless. There then followed a series of informal discussions between the Japanese, House and the British during which little progress was made. Miller discussed the matter with House and Mr Balfour, the British Foreign Secretary, and agreed that the Japanese amendment could not be accepted.[62] House asked Miller to draft an alternative text, which Miller submitted with the comment that 'Any draft which had a real effect would, of course, be impossible.'[63] Miller's objections ran even deeper, however, since any reference would cause it

---

[60] Miller, vol. I, p. 269.

[61] C. Seymour (ed.), *The Intimate Papers of Colonel House,* 4 vols. (London: Ernest Benn, vols. I and II 1926, vols. III and IV 1928), vol. IV, pp. 321–322. The text then read:

> The equality of nations being a basic principle of the League, the High Contracting Parties agree that concerning the aliens in their territories, they will accord them, *so soon and as far as possible,* equal treatment and rights in law and in fact, without making any distinction on account of their race or nationality.

The words italicized were replaced by the words 'as soon as possible' in the text put to the Commission by Baron Makino, thus significantly altering it in a way unacceptable to Wilson and House. See A. S. Link (ed.), *The Papers of Woodrow Wilson,* vol. LIV, (NJ: Princeton University Press, 1986), p. 500.

[62] Miller, vol. I, pp. 193–4. Neither this informal meeting, nor Miller's text, is mentioned in Seymour (ed.), *ibid.*, vol. IV, p. 324 (entry for 9 February 1919).

[63] Miller, vol. I, p. 184. His draft read: 'Recognizing that all men are created equal, the High Contracting Parties agree that the Executive Council may consider any external grievance affecting the nationals of any of the High Contracting Parties, and may make such recommendations in respect thereof as are deemed equitable.'

to become a question of international cognizance, which he considered unacceptable.

House seems to have been preoccupied with ensuring that the Japanese realized that the problem lay not with the US but with the British. He was flattered by the Japanese regarding him as an ally on the matter,[64] yet he did not want the Covenant to contain a substantial legal obligation relating to equality.[65] It is true that the British delegation was the stumbling block in the Commission but the real source of difficulty was Mr Hughes, the Premier of Australia and a member of the British Empire's delegation to the Conference, who saw in the Japanese amendment the threat of mass immigration that would undermine the 'White Australia' policy.

In common with New Zealand and the United States, Australia had enacted legislation limiting immigration from East Asia. They feared that the presence of this clause in the Covenant would be used by Japan as a means of questioning the validity of these rules.[66] The problem of Japanese expansion had been foreseen and acknowledged,[67] but it was clearly felt that no legal obligation to guarantee them equality of treatment abroad could realistically be undertaken. Australia felt itself particularly vulnerable and so was intractable on the issue. This was not the end of the matter, however, and the fate of the 'equality amendment'

---

[64] House records that 'Chinda and Makino said: "On July 8th at Magnolia [House's home] you expressed to Viscount Ishii sentiments which pleased the Japanese Government, therefore we look upon you as a friend and we have come for your advice."' See Seymour (ed.), *The Intimate Papers of Colonel House*, vol. IV, p. 321.

[65] Although House expressed sympathy for the idea to the Japanese, Miller asserts that he knew all along that the texts had no particular legal effect (Miller, vol. I, p. 183). It seems that House was as pleased with the outcome as Miller, although for different reasons. His diary records: 'The result is that the Japanese have expressed to me their profound gratitude . . . It has taken considerable finesse to lift the load from our shoulders and place it upon the British, but, happily, it has been done. This ought to make for better relations between Japan and the United States.' He earlier had recorded that the Japanese proposal ultimately presented was as unacceptable to him as it was to the British. See entry from the Diary of Colonel House for 13 February quoted in Link (ed.) *The Papers of Woodrow Wilson*, vol. LV, p. 155. This passage is not found in the entry for that date in Seymour (ed.), *The Intimate Papers of Colonel House*, vol. IV, p. 325.

[66] See Walters, *A History of the League of Nations*, vol. I, p. 63.

[67] After their meeting on 9 February, Miller recorded in his diary that 'Colonel House said that he did not see how the policy towards the Japanese could be continued. The world said that they could not go to Africa, they could not go to any White country, they could not go to China and they could not go to Siberia; and yet they were a growing nation having a country where all the land was tilled. They had to go somewhere' (Miller, vol. I, p. 183).

must be examined because, as Baron Makino and Mr Veniselos both observed,[68] the questions of racial and religious discrimination were to progress hand in hand.

When the Draft Covenant was presented to the Plenary Session of the Conference on 14 February, Baron Makino, during an occasion that was otherwise almost entirely self-congratulatory in tone, said that he was 'reserving until a later stage . . . a certain proposition . . . for which I shall have to ask favourable and careful consideration'.[69] When Wilson returned from the United States on 14 March the Commission held five more meetings. The Preamble to the Covenant was considered at the very last meeting on 11 April at which Baron Makino proposed that it be amended to include 'the endorsement of the principle of equality of nations and just treatment of their nationals'.[70] This threw the Commission into disarray. This sentiment could hardly be opposed and no legal obligation would be created and it therefore seemed to be almost impossible to avoid voting for it.[71] Nevertheless, some argued the difficulty of including a principle in the Preamble which was not worked out in the Covenant itself,[72] whilst others raised the problem of conflict with the principle of non-interference in internal affairs.[73] Wilson argued that, whilst he fully agreed with the suggestion, its acceptance by the Commission would only lead to trouble in the Plenary of the Conference and therefore he thought it inadvisable to include it.[74] When voted upon, the amendment received eleven out of seventeen votes. Wilson, however, ruled that a unanimous decision was needed for inclusion and therefore the amendment failed.[75]

---

[68] See above, n. 59.   [69] *PPC*, vol. III, p. 225.

[70] Minutes, 15th Meeting, Miller, vol. II, p. 391, and see vol. I, p. 461.

[71] See comments of Mr Larnaude, Minutes, 15th Meeting, Miller, vol. II, p. 390.

[72] Mr Dmowski (Poland), *ibid.*, p. 391.

[73] Lord Cecil, *ibid.*, p. 389 and see Miller, vol. I, p. 466.

[74] Wilson argued that: 'How can you treat on its merits in this quiet room a question which will not be treated on its merits when its gets out of this room?' (Miller, vol. I, p. 463 and vol. II, p. 391.) This rather disingenuous piece of chicanery overlooked the point that the Plenary Sessions of the Conference were almost entirely formal in nature. See H. W. V. Temperley, *HPC*, vol. I, pp. 249–250. The only amendment accepted by the Plenary to the Covenant was proposed by Wilson. See Miller, vol. I, p. 497. The Plenary was, in reality, unable to effect real change once the Commission's proposals had been approved by the Council of Four (which by March had superseded the Council of Ten as the real power behind the Conference).

[75] The Minutes record only the number of affirmative votes cast (and only did this on the insistence of the Japanese) and thereby avoided putting Wilson and House in the difficult position of being seen to have voted against. Lord Cecil certainly voted against but he was under strict instructions to do so and was clearly unhappy with his

If the principal stumbling block was the Australian objection – although pressure to resist measures that would facilitate Japanese immigration had also been growing in the United States – a further problem was the linkage between the Australian position and the inclusion of the Monroe Doctrine within the Covenant. Mr Hughes argued that if the Monroe Doctrine was to be recognized within the Covenant[76] then there was no reason why the 'white Australia' policy should not be similarly recognized.[77] Miller observed that 'however unobjectionable the words, as words, might be, their very vagueness could only mean that they were a sort of curtain behind which was the question of White Australia and of immigration of Eastern peoples into countries which regarded the possibility of such immigration as impossible to discuss'.[78]

Thus the door was finally closed on the Japanese 'equality amendment'[79] and with it the chance for a possible revival of the religious

position. Miller says that this was one of the few occasions on which Lloyd George instructed Cecil on how to act. See Miller in House and Seymour (eds.), *What Really Happened at Paris*, p. 403. Wilson attempted to save face by insisting that the vote did not represent a defeat for the principle (Miller, vol. II, p. 392).

[76] This was achieved by Article 21 of the Covenant and was seen as the price for the support of the United States which did not, in fact, materialize.

[77] See Temperley, *HPC*, vol. VI, p. 352.

[78] Miller, vol. I, p. 461. He might have added that its ramifications were coming too close to home for comfort. House records that even before the matter was taken back to the Commission, he had made it clear to Makino that he would only support him if Prime Minister Hughes dropped his objections. Hughes was threatening to take the matter to the Plenary and to 'raise a storm of protest . . . in the Western parts of the US'. Once again, House was anxious to deflect Japanese criticism from the US. See Seymour (ed.), *The Intimate Papers of Colonel House*, vol. IV, pp. 430–431.

[79] Baron Makino raised but did not press the matter at the Plenary on 28 April (see *PPC*, vol. III, p. 285 at pp. 189–91 and Miller, vol. I, p. 497 and vol. II, pp. 701–704. There were, however, other reasons for this. A controversial issue at the Conference related to Japan's claim to German concessions in the Shantung Peninsula which had been promised to Japan by Britain and France in a secret agreement concluded in 1917. The claim was opposed by China, which was supported by the United States. Since Britain realized that Japan held them responsible for the failure of the equality amendment, they were anxious to satisfy them over the Shantung issue and brokered an arrangement that secured for Japan what she sought. See Seymour (ed.), *The Intimate Papers of Colonel House*, vol. IV, pp. 465–471 and Temperley, *HPC*, vol. VI, pp. 378–382. The threat of Japan not signing the treaty also influenced the Americans. The Italians had just withdrawn from the Conference over the Fuime issue and Wilson could not afford another blow. Given the resolution of the Shantung issue, it was not surprising that Makino let the equality issue fall. There was clearly a trade off between the issues, with Makino agreeing to the Shantung compromise on the very day that the Plenary was due to meet to discuss the Covenant. Some commentators argued that the compromise should have been the other way around. See, e.g. , H. Wilson Harris, *The Peace in the Making* (London: Swarthmore Press Ltd, 1919), pp. 158–159: 'It was not a

liberty proposal. When the wording of the Preamble was being considered it was pointed out that if racial equality was mentioned some reference to religious liberty might be reintroduced, since it was the linkage between the two issues that had led to the deletion of the original proposal.[80] There was, however, no way back. Lord Cecil, in opposing the Japanese amendment, noted that 'it had been found impossible to include within the text matters so unquestionably right as those of religious liberty . . . because they would result in infringements of the sovereignty of states'.[81] He could have added that Britain had already proposed to the Drafting Committee at the end of the eighth meeting of the Commission that the Preamble include a clause reading: 'They [the High Contracting Parties] unite in solemn recognition of the principle of freedom of conscience and religion', but that this had not been adopted.[82] Lord Cecil felt 'it was better that the Covenant should be silent on these questions of right. Silence would avoid much discussion.'[83]

This observation is illustrative of the major shift in attitude that had taken place during the course of the Conference. The bulk of the delegates were chiefly preoccupied, at this late stage in the evolution of the text, with producing a Covenant that would be acceptable to both the Conference and to their governments and which would work on its own terms. No matter how pertinent a matter might be to the overriding aim of preserving the peace of the world, if silence or the exclusion from the Covenant of clauses relating to religious freedom or national equality would increase the acceptability – and workability – of the League, then it was a price worth paying. The mood was summed up by Wilson who said that although no one could dream of interpreting the vote on the Japanese amendment to the Preamble as condemnation of the principle, the proposed clause would raise objections in the United States and it would be better not to insist upon it.[84] The heady idealistic atmosphere of

---

great deal to ask that . . . the League should formally declare that in its eyes a yellow man was as good as a white. For that was really all that Japan wanted.'

[80] This was raised by Mr Veniselos, who considered himself largely responsible for the deletion of draft Article 19 at the tenth meeting of the Commission. See Miller, vol. II, pp. 390–391.

[81] Miller, *ibid.*, p. 389.   [82] Miller, vol. I, p. 218.

[83] Miller, vol. II, p. 392. Walters, (*A History of the League of Nations*, vol. I, p. 64) perhaps best sums up the matter: 'The Japanese argument combined disconcertingly, from the British and American point of view, the qualities of being unanswerable and unacceptable. The only course, therefore, was to abandon both suggestions.'

[84] Miller, vol. II, p. 392. It would indeed be difficult to construe the vote as a rejection of the principle, since it was accepted by a clear majority. The acceptability to Japan of a Covenant not containing provisions on national equality does not seem to have

the Commission's earlier days had yielded to the pressures of domestic interests and the preservation of State sovereignty. Under such circumstances there was little future for an international obligation concerning the freedom of religion, irrespective of its linkage to the more immediately controversial issue of discrimination between nations and races.

As this account illustrates, few apart from Wilson possessed any real enthusiasm for the article on religious liberty and Wilson's own closest advisors on Covenant issues, Miller and House, were themselves opposed. Despite these handicaps it is probable that, but for the Japanese equality amendment, Article 21 of the Drafting Committee's text would have found its way into the Covenant. Its linkage with the equality amendment, however, effectively ended any hope of the Covenant containing an international obligation or even an endorsement of religious freedom. It is ironic that in recent years religious and racial issues have again been linked but this time, whilst the former again floundered, the latter matured into an international covenant.

weighed so heavily, despite Makino suggesting that it might result in Japan refusing to join the League at all (*ibid*. p. 390). American ambivalence is further reflected in a secret dispatch sent to the US Ambassador in Tokyo which said that the US would have accepted the Preamble, but the British flatly refused. This was designed to counter criticism of the US's attitude in the Japanese press. See D. H. Miller, *My Diary at the Peace Conference* (privately published), vol. I, pp. 257–258.

4　The Polish Minorities Treaty

Introduction

The attempt to include a provision concerning religious liberty in the Covenant of the League of Nations failed. However, a second route opened up with the conclusion of a series of minorities treaties which did embrace the concept. These treaties were drafted in the New States Committee which was established by the Council of Four on 1 May 1919.[1] The work of the Committee was, however, preceded by a series of discussions between those representing the principal Allied Powers who were most informed – or, rather, the most lobbied[2] – on the question of the Jews in Poland. As the work of the Committee progressed and broadened out to embrace the problem of minorities in all of the newly constituted and enlarged States in Central and Eastern Europe, it did become more formalized and experts were brought in to help. In the initial stages, however, the decision-making process was concentrated in the hands of a very small circle, comprising the Committee members and the Supreme Council.[3]

---

[1] The background to, and the establishment of, the New States Committee is considered below at p. 114.

[2] One of the most active of American Jewish lobbyists, Louis Marshall, wrote that: 'I am perhaps more responsible for the Minorities Treaties than any other man' (letter to Isaac Franc in C. Reznikoff (ed.), *Louis Marshall: Champion of Liberty* (Philadelphia: The Jewish Publication Society of America, 1957), vol. II, p. 556). For activities of Jewish pressure groups at the Paris Peace Conference see J. Fouques-Duparc, *La Protection des Minorités de Race, de Langue et de Religion* (Paris: Librairie Dalloz, 1922), pp. 159–177; N. Feinberg, *La Question des Minorités à la Conference de la Paix de 1919–1920 et l'action Juives en faveur de la Protection International des Minorities* (Paris: Rousseau et Cie, 1929), and O. I. Janowsky, *The Jews and Minority Rights (1898–1919)* (New York: Columbia University Press, 1933).

[3] When the question of the Jewish minority in Poland was first raised, the Supreme

104

Moreover, the very existence of the New States Committee remained secret during the initial phase of its activities.[4] Although the members had no shortage of information from their advisors, and kept up a constant dialogue with the Jewish and Polish groups, formal consultations only took place at a very late stage by which time the basic structure of the Polish Treaty, which served as a model for the others, was well advanced.[5] The Polish Treaty, then, established the pattern of minorities protection during the inter-war years and exerted a powerful influence on the development of human rights protection following the Second World War. Indeed, the experience of these treaties still influences the debate surrounding the very issue of the international protection of minority rights.

Yet it must be stressed that the very description of the Polish Treaty as a *minorities* treaty is potentially misleading and disguises its origins and function. Above all else, it was designed to protect the Jewish population in the new State of Poland[6] and it was the Jewish lobby that made the treaty a reality.[7] Its applicability to other minority groups was little more than a side effect. Although concern was expressed for other minorities and their needs made known, they had little impact upon the discussions and some amendments distinctly disadvantageous to other minorities were accepted in order to placate Polish unease at the extent of the protection being offered to the Jews.[8]

The focus of the treaty upon Jewish interests makes it difficult to distinguish between those parts which deal with what might be called 'religious liberties' *per se* and those aspects which seek to preserve the distinctive cultural and social patterns of Jewish life which bound them

Council, normally known at this stage of the Conference as the Council of Four, consisted of only Wilson, Lloyd George and Clemenceau and was thus occasionally referred to as the Council of Three. Orlando of Italy had withdrawn from the Council as a consequence of the dispute over Fiume and Trieste. He rejoined the Council on 7 May.

[4] Lloyd George told Sir Herbert Samuel of its existence on 4 May, whence news quickly spread. See D. H. Miller, *My Diary at the Peace Conference* (privately published), vol. I, p. 289.

[5] See below, p. 119.

[6] As late as 17 May, Headlam-Morley, the British member of the Committee, was describing the draft treaty as the 'Report of our Committee on the Jews, etc.'. Letter to Namier, A. Headlam-Morley, *Sir James Headlam-Morley: a Memoir of the Paris Peace Conference 1919* (London: Methuen & Co., 1972), p. 111.

[7] See the comments of M. O. Hudson in E. M. House and C. Seymour (eds.), *What Really Happened at Paris* (London: Hodder & Stoughton, 1921), p. 473.

[8] An example being the decision to restrict the application of Article 9 to those parts of Poland that had been a part of Germany prior to 1914, thus debarring German-speaking minorities in the rest of Poland from its scope. For Article 9 see below, pp. 121, 136.

together as a 'national' entity. This problem struck at the very root of the principles upon which the post-war settlement was, ostensibly, being conducted – national self-determination.

This tension manifested itself in a number of ways. First, the Jewish world was itself divided between the Zionists, who considered the Jews to be a 'nation' and, whilst calling for the establishment of a Jewish National Home, sought 'national rights' in the States of Eastern and Central Europe, and those who saw themselves as nationals of the States in which they lived but sought protection and guarantees against harassment on account of their religion and religious practices.[9] Secondly, the newly established nation States found it difficult to accept that, as sovereign States, they should be subjected to obligations benefitting minorities when they had not had the benefit of such protection when minorities themselves.

The political background to the treaty

Since the first consideration of minority issues at the Conference centred on the protection of the Jews in Poland, it was inevitable that that should provide the context from which the entire subject was approached.[10] The political background to the Polish Treaty is, then, of critical importance.

By the end of the war the establishment of an independent Polish State had become inevitable.[11] Although the precise demarcation of the new State was by no means certain, it was clear that it would include a large Jewish community. This was a matter of considerable concern to groups of emigré Jews living in the West. Not only were they aware of the sufferings of their co-religionists in the past, but they were also aware of how ineffectual the guarantees contained in the Treaty of Berlin had proved to be in the case of Romania. Poland became the focus of their

---

[9] For the background to this see Janowsky, *The Jews and Minority Rights*, chapters 1–6.

[10] Headlam-Morley, *Memoir*, p. 111.

[11] Although not originally a specific British war aim, Mr Asquith had declared in 1914 that the Allies sought to ensure that 'the rights of the smaller nationalities of Europe are placed on an unassailable foundation', whilst the Russians were more explicit in their aim of establishing an autonomous and united kingdom of Poland, which would include Posnania and Galicia. See H. W. V. Temperley, *HPC*, vol. I, p. 169. Whilst the British claim did not necessarily entail the creation of a Polish State, Russia sought to establish a Polish State based on those parts of the old kingdom in German and Austrian, but not Russian, hands. President Wilson called for the creation of a Polish State in the thirteenth of his 'Fourteen Points'. France sought the establishment of as strong a Polish State as possible.

attention, not only because of its large Jewish population, but because of the strength of anti-Semitic feeling.[12]

It was, therefore, comparatively easy to persuade the Western leaders that special measures were required. The difficulty lay in how this was to be done in the context of the peace settlement. Although the Allies had the option of withholding recognition from the new State unless it took upon itself the relevant obligations,[13] there were other pressures influencing the decision-making process, and the security of the new Europe was considered by many to be conditional upon the creation of a viable Poland. The position was further complicated by the divergent aims of the chief powers and the complexities of the pattern of political power in Poland.

France saw in Poland a power that counterbalanced the German threat to France. France had traditionally looked to Russia to fulfil this role, but following the Revolution a new ally was needed and, therefore, the establishment of a large and powerful Polish State was favoured. This view chimed with those of Dmowski, who saw Germany as the principal threat to Polish independence[14] and, given Dmowski's anti-Semitism, the Jews could expect little help from the French.

The British position was very different. They felt that European security could best be preserved by avoiding the creation of another 'Alsace-Lorraine' and, not wanting to give Germany any grounds for complaint against Poland, generally advocated the principle of ethnocentricity. Although by no means identical, this was closer to views of General Pilsudski, who had taken over the Government of Poland in 1918 and was the political opponent of Dmowski.[15]

The United States was less interested in the particulars of the settle-

---

[12] The leader of the Polish National Democrats, Dmowski, had instigated a campaign of boycotting Jewish shops in 1912 and during the course of a visit to the United States in the autumn of 1918 antagonized Jewish leaders by arguing that this economic boycott was justified by the pro-German attitude of the Jewish communities. See K. Lundgreen-Nielson, *The Polish Problem at the Paris Peace Conference* (Odense University Press, 1979), p. 42. For a record of the stormy meeting between Dmowski and Louis Marshall see Reznikoff, *Louis Marshall: Champion of Liberty*, vol. II. pp. 585–593.

[13] Though in some ways this was more of a theoretical than a practical proposition. When the question was discussed by the Council of Three, Miller suggested this as a possibility, but Wilson and Lloyd George do not appear, from the records, to have taken this up. See P. Mantoux, *Les Délibérations du Conseil des Quatres, 24 Mars – 28 Juin 1919* (Paris: Éditions du Centre National de la Recherche Scientifique, 1955), vol. I, p. 475 (hereafter cited as 'Mantoux').

[14] Lundgreen-Nielson, *The Polish Problem*, pp. 70–78.

[15] As such, they were the chief advocates of Ruthenian independence and resisted Polish eastern expansionism, although this was later compromised in order to provide a bulwark against Russian Bolshevism. Lundgreen-Nielson, *ibid.*, pp. 58–78. British policy

ment than in its overall philosophy and Wilson was quicker to advocate the principle of self-determination than translate it into boundaries. He saw the League of Nations as the ultimate arbiter of future problems. In general, his views were closer to the British than the French. The chief influence upon US policy had been Paderwski, who represented Dmowski's National Democrats in the US and had toned down his party's anti-Jewish sentiments in the face of the powerful Jewish lobby.[16]

The problem of dealing with Poland was complicated by the failure of the Poles to speak with one voice. Paderwski returned to Warsaw early in 1919 and reached an accommodation with Pilsudski, by which he, Pilsudski, would retain his position as Chief of State but Paderwski would become Prime Minister and Foreign Minister, with Dmowski remaining in Paris as the chief Polish representative at the Peace Conference. Paderwski later came to Paris himself. When this background is added to the divergent strategies of the Allies with regard to the Poles and account is taken of the rapidly developing political and military situation in the region, a thoughtful and cogent response to the problem of the Jews and other minorities was hardly to be expected, even if it was desired.

On the other hand, the Polish leaders were themselves acutely aware of the need to accommodate the Western-backed Jewish interest groups, if only for economic reasons. The new Poland would need substantial economic assistance and the influence of the Jews in Western banking and financial circles was considerable. It is against this background that the activities of the various Jewish pressure groups must be traced.[17]

These groups were also divided in their aims. Broadly speaking, the British Group, the Joint Foreign Committee (the Secretary and principal figure in which was Lucien Wolf) and the French Alliance Israélite Universelle were more moderate in their aims than the Zionist Americans of the American Jewish Congress, the leading figures of which were Judge Mack and Mr Louis Marshall. Mack and Marshall represented the Congress at Paris[18] where they found common cause with the representatives of the

---

was profoundly influenced by the work at the Foreign Office of Lewis Namier who opposed Polish expansionism and was a Jew of Eastern Galician extraction.

[16] Wilson's aides, especially the US expert on Poland, Professor Lord, and the US Secretary of State Lansing, were markedly more pro-Polish. Lundgreen-Nielson, *The Polish Problem*, pp. 79–89.

[17] See Janowsky, *The Jews and Minority Rights*, pp. 264–319.

[18] The American Jewish Congress had been formed in December 1918 with the purpose of preparing and presenting proposals concerning the civil, religious and political rights of minorities to the Peace Conference – although the focus was, naturally, upon the situation of Jews in Eastern Europe. Louis Marshall was President of the American

Eastern European Jews and together formed the 'Comité des Délégations Juives auprès la Conférence de la Paix' and Judge Mack was elected its Chairman.[19]

Marshall, in common with many other Jewish figures, had already been active in promoting Jewish interests. Following his meeting with Dmowski on 6 October 1918, he wrote a series of letters to President Wilson urging the importance of securing means of protecting the Jewish minorities in Eastern Europe[20] and, with other leaders of the Congress, met Wilson to press the issue on 2 March 1919 during Wilson's visit to the United States and then proceeded to Paris to continue their efforts.

Preliminary manoeuvres

Once in Paris, Mack and Marshall contacted Miller, who was already known to them and was then working on the Covenant of the League of Nations. Mack asked Miller whether it was possible to insert a clause on religious equality in the Covenant of the League, but Miller told him this was unlikely[21] and a few days later advised him to contact those involved with the Polish question,[22] since news of anti-Jewish pogroms in Pinsk had raised the Jewish issue at a crucial moment in the negotiating process and gave added weight to the calls for some form of protection for the Jewish minority in Poland.

Rather than the matter being formally taken up by the Conference, the issue was addressed first of all in a series of private meetings which did not produce any concrete results.[23] Paradoxically, the National Democrats

---

Jewish Committee, one of the groups participating in the Congress. See Reznikoff, *Louis Marshall: Champion of Liberty*, vol. II, pp. 505–580. Of particular interest is the letter of Marshall to Manley Hudson at pp. 551–556 (dated 1921).

[19] Feinberg, *La Question des Minorités à la Conférence de la Paix*, pp. 32–44.

[20] Feinberg, pp. 593–597. Wilson's responses are of some interest as they shed some light upon his desire to see a general clause concerning religious liberty in the Covenant of the League of Nations. He wrote to Marshall saying 'I shall keep the highly important matter . . . in my thoughts whenever I have the opportunity to deal with it' (letter of 16 November 1918, Feinberg, p. 596) and 'I have no doubt that there will be many opportunities to impress upon the Peace Council the serious aspects of the very great and appalling problem upon which you dwell, and I shall deem it a privilege to exercise such influence as I can' (letter of 20 November 1918, *ibid.*, p. 599).

[21] On 1 April 1919. See Miller, *My Diary*, vol. I, p. 217.

[22] On 5 April 1919. *Ibid.*, p. 222.

[23] See Lundgreen-Nielsen, *The Polish Problem*, p. 305. Namier came to Paris to discuss the matter on behalf of the British. He stayed until the draft text was prepared on 13 May and continued to liaise between the Jews and Poles. See Headlam-Morley, *Memoir*, p. 99 and J. Namier, *Lewis Namier: a Biography* (Oxford University Press, 1971), p. 142.

were prepared to recognize the national status of the Jews within Poland but were opposed in this by Paderwski who thought it a ploy to arouse anti-Semitic sentiments.[24] It was against this background that the matter was raised by Wilson in the Council of Three on 1 May 1919.[25]

Whilst these discussion had been taking place, Mack and Marshall had been engaged in intensive discussions with Miller. Manley Hudson, Miller's assistant, had dinner with Mack and Marshall on the evening of 18 April and asked them to submit to Miller a draft concerning 'the protection of minorities in Poland and other places'.[26] This paper was delivered the next day[27] and embodied the principle that:

each national minority . . . composed of at least one per centum of the entire population shall constitute an autonomous organization on a footing of equality with the right of establishing and managing its national, religious, educational, charitable and social institutions . . . For the purposes of this article the Jewish population . . . shall be regarded as a national minority with all the rights specified above.[28]

Each 'national minority' would be entitled to proportional representation at all levels of government, these representatives being chosen by independent electoral colleges. State funds would also be made available to national minorities to fund their exercising of governmental functions.[29] Other clauses provided for the enjoyment of equal civil, religious, political and national rights without abridgment or discrimination on the grounds of race, nationality or religion,[30] the unfettered use of languages by national minorities[31] and a special clause protecting the Sabbath, which

---

[24] Lundgreen-Nielsen, *The Polish Problem*, p. 305.
[25] Mantoux, vol. I, p. 440.   [26] Miller, *My Diary*, vol. XIII, p. 259.
[27] *Ibid.*, p. 262. This was headed 'Proposals for the Protection of Minorities' (p. 422). These were derived from the articles under discussion by the Comité des Juives. The Comité ultimately produced a draft and explanatory memorandum which were submitted to the Conference on 10 June 1919, but bore the date 15 May 1919 (see *ibid.*, vol. IX, p. 191). Most commentators (e.g. Janowsky, *The Jews and Minority Rights*, pp. 314 and 336) take the view that this time lag was of little importance since the substance of the draft had already been presented to the Committee informally by Mack and Marshall. Marshall, however, relates in a letter to Cyrus Adler (of the American Jewish Committee) that the Comité did not finalize its draft proposals until after the New States Committee had finished the substance of its work and it deliberately backdated its submission to obscure its ineffectiveness. See Reznikoff, *Louis Marshall: Champion of Liberty*, p. 568. For both an analysis of the articles and a comparison with the final text of the Polish Treaty see Feinberg, *La Question des Minorités à la Conférence de la Paix*, pp. 76–94.
[28] 'Proposals for the Protection of Minorities', Section I, Article 3. Miller, *My Diary*, vol. VIII, p. 422.
[29] *Ibid.*.   [30] *Ibid.*, Section I, Article 2.   [31] *Ibid.*, Section I, Article 4

provided that: 'Those who observe any other day than Sunday as their Sabbath shall not be required to perform any acts on their Sabbath or holy days which by the tenets of their faith are regarded as a desecration; nor shall they be prohibited from pursuing their secular affairs on Sunday.'[32]

The acquisition of territorial rights by the State in question was to be dependent upon its adopting these provisions as an integral part of its constitution[33] and subject to the guarantee that:

Any of the Signatories of the Treaty of which this article shall constitute a part and any group that may be affected by a failure to observe or to effectuate any of the provisions of this article shall be entitled to submit their complaint for adjudication to the League of Nations or to such tribunal as it may establish and upon such conditions as it shall prescribe.[34]

The three most significant features of this proposal were, first, the creation of 'national minorities' which were to be the recipients of large measures of autonomy within the State, coupled with proportional participation in governmental activities; secondly, the granting to 'groups' within the State the right of complaint to the League of Nations; thirdly, the specific protection of the Sabbath, this being the only provision that explicitly provided for the protection of purely Jewish interests.

Miller had also been drafting a proposal. After discussing the matter with Hudson, he prepared a draft which read:

The protection of life and individual liberty to all inhabitants of Poland is assumed by Poland as an obligation which it recognizes to be of international concern and which it undertakes as such with the other Allied and Associated Powers to carry out so that there shall be no discrimination against any inhabitant of Poland because of race or religion, and so that there shall be fair proportional representation for minorities in all its representative institutions, and so that any public funds used for religious, charitable, educational or social purposes shall be fairly applied in accordance with the aspirations, customs, and language of the various classes of the population so as to benefit all the inhabitants equitably and proportionally, and so that the freedom of language and religion shall be universally enjoyed.

The foregoing provisions shall not only be a matter of individual obligation on the part of Poland but shall also be embodied in the fundamental law of Poland as an irrevocable bill of rights, with which no law or regulation shall conflict or interfere and as against which no law or regulation shall have validity or effect.[35]

[32] *Ibid.*, Section I, Article 5.　　[33] *Ibid.*, Section I.　　[34] *Ibid.*, Section II.
[35] *Ibid.*, p. 455.

This proposal was far less specific. It tied the use of public funds to the good of the population as a whole, rather than to that of the minority in question. There was no general requirement that governmental institutions be based on principles of proportionality, simply an obligation to apply that principle fairly where it was operative. Moreover, the proposal could be taken as subordinating these rights, along with the principles of non-discrimination and freedom of language and religion, to a general requirement to protect the life and liberty of *all* inhabitants of Poland. Finally, there was no specific mechanism for international supervision.

The gulf between these two sets of proposals was narrowed in a series of meetings between Miller and Mack and Marshall,[36] and Miller forwarded the final version of the agreed draft to Colonel House on 29 April.[37] This was much closer to the original Jewish proposals than to his own, although two of the three features of the Jewish draft highlighted above were absent. There was no specific protection of the Sabbath, although it was provided that Poland would 'assure to all inhabitants . . . freedom of religion and the outward exercise thereof'.[38] Similarly, although the general jurisdiction of the League of Nations was admitted, there was no mention of a right of appeal to the League by concerned groups. On the other hand, Miller was convinced by the argument in favour of recognizing the Jews as a national minority. The sole remaining point of disagreement concerned the question of whether proportional representation in elections to public office should be conducted on the basis of the national group or on electoral districts.[39]

Mack and Marshall met with House to discuss this draft on 30 April and they were unhappy with their reception.[40] The draft was, however, passed on to Wilson who, as mentioned above, raised the matter the following day in the Council of Three. If there were to be any protective clauses inserted into the German Treaty, the matter could not wait any longer

---

[36] Held on 21 and 22 April. *Ibid.*, vol. I, pp. 263–265 and 267.

[37] Miller had liaised with House during these discussions, which House thought it best not to make public, although he sanctioned discussion with Britain and France. *Ibid.*, vol. I, p. 270 and vol. VIII, pp. 182–185.

[38] *Ibid.*, Article 3(b).

[39] Alternative versions were presented to House (*ibid.*, Article 6). There were many other changes in the draft, but these were often of style, rather than substance, although often representing not insubstantial improvements. Since the draft was substantially altered in later discussions, these changes will not be examined further.

[40] Miller records that 'afterwards Judge Mack came in and told me of his conversation and said he was hoping to try to get the matter to Lloyd George through Sir Herbert Samuel'. Miller, *My Diary*, vol. I, p. 283. But *cf.* Janowsky, *The Jews and Minority Rights*, p. 340.

since the final text of the treaty was due to be transmitted to the Germans.[41]

Wilson introduced the subject by observing that the persecution of Jews in Poland and Romania posed a threat to world peace and, in consequence, guarantees for national and religious minorities should be included in the German Treaty. He proposed that general articles be inserted into the treaty which would apply to all of the new States that would become a party to the treaty and apply to all minority groups within them.[42] It provided:

1. The State of . . . covenants and agrees that it will accord to all racial or national minorities within its jurisdiction exactly the same treatment and security, alike in law and in fact, that is accorded the racial or national majority of its people.
2. The State of . . . covenants and agrees that it will not prohibit or interfere with the free exercise of any creed, religion or belief whose practices are not inconsistent with public order or public morals, and that no person within its jurisdiction shall be molested in life, liberty or the pursuit of happiness by reason of his adherence to any such creed, religion or belief.[43]

Wilson requested that a small committee of experts be established: 'To consider the question of international obligations to be accepted by Poland and other new states to be created by the Treaties of Peace, including the protection of racial and religious minorities'. At the same time, it was drawn to their attention that 'President Wilson's draft in regard to the protection of religious minorities was generally agreed to be satisfactory.'[44]

---

[41] This finally took place on 7 May. See Temperley, *HPC*, vol. II, p. 1.

[42] See Mantoux, vol. I, pp. 440–442. Wilson drew particular attention to the presence of former German subjects within the new Poland.

[43] *PPC*, vol. V, p. 393. The second paragraph was essentially the same as the text Wilson proposed for inclusion in the League Covenant at the 7th Meeting of the Commission on the League of Nations on 10 February 1919. See D. H. Miller, *The Drafting of the Covenant* (New York: G. P. Putnam's Sons, 1928), vol. II, p. 282 and see above, p. 95.

[44] Mantoux, vol. I, p. 441; and 1st Meeting of New States Committee, Annex A. Miller, *My Diary*, vol. XIII, pp. 13–14. It should be noted that Wilson did not suggest that Miller's draft be adopted. It is probable that, like House, he was not happy with it and felt it would be easier to amend it by working in conjunction with the British, whose attitude he knew to be less extreme than the Zionism still evident in Miller's proposals. Both Wilson and Lloyd George were opposed to the creation of a Jewish 'State within a State' in Poland. See Mantoux, vol. I, p. 440.

The Polish Treaty in the New States Committee

The New States Committee was initially[45] composed of Headlam-Morley (Britain), Miller (USA) and Berthelot (France). Miller and Headlam-Morley met for two and a half hours on the afternoon of Friday 2 May.[46] The first matter to be decided was whether they ought to adopt substantive articles for inclusion in the German Treaty, as advocated by Miller, or merely to insert a clause binding Poland to accept a separate treaty with the Allies, this being Headlam-Morley's view.

From the start, Miller and Headlam-Morley were at odds with each other. Headlam-Morley felt that Miller's proposals were unacceptable and needed to be discussed with the Poles. He drew up a draft report which he planned to submit even if Miller disagreed and also sent Hankey a series of arguments that Lloyd George could raise should Wilson question the rejection of Miller's proposals[47] However, after a further two-hour meeting that evening they adopted a Report which read that: 'It was agreed that the question, in particular so far as it affects the Jews in Poland, is so contentious and so difficult that it is impossible to come to precise conclusions about it in the short time available before the text of the treaty with Germany is closed.'[48]

Miller sent Wilson a memorandum outlining the contents of the Report[49] so that when Miller and Headlam-Morley presented their opinions to the Council of Four the next day (3 May) both sides had been briefed on the disagreement.[50] The Council decided in favour of the British point of view[51] and agreed that a 'holding clause' be inserted into

[45] Following Orlando's rejoining the Council of Four an Italian member, de Martino, was appointed, as was later a representative of Japan. They did not, however, make any significant impact upon the discussions.

[46] Berthelot was not appointed until later that evening, and did not attend any of that day's meetings.

[47] He thought that: 'What Mr Miller . . . has done is simply to take in their crude form certain Jewish suggestions, which we . . . have been trying to persuade the Jews to withdraw.' Letter to Sir Maurice Hankey, in Headlam-Morley, *Memoir*, p. 92.

[48] 1st Report to the Council of Three, Annex B. Miller, *My Diary*, vol. XIII, p. 21; *PPC*, vol. V, p. 441.

[49] See Miller, *My Diary*, vol. XIII, p. 286 and Doc. 914 (vol. IX, p. 255).

[50] As an antidote to those who have dwelt upon the sagacity of the peacemakers with regard to minorities, it is worth noting that Headlam-Morley (*Memoir*, p. 115) records: 'We were very lucky in getting the new states matter taken, as there was an immense crowd waiting, consisting of financial and reparation people. However, Hankey got us quarter of an hour.'

[51] See 60th Meeting, Mantoux, vol. I, pp. 474–475. Headlam-Morley (*Memoir*, p. 114) records that Lloyd George 'said that he did not know how long it took to draw up the

the draft treaty[52] with Germany that would allow the treaty to be closed and forwarded to the Germans for their comments and give the Committee more time to consider the Jewish question.[53] There was no intention of entering into the German Treaty without the Polish treaty of guarantee being in position.

This decision, however, had a wider significance. By gaining time for further discussions, it became possible to cement the rejection of the American Jewish-inspired proposals drafted by Miller. This had the advantage of enabling a more balanced and realistic treaty to be produced but it also meant that the origins of the treaty, and the issues that underpinned it, became obscured. If obligations entered into by Poland had been based on Miller's submission to House, it is unlikely that it could have served as a model for use elsewhere.[54]

As its work ultimately evolved, the Committee took upon itself the task of drafting what might best be described as a set of constitutional principles upon which the new Polish State was to be founded. Miller became more interested in transporting the ideals of the US Constitution to Central Europe and seems to have lost some of his initial sympathy for the Jewish question which became marginalized.[55] It was decided that, since the treaty was to be of general application, it should be drafted in general terms to eliminate the risk of overlooking some minorities.[56] Consideration was also given to the idea of drafting the entire treaty without specifically mentioning the Jews, but this was abandoned since it was felt that without special provisions 'it would not be possible to give

---

American Constitution, but he imagined that it took up some months, and the scheme before us evidently aimed at drawing up a Constitution for Poland within two hours'. See also *PPC*, vol. V, pp. 439–440.

[52] This ultimately became Article 93 of the Treaty of Versailles and provided that:
> Poland accepts and agrees to embody in a Treaty with the Principal Allied and Associated Powers such provisions as may be deemed necessary by the said powers to protect the interests of the inhabitants of Poland who differ from the majority of the population in race, language or religion.

[53] See Temperley, *HPC*, vol. V, p. 125.

[54] Miller, however, had thought this possible: 'If these clauses are accepted for Poland, similar clauses will be adopted for the protection of minorities in other countries, such as Czechoslovakia and Romania, varying somewhat according to the circumstances therein.' (Letter to House, *My Diary*, vol. VIII, p. 182.)

[55] In the end, it was Headlam-Morley (*Memoir*, p. 117) who declared that he 'really had to fight the battle of the Jews almost alone'.

[56] The Committee identified Germans, Ruthenians (or Little Russians), White Russians and Lithuanians as the minorities to which the treaty would apply. At this stage, the Committee did not rule out the possibility of specifying the relevant groups in the treaties with other States. See Headlam-Morley, *Memoir*, p. 54.

them the protection which the information available as to the actual situation in Poland at this moment shows is clearly necessary'.[57] It was also felt it would be neither 'safe nor just' to extend these extra protections to groups other than the Jews.[58] Thus the specific measures relating to the Jews were considered to be the minimum supplement necessary to ensure adequate protection beyond the maximum legitimate level of protection applicable to all.

The Committee finished the first stage of its work on 13 May and sent its second Report to the Council of Four, consisting of a draft treaty and commentary.[59] Articles 2–5 dealt with questions of citizenship.[60] Article 6 contained a general undertaking to protect the life and liberty of all inhabitants of Poland, and specifically granted the free exercise of religion, provided that its practices 'are not inconsistent with public order or public morals'. This article, which applied to all inhabitants, rather than citizens of Poland, was ultimately adopted as Article 2 of the treaty.

Articles 7 and 8 of the draft only applied to citizens and ensured to minorities the right to equality before the law and the free use of any language[61] and the right to establish and maintain, *inter alia*, religious and educational establishments was set out. Article 9 obliged Poland to provide such education as was publicly provided in the language of groups which formed a 'considerable proportion' of the population and to ensure that such groups enjoyed an equitable share of funds made available for educational, religious or charitable purposes. The 'enforcement' of these obligations was addressed by Article 12, which required that the rights created be entrenched within the Constitution, and Article 13, which placed the provisions concerning the protection of racial,

---

[57] *Ibid.*. The Committee justified this decision by commenting upon the widespread geographical distribution of the Jews in Poland and the 'strong anti-Semitic feeling in Poland, which is not even denied by the Poles themselves' which 'throws upon the Allies an obligation to provide safeguards which, it is hoped, will not be necessary for the other minorities'. A further justification was that: 'The Jews are both a religious and a racial minority, and special questions therefore arise in their case which do not arise in the case of other minorities' (*ibid.*, pp. 55–56).

[58] *Ibid.*, p. 56.

[59] See Minutes of 8th Meeting of the New States Committee, Annex B. Miller, *My Diary*, vol. XIII, pp. 53–63.

[60] The most important feature was the requirement that it be conferred 'without any requirement of special proceedings' (Chapter II, Article 2). This was in response to the experience of Romania's having evaded the terms of the Treaty of Berlin. See Miller, *My Diary*, vol. XIII, p. 54 and Headlam-Morley before the Council of Three on 3 May (Mantoux, vol. I, p. 475).

[61] Under Article 11, however, the compulsory teaching of Polish was sanctioned.

religious or linguistic minorities under the protection of the League of Nations.

There were two articles which provided particular guarantees for the Jews.[62] Article 10 provided that:

One or more educational Committees appointed by the Jewish communities of Poland will, under the general control of the State, provide for the distribution of the proportional share of public funds allocated to the Jewish Schools and for the organization and management of these schools.

The purpose of this article was to ensure that the Jewish community retained full control of its schools, a privilege not extended to other minorities, who had to look to the Polish authorities to ensure their enjoyment of funding under Article 9. The justification offered for this was 'the close relations existing among Jews in Poland between education and religion'.[63] It was, then, as an element of religious protection that this proposal was advanced.

The second measure of special protection concerned the Sabbath and was the subject of much dispute within the Committee. Headlam-Morley proposed the following text:

Jews shall not be compelled to perform any act which constitutes a violation of their Sabbath, nor shall they be placed under any disability by reason of their refusal to attend Courts of Law or to perform any judicial act on the Sabbath.

The Jews who observe their Sabbath and Holy days shall not be prohibited from pursuing their secular affairs on Sunday.[64]

Both Miller and Berthelot, along with de Martino, the Italian representative, opposed such a clause but Headlam-Morley was insistent.[65] He agreed to amend the second paragraph[66] so that it read:

---

[62] See Minutes of 8th Meeting of the New States Committee, 2nd Report to the Council of Four. Miller, p. 53.

[63] Minutes of 5th Meeting of the New States Committee, Annex A, Draft Article 6. Miller, *ibid.*, p. 40. There is no indication that the other members of the Committee demurred from this.

[64] *Ibid.*, Article 7.

[65] He wrote to Hankey: 'Everyone who knows Poland, even including those who tend to be anti-Semitic, assures me that the matter is of real pressing importance, and I could not therefore give way on this point.' Headlam-Morley, *Memoir*, p. 106.

[66] He noted that: 'There was some difficulty in persuading Mr Miller that the Christians of Warsaw would not have their religious feelings offended by seeing Jews working on a Sunday; he seemed to think that the Continental Sunday was that to which he is accustomed in Boston or in New York.' *Ibid.*, p. 117. When sending Wilson the final texts approved by the Committee, Miller had observed that the British proposal 'would make by Treaty the Jewish Sabbath a more sacred day than Sunday'. (Miller, *My Diary*, vol. IX, p. 322.) This comment would seem more apposite to the original version of the British proposal, rather than that actually presented.

Poland hereby declares its intention to refrain from ordering or permitting elections, whether general or local, to be held on a Saturday, nor will registration for electoral or other purposes be compelled to be performed on a Saturday.[67]

Nevertheless, a consensus could not be reached.[68] However, when the Committee's Report, which included the amended British proposal in an annex, was considered by the Council of Four on 17 May Headlam-Morley recorded that he 'had very little difficulty in persuading them to agree to it'[69] and it was accepted into the text as Article 12.

The remaining point of controversy at this stage concerned the League of Nations guarantee. The original Jewish proposals would have allowed any party to the treaty or any affected group to submit complaints directly to the League,[70] but, like the Sabbath article, this had not found its way into Miller's first draft. Article 13 of the New States Committee's draft simply proposed that 'the protection of racial, religious or linguistic minorities shall be under the protection of the League of Nations'[71] but did not grant a right of appeal to the minorities themselves.

Headlam-Morley was, at first, in favour of allowing direct appeals from members of minority groups to the League,[72] but neither Miller nor Berthelot were enthusiastic and he changed his mind, believing that the competence of both the Court and the League should be limited to

---

[67] See 2nd Report of the New States Committee, Miller, vol. XIII, p. 63. The reference to 'Courts of Law' was also amended to read 'legal business'.

[68] Miller wrote to Wilson that 'Headlam-Morley has shown an extraordinary change from the time of my first discussions with him. He was then anti-Jewish and pro-Polish, but changed to the extent of his being willing to go farther in favour of the Jews than I thought reasonable' (Miller, vol. IX, p. 304). He attributed this to pressure put on Lloyd George by Sir Herbert Samuel, but there is no evidence to support this. What Miller does not explain is his own quite extraordinary change of mind: his draft articles of 29 April endorsed the notion of Jewish 'national rights', which were subsequently rejected by all concerned.

[69] Headlam-Morley, Memoir, p. 107 and see Mantoux, vol. II, p. 88 at pp. 92–95 and PPC, vol. V, p. 678.

[70] See Miller, vol. IX, p. 424 (proposal of 20 April) and p. 194 (proposal of 10 May).

[71] 2nd Report of the New States Committee, Article 13. Miller, vol. XIII, p. 63.

[72] He sought the assistance of Lord Robert Cecil, who drafted a text which would have allowed any member of the Council of the League or any aggrieved Polish citizen or group of citizens to appeal to the Permanent Court of International Justice (PCIJ). See 15 Meeting of the New States Committee, Annex B, Drafts of proposed Articles 13 and 14. Miller, ibid., p. 103. Had this proposal been accepted it would have meant that the PCIJ would have had to have been endowed with the capacity to hear disputes between individuals and States, rather than being limited to interstate disputes. This would have had far-reaching consequences.

disputes between States.[73] The Committee was still divided over the question of whether any member of the League or only members of the League Council should be able to seize the League machinery of a complaint, the former being the American position, the latter being that of Britain and France. This was referred to the Council of Four, who decided to ask for the views of the States concerned.[74] The latter solution was ultimately decided upon and was embodied in Article 12 of the treaty.[75]

The Polish response and the finalizing of the text

Thus far, the Poles had not been formally involved in the drafting process.[76] The text of the draft treaty was finally sent to the Polish Government (thus bypassing the hostile Dmowski) following the meeting of the Council of Four on 6 June. The Polish reply was not received, however, until 17 June[77] and took the form of a lengthy Memorandum from Paderwski which renewed general complaints concerning the policy of placing obligations upon a sovereign State regarding its treatment of its citizens and argued that any system which gave special privileges to minorities would create ill feeling against them.[78] The 'Jewish clauses',

---

[73] He accepted that allowing individuals to appeal against their government would be a 'serious infraction of sovereignty, which would inevitably draw forth most energetic protests'. He was also concerned that: 'These protests would be dangerous because they could point out that the Great Powers themselves did not allow such an appeal to their own nationals.' Clearly, this was considered to be out of the question. Memorandum dated 5 June in Headlam-Morley, *Memoir*, p. 139.

[74] Mantoux, vol. II, pp. 331–332; *PPC*, vol. VI, pp. 221–222.

[75] See Mantoux, vol. II, pp. 441 and 450; *PPC*, vol. V, p. 514. Both the Greeks and the Czechoslovaks had expressed a preference for the more restrictive approach. The hostility of both Poland and Romania to the more liberal suggestion was already well known.

[76] Officially, neither had the Jewish groups. Miller, however, showed the final Draft Report to Mack and Marshall, earning a strong rebuke from Headlam-Morley. All sides, however, had been privately discussing the matter during the previous week. The objection was one of 'form'. It seemed inappropriate that the Jewish groups should see the Report before it had been transmitted to the Polish Government. See Headlam-Morley, *Memoir*, p. 111 and Janowsky, *The Jews and Minority Rights*, pp. 344–353.

[77] The Reply was dated 15 June. See Annex D to Minutes of 23rd Meeting of the New States Committee. Miller, *My Diary*, vol. XIII, p. 171; *PPC*, vol. VI, p. 535. There was some suggestion that the tardiness of the Polish response was in some way prompted by the French as a delaying tactic, designed to halt progress and, perhaps, sabotage the signing of the treaty. See Lundgreen-Nielson, *The Polish Problem*, p. 378 and Headlam-Morley, *Memoir*, p. 145.

[78] Poland joined with the other States upon whom minority treaties were to be imposed in mounting a fierce assault upon the principles underlying them when the Austrian Treaty, which contained in Article 86 a holding clause identical in substance to that

Articles 10 and 12, were the subject of particular criticism and Paderwski claimed that, 'by distinguishing with the aid of special privileges the Jewish population from their fellow citizens', the Great Powers were 'creat[ing] a new Jewish Problem' and 'assuming thereby before humanity a heavy responsibility'. He was, in effect, both threatening them with, and absolving the Poles from, responsibility for any deleterious consequences of the treaty in Poland. He concluded with the threatening warning that:

it is to be feared that the Great Powers may be preparing themselves unwelcome surprises, for taking into account the migratory capacities of the Jewish population, which so readily transports itself from one State to another, it is certain that the Jews, basing themselves on precedent thus established, will claim elsewhere the national principles which they would enjoy in Poland.[79]

This careful and clever response struck a responsive chord by emphasizing the elements of Jewish nationalism reflected in the treaty and raised the spectre of the Allies themselves becoming subject to similar forms of minority obligations, a possibility that they had resisted, and were continuing to resist, at the cost of some considerable embarrassment. The Council referred it to the New States Committee 'in order to see whether some of the objections raised could not be met'.[80] It was clear that the general tide was turning against the Jewish demands and in favour of the Polish objections.[81]

The New States Committee disowned the assault upon the general principles of the treaty, which they considered to be a matter for the Supreme Council.[82] It re-examined the Jewish clauses, and affirmed their

found in Article 93 of the German Treaty, came up for discussion in the 8th Plenary Session on 31 May 1919. This is considered further below. Nevertheless, this did not prevent Poland from subsequently providing for the linguistic and cultural rights of Polish minorities in the Ukraine and Russia, and recognizing the equivalent rights for Russians, Ukrainians and White Ruthenians in Poland. See Article 7 of the Treaty of Peace between Poland, Russia and the Ukraine, signed at Riga, 18 March 1921 (LNTS No. 149) and Article IV of the Preliminary Treaty of Riga, 12 October 1920 (LNTS No. 101).

[79] Miller, My Diary, vol. XIII, p. 177; PPC, vol. VI, p. 539.
[80] Letter of Hankey, Minutes of 23rd Meeting of New States Committee, Annex C. Miller, My Diary, vol. XIII, p. 170.
[81] See Lundgreen-Nielsen, The Polish Problem, pp. 380–381.
[82] 24th Meeting, Annex B. Miller, p. 189 at p. 190. Lundgreen-Nielsen (The Polish Problem, pp. 380–381) argues that although the Report to the Council on Paderwski's Memorandum bears Berthelot's name (he was Chairman of the Committee), he was in favour of abandoning the treaty altogether and simply accepting a series of declarations by Poland regarding its minorities. This claim is supported by the general policy of France towards Poland and Paderwski's allegedly French-inspired delay in submitting their response to the treaty.

belief that they were needed.[83] However, Article 12 was amended so that Jews could not claim exemption from army service, Article 9 was amended so that it would only apply to German-speaking minorities in former German territories and Article 1 was amended so as to exclude Articles 9–12 from the list of those articles of the treaty recognized as 'fundamental laws' over which no internal law or regulation could prevail.[84] The effect of this was that legislative violations of the Jewish clauses could only be challenged on the international plane.

Headlam-Morley presented these amendments to the Council of Four on 21 June, where they were accepted with little discussion.[85] He also raised a further matter. This was the question of whether allowing the Jews control of their schools would encourage the use of Yiddish, the form of Germanic Hebrew spoken by many Jews in Poland. The Committee was again asked to consider alterations to ensure that the obligation placed upon Poland by Article 9 to provide education in Yiddish was restricted to primary schools. Miller refused to agree to this[86] and Headlam-Morley referred the matter back to the Council of Four where it was considered at length.[87] Wilson was again reluctant to sanction any change but Lloyd George, supported by Headlam-Morley, pressed strongly for the change. They both believed that if Yiddish was used as the medium of secondary and higher education it would foster the creation of a State within a State, which they sought to resist at all costs.[88] Thus it was agreed that the

[83] 'The immense majority of the Jews in Poland demand precise guarantees, and . . . the information as to the present situation of the Jews in Poland and the attitude towards them seems to justify special privileges'. Miller, *ibid.*, p. 191.

[84] *Ibid.*, p. 192.

[85] Mantoux, vol. II, p. 471; *PPC*, vol. VI, pp. 569–570. Paderwski had already raised the use of Yiddish with Lloyd George. He had opposed granting a minority the right to use their own language and had argued that since Yiddish was a form of German, such a right would be 'almost to make German a second official language'. See *PPC*, vol. VI, p. 241.

[86] This opposition seems to have been due to pressure from the American Jews groups who were anxious about the watering down of the treaty. See Lundgreen-Nielson, *The Polish Problem*, p. 381.

[87] See Mantoux, vol. II, pp. 486–490; *PPC*, vol. VI, pp. 624–628.

[88] Headlam-Morley wrote to Sir Maurice Hankey (*Memoir*, pp. 158–159): 'We remain of the opinion that it is right and desirable that the Polish Jews should have the right as a religious community to their own schools. There is, however, a real danger that if these schools are placed under Jewish management, the more extreme national elements among the Jews may use these schools in order artificially to foster the use of the Yiddish language in such a way as to increase the separation which the use of this language produces between the Jews and other citizens of Poland.' Lloyd George expressed similar views. See Mantoux, vol. II, p. 487; *PPC*, vol. VI, p. 627.

treaty should only guarantee the use of Yiddish at the level of primary education and the text of Article 9 was amended so as to read:

Poland will provide in the public educational system in towns and districts in which a considerable proportion of Polish nationals of other than Polish speech are resident adequate facilities for ensuring that in the primary schools the instruction shall be given to the children of such Polish nationals through the medium of their own language . . . [89]

The effect of this alteration, however, went further than allowing restriction on the use of Yiddish. It meant that all secondary education could be conducted in Polish, thus removing the protection previously offered to other minority groups, whose interests seem to have been simply forgotten,[90] underlining once again the importance of the Jewish problem in drafting this treaty.

The final text was sent to Paderwski on 24 June, accompanied by a covering letter from Clemenceau in which he set out the Allies' case for seeking to impose a treaty of guarantee upon Poland. It also set out at length, in a passage worthy of full quotation, the philosophy and purpose underlying the measures of special protection for the Jewish community:

Clauses 10 and 12 deal specifically with the Jewish citizens of Poland. The information at the disposal of the Principal Allied and Associated Powers as to the existing relations between the Jews and the other Polish citizens had led them to the conclusion that, in view of the historical development of the Jewish question and the great animosity aroused by it, special protection is necessary for the Jews in Poland. These clauses have been limited to the minimum which seems necessary under the circumstances of the present day, viz., the maintenance of Jewish Schools and the protection of the Jews in the religious observance of their Sabbath. It is believed that these stipulations will not create any obstacle to the political unity of Poland. They do not constitute any recognition of the Jews as a separate political community within the Polish State. The educational provisions contain nothing beyond what is in fact provided in the educational institutions of many highly organized modern states. There is nothing inconsistent with the sovereignty of the State in recognizing and supporting schools in which children shall be brought up in the religious influences to which they are accustomed in their home. Ample safeguards against any use of non-Polish languages to encourage a spirit of national separation have been provided in the express acknowledgment that the

---

[89] An additional phrase was added to Article 10 which made it clear that the language provisions of Article 9 applied to schools run by the local Jewish Education Committees.

[90] See C. A. Macartney, *National States and National Minorities* (London: Oxford University Press, 1934), pp. 236–237.

provisions of the treaty do not prevent the Polish State from making the Polish language obligatory in all its schools and educational institutions.[91]

No further alterations of substance were made[92] but the 'Sabbath' article was renumbered to become Article 11 of the Treaty which was finally signed on 28 June 1919, along with the Treaty of Versailles. Thus the guarantees were in place at the moment Poland received its formal recognition.

Before turning to the manner in which the Polish Treaty was adopted and adapted for use in other contexts, it is appropriate, by way of conclusion, to reflect upon the extent to which the final version of the text reflected the concerns of the lobbyists. Three elements of the original American Jewish proposals have been highlighted above. The first of these, recognition as a minority possessing 'national rights', though originally accepted by Miller, was unacceptable to the Council of Four and found no place in the final treaty.[93] However, the Poles resurrected the issue by alleging that the special educational privileges assigned to the Jews tended towards their being granted such a status,[94] thus reintroducing the question and resulting in the weakening of Article 9.

There was certainly an element of truth in the Polish claim. The Jews had sought 'national minority' status in order to preserve their control over those matters essential to the maintenance of their separate identity within the State, including educational establishments.[95] It was, there-

---

[91] See New States Committee, Minutes, 27th Meeting, Annex C. Miller, *My Diary*, vol. XIII, pp. 220–221; *PPC*, vol. VI, p. 633.

[92] Paderwski made a further attempt to effect changes when he spoke at the Council of Four on 27 June, suggesting that Yiddish be an 'auxiliary language' for the purposes of primary education under Article 9, but this was rejected. See Mantoux, vol. II, p. 546; *PPC*, vol. VI, p. 725.

[93] This might be contrasted with the treatment of the Sub-Carpathian Ruthenes, an important minority group within the Czechoslovak State. They were given an autonomous Diet that would have legislative powers over, *inter alia*, religious questions. See Czechoslovak Minority Treaty, considered below at pp. 129–130, Articles 10–13.

[94] Paderwski had argued that the special educational and linguistic privileges were ill conceived because the Jews themselves were divided on the merits of the issue and they would cause friction within the Jewish community by implicitly supporting those who sought to 'transform the Jews into an autonomous nation'. Article 10 would 'tend to the creation of a strictly religious education which would contribute to deepen religious divergencies in Poland' and was 'contrary to the modern tendency of all States in using schools as a means of producing citizens brought up in a certain spirit of unity and social solidarity'. See Miller, *My Diary*, vol. XIII, p. 176; *PPC*, vol. VI, p. 539.

[95] They had argued that: 'Without minority rights, Jews, Ukrainians, Lithuanians and others . . . would incur the danger of the annihilation of their ancient civilization, the destruction of their schools and the suppression of their languages. In a word, they would be compelled to submit to complete absorption.' Memorandum from the Comité de Juives accompanying their proposals, dated 10 May 1919. Miller, *My Diary*, vol. IX, p. 197.

fore, easy for the Poles to argue that the special educational (and linguistic) provisions preserved much of the substance of Jewish demands to which the Allies were ostensibly opposed.

The second feature of the Jewish proposals concerned the protection of the Sabbath. Despite Miller's opposition, Headlam-Morley had reintroduced this, although in a weaker form than originally proposed. The Jews had originally sought the freedom to conduct their secular affairs on a Sunday,[96] but this was rejected. Given that military service could now be required of them, this provision did not go as far as the Jews would have wished. The third feature concerned mechanisms of guarantee. Once again, the proposal to allow affected groups to make a direct appeal to the League of Nations was rejected.

Thus the American Jews had every reason to be disappointed with the result of the deliberations in so far as they concerned specific measures of protection for Jews. However, their proposals had always embraced elements aimed at the general protection of individual rights and these aspects, as finally embodied in Articles 2–8 of the treaty, were not only adopted but they established what turned out to be the framework for the entire minorities treaty process. The following chapter will consider how this came about.[97]

---

[96] This was advanced as a question of economic equality: since Jews did not work on Saturdays, they would be deprived of one-sixth of their economic power vis-à-vis non-Jews if they were also precluded from working on Sundays (ibid.).

[97] Articles 1, 2, 3, 6, 7, 8, 9 and 12 of the Polish Treaty were identified as the 'core' of the treaty system in a Memorandum, submitted by Estonia to the Council of the League of Nations in 1923 (see below, pp. 141–142). A description and evaluation of this 'core' as it relates to religious liberty is given in chapter 6, where it serves to introduce the examination of the practice of the League.

5   The extension of the minorities system

The Allied and Associated Powers ultimately entered into five minorities treaties. In addition to that with Poland, treaties were also concluded with Czechoslovakia and the Serb-Croat-Slovene State on 10 September 1919, with Romania on 9 December 1919 and with Greece on 10 August 1920. Since they were all based upon the Polish Treaty, only the differences need be noted. There was, however, a preliminary point of great importance concerning the range of application of the minorities treaty system.

The principle of application

When Wilson first raised the Jewish question in the Council of Four it was assumed that whatever was agreed for Poland would equally apply to Czechoslovakia, as both of them were to be accorded recognition by the treaties[1] and, as its name suggests, the mandate of the New States Committee was restricted to the States which were to be created by the treaties.[2]

From the first, the New States Committee proceeded on the basis that the draft articles it was producing for Poland would apply to Czechoslovakia,[3] but on 6 May the Council of Four agreed to the Committee's request that it be authorized to consider treaties with the Serb-Croat-Slovene State, Romania and Greece.[4] The position concerning the Serb-Croat-Slovene State was complex, since opinions differed as to whether it

---

[1] *PPC*, vol. V, p. 393.
[2] See Letter of Sir Maurice Hankey to the New States Committee, D. H. Miller, *My Diary at the Peace Conference* (privately published), vol. XIII, p. 13.
[3] See Report to the Council of Three (2 May 1919), *PPC*, vol. V, pp. 440–442.
[4] *PPC*, vol. V, p. 483.

was a new State, and thus to be treated in the same way as Poland and Czechoslovakia, or whether it was an extension of the Kingdom of Serbia. A case could be made out either way. The reason for seeking to include Greece and Romania within the proposed treaty system was to offer the same order of protection to the Jews in Romania and Muslims in Thrace as was to be made for the Jews in Poland. There was no question but that this was a departure from the principle that such guarantees would be sought as an adjunct to the question of recognition, for these States were already recognized.

This change of policy did not go unchallenged. Romania in particular strongly objected to the principle of their being made subject to a minority treaty, since they had fought with the Allies in the war, albeit ineffectually. [5] Bratianu, the Premier of Romania, wrote to the New States Committee on 27 May in uncompromising terms, asserting that all citizens enjoyed a complete equality of rights and liberties both religious and political, and declared that: 'Romania is ready to accept all the provisions that all states members of the League of Nations accept for their own territories in this matter. Under any other condition Romania could not admit the intervention of foreign Governments in the application of her domestic laws.'[6] Bratianu was well aware that the principal Allied and Associated Powers had no intention of subjecting themselves to any such obligations. His position amounted to a robust rejection of the general principle of the minorities treaties, and not merely an objection to their being extended to an already recognized State.

The New States Committee, alarmed by this response, urged the Council of Four to bind Romania to accept a minorities treaty by including a clause akin to Article 93 of the Treaty of Versailles in the draft Austrian peace treaty.[7] The draft was discussed at the eighth Plenary

---

[5] Of course, there was nothing new in this, since Romanian independence had been conditional upon the religious and minority rights provisions contained in the Treaty of Berlin. Moreover, proposals advanced for the territorial settlement of the area following a collapse of the Austria-Hungarian Empire had always envisaged some form of minority protection for Hungarians placed within an enlarged Romania. See the survey of US, British and French proposals in S. D. Spector, *Romania at the Paris Peace Conference* (New York: Bookman Associates Inc., 1962), pp. 98–101.

[6] Miller, *My Diary*, vol. XIII, p. 89.

[7] Miller, *ibid.*, vol. XIII, p. 88; *PPC*, vol. VI, p. 84. It provided: 'Romania accepts and agrees to embody in a Treaty with the Principal Allied and Associated Powers such provisions as may be deemed necessary by the said powers to protect the interests of inhabitants of Romania who differ from the majority of the population in race, language, or religion.' Although it was already the intention to insert a similar clause in the Hungarian Treaty, that was not ready to be presented to the Conference. It was hoped that gaining an earlier

meeting, held on 31 May 1919.[8] At that meeting a vigorous attack was launched against the very principle of the treaties. This was led by Bratianu – and joined by Paderwski, Kramar and Trumbitch for Poland, Czechoslovakia and the Serb-Croat-Slovene State – who argued that the imposition of minorities treaties offended against the sovereign equality of States[9] and, by threatening internal dissention, jeopardized international peace, claiming that: 'History is there to prove that the protection of minorities ... has done more to disintegrate States than to consolidate them.'[10]

By way of response[11] Wilson suggested that an obligation guaranteed by the League, rather than by other States, did not offend Romanian sovereignty. When Bratianu pointed out that this was simply untrue[12] Wilson resorted to arguments that showed little regard for the lofty ideals he usually espoused[13] but which also revealed a very real tension. The Great Powers took the view that the ill treatment of minorities could

---

Romanian acceptance of the principle would facilitate the work of the New States Committee and prevent Bratianu from persisting in his opposition.

[8] The treaty had been due to be presented orally at the seventh Plenary two days earlier. Bratianu requested that the text be given them and that they be allowed forty-eight hours in which to study it. This request was acceded to and the debate deferred. *PPC*, vol. III, pp. 393–394.

[9] 'An independent State ... cannot ... accept a special regime to which other sovereign States are not subjected' (*ibid.*, p. 397).

[10] 'If minorities are conscious of the fact that the liberties which they enjoy are guaranteed to them not by solicitude for their welfare of the State to which they belong but by the protection of a foreign State, whatever it may be, the basis of that State will be undermined. At the very basis of the new state of things which it is sought to establish, the seed is sown of unrest, which is in contradiction with the aims which this conference pursues' (*ibid.*, pp. 400–401).

[11] Headlam-Morley, who attended the Plenary, observed: 'He [Wilson] avoided everything which could appear invidious; no mention was made of the Jews, but he said enough to indicate what was in his mind.' A. Headlam-Morley, *Sir James Headlam-Morley: A Memoir of the Paris Peace Conference 1919* (London: Methuen & Co., 1972), p. 136,

[12] *PPC*, vol. III, p. 399.

[13] He pointed out that it was the Great Powers, not the small powers, who had won the war and that it was they, the Great Powers, who would, in reality, have to guarantee the peace of the world. Since they would only police a settlement they approved of, the peace of the world depended not upon the justice of the settlement but upon the degree to which it conformed to their wishes. It was generally believed that Romania was doing very well out of the settlement, and had done very little in military terms to justify its great territorial extension. *Ibid.*, pp. 406–407 and see Spector, *Romania at the Paris Peace Conference*, p. 143. Lloyd George was decidedly unsympathetic: Headlam-Morley, *Memoir*, p. 136, recalled 'Lloyd George turned round, and in a very loud aside said: "This damned fellow; he cannot even get coats for his soldiers without us!", an observation which, though it presents a substantial truth, might perhaps have been expressed more discreetly.'

threaten international peace and security and this made it a matter of international concern. Romania saw the danger to international peace and security in a minority looking not to the State but to the international community for its security.[14]

During this exchange Trumbitch argued that, since Serbia was already recognized as a sovereign State, the minority provisions ought at most to apply only to those areas now ceded to the Serb-Croat Slovene State, rather than to the whole.[15] Wilson retorted that Serbia was seeking recognition as a new entity and so was in the same position as a new State, whilst Romania was being greatly expanded by virtue of the Allies' victory, which entitled him to say: 'If we agree to these additions of territory we have the right to insist upon certain guarantees.'[16] This formalized the position that guarantees could be required of enlarged States that applied to the entire territory and not just the newly ceded areas, as had been the previous practice.

Following the Plenary, it was clear that minorities treaties would be concluded with these States. However, the States were able to trade on their discontent and win concessions at critical moments in the overall negotiating process: both Romania and the Serb-Croat-Slovene State refused to sign the Treaty of St Germain because it would have bound them to accept a minorities treaty and they only succumbed after intense pressure had been exerted[17] and significant alterations to the proposed treaty obtained.[18]

Once it had been decided to extend the minorities treaty system to the newly created and greatly enlarged States, it followed as a matter of course that similar obligations should be placed upon the enemy States with whom peace treaties were being concluded, with the exception of

---

[14] The willingness of Bratianu to accept a level of international oversight adopted by all members of the League should not be taken too seriously. Not only would it conflict with his basic premise of State sovereignty, but he was well aware that there was no prospect of there being such international oversight. He knew that Article 21 of the draft League Covenant had been rejected and that the Covenant was – and would remain – silent on these issues.

[15] *PPC*, vol. III, p. 404.   [16] *Ibid.*, p. 407.

[17] The Allies threatened to refuse to allow them to sign the Treaty of Neuilly, by which peace was concluded with Bulgaria and under the terms of which both States stood to make considerable territorial gains, but which did not contain a minority stipulation concerning Romania and the Serb-Croat-Slovene State (although Article 46 of the Treaty of Neuilly did oblige Greece to do so). They finally signed the Treaty of Neuilly on 27 November 1919 and the Treaty of St Germain shortly afterwards on 5 December 1919. See above, p. 81 and below, p. 136.

[18] See below, pp. 132–135.

Germany. This exception could be explained on the basis that it would have gone beyond the application of existing principles: Turkey and Bulgaria had long been subject to obligations in respect of their religious minorities and Austria and Hungary were, in a technical sense, new States. Germany, on the other hand, was still a Great Power and the refusal of the Allies to accept similar obligations would be put into bold relief by imposing a general regime of minorities obligations upon her.

The peace and minorities treaties were all concluded with the Allied and Associated Powers, that is, the United States, the British Empire, France, Italy and Japan, but the obligations they contained were to be placed under the guarantee of the League of Nations, which came into being with the entry into force of the Covenant on 10 January 1920. The transfer to the League of each set of treaty obligations was examined by the Council and accepted by a resolution.[19] A further set of responsibilities were assumed by the League by virtue of a series of declarations that were requested of a number of States upon their admission to the organization. The following sections will introduce the salient features of these instruments.

The minorities treaties

The Czechoslovak Treaty

The Czechoslovak Treaty[20] was the first of the additional treaties to be considered by the New States Committee. It was decided to adopt the

---

[19]   The resolution by which the League undertook the guarantee of the Polish Treaty simply provided that:

> The stipulations in Articles 1–11 of the treaty between the United States of America, The British Empire, France, Italy and Japan on the one side and Poland on the other, signed at Versailles on 28 June 1919, so far as they affect persons belonging to racial, religious or linguistic minorities, be hereby placed under the guarantee of the League of Nations (13 February 1920: *LNOJ* (1920), p. 56).

Similar resolutions were passed relating to the other instruments. See Austria (27 October 1920); Bulgaria (27 October 1920); Czechoslovakia (29 November 1920); Kingdom of the Serbs, Croats and Slovenes (29 November 1920); Hungary (30 August 1921); Romania (30 August 1921); Greece (26 September 1924) and Turkey (26 September 1924). See 'Protection of Linguistic, Racial or Religious Minorities by the League of Nations', League of Nations Doc. C.24. M. 18.1929. I., p. 2.

[20]   Treaty between the Principal Allied and Associated Powers (the British Empire, France, Italy, Japan and the United States) and Czechoslovakia, signed at St Germain-en-Laye, 10 September 1919 (226 CTS 170; LNTS No. 38). See C. A. Macartney, *National States and National Minorities* (London: Oxford University Press, 1934), p. 240: H. W. V. Temperley, *HPC*, vol. V, pp. 144 and 461–470.

minorities clauses of the Polish Treaty, but without the 'Jewish Clauses'.[21] The Czechoslovaks adopted a generally positive attitude towards the treaty,[22] which suggested that special measures for the Jews were unnecessary.[23] The Committee took the view that, in contrast to Poland, the Jews formed a comparatively small element of the population, were not formed into separate communities and did not form a significant element of any given town or district and the general attitude of the population was not hostile.[24] The text of the treaty was finalized on 7 August and was signed on 10 September 1919, and entered into force on 16 July 1920.

---

[21] Ninth meeting, 19 May 1919. Miller, *My Diary*, vol. XIII, p. 64. Thus Articles 1–9 of the Polish Treaty were duplicated, with Article 12 becoming Article 15 of the Czechoslovak Treaty. The details of the articles dealing with citizenship were, naturally, different. The only other significant variation between these articles in the two treaties concerned Article 9, the obligation to provide State education in the minority language, which, following Polish pressure to curtail the extent of Jewish rights, was limited in the Polish Treaty to the provision of primary schools. This was not carried over into the Czechoslovak Minorities Treaty and so the German minority in Czechoslovakia acquired greater rights than the German minority in Poland.

[22] The Czechoslovak Foreign Minister, Mr Beneš, submitted a memorandum explaining that Czechoslovakia intended to adopt a constitution which provided more extensive minority rights than those contemplated by the Committee. Miller, *ibid.*, p. 69. Nevertheless, this liberal attitude did not prevent Mr Kramer from joining in the assault upon the concept of the treaties in the eighth Plenary ten days later. Temperley, *HPC*, vol. V, p. 144, asserts that they did not do so, but the minutes of the Plenary show this to be the case. See *PPC*, vol. III, p. 402.

[23] Headlam-Morley was in correspondence with R. W. Seton-Watson, who had gone to Czechoslovakia early in May and was sending favourable reports of the Czech attitude towards minorities to the British delegation in Paris. See H. and C. Seton-Watson, *The Making of a New Europe: R. W. Seton-Watson and the Last Years of Austria-Hungary* (London: Methuen, 1981), p. 368.

[24] Miller, *My Diary*, vol. XIII, p. 80. Mr Beneš claimed that: 'There would be no religious difficulties, as no religious questions existed.' Memorandum of Mr Beneš, Annex A to 10th Meeting of the New States Committee, in Miller, p. 69. The history of the Jews in Prague does not entirely support the thesis of religious toleration (for a literary exposé of racial tensions in Prague in the nineteenth Century see A. Trollope, *Nina Balakta* (first published 1867) (London: Oxford University Press, 1946). Jewish groups appealed, unsuccessfully, to Beneš for the articles to be included, not because they felt them necessary in the context of Czechoslovakia, but because their omission would assist Romania to resist their inclusion in the Romanian Treaty. See O. I. Janowsky, *The Jews and Minority Rights (1898–1919)* (New York: Columbia University Press, 1933), pp. 374–375.

The Greek Treaty

The Greek Minorities Treaty[25] was signed alongside the Peace Treaty concluded at Sèvres on 10 August 1920[26] and by which it was to acquire Western Thrace from Bulgaria and, from the Ottomans, Eastern Thrace, sovereignty over the bulk of the Aegean Islands and the administration of the town of Smyrna (Izmir) and its hinterland for a five-year period, to be followed by a plebiscite.[27] Although, once again, the treaty followed the Polish model, there was a comparatively large number of special provisions, reflecting the diverse minorities that it was originally thought would come under Greek control.[28]

It was decided to retain the Jewish Clauses[29] and a number of other groups received special measures. In particular, the religious freedom and social usages of the Muslims were safeguarded[30] and the rights of the monastic communities on Mount Athos were confirmed.[31]In addition, the Valchs of Pindus were assured local autonomy in religious and related matters.[32]

---

[25] Treaty between the Principal Allied and Associated Powers (the British Empire, France, Italy, Japan) and Greece, signed at Sèvres, 10 August 1920 (LNTS No. 711). See Macartney, *National States and National Minorities*, pp. 246–249; Temperley, *HPC*, vol. VI, pp. 99–106; Janowsky, *ibid.*, pp. 375–376.

[26] The Greek Treaty was the last of the minorities treaties to be drafted. Work began on 14 June 1919 and the text was approved in November 1919. Its signature was delayed, pending the negotiation of the Peace Treaty with Turkey. One consequence of the delay was that the United States did not become a party to this treaty.

[27] Greece also received Western Thrace under the terms of a treaty concluded with the Allied powers, to whom it had already been ceded.

[28] The Treaty of Sèvres itself never entered into force, since it was concluded with the Ottoman authorities which were in the throes of losing control in the civil war that would ultimately lead to the Nationalist Government of Kemal Atatürk. Following the military rout of the Greek forces in Asia Minor, the Treaty of Sèvres was abandoned and replaced by the Treaty of Lausanne.

[29] Greece objected to the inclusion of all of Article 10 and the second part of Article 11, the Sabbath clause. Following assurances from Venezilos, the Greek Prime Minister, that it was not necessary, the second part of Article 11 was omitted and the remainder combined to form a single Article 10. Miller, *My Diary*, vol. XIII, pp. 396–397, 427. But for American pressure, these clauses would have been dropped in their entirety. Janowsky, *The Jews and Minority Rights*, p. 376, n. 42. It was suggested that specific mention be made of the Jews living in Salonica but this was resisted by the Greek Prime Minister and not insisted upon.

[30] Article 14. This recalled Article 10 of the Treaty with the Serb-Croat-Slovene State (see below, n. 51). See Miller, *ibid.*, p. 260.

[31] Article 13. See Miller, *Diary*, Vol XIII, p. 260. The rights of the Russian and Bulgarian Orthodox communities had been similarly assured by Article LXII of the Treaty of Berlin (1878). See above at p. 71.

[32] Article 12. Other additional clauses related to land holding in newly acquired areas

The Romanian Treaty

The Romanian Treaty[33] proved to be altogether more difficult. The Allies thought that Romania posed as great a problem as Poland, if not greater. Romania had flouted the protective clauses in the Treaty of Berlin and the need for the adequate protection of the Jewish community was obvious.[34] Although Bratianu wrote to the Committee at the outset of its work opposing the very idea of the treaty,[35] it paid no attention and produced a draft treaty which was modelled on the Polish Treaty and which included the 'Jewish Clauses'.[36] The Report solemnly observed that: 'As signatories

(Article 11) and the racial composition of local government in Adrianople (article 15), the latter being abandoned following the Treaty of Lausanne. See Protocol of 24th July 1923.

[33] Treaty between the Principal Allied and Associated Powers and Romania (the British Empire, France, Italy, Japan and the United States), signed at Paris, December 9, 1919 (226 CTS 435; LNTS No. 140). See Macartney, *National States and National Minorities*, pp. 244–247; Temperley, *HPC*, pp. 148–149 and 454–460.

[34] Once again, although the general clauses applied to all minority groups, including the substantial Hungarian minority in Transylvania, the Muslims, Saxons and Seltzers, the Romanians themselves considered the principal purpose of the treaty to be to provide guarantees to the Jewish community. For the situation of the Jews in Romania see J. Fouques-Duparc, *La Protection des Minorities de Race, De Langue at de Religion* (Paris: Librairie Dalloz, 1922), pp. 98–113 and see above, p. 72. In an attempt to pre-empt the discussions, Romania introduced a Decree Law on 22 May 1919 that purported to facilitate the extension of citizenship to Romanian Jews, but this did not have the desired effect, and served only to demonstrate just how precarious their situation was. See Janowsky, *The Jews and Minority Rights*, pp. 373–4. For the text of the decree see Miller, *Diary*, Vol. XIII, pp. 100–102. However, the New States Committee simply did not trust the Romanians to keep their word:

> the praiseworthy legislative and administrative reforms projected by the Romanian Government, while evincing a growing spirit of liberalism that promises much for the future, cannot of themselves entirely suffice to reassure all of the racial and religious minorities . . . The responsibility of the Principal Allied and Associated Powers cannot be discharged by leaving the protection of Romanian Minorities to such internal legislation as the Kingdom of Romania may have enacted or may hereafter enact (Miller, vol. XIII, p. 277).

The long outstanding nature of US concern for Jews in Romania is outlined by N. Feinburg, 'The International Protection of Human Rights and the Jewish Question (An Historical Survey)', *Is.LR* 3 (1968), 487, at pp. 494–495.

[35] Letter from Bratianu to the New States Committee, 27 May 1919. See Miller, vol. XIII, pp. 88–89.

[36] Report and Draft Articles, 16 July 1919. Annex (A) to 34th Meeting of the New States Committee, Miller, vol. XIII, p. 269. The Report (prepared by Manley Hudson) took the view that: 'The Jewish problem is common to Romania and to Poland. In both countries the Jews are diffused over practically the whole of the land. They constitute both a religious and a racial minority. They have been subject, in the past, to anti-Semitic antagonism. All of these factors appear to necessitate special provisions with regard to schools and the observance of the Jewish Sabbath . . .'

of the Treaty of Berlin, Great Britain, France and Italy cannot divest themselves of the responsibility which they assumed in 1878 for assuring to the Romanian people religious equality in substance and in spirit, as well as in form.'[37]

The final shape of the treaty was, however, ultimately dictated by other factors. Bratianu continued to press for changes in both the territorial settlement and in the Minorities Treaty throughout the summer and autumn of 1919, by which time the mounting sense of crisis that marked the latter stages of the Conference took its toll and it was decided to re-open discussions on the Minorities Treaty in an attempt to secure Romania's signature to the principal peace treaties.[38] In an effort to make progress, it was suggested that the Jewish Clauses be omitted from the treaty.[39] The British, French and Italian delegates on the Council were quite content with this and, though they resisted,[40] the Americans ultimately yielded in the face of pressure from France.[41]

The Americans finally agreed to these changes on the eve of their departure from the Conference on 9 December. They signed the text and then left immediately, in order to deny the Romanians the satisfaction of signing the treaty in their presence. The Romanian signature was added the next day, but at their request the final document was dated 9

---

[37] Ibid., p. 278. The draft also gave some recognition to the position of non-Jewish minorities, providing that local communities of Saxons and Szeklers in Transylvania would have 'local autonomy in regard to scholastic and religious matters, subject to the control of the Romanian State' (draft Article 13, later Article 11 of the treaty). Although the Report had acknowledged the difficulties that Muslims might face, no specific measures were introduced for their benefit.

[38] Bratianu had also suffered an electoral defeat in November 1919 although his political opponents were no more sympathetic than he. For the background see Spector, Romania at the Paris Peace Conference, pp. 130–226.

[39] As something of a sop, a new article was added that was designed to offer some general protection for the problem of statelessness: Article 7 provided that 'Romania undertakes to recognize as Romanian Nationals ipso facto and without the requirement of any formality Jews inhabiting any Romanian territory, who do not possess another nationality.'

[40] Louis Marshall had been forcefully lobbying Secretary of State Lansing on the matter. As late as 25 November he was urging the adoption of new articles going beyond those which were already doomed. See C. Reznikoff (ed.), Louis Marshall: Champion of Liberty (Philadelphia: The Jewish Publication Society of America, 1957), pp. 635–645.

[41] Berthelot, who claimed never to have been in favour of them anyway, made much of the Romanian Decree Law of 22 May, which had so singularly failed to impress him, as a member of the New States Committee, when the matter had first been raised. When the Americans argued for consistency of treatment with Poland, he expressed the view that the treatment of the Jews in Romania had not been so bad as it had been in Poland. See Spector, Romania at the Paris Peace Conference, pp. 207, 217.

December 1919, so as to give the impression that all had been present.[42] Such was the undignified end to the drafting of the Romanian Treaty, which entered into force on 4 September 1920.

The Serb-Croat-Slovene Treaty

The position concerning the Serb-Croat-Slovene Treaty[43] was complex. Like Romania, Serbia was subject to the obligations imposed by the Treaty of Berlin. In addition to its obligations under that treaty, Serbia had also acquired much of Macedonia from Turkey at the conclusion of the Balkan Wars of 1912–1913 and religious liberties of the Muslim population of the area were protected by Articles 7–9 of the Treaty of Constantinople of 1914.[44] Britain, however, was not a party to this later treaty and still recognized the boundaries established by the Treaty of Berlin[45] and wanted guarantees concerning Macedonia in the treaty by which it would recognize Serbian control of the area.

Serbia was only prepared to accept minorities obligations, but not international supervision, in respect of newly acquired areas (which would not include Macedonia) and to the extent that the principal Allied and Associated Powers themselves accepted similar obligations.[46] There-fore, and like Romania, Serbia objected to Article 59 of the Austrian Treaty which, along with the Minorities Treaty, it refused to sign until December 1919.[47] Fully aware of the racial and religious diversity of the region, the Allies pressed for a treaty on the Polish model that would be

[42] Spector, *Romania*, p. 218.
[43] Treaty between the Principal Allied and Associated Powers (the British Empire, France, Italy, Japan and the United States) and the Serb-Croat-Slovene State, signed at St Germain-en-Laye, 10 September 1919 (226 CTS 182; LNTS No. 39). See Temperley, *HPC*, vol. V, pp. 146–148, 446–454; Janowsky, *The Jews and Minority Rights*, pp. 376–377; Macartney, *National States and National Minorities*, pp. 249–250; I. J. Lederer, *Yugoslavia at the Paris Peace Conference: a Study in Frontier-making* (New Haven: Yale University Press, 1963), pp. 239–258.
[44] See above, at p. 74, and see S. J. Shaw and E. K. Shaw, *History of the Ottoman Empire and Modern Turkey* (Cambridge University Press, 1977), vol. II, p. 298.
[45] France, however, did recognize the Serbian acquisition of Macedonia and therefore resisted the Italian suggestion that a special regime be established for Macedonia along the lines of that provided for the Ruthenians in the Czechoslovak Treaty. See Miller, *My Diary*, vol. XIII, pp. 263–266 and 323.
[46] This was aimed at Italy, which refused to accept obligations relating to its newly acquired Slavic minorities.
[47] See Communication from the Serb-Croat-Slovene Government relative to Article 59 of the Conditions of Peace with Austria (24 July 1919), Miller, vol. XIII, p. 337.

applicable throughout the country.[48] The New States Committee finalized the text of the treaty on 9 August 1919.[49]

Once again, it followed the general pattern of the Polish Treaty. Although the Jewish Clauses were not included,[50] special measures were provided for the Muslim minority[51] which were, in some respects, more liberal than the Jewish Clauses themselves.[52] On the other hand, they were much less onerous than the terms of the Treaty of Constantinople, which had previously addressed the rights of Muslims in Macedonia. Nevertheless, the Minorities Treaty did ensure that the obligations, such as they were, would be uniform in content and applicable throughout the new State. In addition, the ineffectual Turkish guarantee was, in common with all the minorities treaty stipulations, replaced by the theoretically more potent League supervision.[53]

The peace treaties

Just as the Polish Treaty served as a model for the other minorities treaties, it was also used as the source for the provisions concerning

[48] With the exception of Article 9, which was to apply only to those territories acquired since 1 January 1913, that is, to all areas outside of the Kingdom of Serbia as recognized in the Treaty of Berlin.

[49] Unlike the Romanian Treaty, it was not subsequently modified to meet the complaints of the Serb-Croat-Slovene State.

[50] The reasons given were that: 'The Jewish population is small and it is not anticipated that any special protection for them will be necessary.' Miller, vol. XIII, p. 435.

[51] Article 10 provided that:

> The Serb-Croat-Slovene State agrees to grant to the Musulmans in the matter of family law and personal status provisions suitable for regulating these matters in accordance with Musulman usage.
>
> The Serb-Croat-Slovene State shall take measures to assure the nomination of a Reiss-Ul-Ulema.
>
> The Serb-Croat-Slovene State undertakes to ensure protection to the mosques, cemeteries and other Musulman religious establishments. Full recognition and facilities shall be assured to Musulman pious foundations (Wakfs) and religious and charitable establishments now existing, and the Serb-Croat-Slovene State shall not refuse any of the necessary facilities for the creation of new religious and charitable establishments guaranteed to other private establishments of this nature.

[52] For example, by obliging the State to protect religious establishments.

[53] The New States Committee, in its Report to the Supreme Council accompanying the treaty, pointed this out but mentioned that the purpose of Article 10 was to 'place the minimum rights under a safe and inviolable guarantee'. See Miller, vol. XIII, p. 434. The continuance of obligations under the Treaty of Constantinople (concluded between Turkey and the Kingdom of Serbia) as between Turkey and the Serb-Croat-Slovene State was left unclear.

minority protection in the peace treaties. What might be called the 'standard articles' – Articles 1, 2, 6, 7, 8, 9 and 12 – were included (amended as necessary) in the treaties with Austria,[54] Hungary[55] and Bulgaria.[56] There were two principal differences. First, whereas in the Polish Treaty only Articles 2–8 were, by virtue of Article 1, to be recognized as 'fundamental laws', all of the equivalent articles in the peace treaties were 'fundamental'.[57] Secondly, whereas Article 9 of the Polish Treaty only applied to German-speaking communities in areas that had, prior to 1914, been a part of Germany, the equivalent clauses in the peace treaties were of general application. The 'Jewish Clauses' were not included in any of these treaties, but, in common with the Polish Treaty, the scope of the articles equivalent to Article 9 was limited to primary education. Like the minorities treaties, the minority obligations in the peace treaties were placed under the guarantee of the League of Nations.

Peace was to be concluded with Turkey by the Treaty of Sèvres, signed by the Ottomans on 10 August 1920. Once again, the treaty contained provisions for the protection of minorities which were modelled upon the Polish Treaty.[58] Article 141 differed from Article 2 of the Polish Treaty, however, by simply providing that: 'All inhabitants of . . . shall be entitled to the free exercise, whether public or private, of any creed, religion or belief' and omitted the qualification that its practice be 'not inconsistent with public order or public morals'. There is more than a mere implication that Ottoman public order and morals were not to be weighed against religious practice. In addition, the treaty reimposed the Capitulations as they had been at the outbreak of the war.[59] Special clauses provided for the protection of specific minority groups.[60]

The Turkish Nationalists reacted with fury to the terms of the treaty as a whole, but accepted the principle of minority rights.[61] Following the

---

[54] Treaty of St Germain, Articles 62, 63, 65, 66, 67, 68 and 69.

[55] Treaty of Trianon, Articles 54, 55, 57, 58 (combined Articles 7 and 8 of the Polish Treaty), 59 and 60.

[56] Treaty of Neuilly, Articles 49, 50, 52, 53 (but replacing 'differences of religion, creed or confession' with the phrase 'differences of religion, creed or profession'), 54, 55 and 57.

[57] Treaty of St Germain, Article 62; Treaty of Trianon, Article 54; Treaty of Neuilly, Article 49.

[58] Articles 140, 141, 145, 147, 148, and 150.

[59] Article 261 even extended the benefit of them to all of the Allied powers. The motive was to re-establish and consolidate the economic advantages which these gave. The religious aspects of the Capitulations were not of any particular interest or significance. See Temperley, *HPC*, vol. VI, pp. 96–102.

[60] Articles 142–144, concerning the Greek and Armenian minorities.

[61] Article 5 of the National Pact of Angora provided:

collapse of the Ottoman Government, the Peace had to be renegotiated with the new Turkish Government which, moreover, had successfully expelled the Greek forces which had occupied Izmir and had been operating in other parts of Anatolia and Thrace. The Treaty of Lausanne marked a radical break with the past in a number of ways. For the first time in 200 years, the Turks, having transformed themselves into a nation State, entered into a treaty on something approaching an equal footing with the western European powers, who could no longer take advantage from dealing with an Empire premised upon a different philosophy of governance and jurisdiction.

The extra-territorial Capitulations were abolished in their entirety[62] but the minority guarantees found in the Treaty of Sèvres were carried over into the new treaty and took the place of the *millet* system. As a recognition of the new situation, the free exercise of religion was, as in all the other treaties, subject to the requirement that its exercise be not incompatible with public order or morals.[63] However, the distinction applied throughout the treaty was that between Muslim and non muslim inhabitants (for the purposes of Articles 38 or 42) or nationals (for the purposes of the remainder), as opposed to that between the national group and 'racial, religious or linguistic' minorities (either inhabitants or nationals, as appropriate) used in the other treaties. This had the serious consequence of excluding the Kurds from the scope of the minority obligations, since, although a minority, they were also Muslim.

The practical importance of the minorities provisions had, however, already been reduced by what was the most dramatic element of the settlement: a compulsory exchange of populations, which had been agreed upon at Lausanne in January 1923.[64] Article 1 of the Convention concerning the Exchange of the Greek–Turkish Populations provided that:

> The rights of minorities will be confirmed by us on the same basis as those established to the profit of minorities in other countries by the *ad hoc* conventions concluded between the Entente powers, their adversaries, and certain of their associates. On the other hand, we cherish the firm conviction that Muslim minorities in neighbouring countries will enjoy the same guarantees where their rights are concerned.

This was consistent with the repudiation of the *millet* system as the basis of inter-communal relations within a new Turkey conceived in terms of a Western nation State. See Temperley, *HPC*, vol. VI, pp. 102–103.

[62] The practical impact of this was not fully realized until 1929. See Shaw and Shaw, *History of the Ottoman Empire and Modern Turkey*, p. 367.

[63] Treaty of Lausanne, Article 38.

[64] This 'solution' to the minority problem had already been foreshadowed by the Convention between Bulgaria and Greece Respecting Reciprocal Emigration of

As from 1 May, 1923, there shall take place a compulsory exchange of Turkish nationals of the Greek Orthodox religion established[65] in Turkish Territory, and of Greek nationals of the moslem religion established in Greek Territory.[66]

In some ways, this simply provided a legal framework for what had already happened by force of arms. The Greek population of the Smyrna (Izmir) district had already fled in large numbers. The expulsion of Muslims from all of Greece excluding Western Thrace was harder to justify but probably saved them from revenge at the hands of the displaced refugees from Anatolia. Moreover, it was underpinned by Kemal's desire to establish a Turkish national homeland.[67] Nevertheless, it was a solution that was at odds with the fundamental presuppositions upon which all of the minority instruments were based.[68]

Minorities, signed at Neuilly-sur-Seine, 27 November 1919 (226 CTS 435, LNTS No. 41) at the same time as the Peace Treaty with Bulgaria. Article 1 provided that:
> The High Contracting parties recognize the right of those of their subjects who belong to racial, religious or linguistic minorities to emigrate freely to their respective territories.

Article 6 §2 further specified that:
> in cases where the right of emigration is exercised by members of communities (including churches, convents, schools and hospitals or foundations of any kind whatever) which on this account shall have to be dissolved, the mixed commission provided for in Article 8 shall determine whether and in what circumstances such members shall have the option of freely taking with them or having transported the moveable property belonging to the communities.

The application of this Convention gave rise to considerable friction, resulting in a number of appeals to the Council of the League of Nations and, as regards the meaning of 'community' in Article 6, an Advisory Opinion from the PCIJ. See *Greco-Bulgarian 'Communities'*, Advisory Opinion, 1930, PCIJ, Series B, No. 17, pp. 21–23. See generally S. P. Ladas, *The Exchange of Minorities: Bulgaria, Greece and Turkey* (New York: Macmillan, 1932). For a moving literary account of the impact of this Convention, see N. Kazantsakis, *The Fratricides* (trans. A. G. Dallas), (London: Faber and Faber, 1974), chapter 1.

[65] The meaning of the word 'established' proved to be controversial and was the subject of an Advisory Opinion of the PCIJ. See *Exchange of Greek and Turkish Populations*, Advisory Opinion, 1925, PCIJ, Series B, No. 10. This and other outstanding questions were finally resolved by the Greek–Turkish Convention signed at Ankara on 10 June 1930 (108 LNTS 233). For the background see H. J. Psomiades, *The Eastern Question: the Last Phase* (Thessalonika: Institute for Balkan Studies, 1968), pp. 73–86.

[66] Article 2 excluded the Greek inhabitants of Constantinople and the Muslim inhabitants of Western Thrace from the compulsory exchange. This meaning of 'inhabitant' also proved controversial, particularly when an attempt was made to expel the Ecumenical Patriarch of the Greek Orthodox Church from Constantinople under this provision. See further below at p. 157, n. 41.

[67] See Psomiades, *The Eastern Question: the Last Phase*, p. 66; Shaw and Shaw, *History of the Ottoman Empire and Modern Turkey*, p. 368.

[68] In effect this was 'ethnic cleansing' under the auspices of international law, which is now considered to be a crime against humanity (see, for example, Article 5(e) of the

Declarations on admission to the League

The first meeting of the League Assembly took place in December 1920, when it was called upon to consider the terms on which new States might be admitted to the League. Jewish lobbyists were again instrumental[69] in persuading Lord Cecil to propose that: 'The Assembly is not prepared to admit any new state to the League unless it will give an undertaking to enter into agreements corresponding with the Minorities Treaties already accepted by several other States.' Following discussions in the Assembly this was watered down and the recommendation finally adopted provided that:

In the event of the Baltic and Caucasian States and Albania being admitted to the League, the Assembly requests that they should take the necessary measures to enforce the principle of the Minorities Treaties, and that they should arrange with the Council the details required to carry this object into effect.[70]

Rather than require that such an undertaking be given as a condition for membership, these States were simply called on to apply the principles of the treaties without any particular mode being specified. On admission, however, the Baltic States were asked to give an undertaking that they would adhere to the recommendation and would negotiate with the Council concerning 'the scope and details' of the application of their

Statute of the International Tribunal for the Former Yugoslavia). It is particularly interesting to see how the PCIJ reconciled this with measures relating to the protection of minorities, albeit in the context of a convention concerned only with 'voluntary' exchanges. In the *Greco-Bulgarian 'Communities'* Advisory Opinion, the Court said:

> The general purpose of the instrument is thus, by as wide a measure of reciprocal emigration as possible, to eliminate or reduce in the Balkans the centres of irredentist agitation which were shown by the history of the preceding periods to have been so often the cause of lamentable incidents or serious conflicts, and to render more effective than in the past the process of pacification in the countries of Eastern Europe. (PCIJ Series B, No. 17, p. 19.)

The Court also gave Advisory Opinions relative to the compulsory exchanges between Greece and Turkey (*Exchange of Greek and Turkish Populations*, Advisory Opinion, 1925, PCIJ, Series B, No. 10 and the *Interpretation of the Greco-Turkish Agreement of 1 December 1926 (Final Protocol, Article IV)*, Advisory Opinion, 1928, PCIJ, Series B, No. 16). Presumably the ICJ would today decline to consider such a treaty at all on the grounds that it was void for its violating a norm of *ius cogens* (Articles 55 and 64, Vienna Convention on the Law of Treaties (1969), 1155 UNTS 311).

[69] See Janowsky, *The Jews and Minority Rights*, pp. 381–382; L. P. Mair, *The Protection of Minorities* (London: Christophers, 1928), p. 49.

[70] Recommendation adopted by the First Assembly of the League of Nations, 15 December 1920.

'international obligations for the protection of minorities' and all signed declarations to that effect.[71]

The first State[72] to make a minorities declaration was Albania which had joined the League in 1920. The Albanian Declaration of 2 October 1921 embodied the minorities provisions of the Polish Treaty and the Council undertook the guarantee by means of a resolution of the same date.[73] There were a number of modifications. The equivalent of Article 2 was expanded to make it clear that all inhabitants of Albania had 'the right to change their religion'. Secondly, a clause similar to that in the Serb-Croat-Slovene Treaty regarding the regulation of family and personal status of Muslim communities was incorporated as Article 3, whilst Article 4 included the requirement that 'an electoral system giving due consideration to the rights of racial, religious and linguistic minorities will be applied'. The most innovative addition was the requirement that, within six months of the date of the declaration, Albania was to present the League Council with detailed information concerning 'the legal status of the religious communities, churches, convents, schools, voluntary establishments and associations of racial, religious and linguistic minorities' and agreed to 'take into consideration any advice it might receive from the League of Nations with regard to this question'. [74]

The three Baltic States became members of the League at the Second Session of the League Assembly in 1921. Lithuania was the first to make its declaration, on 12 May 1922, and its minorities clauses were identical to

[71] Estonian Declaration of 13 September 1921 and Latvian and Lithuanian Declarations of 14 September 1921.
[72] Finland also made a declaration (accompanied by a Council Resolution on 27 June 1921) by which it placed guarantees concerning the preservation of the Swedish language, culture and traditions in the Aaland Islands under League supervision. Complaints were to be forwarded to the Council via the Finnish Government. When Estonia tried to draw on this example before the Council, Lord Cecil insisted that: 'The case of Finland was exceptional and unique and must not be cited as a precedent' (*LNOJ*, vol. IV (1923), p. 1269; see also vol. III (1922), p. 1237). Given the limited nature of this guarantee, and the *sui generis* nature of the Aaland Islands regime, it will not be given any further consideration.
[73] Declaration and Council Resolution of 2 October 1921. See *LNOJ*, vol. II (1921), pp. 1161–1165. Greece had asked that, because of its particular interest in the situation of Greeks in Albania, it be empowered to place information before the League Council. This was rejected.
[74] Article 5 (§2). In fact, Albania was unable to do this in the time available (see *LNOJ*, vol. III (1922), p. 523) and its subsequent legislation prompted a number of petitions to the League, and culminated in a request for an Advisory Opinion from the PCIJ (*Minority Schools in Albania*, 1935, PCIJ, Series A/B, No. 64, p. 4). See below at p. 159.

those of the Polish Treaty and included the 'Jewish Clauses'.[75] Discussions with Estonia and Latvia were, however, prolonged and acrimonious since they objected to being subjected to the obligations, and, unlike Lithuania, were not due to receive anything from the League other than membership. Moreover, they also claimed that their constitutions already went beyond the provisions of the treaties.[76] A compromise was devised which had the practical effect of rendering both Latvia and Estonia subject to the obligations and enforcement mechanisms of the minorities system but without obliging them to make a formal 'minorities' declaration as such. They both submitted detailed documentation in support of their claim that their domestic laws already complied with the minorities treaties and which the Council, once satisfied, accepted, although reserving the right to examine minorities questions further should the need arise.[77]

Since the declarations and resolutions relating to Estonia and Latvia did not specify which of the various articles of the minorities treaties was to apply, it became necessary to determine the precise extent of their obligations. Estonia produced a concordance of the various minorities and peace treaties, and distilled from them the common articles, which it considered represented the 'fundamental principles' of the system, and it

[75] Declaration of 12 May 1922. See LNOJ, vol. III (1922), pp. 524 and 584–588. The Council undertook the guarantee by Resolution on 15 May 1922 (ibid., pp. 536–537) but ratification was delayed until 11 December 1923. By virtue of Article 11 of the Paris Convention of 8 May 1924, this declaration was to apply within the Memel Territory. See LNOJ, vol. V (1924), pp. 1201–1207.

[76] The Memoranda relating to Latvia are set out in LNOJ, vol. III (1922), pp. 248–252, 479–483, 733–750, 1035–1037, 1092–1094 and 1419–1424 (this being the Report to the Council by the Rapporteur, and including the text of a draft declaration modelled on the Polish Treaty, including the Jewish Clauses); vol. IV (1923), pp. 111–112. The Memoranda relating to Estonia are set out in LNOJ, vol. III (1922), pp. 483–485 and vol. IV (1923), pp. 1361–1373 (Annex 545). The Reports from the Council's Rapporteur are found at vol. III (1922), pp. 1231–1238 and vol. IV (1923), pp. 379–380 (Annex 470) and 992–998 (Annex 529: this included a draft declaration modelled on the Polish Treaty, but excluding the Jewish Clauses).

[77] The Latvian Declaration of 7 July 1923 provided that, whilst the consideration of the question was closed: 'The council will nevertheless have the right to take up the question anew and to reopen the negotiations if the situation of the minorities in Latvia does not appear to it to correspond to the general principles laid down in the various so-called minorities treaties.' It also specified that any petitions submitted should be screened and referred to Latvia for comment before being put to the Council. Although this looks like a major concession it was, in fact, merely a recapitulation of the procedural rules already adopted. See LNOJ, vol. IV (1923), p. 933 and below at p. 154.

As regards Estonia, the Council adopted a resolution affirming that it 'will be entitled to consider afresh the status of minorities in Estonia, should the latter cease to enforce these general principles'. See LNOJ, vol. IV (1923), p. 1311.

was only in relation to these that it was prepared to submit itself to scrutiny. These were Articles 1, 2, 3, 6, 7, 8, 9 and 12 of the Polish Treaty.[78] The Council impliedly accepted this analysis of the core obligations of the minorities system when it adopted its resolution concerning Estonia and, in consequence, the Jewish Clauses were not applicable either to Latvia or Estonia. It is ironic, to say the least, that it was only in one of the final pieces of the minorities system jigsaw that its core was finally determined. Only one further minorities declaration was ever made, by Iraq in May 1932.[79]

Other League-sponsored instruments

Mention has already been made of the Convention concerning the Memel Territory.[80] The final instrument which placed minority rights under the protection of the League of Nations was the German–Polish Convention of 15 May 1922 concerning Upper Silesia. This had three sections. The first repeated the minorities provisions of the Polish Treaty, which Poland agreed to extend to its portion of Upper Silesia and Germany agreed to apply within its portion for a fifteen year period. The second section amplified these general provisions, whilst the third permitted individual members of a minority to submit petitions to the League Council, this being the only incidence of an 'individual petition' procedure within the League system.

Conclusion

Further attempts were made to extend the scope of the system to all League members, but without success. During the Second Session of the League Assembly in September 1921 a resolution was adopted which expressed the hope that: 'those states which are not bound by any legal obligation with respect to minorities treaties will nevertheless observe, in their treatment of their own racial, religious and linguistic minorities, at least as high a standard of justice and toleration as is required by any of the treaties and by the regular action of the Council'.[81]

The final attempt was made during the Fifteenth Session of the League

---

[78] See *LNOJ*, vol. IV (1923), pp. 1361–1373 (Annex 545) at p. 1354. Latvia therefore avoided the Jewish Clauses which the Council Rapporteur had suggested be applied to it.

[79] Council Resolution of 11 May 1932.   [80] See above, n. 75

[81] Resolution of 13 September 1921. This had been proposed by Gilbert Murray, a member of the South African Delegation.

Assembly in 1934. Poland proposed a resolution which claimed that 'the present situation in regard to the international protection of minorities is not in harmony with international morality' and that a general minorities convention should be concluded.[82] Although this received degrees of support from other States subject to the system, Poland ultimately withdrew the resolution.[83]

In consequence, it was the instruments considered in the previous sections which formed what became known as the minorities system. It was difficult to defend the minorities treaties as a system because of the inconsistency of their application. It could not be said that obligations were imposed by the victors on the losers since, although the peace treaties with Austria, Hungary, Bulgaria and Turkey contained guarantees for the rights of minorities left within their borders, the Treaty of Versailles did not. Nor was the system uniformly applied to all existing States which received additional territory. Neither Belgium, France nor Denmark were asked to sign a minorities treaty despite having profited territorially at Germany's expense.

More tellingly, guarantees were not required of Italy, which received areas of the Southern Tyrol and of the Istrian Peninsula, and which, had they been awarded to Austria or the Serb-Croat-Slovene State, would have been required of them.[84] The best that can be said is that a certain consistency was sought in the application of the system in Central and Eastern Europe, and subsequently in parts of the Near East, and that this was chiefly dictated by the realization that certain countries were 'bad risks'.[85] Those on the receiving end of these blunt home truths were naturally affronted by the mismatch between the Allies' rhetoric and practice. The lack of a general and uniform system of obligations regarding minorities provided a convenient weapon for those States who wished to avoid their own treaty obligations and Poland ultimately with-

[82] Poland subsequently amended the proposal so that the general treaty would only apply throughout Europe. See *Official Journal*, Special Supplement No. 130, Records of the 15 Ordinary Session of the Assembly. Minutes of the 6th Committee (Political Questions), 8th Meeting, 20 September, 1934, No. 25, pp. 38ff.

[83] Poland had, however, already indicated that it would no longer cooperate with the League's supervision of the treaty. See statement of Colonel Beck (1934) *Official Journal*, Verbatim Record, 15th Ordinary Session of the Assembly, 4th Plenary Meeting, 13 September 1934, p. 2.

[84] However, Italy entered into a number of minorities treaties with the Kingdom of the Serb-Croat-Slovenes. See treaties of 12 November 1920, 23 October 1923, 27 January 1924, 2 July 1924; and 20 July 1925.

[85] Macartney, *National States and National Minorities*, p. 289.

drew from the supervisory mechanisms of the League on this basis, undermining the entire system.[86]

Beyond this lay the fundamental problem that the system had no consistent overall purpose. Different claims were made on behalf of the various instruments at the various stages of their development in order to assure their adoption and, as the claims became more extravagant, the original purpose of the Polish Treaty was eclipsed. In effect, the treaties grew out of control and the Allies made the best of it by foisting upon them a new role that they were not designed to fulfil. Later commentators, following the lead of the League of Nations itself, continued the trend, and it has become customary to regard them as having been intended to protect the national minorities left 'stranded' in States other than their own by the peace settlement – and to condemn them for their failure to do so.

In reality, Wilson and Lloyd George were kick-started into taking note of minority problems at the eleventh hour[87] and the Polish Treaty was intended to satisfy the demands, made chiefly by Jews living in the West, that the civil and political rights of Jews living in the newly constituted Poland be respected and their freedom of religion assured. They were not originally motivated by a desire to protect 'transferred' nationals of pre-existing States and were, at first, simply continuing the tradition of inserting clauses seeking guarantees of certain rights in treaties conferring recognition on new States which had been adopted in the Treaty of Berlin and recognized as an element of the 'public law of Europe'.[88]

---

[86] Poland argued that the system had 'largely served as a means of spreading defamatory propaganda against the States subject to the system, and also as a means of exercising political pressure by States which, without being bound themselves, have used their prerogative to participate in the system of supervision'. See statement of Colonel Beck, n. 83 above.

[87] The New States Committee was established on 1 May 1919 and the draft treaty was scheduled to be presented to Germany on 7 May. If minority issues were truly as significant as apologists of the Peace have claimed it is inconceivable that their consideration would have been left so late. This is not to say that the Allies were unaware of the problems that would face minorities throughout Central and Eastern Europe, nor that they were indifferent towards them. It was simply that up until this time nothing had been done about it (see Headlam-Morley, *Memoir*, p. 113 and Temperley, *HPC*, vol. V, p. 123).

[88] Or, of the public law of dealing with Eastern Europe. It was one thing for the Great Powers to grant territory to others, another when they took it for themselves. See Temperley, *HPC*, vol. V, p. 116. This was why it was considered essential to include some form of minorities clause in the Treaty of Versailles, by virtue of which the Great Powers would be granting recognition to Poland, since once Poland was recognized it might be too late to insist.

6 The experience under the League

The scope of protection

The previous chapters have chronicled the development of the minorities system. All of the instruments shared a common framework which had four basic components: clauses relating to nationality; to equality of rights; general measures concerning minorities; and, where appropriate, specific measures for particular minority groups. The nationality provisions varied in length and detail according to the States concerned and need not be given any further consideration. The 'equality' clauses were standard, varied only in the Albanian Declaration and the Treaty of Lausanne, as were the general minorities clauses. The special minorities clauses comprised the 'Jewish articles' of the Polish Treaty which were either combined with, or replaced by, other particular measures of protection as considered appropriate. Thus religious issues were embraced by this general scheme in a number of ways and the Polish Treaty will be used as a model to demonstrate this.

The 'equality' clauses operated in different fashions. First, Article 2 of the Polish Treaty provided an undertaking to: 'assure full and complete protection of life and liberty to all inhabitants of Poland without distinction of birth, nationality, language, race or religion'. To this general provision was added the specific obligation that: 'All inhabitants of Poland shall be entitled to the free exercise, whether public or private, of any creed, religion or belief, whose practices are not inconsistent with public order or public morals'.

Thus all inhabitants of the State, and not just minorities, were guaranteed the freedom to exercise their religious beliefs – albeit subject to the requirement that its practices were not inconsistent with public order or public morals: there was no unfettered right to the exercise of one's

145

religion – and the clause which was originally intended to apply throughout the States party to the League of Nations Covenant finally became applicable to a mere sub-set of States. However, its association with the minorities system meant that it was not generally perceived as a right applicable to all.

The League of Nations guarantee, established by Article 12, extended only to those stipulations affecting 'persons belonging to racial, religious or linguistic minorities'. On the face of it, this would not seem to extend to Article 2 at all and this reinforced the idea that Article 2 was not a source of real constraint upon the actions of States.[1] However, the scope of Article 12 was a matter of some controversy. In the case concerning *Acquisition of Polish Nationality* Poland argued before the PCIJ that only Polish nationals were capable of forming minorities as defined in the treaty and that, in consequence, questions concerning the interpretation of Article 4, which concerned the right to Polish nationality, were not covered by the League's guarantee.[2]

The Court took the view that the League's guarantee under Article 12 extended to all minorities within Poland, irrespective of nationality, and so encompassed the claims of the German colonists under Article 4.[3] However, the Court also said that the very fact that Article 12 referred to 'the clauses preceding this Article' entailed its application to Article 4.[4] The logic of this is that the League's guarantee would also embrace the right of minorities to the free exercise of religion under Article 2, although the rights of inhabitants not members of a relevant minority would not be embraced.[5] This would be in addition to their right to equality of treatment under Article 8.

It is not, however, entirely clear that this is what the Court intended. It also said that: 'Poland, by consenting, in Article 12 of the Treaty, to the preceding articles being placed under the guarantee of the League of Nations in so far as they concern persons belonging to racial or linguistic

---

[1] Article 12 specified that the stipulations to which it applied were 'obligations of international concern'. This carried an implication that the fulfilment of other obligations was of a different order and that it was, at the very least, inappropriate to submit them to the same degree of international supervision.
[2] *Acquisition of Polish Nationality*, Advisory Opinion, 1923, PCIJ, Series B, No. 7, pp. 12–13.
[3] *Ibid.*, pp. 14–17.   [4] *Ibid.*, p. 17.
[5] This was the view of the former Director of the Minorities Questions section of the League. See P. de Azcárate, *League of Nations and National Minorities: An Experiment* (trans. E. E .Brooke) (Washington: Carnegie Endowment for International Peace, 1945), pp. 58–59.

minorities, also consents to the extension of this protection to the application of Articles 3 to 6 [i.e., the nationality clauses]'.[6]

Given that the Advisory Opinion was only concerned with the acquisition of nationality, this observation does not preclude the extension of the principle to embrace Article 2, but it cannot be confidently stated that it did.[7] However, in a later Judgment the Court drew on this Opinion when concluding that the guarantee in Article 12 was 'given "in so far as they" (the provisions of Articles 1–11) "affect persons belonging to racial, religious or linguistic minorities"'.[8] Thus the rights of minorities under Article 2 were within the scope of the League's guarantee.

Article 7 applied to all Polish nationals[9] and, by virtue of Article 1,[10] was to be a 'fundamental law'. It specified that:

All Polish nationals shall be equal before the law and shall enjoy the same civil and political rights without distinction as to race, language or religion. Differences of religion, creed or confession shall not prejudice any Polish national in matters relating to the enjoyment of civil or political rights . . . No restriction shall be imposed upon the free use by any Polish national of any language in . . . religion . . .[11]

Once again, although this was not a 'minority' right as such it was perceived as one. Indeed, the second sentence was described by one observer as being intended 'to assure that members of religious minorities would not be discriminated against because of their failure to appear for work or to keep their establishments open on their holidays', whilst viewing the third as an example of a general minorities provision.[12]

It was, in fact, Articles 8 and 9 which introduced 'minority rights' into the minorities treaty. Article 8 applied to 'Polish nationals who belong to

---

[6] *Ibid.*, p. 16.
[7] *Cf.* the Observations of Lord Finlay, who took the view that if the protection of life and liberty of an unpopular minority was refused, 'the minority would be one of a mass of inhabitants, whether Polish nationals or not' (Azcárate, *ibid.*, p. 25). This would seem to suggest that the guarantee did not extend to Article 2. It should also be noted that the Court mentioned only racial and linguistic, and not religious, minorities although, once again, this might be explained by the context.
[8] *Treatment of Polish Nationals and Other Persons of Polish Origin or Speech in the Danzig Territory*, Advisory Opinion, 1932, PCIJ, Series A/B, No. 44, p. 4 at p. 39.
[9] In the original draft, they applied to 'citizens of Poland'.
[10] Formerly draft Article 12.
[11] Since Article 7 only applied to nationals, it was unclear whether restrictions on the use of language in worship could be imposed on non-nationals exercising their rights under Article 2, assuming that its use was not contrary to public order or morals.
[12] J. Robinson, *Were the Minority Treaties a Failure?* (New York: Institute of Jewish Affairs, 1943), p. 37.

racial, religious or linguistic minorities' and ensured to them 'the same treatment and security in law and in fact as the other Polish nationals',[13] whilst specifying that: 'In particular they shall have an equal right to establish, manage and control at their own expense charitable, religious and social institutions, schools and other educational establishments, with the right to use their own language and to exercise their religion freely therein.'

On one level, Article 8 added nothing to the treaty. Article 7 prevented Polish nationals from being discriminated against on account of their religious beliefs in the enjoyment of their civil and political rights and Article 8 simply confirmed the equal right of nationals who were also members of racial, religious and linguistic groups to the enjoyment of them. Nevertheless, the very fact that this was spelt out underlines the real purpose of these articles and, just as Article 8 illuminates the real purpose of Article 7, so does Article 9 illuminate the principal thrust of Article 8.

The first part of Article 9 required the State to provide adequate facilities for primary education in the language of the minority group 'in towns and districts where a considerable proportion of Polish nationals of other than Polish speech are residents'.[14] It has already been seen that the wording of this Article was devised in the light of its impact upon the Jewish communities, as was the second part of the article, which obliged the State to ensure that they enjoy an equitable share of resources devoted to religious activities in those towns and districts where such a minority formed a considerable proportion of the population. Again, there was no obligation to provide such resources, merely to ensure equitable enjoyment of those which were provided, and it could be seen

---

[13] In the *Minority Schools* case, in which Germany alleged that Poland was in breach of its obligations under the minority clauses which had been included in the 1922 Geneva Convention concerning Upper Silesia, the Court elaborated slightly on this and commented that 'a generally hostile attitude on the part of the authorities in regard to minority schools, an attitude manifested by more or less arbitrary action, is not compatible with the principle laid down in Article 68 [Article 8 of the Polish Minority Treaty]'. However, it did not have to decide whether the actions of the Polish Government had in fact been discriminatory for the purposes of the Judgment. See *Rights of Minorities in Upper Silesia (Minority Schools)*, Judgment No. 12, 1928, PCIJ, Series A, No. 15, pp. 45–46.

[14] Azcárate (*League of Nations and National Minorities*, pp. 60–61) described this clause as being 'so confused and sibylline that we were never able to discover its real meaning, nor the value of its practical application'. See also I. Evans, 'The Protection of Minorities', *BYIL* 4 (1923–1924) 95, at pp. 106–109.

as simply another specific manifestation of the general requirement of non-discrimination.

However, this again would miss the point that it was intended to do more.[15] The next Article of the Polish Treaty, Article 10, was the first of the 'Jewish Clauses' and confirmed the application of Article 9 to the Jewish communities and explicitly provided for the distribution of such funds via Education Committees appointed by the Jewish communities. What emerges is a picture of a treaty framed in general terms – and acknowledged to be of general application – but constructed in such a way that the particular purposes which it was designed to achieve are highlighted by the progression of specificity within it. If there was no doubt that the Jewish community would share in an even-handed applica- tion of the 'equality' clause then there would have been no need to confirm its application in the general minorities clause, Article 8. If the application of Article 8 had not been in doubt, there would have been no reason to underline its application in the relevant context in Article 9. And the special minority articles, 10 and 11 (sabbath observance), were again necessary only because of the need to close any possible loophole.

The result is that the very real, though qualified, right to the free exercise of religion in Article 2 was obscured by the 'minority' thrust of the treaty. Yet the 'minority' nature of the treaty was secondary to its real purpose. Moreover, the generalization of the minority rights also drew attention away from their primary purpose. The result was that a treaty intended to guarantee the religious freedoms of vulnerable groups became a vehicle for the advancement of general categories of minority rights and religious questions *per se* assumed no real importance under the League.

The history of the evolution of the Polish Treaty is significant for a number of reasons. The final text represented a package that attempted to balance the conflicting aspirations and fears of the various interested parties, not only between the Poles and the Jews but between the British, French and Americans, each of whom considered the others unduly receptive to outside interests.[16] Although the treaty purported to lay

---

[15] *Cf.* the *Minority Schools* case, in which the Court observed that 'Article 69 [Article 9 of the Polish Minority Treaty], in fact, bestows an advantage which is dependent on the fulfilment of certain conditions' and was not itself conditioned by the need for equality of treatment provided for in Article 67 (Article 7 of the Polish Minority Treaty). See *Rights of Minorities in Upper Silesia (Minority Schools)*, Judgment No. 12, 1928, PCIJ, Series A, No. 15, p. 43.

[16] The only point on which any real consensus can be detected between the Allies concerned their rejection of the extreme 'national rights' theory originally advanced by the American Jews, although this, for a time, was reflected in American thinking.

down principles of liberal government, the inherent contradiction of seeking to achieve such an end by means of a diktat was never seriously considered. The humanitarianism that allegedly underpinned the very concept of seeking guarantees from newly created, or greatly enlarged, States was not absolute and was in practical terms always subject to wider issues of security. The Allies were, in effect, seeking to establish a system that would defuse the racial tensions that they foresaw would arise in the new Poland by subjecting Poland to the maximum degree of international supervision that was both practical and prudent.

In short, the Allies wanted to protect the peoples of Poland but did not want to undermine the State. It is difficult to imagine a more awkward case in which to construct a precedent. The existence of a strong Polish State was seen as a political and strategic necessity. The Poles were, on their own admission, strongly nationalistic and anti-Semitic. Recent events amply demonstrated the need to protect the Jewish minority and powerful voices in the West insisted upon effective action. The presence of other national minorities rendered action at the same time both more imperative and more difficult.

Nevertheless, it is worth emphasizing that the generalized right to religious freedom embodied in Article 2 was never a matter of controversy. It was originally proposed by Wilson in the Council of Three, transmitted to the New States Committee and not questioned by them and appeared in the final text in its original form. Secondly, the treaty firmly established the practice of outlawing discrimination on grounds of religion. Although the catalogue of rights which are subject to the principle of non-discrimination has changed out of all recognition from those limited rights covered in the Polish Treaty, this fundamental tenet has remained inviolate.[17]

The means of protection

It is beyond the scope of this current work to consider the full impact of either the Polish Treaty or those instruments based upon it. Its importance for the study of religious freedom under international law is, however, profound. As has been seen, the pre-existing practice of European States had been to require guarantees of religious toleration as a condition of recognition of new States. The Polish Treaty represented the

---

[17] See W. McKean, *Equality and Discrimination under International Law* (Oxford: Clarendon Press, 1983).

culmination of this tradition. Yet at the same time it both breached and broadened previous practice. Rather than address the specific problem of the particular religious minority which formed the focus of attention, the treaty attempted to protect religious freedom by ensuring the generalization of rights: by seeking to ensure, *inter alia*, religious liberty for all, the rights of the individuals which comprise the minority group in question would be assured. Thus the rights of all are protected, eliminating the element of discrimination inherent in previous instruments.

At the same time, however, the treaty clearly acknowledged that this type of protection would not always be sufficient. Hence the reintroduction of specific rights for identifiable minorities. The animosity that these provisions aroused, however, demonstrates the problems inherent in seeking to grant extra protection to particular groups above and beyond that offered to the nationals of the State as a whole. Such problems are further exacerbated when account is taken of the enforcement mechanisms provided in Article 12 of the treaty.

One of the principal innovations of the treaty was that it placed the obligations assumed by Poland to its minorities under the guarantee of an international organization, the League of Nations, rather than under the guarantee of the Great Powers. Thus, rather than it falling to other States to seek redress on behalf of a wronged minority, which they might be either unwilling or unable to do, the matter became the concern of the international community as represented by the League. This, at least, was the theory.

Article 12 of the treaty provided that:

Poland agrees that any member of the Council of the League of Nations shall have the right to bring to the attention of the Council any infraction, or any danger of infraction, of any of these obligations, and that the Council may thereupon take such action and give such direction as it may deem proper and effective in the circumstances.

This meant that, formally speaking, only members of the Council could seize the League machinery. This was a poor application of the underlying principle, but the acceptance of that principle – of international rather than national enforcement of the treaty obligation – was in itself of great significance. However, although it had seemed prudent to limit this right to Council Members when the treaty was drafted, opinions changed when the Council met to consider the practical manner in which the guarantee might operate.[18]

---

[18] The British member of the Council, Lord Balfour, observed that this was a thankless

Article 12 also provided:

> that any difference of opinion as to questions of law or fact arising out of these Articles between the Polish Government and any one of the Principal Allied and Associated Powers, or any Power, a member of the Council of the League of Nations, shall be held to be a dispute of an international character under Article 14 of the Covenant of the League of Nations.[19] The Polish Government hereby consents that any such dispute shall, if the other party thereto demands, be referred to the Permanent Court of International Justice. The decision of the Permanent Court of International Justice shall be final and shall have the same force and effect as an award under Article 13 of the Covenant.

In effect, the PCIJ was to have compulsory jurisdiction over disputes referred to it concerning the minority obligations in the relevant instruments and, in addition, act as the Council's advisor on legal questions. The intention was to allow the guarantor powers to remove disputes from the political to the legal arena[20] and further reduce the possibility of the Treaty being used to justify the intervention by one country in the affairs of another.[21] The Court was called upon to consider questions relating to the minorities treaties on numerous occasions, and, although it was not able to sustain the system once its decay had set in, it is generally agreed that the Court was the one institution which enhanced its reputation by its involvement with minority protection.[22] Moreover, the endorsement of the principle that judicial means should be used to resolve legal disputes was, however – and, indeed, remains – of cardinal importance.

The foundations of the mechanisms by which the League gave

---

task and wondered whether the Council could refuse to accept the guarantees foreseen in the treaties. The Belgian representative, Mr Hymans, subsequently echoed this and proposed that a procedure be established which allowed for this to be done by a committee.

[19] Article 14 of the Covenant provided that:

> The Court shall be competent to hear and determine any dispute of an international character which the parties thereto submit. The Court may also give an advisory opinion upon any dispute or question referred to it by the Council or by the Assembly [of the League of Nations].

[20] *Cf.* Robinson, *Were the Minority Treaties a Failure?*, p. 123, where it is argued that the Council was generally reluctant to exercise its powers in difficult cases and tended to 'retreat behind the authority of the Court'.

[21] The possibility of German intervention in Poland was specifically alluded to (*ibid.*, pp. 140–141). It should be noted that those bound by the minority obligations could not insist upon a dispute with the guarantor being referred to the Court.

[22] E.g., *ibid.*, pp. 149–150.

substance to its guarantee were laid in the Tittoni Report,[23] in which it was interpreted in such a way as to permit non-Council members and minorities themselves 'to call the attention of the League of Nations to any infraction or danger of infraction. But this act must retain the nature of a petition, or a report pure and simple: it cannot have the legal effect of putting the matter before the Council and calling upon it to intervene.' It was therefore proposed that 'when a petition with regard to the question of minorities is addressed to the League of Nations, the Secretary General should communicate it, without comment, to the Members of the Council for information. This communication does not yet constitute a judicial act of the League or of its organs. The competence of the Council to deal with the question arises only when one of its members draws its attention to the infraction or danger of infraction which is the subject matter of the petition or report.' When the Tittoni Report was considered by the Council, the consequences of the minority guarantee were at last appreciated: the British representative, Lord Balfour, expressed concern that 'if it were necessary to protect a minority, one of the members of the Council would have to take upon itself the duty of accusing the State which had not fulfilled its undertakings'.[24] At the following meeting, the Belgian representative, Mr Hymans, took up this theme and, noting the 'invidious position of a Member of the Council charging another Power with an infraction of the Minorities Treaties', suggested that the Council should delegate the consideration of petitions to a committee.[25]

[23] Report of 22 October 1920, reproduced in 'Protection of Linguistic, Racial or Religious Minorities by the League of Nations', League of Nations Doc. C.24.M.18.1929.I, pp. 9–11. This publication includes all the Reports and relevant extracts of the Council's minutes relating to the development of the petition system prior to the 'Madrid Resolution' of 1929. For the development of the petition system see Azcárate, *League of Nations and National Minorities*, pp. 102–123, pp. 163–209; Robinson, *Were the Minority Treaties a Failure?*, pp. 85–108; M. G. Jones, 'National Minorities: A Case Study in International Protection', *Law and Contemporary Problems* 14 (1949), 599, 610–614.

[24] Minutes of the 10th Session of the Council, Brussels, 22 October 1920, League of Nations Doc. C.24.M.18.1929.I, p. 9. In the light of this, he even questioned when the League was obliged to undertake the guarantees and, although the Council decided that it could in theory refuse to accept the obligations, it concluded that: 'As the treaties had been concluded with the utmost difficulty, it was necessary to avoid further reducing their authority' (*ibid.*).

[25] *Ibid.*, p. 11. On 25 October the Council adopted a Resolution which provided:
> With a view to assisting members of the Council in the exercise of their rights and duties as regards the protection of minorities, it is desirable that the President and two members appointed by him in each case should proceed to consider any petition or communication addressed to the League of Nations with regard to an infraction or danger of infraction of the clauses of the treaties for the Protection of Minorities. This enquiry would be held as soon as

In its final form, the petition system was as follows. First, all petitions would be examined by the Secretariat and those which were deemed 'not receivable' were given no further consideration.[26] Those deemed 'receivable' were communicated to the government against whom an allegation had been raised. The government was given three weeks within which to indicate whether it wished to put forward its observations, and granted a further two months in which to do so if it did.[27] The petition was then forwarded to all members of the Council for information, who were to consider whether to place the matter before it. However, at the very outset – and following the suggestion of Mr Hymans – the Council adopted a resolution which placed the primary responsibility[28] in the hands of an *ad hoc* Committee of Three, constituted separately for each petition and from which representatives of States directly concerned were excluded.[29] These 'Minority Committees' became the normal forum for

the petition or communication had been brought to the notice of the Members of the Council (*ibid.*, p. 6).

[26] Following pressure from Poland and Czechoslovakia, the Council adopted the recommendations contained in the Rio Branco Report (*LNOJ*, vol. IV (1923), pp. 1426–1432; League of Nations doc. C.24.M.18.1929.I, p. 20) in a Resolution of 5 September 1923 which provided that, in order to be 'receivable', a petition:
  (a) Must have in view the protection of minorities in accordance with the treaties;
  (b) In particular, must not be submitted in the form of a request for the severance of political relations between the minority in question and the State of which it forms a part;
  (c) Must not emanate from an anonymous or unauthenticated source;
  (d) Must abstain from violent language;
  (e) Must contain information or refer to facts which have not recently been the subject of a petition submitted to the ordinary procedure.
  (*LNOJ*, vol. IV (1923), pp. 1290–1294; League of Nations Doc. C.24.M.18.1929.I, pp. 7, 15–19.)
  These are very similar to the admissibility criteria for individual petitions found in modern human rights instruments, except for the lack of an equivalent of the modern requirement that local remedies be exhausted. *Cf.*, for example, European Convention on Human Rights and Fundamental Freedoms (1950), Articles 26 and 27; First Optional Protocol to the International Covenant on Civil and Political Rights, 1966 (999 UNTS 302), Articles 3 and 5; and see generally T. Zwart, *The Admissibility of Human Rights Petitions* (Dordrecht: Martinus Nijhoff, 1994).

[27] Granting the 'accused' State time to respond was introduced by a Resolution of 27 June 1921 following pressure from Poland and Czechoslovakia (see *LNOJ*, vol. II (1921), pp. 749–750; League of Nations Doc. C.24.M.18.1929.I, pp. 6, 12–14).

[28] All Council members retained the right to place the matter before the full Council if they wished.

[29] See Resolution of 10 June 1925 which provided that:
  The President . . . shall not appoint either the representative of the State to which the persons belonging to the minority in question are subject, or the representatives of a State neighbouring the State to which these persons are

the consideration of minority questions, although following the final alteration to the Rules of Procedure in 1929 all members of the Council were informed of the outcome of their examinations, making it easier to re-open them before the Council.[30]

The Committee, assisted by the Secretariat, would investigate the background and, if it was unable to satisfy itself that the matter had been explained satisfactorily, it would be referred to the Council, thereby seizing it of the petition 'officially'.[31] The Council would appoint a Rapporteur who, sometimes assisted by two members of the Council, would engage in further discussion. The difference between negotiations conducted by the intermediate 'Committee of Three' and the Rapporteur appointed by the Council was that the former were private, the latter public.[32]

The League 'system' also included a number of other instruments which established their own special mechanisms for minorities protection. The 1922 Geneva Convention concerning Upper Silesia[33] established a Minorities Office in each of the areas of the territory to which petitions could

> subject, or the representative of a State the majority of whose population belong from the ethnical point of view to the same people as the persons in question (*LNOJ*, vol. VI (1925), pp. 878–879; League of Nations Doc. C.24.M.18.1929.I, pp. 8, 27–28).
> This aroused great hostility from Hungary and Germany (which was shortly to join the League) and it was pointed out that this had the practical consequence of rendering all European States except Great Britain potentially unable to sit. See Robinson, *Were the Minority Treaties a Failure?*, pp. 99–100 and n. 30 on p. 288.

[30] This was one of the recommendations adopted in the 'Madrid Resolution' of 13 June 1929 (for which see *LNOJ*, vol. X (1929), pp. 1005–1011). This was adopted after a wide-ranging review of the procedures which had been prompted by clashes between Canada and Germany, who sought liberalization and who were opposed in this by many of the States bound by the treaties, notably Poland and Romania. Other changes included informing petitioners of the result of their petitions and permitting the establishment of a 'Committee of Five' to deal with difficult cases. The 'Madrid Resolution' drew on the Report of the London Conference established to examine these issues (*ibid.*, pp. 1133–1155; also reproduced as an Appendix to Azcárate, *League of Nations and National Minorities*).

[31] When the Council asked the PCIJ for an Advisory Opinion in the case concerning *German Settlers in Poland*, Poland objected to Council Members hiding behind the anonymity of the Committees of Three and argued that they were unable to seize the Council of a petition (PCIJ, Series C, No. 3, vol. I, pp. 426–427) but the practice was upheld by the Court (1923, PCIJ, Series B, No. 6, pp. 21–23).

[32] See Azcárate, *League of Nations and National Minorities*, pp. 119–120. He points out that publicity was not always helpful, but some States, particularly Germany and Hungary, wished petitions to be placed before the Council for this very reason.

[33] See Division III of the Geneva Convention. For an overview of the procedure see G. Kaeckenbeeck, *The International Experiment of Upper Silesia: a Study in the Working of the Upper Silesian Settlement 1922–1937* (London: Oxford University Press, 1942), pp. 229–232.

be submitted. In default of satisfaction, the petition would be forwarded to the President of the Mixed Commission (which exercised oversight over a wide range of questions) who, after consultations, would remit it to the Minorities Office with his opinion. This opinion would be forwarded to the relevant authority, which would inform the President of the Mixed Commission of whether it had decided to act upon it.[34] An appeal from this procedure lay, through the Minorities Office, to the Council of the League.[35] As an alternative to this cumbersome 'local procedure', there was the radical alternative of submitting a petition directly to the League Council under Article 147 of the Convention without the need for it to be presented by a Council member.[36]

Another special procedure related to the Free City of Danzig, the status of which was under the guarantee of the League.[37] The post of League of Nations High Commissioner was established by the Treaty of Versailles with responsibility for determining disputes between Poland and Danzig 'in the first instance' and establishing a constitution which would be placed under the guarantee of the League.[38] It was subsequently agreed that appeals from his decisions could be made direct to the League Council.[39] More significantly, the High Commissioner could place questions concerning infringements of the Constitution on the Council Agenda, a procedure often invoked in 1935 and 1936.[40]

Finally, it should be noted that Article 11(2) of the Covenant of the League of Nations provided that it was 'the friendly right of each member of the League to bring to the attention of the Assembly or of the Council any circumstance whatever affecting international relations which threatens to disturb international peace or the good understanding between nations upon which peace depends'. This, then, allowed any member to

---

[34] Articles 149–154.   [35] Article 157.

[36] In consequence, the Council was obliged to consider an inordinate number of petitions relating to Upper Silesia, many of an extremely trivial nature. By way of example, and from the sphere of religious concerns, one petition concerned the 'tit for tat' refusal of the authorities to issue collective passports for groups attending religious ceremonies, thus requiring more expensive and bureaucratic individual applications. The Council's diplomatic request that they try to conclude some arrangement that would obviate the difficulty was little more than a diplomatic way of telling both sides to 'grow up'. See *LNOJ*, vol. X (1929), pp. 558–559 and pp. 770–773 (Annex 1120 and 1120a).

[37] Treaty of Versailles, Article 102.

[38] Treaty of Versailles, Article 103. The Constitution was adopted on 11 May 1922.

[39] See Treaty between Poland and the Free City of Danzig, 27 October 1920.

[40] See below, pp. 169–170. At the request of the High Commissioner, this power was placed in the hands of a Committee of Three in 1936, in an attempt to depoliticize the office. See *LNOJ*, vol. XVIII (1937), pp. 112–113.

place a situation before the Council, and a number of cases in which minority issues were prominent were examined under this article. However, the minority aspects of these situations were often secondary to the general issues raised, and these incidents, though rich in details concerning the plight of minorities, will not be considered further since they did not bear directly upon the system of minority protection as such.[41]

The practice of protection

Despite the rather narrow formulation of the treaties, there was, in practice, considerable potential for petitions to be lodged and to receive a form of consideration within the League system. It is against this background that the use of the procedures must be judged. It is difficult to give precise details concerning the use of the petition system in its early years since only those which were referred to the Council would necessarily be made public.[42] Between 1920 and 1929, however, it is estimated that 345 petitions were submitted to the League, representing 208 different complaints. Twenty were inapplicable *ratio temporis* and, of the remaining 188, 143 were declared 'receivable'. Following consideration by the Committees of Three, eighteen were forwarded to the Council for consideration.[43] Following the changes ushered in by the 'Madrid Resolution', the entire petition system became more transparent and statistics were published annually from 1930[44] and show that in the remaining ten

[41] For example, Greece used Article 11(2) as a vehicle to refer aspects relating to the situation in Albania to the Council. At first sight, the reference concerning the threat to expel the Ecumenical Patriarch from Constantinople under the terms of the 1923 Population Exchange Convention seems closer to a case of minority protection. This was to be referred to the PCIJ for an Advisory Opinion, but a settlement was reached between the parties before this was done. See *LNOJ*, vol. VI (1925), pp. 482–487, 578–581 (Annex 576(a) and (b) 854–855 and 895). In fact, it was an incident within a long-running tussle between Turkey and Greece over the role of the Patriarchate and its relationship with the new Turkish State. See H. J. Psomiades, *The Eastern Question: the Last Phase* (Thessalonika: Institute for Balkan Studies, 1968), pp. 89–105. Greece also attempted to raise the question before the PCIJ when it was considering the Council's request for an Advisory Opinion relating to the Population Exchange Convention, but the Court considered it outside the scope of the request (*Exchange of Greek and Turkish Populations*, Advisory Opinion, 1925, PCIJ, Series B, No. 10 at p. 17).

[42] Details of others might be published in the *Official Journal* if the Government against which the petition had been made permitted.

[43] See *Minorities* (publication of the League of Nations Union), p. 35.

[44] This was one of the proposals put forward by the 1929 London Conference and adopted in the 'Madrid Resolution'. See *LNOJ*, vol. X (1929), pp. 1005–1006. The results of all

years of its existence, 585 petitions were submitted, of which 247 were deemed 'non-receivable' and 338 'receivable'.[45]

Numbers alone say very little about the system, and it is beyond the scope of this work to give a detailed examination of the workings of the League system.[46] However, the most cursory examination reveals that very few of the petitions examined were directly concerned with religious questions. Although the monks of Mount Athos submitted a large number of petitions, these were almost all concerned with traditional privileges, land rights and questions of agrarian reform[47] rather than the free exercise of their religion or discrimination on account of their religion.

Similarly, the Catholic bishops in Armenia also submitted a number of petitions which concerned their general status, issues of family law, the capacity to buy and sell immovable property and the distribution of public funds to schools in accordance with Article 41(2) and (3) of the Treaty of Lausanne.[48] The Catholic, Reformed and Unitarian Churches of Transylvania also submitted a petition concerning Romanian legislation relating to the regulation of private education which, although relating

---

Committee of Three deliberations were henceforward to be circulated to all Council Members for information and consideration was to be given to the publication of the details in the *Official Journal*, if the Government concerned consented.

[45] A table collating the annual figures published in the *LNOJ* is found in Robinson, *Were the Minority Treaties a Failure?*, p. 128.

[46] For a general overview, see, in addition to other works cited, Jones, 'National Minorites: a Case Study in International Protection', pp. 614–619.

[47] Most of these were not referred to the Council and so were only officially recorded after 1929. Most of them were rejected, but took up a considerable amount of time. Examples of petitions are found in *LNOJ*, vol. XI (1930), pp. 829–832 and 1821; vol. XIII (1932), pp. 155–156, 1107–1108; vol. XIV (1933), pp. 426–427; vol. XV (1934), pp. 1118–1119, 1239–1241; vol. XVI (1935), pp. 533–534. *Cf.* Azcárate, *The League of Nations and National Minorities*, pp. 53–54 and 86–87, where he admits to having sympathy with the attitude of the Greek Government that it was impossible to respect these privileges in the light of the arrival of approaching half a million refugees from Anatolia.

[48] *LNOJ*, vol. XI (1930), pp. 1823–1824. The Reports of the Committees do suggest that they were fairly easily satisfied: the final point of the Armenian bishops' petition alleged that: 'As regards the Government and municipal grants provided for in Article 41 in favour of the non-Moslem minorities, we need hardly say that the question has not even been considered.' The Committee was satisfied with the reply that: 'The Ministry of Education draws the grants for minority schools from the funds allotted for that purpose. The figure is fixed according to the needs of the schools and the funds available. The grants are paid to the communities in question for the proper purposes.' Governmental denials or assertions to the contrary were often sufficient to ensure the rejection of a complaint without further evidence.

to confessional schools, was really a part of the general question of the treatment of the Hungarian minority.[49]

Religious freedom as the object of petitions

A small number of petitions did, however, centre upon religious freedoms. The Catholic archbishop and bishops in Albania petitioned against a number of legislative and other acts but these were not pursued by the Committee of Three following the receipt of further information from the Government.[50] The petition also claimed that Article 5 of the Albanian Minorities Declaration had been contravened by Articles 206 and 207 of the 1933 Albanian Constitution, which prohibited the continuance of any private schooling in Albania.[51] A similar complaint had been lodged by Greece under Article 11(2) of the Covenant of the League of Nations concerning the position of linguistic minorities and had already been placed on the Council's agenda. An Advisory Opinion was eventually sought from the PCIJ which concluded that Albania was in violation of its obligations as regarded the schools of both the linguistic and religious minorities.[52] In consequence, Albania amended its laws so as to permit private schools and other educational establishments.[53]

The freedom of the Russian minority in Bessarabia to the free exercise of their religion was raised in a petition submitted in 1932.[54] It was

---

[49] For the Report of the Committee of Three see *LNOJ*, vol. VII (1926), pp. 741–742. The Committee recognized the potential for a violation of Article 9 of the Minorities Treaty in the legislation, but did not feel that a violation had yet occurred, or was inevitable. The background to this petition is examined by L. P. Mair, *The Protection of Minorities* (London: Christophers, 1928), pp. 163–170, who also says that it had been preceded by other petitions which had not been taken up, and which alleged that one of the reasons for imposing restrictions upon Romanians attending confessional schools was to prevent proselytizing (*ibid.*, p. 162). The actual practice under the Act led to a flood of later petitions from other sources. See, for example, *LNOJ*, vol. XIV (1933), pp. 428–466.

[50] These concerned the promulgation of a law on divorce, the closing of an Orthodox Church, and a Decree Law concerning religious communities. See *LNOJ*, vol. XVI (1935), pp. 560–561 and vol. XVII (1936), pp. 927–928.

[51] Article 206 provided that:
> The teaching and education of Albanian subjects are reserved to the State, which will make itself responsible for them in its schools. Elementary education is compulsory for all Albanian nationals, and will be given without charge. Private schools, of all categories, now in existence will be closed.

[52] *Minority Schools in Albania*, Advisory Opinion, 1935, PCIJ, Series A/B, No. 64, p. 4.

[53] See *LNOJ*, vol. XVII (1936), pp. 560–562 and 741–743.

[54] *LNOJ*, vol. XIII (1932), pp. 1490–1492. This was submitted by an individual, M. Tzamoutali, a member of the 'Union of the Russian Minority'. Romania claimed that there was no such legally constituted organization and that the petitioner was not, in fact, Russian. Neither point, however, affected the capacity of the Committee to receive a petition.

alleged that Romania had placed the Russian Orthodox community under the jurisdiction of the Romanian Church in an attempt to sever its links with the Patriarchate of Moscow and to have the Russian language and rites replaced with Romanian. Permission to establish a new Russian Orthodox Church had been refused and private meetings, where worship was conducted in Russian, were banned and several priests prosecuted.

The government response was that the canons of the Orthodox Church forbade the establishment of a new community in a territory where a national orthodox church was already established and, since the transfer of Bessarabia from Russia, that national church was Romanian. It was claimed that the rites were identical but for the dates of the major feasts: the Russian Orthodox Church, unlike all others, had not changed from the Julian to the Gregorian calendar. The allegations concerning the imposition of the Romanian language were denied and the action taken by the civil authorities against the priests was claimed to be merely the execution of procedures stipulated by canon law.

The Committee claimed that it had examined these allegations in the light of the general right to the free exercise of religion (Article 2 of the Minorities Treaty) as well as the right to the free use of language in worship (Article 8(3)). However, the summary presented to the Council only alluded to the linguistic dimensions of the petition and felt justified in closing the examination of the question submitted to it without bringing it to the attention of the Council.[55] This case illustrates one of

---

[55] As one of the few petitions that was directly focused upon a religious question, it is worth quoting from the information placed before the Council at some length. The Committee of Three concluded that:

> the Romanian Government has communicated, at the Committee's request, certain supplementary information, stressing the liberal spirit in which the Romanian Church has always treated the question of the language employed in religious services or preaching. The Romanian Government mentions, as an example, that in the diocese of Hotin there are thirty-seven priests of Slav origin who use their own language in the exercise of their ministry, and that in the town of Chisinau there are two churches in which the Office is said in old Slavonic, while in the Metropolitan Cathedral itself the Metropolitan performs the Office partly in Slavonic. With reference to the information furnished by the Holy Synod of the Romanian Church, the Government informed the Committee that, with the exception of [the current] petition, the Holy Synod has up till now received no complaints from the Russian minority in Bessarabia concerning the question of the language used in religious worship or preaching.
>
> The Committee took note with satisfaction of the information resumed above, in particular of the examples given by the Romanian Government as a

the limitations of the minorities system: it could not – or was not – used to penetrate beyond the surface legal structures. In particular, the Committees of Three felt themselves unable to consider cases which turned on the application of internal church rules. As was observed in the instant case, if believers wished to leave the Church, they were free to do so.

However, this overlooked the point that the various Orthodox churches in Eastern Europe were the product of national consciousness.[56] It was inherently contradictory to attempt to protect the rights of national minorities in disregard of the new national boundaries whilst at the same time denying them the freedom to worship within the appropriate tradition, even if that was a nationalist tradition. The tendency for questions of internal church order to mask wider nationalist tensions provided a good reason for this.[57] Nevertheless, the balance was struck in favour of the nation State and not the national church.[58]

It might be concluded that possibly the only general principle that emerged from the petitions concerning the exercise of religious freedom was that questions regarding the internal order of a church system operating within a nation state would not be discussed[59] but the language

> proof of the liberal spirit in which several cases of the same kind have been settled. The Committee feels justified in believing that, animated by the same spirit, the Romanian Government and the Romanian religious authorities will ensure that populations of a language other than the official language enjoy, as far as is practically possible, facilities with regard to the use of their mother-tongue, particularly in preaching and religious instruction. It relies on the Romanian Government's spirit of tolerance to find a way to apply this principle.

[56] Nationalism had underpinned the development of the Orthodox Church since Ottoman times.

[57] *Cf.* the problems faced within the Silesian system. The United Evangelical Church in Polish Upper Silesia was perceived as an agent of germanization and was hostile to the incorporation of Polish Evangelicals. When the 1922 Geneva Convention lapsed in 1937 the Polish authorities imposed their authority upon the Church, it no longer being able to have recourse to the international petition mechanisms. Against this background attempts to apply the details of the Convention concerning religious issues *qua* religious issues were doomed to fail. See Kaeckenbeeck, *The International Experiment of Upper Silesia*, pp. 288–298.

[58] This is clear in the 1922 Geneva Convention concerning Upper Silesia, which tolerated relations between a church and others outside of the territory only if the contacts were of a purely ecclesiastical nature and conducted with a view of cooperation in regard to creed, doctrine, worship and charity (Articles 87(2) and 88). Gifts could also be received from co-religionists abroad.

[59] See the consideration of the petition submitted by various prelates concerning the situation of the Bulgarian minority in Greece. Like the petition concerning the Russian minority in Bessarabia, the allegation was that Greece had dissolved the Bulgarian

in which services were conducted and priests communicated with their congregations should be a matter for the minority concerned.[60]

If religious freedom was one of the driving impulses behind the minority treaties, it can only be concluded that it received little advancement through the international petition system. Of course, it could be argued that this was a sign of its success: that States were abiding by their international obligations, rendering petitions unnecessary. Certainly, some countries did honour some of their treaty obligations,[61] but many did not and it would be naive in the extreme to interpret the lack of petitions as signifying a generally satisfactory situation.

Religious questions as adjuncts to petitions

Although religious questions formed the core of comparatively few petitions, they were more frequently used to support general claims of ill treatment. For example, several complaints relating to the situation of the Polish minority in the Kovno region of Lithuania were received by the League, the first in 1921 from Polish deputies in the Kovno Diet and

---

religious communities and was forcing them into the Greek Orthodox Church. Although the linguistic aspects of this petition were examined and tested in a somewhat more exacting fashion than was often the case (see n. 60 below), the Report of the Committee said: 'Though taking into account the provisions of the Greek Minority Treaty concerning freedom of conscience and worship, the Committee considered that, *in accordance with the precedent set in similar cases*, it could not examine the ecclesiastical or canonical aspect of the problem' (*LNOJ*, vol. XV (1934), pp. 1674–1675; emphasis added). The (much earlier) Report concerning the Petition of the Union of Evangelical Churches in Poland, considered below at p. 164, implied that this might be a possibility.

[60] In addition to the petitions already cited, see also that submitted by the 'Union of Intellectuals from the District of Neustadt' and the 'Union of Intellectuals from the District of Leobschütz', concerning the use of the Polish and Moravian languages in worship. The Committee of Three, in terminating its consideration of the petition, 'expressed the wish that the competent authorities should allow the majority language to be substituted for the minority language at divine service only in cases where, as at Olbersdorf, this was the express desire of the congregation' (*LNOJ*, vol. XI (1930), p. 388).

[61] This topic is fully examined in Robinson, *Were the Minority Treaties a Failure?*, pp. 194–239, especially pp. 204–205 and 236–238 where it is concluded that: 'As a rule . . . discriminatory measures against specific nationalities or religions . . . were never incorporated into the text of laws or decrees, but their absence did not prevent such discrimination in fact' (*ibid.*, p. 239). The principal exceptions to this general rule concerned the Hungarian *numerus clausus* legislation, the Romanian citizenship laws and the Nazi legislation which are considered below.

supported by the Polish Foreign Minister.[62] This was not a minority petition as such, since Lithuania had not as yet made its declaration concerning minorities. The situation of the Polish minority in Lithuania was examined by a Committee of Three following the submission of a series of petitions from a group of Polish exiles. The Secretariat drew up a summary of the complaints received by 1 March 1925 and recorded that:

The petitioners allege that the Lithuanian authorities have connived at the action of certain groups of individuals who have systematically hindered the priests from conducting religious services in the Polish tongue, have prevented the congregations from offering prayers in Polish in the Catholic churches of Kovno and have outraged religious sentiments in other ways.

The Lithuanian Government points out that the use of the Polish tongue in the Churches at Kovno has never been prohibited either by the civil or by the ecclesiastical authorities; it admits that painful incidents have occurred, but says that these incidents were the result of Polish propaganda. The Polish language is allowed in six Catholic churches out of a total of seven churches.[63]

---

[62] *LNOJ*, vol. II (1921), pp. 872–878. This alleged, *inter alia*, that:

> The use of the Polish language is being systematically eliminated in the churches, in sermons and even in the confessional. In parishes containing a Polish minority, this language has been totally abolished. Polish priests are usually sent to parishes which are purely Lithuanian, while those where the Polish element predominates are ministered to by Lithuanian priests.
>
> The Government, instead of trying to check the partiality of the Lithuanian clergy, only aggravates the situation by dismissing and departing the best Polish priests and, above all, those who are dearest to and most highly esteemed by the people (for example, the banishment of the Prelate Pacewicz and the Abbé Savicki). (*Ibid.*, at p. 876.)

The Lithuanian Government in reply quoted:

> circular No. 4477 of the year 1921 . . . according to which the two languages are admitted in all Churches, even in Kowno, except for the Liturgy, which, in Lithuania, as in all other Catholic countries, is read in Latin. An exception only is made in the case of the non-parochial churches of Vyauto, of the College of Kowno and the garrison church. The two churches of St Gertrude and the Convent of the Benedictines enjoy the privilege of using only Polish. As regards the Prelate Pazewitch and the Abbé Sawicki, to whose 'deportation' the memorandum devotes a whole paragraph, they were only sentenced to temporary banishment from that town for the non-execution of an order of the military commandant of Kowno. (*Ibid.*, pp. 1000–1005 at 1003.)

This is quoted in full as it typifies the nature of complaints and responses. It is also typical in that the background lies in the dispute between Poland and Lithuania over the District of Vilna: Poland wished to emphasize before the League the perils of Poles being subject to Lithuanian jurisdiction, whilst Lithuania wished to refute all such allegations as propaganda. See also *LNOJ*, vol. III (1922), pp. 93–95 and 138 (Annex 295c) where Poland urged the Council that Lithuania 'should recognize that the Polish Minorities . . . have a fundamental and perpetual right freely to perform their religious rites in their own language'.

[63] *LNOJ*, vol. VI (1925), p. 584.

The Committee of Three seems to have been satisfied with this response, and did not suggest that this aspect of the petition be examined further.[64] The Council's Rapporteur did, however, make a passing reference, but merely to observe that these incidents 'were engaging the attention of the Lithuanian Government' which 'no doubt would take the necessary steps to prevent the churches from becoming the scene of disputes between different sections of the population and to see that none of them are prevented from practising their religion in their mother tongue, provided they respect the same right for others'.[65]

In November 1921 the Germanic League in Poland submitted a stream of petitions concerning the situation of the German 'colonists' in what had been East Prussia. These raised difficult questions which were ultimately referred to the PCIJ.[66] The Report of the Committee of Three included a number of subsidiary matters, two of which related to religious questions. The first concerned a claim that the activities of the Institute of Sisters (Deaconesses) at Posen had been curtailed, in response to which Poland had claimed that sections of this society were a source of danger to public order.[67] The Council Rapporteur subsequently recorded that 'the Polish Government, during the Russo-Polish war, had to supervise the activities of this association, but that the Deaconesses Institute was not in any way interfered with in carrying out its ordinary duties' and this seems to have concluded the matter.[68]

The second complaint concerned the position of the United Evangelical Church in East Prussia, which objected to the Polish Government appointing members to its governing institutions. Poland claimed that the Church statutes placed the Church under the supreme authority of the

---

[64] *Ibid.*, pp. 484–485 and 581. Some of the Committees of Three were willing to accept at face value assertions by governments that the facts alleged were untrue, particularly if supported by official statistics or legislative acts. See also the petition concerning the situation of the Albanian minority in Yugoslavia, in which it was alleged that restrictions were placed upon the use of the Albanian language in worship. The Committee of Three accepted the Government's assertion that this was untrue. The evidence supporting this claim was that the majority of fourteen Catholic churches in Southern Serbia had been built since the coming to power of the Government, whilst Muslim emigration had been prompted by their own 'religious fanaticism which impels them to sell their property and settle in Turkey' (*LNOJ*, vol. XIV (1933), pp. 680–687 at p. 681 and *cf.* also pp. 684–685).

[65] *LNOJ*, vol. VI (1925), p. 866. The Council was ultimately satisfied with the Lithuanian response to the other aspects of the petition. *Ibid.*, pp. 1339–1341 and pp. 1452–1454 (Annex 792).

[66] See *German Settlers in Poland*, Advisory Opinion, 1923, PCIJ, Series B, No. 6.

[67] *LNOJ*, vol. III (1922), pp. 555 and 702–707 at p. 705 (Annex 366).

[68] *Ibid.*, pp. 1181–1182 and 1293–1298 at p. 1296 (Annex 414).

Head of State and that this right, formerly exercised by the King of Prussia, had now passed to the Polish Republic.[69] Following the receipt of further information, the Council's Rapporteur noted that this was a temporary situation pending the enactment of legislation to be framed 'on the basis of proposals submitted by the religious body concerned' and that 'any action opposed to the interests of the Church is out of the question'. Once again, this was sufficient to satisfy the Rapporteur and Council.[70]

These cases illustrate how fine is the line – if there really is a line at all – dividing the two categories of cases so far examined. This is particularly so for the petitions submitted to the Council by the Catholic clergy in Danzig, following the coming to power of the National Socialists in 1933.[71] One of their first acts was to pass a Decree Law which granted full powers to the Senate of the City and bypassed the Assembly.[72] The Senate then issued a number of decrees, including that of 4 April 1933 which forbade the unauthorized wearing of uniforms in public. The Organization of Catholic Youth was not granted permission, and it was claimed that this violated their right to freedom of expression.

The response of the Senate was that: 'The negative attitude of these organizations towards the State as it is today is known to the overwhelmingly National Socialist population of Danzig: it regards the public emphasis given to this hostile attitude by the wearing of a distinctive uniform as a provocation.'[73] As this clearly demonstrates, what was really at issue was the implementation of Nazi policy within the Free City and its compatibility with Article 73 of the Constitution,[74] the city's Polish

---

[69] *Ibid.*, pp. 555 and 702–707 (Annex 366) at pp. 705–706. This complaint had originated in complaints received back in August 1920.

[70] *Ibid.*, pp. 1181–1182 and 1293–1298 (Annex 414) at p. 1296.

[71] See petition of 30 August 1934, *LNOJ*, vol. XVI (1935), pp. 762–788.

[72] Decree Law of 24 June 1933, 'Law for the Relief of the Distress of the People and State'. An opportunity to raise the constitutionality of this Decree occurred when subsequent petitions concerning penal laws enacted in August 1935 led the Council to request an Advisory Opinion from the PCIJ but the scope of the request was limited to the compatibility of the Decrees issued under them, thus preventing the Court from exploring this question. Since the Court concluded that the penal laws themselves violated the Constitution it did not find it necessary to pass upon the question. See *Consistency of Certain Danzig Legislative Decrees with the Constitution of the Free City*, Advisory Opinion, 1935, PCIJ, Series A/B, No. 65, p. 41 at p. 54. *Cf.* the Declaration of Count Rostworowski, Judge, who argued that the Decrees of 1935 were invalid because the 1933 Enabling Law was unconstitutional (*ibid.*, p. 59).

[73] See *LNOJ*, vol. XVI (1935), p. 767.

[74] Article 73 provided that:
    All nationals of the Free City shall be equal before the Law. Exceptional law

population being predominantly Catholic.[75] After lengthy exchanges and a report from a Committee of Jurists, the Council ultimately adopted a Report which declared this, and other, pieces of legislation unconstitutional and called upon the Senate to ensure that its legislation be brought back into conformity.[76]

Petitions from Jewish groups

The force behind the construction of the entire minority system was the desire to afford protection to the Jews in Central and Eastern Europe. Given the history of the evolution of the treaties, it was ironic that very few petitions were submitted from Jewish sources. The reason for this was conclusively summed up as being that 'long experience has taught them that winning a case against their Government was often a pyrrhic victory at best'.[77] Moreover, although the two petitions examined by the Council emanating from Jewish groups[78] did result in 'victories', the League was, ultimately, unable to exert the pressure necessary to render them genuine or lasting.

The first of the petitions considered by the Council concerned the so-

---

shall be inadmissible . . .

Men and Women shall have the same civil rights and duties . . .

There shall be no legal privileges or disqualification due to birth, position or creed . . .

Unlike the legislation relative to German Upper Silesia (for which see below at p. 168), the Decrees were not discriminatory in language but it was claimed that they were in fact interpreted exclusively with the object of protecting the organizations of National Socialism.

[75] The Senate claimed that its Decrees were not aimed at religious activities, and pointed to Section 2(b) of its Decree concerning School Pupil Membership of Associations which provided that 'pupils may, however, become members of religious associations, if the latter confine themselves to giving their members religious teaching and if their activities are limited to matters of religion (Bible study, devotional exercise, etc.)'. This again acknowledges the potential political dimensions of religious affiliation.

[76] LNOJ, vol. XVI (1935), pp. 139–141, 648–649, 1187–1197.

[77] Robinson, *Were the Minority Treaties a Failure?*, p. 248; see also J. Robinson, 'International Protection of Minorities: A Global View', *Is.YHR* 1 (1971) 61, 71–73.

[78] Other petitions were submitted by Jewish groups which were either declared 'non-receivable' or not reported to the Council. See, for example, League of Nations Doc. C.198.M.110.1922.I (concerning the position of Jewish 'optants' under Article 80 of the Treaty of St Germain, submitted by the Joint Foreign Committee and the Alliance Isráelite Universelle on 17 November 1921: Mair, *The Protection of Minorities*, p. 131); a communication concerning the extension of the Sunday Closing Law in Greece to the Jewish community was also declared non-receivable (Mair, *ibid.*, p. 205).

called Hungarian *numerus clausus* law.[79] This provided that only those 'known to be of absolutely unimpeachable national loyalty and morality' would be entered on the rolls of universities and other higher educational institutions and of these, a limited number would be admitted for higher education, bearing in mind both their intellectual qualities and that the number of students of different races and nationalities permitted to enter universities should be in proportion to the number of inhabitants of the races and nationalities in the country. Hungary claimed that the law had a twofold object: 'to reduce the number of the educated working class' and 'to guarantee the rights of the minority groups'.[80]

The Council adopted the recommendation of the Committee of Three that it request information to determine whether the application of the law did, in practice, disregard 'the legitimate rights of minorities'. The Hungarian representative immediately pointed out that Jews formed 33 per cent and 42.5 per cent of the student population of the universities at Szeged and Pécs respectively, whilst forming only 6 per cent of the total population of Hungary.[81] Further statistical information was provided, but in January 1925 a further petition was submitted, in which it was argued that the practical effect of the law was to 'expatriate Jews' seeking education to other countries. Hungary insisted that the law simply ensured equality of access and that its abrogation would place the Jews in a privileged position that was contrary to the spirit of the treaty obligations. They also objected to this matter being raised by external groups, rather than Hungarian Jews themselves.[82] Nevertheless, Hungary also pointed out that the law was a temporary measure to deal with an abnormal situation and would be amended when possible and, in the light of this, the Council decided to take no further action, but to wait upon events.[83] A further petition was received in 1927 but the law was

---

[79] Law XXV of 1920. The petitions were submitted in November 1921 by the Joint Foreign Committee of the Jewish Board of Deputies of the Anglo-Jewish Association and the Alliance Israélite Universelle, the latter organization also objecting to the law's failure to apply to religious minorities, which they considered the Jews to be. See generally Mair, *The Protection of Minorities*, pp. 138–142, and H. Rosting, 'Protection of Minorities by the League of Nations', *AJIL* 17 (1923), 641, 659.

[80] See the Report of the Committee of Three, 22 September 1922, *LNOJ*, vol. III (1922), pp. 1204 and 1425–1426 (Annex 427). When considering the first of these objects, it should be recalled that the law was passed shortly after the collapse of Bela Kun's workers revolution, in consequence of which Hungary wished 'to obtain guarantees of the patriotic loyalty of its future officials'.

[81] *Ibid.*, pp. 1204–1205.

[82] *LNOJ*, vol. VII (1926), pp. 145–153.   [83] *Ibid.*, p. 171.

amended in March 1928 and the Committee accepted this as a final settlement of the matter and did not refer or report this to the Council.[84]

The second of the two 'Jewish' petitions considered by the Council concerned the application of Nazi racial legislation to Upper Silesia.[85] As has already been explained, Upper Silesia was the only area of Germany formally bound by minority clauses and was subject to the League's supervision. The Geneva Convention of 1922, which governed the Silesian settlement, had established a two-tier structure for complaints, a local procedure under Article 149 and a direct right to petition the Council of the League under Article 147, thereby avoiding the filter of the Committees of Three. In April 1933 the new Nazi Government in Germany enacted a series of discriminatory laws debarring non-Aryans from employment in government service[86] and in a number of the professions,[87] and restricting access to German schools.[88]

The petitioner was a German national of Jewish origin who had been living in German Upper Silesia and had been dismissed from his job. His petition, however, related not only to his own situation, but to that of all Jews in Upper Silesia. At the outset, the German Government accepted that 'international conventions concluded by Germany cannot be affected by internal German legislation. Should the provisions of the Geneva

---

[84] See League of Nations Union, *Minorities*, pp. 38–39.

[85] Petition of Franz Bernheim, 12 May 1933. See *LNOJ*, vol. XIV (1933), pp. 844–849 and 930–933 (Annex 1451, containing the text of the petition). See Kaeckenbeeck, *The International Experiment of Upper Silesia*, pp. 262–267.

[86] Law No. 34 of 1933, Statute on the 'Reorganization of the Civil Service'. Section 3 (1) provided 'Officials who are of non-Aryan descent are to be placed in retirement'.

[87] Law No. 36 of 1933, 'Admission to the Legal Profession'. Section 1 provided that: 'The admission of lawyers who are of non-Aryan descent can be cancelled up to 30 September 1933'; Section 2 provided that: 'Admission to legal practice can be refused to persons . . . of non-Aryan descent'. An administrative circular from the Prussian Ministry of Justice explained that 'the maintenance of public order and security will be exposed to serious danger if Germans are still liable to be served with documents in legal proceedings which have been drawn up or certified by Jewish notaries. I accordingly ask that Jewish notaries should be urgently recommended, in their own interests, to refrain until further notice from exercising this calling . . . [S]hould they refuse to comply with this recommendation, they will expose themselves to serious dangers in view of the excited state of public opinion.' Similar measures were also taken against doctors. A Decree from the Ministry of Labour provided that: 'Doctors on the panel of insurance funds of non-Aryan descent shall . . . no longer be allowed to practice. New entries of such doctors on the panel of insurance funds shall not be allowed.'

[88] Law No. 35 of 1933 provided that since the Jews represented only 1.5 per cent of the German population, no school should have more than that percentage of Jewish pupils.

Convention have been violated in German Upper Silesia, this can only be due to mistakes on the part of subordinate organs acting under a mistaken interpretation of the laws.'[89] Nevertheless, they objected that the Council had no jurisdiction to consider petitions from individual members of a minority which raised general questions rather than personal grievances. It was also claimed that no 'definite *de facto* situation had yet arisen in Upper Silesia as to the applicability of these laws'.[90] These objections were rejected by a Committee of Jurists to which they were referred[91] and the Council, taking note of the German declaration, adopted a Report which expressed the conviction that Germany would act in accordance with its obligations[92] and called for the reinstatement of those who had been dismissed.[93]

Jewish groups also joined in the attempts to challenge the implementation of pro-Nazi policies in the Free City of Danzig, considered above.[94] Because the allegations raised in the petitions were not proven, the Commission of Jurists could not comment directly upon the specific incidents but, as has already been mentioned, the Report submitted to the Council left no room for doubt that the actions of the City's Senate were in violation of Article 73 of the Constitution. For example, when considering the allegations of defamation and boycotts, the Committee, though recognizing that the authorities were 'neither entitled nor bound to intervene unless public security is disturbed or endangered, and that it is not its business to interfere in the clash of political opinions . . . wonders whether there is not, in a sense, a disturbance of public security when a whole section of the population is subject to constant and serious

---

[89] *LNOJ*, vol. XIV (1933), p. 823.

[90] *Ibid.*, pp. 823, 838–840.

[91] *Ibid.*, pp. 934–935 (Annex 1451a).

[92] *Ibid.*, pp. 844–849. The Report observed that: 'The mere perusal of the laws and administrative orders mentioned in the petition . . . shows that, in so far as some at any rate of the stipulations have been applied in the territory of Upper Silesia, this application cannot have taken place without conflicting with a number of clauses of . . . the Geneva Convention.'

[93] Bernheim's case was referred back to the local procedure for settlement. The Mixed Commission in fact concluded that Bernheim had been dismissed because of his poor workmanship and Communist sympathies but he was ultimately awarded 1,600 marks in compensation. Forty-seven similar cases, concerning lawyers, doctors and other public or private employees, were subsequently settled. See Kaeckenbeeck, *The International Experiment of Upper Silesia*, p. 266.

[94] Petitions were submitted by the 'Verein Jüdischer Akademiker' on 8 April 1935 and the 'Vereinigung Selbständiger Jüdischer' on 14 May 1935. See *LNOJ*, vol. XVI (1935), pp. 830–862 (Annex 1551). Further petitions were lodged on 27 August 1935, *ibid.*, pp. 1321–1328 (Annex 1566).

defamation on the sole ground of its race or religion'.[95] The offending decrees were subsequently amended,[96] although a flood of petitions continued to be referred to the Council.[97] Until 1936, the League High Commissioner was able to exert sufficient pressure to fend off the strict application of much of the Nazi legislation applied elsewhere and during 1937 and 1938 the implementation of the anti-Jewish 'Nuremberg Laws' was being announced only to be postponed (to be finally introduced in December 1938). The formal connection between Danzig and the League was severed in September 1939.[98]

Conclusion

Although it would be wrong to lay the blame for the collapse of the inter-war system for minority protection on any one factor, its inability even to address, let alone influence, the rising tide of anti-Semitism demonstrated how ineffectual it really was. The practical impossibility of ensuring that States fulfilled their international obligations regarding their treatment of minorities was overtaken by the increasing difficulty in even calling them to account for these violations before the League. Germany, which had only joined the League in 1926, withdrew in October 1933 and in September 1934 Poland announced that it would no longer cooperate with the League in matters concerning minority protection. The Geneva Convention on Upper Silesia expired on 15 May 1937. In consequence, the numbers of petitions addressed to the League plummeted from its peak of 204 in the period July 1930–June 1931, to four in 1938–1939.[99] Likewise, the number of receivable petitions fell from a peak of eighty in 1931–1932, to one in its final year, and only thirty-two from June 1935 to its end.

Rightly or wrongly, the experience of a system of minority protection based upon treaties and declarations under the direct protection of the League Council was considered to have failed and no trace of it was found in the proposals for the establishment of its successor, the United Nations

---

[95] *Ibid.*, pp. 1190–1191.
[96] See *LNOJ*, vol. XVII (1936), pp. 121–124 and 511–516.
[97] See *LNOJ*, vol. XVII (1937), pp. 174–232 (Annexes 1582–1585).
[98] See F. P. Walters, *A History of the League of Nations* (London: Oxford University Press, 1952), vol. II, pp. 617–622 and 793–797.
[99] The Minorities Section was merged with the Political, Disarmament and Mandates Divisions into a single unit in 1939, the Secretary General observing that 'At the present time the execution of these obligations did not overtax anyone' (*LNOJ*, vol. XX (1939), p. 94).

Organization. Nevertheless, many of its procedural innovations found a new life in the European Convention on Human Rights and Fundamental Freedoms which, although following the path of the United Nations in eschewing the direct protection of minorities, stands as the intellectual heir to the League's minorities system: and this is fitting, for it was Europe which provided the forum within which the system was devised and developed.

7   The UN system

Introduction

For some, the serious study of human rights begins with the creation of the United Nations in 1945 and the adoption of the United Nations Declaration of Human Rights in 1948. It is, with hindsight, easy to see the post-Second World War settlement as a watershed: a moment of universal revulsion at the horrors that had recently been endured and inflicted, coupled with a desire to ensure that similar events would never again come to pass. Certainly, the peace settlement was very different to the 1919 Paris Peace Conference, but it would be a mistake to view the inter-war practice as being of only historic interest, since those involved in its construction drew upon their collective experience of it when determining the future shape of 'human rights' protection in international law.

Indeed, the move from the minorities treaty approach to that of a system based upon generalized and individually orientated rights occurred more by way of natural evolution than as a 'fresh start'. For example, on 10 February 1947, the Allied and Associated Powers concluded Peace Treaties with Italy, Finland, Hungary, Bulgaria and Romania which included a general clause providing that the State in question:

shall take all measures necessary to secure to all persons under [their] jurisdiction, without distinction as to race, sex, language, or religion, the enjoyment of human rights and fundamental freedoms, including freedom of expression, of press and publication, of religious worship, of political opinion and of public meeting.[1]

---

[1] Treaty of Peace between the Allied and Associated Powers and: Italy, Article 15 (see also Article 21 and Article 4 of Annex VI, the Permanent Statute of the Free City of Trieste); Finland, Article 6; Hungary, Article 2(1); Bulgaria, Article 2; Romania, Article 3(1). Texts in *AJIL Supp.* 42 (1948), pp. 47 (Italy), 179 (Bulgaria), 203 (Finland), 225 (Hungary), 252

This was in the mould of the minorities treaties, in that this obligation was imposed upon the defeated States by the victors, rather than assumed by all. Moreover, the vulnerable position of some minority groups remained a motivating factor.[2] Nevertheless, by focusing upon the rights of the individual it illustrates a move away from the path of minority rights protection.[3]

Just as religious freedom had previously been bound up with minority rights, since the 1940s the international protection of religious freedom has been bound up with the development of the concept of individual human rights as an object of international legal concern. Indeed, one of the first manifestations of the system devised under the auspices of the United Nations recognized the freedom of worship as an essential component. In his since famous Annual Address to Congress in 1941,

(Romania). See also *UN Year Book of Human Rights*, 1947, pp. 390–397. These articles are examined in S. D. Kertesz, 'Human Rights in the Peace Treaties', *Law and Contemporary Problems*, 14 (1949), 627 at 636. See also *Paris Peace Conference 1946 Selected Documents* (Washington DC: US Department of State, 1946).

[2] Italian minorities in territories transferred to France, Greece (in respect of the Dodecanese Islands) and Yugoslavia were to enjoy similar rights (Italian Treaty, Article 19(4)). The UK also ensured that the treaties with Hungary (Article 2(2)) and Romania (Article 3(2)) also included an undertaking that:

> the laws in force in [Hungary/Romania] shall not, either in their content or in their application, discriminate or entail any discrimination between persons of [Hungarian/Romanian] nationality on the ground of their race, sex, language or religion, whether in reference to their persons, property, business, professional or financial interests, status, political or civil rights or any other matter.

The object of this was said to be 'to relieve the suffering of Jews in Eastern Europe'. See Kertesz, 'Human Rights', p. 636.

[3] These treaties proved no more effective in securing to individuals the freedoms they proclaimed than had the minorities treaties. The US and the UK argued that the suppression of democratic government in Bulgaria, Hungary and Romania had brought with it violations of the treaties. Specific allegations included actions taken against religious leaders in Hungary and Bulgaria and the suppression of the Uniate and Greek Orthodox Church in Romania. Following the refusal of these States to appoint members of a Commission to consider the dispute between the parties, as required by Articles 36, 40 and 38 of the respective treaties, – and acrimonious debate in which the actions of the three States were condemned – the UN General Assembly requested an Advisory Opinion from the ICJ since, under the treaties, the UN Secretary General could appoint a third and neutral member of a Commission if the parties had been unable to agree. The ICJ advised that an appointment by the Secretary General was contingent upon the appointment of national members. See *Interpretation of Peace Treaties with Bulgaria, Hungary and Romania*, Second Phase, Advisory Opinion, *ICJ Reports 1950*, p. 221. In effect this meant that the system could not be made to work without the cooperation of the States concerned and the treaty obligations were practically worthless. The General Assembly debates and the background to the Request are examined in Y.-L. Liang, 'Observance in Bulgaria, Hungary and Romania of Human Rights and Fundamental Freedoms: Request for an Advisory Opinion on Certain Questions', *AJIL* 44 (1950), 100.

President Roosevelt outlined four basic freedoms: the freedom of speech and expression, freedom of worship, freedom from want and freedom from fear.[4] These ideals were to provide the basis for the Atlantic Charter concluded between Roosevelt, as President of the USA, and Churchill, Prime Minister of the United Kingdom.

The Atlantic Charter, however, only made explicit reference to the freedoms from fear and want.[5] This occasioned some criticism in the United States and prompted Roosevelt to report to Congress that: 'it is unnecessary for me to point out that the declaration of principles includes of necessity the world need for freedom of religion and freedom of information. No society of the world organized under the announced principles could survive without these freedoms which are a part of the whole freedom for which we strive.'[6] The Declaration by the United Nations of 1 January 1942 took this further by stating in its preamble that: 'complete victory over their enemies is essential to defend life, liberty, independence and religious freedom, and to preserve human rights and justice'.[7]

This placed religious freedom on a par with the most basic needs of the individual, all of which were separated off from other forms of 'human rights', making the centrality of religious freedom strikingly clear. The first drafts of what was to mature into the United States' Dumbarton Oaks Proposals included a bill of rights which provided for the freedom of conscience and worship, subject to restraints of public order and good morals.[8] However, this was dropped at a comparatively early stage[9] and the proposals presented to the Dumbarton Oaks conference did not

---

[4] US Senate Doc. No. 188, 77th Congress, 2nd Session, pp. 86–87.

[5] Point 6 provided that: 'they hope to see established a peace which will afford to all nations the means of dwelling in safety within their own boundaries, and which will afford assurance that all men in all lands may live out their lives in freedom from fear and want.' See H. Doc. 358/77C1/1941, reproduced in R. B. Russell, *A History of the United Nations Charter: the Role of the United States 1940–1945* (Washington DC: The Brookings Institute, 1958), p. 975 (Appendix B). For a discussion of the background to the Charter see *ibid.*, pp. 34–43.

[6] See *ibid.*, pp. 41–42.

[7] The Declaration was concluded by the USA, the UK, the USSR, China, Australia, Belgium, Canada, Costa Rica, Cuba, Czechoslovakia, the Dominican Republic, El Salvador, Greece, Guatemala, Haiti, Honduras, India, Luxembourg, the Netherlands, New Zealand, Nicaragua, Norway, Panama, Poland, South Africa and Yugoslavia. See US Exec. Agreement Ser. 236, January 1 1942. The text is reproduced in Russell, *ibid.*, p. 977 (Appendix C) and considered at pp. 50–58.

[8] See *ibid.*, p. 324.

[9] See *ibid.*, pp. 323–329 and see the Memorandum prepared for Roosevelt reproduced on p. 990 (Appendix F).

include the promotion of human rights among the purposes of the organization to be created.[10] Latin American States were at the forefront of those pressing for this to be addressed[11] and the sponsoring powers subsequently amended the proposed draft of Article 1(3) of what was to become the UN Charter by the addition of the words: 'and promotion and encouragement of respect for human rights and fundamental freedoms for all without distinction as to race, language, religion or sex'.[12]

However, a number of States sought to go beyond this and at the San Francisco Conference proposed that a 'declaration' setting out basic human rights should form an integral part of the Charter.[13] The most important of these proposals was that presented by Panama,[14] which

[10] Dumbarton Oaks Proposals for a General International Organization, Doc. G/1, *UNCIO*, vol. 3, p. 2 and vol. 6, p. 534. See also Russell, *A History of the UN Charter*, pp. 411–477 and 1019 (Appendix I).

[11] See, for example, the joint amendment of Brazil, the Dominican Republic and Mexico, G/25, vol. 3, p. 602. See also Mexico, G/7 (c)(1), vol. 3, p. 175 at p. 178; Venezuela, G/7 (d)(1), vol. 3, p. 189 at p. 224. The importance of including such a reference had been affirmed in the Final Act of the Inter-American Conference on Problems of War and Peace at Chapultepec, 7 March 1945 (for which see Russell, *A History of the UN Charter*, pp. 559–569). They were joined in this call by Egypt, G/7 (q)(1), vol. 3, p. 453; France, G/ 7 (o), vol. 3, p. 376 at p. 383; India, G/14 (h), vol. 3, p. 527; Norway, G/7 (n), vol. 3, p. 353 at p. 355. Whereas the proposals listed above concerned the statement of 'Purposes' in Article 1, some States suggested that similar wording be inserted into both the Preamble of the Charter (e.g. Lebanon, G/14 (a), vol. 3, p. 474; South Africa G/14 (d), vol. 3, p. 476) or into the statement of 'Principles' in Article 2 (e.g. Chile, G/2 (i)(1), vol. 3, p. 292 at p. 294.

[12] See Doc. G/29, 5 May 1945, UNCIO, vol. 3, p. 622 and vol. 6, p. 555. This was very much at the behest of the United States, which pressured the USSR and UK into accepting such a reference. See Russell, *A History of the UN Charter*, pp. 423–424 and 778–779. The United States' position was itself influenced by the forty-two private organizations admitted to the Conference by the United States as its 'consultants'. See J. P. Humphrey, 'The UN Charter and the Universal Declaration of Human Rights', in E. Luard (ed.), *The International Protection of Human Rights* (London: Thames and Hudson, 1967), p. 39 at pp. 40–46. The Four Power amendment also inserted the word 'cultural' after 'social' in the first part of the subsection.

[13] Some States, whilst not suggesting that a full list of rights be drawn up for inclusion in the Charter, proposed texts which made mention of some, including religion. See, for example, Norway: 'All Members of the UN undertake to defend the life, liberty, independence and religious freedom and to preserve human rights and justice' (G/7 (n), vol. 3, p. 353 at p. 355); New Zealand: 'All members undertake to preserve, protect and promote human rights and fundamental freedoms and in particular the rights of freedom from want, freedom from fear, freedom of speech and freedom of worship' (G/ 4 (f), vol. 3, p. 486); Chile: 'Every State must recognize for the individual the right to the free exercise, both in public and in private, of his religion and his profession, science or art, as long as the practice thereof is not incompatible with public morals (G/2 (i)(1), vol. 3., p. 292 at p. 294.

[14] The Panamanian draft was, in fact, the text which had been drawn up by Dr Ricardo

put forward the text of a draft 'Declaration of Essential Human Rights', the first article of which provided that: 'Freedom of belief and of worship is the right of everyone. The State has a duty to protect this freedom.'[15]

Cuba also advocated the adoption of a declaration and submitted the draft of a 'Declaration of the International Rights and Duties of the Individual' to serve as a basis for discussion. Article IV(c) of that draft provided for: 'Liberty to profess any religion which he may freely choose and to practise its worship without any limitation other than respect for public order and morals.'[16]

Similarly, Uruguay urged that liberties and rights 'be defined in a special charter' but, rather than offer a text for consideration, suggested that the Charter of the Organization should itself require that both a declaration and 'a system of effective international juridical guardianship of those rights' be submitted to the Organization within six months of its coming into being.[17]

At the San Francisco Conference there was a good deal of sympathy for the idea of a declaration but it was decided that there was simply no time to formulate a text and it was agreed that this task should be left to the new Organization.[18]

Alfaro, an ex-President of Panama and director of the American International Law Institute who represented Panama at the San Francisco Conference. He had been requested to do so by the American Law Institute (ALI), which was interested in examining ways in which Roosevelt's 'Four Freedoms' might be given effect. It was adopted by the ALI in 1944. See L. B. Sohn, 'How American International Lawyers Prepared for the San Francisco Bill of Rights', *AJIL* 89 (1995), 540. Panama also called for the inclusion within the Charter of the Declaration of the Rights and Duties of Nations adopted by the American Institute of International Law on 6 January 1916. See *UNCIO*, vol. 3, pp. 266 and 272–273; vol. 6, pp. 546 and 549–551.

[15] All of the rights set out in the Declaration were, however, subject to Article 18 which provided that: 'In the exercise of his rights every one is limited by the rights of others and by the just requirements of the democratic state.' Doc. G/7 (g)(2), *UNCIO*, vol. 3, p. 265–269; vol. 6, pp. 545–549.

[16] G/14 (g), vol. 3, p. 493 at p. 500. There is a suggestion, however, that Article IV of this draft was primarily concerned with ensuring equivalence of treatment with nationals and, if so, this is more a matter of anti-discrimination than of religious liberty *per se*.

[17] Uruguay, G/7 (a)(1), *UNCIO*, vol. 3, pp. 34–35; vol. 6, p. 552. Mexico also called for the inclusion of a Declaration, but did not put forward a text. See G/7 (c)(1), *UNCIO*, vol. 3, p. 175 at p. 176.

[18] See, e.g., Report of the Rapporteur of Committee I, I/1/34(1), UNCIO, vol. 6, p. 446 at p. 456; B. Simma (ed.), *The Charter of the United Nations: A Commentary* (Oxford: Clarendon Press, 1994), p. 53.

The separation of the freedom of religion from the framework of minority rights

One of the principal differences between the Covenant of the League of Nations and the UN Charter is that whilst the former made no mention of human or minority rights, the latter explicitly provides that 'promoting and encouraging respect for human rights and for fundamental freedoms for all' is to be one of the very purposes of the Organization.[19] Article 55 takes this further and obliges the UN, as an organization, to 'promote . . . universal respect for, and observance of, human rights . . . '[20] whilst, by virtue of Article 56, Member States 'pledge themselves to take joint and separate action in co-operation with the organization' in order to assist it in achieving its purposes.[21]

The UN Charter vests responsibility for discharging these functions in the General Assembly and the Economic and Social Council (ECOSOC).[22]

---

[19] UN Charter, Article 1(3) and see L. M. Goodrich, E. Hambro and P. Simons (eds.), *Charter of the United Nations*, 3rd and rev. edn (New York: Columbia University Press, 1969), p. 10.

[20] The original Dumbarton Oaks Proposals provided that 'the organization should facilitate solutions . . . and promote respect for human rights and fundamental freedoms'. The final version is stronger in that it mentions the 'observance' of such rights. The reason for this change is unclear. Russell comments that it was probably derived from an Australian proposal to add to the original 'respect for Human Rights and the observance by all members of fundamental freedoms'. See Russell, *A History of the UN Charter*, p. 783 and UNCIO, vol. 6, p. 306. Panamanian attempts to include the 'protection' of human rights, however, failed. See Russell, *ibid.*, pp. 777–780 and UNCIO, vol. 6, p. 535.

[21] See Goodrich, Hambro and Simons, *Charter of the United Nations*, pp. 372–374; Simma, *The Charter of the United Nations*, pp. 776–780, 793–794. Formally speaking, the combined effect of these articles is to oblige States to cooperate with the UN in its quest to promote universal respect for human rights. The early debates surrounding Articles 55 and 56 focused upon whether a 'pledge' under Article 56 implied a legal obligation, rather than upon the content of the obligation, if any, assumed (e.g. H. Kelsen, *The Law of the United Nations* (London: Stevens, 1950), p. 29; H. Lauterpacht, *International Law and Human Rights* (London: Stevens, 1950), p. 148) and the consequences of this upon the scope of domestic jurisdiction and Article 2(7) of the Charter (see, e.g., R. Higgins, *The Development of International Law through the Political Organs of the United Nations* (Oxford University Press, 1963), p. 128). For an overview see G. J. Jones, *The United Nations and the Domestic Jurisdiction of States* (Cardiff: University of Wales Press and the Welsh Centre for International Affairs, 1979), pp. 33–64. Nevertheless, the ICJ has expressed the view that, taken together, these articles equate to an obligation to observe and respect human rights. See *Legal Consequences for States of the Continued Presence of South Africa in Namibia (South West Africa) notwithstanding Security Council Resolution 276 (1970)*, Advisory Opinion, *ICJ Reports 1971*, p. 16 at paras.128–131.

[22] UN Charter, Article 60. The powers of the General Assembly are set out in Chapter IV (Articles 9–22) of the Charter and those of ECOSOC in Chapter X (Articles 61–72). The functions of the General Assembly and ECOSOC in relation to human rights are examined by A. Cassese, 'The General Assembly: Historical Perspective 1945–1989',

ECOSOC is to 'make or initiate studies and reports with respect to international economic, social, cultural, educational, health and related matters' and is empowered to 'make representations with respect to such matters to the General Assembly, to Members of the UN, and to the specialist agencies concerned'.[23]In addition, it is expressly provided that 'it may make recommendations for the purposes of promoting respect for, and observance of, human rights and fundamental freedoms for all'[24] and that 'it may prepare draft conventions for submission to the General Assembly, with respect to matters falling within its competence'.[25] As will be seen, it is in the fulfilment of this latter function that ECOSOC has done most to develop international standards concerning human rights.

In order to assist it in its tasks, the Charter required ECOSOC to establish 'Commissions in economic and social fields and for the protection of human rights'[26] and, at its First Session, held at Church House, Westminster in January 1946, ECOSOC adopted a resolution which provided that: 'The ECOSOC, being charged under the Charter with the responsibility of promoting universal respect for, and observance of, human rights and fundamental freedoms for all without distinction as to race, sex, language or religion, and requiring advice and assistance to enable it to discharge this responsibility, Establishes a Commission on Human Rights.'[27]

The work of the Commission on Human Rights (CHR)[28] was to be directed towards submitting proposals and recommendations and reports to the Council regarding a broad, but finite, set of questions, these being:

(a)   An international bill of rights.
(b)   International declarations or conventions on civil liberties, the status of women, freedom of information and similar matters.
(c)   The protection of minorities.
(d)   The prevention of discrimination on grounds of race, sex, language or religion.
(e)   Any other matter concerning human rights not covered by items (a), (b), (c) and (d).[29]

pp. 25–54; J. Quinn, 'The General Assembly into the 1990s', pp. 55–106 and D. O'Donovan, 'The Economic and Social Council', pp. 107–125, in P. Alston (ed.), *The United Nations and Human Rights: A Critical Appraisal* (Oxford: Clarendon Press, 1992).
[23] Article 62(1).   [24] Article 62(2).   [25] Article 62(3).   [26] Article 68.
[27] E/20 (15 February 1946), Off. Rec. 1st Session, p. 147, Annex 5 (subsequently E/27 of 22 February 1946).
[28] For an overview of the work of the CHR see P. Alston, 'The Commission on Human Rights' in P. Alston (ed.), *The United Nations and Human Rights*, pp. 126–210.
[29] E/20. The original proposal was somewhat more limited in scope, being restricted to the first four heads. The final residual category was added by ECOSOC Res. E/56/Rev. 1. The original was substantially similar to the proposals contained in the Report by the

ECOSOC had determined that a 'nuclear commission', comprising nine members appointed in their individual capacities, should meet and make recommendations concerning the definitive composition of the Commission.[30] Not surprisingly, therefore, much of the work at this first session was concerned with organizational matters.[31] Nevertheless, it considered its chief priority to be the drafting of an international bill of rights, believing that this might be found to cover substantially items (b), (c) and (d), and recommended that the full Commission, once established, undertake this task as soon as possible.[32] Thus the protection of minorities and the prevention of discrimination were, from the outset, seen as secondary to the wider concept and framework.

At this stage, however, the substance of an international bill of rights was entirely unclear and there was a tension between advocates of the nebulous concept of 'human rights' found in the UN Charter, but which was yet to be defined, and the more concrete concept of minority rights, which had a proven track record, even if that record was by no means entirely satisfactory.[33] Indeed, some on the ECOSOC took the view that minority rights formed a separate category, distinct from 'human rights and fundamental freedoms'[34] and the Nuclear Commission had itself

Executive Committee to the Preparatory Commission of the UN, UN Doc. PC/EX.113/Rev.1 and the Report of the Preparatory Commission of the United Nations, UN Doc. PC/20.

[30] E/27, pp. 6–7. In fact, only six members of the Nuclear Commission were present at the first session.

[31] See Report of the CHR (Nuclear Commission) to the 2nd Session of ECOSOC, May 1946, E/38/Rev. 1. The most contentious issue concerned the status of the members of the Commission. The 'Nuclear Commission' recommended that CHR members serve in an individual capacity but ECOSOC ultimately decided that the CHR 'shall consist of one representative from each of 18 members of the UN selected by the Council' (E/56/Rev.1, para. 2(a)). This had the effect of making the CHR a more political body than the Nuclear Commission had intended from the very outset.

[32] Report of the CHR (Nuclear Commission) to the 2nd Session of ECOSOC, Doc. E/38/Rev.1, pp. 160–161.

[33] When considering the Report of the Nuclear Commission, the Belgian representative on ECOSOC, Mr Dehousse, compared the Covenant of the League of Nations with the UN Charter and pointed out that whilst the Charter remedied the problem posed by the territorial limitation of the minority treaty system, 'the League Covenant provided for a system of control and guarantee, while the Charter did not contain any methods for supervision'. This, he felt, was a 'grave omission' (ECOSOC, 2nd Session, Off. Rec. p. 37). If the absence of mechanisms of oversight was the price that had to be paid to secure acceptance of the Charter provisions concerning human rights then, at the time, it was a fairly bad bargain. The Charter provisions were merely enabling, and the substance of the concept which members were to assist the organization in promoting remained to be defined.

[34] This is implicit in the comments of Mr Feonov (Soviet Union), ECOSOC, 2nd Session, Off. Rec. p. 35; Mr Dehousse (Belgium), ibid., p. 37.

recommended that the Secretariat should collect all documentation concerning items (c) and (d) of its terms of reference 'as a preliminary step to future consideration of the question of establishment of sub-commissions on these subjects'.[35]

Thus although the Charter did not expressly raise the issue of minority protection, it did find recognition within the system and ECOSOC empowered the CHR to establish separate sub-commissions to consider issues relating to minorities and discrimination.[36] Instead of doing this, however, the CHR ultimately decided to establish a single 'Sub-Commission on Prevention of Discrimination and the Protection of Minorities', whose members would serve in an individual capacity.[37] Although something of a generalization, this marked the practical downgrading of the minority approach as a separate strand of human rights protection within the UN system.[38]

---

[35] Report of the CHR (Nuclear Commission) to the 2nd Session of ECOSOC, E/38/Rev.1, *ECOSOC Journal*, No. 14, p. 163.

[36] E/56/Rev.1 and E/84, paras. 8–10. The functions of these sub-commissions was to be 'to examine what principles should be adopted in the definition of the principles which are to be applied in their respective fields' and 'to deal with the urgent problems' in these fields 'by making recommendations to the Commission'.

[37] See the First Report of the CHR to ECOSOC, E/259, paras. 18–19. These decisions were subsequently endorsed by ECOSOC. See ECOSOC Off. Rec., 2nd Year (4th Session), pp. 103–113. Both the Soviet Union and Czechoslovakia opposed these decisions (*ibid.*, pp. 104 and 110). For a general analysis of the work of the Sub-Commission see A. Eide, 'The Sub-Commission on Prevention of Discrimination and Protection of Minorities', in P. Alston (ed.), *The United Nations and Human Rights*, pp. 211–264.

[38] See P. Thornberry, *International Law and the Rights of Minorities* (Oxford: Clarendon Press, 1991), pp. 124–132. This tendency culminated with the 1950 Secretariat Study ('Study of the Legal Validity of the Undertakings Concerning Minorities', E/CN.4/367) which concluded that the minorities treaties were no longer to be considered in force. Likewise, the declarations made on admission to the League were also considered to have lapsed, with the exception of those made by Iraq and Albania which could be reactivated should the UN choose to undertake the guarantee (which has not occurred). The obligation entered into by Finland with respect to the Aaland Islands was considered to remain in force, since it was contained in a bilateral treaty and was not contingent upon the League's acceptance of the guarantee. Similarly, the obligations undertaken by Greece and Turkey in the Treaty of Lausanne were considered to remain in force. The minority provisions in the other post-WWI peace treaties were, of course, superseded by those concluded in 1947 (for which see above at p. 172). See M. Ganji, *The International Protection of Human Rights* (Geneva: Librairie E. Droz, 1962), pp. 77–81; Thornberry, *ibid.*, pp. 53–54. It is, then, surprising that the ICJ should have left the question open when, in 1993, Bosnia-Herzegovina argued that Article 11 of the 1919 Serb-Croat-Slovene Treaty provided it with a basis for exercising jurisdiction in the case brought by it against Yugoslavia (Serbia-Montenegro). See *Application of the Convention on the Prevention and Punishment of the Crime of Genocide, Provisional Measures, ICJ Reports 1993*, p. 325 at para. 31. But *cf.* J. P. Humphrey, *Human*

The First Session of the CHR opened in January 1947 at Hunter College, New York. Its principal business was the drafting of the international bill of rights. It was decided that the Chairman (Mrs Roosevelt, USA), Vice-Chairman (Mr Chang, China) and Rapporteur (Mr Malik, Lebanon) should prepare a draft to be examined by the full Commission at its next session. Thus the primary responsibility for framing the document that would 'set the agenda' for the subsequent development of the code of human rights was to have rested with just three members of the Commission. However, this was challenged in the ECOSOC[39] and the group was ultimately widened to include the representatives of Australia, Chile, China, France, Lebanon, USA, UK, and the USSR.[40] This Drafting Committee met in June 1947 and adopted a text which leant heavily upon the 'Secretariat Outline' which had been produced by John Humphrey, the Director of the UN Human Rights Division.[41] The Report presented to the Second Session

Rights and the United Nations: A Great Adventure (Dobbs Ferry, NY: Transnational Publishers, 1984), pp. 47–48, who, as Director of the Human Rights Division, expressed regret that the ICJ had not been asked to consider this matter in the first place, and questioned the role of the Secretariat in producing this Report. For general surveys of the work of the UN relating to minority rights see, in addition to the works already cited, F. Ermacora, 'The Protection of Minorities before the United Nations', *HR* 182 (1983), 250; G. Alfredsson and A. de Zayas, 'Minority Rights: Protection by the UN', *HRLJ* 12 (1993), 1. See also below, p. 370.

[39] The Soviet Union argued that the group was both too small and its responsibilities too great, and further objected to there being no representation from European countries (ECOSOC Off. Rec., 2nd Year (4th Session), p. 104).

[40] CHR Res. E/325 and ECOSOC Res. E/437 (46(IV)). Humphrey observed that the larger group was created by Mrs Roosevelt in a fashion which 'although politically realistic probably had no legal basis'. See Humphrey, 'The UN Charter and the Universal Declaration of Human Rights', in E. Luard (ed.), *The International Protection of Human Rights*, p. 48. The advantage of a very small group would have been that its very compactness would have undermined any attempt at politicization. The Commission still saw itself as an advisory body of experts, whilst ECOSOC viewed it as a politically representative forum. *Cf.* the proposal of the Nuclear Commission that its membership be independent.

[41] The Secretariat Outline (E/CN.4/AC.1/3). This was reproduced as Annex A to the Report of the Drafting Committee (E/CN.4/21) and is reproduced in the *UN Yearbook on Human Rights* for 1947, p. 484. Humphrey, *Human Rights and the United Nations*, pp. 29–76 provides a compelling account of the drafting process from the stance of the Secretariat. He records that it was decided that he should 'absent myself from the office for a week and devote my full attention to the declaration. It was therefore at the Lido Beach Hotel that, with some help from Emile Giraud, I prepared the first draft of the UDHR.' He goes on to record that he worked off a number of drafts collected by the Secretariat which, with two exceptions, were all from the English-speaking sources in the democratic West. He added that: 'The documents which the secretariat brought together ex post facto in support of my draft included texts extracted from the constitutions of many countries. But I did not have this before me when I prepared my draft' (*ibid.*, pp. 31–32).

of the CHR by the Drafting Committee identified three distinct components of an 'international bill of rights'[42] and, following consideration of the Report by the CHR, it became settled that the 'international bill of rights' would be composed of a declaration, a convention and means of implementation.[43]

It is well known that the Universal Declaration of Human Rights (UDHR) does not contain any mention of minority rights.[44] Although draft articles relating to the rights of minorities were submitted by both the Human Rights Division of the UN Secretariat[45] and the Sub-Commission[46] during the initial phases of its development, and were subsequently pressed by a number of States in the Third Committee of the General Assembly, these suggestions came to nothing. Mrs Roosevelt, the Chairman of the CHR, was fundamentally opposed to the concept of minority rights, believing

---

[42] E/CN.4/21, paras.12 and 19.

[43] Report of the CHR, 2nd Session, 1947, E/600, paras. 16–18.

[44] See Thornberry, *International Law and the Rights of Minorities*, pp. 133–137 for an examination of the background to this. GA Resolution 217C (III), adopted on the same day as the UDHR, provided:

> *Considering* that the United Nations cannot remain indifferent to the fate of Minorities,
>
> *Considering* that it is difficult to adopt a uniform solution of this complex and delicate question, which has special aspects in each State in which it arises,
>
> *Considering* the universal character of the Declaration of Human Rights,
>
> *Decides* not to deal in a specific provision with the question of minorities in the text of this Declaration.

The Resolution went on to request the CHR and Sub-Commission to undertake a 'thorough study of the problems of minorities'.

[45] Article 46 of the 'Secretariat Outline' had proposed:

> In States inhabited by a substantial number of persons of a race, language or religion other than those of the majority of the population, persons belonging to such ethnic, linguistic or religious minorities shall have the right to establish and maintain, out of an equitable proportion of public funds available for the purpose, their schools and cultural institutions, and to use their language before the courts and other authorities and organs of the State, and in the press and public assembly.

The similarity between this and Articles 9 and 10 of the Polish Minority Treaty is striking.

[46] The Sub-Commission proposed that:

> In States inhabited by well defined ethnic, linguistic or religious groups which are clearly distinguished from the rest of the population and which want to be accorded differential treatment, persons belonging to such groups shall have the right as far as is compatible with public order and security to establish and maintain their schools and cultural or religious institutions, and to use their own language and script in the press, in public assembly, and before the courts and other authorities of the States, if they so choose. (UN Doc. E/CN.4/SR.52, p. 9).

Thornberry, *International Law and the Protection of Minorities*, p. 134, aptly characterizes this as a 'less than enthusiastic provision'.

that 'the best solution of the problem of minorities was to encourage respect for human rights'.[47] Rather than see minority rights as different but complementary, Mrs Roosevelt and the CHR saw them as being simply inferior.[48] Irrespective of whether this was right or wrong, the consequence of this approach was that minority protection ceased to be the primary vehicle through which religious freedoms were addressed on the international plane.[49]

Religious freedom and the Universal Declaration of Human Rights

Article 18 of the UDHR provides that:

Everyone has the right to freedom of thought, conscience and religion: this right includes freedom to change his religion or belief, and freedom, either alone or in community with others and in public or private, to manifest his religion or belief in teaching, practice, worship and observance.

This has been described as an ' "easy case" in the human rights catalogue'[50] and it is true that it occasioned less debate than other provisions of the UDHR. The discussion that did take place suggests that the substance of the right to religious freedom was far from straightforward.[51] If the adoption of the text proved to be comparatively unproblematic, this reflected a willingness to compromise, rather than a common understanding of what was embraced by such a right.

The Secretariat Outline had proposed that: 'There shall be freedom of conscience and belief and of private and public religious worship.'[52] When it met in June 1947, the Drafting Committee opted for a more expansive approach and ultimately presented alternative drafts to the CHR.[53] The first provided: 'Individual freedom of thought and conscience, to hold and change beliefs, is an absolute and sacred right. The practice of a private or

---

[47] A/C.3/SR.161, p. 726.

[48] See Thornberry, *International Law and the Rights of Minorities*, p. 136.

[49] For an examination of the role played by minority rights in the protection of religious freedom see Y. Dinstein, 'Freedom of Religion and the Protection of Religious Minorities', *Is.YHR* 20 (1990), 155–181; reprinted in Y. Dinstein and M. Tabory (eds.), *The Protection of Minorities and Human Rights* (Dordrecht: Martinus Nijhoff, 1992), pp. 145–169.

[50] M. Scheinin, 'Article 18', in A. Eide (ed.), *The Universal Declaration of Human Rights: A Commentary* (Oslo: Scandinavian University Press, 1992), p. 263. The drafting of Article 18 is considered at pp. 262–266.

[51] *Cf.* Humphrey, *Human Rights and the United Nations*, pp. 67–68, who says that 'much thought and discussion was given at every stage of the drafting to Article 18'.

[52] E/CN.4/AC.1/3, Article 14.

[53] Report of the Drafting Committee, E/CN.4/21, paras. 13–17 and Annex F, Article 20.

public worship, religious observances, and manifestations of differing convictions, can be subject only to such limitations as are necessary to protect public order, morals and the rights and freedom of others.'[54]

The UK had submitted a series of draft articles which were designed to form the basis of a legally binding instrument (the division of the 'international bill of rights' into a declaration, covenant and measures of implementation not having yet been decided upon). Its proposed article on religion or belief formed the alternative proposed by the Drafting Committee and provided:

1. Every person shall be free to hold any religious or other belief dictated by his conscience and to change his belief.
2. Every person shall be free to practice, either alone or in community with other persons of like mind, any form of religious worship and observance, subject only to such restrictions, penalties or liabilities as are strictly necessary to prevent the commission of acts which offend laws passed in the interests of humanity and morals, to preserve public order and to ensure the rights and freedoms of other persons.
3. Subject only to the same restrictions, every person of full age and sound mind shall be free to give and receive any form of religious teaching and to endeavour to persuade other persons of full age and sound mind of the truth of his beliefs, and in the case of a minor the parent or guardian shall be free to determine what religious teaching he shall receive.[55]

These drafts were considered by the CHR in December 1947 and were amalgamated and abbreviated to form Article 16 of the Draft Declaration that was adopted and transmitted to the ECOSOC. Draft Article 16 provided:

1. Individual freedom of thought and conscience, to hold and change beliefs, is an absolute and sacred right.
2. Every person has the right, either alone or in community with other persons of like mind and in public or private, to manifest his beliefs in worship, observance, teaching and practice.[56]

---

[54] The Drafting Committee requested a small group of four (comprised of the representatives of the UK, Lebanon, France and the USA) to prepare a text for its consideration, and this group asked the French representative, René Cassin, to prepare a draft. He had already presented a series of articles which had included proposals which were accepted by them and referred back to the full Committee as E/CN.4/AC.1/W.2/Rev.1, Articles 21 and 22. Subject to comparatively minor alterations, they were adopted as the first alternative proposed by the Drafting Committee.
[55] E/CN.4/AC.1/4, Annex 1 (reproduced as Annex B to the Report of the Drafting Committee, E/CN.4/21).
[56] See Report of the CHR, 2nd Session, 1947, E/600, Annex A. René Cassin was Rapporteur

Surprisingly enough, this did not refer to religion directly, although it was clearly understood to fall within its terms since it is implicit in the right to manifest beliefs in worship. The proposal also declared that individual freedom of thought and conscience was a 'sacred' right. This could be taken either to suggest that only religious beliefs were encompassed by the draft, or that all forms of belief were divine in nature. Neither proposition was acceptable and, although the Drafting Committee, which met again in May 1948, did not alter the text,[57] it was changed to meet these concerns by the drafting sub-committee at the Third Session of the CHR in June 1948. The result was the one paragraph draft of Article 16 that was ultimately adopted as Article 18 of the UDHR.[58] This firmly established the 'secular' nature of the freedom of thought and conscience, a trend that has continued and grown in strength.

During the May 1948 session of the Drafting Committee, the Soviet Union had, however, proposed an alternative which provided that: 'Everyone must be guaranteed freedom of thought and freedom to perform religious services in accordance with the laws of the country concerned and the requirement of public morality.' Although not taken up, it was included in its Report[59] and was considered by the CHR, which rejected it by ten votes to five, with one abstention. It was represented[60] when the Draft Declaration was considered in the Third Committee of the General Assembly during its third Session at the end of 1948[61] and considered alongside four other proposed amendments, submitted by Sweden,[62] Saudi Arabia,[63] Cuba[64] and Peru.[65]

The Soviet delegate, Mr Pavlov, stressed the need to sanction freedom of thought, 'in order to promote the development of modern sciences and which took account of the existence of free-thinkers whose reasoning had led them to discard all old fashioned beliefs and religious fanaticism'. He also felt that it was necessary to permit the State to take steps against 'certain religious practices' which were 'contrary to the requirements of

to the working group that considered the Draft Declaration and so it is not surprising to see that it was the version derived from his draft which was the dominant influence.
[57] See Report of the Drafting Committee, E/CN.4/95.
[58] Report of the CHR, 3rd Session, June 1948, E/800, Annex A, Article 16. See text of Article 18 UDHR quoted at the head of this section.
[59] E/CN.4/95.
[60] See Report of the CHR, 3rd Session, June 1948, E/800, p. 33. This was recapitulated, along with the other amendments listed below, in A/C.3/289/Rev. 1.
[61] GAOR, 3rd Session, 1949, Part I, Third Committee, 127th and 128th Meetings (A/C.3/SR.127-128), pp. 390-408 (references to the debates in the following footnotes are given by page number).
[62] A/C.3/252.   [63] A/C.3/247.   [64] A/C.3/232.   [65] A/C.3/225.

morality and could have deplorable effects on society'.[66] Mrs Roosevelt pointed out that draft Article 27 (subsequently Article 29) permitted a State to intervene in the enjoyment of the rights proposed in draft Article 16 on grounds of public morality, and objected to the proposal to subject the right to the provisions of national law.[67] These views were echoed by many of the other delegates[68] and the amendment was rejected.[69]

The Swedish amendment was similar to the first element of the Soviet proposal in that it sought to place limits upon the freedom to manifest religious beliefs. It provided that: 'In order to protect individuals who have religious beliefs different from the officially recognized religion, or who have no religious belief whatever, against manifestations of religious fanaticism, it is proposed that the following words be added to this article after "... worship and observance": "provided that this does not interfere unduly with the personal liberty of anybody else".'

This was criticized for being too vague to be helpful[70] and was rejected for much the same reasons as the Soviet proposal.[71] There was, however, an important difference between them. The Soviet proposal had linked restrictions upon expressions of religious fanaticism with the need to preserve public morality. It would also have permitted the State to prevent believers indulging in ritual practices considered to be an offence but which did not in themselves bear upon the rights of others. By also stressing the primacy of national law, the Soviet proposal reeked of collectivism. The Swedish proposal, on the other hand, was more limited in scope – for example, it would not have affected practices such as personal flagellation or self mutilation – and stressed the importance of preserving the right of the individual in the face of excessive manifestations of religious zeal. This struck a chord with those who were troubled

---

[66] A/C.3/SR.127–128, p. 391. 'Human sacrifice' and 'flagellation and savage mortification' were given as examples of such behaviour.

[67] Ibid., pp. 392–393.

[68] See, for example, Mrs Corbet, (UK, ibid. p. 393); Mr Contoumas (Greece, p. 394); Mr Aquino (Philippines, p. 396); Mr Cassin, (France, pp. 396–397); Mr Beaufort (Netherlands, p. 397); Mrs Ikramullah (Pakistan, p. 399); Mr Azkoul (Lebanon, p. 399); Mr García Bauer (Guatemala, p. 402).

[69] The first clause, 'Everyone must be guaranteed freedom of thought', was rejected by twenty-three votes to nine, with eight abstentions. The second clause, 'and freedom to perform religious services' was rejected by twenty-four votes to nine with eight abstentions. The remainder fell automatically. See ibid. p. 405.

[70] See Mr Dehousse (Belgium, ibid. p. 395).

[71] E.g. Mrs Roosevelt (USA, ibid. p. 393); Mrs Corbet (UK p. 393); Mr Aquino (Philippines, p. 396); Mr Cassin (France, p. 396); Mrs Ikramullah (Pakistan, p. 399); Mr Azkoul (Lebanon, p. 399); Mr García Bauer (Guatemala, p. 402).

by the activities of religious groups but were also wary of giving ground to communist sentiments.

Thus several delegates saw the Swedish amendment as being primarily concerned with the need to guard against the effects of proselytism and expressed considerable sympathy for this.[72] Indeed, Mr Dehousse of Belgium was of the opinion that: 'In professing or propagating a faith one could, to a certain extent, interfere with the freedom of others by seeking to impose an unfamiliar idea upon them. But proselytism was not limited to only one faith or religious group. If it was an evil, it was an evil from which all sides had to suffer.'[73] However, Mr Baroody, the representative of Saudi Arabia,[74] submitted a proposal that challenged the entire question of permitting the manifestation of beliefs. It proposed that the second sentence of Article 16 be deleted in its entirety, so that it would simply provide that: 'Everyone has the right to freedom of thought, conscience or religion.'[75] Although he suggested that the article as proposed was unbalanced because it only included the right to change one's religion and not one's thought or conscience – and tried to suggest that this was the consequence of conflicting political ideologies – it was clear from the outset that the real intention of the Saudi Arabian proposal was to eliminate the reference to the right to change one's religion.[76] He concluded the presentation of his proposal by confirming that Saudi Arabia would be prepared to accept Article 16 if the express reference to the freedom to change religion or belief was omitted and it was subsequently amended in this fashion.[77] For many of the delegates, however,

---

[72] E.g. Mr Contoumas (Greece, pp. 393–394), who questioned whether the freedom to manifest one's religion 'might not lead to unfair practices of proselytizing' and felt that 'while, admittedly, every person should be free to accept or reject the religious propaganda to which he was subjected, he felt that an end should be put to such unfair competition in the sphere of religion'. See also Mr Aquino (Philippines, p. 396).

[73] *Ibid.* p. 395.   [74] Jamil Baroody was, in fact, a Lebanese Christian.

[75] A/C.3/247. The impact of the Islamic States upon the drafting of the UDHR, and the background to it, is examined by J. Kelsey, 'Saudi Arabia, Pakistan and the Universal Declaration of Human Rights', in D. Little, J. Kelsey and A. A. Sachedina (eds.), *Human Rights and the Conflict of Cultures: Western and Islamic Perspectives on Religious Liberty* (Columbia: University of South Carolina Press, 1988), p. 33.

[76] Mr Dehousse had argued that it was essential to permit the 'external manifestations of creeds by which expression was given to beliefs' otherwise it would be pointless to proclaim the freedom of thought, conscience and religion at all. It was for this reason that he opposed the original version of the Saudi Arabian proposal. His comments imply sympathy for the amended version subsequently put forward (A/C.3/SR.127–128, p. 395).

[77] *Ibid.* pp. 391–392 and 396. In support of this view, he observed that: 'throughout history missionaries had often abused their rights by becoming the forerunners of a political

the freedom to change one's religion was an essential part of the freedom of religion.[78]

Nevertheless, the amended proposal attracted some support, though often expressed indirectly by way of a preference for a shorter and less elaborate statement of the right.[79] At base, there was an irreconcilable conflict between the Muslim States which were not prepared to accept the claim that all individuals were entitled to change their religious beliefs and others for whom this was an essential prerequisite.[80] The amended proposal was rejected by twenty-two votes to twelve, with eight abstentions[81] – meaning that very nearly half of the Committee failed to endorse the right to change religions. When, at the conclusion of the debate, the unamended draft was voted on in parts, the phrase 'this right includes freedom to change his religion' was accepted by twenty-seven votes to five, with twelve abstentions – the five States voting against all being Muslim.[82]

The other amendments prompted less discussion. The Peruvian amendment, which was designed to place religious freedoms in a separate article in the interests of better drafting, was withdrawn once the consensual nature of the draft had been made clear.[83] The Cuban amendment was also said to be rooted in the unsatisfactory draftsmanship of Article 16.[84] Whilst not an obvious improvement upon the existing text,[85] the proposal

intervention, and there were many instances where peoples had drawn into murderous conflict by the missionaries' efforts to convert them'. *Cf.* Mr Aquino (Philippines, p. 396), who argued that such incidents supported the call for its inclusion.

[78] E.g. Mrs Roosevelt (USA, p. 393); Mrs Corbett (UK p. 393); Mr Dehousse (Belgium, pp. 394–395); Mr Cassin (France, p. 397); Mr Azkoul (Lebanon, p. 399).

[79] See Mr Anze Matienzo (Bolivia, *ibid.* p. 400); Mr Abadi (Iraq, p. 402); Mr Pavlov (USSR, p. 403); Mr Kaylay (Syria, p. 403).

[80] Mr Baroody challenged the French, Lebanese, British, Belgian and Dutch delegates 'whether they were not afraid of offending the religious beliefs of their Moslem subjects by imposing that article on them.' However, to confuse matters, he then claimed that 'to mention the individual's right to change religion was superfluous, as that particular freedom was implied in the freedom of belief' (*ibid.* p. 404: a view endorsed by Mr Beaufort, Netherlands, p. 397).

[81] *Ibid.* p. 405.

[82] *Ibid.*, these being Afghanistan, Iraq, Pakistan, Saudi Arabia and Syria.

[83] *Ibid.* p. 392. The Amendment provided: 'Every person has the right freely to profess a religious faith, and to express it in thought and in practice, both in public as well as in private.' This has been criticized on the grounds that it might be taken to prohibit the teaching of religion (Mrs Roosevelt, USA, p. 392); and that it excluded freedom of conscience in regard to philosophical and scientific concepts (Mr Dehousse, Belgium, p. 394; Mrs Corbet, UK, p. 393; Mr Aquino, Philippines, p. 395).

[84] Particular attention was drawn to the opening phrase, which was said to 'mean nothing, as it stated a right which was evident, which existed *a priori* and which need not be defended' (Mr Pérez Cisneros, Cuba, p. 404).

[85] As originally recorded in A/C.3/289/Rev.1, the proposal would have amended the opening

did not seem to merit the criticism which it attracted,[86] the real reason for much of which seems to have been the desire to preserve the existing text against any change, and it was rejected by twenty-six votes to five, with ten abstentions.[87]

It was, perhaps, the Bolivian delegate who best typified the mood within the Committee, and who observed that:

article 16 was concerned with a great problem of the human spirit, namely, religious belief and mutual tolerance. That was why the Bolivian delegation felt obliged to give expression to the anxiety it felt on account of the wording of that article, which was more of a sophism than a proclamation of principles. In their desire to keep in line with realities its authors had failed to give it a sufficiently lofty design.

The Bolivian delegation would have liked a brief and eloquent article regarding freedom of thought and belief . . . However, while using the right to express its opinion in the name of the freedom of thought which it intended to defend, the Bolivian delegation also intended to show a spirit of tolerance and would therefore accept article 16 with all that it was meant to imply.[88]

To put the matter briefly, the essential difficulty was that it was entirely unclear what the article was meant to imply, and the discussions surrounding its adoption provide no clarification. This is clearly illustrated by debate concerning the Swedish and Saudi Arabian amendments. Virtually all States agreed that the freedom of thought, conscience and religion should be assured to all.[89] From the first, however, it was understood that restrictions had to be placed upon this right, but there was no consensus concerning either the extent or form that such restrictions should take. Public morality, the rights of others and the dignity of believers themselves were seen as competing interests that could not be reconciled and were best left in a state of unresolved tension, with the Draft Declaration as a whole providing some support for most points of view.[90]

---

sentence so as to read: 'Every person has the right freely to profess a religion or philosophical belief. This right includes . . .'. When put to the vote, the Cuban delegate said that the proposal was to amend it so as to read: 'Every person has the right freely to profess a belief or conviction in any subject. This right includes . . .' (p. 405).

[86] E.g. Mr Aquino (Philippines, p. 396), who thought it 'negative and restrictive'.
[87] *Ibid*. p. 405.   [88] *Ibid.* p.400.
[89] At the request of the Cuban delegate, votes were taken on each part of the text and the first phrase was adopted with forty-four votes in favour, with Cuba abstaining on the grounds that it was meaningless. See *ibid*. pp. 405–406.
[90] Mrs Begtrup (Denmark, p. 407) abstained in the final vote adopting the article as a whole, complaining that 'it could be seen that the various delegations would interpret the provisions of the declaration in different ways and therefore it would have been advisable to have as wide and as general, but as short, a text as possible'.

The discussions also reveal widely divergent views concerning the relationship between the freedom of thought and conscience and the freedom of religion[91] and the meaning of 'belief'.[92] Several delegates expressed concern that the article was too heavily weighted in favour of religion and did not do enough to assure the manifestation of non-religious beliefs.[93] The very nature of religious belief was also a matter on which different views were expressed.[94] Most accepted that the inner realm of private belief and the outward act of manifestation formed a continuum, but differed over the point within the continuum at which interference with the enjoyment of the right was justified.[95] Others, however, drew a clear distinction between the freedom of religion, which concerned the relationship between God and Man, and the freedom of worship, which concerned the relationship of man with society.[96]

[91] E.g. Mr Pavlov (USSR, p. 402, supported by Mr Plaza, Venezuela, p. 400) thought that 'freedom of thought' encompassed scientific, philosophical and religious thought whereas Mr Jiménez de Aréchaga (Uruguay, p. 401) saw a need to extend the 'freedom of thought' to embrace science and politics. He also believed that the freedom of conscience formed a distinct concept that was 'out of place in a legal document'. Mr Encinas (Peru, p. 398) considered all three concepts, though closely connected, to be distinct.

[92] Mr Chang (China, p. 398) endorsed the original view of the CHR that freedom of belief – and by which was meant religious belief – was included within the freedom of thought and conscience whilst Mr Cassin (France, p. 397) seemed to assume that 'belief' was the broader concept, since he thought that the freedom to manifest a 'belief' included the right to manifest one's thought through being able to change one's opinion, a right not otherwise included in the article. *Cf.* Mr Baroody (Saudi Arabia, p. 404) who thought that the right to change one's religion was implied by the freedom of belief, whereas Mr Beaufort (Netherlands, p. 397) thought that the right to change one's beliefs was implicit in the freedom of conscience.

[93] E.g. Mr Pavlov (USSR p. 391); Mr Saint-Lot (Haiti, p. 399); Mr Jiménez de Aréchaga (Uruguay, p. 401) and Mr Cassin (France), who asked that the word used in the French text to equate with 'belief' in the English be changed from *croyance* to *conviction*, since the former term was said to have 'an essentially religious flavour' (p. 397).

[94] E.g. Mr Baroody (Saudi Arabia, p. 392) felt that 'religion was essentially a manifestation of an emotion', whereas for Mr Aquino (Philippines, p. 395) it was the 'expression of faith' and therefore 'inevitable that the definition of freedom of religion should give rise to differences of opinion'. Mr Chang (China, p. 398) explained that the Chinese considered that 'a man's actions are more important than metaphysics'. Naturally, this would place a premium upon 'pluralistic tolerance'. *Cf.* Mr Baroody, who thought that 'a good religion was one which advocated a reciprocal spirit of kindness and tolerance' (p. 392). His attitude towards a 'bad' religion which did not demonstrate these virtues was not made clear.

[95] This was the central issue in the discussions concerning the Saudi Arabian amendment.

[96] Mr Abadi (Iraq, p. 402).

For some the article made the best of a bad job,[97] whilst for others it was all that it should be.[98] In the light of these problems, the prevalent view was that the text as presented was a compromise that should not be picked over and it was on that basis that it was finally adopted by thirty-eight votes to three, with three abstentions.[99] Even if there was now widespread agreement concerning the text, it is clear that there was no real consensus concerning its interpretation. This was hammered home when several of the delegations which had voted in favour of it made statements which reserved their positions, thereby underlining some of the most potent differences between them.[100]

The Draft Declaration was then transmitted to the General Assembly where it prompted little discussion. The right to change one's religion was, however, raised by Egypt, which asserted that 'it was not entirely in agreement with that "right"', suggesting it might encourage 'the machinations of certain missions, well known in the Orient, which relentlessly pursued their efforts to convert to their own beliefs the masses of the

---

[97] E.g. Mr Dehousse (Belgium, pp. 395 and 407).

[98] E.g. Mr De Athayde (Brazil, p. 401), who thought that 'article 16 was the most important in the entire declaration' and that 'the basic text of the article was complete and that the detailed enumeration which followed the declaration of principle constitutes the essence itself of the philosophy which should be at the basis of that article'.

[99] *Ibid.* p. 406. No less than twelve delegates gave the consensus nature of the text as one of the reasons for their support. See Mrs Roosevelt (USA, p. 393); Mrs Corbet (UK, p. 393); Mr Contoumas (Greece, p. 292); Mr Santa Cruz (Chile, p. 395); Mr Aquino (Philippines, p. 395); Mr Cassin (France, p. 396); Mr Kural (Turkey, p. 397); Mr Encinas (Peru, p. 398); Mr Matienzo (Bolivia, p. 400); Miss Bernardino (Dominican Republic, p. 401); Mr Garciá Bauer (Guatemala, p. 401) and, as regards its second part, Mr Pérez Cisneros (Cuba, p. 404).

[100] Of those voting in favour, Mr Contoumas (Greece, p. 406) said that he had voted for Article 16 'on the understanding that it did not authorize unfair practices of proselytism'. Mr Plaza (Venezuela, pp. 400 and 406) said that his country – which had supported the Soviet amendment – reserved its position regarding its application to Venezuela in the light of its Constitution. Mr Pavlov (USSR, p. 406) yielded little and, reiterating the provisions of the Soviet Constitution, expressed the opinion that 'other countries . . . were not as progressive as his own and therefore it would have been too much to expect them to subscribe to the same guarantees as the USSR'. Mr Campos Ortiz (Mexico, pp. 406 407) explained that his vote was premised on the understanding that the freedom to manifest beliefs in teaching 'referred to the freedom of man to instruct others in his beliefs or religion within those necessary limitations, in order to ensure "recognition and respect for the rights of others, requirements of morality, public order and the general welfare" as stated in article 27'. This represents a narrow reading of these texts. Perhaps most startlingly, Mr Aziz (Afghanistan, p. 408) reaffirmed his support for the Saudi Arabian amendment and 'reserved the right to conform to Moslem laws with regard to the question'.

population'.[101] This point was also made by Pakistan, which argued that 'it was undeniable that their activity had sometimes assumed a political character which had given rise to justifiable objections', whilst stressing that 'the Moslem religion had unequivocally proclaimed the right to freedom of conscience and had declared itself against any kind of compulsion in matters of faith or religious practices'.[102]

The General Assembly adopted what had by then become renumbered as draft Article 19 by forty-five votes in favour, with four abstentions. It went on to adopt the UDHR as a whole – with the text now renumbered as Article 18 – by forty-eight votes in favour, with eight abstentions.[103] In consequence, what has proven to be one of the most influential statements of the religious rights of mankind yet devised entered into the international arena with no further light shed upon its meaning.

In itself, this was, perhaps, of no great importance. It is axiomatic that the UDHR was not intended as a source of legal obligation but was, as the Preamble declares, proclaimed as 'a common standard of achievement for all peoples and all nations'.[104] A lack of precision in a declaration which was setting rather than creating rights and imposing obligations meant that there was room for subsequent creative development. The question became more problematic, however, when, as will be seen below, Article 18 of the UDHR was taken as the model for Article 9 of the European Convention on Human Rights and Fundamental Freedoms and, in consequence, has been interpreted and applied by the Strasbourg organs within a Western European context. Because of this, the jurisprudence of the ECHR inevitably reflects back upon an understanding of the UDHR

---

[101] Mr Raafat, GAOR, 3rd Session, 1948, Part I, p. 913.

[102] Sir Mohammad Zafrullah Khan, GAOR, 3rd Session, 1948, Part I, p. 891. This is rather disingenuous, since, if so, it is difficult to understand why some Muslim States sought to place fetters upon their own subjects by restricting their right to change religion, rather than seeking to limit the right of missionaries of other faiths to manifest their faith in proselytism. Perhaps it was because, as he acknowledged, Islam was itself a missionary religion (*ibid.*, p. 890). The dispute between Saudi Arabia and Pakistan is examined by Kelsey, 'Saudi Arabia, Pakistan and the Universal Declaration of Human Rights' in D. Little, J. Kelsey and A. A. Sachedina (eds.), *Human Rights, and the Conflict of Cultures*, pp. 37–50.

[103] GA Res. 217A (III) of 10 December 1948. See GAOR, 3rd Session, 1948, Part I, p. 933.

[104] For an analysis of the effect of the Declaration at the time of its adoption see H. Lauterpacht, 'The Universal Declaration of Human Rights', *BYIL* 25 (1948), 354. Not only did he conclude that it was without legal effect, he expressed the view that 'not being a legal instrument, the Declaration would appear to be outside international law and its provisions cannot properly be the subject matter of legal interpretation . . . There is a tendency – which ought to be resisted – to indulge in a legal interpretation of what is not a legal instrument.' (*ibid.*, pp. 369–370).

itself. On the other hand, the principles enshrined within the UDHR have themselves been subject to development within the UN context, and as a result, there are clear possibilities for tension between the various understandings placed upon the words of the Declaration. Of course, this does no more than replicate the situation at the time that the text was adopted. But there is the crucial difference that this divergence now opens up at the level of international obligation.

8   Article 18 of the International Covenant on Civil and Political Rights

The drafting process

As has been seen, it was not until the Second Session of the CHR in December 1947 that it was decided that the 'international bill of rights' should comprise a declaration, a covenant and means of implementation. The Covenant was to provide both a source of legal obligation and define in detail the rights set out in the Declaration.[1] The original intention was to produce all of the elements of the 'bill' simultaneously. The Drafting Committee, meeting in June 1947, decided to adopt the articles submitted by the UK as the basis for a draft covenant.[2] This was examined by a working group at the Second Session of the CHR and remodelled to provide:

1. Every person shall have the right to freedom of religion, conscience and belief, including the right, either alone or in community with other persons of like mind, to hold and manifest any practice or belief, to change his belief, and to practice any form of religious worship and observance, and he shall not be required to do any act which is contrary to such worship and observance.
2. Every person of full age and sound mind shall be free, either alone or in a community with other persons of like mind, to give and receive any form of religious teaching [and endeavour to persuade other persons of full age and sound mind of the truth of his beliefs][3], and in

---

[1] For an overview of the drafting process see M. J. Bossuyt, *Guide to the 'Travaux Préparatoires' of the International Covenant on Civil and Political Rights* (Dordrecht: Martinus Nijhoff, 1987), pp. 351–371.

[2] Report of the Drafting Committee, E/CN.4/21, para. 14. The UK proposals (E/CN.4/AC.1/4) appear as Annex B to this Report, and, as articles for the Draft Convention, as Annex G. Thus Article 13 of the UK draft was presented to the CHR both as an alternative to the French draft of Article 14 of the Declaration and as Article 8 of the Draft Covenant.

[3] Square brackets not in the original. See below.

the case of a minor the parent or guardian shall be free to determine what religious teaching he shall receive.

3. The above rights and freedoms shall be subject only to such limitations as are prescribed by law and are necessary to protect public order and welfare, morals and the rights and freedoms of others.[4]

This was adopted by the CHR, with the exception of the phrase in the second sub-paragraph indicated in square brackets, which was removed at the suggestion of Egypt.[5] The text was, however, again reworked by the Drafting Committee in May 1948. The first subsection was divided into two parts, separating out the right to hold a belief from the right of manifestation. This brought it closer to the then current version of the Declaration text. The second subsection was broadened by the removal of the opening qualifications. The final subsection was unchanged. The entire article was, however, cast in a negative formulation, and so provided:

1. No one shall be denied freedom of thought, belief, conscience and religion, including freedom to hold any religious or other belief, and to change his belief.

2. No one shall be denied freedom, either alone or in association, to manifest his belief in practice, and in worship and observance, and no-one shall be required to do any act which is contrary to such worship and observance.

3. No one shall be denied freedom, either alone or in association, to give and receive any form of religious teaching, and to endeavour to persuade other persons of the truth of his beliefs.

4. The above rights and freedoms shall be subject only to such limitations as are prescribed by law and are necessary to protect public order and health, morals and the fundamental rights and freedoms of others.[6]

This draft was before the Third Session of the CHR in June 1948 along with the Draft Declaration. However, there was insufficient time to consider

---

[4] Report of the Working Group to the CHR, E/CN.4/56, Art. 15. In fact, the working group, comprising the representatives of Chile, China, Egypt, the Lebanon, the UK and Yugoslavia, decided not to base its work on the UK draft article, but upon an alternative American proposal (E/CN.4/37, Art. 12). This was adopted as the basis of the first sub-paragraph, the final sub-clause of which ('and he shall not be required . . .') being added at the suggestion of Charles Malik of the Lebanon. The second and third sub-paragraphs of the original UK draft were then combined to form the second sub-paragraph.

[5] This was narrowly accepted, by four votes to three, with nine abstentions (see E/CN.4/ SR.37, p. 16). For the final version of the article approved by the CHR see the Report of the CHR, 2nd Session, 1947, E/600, Annex B, Article 16.

[6] E/CN.4/95, Article 16.

both and the CHR decided to press ahead wit the Declaration[7] and it did not return to the Covenant until its Fifth Session in 1949 when, not surprisingly, it provided a further opportunity to raise the issues that had emerged during the discussions leading up to the adoption of Article 18 of the UDHR.[8]

Moreover, the old draft now appeared inadequate. Its use of the fourfold formula of 'thought, belief, conscience and religion' made it clear that religious and non-religious beliefs were embraced by it. However, it only referred expressly to the right to change one's belief, not religion, whereas the right to hold both a belief and a religion received express acknowledgment. This clearly implied that there was no right to change religion. This is not what had been intended: the 1948 wording had been inspired by the French draft, which had treated 'religion' and 'belief' as synonymous whereas the relationship between these concepts had now become a contentious issue.

The CHR brought the text of the Covenant back into line with the UDHR by adopting the joint proposal of the United States and France that the wording of Article 18 of the UDHR be used as the basis of paragraph 1 of the Covenant Article.[9] This also had the effect of bringing about a re-run of the debates that had taken place in the Third Committee. The Soviet amendment, rejected in the context of the Declaration, was again proposed and rejected.[10] Likewise, the freedom to change religion again proved troublesome and Egypt proposed that it be deleted[11] on the grounds that it was implicit within the concept of freedom of religion, and that the Covenant ought not to encourage proselytism, or sow doubts in the minds of believers.[12] The response to

---

[7] Report of the CHR, 3rd Session, June 1948, E/800, para. 14.

[8] Report of the CHR, 5th Session, May–June 1949, E/1371, paras. 16–24.

[9] It was adopted with eleven votes in favour and four abstentions. The USA had originally suggested that the negative formulation be retained ('No one shall be denied the freedom . . .'), but agreed to the French suggestion that the common positive formulation be used. See E/CN.4/SR.117, pp. 11,12.

[10] The voting was nine votes to four, with three abstentions.

[11] See E/CN.4/253.

[12] E/CN.4/SR.116, p. 8. See also Report of the CHR, 5th Session, E/1371, Annex II, p. 33 where Egypt again reiterated its view that 'when it is recognized that everyone has the right to freedom of thought, conscience and religion, and everyone is guaranteed the right to practise or manifest his religion, the concept of freedom of religion is applied and realized'. In addition, it was pointed out that there was little point in forcing the right upon unwilling States since, 'any attempt to deal with non-essential principles in connection with so delicate a question is likely, however, to result in the discussion of contentious problems and lead states not to ratify the covenant, which is a legal document'.

this was somewhat more robust than in the Third Committee on the UDHR[13] and the proposal was defeated, but only by seven votes to two, with seven abstentions, representing a considerable weakening of support for the principle.

At one level, the text of the Covenant seemed to be taking the same path as that of the Declaration and at the Sixth Session of the CHR in the following year the first sub-paragraph was adopted without amendment[14] and transmitted to ECOSOC along with the remainder of the Covenant text. However, differences surrounding all aspects of the text were hardening and, although ECOSOC referred it on to the General Assembly, it requested that a number of fundamental questions relating to its form and content be examined,[15] including the adequacy of the articles already drafted. The text of Article 18 of the UDHR was, therefore, again scrutinized by the Third Committee – albeit now in the context of the Covenant – and the same points were raised as in previous debates.[16] Clearly, some form of compromise was needed and at the Eighth Session of the CHR a proposal was introduced which sought to bridge the gap between the differing points of view. It had two elements. The first was that the second portion of the paragraph be amended so as to read: 'This right shall include freedom to maintain or to change his religion or belief . . .'[17] This compromise was warmly welcomed and adopted unanimously.[18] It had the advantage of placing the right to maintain a religion on an equal footing with the right to change religion. If, as those in favour of deleting the clause had always maintained, the right to change was implicit in the freedom of religion itself, the freedom to hold a religion was similarly protected and little of real substance was to be gained by spelling it out in this fashion.

However, the real impact of the change was the implication that one might be protected in one's right to maintain a religion, and this would justify the adoption of measures against proselytism which might otherwise run the risk of transgressing the missionary rights of other faiths.

---

[13] E.g. France argued that there were religious bodies which discouraged conversion and some States discriminated against non-believers of State religions. E/CN.4/SR.116, p. 11.

[14] E/CN.4/SR.161, §§45–47. The first and third clauses of the paragraph were adopted unanimously, and the second part was adopted by thirteen votes to one.

[15] See D. McGoldrick, *The Human Rights Committee: its Role in the Development of the International Covenant on Civil and Political Rights* (Oxford: Clarendon Press, 1991), pp. 6–7.

[16] Egypt, A/C.3/SR.288, §26; Saudi Arabia, A/C.3/SR.289, §§40–47 and A/C.3/SR.306, §§47–48.

[17] E/CN.4/L.187.

[18] E/CN.4/SR.319, p. 13 and see Egypt, p. 3; France, p. 4; Yugoslavia, p. 10; Greece, p. 11.

This was underscored by the second proposal, which was that a new second paragraph be added to the article which would provide:

> 2. No one shall be subject to any form of coercion which would impair his freedom to maintain or to change his religion or belief.

This caused some concern, since the phrase 'any form of coercion' might include the presentation of arguments or other forms of intellectual debate that sought to undermine the strength of a person's beliefs and it was considered necessary to make it clear that not all forms of activity which might be deemed by some to amount to 'coercion' were to be prohibited. Textually, this concern was acknowledged by the removal of the words 'any form of' from the paragraph.[19] Although not exactly obvious from the resulting text, this went some way towards recognizing that not all forms of coercion were impermissible. Of course, the difficulty remained of distinguishing between those that were and those which were not.

The discussion provided some guidance on this point: 'it was understood that the word "coercion" should not be construed as applying to moral or intellectual persuasion, or to any legitimate limitation of freedom to manifest one's religion or belief'.[20] The point at which persuasion becomes coercion is, however, very much a matter of subjective assessment, as is the point at which restrictions placed upon the manifestation of a belief become coercive. However, coercion which 'impairs' the freedom does embrace indirect as well as direct forms of pressure[21] and so a fairly broad range of possibilities seems to be encompassed by the term.[22]

Despite the adoption of these compromise texts, the matter was not allowed to rest. The inclusion of any mention of a specific right to change religion provoked comment when the Draft was again considered by the

---

[19] E/CN.4/SR.319, p. 13.

[20] A/2929, Chapter VI, §110, summarizing E/CN.4/SR.319, pp. 6–7 (Australia).

[21] It is often difficult to distinguish between forms of pressure which are 'direct' and those which are 'indirect'. The threat of physical force is clearly direct. The promise of advancement in secular society is clearly indirect. The threat of a curse of some sort is difficult to classify.

[22] This point was clarified when Saudi Arabia introduced an amendment which would have replaced 'impairs' with 'deprives' (A/C.3/L.876, for which see below, n. 24). It was pointed out that 'impair' had the broader meaning (Philippines, A/C.3/SR.1025, §3; India, A/C.3/SR.1027, §12). Had Saudi Arabia pressed the amendment it would have been advocating a restriction upon the ability of the State to prevent coercive behaviour, the opposite of what was intended.

Third Committee at its Ninth (1954)[23] and Fifteenth (1960) Sessions. At the Fifteenth Session, and for the last time, Mr Baroody, representing Saudi Arabia, proposed the deletion of the words 'to maintain or to change his religion or belief' from the first paragraph of the article[24] but withdrew this[25] in favour of a compromise proposal put forward by the Philippines and Brazil which replaced these words in paragraphs 1 and 2 of the article with the phrase 'to have a religion or belief of his choice'.[26] Despite this, there was still a considerable divergence of opinion[27] and, in an attempt to secure a compromise, the UK delegation, which felt that the phrase 'to have' implied a static position that did not go far enough, sought to insert the expression 'or to adopt' into the amendment.[28] This was enough to settle the question[29] and the new version of Article 18(1) and (2) was finally adopted.[30] As amended, it provides:

> 1. Everyone shall have the right to freedom of thought, conscience and religion. This right shall include freedom to have or to adopt a religion or belief of his choice, and freedom, either individually or in commu-

[23] See Afghanistan, E/CN.4/SR.565, §§9–16.

[24] A/C.3/L.876. See A/C.3/SR.1021, §§6–14; A/C.3/SR.1022, §27; A/C.3/SR.1023, §11. It received support from Greece (A/C.3/SR.1022, §1); Afghanistan (ibid., §18); Brazil (A/C.3/SR.1023, §16). Canada thought it made no difference whether it was deleted or not, since the right to change religion was inherent in the first phrase of the article (A/C.3/SR.1024, §2).

[25] See A/C.3/SR.1026, §§26–27. He again maintained that the right to change religion was implicit in the first sentence whilst at the same time he felt that if the Philippine/Brazilian proposal were adopted, 'it would no longer be liable to convey the impression that the Committee unwittingly sanctioned interference with beliefs that some people regarded as sacred'.

[26] A/C.3/L.877 and see the Philippines (A/C.3/SR.1024, §8; A/C.3/SR.1025, §§1–4).

[27] E.g. it received support from: Morocco (A/C.3/SR.1024, §11); Argentina (A/C.3/SR.1025, §25); Cyprus (§32); Afghanistan (A/C.3/SR.1026, §1); Spain (§3); United Arab Republic (§13); Ceylon (§20); Indonesia (A/C.3/SR.1027, §15); Yugoslavia (§25); India (§§29–30); Dominican Republic (§32). Several States, however, expressed a strong preference for the original article. See, e.g., Nigeria (A/C.3/SR.1025, §18); Pakistan (§§21–24); Liberia (A/C.3/SR.1025, §§6–7); Netherlands (§43); Israel (§46).

[28] A/C.S/SR.1027, §2.

[29] For some delegations, this tipped the balance in favour of the compromise solution: e.g. Italy (§11). Others, whilst not satisfied, were prepared to accept it in a spirit of compromise: e.g. USA (§20); Yugoslavia (§25). On the other hand, Afghanistan considered that it went too far and abstained on the inclusion of the new phrase, whilst accepting the original version of the amendment (§37). The words 'or to adopt' were adopted by fifty-four votes to none, with fifteen abstentions.

[30] The Brazilian and Philippine amendment was adopted by sixty-seven votes to none, with six abstentions. Article 18(1) was then adopted by seventy votes to none with two abstentions. Article 18(2) was adopted by seventy-two votes to none with two abstentions and, following the adoption of subsections (3) and (4) (for which see below, pp. 200–201), the article as a whole was adopted unanimously. See A/C.3/SR.1027, §36.

nity with others and in public or private, to manifest his religion or belief in worship, observance, practice and teaching.

2.   No one shall be subject to coercion which would impair his freedom to have or to adopt a religion or belief.

Article 29(2) of the UDHR subjected the enjoyment of the freedoms it proclaimed to a series of restrictions. Rather than use a general clause, the Covenant qualified each right in a separate paragraph of each article. Article 18(3) of the Covenant provides:

3.   Freedom to manifest one's religion or beliefs may be subject only to such limitations as are prescribed by law and are necessary to protect public safety, order, health or morals or the fundamental rights and freedoms of others.

Whereas Article 29(2) of the UDHR applied to all aspects of the Declaration, Article 18(3) only applies to the manifestation of religion or beliefs.[31] Since Article 18 is exempt from the scope of Article 4, which permits derogation from Covenant rights in times of 'public emergency which threaten the life of the nation,'[32] this means that the freedom of thought, conscience and religion is absolute and inviolable under the Covenant. Although the interpretation of this paragraph is crucial to the practical application of Article 18, since it permits a State to interfere with the exercise of aspects of the freedom of religion, its development sheds no real light on the content of that right itself[33] and so will not be examined further here.[34]

The final sub-paragraph of Article 18 provides:

The States Parties to the present Covenant undertake to have respect for the liberty of parents and, when applicable, legal guardians to ensure the religious and moral education of their children in conformity with their own convictions.

The inclusion of this provision, the origins of which are found in the original UK proposals of 1947,[35] is something of an anomaly. At both its

---

[31] The differences between the range of permissible restrictions under Article 29 of the UDHR and under Article 18(3) of the ICCPR are set out in J. P. Humphrey, 'Political and Related Rights', in T. Meron (ed.), *Human Rights in International Law* (Oxford: Clarendon Press, 1984), pp. 177–181.

[32] See Article 4(2).

[33] It was the fact that restrictions were possible, rather than the precise grounds upon which they could be justified, that was the important factor. *Cf.* the debates surrounding the rejection of the Soviet amendment to the UDHR considered above, pp. 185–186.

[34] For an overview of the Covenant restriction see A. C. Kiss, 'Permissible Limitations on Rights', in L. Henkin (ed.), *The International Bill of Rights: the Covenant on Civil and Political Rights* (New York: Columbia University Press, 1981), pp. 290–310.

[35] See n. 2 above.

Fifth and Sixth Sessions the CHR rejected a number of proposals that concerned the right of parents to determine the nature of the religious teaching, if any, given to their children, principally on the grounds that the proper place for such a provision was in an article dealing with education.[36] This was realized in Article 14(3) of the International Covenant on Economic, Social and Cultural Rights, but during the Fifteenth Session of the Third Committee in 1960, Greece pressed to include the text of that article, in so far as it applied to religious and moral instruction, within the ICCPR in order to ensure that it would apply to those States which only became a party to the latter instrument.[37] Although there was no real objection to the principle involved there was considerable doubt about its inclusion,[38] which was ultimately approved in a fairly half-hearted fashion.[39]

The unresolved controversies

Although different in several respects from Article 18 of the UDHR, it cannot be said that the text and drafting history of the Covenant article lends much by way of clarification. Both were intended to forge a consensus by avoiding the central point at issue: whether the freedom of religion included the freedom to change religion. For some of the Muslim States,[40] the very idea that it might be legitimate to abandon Islam for another faith was an affront that could not be countenanced, whilst for others the freedom to change one's religion was so fundamental that the freedom of religion shorn of this attribute would not be a freedom worthy

---

[36] See A/2929, chapter VI, §115.

[37] A/C.3/SR.1022, §3; A/C.3/SR.1023, §7 and A/C.3/SR.1025, §58.

[38] A number of States were strongly in favour: e.g. UK (A/C.3/SR.1022, §8); Liberia (A/C.3/SR.1023, §9); Ghana (A/C.3/SR.1025, §18); Argentina (§25); Cyprus (§34); Lebanon (§39); Israel (§48); Nigeria (§52); USA (A/C.3/SR.1027, §21). Others felt that it was inappropriate to include a right pertaining to a third party in an article setting out the rights of an individual: e.g. Philippines (A/C.3/SR.1022, §12); Poland (A/C.3/SR.1023, §17); Pakistan (A/C.3/SR.1024, §26); USSR (A/C.3/SR.1025, §57); United Arab Republic (A/C.3/SR.1026, §15); Yugoslavia (A/C.3/SR.1027, §27). The Netherlands considered the proposal redundant (A/C.3/SR.1025, §43) whereas Ceylon thought it ran counter to the very purpose of the article as a whole (A/C.3/SR.1022, §23). Most States foresaw problems of definition and difficulties where orphans or adopted children were concerned.

[39] It was adopted by thirty votes to seventeen, with twenty-seven abstentions. See A/C.3/SR.1027, §36.

[40] Pakistan once again took the view that Islam was a missionary religion (a point denied by Saudi Arabia, see A/C.3/SR.1021, §15; see also A/C.3/SR.289, §§40–47 and above, p. 192, n. 102) and did not seek to deny others the free right of conversion (A/C.3/SR.571, §45; A/C.3/SR.1024, §21).

of legal recognition at all.[41] The wording finally adopted might seem to anchor the article within comfortable proximity of the right to change one's religion. Yet precise wording to this effect was expressly excluded from the text[42] and it is open to the interpretation that it allows an individual to continue in a faith, to adopt a faith, but not abandon a faith already held.[43] It has, however, become generally accepted that Article 18 does embrace the right to change religion, although the evidence advanced in support of this is not wholly convincing.[44]

With this once again forming the focus of discussion, it is easy to miss the fact that none of the doubts and confusions concerning the meaning and relationship between the various concepts embraced by the article were resolved.[45] They were, if anything, accentuated. Indeed, the very purpose of the article itself became a subject of disagreement. The Argentine delegate argued that Article 18 was primarily concerned with freedom of religion and that 'although thought and conscience were also

[41] E.g. before the CHR, see France (E/CN.4/SR.116, p. 11); Philippines (p. 8); USA (E/CN.4/ SR.161, §§10, 27); Yugoslavia (§26). Before the Third Committee see Liberia (A/C.3/ SR.1023, §8); Pakistan (A/C.3/SR.1024, §§23–25); Philippines (A/C.3/SR.1025, §2); Netherlands (§43); Israel (§46); France (ibid., §6); Cuba (§9); Yugoslavia (A/C.3/SR.1027, §23).

[42] Cf. the comments of the UK delegate who pointed out that since the UDHR explicitly mentioned the right to change religion it was 'necessary to consider very carefully before accepting an amendment to delete it' (A/C.3/SR.1022, §5).

[43] That the resulting text is not clear either way is amply demonstrated by the divergence of views expressed by two contributors to L. Henkin (ed.), The International Bill of Rights. V. Pechota ('The Development of the Covenant on Civil and Political Rights', p. 32 at p. 59) thought that the Third Committee 'accepted a formula which dodged the issue', whereas K. F. Partsch ('Freedom of Conscience and Expression and Political Freedoms', p. 209 at p. 211) thought 'it clearly implies the right to abandon a religion to which one adhered previously as well as the right to adopt a different religion'. It must be said that it is difficult to reconcile Partsch's view with the drafting history. In support of his proposition he cites (p. 447, n. 10) the views expressed by governmental experts of the Council of Europe (CE/H(70)7, para. 165) but their agreement is hardly surprising.

[44] The Krishnaswami Study (E/CN.4/Sub.2/200/Rev.1) pointed out that 'the consensus of world opinion, as expressed in the UDHR, is unequivocally in favour of permitting an individual not only to maintain but also to change his belief' (p. 25). The Odio Benito Report (paras. 20–21) argued that, despite the differences in wording between the UDHR and the ICCPR (and, indeed, the UN Declaration), 'all meant precisely the same thing', because such a right was 'implicit, . . . regardless of how that concept is presented'. The Human Rights Committee have also understood Article 18 to embrace the right to change one's religion or belief. See below, p. 221.

[45] Partsch, 'Freedom of Conscience', in L. Henkin (ed.), The International Bill of Rights, p. 210 suggests that the wording was sufficiently 'diplomatic' as to embrace all shades of interpretation.

mentioned in the first sentence, they were obviously to be interpreted in the light of the third term, religion. The meaning of the first sentence was, therefore, that everyone should be free to follow his conscience in spiritual matters.'[46] Others argued that 'thought', 'conscience' and 'religion' were separate concepts, each of which was to be accorded equal importance.[47]

The central difficulty concerned the meaning of the word 'religion'. For Saudi Arabia, what distinguished a religion from 'thought' or 'conscience' was its 'dogmatic and relatively stable nature',[48] whilst for others it was the belief in some 'divine ruling power'.[49] Nigeria argued for religion to be defined in such a way as would make it clear that it was more than simply a 'formal way of worship' and, objecting to 'missionaries who held that those whose religion was not based on some holy book had no religion', argued that: 'Every individual should have the right to worship as he saw fit, even if he chose to worship a rock or a river.'[50] In the light of this, others took the view that it was best not to attempt to define the term at all.[51]

The relevance of this is related to the meaning of the word 'belief', another important term that remained undefined. The first phrase of Article 18(1) refers to the freedom of 'thought, conscience and religion'. The second phrase deals with the right to manifest a 'religion or belief'. Since 'belief' was not mentioned in the first phrase, it had to equate with one of the concepts mentioned. Some considered 'belief' to be synonymous with 'thought', which meant that the second phrase of Article 18(1) included the right to manifest non-religious ideas. Others took it to be synonymous with 'religion', thereby excluding the right to manifest non-religious beliefs.

The second viewpoint relates more comfortably to the overall structure both of Article 18 and of the Covenant as a whole. It should be remembered that Article 19 provides for the freedom of expression, which might be considered a more appropriate conceptual vehicle through which to consider the manifestation of non-religious beliefs. Nevertheless, it is

---

[46] A/C.3/SR.1025, §22. For this reason, it was felt that the article 'should consist merely of an enunciation of the right to freedom of religion' (§24). This position was endorsed by Spain (A/C.3/SR.1026, §§2–5).

[47] E.g. Saudi Arabia (A/C.3/SR.1021, §8); Ceylon (A/C.3/SR.1026, §18).

[48] A/C.3/SR.1021, §9.

[49] Cyprus (A/C.3/SR.1025, §30).   [50] Nigeria (A/C.3/SR.1023, §23).

[51] E.g. Uruguay (A/C.3/SR.1023, §24); El Salvador (A/C.3/SR.1024, §15).

symptomatic of the terminological inexactitude that besets this article that, when the Yugoslav delegate asked the representative of the Secretary General whether the term 'belief' had purely religious connotations or whether it included secular convictions,[52] he replied that 'he would not presume to give any personal interpretation to the Committee of the term "belief", or even to indicate what interpretation might currently be held in the secretariat'.[53]

He did, however, point out that the *Krishnaswami Study*, then only recently published, had commented that: 'In view of the difficulty of defining "religion" the term "religion or belief" is used in this study to include, in addition to various theistic creeds, such other beliefs as agnosticism, free thought, atheism and rationalism.'[54] This drew attention to the fact that some non-theistic philosophies could be equated with religious beliefs and treated in a similar fashion. It did not suggest that all forms of 'secular' thoughts were beliefs the manifestation of which were protected. Nor did it say they were not (although it did carry a certain implication to that effect). In short, it simply underlined that not only was the meaning of the term 'belief' not beyond doubt, but that the definition of 'religion' was also a potential source of disagreement.

Discussion centred on the position of atheists. The Soviet delegate argued that atheism was not a religion but was nevertheless within the scope of the article since the term 'belief' had a broad meaning.[55] Those that equated 'belief' with religion denied that atheism was within the scope of the article at all.[56] Although this matter remained unresolved, the general tenor of the discussion leant towards the inclusive interpretation that had received mild endorsement from the Secretariat.[57]

---

[52] A/C.3/SR.1027, §26.

[53] A/C.3/SR.1027, §34.

[54] *Ibid.*, quoting the *Krishnaswami Study*, p. 1, n. 1.

[55] USSR (A/C.3/SR.1025, §55): 'Atheism . . . was an outlook on life which rejected the existence of any supernatural controlling power . . . There was no doubt that it was an outlook which merited respect and protection along with all others.' See also Saudi Arabia (A/C.3/SR.1021, §8); Japan (A/C.3/SR.1026, §23). *Cf.* the position of Cyprus, which took the view that atheism was not a religion but that all three elements had an equal importance (A/C.3/SR.1025, §30).

[56] Argentina (A/C.3/SR.1025, §27); Spain (A/C.3/SR.1026, §2); Venezuela (A/C.3/SR.1026, §14). The Spanish delegate argued that:

> Article 18 was not designed to protect unbelievers or sceptics, who could more properly rely on article 19. Article 18 was not an atheist's manifesto . . . those who renounced their belief or who felt no need for it should not try to distort the meaning of article 18 or to use it in order to try to arrogate to themselves privileges and advantages which the article was not designed to accord them.

[57] The relationship between the definition of 'religion', the relationship of 'religion' to

The emphasis upon the right to change one's religion meant that other questions relating to the manifestation of religion received comparatively little consideration. The original draft Article 16(2) had provided that:

No one shall be denied the freedom, either alone or in association, to manifest his belief in practice, and in worship and observance.

This had been amplified by the addition that 'no one shall be required to do any act which is contrary to such worship and observance'. This was lost when the text of the UDHR was adopted at the Fifth Session of the CHR.[58] The implication is that a person could be required to act in a fashion contrary to the *practice* of the belief, that is, in acting in accordance with the impulses which flowed from the religious convictions that he held. In consequence, the word 'observance' would take on a fairly narrow meaning, closely allied to worship.

On the other hand, the summary of the debates in the CHR record the discussion as being concerned with proposals concerning acts contrary to 'religious observance and practice'.[59] Presumably 'worship' was subsumed within one of these, but it is unclear which. Whilst the division implicit in the original draft was conceptually coherent, the discussion again shows a general confusion between the terms 'practice', 'worship' and 'observance'. The one point that was clear was that the right to manifest a religion did not, even as a matter of definition, preclude the possibility of

---

'belief' and the consequences of them was well put by the delegate of Pakistan (A/C.3/SR.1024, §24):

> there was a distinction between religion and philosophy or ethics. The essence of religion might best be characterized as the human recognition of a superhuman controlling power. Thus atheism, which denied the existence of such a power, and agnosticism, which held that nothing about its attributes or even its existence could be known, were hardly to be regarded as religions, no matter how honestly and sincerely those beliefs might be held. At the same time, if there were beliefs which could not be termed religion, it followed that freedom of religion did not in itself cover freedom to maintain or change such beliefs as atheism or agnosticism. The second sentence of paragraph 1 clearly protected that right for both religion and belief, but the first sentence alone, in her delegation's view, did not.

This suggests that the first sentence – the bare statement of the right – is both passive and static. Any right to change one's religion or belief, however defined, flows from the second sentence. This, of course, was contested by those delegates who thought that the bare freedom of thought, conscience and religion implied the right of change.

[58] Although it was suggested that it be reinserted, France thought 'it might not always be possible to apply such a provision, especially in countries where many different religions were practised'. See A/2929, chapter VI, §117, drawing on E/CN.4/SR.116, p. 19.

[59] *Ibid.*

a person being required to act in a manner that raised conflicts with their faith,[60] irrespective of Article 18(3).

Once again, a text was adopted which successfully circumvented the very real differences that had been revealed. Yet in doing so it shifted ground in an important respect. The very search for a consensus solution to the contentious issues caused the delegates to compromise. In an area concerning fundamental beliefs, compromise relating to the content of the beliefs held was always going to be an impossibility. Consciously or unconsciously, the ground for compromise became the acceptance of diversity and, rather than promote religious freedom, the emphasis shifted towards toleration of religion or belief.[61] Indeed, the unalloyed freedom of religion was, at times, portrayed not as a good that was to be safeguarded but more as a potential evil.[62]

This was encouraged by, and threw into bold relief, the question of change of religion and of proselytism. Toleration and respect would place boundaries upon exercises of religious freedom which imperilled the equivalent rights of others. The application of these principles would be very much within the appreciation of the State concerned. Even here, however, disagreement was already apparent. For Saudi Arabia: 'if the individual was to enjoy true religious freedom, he had to be protected against pressure, proselytism and also against errors and heresies. Men could be induced to change their religion not only for perfectly legitimate intellectual or moral reasons, but also through weakness or credulity.'[63] The role of the State was to ensure that religious freedom could be enjoyed by taking steps to prevent such actions. As the Italian delegate, Mr Capotorti, put it, 'its task was to ensure the possibility of a peaceful rivalry between faiths and respect for the beliefs of others'.[64] In reality,

---

[60] This is again illustrated by the withdrawal by the Philippines of a proposal (E/CN.4/365) that conscientious objectors be exempted from military service. See E/CN.4/SR.161, §57. See also Republic of China (§51); USA (§52); UK (§53); Uruguay (§54); Australia (§55); India (§56).

[61] See, e.g., United Arab Republic (A/C.3/SR.1026, §12): 'the principles underlying article 18 . . . enshrined the spirit of tolerance that was a sign of progress and civilization'.

[62] E.g. Ceylon (A/C.3/SR.1026, §19): whilst admitting that freedom of religion was, along with freedom of thought and conscience, good in itself, the delegate also maintained that 'as soon as a religion became organized and wished to impose itself it perfected techniques which were perhaps more discreet than those employed in the Middle Ages but just as dangerous'.

[63] A/C./SR.1022, §27.

[64] A/C.3/SR.1027, §9. See also Bolivia (A/C.3/SR.1025, §36): 'The freedom of religious sects or communities to practise their religion should not be interpreted as giving them the right to act in a way which was offensive or detrimental to other religious groups'; and the Netherlands (ibid., §41): 'Article 18 also contained a legal check against excessive

the article was being seen not as primarily concerned with the religious freedom of believers, but with maintaining order between those espousing different points of view[65] within the framework of a liberal society.[66]

The subsequent interpretation of Article 18

If the purpose of the Covenant was to lend definition and clarity to the general statement of principles to be found in the UDHR then it cannot be said to have been a success. The Covenant did, however, translate the essence of the UDHR Article 18 into a source of legal obligation. It also established the Human Rights Committee (HRC) as a treaty-monitoring body with power to receive, examine and comment upon reports which States party to the Covenant were obliged to submit and which set out their record of compliance with the obligations assumed.[67] States could also agree to the HRC considering communications concerning their record which had been submitted by other State Parties which had themselves accepted this procedure.[68] Above all, and for those States which accepted it, the First Optional Protocol to the Covenant established a mechanism by which individuals claiming to be victims of a violation of the Covenant could submit a communication to the HRC.

Unfortunately, the HRC's examination of State reports and its consid-

---

manifestations of religious proselytism, in that all attempts on the part of believers and churches alike to promulgate certain religious beliefs were subject to the limitation that they must not encroach upon freedom of thought in any manner contrary to the spirit of the article.'

[65] Cf. Nepal (A/C.3/SR.1023, §4): 'If the article was properly implemented, it should put an end to the persecutions now being carried on in the name of certain ideologies and lead to the peaceful coexistence of all individuals, whatever their convictions or religious beliefs.'

[66] Cf. Liberia (A/C.3/SR.1023, §8): 'The first sentence of paragraph 1 seemed at first sight perfectly clear, but it was open to subjective interpretations. It was intended to proclaim the moral right of the individual to follow his conscience and adopt any religion he saw fit, *but difficulties could arise if the religion he adopted was itself intolerant and opposed to the freedoms laid down in that sentence*' (emphasis added). According to such a view, the content of one's belief was of less importance than the philosophical basis underlying the code by which it was to be protected.

[67] ICCPR, Article 40.

[68] ICCPR, Article 41. The State in relation to which a communication has been submitted can also agree to the establishment of an *ad hoc* Conciliation Commission, to assist in the search for an 'amicable solution' and, if unsuccessful, report on the facts and present its views on the possibility of such a solution ultimately being achieved (Article 42). Neither article has been used.

eration of individual communications has shed little further light on the meaning to be accorded to Article 18. On the other hand, in 1993 the HRC adopted General Comment No. 22(48) which provides an authoritative statement of their understanding of the article.[69] Throughout all its work, however, the HRC fails to distinguish adequately between the right to freedom of thought, conscience and religion and the question of discrimination on these grounds. Once issues primarily (but not exclusively) relating to discrimination and minority rights are stripped away, the relative paucity of the interpretive material relating to Article 18 *per se* is all the more apparent. This would not in itself be a matter for concern if it were not for the tendency to interpret Article 18 from within the framework provided by these other Covenant rights. From the point of view of the State or individual concerned, this may not make any practical difference, since any particular situation is an amalgam of competing and interacting factors. Nevertheless, it once again tends to switch attention away from the search for an autonomous understanding of the content of religious freedom.

For example, after having stressed that Article 18 applies to all forms of belief, religious or otherwise,[70] the General Comment draws the conclusion that:

The Committee *therefore* views with concern any tendency to discriminate against any religion or belief for any reasons, including the fact that they are newly established, or represent religious minorities that may be the subject of hostility by a predominant religious community.[71]

Though doubtless subjects for concern, these questions do not flow from the recognition of the breadth of the concept of 'religion or belief' under the Covenant. Similarly, a number of other matters which are potentially

---

[69] CCPR/C/21/Rev.1/Add.4, adopted on 20 July 1993 (reproduced in *HRLJ* 15 (1994), 233) and see M. Nowak, 'The Activities of the UN Human Rights Committee: Developments from 1 August 1992 through 31 July 1995', *HRLJ* 16 (1995), 377 at pp. 379–380, who described it as a 'far reaching universal interpretation'. M. Nowak, *UN Covenant on Civil and Political Rights: CCPR Commentary* (Kehl am Rhein: N. P. Engel, 1993), pp. 309–334 surveys the work of the HRC relating to Article 18 prior to the drafting of the General Comment. The work of the HRC in its early years (from 1977 to 1979) is surveyed by Partsch, 'Freedom of Conscience', in L. Henkin (ed. ,) *The International Bill of Rights*, pp. 214–216.

[70] See below, pp. 213–214.

[71] General Comment No. 22, para. 2 (emphasis added).

related to the freedom of religion *per se* are seen as raising issues of discrimination, such as education and conscientious objection.[72]

Similarly, the General Comment explicitly points to the potential dangers posed by a State religion in the following terms:

The fact that a religion is recognized as a State religion or that it is established as official or traditional or that its followers comprise the majority of the population, shall not result in any impairment of the enjoyment of any of the rights under the Covenant, including articles 18 and 27 [minority rights], nor in any discrimination against adherents of other religions or non-believers. In particular, certain measures discriminating against the latter, such as measures restricting eligibility for government service to members of the predominant religion or giving economic privileges to them or imposing special restrictions on the practice of other faiths, are not in accordance with the prohibition of discrimination based on religion or belief and the guarantee of equal protection under article 26.[73]

Here the HRC itself recognizes that this is a matter under Article 26, rather than Article 18, and this illustrates the point that much of the work of the HRC in relation to Article 18 says little about its core meaning. In the various comments on State reports, concern is expressed about the prominent position of one form of religious persuasion within

---

[72] See, for example, Mr Opsahl (who noted with respect to the 2nd Periodic Report of Hungary that only some religious groups were exempted from military service and questioned the justification of according differing treatment to individuals with equally serious convictions), *Yb.HRC* 1985/86 I, 493; Mr Cooray (who, with respect to the 2nd Periodic Report of Norway, asked whether conscientious objectors who performed alternative service received the same pay as those performing military service and, if not, how that was reconciled with the right to non-discrimination enshrined in the Covenant), *Yb.HRC* 1988/89 I, 22. See also the concerns expressed with respect to Belgium (*Yb.HRC* 1987/88 I, 208); Portugal (*Yb.HRC* 1989/90 I, 68); Spain (*Yb.HRC* 1990/91 I, 77); Cyprus (*IHRR* 2(1) (1995), 173). *Cf. Brinkhof v. the Netherlands*, Comm. No. 402/1990: Views adopted on 27 July 1993, *IHRR* 1(2) (1994) 92, para. 9.3, where the HRC expressed the view that 'the exemption of only one group of conscientious objectors [Jehovah's Witnesses] and the inapplicability of exemption for all others cannot be considered reasonable'.

[73] General Comment, para. 9 and *cf.* the Concluding Observations of the HRC with respect to the Interim Report of Iran, para. 22, which adopt the wording of the General Comment: 'In that regard, the Committee wishes to emphasize that recognition of a religion as a State religion should not result in any impairment of the enjoyment of any of the rights under the Covenant, including articles 18 and 27, nor in any discrimination against adherents of other religions or non-believers since the right to freedom of religion and belief and the prohibition of discrimination cannot be abrogated by the recognition of an official religion or belief' (*IHRR* 2(1) (1995), 204). It should, however, be noted that the HRC here says that recognition of a State religion 'should' not impair rights, whereas the General Comment says that it 'shall' not. The compatibility of a State Church with Article 18 is not a matter of doubt.

a State and the consequential advantages and privileges, financial and non-financial, that it enjoys.[74] A problem that is closely connected to this concerns the recognition of religions: not only is there the risk of discrimination in giving recognition to some religions and not to others, there is also the risk of discrimination against those individuals that adhere to a non-recognized religion. Paradoxically, these questions, which would appear to be obvious candidates for consideration under Article 26, are often raised under Article 18, thus exacerbating the confusion between them.[75]

What holds for State religions applies equally to State beliefs. The General Comment provides that:

If a set of beliefs is treated as official ideology in constitutions, statutes, proclamations of the ruling parties, etc., or in actual practice, this shall not

[74] See, for example, the comments of Mr Cooray (who, with respect to the 2nd Periodic Report of Sweden, asked whether the apparent advantages and privileges enjoyed by the Church of Sweden did not amount to discrimination), Yb.HRC 1985/86 I, para. 11; Mr Lallah (who enquired whether State funds were made available to religious denominations in Trinidad and Tobago, and to religious educational establishments in Norway, in a non-discriminatory fashion), Yb.HRC 1987/88 I, 37 and Yb.HRC 1988/89 I, 23. General questions concerning the consequences of the pre-eminence of the Roman Catholic Church vis-à-vis other denominations have also been raised. See, for example, the consideration of the Initial Reports of Bolivia (Yb.HRC 1988/89 I, 233, 241) and Argentina (Yb.HRC 1989/90 I, 123); the 3rd Periodic Report of Costa Rica (IHRR 1(3) (1994), 197); and the 2nd Periodic Report of Portugal (Yb.HRC 1989/90 I, 68: in this case the HRC went further and asked the State to comment on the main differences in the status of the Catholic Church and other religious denominations and explain 'How is the right to equal treatment [emphasis added] of the latter ensured?').

[75] In addition to the instances quoted in the previous footnote see also Mrs Higgins (who, with respect to the 2nd Periodic Report of Czechoslovakia, noted that some religions were prohibited, and citizens refused access to certain professions because of their religious convictions, and asked to know the reason for such State interference in religious matters, 'which was incompatible with the provisions of article 18 of the Covenant'), Yb.HRC 1985/86 I, 469; Concluding Observations with respect to the Interim Report of Iran, para. 15 (which expressed the view that 'contrary to the provisions of articles 18 and 19 of the Covenant, members of certain political parties who did not agree with what the authorities believe to be Islamic thinking or who expressed opinions in opposition to official positions have been discriminated against'), IHRR 2(1) (1995), 203. This might be contrasted with the comment of Mr Cooray with respect to the 2nd Periodic Report of Denmark. He noted the king had to be a member of the Evangelical Lutheran Church and 'was not clear how that article could be reconciled . . . with article 18, paragraph 1, or article 26 of the Covenant' (Yb.HRC 1987/88 I, 84). This places the emphasis upon the freedom of thought, conscience and religion of the individual, rather than upon the discriminatory consequence of the restriction. It recognizes the relevance of Article 26 but does not seek to raise the issue of discrimination within the framework of Article 18. See also Mr Cooray, with respect to the 2nd Periodic Report of Norway, Yb.HRC 1988/89 I, 22.

result in any impairment of the freedoms under article 18 or any other rights recognized under the Covenant nor in any discrimination against persons who do not accept the official ideology or who oppose it.[76]

This concern relates back to the consideration of reports from the former communist countries, where there tended to be more freedom to propagate atheist beliefs than religious faith.[77]

Another example is provided by the manner in which the General Comment addresses discrimination against conscientious objectors on the grounds that they did not perform military service, even though they performed alternative service. It provides that:

When [the right of conscientious objection] is recognized by law or practice, there shall be no differentiation among conscientious objectors on the basis of the nature of their particular beliefs; likewise, there shall be no discrimination against conscientious objectors because they have failed to perform military service.[78]

The holistic approach to the enjoyment of the rights provided for in Article 18 is well reflected in paragraph 9 of the General Comment:

The measures contemplated by article 20, paragraph 2, of the Covenant constitute important safeguards against infringements of the rights of religious minorities and of other religious groups to exercise the right guaranteed by articles 18 and 27, and against acts of violence or persecution directed toward those groups. The Committee wishes to be informed of measures taken by States parties concerned to protect the practices of all religions or beliefs from infringement and to protect their followers from discrimination. Similarly, information as to respect for the rights of religious minorities under article 27

---

[76] General Comment, para. 10.

[77] Once again, this was often expressed in terms which emphasized the discriminatory aspects of the situation. See, for example, the comments of Mr Tomuschat (who, with respect to the 2nd Periodic Report of the USSR, noted 'what appeared to be a startling discrepancy between atheism and religious beliefs inasmuch as religious communities apparently did not have the same rights as atheists to engage in propaganda'), Yb.HRC 1985/86 I, 88; Mrs Coté-Harper (who, with respect to the 2nd Periodic Report of the Byelorussian SSR, noted that it 'stated that citizens with atheistic convictions were entitled to express them freely and to conduct propaganda but that it contained no similar statement in regard to the expression of religious convictions'), ibid., 105; Mrs Higgins (who, with respect to the 2nd Periodic Report of Czechoslovakia, noted that 'while it was forbidden to propagate religious faith, atheist propaganda was permitted'), ibid., 469. See also the comment of Mr Wennergren in relation to the 3rd Periodic Report of Finland (who noted that atheist organizations did not have the right to engage in anti-religious propaganda and 'wondered what specific reasons there could be for only atheists to be affected and whether such a provision was compatible with articles 18 and 19 of the Covenant' Yb.HRC 1990/91 I, 52.

[78] General Comment, para. 11.

is necessary for the Committee to assess the extent to which the freedom of thought, conscience, religion and belief has been implemented by States parties. States parties concerned should also include in their reports information relating to practices considered by their laws and jurisprudence to be punishable as blasphemous.

It is worth recalling that this is a General Comment on Article 18 of the Covenant. This section of the Comment suggests that, in terms of practical application, Article 18 is seen as being as much a vehicle for ensuring that the religious dimension of rights provided for elsewhere within the Covenant is raised and adequately addressed, as it is a source of obligation regarding the freedom of thought, conscience and religion. It is, then, not surprising that the work of the HRC has not substantially clarified its meaning. The next section will provide an overview of that which has been achieved.

The key elements

In the abstract, the freedom of conscience, thought and religion is highly valued by the HRC.[79] The General Comment describes it as being

far reaching and profound; it encompasses freedom of thoughts on all matters, personal conviction and the commitment to religion or belief, whether manifested individually or in community with others.[80]

At the same time, and (at least in part) for the reasons given above, little has been said about the key issues relating to the article itself. Answers to questions such as 'what is a religion or belief?', 'what is a manifestation of a religion or belief?' and 'what restrictions on the freedom of conscience, thought and religion are to be allowed?' are left surprisingly opaque. It is somewhat disquieting to find a member of the HRC taking the view that 'everyone was free to interpret article 18 of the Covenant as he wished'.[81] Although firm answers to these questions are not to be expected – nor, indeed, welcome – clearer guidance concerning its parameters, and more pointers to the issues upon which meaningful debate could usefully be focused, might not be an unrealistic expectation.

---

[79] The importance was emphasized by Mr Tomuschat, when he said that 'article 18 of the Covenant was a corner-stone of human dignity, for only if a person enjoyed freedom of conscience could he develop his personality and establish his identity' (*Yb.HRC* 1985/86 I, 88). See also Nowak, *CCPR Commentary*, pp. 309–310.

[80] General Comment, para. 1.

[81] Mr Lallah (comments with respect to the 2nd Periodic Report of Sweden), *Yb.HRC* 1985/ 86 I, 338.

Both the wording of Article 18 and the work of the HRC revolve around three distinct elements: (1) the freedom of conscience, thought and religion (2) the right to manifest one's religion or belief, and (3) the possibility of certain restrictions on these freedoms. Each of these elements raises certain questions: What is a religion or belief? What is a manifestation? What restrictions are possible? These questions will be examined below. In addition, and since it gave rise to so much controversy during the drafting process, the question of the right to change one's religion or belief will also be considered.

The freedom of thought, conscience and religion

The first set of problems relating to Article 18 concerns its scope of application. It should be noted at the outset that members of the HRC have expressed the view that Article 18 dealt with the right of the individual to freedom of thought and religion and 'did not deal with the freedom of churches or religious organizations with which religion could not be identified'.[82] On this basis, it would seem that religious and other organizations are not within the scope of the article. Even if they were,[83] a church or similar organization could not utilize the communications procedure under the First Optional Protocol since this is only open to individuals.[84]

A further question concerns the forms of belief to which it applies. The General Comment provides that:

Article 18 protects theistic, non-theistic and atheistic beliefs, as well as the right not to profess any religion or belief. The terms belief and religion are to be

---

[82] Mr Graefrath (comments with respect to the 2nd Periodic Report of the Ukrainian SSR), *Yb.HRC* 1985/86 I, 266. Hence it did not entail 'any freedom for the churches from domestic law, not to speak of any particular Church' (Mr Graefrath (comments with respect to the 2nd Periodic Report of Czechoslovakia), *ibid.*, 470; also Mr Tomuschat, *ibid.*). See also Mr Opsahl (who noted with respect to the 2nd Periodic Report of Hungary that Article 18 'provides for the rights of individuals and not religious groups'), *ibid.*, 493. This contrasts with the position under the European Convention on Human Rights, for which see below, p. 286.

[83] On the other hand, members of the HRC have themselves acknowledged that measures taken against a Church risked undermining the right of the individual to freedom of religion (see Mr Tomuschat (with respect to the 2nd Periodic Report of Czechoslovakia), *Yb.HRC* 1985/86 I, 470; Mr Opsahl (with respect to the Report of Hungary), *ibid.*, 493. Cf. Nowak, *CCPR Commentary*, p. 658 who takes the view that Article 18 ensures rights to groups of persons.

[84] In *Hartikainen v. Finland*, Comm. No. 40/1978 (Views adopted on 9 April 1981), *SD* I, 74 the General Secretary of the Union of Free Thinkers was not able to submit a communication alleging a violation of Article 18(4) in his official capacity but only as a representative of other individuals.

broadly construed. Article 18 is not limited in its application to traditional religions or to religions and beliefs with institutional characteristics or practices analogous to those of traditional religions.[85]

Although this makes it clear that Article 18 ranges beyond conventional forms of religion and belief, it gives no guidance concerning how broad a construction is to be placed upon them. It is clear that the Comment assumes that traditional religions will have 'institutional characteristics'. It is unclear whether the Comment means that non-traditional religions or beliefs need not possess institutional characteristics or practices *similar* to those of the traditional religions, or whether it means that they need not have any such characteristics at all. The former implies at least a degree of formal organization and structure whereas the latter potentially would embrace the most idiosyncratic of personal patterns of belief. The wording itself leans towards the former view. Yet if this is so, it would exclude well-established forms of belief, such as pacifism, which are not necessarily exercised within an institutional framework, and it is clear that this is not the case.[86] Indeed, atheism would also not be included on this basis, but – as the opening words of this paragraph of the Comment make clear – this is not the case. Adopting the latter view, however, necessitates further refinement.[87]

---

[85] General Comment, para. 2. The emphasis within the HRC upon organized religion contrasts with the view that religious organizations are not themselves capable of enjoying rights under the Covenant. If Article 18 does provide for the rights of individuals and not religious groups it is a little surprising that the only touchstone offered for interpreting its reach draws upon the comparison with the structures of organized religion.

[86] Conscientious objectors are clearly accepted as comprising a category whose beliefs fall within the scope of Article 18, even though this is not necessarily related to a religious belief nor pursued through institutional structures. See, for example, *Muhonen v. Finland*, Comm. No. 89/1981 (Views adopted 8 April 1985), *SD* II, 121, and below, p. 216.

[87] The practice of the HRC does not lend much assistance. Questioning focuses upon organized religions and, when asked about the different religious groups within each country, States' representatives usually respond by giving an account of the most important forms of belief and merely note that other, smaller and unspecified, groups also exist. Since the Committee rarely follows this up, no real light is shed upon the question. It is, however, clear that State practice varies enormously, with the number of recognized religions ranging from single figures to, in the case of Argentina, some 2,730 registered religious organizations (*Yb.HRC* 1989/90 I, 138). In response to a question concerning the scope of its Article 2 of its Organic Law No. 7/1980 on religious freedom, Spain explained that it did not extend to 'groups interested in psychic or parapsychological phenomena, spiritualism or humanism' (*Yb.HRC* 1985/86 I, 169).

Freedom to manifest religion or belief

Whilst Article 18 grants to the individual the freedom to hold patterns of thought, conscience and religion, the right of manifestation is limited to religion or belief. Given that the concept of a religion or belief, for the purposes of the Covenant, remains unclear, it is not possible to consider in a meaningful fashion the question of whether,[88] and how, a distinction should be drawn between, on the one hand, 'religion and belief' and, on the other, 'thought and conscience', the manifestation of which would not be embraced by Article 18.[89] With that proviso, the following sections will give an overview of the meaning placed upon the concept of a 'manifestation'.

What is a manifestation?

The General Comment gives an extensive description of what is meant by the term 'manifestation':

The freedom to manifest religion or belief in worship, observance, practice and teaching encompasses a broad range of acts. The concept of worship extends to ritual and ceremonial acts giving direct expression of belief, as well as various practices integral to such acts, including the building of places of worship, the use of ritual formulae and objects, the display of symbols, and the observance of holidays and days of rest. The observance and practice of religion or belief may include not only ceremonial acts but also such customs as the observance of dietary regulations, the wearing of distinctive clothing or headcoverings, participation in rituals associated with certain stages of life, and the use of a particular language customarily spoken by a group. In addition, the practice and teaching of religion or belief includes acts integral to the conduct by religious groups of their basic affairs, such as, *inter alia*, the freedom to choose

---

[88] The views adopted by the HRC in *MA v. Italy*, Comm. No. 117/1981 (Views adopted on 10 April 1984), *SD* II, 31 suggest that there is a need. The author of the communication argued that his political opinions were violated by his conviction for attempting to re-establish the fascist party in Italy. Although this was submitted under Article 19, the HRC, in finding the restriction upon his right justified under Article 19(3), also observed that Article 18(3) similarly provided a justification. Since Article 18(3) only relates to restrictions upon manifestations of religion or belief, this would suggest that fascist views were to be equated with a 'belief'. If correct, this would dramatically extend the scope of Article 18(1). It would be better to conclude that such political beliefs, though doubtless encompassed by Article 18(1), were not such as to give rise to a right of manifestation at all, not being a 'religion or belief'. Similar problems under the ECHR are considered in chapter 10.

[89] This question will, however, be examined in relation to the European Convention on Human Rights and the conclusions reached would seem to apply with equal force to the Covenant. See below, p. 289.

their religious leaders, priests and teachers, the freedom to establish seminaries or religious schools and the freedom to prepare and distribute religious texts or publications.[90]

Although said to be broad in scope, this is a comparatively restrictive formulation. First, the four forms of manifestation – worship, observance, practice and teaching – provide an exhaustive catalogue. Secondly, and more significantly, the interpretation placed upon those four heads limits their scope to acts closely and directly connected with the formal practice of religious rites and customs. Forms of behaviour and activities which flow from religious convictions are not seen as manifestations of belief. This reflects the practice under the reporting procedure. Although little is said concerning what amounts to a 'manifestation' in the examination of country reports, the little that there is confirms the narrow approach found in the General Comment.[91]

Against this stands the question of conscientious objection and parental rights concerning the religious education of their children, both of which appear to be treated as a form of manifestation and, as such, suggest a broader understanding of the term which embraces activities flowing from, as opposed to directly connected to the practice of, one's religion or belief.

These will be considered in the following sections, which will show that conscientious objection is a *sui generis* issue and that, since religious education is expressly provided for in Article 18(4), neither justifies extending the scope of the term 'manifestation' beyond the limited range outlined in the General Comment.

Conscientious objection

A right to conscientious objection can only be sustained under Article 18 if it is considered to be a form of manifestation of a religion or belief.[92] The General Comment is not clear about this. It provides that:

---

[90] General Comment, para. 4.

[91] As might be expected, States take differing views. For example, the Ukrainian SSR expressed the view that 'literature . . . necessary for . . . services was permitted, but religious associations could not organize libraries because they did not come within the purview of activities which met the needs of believers' (*Yb.HRC* 1985/86 I, 266), whilst the Netherlands expressed the view that: 'The term "manifest" includes not only holding certain religious or ethical beliefs but also acting in accordance with them' (2nd Periodic Report (1988), CCPR/C/42/Add.6, para. 123).

[92] See Partsch, 'Freedom of Conscience', in L. Henkin (ed.), *The International Bill of Rights*, p. 212.

Many individuals have claimed the right to refuse to perform military service (conscientious objection) on the basis that such a right derives from their freedoms under article 18. In response to such claims, a growing number of States have in their laws exempted from compulsory military service citizens who genuinely hold religious or other beliefs that forbid the performance of military service and replaced it with alternative national service. The Covenant does not explicitly refer to a right of conscientious objection, but the Committee believes that such a right can be derived from article 18, in as much as the obligation to use lethal force may seriously conflict with the freedom of conscience and the right to manifest one's religion or belief. When this right is recognized by law or practice, there shall be no differentiation among conscientious objectors on the basis of the nature of their particular beliefs; likewise, there shall be no discrimination against conscientious objectors because they have failed to perform military service. The Committee invites States parties to report on the conditions under which persons can be exempted from military service on the basis of their rights under article 19 and on the nature and length of alternative national service.[93]

At first sight, it seems to acknowledge a right of conscientious objection without hesitation. However, the subsequent use of the phrase 'when this right is recognized by law or practice' suggests that the right does not automatically follow from the right to manifest religion or belief. The HRC has expressed concern in cases where there was a lack of provision for conscientious objection,[94] and raised issues of discrimination regarding conscientious objectors in the context of Article 18.[95]

Whilst this suggests some recognition of the right, it has been tentative in its practice under the Optional Protocol. After having found it unnecessary to answer the question in *Muhonen v. Finland*,[96] the HRC endorsed the view that the Covenant did not provide the right of conscientious objection in *LTK v. Finland*, saying: 'The Covenant does not provide for the right to conscientious objection; neither article 18 nor article 19 of the

---

[93] General Comment, para. 11.

[94] See, for example, Mr Prado Vallejo (who, with respect to the 2nd Periodic Report of Finland, asked what was being done to respect the wishes of those who were prepared to perform substitute civilian service), *Yb.HRC* 1986/86 I, 361; Mr Aguilar Urbina (who, with respect to the Initial Report of St Vincent and the Grenadines and in the context of Article 18, asked for information regarding protection of conscientious objectors), *Yb.HRC* 1989/90 I, 129); Concluding Observations with respect to the 2nd Periodic Report of the Libyan Arab Jamahiriya, para. 13, *IHRR* 2 (1995), 438. However, this was not a unanimous view even at the time. See, for example, Mr Opsahl, who, whilst accepting that this was the generally accepted interpretation, noted that 'many held the contrary view' (*Yb.HRC* 1985/86 I, 361, 493).

[95] See n. 72 above.

[96] Comm. No. 89/1981 (Views adopted on 8 April 1985), *SD* II, 121, para. 3.

Covenant, especially taking into account paragraph 3(c)(ii) of article 8,[97] can be construed as implying that right.'[98]

However, although it has maintained this position,[99] in *JP v. Canada*, and whilst holding that 'the refusal to pay taxes on grounds of conscientious objection clearly falls outside the scope of the protection of this article', the HRC expressed the view that 'Article 18 . . . certainly protects the right to hold, express and disseminate opinions and convictions, including conscientious objection to military activities and expenditures.'[100] This does not go so far as to say that individuals have the right to manifest their conscientious objection to military service by abstaining from it but it lends further credence to the claim.[101]

---

[97] Article 8 (3) provides:

   3. (a) No one shall be forced to perform forced or compulsory labour.

      (b) . . .

      (c) For the purpose of this paragraph, the term, forced or compulsory labour shall not include:

         (i) . . .

         (ii) any service of a military character and, in countries where conscientious objection is recognized, any national service required by law of conscientious objectors.

[98] Comm. No. 185/1984 (Decision of 9 July 1985), *SD* II, 61, para. 5.2.

[99] See *RTZ v. the Netherlands*, Comm. No. 245/1987 (Decision of 5 November 1987), *SD* II, 73, para. 3.2; *MJG v. the Netherlands*, Comm. No. 267/1987 (Decision of 24 March 1988), *SD* II, 74, para. 3.2; *Järvinen v. Finland*, Comm. No. 295/1988 (Decision of 25 July 1990), *HRLJ* 11 (1990), 324, para. 6.1; *CBD v. the Netherlands*, Comm. No. 394/1990 (Decision of 22 July 1992), A/47/140, Annex (P), para. 6.3; *JPK v. the Netherlands*, Comm. No. 401/1990 (Decision of 7 November 1991), A/47/40, Annex (T), para. 6.5. See also *Brinkhof v. the Netherlands*, Comm. No. 402/1990 (Views adopted on 27 July 1993), *IHRR* 1(2) (1994), 92, para. 6.2, in which the HRC recalled its refusal to declare admissible the claim that, because the author would be required to participate in plans which envisaged the use of nuclear weapons, he was being required to conspire in plans to commit crimes against humanity, illegal under international law, and hence his domestic conviction breached Articles 6 and 7 of the Covenant. This line of reasoning was again rejected by the HRC in *ARU v. the Netherlands*, Comm. No. 509/1992 (Decision of 19 October 1993), *IHRR* 1(2) (1994), 55.

[100] *JP v. Canada*, Comm. No. 446/1991 (Decision of 7 November 1992), A/47/40, Annex X, sect. Y, para. 4.2. This was endorsed by the HRC in *JvK and CMGvK-S v. the Netherlands*, Comm. No. 483/1991 (Decision of 23 July 1992), A/47/40, Annex X, sect. cc, para. 4.2 and *KV and CV v. Germany*, Comm. No. 568/1993 (Decision of 8 April 1994), *IHRR* 1(3) (1994), 54, para. 4.3.

[101] But *cf.* Nowak, *CCPR Commentary*, p. 324 who paraphrases this as having stated 'that "conscientious objection to military activities and expenditures" was "certainly" protected by Article 18'. This seems to read a little too much into the comment. See also the Individual Opinion of Mr Wennergren in *Järvinen v. Finland*, Comm. No. 295/ 1988 (Decision of 25 July 1990), *HRLJ* 11 (1990), 324 which also supports this view. See also Nowak, 'The Activities of the UN Human Rights Committee: Developments from 1 August 1992 through 31 July 1995', 379 who characterizes the General Comment as

The Commission on Human Rights has also hesitated. In Resolution 1995/83 it drew attention to 'the right of everyone to have conscientious objections to military service as a legitimate exercise of the right to freedom of thought, conscience and religion as laid down in Article 18 of the Universal Declaration of Human Rights as well as Article 18 of the International Covenant on Civil and Political Rights'.[102] This stops short of declaring that those who do have such objections have the right to be exempted from compulsory military service, and this is reinforced by the Resolution 'appealing' to States to enact legislation to this effect.[103]

Even if conscientious objection is recognized as a right under the Covenant, this should not be taken as having any impact upon an understanding of the general right to manifest a religion or belief. The General Comment argues that conscientious objection is linked to Article 18 by the need to respect the right of an individual not to be forced to use lethal weapons. If of general application, such a principle would allow an individual to argue that any form of activity that required him to act in a fashion contrary to his religion or belief would result in a violation of Article 18. This is clearly at odds with the understanding of the right of manifestation as set out in the General Comment and leads to the conclusion that, to the extent that the HRC has come to acknowledge a right of conscientious objection under the Covenant, this is of a *sui generis* nature and does not impact upon the broader issues under Article 18.

Education

Although worded in a separate section, the freedom of parents to ensure that the religious education of their children is in accord with their own convictions can be seen as a specific form of manifestation. The General Comment links Article 18(4) with the freedom of manifestation under Article 18(1):

The Committee is of the view that article 18(4) permits public school instruction in subjects such as the general history of religions and ethics if it is given in a neutral and objective way. The liberty of parents or legal guardians to ensure that their children receive a religious and moral education in conformity with

'a modern approach departing from its earlier jurisprudence on individual communications'.

[102] See also CHR Res. 1987/46, 1989/59 and 1993/84, the Reports by Mr Eide and Mr Mubanga-Chipoya (E/CN.4/Sub.2/1983/30) and of the Secretary-General (E/CN.4/1985/25; E/CN.4/1989/30; E/CN.4/1991/64; E/CN.4/1993/68 and E/CN.4/1995/99).

[103] But *cf*. Nowak, *CCPR Commentary*, p. 323 (n. 70), who described CHR Res. 1993/84 (which used identical language) as 'the definitive recognition of the right to conscientious objection by the Commission on Human Rights'.

their own convictions, set forth in article 18(4), is related to the guarantees of the freedom to teach a religion or belief stated in article 18(1). The Committee notes that public education that includes instruction in a particular religion or belief is inconsistent with article 18(4) unless provision is made for non-discriminatory exemptions or alternatives that would accommodate the wishes of parents and guardians.[104]

This suggests that Article 18(4) is considered as a specific application of the principle of manifestation found in Article 18(1). This, however, would be at odds with the drafting history[105] and would fail to recognize that the close connection between the freedom to teach under Article 18(1) and the duty to respect parental wishes under Article 18(4) has caused confusion. Parental rights under Article 18(4) are not to be equated with the freedom to manifest one's religion or belief in teaching. There is a very obvious difference between giving and receiving.[106] Even if it were to be taken as a form of manifestation under Article 18(1), the very limited nature of the parental right[107] would make this a very weak base upon which to mount an argument for the recognition of a more expansive freedom of manifestation.

---

[104] General Comment, para. 6. See also, for example, Mrs Coté-Harper (who, with respect to the 2nd Periodic Report of the USSR, observed that since parents could not receive religious instruction in an institution, 'Soviet law seemed to be in violation of article 18, paragraph 1, of the Covenant which provided for the right to manifest one's religion'), Yb.HRC 1985/86 I, 88 (emphasis added).

[105] See above, pp. 200–201.

[106] This confusion has also operated in the other direction and the freedom to manifest religion or belief in teaching has been seen as a breach of Article 18(4). See, for example, Mr Tomuschat (who, with respect to the 2nd Periodic Report of the Byelorussian SSR, considered that 'if . . . no one was allowed to teach religion to children other than his own children, that constituted a restriction that could hardly be reconciled with article 18, paragraph 4, of the Covenant'), Yb.HRC 85/86 I, 100.

[107] There is no positive right to have a child educated in the tenets of a particular religion or belief. Education which includes religious instruction is permitted as long as provisions are made for those who do not want to be instructed. Moreover, Article 18(4) does not preclude a child being exposed to general education about various forms of religion or belief, provided that it is given in a neutral way. See, for example, Hartikainen v. Finland, Comm. No. 40/1978 (Views adopted 9 April 1981), SD I, 74 and Nowak, CCPR Commentary, pp. 330–334. The position under the ECHR is considered in chapter 11. There is also the intractable problem of reconciling the wishes of the parent with the right of the child. This may lie behind the comment of the Committee with respect to the 3rd Periodic Report of Norway, para. 10, when it observed 'that article 2 of the Constitution which provides that individuals professing the Evangelical–Lutheran religion are bound to bring up their children in the same faith is in clear contradiction with article 18 of the Convention, (IHRR 1(2) (1994), 273). Alternatively, the Committee might have been so scrupulous as to ensure that parents were free to bring up their children in a manner not in accordance with their own beliefs, a rather bizarre position.

Is there a right to change one's religion?

The *travaux préparatoires* of Article 18 showed that there was no consensus on the existence of a right to change one's religion. The General Comment, however, asserts that

the freedom 'to have or to adopt' a religion or belief necessarily entails the freedom to choose a religion or belief, including, *inter alia*, the right to replace one's current religion or belief with another or to adopt atheistic views, as well as the right to retain one's religion or belief.[108]

Although this view is widely held[109] and often expressed within the HRC,[110] there cannot be said to be a consensus, with Muslim countries continuing to express their dissent.[111]

Restrictions upon the scope of Article 18(1)

Article 18(1) distinguishes between, on the one hand, the freedom of thought, conscience and religion and, on the other, the freedom to manifest a religion or belief. It is only the freedom of manifestation which is subject to the restrictions set out in Article 18(3). Since Article 4(2) includes Article 18 amongst those articles of the Covenant which cannot be subject to derogation in times of public emergency, the freedom of thought, conscience and religion is absolute, as are also the freedoms set out in Article 18(2) and (4).[112]

---

[108] General Comment, para. 5.   [109] See above, pp. 201–202, and n. 44.

[110] See, for example, Mr Mommersteeg (who, with respect to the 2nd Periodic Report of Tunisia, asked whether freedom of religion included the right to change one's religion, even if it were Islam), Yb.HRC 1987 I, 50); the Concluding Observations of the HRC with respect to the 2nd Periodic Report of the Libyan Arab Jamahiriya, para. 13 (which noted the existence of 'Severe punishments for heresy . . . and the restrictions on the right to change one's religion'), IHRR 2(2) (1995), 438, and with respect to the 3rd Periodic Report of Morocco, para. 14 (which expressed concern 'at the impediment placed upon the freedom to change one's religion'), *ibid.*, 441; the Concluding Observations of the HRC with respect to the Interim Report of Iran, para. 16 (in which it expressed 'concern at the extent of the limitations and restrictions on the freedom of religion and belief, noting that conversion from Islam is punishable and that even followers of the three recognized religions are facing serious difficulties in the enjoyment of their rights under article 18 of the Covenant'), IHRR 2 (1995), 203.

[111] See previous note and *cf.* the Sudanese justification for the retention of the death penalty for apostasy (Yb.HRC 1990/91 I, 291–292 and see also below, p. 256, in the context of the work of the UN Special Rapporteur).

[112] See General Comment, paras. 3 and 8. Para. 1 of the General Comment says that its non-derogable nature reflects 'the fundamental character of these freedoms'. Whilst this may be true of the freedom of thought, conscience and religion in Article 18(1) and the freedom from coercion in Article 18(2), it is more difficult to discern the fundamental nature of the parental freedoms set out in Article 18(4). It is noticeable

The consequence of this is that actions which are directed towards pressurizing individuals to change or abandon their religion or belief[113] are always in violation of the Covenant, since, as the General Comment explains:

Article 18(2) bars coercions that would impair the right to have or adopt a religion or belief, including the use or threat of physical force or penal sanctions to compel believers or non-believers to adhere to their religious beliefs and congregations to recant their religion or belief or to convert. Policies or practices having the same intention or effect, such as for example those restricting access to education, medical care, employment or the rights guaranteed by article 25 and other provisions of the Covenant are similarly inconsistent with article 18(2). The same protection is enjoyed by holders of all beliefs of a non-religious nature.[114]

Paragraph 3 of the General Comment goes even further and expresses the view that:

In accordance with articles 18(2) and 17, no one can be compelled to reveal his thoughts or adherence to a religion or belief.[115]

Article 18(3) provides that:

Freedom to manifest one's religion or beliefs may be subject only to such limitations as are prescribed by law and are necessary to protect public safety, order, health, or morals or the fundamental rights and freedoms of others.

This catalogue differs from others within the Covenant. In some respects it is broader than that found in other articles. For example, Articles 21

that the General Comment refers to Article 18(4) in para. 8 as being beyond the scope of Article 18(3) but does not mention it in para. 3, where the non-derogable nature of Article 18(1) and (2) is considered. See also Partsch, 'Freedom of Conscience', in Henkin (ed.), *The International Bill of Rights*, p. 212. *Cf.* the examination of the Initial Report of Zaire which questioned the meaning of the parents' right to place children in institutions, and provide them with the intellectual, moral and religious education of their choice, 'under the supervision and with the help of the People's Movement for the Revolution'. The legitimacy of a restriction was not itself raised (*Yb.HRC* 1987 I, 110).

[113] But see n. 115 below.   [114] General Comment, para. 5.

[115] All of this assumes, however, that the term 'belief' in Article 18(2) is co-extensive with 'thought and conscience' in Article 18(1). If it were to be accorded a narrower meaning, akin to religion, then forms of activity that would otherwise be prohibited by Article 18(2) might become possible, since they would not deny the right of thought or conscience but place a greater price upon holding to it. For example, would it violate Article 18(1) and (2) if political prisoners were required to recant before release? There would certainly be coercion in relation to 'thought and conscience' but not necessarily 'religion or belief'. See, for example, the examination of the Report of Korea (*Report of the HRC* (A/47/40), para. 484). There would, of course, be a separate issue under Article 19 of the Covenant.

(the right of peaceful assembly) and 22 (the right to freedom of association) require that restrictions be 'necessary in a democratic society'. In
addition, it is not entirely clear whether 'public' qualifies 'order', 'health'
and 'morals', although the better view is that it does.[116] On the other
hand, the grounds of lawful restriction are considerably more limited
than in other articles. Article 18(3) does not include restrictions necessary
for the protection of 'public order (*ordre public*)' and 'national security'.[117]
Moreover, and unlike other Covenant provisions, limitations under
Article 18 are only permissible if they are to protect the 'fundamental'
rights and freedoms of others. One consequence of these differences is
that care is needed when practice relating to other Covenant articles is
considered in the context of Article 18.

The General Comment expands upon Article 18(3) at some length and
explains that:

> In interpreting the scope of permissible limitation clauses, States parties should
> proceed from the need to protect the rights guaranteed under the Covenant,
> including the right to equality and non-discrimination on all grounds specified
> in articles 2, 3 and 26. Limitations imposed must be established by law and must
> not be applied in a manner that would vitiate the rights guaranteed in article
> 18. The Committee observes that paragraph 3 of article 18 is to be strictly
> interpreted: restrictions are not allowed on grounds not specified there, even if
> they would be allowed as restrictions to other rights protected in the Covenant,
> such as national security. Limitations may be applied only for those purposes
> for which they are prescribed and must be directly related and proportionate to
> the specific need on which they are predicated. Restrictions may not be imposed
> for discriminatory purposes or applied in a discriminatory manner. The Com-
> mittee observes that the concept of morals derives from many social, philoso-
> phical and religious traditions; consequently, limitations on the freedom to
> manifest a religion or belief for the purpose of protecting morals must be based
> on principles not deriving exclusively from a single tradition. Persons already
> subject to certain legitimate constraints, such as prisoners, continue to enjoy
> their right to manifest their religion or belief to the fullest extent compatible
> with the specific nature of the constraint. States parties' reports should provide
> information on the full scope and effects of limitations under article 18(3), both
> as a matter of law and of their application in specific circumstances.[118]

This, then, provides the framework within which each situation is to be
assessed. As the application of these principles will depend upon the facts,

---

[116] For a full examination of these issues and of the interpretation of and practice under
Article 18(3), see Nowak, *CCPR Commentary*, pp. 324–329.
[117] Found in Articles 12 (liberty of movement), 14 (press exclusion for court proceedings),
19 (freedom of opinion and expression), 21 and 22.
[118] General Comment, para. 8.

and as the number of instances in which it has been called upon to determine issues under Article 18(3) are comparatively few, it is difficult to distil much further guidance from the work of the HRC with safety. It is, however, clear that restrictions must fall within the prescribed heads of limitation if they are to be acceptable.[119] Beyond this, it is worth concluding by presenting a number of examples of individual communications in which the HRC has considered Article 18(3).

In *Singh Bhinder v. Canada*[120] the author claimed to be a victim of a violation of Article 18 in that, as a Sikh, his religion required him to wear a turban and his refusal to wear protective headgear at work, as demanded by Canadian law, had resulted in the termination of his contract of employment. The HRC was of the view that, 'If the requirement that a hard hat be worn is regarded as raising issues under article 18, then it is a limitation that is justified by reference to the grounds laid down in article 18, paragraph 3.'[121] It is clear that the State is entitled to enforce paternalistic legislation aimed at ensuring health and

---

[119] See, for example, Mr Cooray (who, with respect to the 2nd Periodic Report of Sweden, considered that legislative provisions which prohibited the practice of a religion if it caused public indignation, 'paved the way for abuses and imposed restrictions that went far beyond those referred to in article 18, paragraph 3, of the Covenant'), *Yb.HRC* 1985/86 I, 337; Mr Errera (who, with respect to the 2nd Periodic Report of Czechoslovakia, questioned the requirement that only priests who were 'politically worthy of confidence' could engage in religious activities), *ibid.*, 469; Mr Tomuschat (who, with respect to the 2nd Periodic Report of Czechoslovakia, questioned whether 'narrow and strict State control over the Church . . . was in keeping with the provisions of article 18, paragraph 3'), *ibid.*, 470; Mr Wennergren (who, with respect to the Initial Report of Belgium, took the view that taking account of the fact that salaries and pensions of ministers of religion were paid by the State when considering whether to recognize a religious denomination would not be in accordance with Article 18(3)), *Yb.HRC* 1987/88 I, 209; Mr Tomuschat (who, with respect to the 2nd Periodic Report of the USSR, considered that restrictions on persons under eighteen years of age becoming members of a religious community could not be justified), *Yb.HRC* 1985/86 I, 89. See also Partsch, 'Freedom of Conscience', in Henkin (ed.), *The International Bill of Rights*, p. 215.

[120] Comm. No. 208/1986 (Views adopted on 9 November 1989). See *14 Annual Report of the HRC*, A/45/50, 1990, vol. II, Annex E; *Yb.HRC* 1989/90 II, p. 398.

[121] *Ibid.*, para. 6.2. The HRC also examined the matter in relation to Article 26 (non-discrimination). Although recognizing that it was dealing with legislation which, on the face of it, was neutral but was 'said to operate in fact in a way that discriminates against persons of the Sikh religion', it thought that 'legislation requiring the workers in federal employment be protected from injury . . . by the wearing of hard hats is to be regarded as reasonable and directed towards the objective purposes that are compatible with the Covenant, (paras. 6.1, 6.2). For similar practice under the ECHR, see below, p. 325, n. 39.

safety.[122] The HRC has taken a similarly broad view of what constitutes public order. In *Coeriel and Aurik v. the Netherlands* it expressed the view that: 'With regard to the authors' claim under article 18 of the Covenant the Committee considered that the regulation of surnames and the change thereof was eminently a matter of public order and restrictions were therefore permissible under paragraph 3 of article 18.'[123] This suggests that whilst the Committee is keen to ensure that limitations fall within the permitted heads of restriction, those heads are of considerable latitude.

The HRC has also expressed the view that the State is not in breach of its obligations under Article 18 if religious authorities are permitted to take actions which have the effect of denying an individual the freedom of manifestation.[124] Indeed, to do otherwise would be to invite the State to interfere with the management of religious organizations which would itself raise issues under the Covenant.[125]

Restrictions on propaganda and advocacy of hatred

By way of conclusion, it should be noted that Article 20 of the Covenant requires a State to place some limitations upon the manifestation of religion or belief.[126] Article 20 provides:

1. Any propaganda for war shall be prohibited by law.
2. Any advocacy of national, racial or religious hatred that constitutes incitement to hostility or violence shall be prohibited by law.

---

[122] The actual head under which the restriction was justified was not specified. The author had argued that the only risk involved was to himself. Since the relevant heads of restriction relate to 'public' safety and (probably) public health then, if this was indeed the case, it should have had some weight. Equally, although the employer would be bearing a greater risk of having to pay compensation for injuries received, this would not seem to amount to a protection of a 'fundamental' right of others.

[123] Comm. No. 453/1991 (Views adopted on 31 October 1994), *IHRR* 2(2) (1995), 297, para. 6.1.

[124] See *W. Delgardo Páez v. Colombia*, Comm. No. 195/1985 (Views adopted on 12 July 1990), *HRLJ* 11 (1990), 313, para. 5.7: 'The Committee finds . . . that Colombia may, without violating this provision of the Covenant, allow the Church authorities to decide who may teach religion and in what manner it should be taught.' *A fortiori*, in *Coeriel and Aurik v. the Netherlands*, Comm. No. 453/1991 (Views adopted on 31 October 1994), *IHRR* 2(2) (1995), 297, para. 6.1: 'The Committee, moreover, considered that the State party could not be held accountable for restrictions placed upon the exercise of religious offices by religious leaders in another country.'

[125] For similar decisions under the ECHR see below, p. 300.

[126] See General Comment, para. 7, which refers to General Comment No. 11/19 of 29 July 1983 concerning Article 20. The inclusion of Article 20 within the Covenant was controversial and has been the subject of sixteen reservations. See Nowak, *CCPR Commentary*, pp. 359–369.

Naturally, restrictions necessary to achieve these purposes would find a justification under Article 18(3). The difference lies in the obligatory nature of such measures.[127]

---

[127] There is, however, a question over whether a State is entitled to take measures with reference to Article 20 which go beyond those justifiable under the derogation clauses attached to each of the articles. In *JRT and the WG Party v. Canada*, Comm. No. 104/1981 (Decision of 6 April 1983), *SD* II, 25 it was claimed that Canada had infringed Article 19 of the Covenant by preventing members of the Western Guard Party from using the telephone network to disseminate anti-Jewish views. Rather than consider whether this restriction upon their freedom of expression was justified by reference to Article 19(3), the HRC decided that the obligation placed upon the State by Article 20 rendered the communication inadmissible *ratione materiae*. This suggests that Article 20 does more than merely require States to take measures which would otherwise be optional under the derogation clauses. If correct, this would legitimate – indeed, obligate – measures in respect of those elements of the Covenant articles, including Article 18(1), (2) and (4) which are non-derogable under Article 4(2). This might be an attractive interpretation, since it would, for example, prevent parents from using Article 18(4) (if it is, in fact, non-derogable: see n. 112 above) to seek to have their children educated in forms of religion which advocated war or racial hatred. On the other hand, it would also allow States to take measures stricter than those which were strictly necessary in respect of such activities. The general effect of the reservations to this article noted in the preceding footnote is to ensure that the obligation to enact legislation does indeed conform to the restrictions set out in various articles. However, whilst all require conformity with Article 19(3), only the reservations of Belgium and Luxembourg require conformity with Article 18(3).

9 The 1981 Declaration on the Elimination of All Forms of Intolerance and of Discrimination Based on Religion or Belief

The background to the Declaration

In 1956 the Sub-Commission on Prevention of Discrimination and Protection of Minorities decided to undertake a study of discrimination in the matter of religious rights and practices and appointed a Special Rapporteur, Mr Arcot Krishnaswami, to undertake this task.[1] His report, entitled, 'Study of Discrimination in the Matter of Religious Rights and Practices' was finally submitted to the CHR in 1960, after having been revised in the light of comments from States and within the Sub-Commission. Although the opening words of the Study refer to 'religions and beliefs',[2] its title accurately reflects the fact that its prime concern was with religion. However, it went beyond the question of discrimination and considered what was meant by freedom of religion or belief,[3] as found in the UDHR,[4]

---

[1] This followed the completion of a first study into discrimination in education. Such a study had first been suggested in 1953. For the background to, and methodology of, the study see the summary prepared by the Secretariat and included as Annex II to the version of the Study (E/CN.4/Sub.2/200/Rev.1; hereafter, *Krishnaswami Study*) published by the UN in 1960. Although not mentioned in the Secretariat summary, the origins of the Report lay in the initiatives of a Jewish organization. See N. Lerner, 'Toward a Draft Declaration against Religious Intolerance and Discrimination', *Is.YHR* 11 (1981), 82 at 83.

[2] Confusingly, the footnote on p. 1 observes that: 'In view of the difficulty of defining religion, the term "religion *or* belief " is used in this study to include, in addition to various theistic creeds, such other beliefs as agnosticism, free thought, atheism and rationalism' (emphasis added). Given that the text refers to 'religion *and* beliefs' this carries the implication that the forms of belief mentioned are being equated with religion, a subtle difference but a matter which had already aroused controversy and which dogged all discussion within the UN on these questions.

[3] Although often mentioned in those sections examining the evolution of international concern, issues relating to 'thought and conscience' were outside the scope of the Study.

[4] It should be recalled that at this time Article 18 of the ICCPR had not been finalized.

227

and concluded with a series of 'basic rules' which elaborated upon the meaning of Article 18 of the UDHR in the light of the State practice submitted.[5] The Sub-Commission examined these rules and produced its own 'Draft Principles on Freedom and Non-Discrimination in the Matter of Religious Rights and Freedoms', the title of which clearly indicated this dual purpose, and which were transmitted to the CHR along with the *Krishnaswami Study*. The CHR began a detailed examination of the Draft Principles at its Eighteenth Session (1962)[6] and intended to continue this the following year. However, this was overtaken by events.

Mounting Third World pressure against apartheid in South Africa culminated in the General Assembly requesting in 1962 that the CHR prepare a declaration and convention on the Elimination of All Forms of Racial Discrimination.[7] At the same time, and very much as a 'quid pro quo', the General Assembly also asked the CHR to prepare drafts of a declaration and a convention on the elimination of religious intolerance.[8] An ambitious timetable was set: drafts of the declarations were to be submitted to the General Assembly in 1963 and drafts of the conventions in 1964, if possible, but no later than 1965. Inevitably, the instruments concerned with racial discrimination took priority and the Declaration on the Elimination of All Forms of Racial Discrimination was duly presented to, and adopted by, the General Assembly in 1963[9] and the Convention in 1965.[10]

It was not until its Twentieth Session in 1964 that the CHR began its

---

[5] Since States had been asked to submit information not only on matters concerned with discrimination but with the substance of the right to freedom of religion – and in particular the right to change and to manifest one's religion or beliefs – this result was not surprising.

[6] See Report of the CHR, 18 Session, 1962, E/CN.4/832/Rev.1, paras. 100–157.

[7] GA Res. 1780 (XVII), 7 December 1962.

[8] GA Res. 1781 (XVII), 7 December 1962. *Cf.* Lerner, 'Toward a Draft Declaration against Religious Intolerance and Discrimination', pp. 84–86 who points out the relevance of concern about increasing incidents of anti-Semitism as a factor in the genesis of the decision to proceed with the Declaration and the reluctance of the Socialist and Arab States to have religious liberty and anti-Semitism examined alongside racial discrimination. See also M. Laligant, 'Le project de Convention des Nations Unies sur l'élimination de toutes les forms d'intolérance religieuse', *Revue Belge de Droit International* 5 (1969), 175.

[9] See GA Res. 1904 (XVIII), 20 November 1963.

[10] See GA Res. 2106 A (XX) of 21 December 1965; 660 UNTS 195. The Convention was opened for signature in March 1966. The drafting of this Convention is examined by E. Schwleb, 'The International Convention on the Elimination of all forms of Racial Discrimination', *ICLQ* 15 (1966), 996. See generally N. Lerner, *The UN Convention on the Elimination of all Forms of Racial Discrimination*, 2nd edn (Alphen aan den Rijn, The Netherlands: Sijthoff & Noordhoff, 1980).

work on the draft instruments concerning the elimination of religious intolerance. During its nineteenth Session in 1963 the CHR had, however, requested the Sub-Commission on the Prevention of Discrimination and Protection of Minorities to prepare a draft declaration and this formed the basis of discussion the following year.[11] The CHR was unable to complete its examination of this draft at its Twentieth Session but, rather than continue with it at the following session, it decided to turn to the Draft Convention and, once again, requested the Sub-Commission to prepare a draft.[12] This decision was endorsed by the General Assembly, which expressed the hope that it could receive the final draft of a convention in order that it might be adopted and opened for signature 'before 1968'.[13] The CHR worked on the Convention during its Twenty-Second and Twenty-Third Sessions (1966 and 1967) but was only able to finalize twelve draft articles[14] which were considered that year by the Third Committee of the General Assembly. In consequence, the draft of the Convention was prepared before the Declaration, an odd procedure which did nothing to improve its chances of being adopted. The Preamble and Article 1 of the Draft Convention were approved by the Third Committee in 1967[15] but since then no further progress has been made towards its completion.[16]

With progress on the Covenant stalled, attention shifted back to the Declaration and, following the adoption of GA Res. 3027 (XXVII) of 1972 and 3069 (XXVIII) of 1973, in which the General Assembly asked the CHR to give the Declaration priority over the Convention, the CHR resumed work upon it at its Thirtieth Session in 1974. The Declaration, now entitled the 'Declaration on the Elimination of All Forms of Intolerance

[11] See CHR Res. 10 (XIX). The Draft Declaration prepared by the Sub-Commission is found in Report of the CHR, 19 Session, 1963, E/CN.4/873, chapter III.
[12] CHR Res. 2 (XX). The draft prepared by the Sub-Commission is found in E/CN.4/882 and Corr.1, para. 321; Res. 1 (XVII), Annex. It is also set out in the presentation of the discussions on the Draft Convention in the Report of the CHR, 21st Session, E/CN.4/891 (E/4024), para. 326.
[13] GA Res. 2081 (XX).
[14] See Report of the CHR, 22nd Session, 1966, E/CN.4/916 (E/4184) chapter II; Report of the CHR, 23rd Session, 1967, E/CN.4/940 (E/4322) chapter II and CHR Res. 3 (XXIII), Annex A of which contains the twelve Draft Articles upon which agreement had been reached.
[15] For a detailed examination of the work on the draft Convention see J. Claydon, 'The Treaty Protection of Religious Rights: UN Draft Convention on the Elimination of All Forms of Intolerance and of Discrimination based on Religion or Belief', *Santa Clara Lawyer* 12 (1972), 403; H. Jack, '58 Words, Two Commas: Snail-like Motion Toward a UN Declaration for Religious Freedom' (1976), reprinted in R. Woito (ed.), *International Human Rights Kit* (Berkeley, CA: World Without War Council, 1977), p. 154.
[16] Nor is there any likelihood of any progress in the near future. See below, p. 257.

and of Discrimination Based on Religion or Belief '[17] was finally adopted without a vote in GA Res. 36/55 of 25 November 1981.

Given that nearly thirty years have passed since they were last considered, and that they have not yet passed into a finalized convention text, it would be imprudent to dwell at length upon the work surrounding the Draft Convention. The Declaration is of much greater importance but it is not, in itself, a direct source of legal obligation and, as will be evident from the examination conducted below, its drafting was heavily influenced by cold war pressures and prejudices, as well as – in its last phase – the first stirring of emergent Islamic fundamentalism. Moreover, it must be remembered that the primary purpose of the Declaration and Convention was to eliminate intolerance and discrimination. Indeed, they were not intended to promote religious freedom as such, and were aimed at intolerance and discrimination not only against but by the religious and the non-religious on account of their beliefs. To that extent, they have more to do with the question of non-discrimination than with freedom of religion *per se*[18] – and given that their origins lie alongside the Declaration and Convention on the Elimination of All Forms of Racial Discrimination, this is hardly surprising.

The emphasis upon discrimination has had its inevitable effect of distorting the perception of religious freedom in much the same way as its association with minority rights distorted it during the inter-war years.[19] In the following sections, the work surrounding the formulation of the Declaration and Draft Convention will be examined in order to see what light, if any, they shed upon the substance of the concepts and rights of manifestation of religion and belief, as set out in the UDHR and the ICCPR. It also provides further illustrations of the drift away from the

---

[17] This change, intended to harmonize the title of the Declaration with the wording of Article 18 of the UDHR, was proposed by Morocco in the Third Committee in 1973. See A/C.3/SR.2012 and Lerner, 'Toward a Draft Declaration against Religious Intolerance and Discrimination', p. 90. A similar change had been made to the title of the Draft Convention in 1967. See Claydon, 'The Treaty Protection of Religious Rights', pp. 415–416.

[18] But *cf.* the criticism levelled at the text of the Declaration in the Third Committee by Bulgaria, that 'instead of dealing with the question of the elimination of intolerance and discrimination based on religion or belief, it concentrated in fact on freedom of religion' (A/C.3/36/SR.43, §73; see also A/C.3/36/SR.35, §43).

[19] See, for example, M. S. McDougal, H. D. Lasswell and L.-C. Chen, *Human Rights and World Public Order* (New Haven: Yale University Press, 1980), pp. 653–689, where much of the material considered in this and preceding chapters is examined from the viewpoint of discrimination and religious liberty *per se* is largely unexplored. Indeed, much of this chapter had previously appeared as 'The Right to Religious Freedom and World Public Order: The Emerging Norm of Nondiscrimination', *Mich. L. Rev.* 74 (1976), 865.

protection of *religious* freedom and the move towards non-discrimination and relativist thinking.

The freedom of religion or belief in the Declaration and Draft Convention

Article 1 of the 1981 Declaration proclaims the right to freedom of thought, conscience and religion and is closely modelled on Article 18 of the International Covenant on Civil and Political Rights, the background to which has been considered above and the wording of which had been current since 1960. However, it was not adopted as the basis for the article until a comparatively late stage in the development of the Declaration and only then in the face of considerable opposition. More importantly, its inclusion was prompted by the inability of the CHR to agree upon a definition of the concepts it proclaimed.

Although the *Krishnaswami Study* had adopted a working definition of 'religion or belief' this was not formally set out as one of the 'basic rules' identified, and it seemed at first as if progress could be made towards the completion of the Declaration without a definition being provided.[20] The Draft Declaration submitted to the CHR by the Sub-Commission in 1964 simply provided that:

Everyone has the right to adhere, or not to adhere, to a religion or belief and to change in accordance with the dictates of his conscience – without being subjected to any pressure, inducement or undue influence likely to impair his freedom of choice or decision in this matter.[21]

The CHR established a working group to study this draft and its version of what was now draft Article 1 provided:

Everyone has the freedom of thought, conscience and religion. This right shall

---

[20] When the CHR was considering the Sub-Commission's Draft Principles in 1962 it was generally felt that it 'should not attempt to examine theoretical religious concepts, but should concentrate upon the elaboration of practical rules for freedom of religion and other beliefs which could be universally supported' (Report of the CHR, 18th Session, 1962, E/CN.4/832/Rev.1, para. 110).

[21] See Report of the CHR, 19 Session, 1963, E/CN.4/874, §294. This was a conflation of Part I(1) and (3) of the Sub-Commission's Draft Principles of 1960, which were based on the first of the 'Basic Rules' set out in the *Krishnaswami Study*. This appeared as draft Article IV, presumably to highlight the fact that non-discrimination was its primary purpose. However, all subsequent drafts moved this to the head of the Declaration. The chief difference between, on the one hand, the Sub-Commission's 1964 draft and, on the other, the *Krishnaswami* Rules and the 1960 Draft Principles version is that it places a greater emphasis upon the right to change religion.

include freedom to adhere or not to adhere to any religion or [to any religious or non-religious] belief and to change his religion or belief in accordance with the dictates of his conscience, without being subjected to any coercion likely to impair his freedom of choice or decision in the matter.[22]

As the bracketed words suggest, disagreement had arisen within the working group concerning the status of non-religious beliefs. It was generally agreed that the Declaration should protect religious and other forms of belief equally, but whereas some thought that the text achieved this, others sought to have this spelt out in clearer language. The working group left this to be decided by the Plenary of the CHR, along with a number of definitions which had been proposed for inclusion within the Declaration,[23] but because of the shortage of time these were not considered.

At its next sessions the CHR did consider the definitions of 'religion' and 'belief', but not in the context of the Declaration. It had decided to move on to a consideration of the text of the Draft Convention submitted by the Sub-Commission. Given that this was to be a source of legal obligation, it was necessary to ensure that the meaning and relationship of the terms 'religion' and 'belief' were adequately explained and Article 1 of the draft provided that:

For the purposes of this Convention:
  (a) The expression 'religion or belief' shall include theistic, non-theistic and atheistic beliefs.

This wording had been used in the explanatory footnote at the beginning of the *Krishnaswami Study*. Although more of a confirmation that certain forms of belief were within the scope of the Convention than a definition of what a religion or belief actually was, it was adequate for the limited purpose in hand. Nevertheless, it provoked a lively discussion in the CHR, the essence of which concerned the question of whether atheism should receive special mention, particularly since it was only one form of non-religious belief.[24] The United States proposed an amendment which

---

[22] E/CN.4/L.713/Rev. 1.
[23] *Ibid.* These were:
  (a) Austria: 'For the purpose of this Declaration the term "belief" is understood as expression for the various theistic creeds or such other beliefs as agnosticism, free thought, atheism and rationalism.'
  (b) Ukrainian SSR: 'In this Declaration the term "religion or belief" means both religious beliefs and atheistic convictions.'
  (c) UK: 'In this Declaration the term "belief" includes both religious and non-religious beliefs.'
[24] Thus France proposed (E/CN.4/L.727) that agnosticism should also be mentioned. It

avoided the use of the term 'atheist' and withdrew this only on the express understanding that the original version would guarantee an absolutely equal treatment in law for all religions and beliefs, without preference for any, and that this was understood by States which had adopted atheistic ideologies – that is, the Soviet bloc.[25] Israel raised the objection that the definition did not make it clear whether the terms 'theistic, non-theistic and atheistic' were forms of religion or forms of belief and, in order to clarify that these were forms of 'belief', proposed an amendment which excluded 'religion' from the definition altogether,[26] justifying this on the ground that the meaning of 'religion' was generally well understood.[27]

Underlying all these exchanges was a tension between those States who saw the Convention as a means of enshrining the primacy of religious belief over Socialist atheism and the Socialist States which sought to achieve parity for their dogmas in a convention ostensibly aimed at the protection of religious belief. The solution was to deprive the draft of any doctrinal bias by making its non-discriminatory aspects even more prominent than was already the case. Thus it was comparatively easy to forge a consensus around an understanding that: 'The Convention imposed the obligation to respect the conviction of all people in the field of religion or belief without any distinction. This was acceptable because if anyone claimed respect for his personal feelings, for his conscience, then he had to accept and to recognize the same freedom for others.'[28] Against this background the wording proposed by the Sub-Commission was approved unanimously. It was also accepted by the Third Committee when it considered the Draft Convention in 1967, but for a rather different reason.

An attempt was made to remove the words 'non-theistic' from the text on the grounds that they were unnecessary and raised the prospect of according protection to political beliefs but, along with most other

subsequently withdrew this proposal when it became clear that most thought it was embraced by the word 'belief' (Report of the CHR, 21st Session, 1965, E/CN.4/891, §§106, 121).

[25] *Ibid.*, paras. 105 and 120. The proposed text (E/CN.4/L.722) provided that: 'The expression "religion or belief" shall embrace theistic and non theistic religion, or belief concerning religion, including rejection of any or all such religion or belief.'

[26] After several amendments, the final version of the proposal (E/CN.4/L.728) provided that: 'The expression of "belief" shall include atheistic or agnostic philosophies and convictions.'

[27] Report of the CHR, 21st Session, 1965, E/CN.4/891, §122. Like the other amendments, this was also subsequently withdrawn.

[28] *Ibid.*, §126.

amendments, this proposal was withdrawn.[29] A Syrian proposal remained to be considered which proposed to replace the text with the following definition:

In the expression 'religion or belief' the word 'belief' shall mean metaphysical or ideological beliefs of an all-inclusive nature, whether theistic, non theistic or atheistic.[30]

This left religion undefined, but it was again argued that this was unimportant.[31] This provoked a number of disagreements but the discussion ultimately descended into what can best be described as a procedural nightmare and resulted in the amendment being withdrawn and the original draft, as first proposed by the Sub-Commission, being adopted.[32] This is the closest that the United Nations, as an organization, has yet come to defining this central phrase. Although it was not adopted for inclusion in the Draft Convention, this definition came close to being adopted for the Declaration ten years later.

The CHR resumed work on the Draft Declaration in 1974 but it was not until 1977 that it began consideration of its first article.[33] The working group established to examine the issue[34] was confronted with an array of drafts, one of which proposed that Article 1 of the Covenant be used as the basis of the opening article of the Declaration.[35] This was soon lost in an avalanche of proposals and amendments. As in all previous discussions,

---

[29] The proposal was submitted by the Byelorussian SSR and was somewhat self serving: since the Soviet States embraced atheism as a political dogma, their political stance was already protected by the definition. See A/C.3/SR.1507, §4 and Bulgaria, §6.

[30] A/C.3/L.1484 and Corr. 1.

[31] But for different reasons. For example, the Syrian representative thought its meaning self evident (A/C.3/SR.1509, §2). In a different context, the Italian representative had thought that religion was ultimately defined by 'belief' (A/C.3/SR.1508, §17).

[32] A vote was taken on the first word of the proposal, 'In', which was defeated. The propriety of taking this vote at all was challenged, and Italy further proposed a separate vote on the words 'metaphysical or ideological beliefs of an all-inclusive nature, whether', which were deleted. Syria then attempted to withdraw its amendment but Italy reintroduced it, only to withdraw it again. The original wording was then adopted by ninety-four votes to none, with four abstentions (see A/C.3/SR.1510, §§6–49).

[33] The title and Preamble of the draft Declaration were discussed and adopted during the 1974–1976 sessions. See Reports of the CHR, 30th Session, 1974, E/CN.4/1154, paras. 51–58; 31st Session, 1975, E/CN.4/1179, paras. 169–176; and 32nd Session, 1976, E/CN.4/1213, paras. 171–177.

[34] The Report of the working group for 1977 is contained in E/CN.4/L.1357 and reproduced in the Report of the CHR, 33rd Session, 1977, E/CN.4/1257, §197. The Report of the working group for 1978 is contained in E/CN.4/L.1401 and reproduced in the Report of the CHR, 35th Session, 1978, E/CN.4/1292, §259.

[35] E/CN.4/L.1401, para. 4.

the principal difficulties were the inclusion of an express reference to atheism and, whether or not it was mentioned, the relationship between 'religion' and 'belief'. In addition, new problems emerged when it was suggested that the Declaration should contain a positive endorsement of the right to criticize religion[36] and draconian limitation clauses.[37] Express mention of animistic, polytheistic beliefs was also canvassed.[38] In an attempt to break out of this downward spiral, Austria proposed that Article 1 of the Declaration should adopt Article 18(1) – (3) of the ICCPR, but even this was unable to secure a consensus.[39]

However, this fundamentally changed the nature of the debate. The purpose of Article 18 of the ICCPR was to place a statement concerning religious freedom in a covenant that would act as a source of legal obligation. It did not seek to define its terminology. A declaration and convention concerned with 'religion' and 'belief' ought to do so. The text of the ICCPR had the advantage of having been already adopted by the General Assembly but it was inadequate for the function for which it was now being suggested. At the next session of the CHR in 1979 the same issues dominated discussion in the working group and Austria again proposed the use of the first three paragraphs of Article 18 of the ICCPR, but subsequently agreed to the addition of a Soviet proposal as a new first paragraph, which provided:

1. No one shall be subject to discrimination by any State, institution, group of persons or person on grounds of religion or theistic, non-theistic or atheistic convictions.[40]

Even this did not suffice, since some thought that the final phrase should refer to theistic, non-theistic or atheistic 'beliefs' rather than 'convictions', whilst others thought that the entire phrase should be replaced by an

---

[36] E.g. , the proposals of the Byelorussian SSR (E/CN.4/L.1357, para. 13) and the USSR (E/CN.4/L.1401, paras. 12, 33).
[37] Bulgaria proposed (E/CN.4/L.1401, para. 14) that:
The right to freedom of religious belief shall not be used for purposes of endangering the security of the society or for any kind of activity which may cause harm to the health of citizens or encroach on the personality or rights of citizens, or which may incite citizens to refrain from public activity and from performing their obligations as citizens or which may lead to the involvement of minors in any such activities.
[38] Ibid., para. 29.
[39] Ibid., paras. 35–41. This was noted with disquiet when the Report of the working group was considered by the CHR, given that over forty States had by that time ratified the Covenant (E/CN.4/1292, §260). See also the comments of the Netherlands in the Third Committee of the General Assembly in 1978 (A/C.3/33/SR.61, § 3).
[40] Report of the CHR, 35th Session, 1979, E/CN.4/1347, §274 at para. 13.

unqualified reference to 'beliefs' alone. Rather than pursue this any further, the working group referred this draft to the plenary of the Commission.[41] Canada and Colombia proposed that Article 1 of the Declaration should only consist of the paragraphs from the ICCPR.[42] Although some States wanted further discussion,[43] the proposal was ultimately adopted[44] and passed to the General Assembly.

The discussion of the Declaration in the Third Committee of the General Assembly in 1981 proceeded along predictable lines: most States welcomed the Declaration whilst maintaining that its provisions were already faithfully reflected in their constitutions and domestic legislation or traditions. The Eastern European States complained that the Declaration had not been adopted by consensus and failed to give adequate expression to the equal rights of atheists and others espousing non-religious beliefs,[45] whilst Iran made a vehement attack upon the entire concept of the Declaration.[46] If the text was to be adopted by consensus it was clear that some movement would have to take place and, following a series of consultations, the Chairman announced that a number of changes had been made to the text which were intended to confirm the application of the Declaration to non-religious beliefs.[47]

At the same time, he also announced a series of changes that reflected

---

[41] *Ibid.*, para. 28.   [42] E/CN.4/L.1464.

[43] A proposal to continue the discussions at the next session was defeated with only six votes in favour (Bulgaria, Cuba, Iraq, Poland, Syrian Arab Republic and the USSR) to twelve against, but with fourteen abstentions. See Report of the CHR, 35th Session, 1979, E/CN.4/1347, §279.

[44] CHR Res. 20 (XXXV). *Ibid.*, § 279 and pp. 125–137.

[45] E.g. GDR (A/C.3/36/SR.32, §2); Byelorussian SSR (*ibid.*, §60); Ukrainian SSR (A/C.3/36/SR.34, §31); Hungary (*ibid.*, §35); Bulgaria (A/C.3/36/SR.35, §43); USSR (A/C.3/36/SR.36, §20).

[46] Iran maintained that: 'The UN was a secular body and the UDHR a secular instrument which permitted the vapid fabrication of Zionism and Western and Eastern Imperialism to break the united front of the followers of divine faiths.' but argued that 'the malicious secularism of the United Nations was no longer a characteristic of all Member States. Muslims . . . did not ask for toleration: what mattered was respect. Believing that secular bodies were not qualified to deal with religious matters, they respectfully requested such bodies not to attempt it, since their efforts were out of place' (A/C.3/36/SR.29, §§11–14). Iran also pointed out that Article 18(2) of the ICCPR, which precluded coercion impairing freedom of choice, 'could never apply to Muslims, who were not permitted to adopt another religion' (*ibid.*, §16).

[47] The phrase 'religion or belief' was altered to 'religion or whatever belief' in the third preambular paragraph and in Article 1(1), second sentence. See A/C.3/36/SR.43, §40. Although this was enough to secure approval, the Eastern bloc States still expressed concerns over its scope. The USSR insisted that 'protection for freedom of religion and belief should also be interpreted as freedom not to profess any religion, to have atheistic beliefs and to propagandize them without restrictions' (*ibid.*, §69). See also GDR (§61); Bulgaria (§74); and Czechoslovakia (§85).

concerns that had been long held but had not been openly addressed in the public sessions, although hinted at by the Iranian representative: the freedom to change one's religion or belief.[48] Following discussions with the Chairman of the Islamic Conference,[49] it was decided that the words 'or to adopt' were to be deleted from Article 1 paragraphs (1) and (2) and the phrase 'including the right to choose, manifest and change one's religion or belief' was to be deleted from the second preambular paragraph,[50] which had provided that:

Considering that the Universal Declaration of Human Rights and the International Covenants on Human Rights proclaim the principles of non-discrimination and equality before the law and the right to freedom of thought, conscience, religion and belief, including the right to choose, manifest and change one's religion or belief'.

The Chairman also announced the inclusion of an additional Article 8, which provided that:

Nothing in the present Declaration shall be construed as restricting or derogating from any right defined in the Universal Declaration of Human Rights and the International Covenants on Human Rights.

The result is unsatisfactory on a number of counts. First, the Declaration again avoided defining what was meant by 'religion' and 'belief' and, even if the meaning of these terms is generally understood, this is difficult to justify. Moreover, and perhaps unwittingly, the text as adopted had a potentially damaging impact upon the UDHR. The UDHR makes express mention of the right to change one's religion or belief. The ICCPR adopted a compromise formula which was wilfully obscure on this point. All of the draft texts of Article 1 of the Declaration considered in the CHR had included the right to change religion, although some warning notes had been sounded: Egypt had proposed that the words 'to change' be deleted from one proposal under discussion on the ground that they were already implicit in the words 'to choose' that were also present.[51] The decision to

---

[48] See N. Lerner, 'The Final Text of the UN Declaration against Intolerance and Discrimination based on Religion or Belief', Is.YHR 12 (1982), 185, 187.

[49] See A/C.3/36/SR.43, §§50, 64.

[50] The final clause, now deleted, had been added at the suggestion of Ghana to the original draft of the Preamble submitted by Byelorussian SSR in 1975. It had prompted little discussion either then or since. See Report of the CHR, 31st Session, 1975, E/CN.4/1179, §173 at paras. 9–10.

[51] Report of the CHR, 34th Session, 1978, E/CN.4/1292, §27. This was supported by the Libyan Arab Jamahiriya as 'reflecting the Islamic point of view' (ibid., §30). It had also been observed that there were insufficient Islamic States on the working group 'to ensure a fully satisfactory text' (§26).

remove the compromise wording of the ICCPR from the text of the Declaration meant that the Declaration became the weakest of the three instruments in this regard and that twenty-four years of discussion surrounding them had resulted in the diminution of what for many had always been a key element of their conception of religious freedom. Ironically, the *Krishnaswami Study*, which provided the original impetus for developing freedom of religion or belief within the context of non-discrimination, had strongly supported the right to change one's religion.[52]

Article 8 does not redress this since it only relates to conflicts between rights proclaimed.[53] Since it does not include the right to change one's religion there is nothing *in* the Declaration which restricts or derogates from the UDHR or ICCPR: the problem stems from its not being included. Naturally, the text of the UDHR remains, but doubt is surely cast upon it by the decision of the General Assembly to exclude the right from the 1981 Declaration, particularly in view of the weakening already evidenced by the adoption of Article 18 of the ICCPR.[54] If this was the fate of the Declaration, it seems clear that a similar fate would have befallen the draft of the Convention if it had been considered at the time, since this also included a reference to the right to change one's religion. In sum, the impact of the Declaration upon an understanding of the meaning of the terms 'religion' and 'belief' in international instruments has been negative, in the sense of adding to doubt rather than lending certainty.

---

[52] The Study claims that 'the consensus of world opinion, as expressed in the UDHR, is unequivocally in favour of permitting an individual not only to maintain but also to change his religion or belief in accordance with his convictions' (*Krishnaswami Study*, p. 25).

[53] But *cf.* D. J. Sullivan, 'Advancing the Freedom of Religion or Belief Through the UN Declaration on the Elimination of Religious Intolerance and Discrimination', *AJIL* 82 (1988), 487 at 495, who, whilst taking the view that the right to change religion is inherent, considers that Article 8 supported this by 'saving' the right to change as set out in the UDHR.

[54] An entirely different conclusion was drawn by Mrs Odio Benito in her 1987 study 'Elimination of all Forms of Intolerance and Discrimination based on Religion or Belief' (hereafter the *Odio Benito Report*). She argued that the mention of the freedom 'to have a religion or whatever belief of his choice' 'implies that the 1981 Declaration, without repeating the UDHR or the ICCPR word for word, encompasses the right to change one's religion or belief . . .' (para. 200). It is difficult to see how this conclusion can be reconciled with the drafting history. The *Krishnaswami Study* itself had pointed out that 'it does not follow from the mere acknowledgment of one's right to maintain a religion or belief that the right to change it is also conceded' (*Krishnaswami Study*, p. 16).

The content of the right to freedom of thought, conscience or religion

For many, the most important question is neither the manner in which the right to freedom of thought, conscience, religion or belief is expressed, nor the definition of 'religion or belief' that is provided, but its practical implications. There was never any real doubt that both the Declaration and Covenant would contain a separate article providing for this. The principal questions that needed addressing concerned the level of detail that would be provided, and the restrictions to which it would be subjected. Once again, the *Krishnaswami Study* provides the starting point.

The *Krishnaswami Study* saw the freedom to manifest a religion or belief as having two basic elements, the freedom to comply with what was prescribed or authorized by a religion or belief and the freedom from performing acts incompatible with the prescriptions of a religion or belief. The 'freedom of action' included worship, processions, pilgrimages, the use of equipment and symbols, arrangements for disposal of the dead, observance of holidays and days of rest, dietary practices, the celebration of marriage and its dissolution by divorce, the dissemination of religion or belief and training of personnel.[55] The 'freedom from forced participation' included the taking of oaths, issues relating to military service, participation in religious or civic ceremonies, divulging the secrets of the confessional and compulsory prevention or treatment of disease.[56]

The Part II of the 1960 Draft Principles substantially followed this classification and catalogue, clarifying some aspects and adding the right to manifest a religion or belief through teaching.[57] The Draft Declaration prepared by the Sub-Commission in 1964 contained an even longer and more detailed catalogue of the 'freedom of action' in Article VI,[58]

---

[55] *Ibid.*, pp. 31–42.   [56] *Ibid.*, pp. 42–45.

[57] Draft Principles, Part II, 8(a). This was noted by Krishnaswami when he presented his *Study* to the CHR. See Report of the CHR, 16th Session, 1960, para. 19.

[58] Article VI provided:

Everyone has the right to comply with what is prescribed by his religion or belief and shall be free to worship, and profess, in public or in private, without suffering any discrimination on account of his religion or belief and specifically:

1. Every person and every group has the right to worship, either alone or together with others, in public or in private, and to maintain houses of worship in accordance with the prescription of their beliefs.
2. (i) Every individual has the right in association with others, without any limitation based on the number of members, to form and maintain religious communities and institutions.
   (ii) Every religious community and institution has the right, in association with

supplemented by aspects of the 'freedom from compulsion' in subsequent articles.[59] However, the CHR working group rejected such a detailed approach and, instead, substituted the following succinct proposal:

Every person and every group or community has the right to manifest their religion or belief in public or in private, without being subjected to any discrimination on the grounds of religion or belief; this right includes in particular:

    (a)   freedom to worship, to assemble and to establish and maintain places of worship or assembly;

    (b)   freedom to teach, to disseminate [at home or abroad], and to learn their religion or belief, and also its sacred language or traditions;

    (c)   freedom to practise their religion or belief by establishing and main-

      similar religious communities and institutions, to form territorial federations on a national, regional or local basis.

3. Everyone has the right to teach and to learn his religion or belief, his sacred language and religious traditions, either in public or in private. No one shall be compelled to receive instruction in a religion or belief contrary to his convictions or, in the case of children, contrary to the wishes of their parents, or legal guardians. All education shall be directed to promote understanding, tolerance and friendship among all religions and beliefs.

4. Every religious group or community has the right to write, to print and to publish religious books and texts and shall be permitted to train personnel required for the performance of its practices or rites. No religious group or community shall be prevented from bringing teachers from abroad for this purpose. Every religious group or community shall be enabled to have contacts with communities and institutions belonging to the same religion abroad.

5. (i) Everyone has the right to observe the dietary practices prescribed by his religion or belief. Any individual or any religious community shall be permitted to acquire and produce all materials and objects necessary for the observance of prescribed ritual or practices, including dietary practices.

    (ii) Where the State controls the means of production and distribution, it shall help to provide the above mentioned materials, or the materials and means necessary for their production, to religious communities of the religions concerned and to its members, and if necessary allow them to be imported.

6. Everyone has the right to make pilgrimage to sites held in veneration, whether inside or outside his country, and every state shall grant freedom of access to these places.

7. Equal legal protection shall be accorded to all forms of worship, places of worship and institutions. Similar guarantees shall be accorded to ritual objects, language or worship and sacred books.

8. Due account shall be taken of the prescriptions of each religion or belief relating to holy days and days of rest, and all discrimination in this regard between persons of different religions or beliefs shall be prohibited.

[59] Other freedoms, and aspects of the freedom from compulsion, were addressed in the Sub-Commission's draft Articles VII (Marriage Rites), VIII (Burial Customs) and X (Oaths) but were not considered by the CHR at this time. See Report of the CHR, 19 Session, 1963, E/CN.4/874, §294.

taining charitable and educational institutions and by expressing the
implications of religion or belief in public life;

(d)   freedom to observe the rites or customs of their religion or belief.

Although radically different in style, the content of the working group
draft was not necessarily more restrictive since much of what was no
longer expressly mentioned could be taken to be implicit in what
remained. However, and as the controversy over the bracketed words
suggests, real differences of substance were contemplated, and this led
the United States to propose additional articles concerning, *inter alia*,
ritual and dietary practices, holy days, pilgrimages, burial places, the
formation of international associations and of international communication with co-religionists. The CHR never gave these proposals detailed
consideration. At the following session it turned to the Draft Convention
that had been prepared by the Sub-Commission and, when it returned to
the formulation of the Declaration, worked from an entirely different set
of proposals submitted by the United States.

The text of the Draft Convention prepared by the Sub-Commission in
1964 contained, in Article III, a listing which followed the basic contours
of its proposed Declaration, although expressed in a more direct fashion.
Some argued that it was excessively detailed and all that was needed was
an affirmation of the right of manifestation,[60] but this was rejected by the
majority who thought it should 'contain specifications of rights in the
greatest possible detail'.[61] At the same time, it was also accepted that 'in
view of the diversity of religions and beliefs ... [it] ... should be as
general and concise as possible'.[62] It is, therefore, not unreasonable to
assume that the resulting draft reflects the product of these tensions.
However, since it was never considered in detail by the Third Committee
in 1967,[63] the text must be treated with extreme caution. Consequently,
all that will be done here is to set out the text proposed by the Sub-
Commission as subsequently amended by the CHR. This will indicate the
general areas of agreement and of controversy whilst also giving a reasonable indication of the parameters of future debate.[64] Elements of the Sub-

---

[60] See, for example, the proposal of Poland (E/CN.4/L.738) in the Report of the CHR, 21st
Session, 1965, E/CN.4/891, §§191 and 229.

[61] *Ibid.*, §§230–234 at §233.   [62] *Ibid.*, §236.

[63] Many delegations did, however, comment on it during the general debate. See GAOR,
22nd Session (1967), A/C.3/SR.1486–1511 and R. S. Clark, 'The United Nations and
Religious Freedom', *New York Univ. Journal of Int. Law and Pol.* 11 (1978), 197 at 210–214.

[64] The prospects for a convention are considered below, at pp. 257–261.

Commission draft that were not accepted by the CHR appear in square brackets. Wording added by the CHR is italicized.

1. States Parties undertake to ensure to everyone *within their jurisdiction* the right to freedom of thought, conscience or religion. This right shall include:
    (a) Freedom to adhere or not to adhere to any religion or belief and to change his religion or belief in accordance with the dictates of his conscience without being subjected *either to any of the limitations referred to in article XII or* to any coercion likely to impair his freedom of choice or decision in the matter, *provided that this subparagraph shall not be interpreted as extending to manifestations of religion or belief*; and
    (b) Freedom to manifest his religion or belief either alone or in community with others, and in public or in private, without being subjected to any discrimination on the grounds of religion or belief.
    (c) Freedom to express opinions on questions concerning a religion or belief;
2. [Subject to the limitations contained in articles IX, XI and XII], States Parties shall, in particular, ensure to everyone *within their jurisdiction*:
    (a) Freedom to worship, to [assemble] *hold assemblies related to religion or belief* and to establish and maintain places of worship or assembly *for these purposes*;
    (b) Freedom to teach, to disseminate and to learn his religion or belief and its sacred languages or traditions, *to write, print and publish religious books and texts,* and to train personnel intending to devote themselves to the performance of its practices or observances;
    (c) Freedom to practice his religion or belief by establishing and maintaining charitable and educational institutions and by expressing *in public life* the implications of religion or belief [in public life];
    (d) Freedom to observe the rituals, dietary and other practices of his religion or belief and to produce or if necessary import the objects, foods and other articles and facilities customarily used in its observances and practices;
    (e) Freedom to make pilgrimages and other journeys in connection with his religion or belief whether inside or outside his country;
    (f) Equal protection for [his] *the* places of worship *or assembly,* for his rites, ceremonies, and activities, and for the [burial places] *places of disposal of the dead* associated with his religion or belief;
    (g) Freedom to organize and maintain local, regional [and] national *and international* associations[, and to participate in international associations] in connection with his [activities] *religion or belief, to participate in their activities,* and to communicate with his co-religionists and believers;
    (h) Freedom from compulsion to take an oath of a religious nature;
    [(i) Freedom from compulsion to undergo a religious marriage ceremony not in conformity with his religion or belief.]

The most important of these changes related to the application of the limitation clauses. In the Sub-Commission's draft, Articles IX, XI and XII were said to apply only to the provisions of subsection (2) of Article III. In fact, this was unnecessary since those articles applied to the entire convention anyway. However, the CHR amended the text so that paragraph 1(a) should be subject to no limitation at all.[65] This was only possible once the question was answered of whether the bare statement of the right of thought, conscience or religion in paragraph 1(a) implied a right to manifest it in some way. Some took the view that adherence to any religion or belief meant adherence to certain rules and rituals which equated to forms of manifestation. Others took the view that paragraph 1(a) referred only to 'internal matters', as was made clear by the phrase 'in accordance with the dictates of his conscience', and that any form of manifestation fell within the scope of paragraphs 1(b) and 2.[66] In order to make it clear that expressions and manifestations of belief were still subject to limitation it was expressly provided that paragraph 1(a) was not to be interpreted as implying a right of manifestation.[67] This was a significant clarification of a troublesome issue.[68]

When the CHR resumed its consideration of the Declaration, there was further disagreement concerning the need for a detailed catalogue but, once again, it was decided that this be done.[69] Discussion was based around a series of texts submitted by the United States and which closely followed the substance of the text adopted by the CHR for the draft Convention. In what follows, the US proposals are set out and those elements added appear in italic, whilst the deletions are placed in square brackets. The sections appearing in bold are those on which no agreement could be found.

In accordance with article I, and subject to the provisions of paragraph 3 of article I, the right to freedom of thought, conscience, religion and belief shall include, *inter alia*, the following freedoms:

---

[65] See Report of the CHR, 21st Session, 1965, E/CN.4/891, §§240–254 and 297.

[66] *Ibid.*, §240.   [67] This was at the suggestion of India. *Ibid.*, §239.

[68] The addition of paragraph 1(c) also sheds light on the CHR's thinking concerning the nature of a 'manifestation' of religion or belief. It was intended to 'secure the right of individuals to express their ideas on religious matters or on matters relating to religion independently of religious manifestations in the sense of worship' and, in that sense, its basic purpose was 'eliminating restrictions on freedom to express opinions' (*ibid.*, §§255, 257). This suggests that 'manifestation' did not extend beyond the actual practice of one's religion or belief, a fairly narrow interpretation.

[69] See Report of the CHR, 37th Session, 1981, E/CN.4/1475, §343 at paras. 35–36. The Soviet and Byelorussian representatives expressly reserved their position on this question.

(a) [To assemble] *To worship or assemble in connection with a religion or belief,* and to establish and maintain places [of worship or assembly] *for these purposes;*

(b) To establish and maintain *appropriate* charitable [and educational] *humanitarian* institutions [affiliated with religion or beliefs];

(c) To make, [distribute, and import where not available locally,] *to acquire and to use* to an adequate extent[,] the necessary articles and materials related to the rites or customs of a religion or belief;

(d) To [teach,] write, publish and to disseminate *relevant* publications [in the field of religion or beliefs] *in those areas;*

(e) To teach [in the matter of] *a* religion or belief *in places suitable for these purposes;*

(f) To solicit and receive *voluntary* financial and other contributions from individuals and institutions **designed solely for the purposes of supporting a religion or beliefs and not motivated by any political aim;**

(g) To train [and], *to* appoint [in adequate numbers ministers or others], *to elect or to designate by succession* appropriate leaders called for by [a] *the requirements and standards of any* religion or belief;

(h) *To observe days of rest and* to celebrate holidays and ceremonies in accordance with the [precepts] *customs* of one's religion or belief;

(i) **To establish and maintain communications with individuals and communities in matters of religion and belief at the national and international level.**

The position of States which were the sole provider of education, and that of a secular nature, was met by the amendments to sub-paragraphs (b) and (e). Of the remaining changes, the chief points of controversy surrounded sub-paragraphs (f) and (i). The USSR had proposed the addition of the last section of (f) which was said to be 'designed to prevent the provision from being used as a pretext for contributions to fascist, nazi or anti-democratic movements or for interference by a foreign power in the internal affairs of a State'.[70] The working group could not agree on the wording of the section, which was referred to the plenary of the Commission which decided to delete it.[71] Sub-paragraph (i) was similarly referred to the Commission and accepted by it.[72]

With disagreement still surrounding its adoption, this text was transmitted via ECOSOC to the General Assembly. The general complaints of the Eastern European States to the text in the Third Committee has already been noted.[73] The USSR argued that Article 6 'bore no direct relation to the theme of the declaration'.[74] In addition, particular objec-

---

[70] *Ibid.*, para. 67.   [71] *Ibid.*, §§346–348.   [72] *Ibid.*   [73] See above, p. 236.
[74] *Ibid.*, §70.

tions were lodged by Romania in relation to sub-paragraphs (d), (h) and (i),[75] Yugoslavia in relation to (b) and (h)[76] and the Syrian Arab Republic in relation to (f).[77] Nevertheless, the text was not amended and it was subsequently adopted by the General Assembly in GA Res. 36/55.[78]

As has already been pointed out, several Eastern European States took the view that the Declaration had failed in its purpose. They claimed that its failure to place religious and other forms of belief on a strictly equal footing gave too great an advantage to religious adherents. It was also claimed that it was about discrimination in favour of religion, rather than non-discrimination in the enjoyment of religious freedoms. This might seem an odd charge to level at a Declaration that was regarded by many as being *about* religious freedom in the first place, but such an under- standing is itself misconceived. In a sense, the Declaration was about neither religion or belief nor discrimination, but about the political and ideological rivalries of the principal power blocs and for which the debates simply provided another forum. It would, however, be overly simplistic to write off the entire experience of the evolution of the Declaration on this basis, although it does justify treating it with extreme caution. There are important lessons to be drawn from the way in which the discussions evolved, the most important of which concerns the way the discussions veered away from the central problems posed by the definition of a religion or belief and the content of the freedom of manifestation. This demonstrates the extreme difficulty – some might say impossibility – of setting the power of religious and other life-defining concepts within the framework of a system of human rights which is premised upon universalist presuppositions with which they are not necessarily in harmony.

Subsequent elaboration and the work of the Special Rapporteur

In 1983, the CHR and the Sub-Commission requested that a Special Rapporteur be appointed to prepare a report which would, *inter alia*, comment upon 'the various manifestations of intolerance and discrimina- tion on the grounds of religion or belief in the contemporary world and on specific rights violated, using the Declaration as a standard'.[79] The

---

[75] A/C.3/36/SR.43, §§52–53.   [76] A/C.3/36/SR.35, §31.
[77] A/C.3/36/SR.43, §65. It also objected to Article VII.
[78] For an overview of Article 6 as ultimately adopted see Lerner, 'Toward a Draft Declaration against Religious Intolerance and Discrimination', pp. 92–97.
[79] CHR Res. 1983/40 and Sub-Commission Res. 1983/31.

resulting Report, compiled by Mrs Elizabeth Odio Benito, included numerous examples of situations which she deemed to violate the convention standards, but in a non-country specific fashion.[80] Valuable though the Report is, its observations concerning the nature of the standards set out in the Declaration have been overshadowed by the more detailed and ongoing work of the UN Special Rapporteur on Religious Intolerance.

In 1986 the CHR decided to appoint for one year a Special Rapporteur to examine incidents and governmental actions in all parts of the world inconsistent with the provisions of the Declaration, and to recommend measures to be taken in response to such situations.[81] This mandate was extended for a further year in 1987, for two yearly periods in 1988 and 1990 and for three yearly periods in 1992 and 1995.[82] The Special Rapporteur has submitted annual reports to the Commission on Human Rights[83] and an interim report on the first ten years of the mandate to the Fiftieth Session of the General Assembly.[84]

---

[80] E/CN.4/Sub.2/1986/26, paras. 41–82. The Report was reprinted as vol. 2 of the UN Human Rights Study Series in 1989 (UN Sales No. E.89.XIV.3). The problems posed in producing this Report, including the limited numbers of responses to questionnaires, the poor quality of replies and of the assistance provided by the Centre for Human Rights, are set out in E. Odio-Benito, 'Keynote, Address, in L. Swindler (ed.), *Religious Liberty and Human Rights in Nations and Religions* (Philadelphia: Ecumenical Press, Temple University and New York: Hippocrene Books, Inc., 1986), pp. 3–6.

[81] CHR Res. 1986/20, para. 2. The background to this is examined by D. Weissbrodt, 'The Three "Theme" Special Rapporteurs of the UN Commission on Human Rights', *AJIL* 80 (1986), 685 at 696–697 and B. Dickson, 'The UN and Freedom of Religion', *ICLQ* 44 (1995), 327 at 347–354. P. Alston, *The United Nations and Human Rights: a Critical Appraisal* (Oxford: Clarendon Press, 1992), p. 174, says that this mandate was at least in part the result of a US desire to 'focus the spotlight on Eastern Europe' and the Soviet Union, Byelorussia, the GDR, Bulgaria and Syria opposed the establishment of the mandate. This mirrors the moves to embark upon the drafting of the Convention in the early 1960s.

[82] See CHR Res. 1987/15; 1988/55; 1990/27; 1992/17 and 1995/23. In consequence, the mandate of the current Rapporteur will expire in 1998. The position of Special Rapporteur was held by Mr Angelo Vidal d'Almeida Ribeiro until 1993 when, following his resignation, he was succeeded by Mr Abdelfattah Amor.

[83] 1st Annual Report, E/CN.4/1987/35; 2nd Annual Report, E/CN.4/1988/45 and Add.1; 3rd Annual Report, E/CN.4/1989/44; 4th Annual Report, E/CN.4/1990/46; 5th Annual Report, E/CN.4/1991/56; 6th Annual Report, E/CN.4/1992/52; 7th Annual Report, E/CN.4/1993/62 and Add.1 and Corr.1; 8th Annual Report, E/CN.4/1994/79; 9th Annual Report, E/CN.4/1995/91 and Add.1; 10th Annual Report, E/CN.4/1996/95. Unlike previous Reports, and for financial reasons, the latest document does not include the full texts of communications sent and replies received.

[84] A/50/440 of 18 September 1995. This had been requested by the General Assembly in GA Res. 49/188 of 23 December 1994. This Report provides an authoritative overview of the work of the Special Rapporteur and is the source of much of the factual material presented in this section. The 10th Annual Report, E/CN.4/1996/95, is a summarized

Although the Reports are described as being concerned with the 'implementation' of the Declaration, the Special Rapporteur is not an agent of enforcement. Rather, his role is to investigate, comment and advise upon the manner in which States adhere to the standards set out in the Declaration. To this end, he gathers information on the legislative and constitutional guarantees relating to his mandate[85] as well as communicating with States regarding particular allegations of religious intolerance or discrimination. He can also make *in situ* visits to States, either at the request, or with the consent, of the State concerned.[86]

Given the scope of the mandate and its relationship with the Declaration, it is not surprising that the work of the Special Rapporteur tends not to address directly questions such as the definition of religion or belief or of the legitimate scope of the freedom of manifestation. Moreover, to the extent that the mandate is bound up with questions of discrimination in the enjoyment of rights, attention is drawn away from these questions. That being said, 116 of the allegations communicated to States have raised issues under Article 1 of the Declaration and 102 issues under Article 6, whilst only seventy raised issues of discrimination as such.[87] Paradoxically, the work of the Special Rapporteur, whose mandate under the Declaration is directed at discrimination and intolerance, has as much, if not more, to say about violations of the freedom of religion *per se* than has the Human Rights Committee when considering Article 18 of the Covenant.

The 1995 Interim Report to the General Assembly records that the Special Rapporteur has communicated a total of 232 allegations of practice inconsistent with the Declaration to a total of seventy-four different countries since the establishment of the mandate. Seven of these

and updated version of this document. The work of the Special Rapporteur is considered by Dickson, 'The UN and Freedom of Religion', pp. 347–354. Special Rapporteur Ribeiro also commented on the operation of his mandate in 'The Special Rapporteur for Religious Intolerance', *Bulletin of Human Rights*, 90/1 (1991), 1.

[85] For the summaries of replies received to requests for information see E/CN.4/1991/56, paras. 16–31; E/CN.4/1992/52, paras. 76–164; E/CN.4/1995/91/Add.1, paras. 22–49; A/50/440, paras. 19–26.

[86] The working methods of the Special Rapporteur are set out in the opening section of the annual reports. Mr Amor places greater emphasis on *in situ* visits than his predecessor (who conducted only one such visit, to Bulgaria in 1987: see E/CN.4/1988/95) and has already conducted visits to China in 1994 (see E/CN.4/1995/91, pp. 110–143) and, in 1995, to Pakistan (see E/CN.4/1996/95/Add.1) and Iran (see E/CN.4/1996/95/Add.2). Visits to Greece and India are planned for 1996 and visits are also being sought to the Sudan, Vietnam and Turkey. See also E/CN.4/1994/79, paras. 13–15; E/CN. 4. 1995/91, pp. 5–6; A/50/440, paras. 27–34 and E/CN.4/1996/95, paras. 11–17.

[87] A/50/440, paras. 56–67.

communications were 'urgent appeals', to which others have since been added. This procedure was introduced by Mr Amor in 1994 and is reserved for 'particularly serious situations or cases'. Such appeals usually relate to threats to the life or liberty or physical integrity of individuals and are a way of extending a 'protective mantle' towards them.[88] Although the threat has arisen as a consequence of their religion or belief, the concern is not restricted solely – or, indeed, primarily – to that aspect of the situation and the Rapporteur's action provides evidence of a general climate of intolerance or discrimination that transcends the question of definition.[89]

Much the same comment can be made in relation to many of the other allegations communicated to States. Of the 225 other communications, 184 have raised, *inter alia*, questions concerning the right to life, physical integrity and the security of the person, a set of rights not expressly found within the Declaration but, naturally, bound up within it.[90] Whilst this again points to the seriousness of the allegations, it also means that the thrust of the communications does not necessarily lie in the infringement of the Declaration standard but in the nature of the threat that faces the individuals concerned as a consequence of that breach: the nature of the standard breached serves to place that consequence within the scope of *this* Rapporteur's mandate[91] but may not require particularly detailed

---

[88] One Urgent Appeal has been sent to each of Bangladesh, Pakistan and Saudi Arabia and two to Iran, Iraq and China. See A/50/440, para. 54 and Annex II and E/CN.4/1996/ 95, paras. 39–40. These have concerned, *inter alia*, 'the murder of the reverend Tatavous Mikaelian, in the Islamic Republic of Iran, the death of members of the Al Khoei family, in Iraq, the death threats for blasphemy against human rights advocates and priests, in Pakistan' (A/50/440, *ibid.*); 'the case of Professor Nassar Hamed Abou Zid, who was declared a heretic because of writings' (E/CN.4/1996/95, para. 39) and, in China, Father Chandral Rimpoché, head of the Committee seeking to identify the successor to the Panchan Lama and a Tibetan Monk held in incommunicado detention (*ibid.*, para. 40).

[89] The Special Rapporteur has recorded that he 'had difficulty in establishing a clear distinction between religious conflicts and ethnic conflicts, and between religious intolerance and political persecution. However, he transmitted the allegations to the Governments concerned and invited them to furnish information on the cases reported'. See E/CN.4/1995/91, p. 146.

[90] Other heads not strictly speaking within the scope of the mandate, but germane to its operation and, as such, used for classifying the nature of the communications, are the right to freedom of movement and to freedom of expression and opinion. The relevance of these forms of human rights infringements to the work of the Special Rapporteur was explained in the first Annual Report. See E/CN.4/1987/35, paras. 72–87.

[91] It also could lie concurrently within the mandate of other thematic or country Rapporteurs. See, for example, E/CN.4/1993/62, paras. 69–70 in which he explained that no communications had been addressed to the governments in the former Yugoslavia

consideration. Although generally illustrative of the range of violations of the Declaration standards, the gravity of many of the allegations means that there is neither need nor scope for developing a firmer understanding of its more opaque elements.

For example,[92] the final Report of Special Rapporteur Ribeiro, covering action taken in 1992, recounts numerous communications concerning allegations of wholesale violations of the most basic rights of entire communities of believers as human beings, such as extra-judicial killings, torture and rape.[93] Many others raise allegations of repression which, whilst less wholesale, often includes violence and forced conversion.[94] Usually, such communications also raise claims directly related to the freedom to exercise a religious belief, liberties, including the destruction of places of worship and religious sites, which are also the object of communications in their own right.[95] Such complaints also form an element of many other communications alleging legislative or administrative restraints upon, or interference with, the free practice of religious worship.[96] The Reports covering the following years, whilst addressing

because the widespread destruction of places of worship and other religious sites had already been noted by the Special Rapporteur specifically appointed by the CHR to examine the situation of human rights in the former Yugoslavia (A/47/666, S/24809, paras. 26 and 71). See also E/CN.4/1994/79, paras. 84–93 and E/CN.4/1995/91, p. 110. Unlike the other Reports, the 1994 Report did, however, provide details of alleged violations.

[92] It should be stressed that the examples in the following footnotes are given by way of general illustration. No attempt has been made to classify and catalogue the nature of all communications comprehensively. Similarly, they relate to allegations which have often – indeed, usually – been comprehensively rejected (where replies have been given) by the States concerned.

[93] See, for example, communications to Ethiopia, concerning the Orthodox Christians in the Arba Gugu region (E/CN.4/1993/62, para. 29); Iraq, concerning the position of the Shi'ia Muslims (E/CN.4/1992/52, para. 55; E/CN.4/1993/62, paras. 39–40); Myanmar, concerning the position of the Muslim population of the Rakhine State (Arakan) and the Christian communities of the Irrawaddy delta (paras. 45–46).

[94] See, for example, allegations concerning the treatment of Buddhist monks and nuns and of Christians in China (E/CN.4/1993/62, para. 22); of the Copts in Egypt (ibid., paras. 25–26); of the forced conversion of Christians in India (ibid., para. 34); the treatment of Baha'is in Iran (ibid., paras 37–38: including sentences of death for the refusal to change religion. See also the Report of the Special Rapporteur Visit to Iran, E/CN.4/1996/95/Add.2, paras. 69–70 and, as regards Protestant Christians, paras. 79–85); of the expulsion of Jehovah's Witnesses from Malawi (ibid., para. 43); of Ahmadis and Christians in Pakistan (ibid., paras. 48–49: including the introduction of the death penalty for blasphemy. See also the Report of the Special Rapporteur Visit to Pakistan, E/CN.4/1996/95/Add.1, paras. 65–66); of Christians and Animists in the Sudan (ibid., para. 57); of Orthodox Christians in the Ukraine (ibid., para. 65).

[95] See, for example, the communication to Sri Lanka (E/CN.4/1993/62, para. 54).

[96] See, for example, allegations concerning interference with the procedures for finding

concerns in an increasing number of countries, continue to be dominated by allegations of grave violations, often in situations of more general international concern.[97]

What is a 'religion'?

The Special Rapporteurs have taken a rather expansive view of what constitutes a religion. The Interim Report to the General Assembly records the percentage of communications made by the Special Rapporteur which raise issues relating to various religions. These are as follows: Christianity 59 per cent; Islam 33 per cent; Buddhism 11 per cent; Hinduism 3 per cent; Judaism 4 per cent; 'Other religions and religious groups' 37 per cent.[98] The second Annual Report made clear that 'new religious movements' fell within the scope of the mandate, and observed that 'freedom of religion and belief is indivisible and all religious or belief-based movements, regardless of their length of existence, geographical origin or ideological foundations, must benefit from all the guarantees attaching to respect for the right to freedom of thought, conscience, religion or belief'.[99] In consequence, this latter category includes religions such as 'Ahmadis, Baha'is, Pentecostals, Jehovah's Witnesses, Seventh Day Adventists, spiritualist religions, Hare Krishna, Scientology and the "Family of Love." '[100]

reincarnations of Tibetan religious figures by China (E/CN.4/1993/62, para. 18); of members of the 'New Testament' Church in Malaysia (ibid., para. 44); the general disabilities of Jehovah's Witnesses in Cuba (ibid., paras. 23–24) and Greece (ibid., paras. 30–33); and the Uniate Church in Romania (ibid., para. 50).

[97] See, for example, China (E/CN.4/1994/79, paras. 41–42); India (paras. 55–57); Iran (paras. 58–59: details withheld to allow a reasonable time for a response); Iraq (paras. 60–61); Myanmar (para. 64); Pakistan (paras. 67–68: details withheld to allow a reasonable time for a response); Sudan (paras. 75–76); Viet Nam (paras. 79–83). All these countries are again mentioned in the Report for the following year, E/CN.4/1995/91 (China: Report of Visit, pp. 110–143; India, p. 42; Iran, p. 50; Iraq, p. 53; Myanmar, p. 64; Pakistan, p. 66; Sudan, p. 80 and Viet Nam, p. 104 and also Turkey, p. 102). These are joined by others such as Ghana, p. 38; Liberia, p. 58 and Rwanda, p. 77. In addition, the tenor of the communications to other countries, many addressed in previous years, indicates concern about the growth of religious intolerance. See, for example, Algeria, p. 9; Saudi Arabia, p. 13; Egypt, p. 34; Ethiopia, p. 37; Kenya, p. 56; Mexico, p. 61; Mongolia, p. 62; Nigeria, p. 65; Tanzania, p. 102.

[98] A/50/440, Table 5 (p. 22) and Annex V. Some communications raise multiple issues. The dominance of Christianity is explained in the Report as being due to the greater levels of organization and rights awareness among the Christian communities (para. 71).

[99] E/CN.4/1988/45, para. 8; reiterated in E/CN.4/1989/44, para. 17.

[100] A/50/440, para. 70. The Report notes that this group is comprised of 'very diverse religions and religious groups' which are 'numerically quite small' and, in

The inclusion of the latter in this recent Report indicates a shift of focus by the newly appointed Rapporteur from the stance adopted by his predecessor, who sought to differentiate 'new religions' from 'sects and religious associations' which are difficult to distinguish from 'religions'. Mr Ribeiro had observed that:[101]

aspects having to do with the antiquity of a religion, its revealed character and the existence of a scripture, while important, are not sufficient to make a distinction. Even belief in the existence of a Supreme Being, a particular ritual or a set of ethical and social rules are not exclusive to religions but can also be found in political ideologies.

The activities of sects and religious associations were clearly viewed with some suspicion,[102] and the Special Rapporteur indicated that he would be slow to take up complaints concerning individuals who claimed that legal action taken against followers of such a sect or religious association on an individual basis, and alleging breaches of legal norms of general application, violated the Declaration standards.[103] Similarly, whilst the Special Rapporteur acknowledged that the Declaration 'protects not only religions but also theistic, non-theistic and atheistic beliefs',[104] non-religious beliefs have rarely given rise to communications.[105] The first Report of Mr Amor raised numerous concerns relating to the situation of the 'Family of

consequence, 'these are cases where minorities are being subjected to religious intolerance' (para. 72).

[101] E/CN.4/1990/46, para. 110. See also Ribeiro, 'The Special Rapporteur for Religious Intolerance', pp. 4–5.

[102] He has commented that: 'Experience has shown that many newer sects and religious associations seem to engage in activities which are not always of a legal nature' and suggests that the Declaration can play a role in differentiating between the legal and illegal activities of such groups, presumably by reference to the standards set out in Article 6. There is no suggestion that religions, properly understood, might also engage in activities which might be legitimately labelled as 'illegal'. See E/CN.4/1009/46, para. 110.

[103] The Special Rapporteur has expressed the opinion that 'the possible sentencing of one or more individuals in a criminal trial does not mean a condemnation of the religion or belief that they consider themselves to serve. All religions have already experienced similar situations without being themselves affected' (E/CN.4/1990/46, para. 111).

[104] E/CN.4/1990/46, para. 110; E/CN.4/1995/91, p. 147.

[105] One example of such action concerned the alleged harassment, investigation and prosecution in the United States of Lyndon LaRouche who was 'said to be the founder and leader of a metaphysical association whose beliefs are reportedly centred on the right of all peoples to development and economic justice'. The Special Rapporteur sought the comments of the Government, despite observing that he 'was not able to establish beyond doubt whether Mr LaRouche's association can be considered as falling under the terms of the Declaration'. E/CN.4/1992/52, para. 74; E/CN.4/1993/62, para. 66.

Love',[106] and might indicate a greater readiness to communicate allegations concerning new religious movements, sects and religious associations.[107]

As the Special Rapporteur has acknowledged, it is extremely difficult to differentiate between these categories. It is also potentially counterproductive, since it goes some way towards legitimizing the response of those States who deny groups religious freedoms on the ground that they are not recognized as religions.[108] If the Special Rapporteur is entitled to resort to subjective assessments which result in differential treatment, why should States not be able to do the same?[109]

The nature of the violation

A less expansive approach is taken towards the question of what counts as a 'manifestation' of a religion or belief. The Special Rapporteur has said that the vast majority of the issues raised under Article 1 of the Declaration 'have concerned prohibitions on proselytizing, on possessing certain religious objects and cases of forced conversion', whilst the issues raised under Article 6 have been dominated by 'cases of the forcible closure, destruction and prohibition of the construction of places of worship, prohibition of religious publications, or celebrating religious holidays and violations of the freedom to elect religious leaders'.[110]Article 6 of the Declaration is said not to provide an exhaustive list of possible forms of manifestation[111] and the summaries of allegations received relating to Articles 1 and 6 found in a number of the (earlier) Annual Reports reveal

---

[106] See communications to the Governments of Australia (E/CN.4/1994/79, paras. 34–35; E/CN.4/1995/91/Add.1, paras. 6–7); Spain (E/CN.4/1994/79, paras. 46–47); France (ibid., paras. 51–52).

[107] See, for example, the communication to the Government of Bulgaria concerning twenty-four sects declared illegal, including the 'White Brotherhood, Angels of Salvation, Soldiers of Christ, Soldiers of Justice, Wassan, Emmanuel, Gedeon, Salvation and Jehovah's Witnesses' in his second Report, E/CN.4/1995/91, p. 28.

[108] See, for example, replies to communications concerning the Church of Scientology given by Italy (E/CN.4/1990/46, paras. 55–56), Spain (ibid., paras. 78–79) and Germany (E/CN.4/1994/79, paras. 29–30); the reply to the communication sent to Spain concerning the 'Family of Love' (E/CN.4/1994/79, paras. 46–47); the reply of Bulgaria to the communication concerning sects (E/CN.4/1995/91, pp. 29–30) and the reply of Morocco to a communication concerning the Baha'is (ibid., p. 61).

[109] Mr Ribeiro referred to 'the so called Church of Scientology' in E/CN.4/1991/56 para. 101, although his communications (for which see the previous footnote) did not refer to it in this fashion.

[110] A/50/440, para. 59.

[111] See, for example, E/CN.4/1987/35, para. 18.

that the following situations are seen as violating the Declaration standards:[112]

    a. restrictions on the right to manifest one's religion in public;

    b. restrictions on the right to manifest one's religion in private;

    c. sanctions for belonging to a specific denomination;

    d. refusal to register certain religious communities;

    e. refusal to recognize the right to conscientious objection;

    f. the destruction, enforced closure, evacuation or arbitrary occupation of places of worship or assembly for a religion or belief;

    g. prohibition of the opening of new places of worship or assembly;

    h. refusal to grant permits to build new places of worship or assembly, or repair of existing premises;

    i. restriction of certain activities of a cultural nature relating to a religion or belief;

    j. seizure or confiscation of religious property or articles of worship;

    k. prohibition on importing, possessing, exhibiting or distributing certain articles of worship;

    l. prohibition on publishing, importing or distributing publications relating to a religion or belief;

    m. restriction or prohibition of religious propaganda or of propaganda concerning a belief (proselytism);

    n. censorship of religious publications, sermons or addresses;

    o. use for secular purposes of places considered to be sacred for certain religions or beliefs;

    p. profanation of burial places;

    q. restrictions on the right to set up seminaries to train clergy and on the possibilities for seminarists to receive adequate instruction;

    r. restrictions on the right to appoint sufficient numbers of clergy;

    s. the inability to celebrate holidays and ceremonies in accordance with the precepts of one's religion or belief;

    t. restrictions on the right to change religion.

Despite the length of this non-exhaustive list, these forms of manifestation chiefly relate to the ability of believers to enjoy the practice of their religion in a fairly narrow sense. There has been something of a reluctance to move beyond the forms of manifestation either set out in, or directly flowing from, the Declaration and address wider and more

---

[112] E/CN.4/1988/45, paras. 40–48; E/CN.4/1989/44, para. 96; E/CN.4/1990/46, para. 105; E/CN.4/1991/56, para. 92; E/CN.4/1992/52, para. 107; E/CN.4/1993/6, para. 74; E/CN.4/1994/79, para. 102; E/CN.4/1995/91, p. 146; E/CN.4/1996/95, para. 47. The First Annual Report also contains a section which sets out a series of non-country-specific allegations which demonstrate the existence of violations of each of the sub-sections of Article 6 and illustrates the various forms that such violations can take. See E/CN.4/1987/35, paras. 46–58.

controversial questions concerning the ability of believers to act in accordance with the dictates of their religious beliefs. For example, early in the operation of the mandate, the Special Rapporteur was faced with a claim that it was discriminatory for an employer to question job seekers concerning their religious beliefs when these had no bearing on the skills needed to perform the job in question. He responded by pointing to the comparatively trivial nature of the alleged violation when compared to the situations of discrimination faced by many other believers.[113] Clearly, it seems that the emphasis is upon the more pressing, and basic, needs. This may well be a sensible, pragmatic decision, but it serves to underline the limited usefulness of studying the practice of the Special Rapporteur for guidance concerning the limits of the freedom to manifest one's religion or belief, although the Reports provide a depressing catalogue of the infinite variants surrounding the restriction of even the most basic forms of manifestation.

There is, however, a suggestion that different levels of enjoyment might pertain to some forms of religion or belief but not to others, particularly those classified as 'new religions'. The early Annual Reports indicated that, whilst the right of believers to adhere to such faiths was to be assured, their capacity to manifest those beliefs – even within the terms of Article 6 – was to be the subject of careful scrutiny. It has been observed that 'the secular activities, particularly the financial and medical activities, of some of these movements and the possible effects which membership of them may have on the health and the physical or moral integrity of their followers have to be monitored closely by the Governments concerned'.[114] At the very least this suggests that new religious movements, whilst accepted as religions for the purposes of the mandate, are viewed with some suspicion.[115]

The distinction drawn between the 'secular' and 'non-secular' activities of such movements is, however, not at all clear. As has been seen, the 'mainstream' religious traditions do not themselves derive much protec-

---

[113] 'While the reservations of the Unions, in their concern to avoid any possibility of discrimination, are understandable, it is also obvious that, in other countries, the situation in respect of discrimination based on religion or other beliefs is definitely more disturbing.' E/CN.4/1987/35, para. 63.

[114] E/CN.4/1989/44, para. 17. See also E/CN.4/1988/45, para. 8.

[115] Of course, if expressed in this fashion, this would amount to discrimination of the very sort that the Special Rapporteur is mandated to address. However, this has been achieved with reference to Article 1(3) of the Declaration which permits restrictions upon the enjoyment of the rights set out in the Declaration. See, for example, E/CN.4/1995/91, pp. 147–148.

tion for manifestations of belief falling beyond the narrow sphere of activities connected with the ability to perform acts of religious worship. Whilst the Reports do acknowledge that the effects of intolerance spill over into 'secular life',[116] and that the Declaration is violated by death threats and intimidation directed against clergy 'as a result of the community work performed in parallel with their religious functions',[117] these aspects of intolerance have not been the object of many communications. If the latest Reports are symptomatic of a trend, the number of communications is set to increase and it may be that future Reports will address these issues in a less tangential fashion. Against this, instances of systematic violence against believers seem likely to dominate the work of the Special Rapporteur for the foreseeable future.

In addition, the Reports also demonstrate the continuing lack of consensus surrounding the question of whether the Declaration embraces the right to change one's religion. It has already been seen that, despite the evidence of the *travaux préparatoires*, the *Odio Benito Report* expressed the view that this was indeed the case.[118] The Special Rapporteur is also of this opinion[119] and has communicated several allegations concerning the situation of those who have renounced their beliefs.[120] In

---

[116] A standard recital is that the Special Rapporteur has noted 'the continuation in the application of administrative sanctions against members of certain faiths such as confiscation of property, denial of access to education and employment, exclusion from public service and the denial of salaries and pensions'. See, for example, E/CN.4/1993/62, para. 77; E/CN.4/1994/79, para. 105.

[117] E/CN.4/1993/62, para. 77; E/CN.4/1994/105, para. 77. This does, however, suggest that a distinction exists between the practice (manifestation) of religion and acting in accordance with its dictates which, whilst it might be of no significance in the case of a priest, might still be of relevance to the situation of other adherents to the faith.

[118] See above, pp. 201 and 221.

[119] E.g. E/CN.4/1996/95/Add.1, para. 84; E/CN.4/1996/95/Add.2, para. 91.

[120] See, for example, the arrest of Christian converts in Nepal (E/CN.4/1991/56, para. 79). In response to a subsequent communication, Nepal transmitted a copy of its Constitution, Article 19(1) of which provided: 'Every person shall have the freedom to profess and practise his own religion as coming down to him hereditarily having due regard to the traditional practices, provided that no person shall be entitled to convert the religion of any person.' This was explained as protecting those living in a socio-economically weak society from 'involuntary religious conversion' induced by 'financial enticement and other temptations'. Although not formally a bar to an individual changing their religion, the practical impact is to preclude this possibility. This, however, is seen as 'a source of guarantee to a weak person in protecting and preserving his fundamental right'. See E/CN.4/1994/79, paras. 65–66. See also the communications to the Governments of Bhutan (E/CN.4/1991/91, p. 21); Egypt (*ibid.*, p. 35); Morocco (*ibid.*, p. 60) and Malaysia (*ibid.*, p. 59). *Cf.* the discussion of the *Kokkinakis* case before the European Court of Human Rights considered below, p. 332.

particular, the Special Rapporteur has questioned the imposition of the death penalty for apostasy in the Sudan.[121] The Sudanese response is revealing:[122]

Islam is regarded by Muslims not as a mere religion but as a complete system of life. Its rules are prescribed not only to govern the individual's conduct but also to shape the basic laws and public order of the Muslim State. Accordingly, apostasy from Islam is classified as a crime for which *ta'zir* punishment may be applied (*ta'zir* is a disciplinary, reformative and deterrent punishment).

. . . The punishment is inflicted in cases in which the apostasy is a cause of harm to the society, while in those cases in which an individual simply changes his religion the punishment is not to be applied. But it must be remembered that unthreatening apostasy is an exceptional case . . . Assuredly, the protection of society is the underlying principle in the punishment for apostasy in the legal system of Islam.

Similarly, in response to a communication concerning a comment in a religious ruling (fatwah) that 'Shia are apostates from Islam "for which they deserve to be killed" ', Saudi Arabia maintained that:

freedom of religion . . . has double edges:
   (a)   the freedom of any country to adhere to, protect and preserve its religion.
   (b)   The respect and tolerance towards religious minorities of the country's citizens as long as they respect the constitutional tenets of their country.[123]

This suggests that, despite the programmatic assertions of the Special Rapporteurs and others, there still is no real acceptance of this right by those States which had opposed it throughout the drafting of the Covenant and Declaration. Indeed, in his Report covering activities in 1993, the Special Rapporteur included this right in his list of the more

[121]   E/CN.4/1993/62, para. 55.
[122]   *Ibid.*, para. 56. The problem posed for Islamic States by the relationship between apostasy and public order is examined by A. A. Sachedina, 'Freedom of Conscience and Religion in the Qu'ran', in D. Little, J. Kelsey and A. A. Sachedina (eds.), *Human Rights and the Conflict of Cultures: Western and Islamic Perspectives on Religious Liberty* (Columbia: University of South Carolina Press, 1988), pp. 76–81. M. Talbi, 'Religious Liberty: A Muslim Perspective', in Swindler (ed.), *Religious Liberty and Human Rights in Nations and Religions*, p. 175 at p. 183 says he knew of no implementation of the death penalty for apostasy in the history of Islam before a hanging took place in the Sudan in 1985.
[123]   E/CN.4/1993/62, paras. 51–52. See also E/CN.4/1995/91, p. 16. In reply to a previous communication concerning discrimination against Shia Muslims, Saudi Arabia had observed that if a person 'dislikes its laws and legislation he should not choose to live in it, but if he does he should strictly respect and accept its laws and legislation' (E/CN.4/1991/56, paras. 82–83).

numerous forms of violation.[124] In addition, Article 10 of the Convention on Human Rights and Fundamental Freedoms recently concluded by the Commonwealth of Independent States also fails to make explicit mention of the right to change religion, reflecting the generally restrictive tone of the article as a whole.[125]

Prospects for a convention

It is against this background that the prospects for the success of further attempts to draw up a convention on religious intolerance and discrimination must be assessed. The Declaration is not, strictly speaking, a source of direct legal obligation binding on States since it was adopted as a General Assembly Resolution which under the UN Charter only has a recommendatory status.[126] Nevertheless, declarations adopted by way of a General Assembly Resolution may be presumed to be statements of law, if the circumstances surrounding their adoption suggest that this is warranted,[127] and the *Odio Benito Report* forcefully argued that the Declaration contained 'concrete "obligations of conduct" which, although not directly imposed on States, as is compliance with a convention signed by the State, none the less link it to the achievement of the goals set out in such declarations . . . [T]he refusal to accept United Nations Resolutions on human rights places a state in a position that is incompatible with its status as a Member of the United Nations.'[128]

Of course, obligations in respect of human rights can become binding

---

[124] E/CN.4/1994/79, para. 102. See also Ribeiro, 'The Special Rapporteur for Religious Intolerance', p. 5, where he says that 'the right to abandon one religion or belief for another' was a principle 'that would necessarily be included in a convention'.

[125] Commonwealth of Independent States Convention on Human Rights and Fundamental Freedoms, signed at Minsk, 26 May 1995. Text in Council of Europe Doc. H/INF (96)1, Annex 56 (p. 197). Article 10 provides:

1. Everyone shall have the right to freedom of thought, conscience and faith. This right shall include freedom to choose one's religion or belief and freedom, either alone or in community with others, to engage in religious worship, attend and perform religious and ritual ceremonies and act in accordance with them.

2. Freedom to manifest one's religion or belief shall be subject only to such limitations as are prescribed by law and are necessary in a democratic society in the interests of national security, public safety, public order, public health or morals and for the protection of the rights and freedoms of others.

[126] UN Charter, Article 10. Member States are only formally bound by decisions of the Security Council (Articles 25 and 49).

[127] See B. Sloane, 'General Assembly Resolutions Revisited', *BYIL* 58 (1987), 41 at 140. See also pp. 125–139 for an examination of the relevant factors.

[128] Paras. 193–194.

on all States as a matter of customary international law.[129] Even if this has come about as regards Article 1,[130] it is unlikely that the forms of manifestation itemized in Article 6 have similarly been accepted.[131] Moreover, to the extent that debate still surrounds the question whether the right to change a religion is inherent in Article 1 of the Declaration (or, indeed, Article 18 of the ICCPR), it is clear that even accepting that article as reflective of customary law simply changes the nature of the debate to one of interpretation rather than one of legality. Certainly, the Special Rapporteur uses the language of legal obligation in his communications[132] and those States which do respond to communications do not seem to question the relevance of the Declaration standard, although they will often question its interpretation as well as its application to the facts as alleged. Nevertheless, the question of transforming the Declaration into a legally binding instrument remains.

Following the adoption of the Declaration, the United Nations organized in December 1984 a seminar on the encouragement of understanding, tolerance and respect in matters relating to freedom of religion or belief which recommended that further attention be given 'to the question of drawing up an international convention for the promotion and protection of freedom of religion or belief'.[133] In 1987 the *Odio Benito Report* echoed this call[134] and in March 1988 the CHR requested the Sub-Commission on Prevention of Discrimination and Protection of Minorities

---

[129] For an account of this process in the context of human rights see T. Meron, *Human Rights and Humanitarian Norms as Customary Law* (Oxford: Clarendon Press, 1989), Section II (pp. 79–114).

[130] For example, the *Third Restatement of the Foreign Relations Law of the United States* does not include religious intolerance or discrimination within its list of peremptory or customary norms (§702) but does suggest that a case can be made out for its inclusion (see §702, comment j).

[131] The 1993 World Conference on Human Rights 'called upon' governments to take measures 'to comply with their international obligations . . .to counter intolerance and related violence, . . .recognizing that every individual has the right to freedom of thought, conscience and religion'. However, it then merely 'invited' States 'to put into practice' the provisions of the Declaration (Vienna Declaration and Programme of Action (1993), II, para. 22, *ILM* 32 (1993), 1661). This rather suggests that the Declaration has not attained the force of customary law in itself and, whilst the freedom of thought, conscience and religion might have attained such a status, the freedom of manifestation, and certainly the catalogue in Article 6 of the Declaration, has not yet done so.

[132] But *cf.* the first Report, in which the Declaration was described as a 'morally binding instrument' (E/CN.4/1987/35, para. 9).

[133] ST/HR/SER.A/16, para. 102.

[134] This was described as an 'urgent need'. See *Odio Benito Report*, paras. 213 and 217.

'To examine . . . the issues and factors which should be considered before any drafting of a further binding instrument . . . takes place.'[135]

In pursuance of this, the Sub-Commission requested Mr Theo Van Boven to prepare a report.[136] This Report indicated the general nature of the problems to be faced, but did not attempt to identify particular issues that would need addressing. He did, however, emphasize the need for 'careful preparatory work and research . . . as regards the precise meaning of existing standards'.[137] The central message of the Report was for the need for care and further thought before embarking on such an exercise, and that same message has now been given by the Special Rapporteur, who considered 'the elaboration of an international convention . . . to be a necessary but premature step, given the present circumstances.'[138]

All of the various reports give lists of factors which need to be addressed in order to achieve a world rid of religious intolerance and discrimination, but the chief difficulty is seen to lie in the intolerant attitude of believers themselves. This is seen as a handicap which can be overcome with copious doses of education concerning human rights.[139] The Interim

---

[135] CHR Res. 1988/55. This resolution also called upon the Sub-Commission to be mindful of GA Res. 41/120 of 4 December 1986 which had called for 'UN member States and bodies to bear in mind, when drafting instruments, the need for texts to be sufficiently precise to give rise to identifiable and practicable rights and obligations' and 'attract broad international support'.

[136] Sub-Commission Decision 1988/112, 1 September 1988.

[137] E/CN.4/Sub.2/1989/32, para. 19(c). He expressed the hope that a 'general comment' issued by the HRC might help in this task but, as has been seen, the comment that has been issued does not add much further clarification. See also T. Van Boven, 'Advances and Obstacles in Building Understanding and Respect between People of Diverse Religion or Beliefs', *HRQ* 13 (1991), 438.

[138] A/50/440, para. 85. See also E/CN.4/1994/79, para. 111: 'Such an instrument should not be hastily drafted. Time is still needed to achieve significant progress in respect of religious freedom and to combat intolerance and discrimination based on religion or belief.' This might be contrasted with the views of his predecessor, who called for work to commence on such an instrument in his very first Report and reiterated the importance of making progress towards its realization in all his subsequent Reports. See E/CN.4/1987/35, para. 96; E/CN.4/1988/45, para. 66; E/CN.4/1989/45, para. 103(a); E/CN.4/1990/46, paras. 117–119; E/CN.4/1991/56, para. 107; E/CN.4/1992/52, para. 191; E/CN.4/1993, para. 89. See also Ribeiro, 'The Special Rapporteur on Religious Intolerance', p. 5.

[139] *Cf.* World Conference on Human Rights, the Vienna Declaration and Programme of Action which observed that: 'While the significance of national and religion particularities and various historical, cultural and religious backgrounds must be borne in mind, it is the duty of States, regardless of their political, economic and cultural systems, to promote and protect all human rights and fundamental freedoms' (para. I, 5). This is later amplified when the Conference reaffirmed that: 'States are duty-bound . . . to ensure that education is aimed at strengthening the

Report of the Special Rapporteur makes it clear that a 'culture of tolerance' must be developed, noting that 'religious teaching in primary and secondary schools could constitute the first stage of a process aimed at consecrating a minimum of generally accepted values and principles that might serve as a basis for a common programme of tolerance and non-discrimination . . . It is essential to develop a whole system for promoting human rights and tolerance through education.'[140] In a passage worth quoting at length, he observed that:

The reservations concerning religious freedom that have been expressed, albeit on rare occasions, should be dealt with patiently and deliberately, through further dialogue. Such dialogue should take into account the factors, be based on internationally established principles, involve all the parties concerned, determine the potential for immediate action and set a long-term course without any concessions. Progress in this field is as much a matter of uncovering facts, motivations and concerns as of the need to protect human rights in general and religious freedom in particular. The only way to make progress in promoting religious freedom is to avoid categorical, inflexible attitudes, impulsive and ineffectual initiatives, ill considered behaviours, blind obstinacy, gratuitous accusations, inconsistent judgements and grandiose but futile gestures. In other words, it is time to take a hard look at reality, in all its complexity, and work with it to change it gradually.[141]

If this means anything, it means that the freedom of religion does not include the right to adhere to a religion which is intolerant of the beliefs of others.[142] On this view, 'Human Rights' has itself become a 'religion or belief' which is itself as intolerant of other forms of value systems which may stand in opposition to its own central tenets as any of those it seeks to address.[143] Expressions of such views are not restricted to the UN. The

respect of human rights and fundamental freedoms' (para. II, 33). See also UDHR Article 26(2).

[140] A/50/440, paras. 83–84; E/CN.4/1996/95, paras. 67–68.

[141] A/50/440, para. 86; E/CN.4/1996/95, para. 70

[142] *Cf.* Sullivan, 'Advancing the Freedom of Religion', pp. 510–518 where some problems of conflict between the Declaration standards and others in the human rights catalogue – particularly women's rights – are examined and a system of resolution is proposed which involves balancing a number of factors, including 'the significance of a particular religious practice to the underlying religion or belief'. To the believer, religious practices are not capable of being 'balanced away' in this fashion without undermining their religious freedom.

[143] *Cf.* McDougal, Lasswell and Chen, *Human Rights and World Public Order*, p. 662: 'Even so fundamental a freedom as that of religious inquiry, belief, and communication must, of course, be exercised and protected with due regard for the comparable rights of others and for the aggregate common interest in the preservation of all basic human rights.'

Parliamentary Assembly of the Council of Europe has also observed that: 'There is a recognisable crisis of values (or rather lack of them) in present day Europe. The pure market society is revealed as inadequate as communism for individual well-being and social responsibility. *The recourse to religion as an alternative has, however, to be reconciled with the principles of democracy and human rights.*'[144]

In seeking to assert itself in this fashion, the international community risks becoming the oppressor of the believer, rather than the protector of the persecuted. Clearly, the time is not yet ripe for a convention: not because of the unwillingness of States to adopt such an instrument, but because of the reluctance of the international community to accept that in the religious beliefs of others the dogmas of human rights are met with an equally powerful force which must be respected, not overcome.

[144] Parliamentary Assembly of the Council of Europe, Recommendation 1202 of 2 February 1993, on religious tolerance in a democratic society, para. 9 (emphasis added).

10 Religious freedom under the European Convention on Human Rights: the drafting of Article 9 and of Article 2 of the First Protocol

It is accepted that the ECHR is to be interpreted in accordance with Article 31 of the Vienna Convention on the Law of Treaties, which provides that treaties are to be interpreted 'in good faith in accordance with the ordinary meaning to be given to the terms of the treaty in their context and in the light of its object and purpose'.[1] According to Article 32, preparatory materials are to be examined in order to 'confirm the meaning resulting from the application of article 31' or to determine the meaning where such an interpretation is 'ambiguous or obscure' or 'leads to a result which is manifestly absurd or unreasonable'. Given that the terms of Article 9 of the ECHR and Article 2 of the First Protocol are fairly obscure, the preparatory work should be of some relevance to their interpretation and application.[2] Against this, however, must be placed the manner in which the Court and Commission have adopted a teleological approach to the convention text, which diminishes the impact of the

---

[1] Although the Vienna Convention does not have retrospective effect, the European Court of Human Rights has taken the view that Articles 31–33 are reflective of customary international law. See *Golder v. UK*, Ser. A, no. 18 (1975), para. 29. The Court's methods of interpretation are examined by J. G. Merrills, *The Development of International Law by the European Court of Human Rights*, 2nd edn (Manchester University Press, 1993), pp. 69–97 and D. J. Harris, M. O'Boyle, C. Warbrick, *Law of the European Convention on Human Rights* (London: Butterworths, 1995), pp. 5–18.

[2] Thus in *Kjeldsen, Busk Madsen and Pedersen v. Denmark* (the *Danish Sex Education* cases: Ser. A, no. 23 (1976), para. 50) the Court said that the preparatory material was 'of particular consequence in the case of a clause [Article 2 of the First Protocol] that gave rise to such impassioned debate'. It was also considered relevant to the interpretation of that clause in the *Belgian Linguistics* case (Ser. A, no. 6 (1968), pp. 30–33). However, in *Campbell and Cosans v. UK* (Ser. A, no. 48 (1982), para. 36) the Court thought that 'little assistance as to its precise significance is to be gleaned from the *travaux préparatoires*', with regard to the meaning of the word 'philosophical'. See Merrills, *ibid.*, p. 94, who takes the view that this was motivated by the desire to reach a different conclusion.

debates surrounding their adoption nearly fifty years ago.[3] Moreover, and as will be seen below, the preparatory work tends only to highlight the problems surrounding the texts, rather than resolve them.

Nevertheless, given that the freedom of religion has received comparatively little attention from the Strasbourg organs, the drafting history still has a relevance to its interpretation and application. In addition, the discussions retain their interest because of the light they shed upon the manner in which this aspect of the 'public order of Europe', said to be enshrined within the Convention,[4] came into being. The discussions also take their place in the general development of thinking concerning the freedom of religion.

Introduction

The origins of the ECHR lie in a draft convention drawn up by the International Juridical Section of the European Movement in the summer of 1949.[5] This text contained a rather terse list of rights to be guaranteed to all persons within the territories of the contracting States, including 'Freedom of religious belief, practice and teaching'.[6] In common with all of the rights included in the draft, this freedom was to be subject 'only to such limitations as are in conformity with the general principles of law recognized by civilized nations and as prescribed by law for: (a) Protecting the legal rights of others; (b) Meeting the just requirements of morality,

---

[3] See, e.g., *Tyrer v. UK*, Ser. A, no. 26 (1978), para. 31, where the Court said that 'the Convention is a living instrument which . . . must be interpreted in the light of present-day conditions'. See also Harris, O'Boyle and Warbrick, *Law of the ECHR*, p. 17.

[4] See, e.g., *Loizidou v. Turkey (Preliminary Objections)*, Ser. A, no. 310 (1995), para. 93, where the Court referred to 'the special character of the Convention as an instrument of European public order (*ordre public*) for the protection of individual human beings and its mission . . . "to ensure the observance of the engagements undertaken by the High Contracting Parties"'.

[5] For an overview of the background to, and drafting of, the ECHR see A. H. Robertson, 'The European Convention of Human Rights', *BYIL* 27 (1950), 143; A. H. Robertson and J. G. Merrills, *Human Rights in Europe*, 3rd edn (Manchester University Press, 1993), pp. 1–14; R. Beddard, *Human Rights and Europe*, 3rd edn (Cambridge: Grotius Publications Ltd, 1993), pp. 19–32; R. Goy, 'La Garantie Européenne de la Liberté de Religion', *RDP* 107 (1991), 5, 6–12.

[6] Draft European Convention on Human Rights, Article 1(e). See Council of Europe, *Collected Edition of the 'Travaux Préparatoires' of the European Convention on Human Rights (CETP)*, 8 vols. (The Hague: Martinus Nijhoff, 1975–1985), vol. I, Appendix, p. 296.

public order (including the safety of the community) and the general welfare'.[7] The underlying purpose of the Draft Convention was to ensure that the rights and freedoms already enjoyed by those living in the countries represented within the European Movement would not be subject to any diminution.[8] To this end, Article 6 of the Draft Convention required of each State only that it should guarantee the rights listed in Article 1 'to the extent that such rights were secured by the constitution, laws and administrative practice existing in its country at the date of signing this Convention by such State'.[9] At the same time, it looked towards a 'supplementary agreement' which would define the rights and limitations outlined in Articles 1 and 3.[10] Thus, just as the cold war was developing, the States of Western Europe were being urged to draw a line under their domestic provisions and guarantee the continuance of whatever freedoms were currently recognized: developing and defining standards was to come later.[11] The task of taking this forward fell to the newly established Council of Europe.

Article 9: the freedom of thought, conscience and religion

The Statute of the Council of Europe was signed on 5 May 1949. Article 1(b) of the Statute gave as one of its objects: 'The maintenance and further realization of human rights and fundamental freedoms' and, by virtue of Article 3, all Member States were obliged to accept 'the principles of the rule of law and the enjoyment by all persons within its jurisdiction of human rights and fundamental freedoms'. The First Session of the Consultative Assembly of the Council of Europe took place in August 1949

---

[7] Article 3, p. 298.

[8] Mr David Maxwell-Fyfe (Rapporteur to the International Juridical Section of the European Movement) addressing the First Session of the Consultative Assembly of the Council of Europe. *CETP*, vol. I, p. 120.

[9] Article 6(a). Any additional protection subsequently introduced by a country in respect of the rights included in Article 1 would be similarly guaranteed.

[10] Article 5. If the standards commonly agreed were lower than those existing in a given country, then a greater protection would be offered by this interim arrangement than by a supplementary agreement. See Maxwell-Fyfe, *CETP*, vol. I, p. 120.

[11] See M. Teitgen (Chairman of the International Juridical Section of the European Movement) when placing the draft before the Consultative Assembly of the Council of Europe. *CETP*, vol. I, pp. 44–46.

and its agenda included an item[12] headed 'Maintenance and further realization of human rights and fundamental freedoms'.[13]

Sir David Maxwell-Fyfe and M. Teitgen introduced a motion before the Assembly that called for the immediate conclusion of a convention along the lines of the draft prepared under the auspices of the European Movement.[14] Whilst most delegates endorsed the general sentiments embodied in the draft,[15] there was considerable disagreement over the merits of the 'interim' and 'supplementary agreement' approach. Many were in favour of seeking more precise definitions from the outset,[16]

---

[12] The draft agenda had been considered by a Preparatory Commission, in which Ireland had proposed an additional agenda item concerning 'defence of the basic political, civil and religious rights of man'. This had little to do with human rights as such. It was included alongside 'methods to ensure peaceful settlement of disputes between members' and 'settlement of frontier problems' and was designed to place the dispute with the UK over Northern Ireland before the Assembly. The item was not accepted. See Doc. C/19 of 6 July (pp. 2–4). The question was raised by some delegates in the Assembly in any case. See records of 1st Session, pp. 102–106 (Mr Everett) and 138–144 (Mr MacEntree).

[13] The Preparatory Committee referred the inclusion of this item to the Committee of Ministers (Doc. CP/18 of 5 July 1949 (CETP, vol. I, p. 2) and the Report of the Preparatory Commission, 13 July 1949 (ibid., p. 6)). Before reaching that Committee, however, the proposed item was amended, on the suggestion of the UK, to include the question of the definition of human rights, as well as their maintenance and realization. (See Records of the Preparatory Commission for the 1st Session of the Committee of Ministers, ibid., p. 8.) This proved controversial in its own right and was a factor contributing to the Committee's decision to delete the item from the Assembly's Agenda, the formal reason given being that the same matters were also being examined by the United Nations. (1st Session of the Committee of Ministers, 2nd Meeting, ibid., pp. 10–13.) This decision was roundly condemned in the Assembly, which proposed to the Committee of Ministers that an item on human rights be included. The Committee ultimately acceded to this request, although the final form of the item made it unclear whether the definition of human rights was to be included as a matter of debate. See Consultative Assembly Records, 12 and 13 August 1949 (ibid., pp. 14–21) and Committee of Ministers, 13 August 1949 (ibid., pp. 23–27). See also G. Marston, 'The United Kingdom's Part in the Preparation of the European Convention on Human Rights', ICLQ 42 (1993), 767 at 806–807. This article provides a full analysis of the background to the role played by the UK in the drafting process.

[14] Records of the Consultative Assembly, 19 August 1949, CETP, vol. I, pp. 36–154.

[15] Several delegates made special mention of the significance of religious freedom: M. Teitgen (ibid., p. 46) described it, in common with all the rights listed in Article 1 of the Draft Convention, as 'fundamental, undisputed freedoms'. M. Cingolani (Italy: ibid., p. 62) considered the right 'of religious belief and of the works through which religious faith is manifest' to be 'the most sacred right of all'.

[16] E.g. Mr Lannung (Denmark) p. 50; Mr Edberg (Sweden) p. 78; Mr Ungoed-Thomas (UK) pp. 80–82; M. Fayat (Belgium) p. 88.

whilst others considered this either unnecessary[17] or not sufficiently pressing as to warrant delay.[18]

The matter was referred to the Committee on Legal and Administrative Questions which abandoned the 'twin track' approach outlined in the earlier draft[19] and attempted to meet the arguments of those that had sought greater definition by 'borrowing' from the Universal Declaration of Human Rights as far as it felt this possible.[20] The Committee had no difficulty in accepting the relevance of Article 18 of the UDHR, and Article 2 of its amended draft provided that:

In this convention, the Member States shall undertake to ensure to all persons residing within their territories:

. . .

(5) Freedom of thought, conscience and religion, in accordance with Article 18 of the Universal Declaration.[21]

When the Committee's Report (the *Teitgen Report*) was considered by the Assembly the bulk of the discussion concerned the proposal to establish the European Court and Commission of Human Rights[22] and the questions of whether to recognize property rights and the rights of parents with respect to the nature of their children's education in the catalogue of fundamental freedoms.[23] The proposed text on religious freedom attracted no attention and was not mentioned in the debates. It was duly accepted by the Assembly[24] and forwarded to the Committee of Ministers

---

[17] E.g. Mr Dominedo (Italy) p. 72.

[18] E.g. M. Teitgen (France) p. 46; Mr Foster (UK) p. 92; Sir David Maxwell-Fyfe, pp. 118–120.

[19] This Committee considered the proposal between 22 August and 5 September 1949 under the Chairmanship of Sir David Maxwell-Fyfe, with M. Teitgen acting as Rapporteur. For the records of the Committee see *CETP*, vol. I. pp. 154–214.

[20] This also had the advantage of disarming those who had argued against devising definitions in the European context lest they contradicted those developed by the United Nations. Report of the Committee on Legal and Administrative Questions to the Assembly, 5 September 1949, para. 6. See *CETP*, vol. I, p. 218. See also p. 268 (presentation by M. Teitgen of the Report to the 17th Sitting of the Consultative Assembly).

[21] The proposal, moved by Mr Ungoed-Thomas, was accepted unanimously. See *CETP*, vol. I, p. 174. At this stage the text simply made reference to the UDHR, the relevant provisions of which were included in an annex. It was the Committee of Experts which subsequently decided to utilize the wording of the Declaration in the text, so that the text of the Convention would be complete in itself. See Meetings of the Committee of Experts, Doc. A 783, *CETP*, vol. III, pp. 190–192.

[22] Records of the Consultative Assembly, 18th Sitting, 8 September 1949, *CETP*, vol. II, pp. 142–228.

[23] *Ibid.*, pp. 48–132.

[24] *Ibid.*, pp. 46, 132 and 274. The final version of the text was adopted by sixty-four votes for, one against, with twenty-one abstentions.

which decided to convene a Committee of (legal) Experts to draw up a draft for it to consider.[25]

This Committee met in February and March 1950, and was faced immediately by exactly the same problem as had dogged the earlier stages of the drafting process – the question of how great a degree of definition was necessary. It characterized the difference as being between the 'definition' and 'enumeration' of rights. The Committee of Experts felt itself unable to resolve this fundamental question[26] and so produced two texts. Version 'A' was based upon the 'enumeration' approach, and was modelled upon the draft forwarded to the Committee of Ministers by the Consultative Assembly, whilst version 'B' was based upon a draft submitted by the UK and which sought to provide more precise definitions of the rights.[27] Although the definition of the right, borrowed from the UDHR, remained unaltered in both versions,[28] amendments limiting its impact were introduced by supporters of both the 'enumeration' and the 'definition' approach.

Turkey and Sweden, proponents of the 'enumeration' approach, introduced separate amendments[29] but, after discussion, agreed to move a joint amendment which sought to add to draft Article 2(5) (version 'A') the qualification that: 'This provision does not affect existing national laws

---

[25] See *CETP*, vol. II, pp. 288–297 and 302–305. The Committee of Ministers decided not to involve the Assembly's Committee on Legal and Administrative Questions. The experts were to be directly appointed by the governments of the Member States of the Council of Europe. The Standing Committee of the Consultative Assembly saw this as both a snub and a delaying tactic. Letter to the Chairman of the Committee of Ministers, *ibid.*, p. 300.

[26] The Committee felt that this 'should be decided in the light of political rather than legal considerations'. Report to the Committee of Ministers (Doc. CM/WP 1(50) 15, A 924 of 16 March 1950), *CETP* vol. IV, p. 16.

[27] Report to the Committee of Ministers (Doc. CM/WP 1(50) 15, A 924 of 16 March 1950), *CETP*, vol. IV, pp. 6–49, draft text included as Appendix, Doc. A 925 (*ibid.*, p. 50). The Committee also included as variants of versions 'A' and 'B' texts which did not include provisions establishing a European Court of Human Rights. This Committee felt that this was also a political, rather than a legal, question (*ibid.*, p. 16).

[28] Article 2(5) of version 'A' and Article 9 of version 'B'.

[29] Turkey proposed two amendments, the first adding the words, 'subject to reservations concerning legislative measures to prevent attempts being made once again to suppress these freedoms' (Doc. A 775, *CETP*. vol. III, p. 182); the second adding the words, 'Subject to reservations as regards the measures required for ensuring security and public order, as well as those restrictions which, for reasons of history, it has been considered necessary, by the States, signatory to this Convention, to place on the exercise of this right' (Doc. A 787, *ibid.*, p. 196). Sweden proposed to add: 'This provision does not affect existing national laws as regards rules relating to religious practice and membership of certain faiths.'

which contain restrictive regulations concerning religious institutions and endowments or membership to certain faiths.'[30] This was ultimately incorporated into version 'A' as Article 7(b), the full text of which provided that: 'Nor may these provisions be considered as derogating from already existing national rules as regards religious institutions and foundations or membership of certain confessions'.[31]

Both countries were seeking to ensure that laws currently in force would not be subject to critical examination and it was understood that the article would not justify the imposition of new restrictions.[32] The representatives of both the UK and the Netherlands objected, considering it wrong that special circumstances appertaining to only two States should become the subject of a collective guarantee, and saw problems in reconciling the preservation of the existing legislation with the principle of non-discrimination.[33]

The Report of the Committee of Experts commented that this paragraph 'was intended to cover those reasonable restrictions on the eligibility for public office of members of certain religious faiths which are prescribed in the constitutions of certain states and which, it was recognized, could not be removed immediately'.[34] This is a little difficult to understand. If restrictions upon eligibility were 'reasonable', then there would seem to be no reason for the State to consider removing them. The non-discrimination provision of Article 5 was, like Article 2(5) itself, subject to Article 6 which allowed the enjoyment of rights to be limited 'in order to satisfy the just requirements of public morality and order, national security and territorial integrity, as well as the smooth working of administration and justice in a democratic society'. The entire point of the subsection was to allow the continuation of a state of affairs that was considered to be unreasonable but necessary. This was made even more obvious by the observation that: 'It is also intended to cover similar regulations regarding the membership and the activity of certain religious institutions.'[35] This clearly contemplates the continuation of discriminatory practices.

---

[30] Ibid., p. 200.

[31] Doc. CM/WP 1(50) 15, appendix (A 925 of 16 March 1950), CETP, vol. IV, p. 54.

[32] Report to the Committee of Ministers (Doc. CM/WP 1(50) 15, A 924 of 16 March 1950), CETP, vol. IV, p. 26. The Swedish representative argued that 'the place occupied by the Lutheran faith had its origin in the distant past, and that this did not impede the right, freely recognized in that country, to adopt another faith, provided that the person concerned joined some other religious community . . . [I]t could not be overlooked that there were considerable obstacles, constitutional and others, which would oppose any attempt to modify it' (ibid., p. 28).

[33] Ibid..   [34] Ibid., p. 32.   [35] Ibid..

Equally, there seems to have been no objection made to the principle of restricting eligibility for certain public offices to members of a particular religious community.

Moreover, the representative of the Netherlands expressed his understanding for the reasons which had led Turkey to impose restrictions on certain religious activities in the interests of 'cultural recovery'. Although these remarks were not entirely unambiguous, the Turkish expert took them as an endorsement of his government's policy. In a formal Reply to the Report of the Committee, the Turkish Expert stressed that:

legislative measures relating to . . . the Moslem religious orders are in no way intended to place restrictions on the freedom of religion . . . It must, however, be pointed out that in the course of our history a number of attempts at reform and modernization have been frustrated by stubborn resistance on the part of certain persons or groups of persons who wished to keep the population in ignorance for their own ends . . . Turkey has therefore been obliged to start by abolishing the Moslem orders and their archaic institutions.[36]

As mentioned above, the rights enumerated in the *Teitgen Report*, in the Assembly's draft and the Committee of Experts' version 'A' – all based on the 'enumeration' approach – were subject to the general limitations set out in Article 6. The Turkish and Swedish proposal had sought to provide an extra limitation applicable only to Article 2(5). The alternative 'definition' approach provided a separate limitation clause for each freedom, where deemed necessary. The UK draft proposal dealt with religious freedoms in Article 9(1) and added a new subsection which provided that:

2. Freedom to manifest one's religion or beliefs shall be subject only to such limitations as are pursuant to law and are reasonable and necessary to protect public safety, order, health or morals or the fundamental rights and freedoms of others.[37]

This was subject to some relatively minor alterations but was also amended so as to incorporate the substance of the Turkish and Swedish amendment so that in its final form it read:

2. Freedom to manifest one's religion or beliefs shall be subject only to such limitations as are prescribed by law and are necessary in the interests of public safety, or for the protection of public order, health or morals, or for the protection of the rights and freedoms of others, provided that nothing in this Convention may be considered as

---

[36] Reply of the Turkish Expert to the Comments of the Netherlands Expert (Addendum 2 to Doc. CM/WP 1(50) 15, A 1280 of 27 May 1959) *CETP*, vol. IV, p. 80. *Cf.* the Turkish reservation to Article 2 of the First Protocol, see below, p. 279, n. 94.

[37] Doc. A 798, Article 9, *CETP*, vol. III, p. 206.

derogating from already existing national rules as regards religious institutions and foundations, or membership of certain confessions.[38]

The Committee of Ministers, rather than deal with the issues raised in the Report of the Committee of Experts itself, decided to convene a Conference of Senior Officials to 'prepare the ground' for them and to suggest solutions to the political problems that had been raised by the Experts.[39] The Conference was as split as the Committee of Experts had been on the question of whether to adopt the 'enumeration' or 'definition' approach.[40] This ultimately became interwoven with the question of whether to establish a European Court of Human Rights[41] and a compromise emerged in which the text would be an amalgam of both approaches and a court would be established but with only optional jurisdiction. As far as the freedom of religion was concerned, the text adopted followed the definition approach and Article 9(1) of version 'B' was adopted with neither debate nor comment. Subsection (2) was, however, the subject of some considerable discussion, the result of which had a major impact upon the entire Convention system.

First, the reference to limitations necessary 'in the interests of national security' was replaced with limitations necessary 'in a democratic society'.[42] Secondly, and most significantly, the phrase added to draft Article 9(2) by the Committee of Experts in response to the Turkish and Swedish proposal received further criticism. The UK representative argued that it was illogical to permit expressly the continuance of contradictory legislation and suggested that a new clause be added which would permit

[38] *CETP*, vol. IV, p. 62.
[39] Third Session of the Committee of Ministers, 30 March–1 April 1950. *CETP*, vol. IV, pp. 84–95.
[40] See, e.g., *CETP*, vol. IV, p. 112.
[41] Four States (UK, Netherlands, Greece and Norway) favoured definition. Four States (France, Ireland, Italy and Turkey) favoured enumeration. Two States (Belgium and Luxembourg) favoured enumeration if a court was established but definition if it was not. Denmark and Sweden (the Chairman) were neutral. Generally speaking, those States in favour of definition were opposed to the court, whilst those in favour of enumeration were in favour of it. Both Turkey and Sweden, however, were against the court, thus ensuring there was no majority for either position. See Report of the Conference of Senior Officials, *CETP*, vol. IV, pp. 246–250. See also Marston, 'UK Part in ECHR Preparation', pp. 808–811.
[42] The Report of the Conference to the Committee of Ministers says that these words also replaced the phrase 'in the interests of public safety', but these are still found in the draft article appended to it. See Report of the Conference of Senior Officials, *CETP*, vol. IV, p. 258 and Draft Convention, Article 9 (Doc. CM/WP 4(550) 19 annex; A 1452), *CETP*, vol. IV, p. 278.

reservations.[43] The Swedish representative was happy with this, since 'the discriminatory Swedish legislation on freedom of religion was shortly to disappear'.[44] However, the newly added article was of general application, not limited to religious freedom, and provided:[45]

1. Any State may when signing this Convention or when depositing its instrument of ratification or accession, make a reservation in respect of any particular provision of the Convention to the extent that any law then in force in its territory is not in conformity with that provision. Reservations of a general character shall not be permitted under this Article.

2. Any reservation made under this Article shall contain a brief statement of the law concerned.[46]

This, rather than Article 9(2) itself, now became the focus of discussion. The Committee on Legal and Administrative Questions of the Consultative Assembly expressed its general approval with the text produced by the Officials but objected to Article 60 on the basis that 'such a power would threaten to deprive [the Convention] of this practical effect and . . . moral authority'.[47] Nevertheless the clause remained, now numbered Article 64, in the Draft Convention adopted by the Committee of Ministers on 7 August[48] and was not subsequently challenged when the text was placed before the Second Session of the Consultative Assembly sitting from 11 to 28 August.[49] Nor were any further amendments to Article 9

---

[43] *Ibid.*, p. 258. The illogicality of contradictory legislation being countenanced outside of the text did not seem to be a matter of concern. *Cf.* the Netherlands, which suggested that it be removed to the Protocol of Signature, rather than be the text itself (*ibid.*, p. 172).

[44] *Ibid.*, p. 258. It might be noted that the Swedish representative in the Committee of Experts had, less than four months earlier, thought that this would present grave problems.

[45] Draft Convention, Article 60 (Doc. CM/WP 4(550) 19 annex; A 1452), *CETP*, vol. IV, p. 294.

[46] Norway proved to be the only State which did make a reservation with respect to Article 9, and which provided: 'Whereas Article 2 of the Norwegian Constitution of 17 May 1814 contains a provision under which Jesuits are not tolerated, a corresponding reservation is made with regard to the application of Article 9 of the Convention.' This reservation was withdrawn on 4 December 1956 following the amendment of the Constitution to bring it into conformity with the Convention. Article 9 also prompted Norway to repeal an 1891 statute which had required dissenters (members of non-State churches) to meet in public. See F. Castberg, *The European Convention on Human Rights* (Leiden: Sijthoff, 1974), pp. 26, 146.

[47] Letter from Sir David Maxwell-Fyfe (Chairman) to the Committee of Ministers, 24 June 1950 (Doc. CM (50) 29), *CETP*, vol. V, p. 40.

[48] Draft Convention, Doc. A 1937 of 7 August 1950. *CETP*, vol. V, p. 142.

[49] For the records of the sittings see *CETP*, vol. V, pp. 210–351 and vol. VI, pp. 2–191.

presented.[50] The evolution of these articles was complete and it simply remained for them to be adopted along with the rest of the Convention by the Committee of Ministers on 4 November 1950 at its Sixth Session in Rome.[51]

As finally adopted, Article 9 of the ECHR provides:

1. Everyone has the right to freedom of thought, conscience and religion; this right includes freedom to change his religion or belief and freedom, either alone or in community with others and in public or private, to manifest his religion or belief in worship, teaching, practice and observance.

2. Freedom to manifest one's religion or beliefs shall be subject only to such limitations as are prescribed by law and are necessary in a democratic society in the interests of public safety, for the protection of public order, health or morals, or for the protection of the rights and freedoms of others.

Article 2 of the First Protocol: parental choice in education

One of the issues that attained prominence during the latter stages of the drafting process concerned the right of parents to determine the nature of their children's education.[52] This had been raised by M. Yetkin of Turkey in the First Session of the Consultative Assembly[53] and the catalogue of rights set out in the *Teitgen Report* had included as Article 2(11): 'The rights of parents concerning the education of their children as defined in paragraph 3 of Article 26 of the Declaration of the United Nations'.[54] This proved controversial for a number of reasons.

It was argued in the Assembly that this right, along with the right to marry and to own property (*Teitgen Report*, Article 2(10) and (12)), should be deleted from the text since it was too complex to be dealt with quickly

---

[50] *CETP*, vol. VI, p. 148. The amendments that were suggested by the Consultative Assembly were, with one minor exception, rejected by the Council of Ministers. The French and German members of the Standing Committee of the Consultative Assembly did not attend the ceremony accompanying the signing of the Convention in protest. See Doc. IP/180, *CETP*, vol. VII, p. 46.

[51] *CETP*, vol. VII, pp. 38–40.

[52] See A. H. Robertson, 'The European Convention on Human Rights: Recent Developments', *BYIL* 28 (1951), 359 at 362–364.

[53] *CETP*, vol. I, p. 124.

[54] Proposed by M. Teitgen in Doc. 116 and accepted by the Committee on Legal and Administrative Questions by ten votes to five. See *CETP*, vol. I, pp. 168 and 176. See also the *Teitgen Report*, para. 9, *ibid.*, p. 220 where this was included as one of three 'family rights', the others being freedom from all arbitrary interference in family life (Article 2(4)) and the right to marry and to found a family (Article 2(10)).

and should not be allowed to cause delay.[55] It was decided to refer both Article 2(11) and (12) back to the Legal Committee for further study and report rather than pass it on to the Committee of Ministers,[56] and so the issue became separated from the full text and the process that led up to the adoption of the ECHR in the autumn of 1950.

The Committee on Legal and Administrative Questions reconsidered the question of education and property rights in June 1950. It confirmed its view that these rights ought to be included in the text of the Convention,[57] but the decision of the Conference of Senior Officials to adopt the more 'definition-oriented' approach meant that the simple statement endorsed by the Legal Committee the previous year would no longer suffice and a sub-committee was set up to provide appropriate definitions.[58] This four-member sub-committee met on 8 August 1950 and adopted a text which provided that:

All persons are entitled to education. The responsibilities assumed by the State with regard to education may not encroach on the right of parents to ensure the spiritual and moral instruction of their children in accordance with their own religious and philosophical beliefs.[59]

The chief point of difficulty concerned the relationship between the claim of the State and of the parent. This had been masked by the careful wording of the text[60] but dominated the discussion of it in the Assembly. Although for some the issue remained one of determining whether the

---

[55] The UK representatives were at the forefront of this. Lord Layton argued that the Convention represented the minimum set of acceptable standards to which other States – such as Germany and Spain – would have to conform if they wished to join the Council of Europe and the violation of which would trigger 'intervention' or enforcement. He did not consider these rights to be sufficiently significant as to justify their inclusion in such a 'threshold' document (*CETP*, vol. II, p. 48). As regards education in particular, he observed that: 'How the rights of the parents are to be safeguarded when the State is necessarily assuming major responsibility for education is an extremely complex problem' (*ibid.*, p. 54). See also Mr Ungoed-Thomas, *ibid.*, p. 60.

[56] The vote in favour of reference back was very close, with forty-three in favour and forty against (*ibid.*, vol. II, pp. 4 and 132). Article 2(12) was also referred back but Article 2(10) was accepted.

[57] Lord Layton argued that they ought to be mentioned in the Preamble, rather than the text, but this was rejected. See *CETP*, vol. V, pp. 16 and 24.

[58] Minutes of 24 June 1950, *CETP*, vol. V, p. 26.

[59] Doc. Consultative Assembly No. 30, 8 August 1950. *CETP*, vol. V, p. 208.

[60] The Rapporteur, M. Bastid of France, rather disingenuously claimed that the sub-committee had fully agreed with the principles embodied in the text submitted by M. Rolin of Belgium which had referred to the rights of parents to 'bestow' appropriate training on their children and which had, therefore, given greater prominence to parental rights than the text adopted. See *CETP*, vol. V, pp. 202–204.

rights of the State or of the parent should be paramount,[61] the crux of the matter concerned whether a State would be obliged to provide funding for denominational or confessional schools. Despite the general belief that this was not the case, some still considered that the text implied that the State would be obliged to provide suitable facilities.[62] It was, therefore, referred back to the Committee on Legal and Administrative Questions which adopted an amended version proposed by M. Teitgen which provided that: 'Every person has a right to education. The functions assumed by the State in respect of education and of teaching may not encroach upon the right of parents to ensure the spiritual and moral education and the teaching of their children in conformity with their own religious and philosophical convictions.'[63]

This went beyond the previous proposal in that it recognized the right of the parent to ensure that all teaching, as opposed to simply religious teaching, was 'permeated with a religious spirit'.[64] Replacing the phrase 'responsibilities assumed' with the words 'functions assumed' stressed the volitional nature of the State's involvement in the educational process and was intended to underline the lack of an obligation upon the State to provide facilities.[65] In addition, Sir David Maxwell-Fyfe explained that:

the object of this Article is to meet what we all know was a terrible aspect of totalitarianism, namely, that the youth of the country were brought up so much under the dogmatic teaching of totalitarianism by the agencies or para-agencies

---

[61] E.g. Mr Azara (Italy), *ibid.*, p. 246 and Mr Beaufort (Belgium) p. 328.

[62] This was the view taken by Mr Schmal (Netherlands) p. 250 and Mr MacEntree (Ireland) pp. 304–314.

[63] Doc. AS/JA (2) 6, 16 August 1950; A 2207. *CETP*, vol. VI, p. 6. Adopted by the Committee by seventeen votes to three at its meeting on 17 August 1950 (*ibid.*, p. 20). See also the Report of 24 August submitted by the Committee to the Assembly (*ibid.*, p. 62).

[64] M. Rolin (Belgium), who felt that it was this feature which distinguished denominational instruction from State instruction (*ibid.*, p. 158).

[65] E.g. Mr Schmid (Germany), who said that the text, 'whilst giving parents the right to set up private schools according to their religious and philosophical beliefs, does not compel States to institute, at the request of parents, denominational schools the expense of which are borne by the State' (*ibid.*, p. 158). But *cf.* Mr De Valera (Ireland) who continued to voice Irish objections to this view, arguing that: 'The Article . . . is simply an expression of secularist opinion. It safeguards parents from interference by the State with the religious education of . . . their children. But in many States there are large sections of the population who desire something more than that. These people pay taxes and they desire the education to be given to their children to be much more positively religious than that which they would get in an institution which is purely secularist. They should not have to pay twice' (*ibid.*, p. 152 and *cf.* the Irish Declaration, below, p. 279, n. 96).

of the State that it was impossible for their parents to bring them up in their own religious and philosophic beliefs.[66]

This introduced a further dimension and considerably expanded the scope of the article. Whilst it did not oblige the State to provide schools catering for particular denominational or philosophical groupings, it gave parents the right to object to the child being exposed to forms of tuition which might render the task of educating the child in accordance with parental convictions more difficult. It was adopted in the Assembly by ninety-seven votes, with fifteen abstentions, and forwarded to the Committee of Ministers. At this stage, it would still have been possible to include this in the text of the full Convention but the Committee of Ministers decided not to risk further delay and passed them on to another Committee of Experts, to be examined with a view to drawing up a protocol to the Convention.[67]

There then ensued another round in which various texts were passed between the Committee of Ministers and its Committee of Experts and the Assembly and its Legal and Administrative Committee. The principal concern remained the question of whether the State would be obliged to provide or support teaching in accordance with parental convictions, now joined by concerns that a parent might be able to insist upon a child being educated in accordance with philosophies alien to those underpinning the Convention. Both of these questions were considered by the Committee of Experts in February 1951 when, in addition to the text adopted by the Assembly, it had before it drafts submitted by the UK[68] and by Belgium.[69]

There were three main points at issue. The first concerned whether the right should be stated in the positive or the negative. The Committee

---

[66] *Ibid.*, p. 162.

[67] *CETP*, vol. VII, pp. 22–24, 44. This decision was bitterly condemned in the Assembly at its sitting later that month by M. Teitgen, who singled out the UK as the principal culprit (*ibid.*, p. 96), a charge denied by Mr Mitchison (p. 106) but accepted, at least in part, by Lord Layton (p. 118).

[68] The UK text provided that: 'No person should be denied the right to education. In the exercise of any functions which the State may assume in relation to education and to teaching it shall have regard to the liberty of the parents to ensure the religious education of their children in conformity with their own convictions' (*ibid.*, p. 186).

[69] The Belgian text provided that: 'Every person has the right to education. Parents have the right to ensure the religious education and the teaching of their children in conformity with their own religious philosophical convictions. The State in the organization of public instruction shall respect this right of parents and shall take the necessary measures to ensure its effective exercise' (*ibid.*, pp. 194–196).

remained undecided on this.[70] The second concerned whether the article should concern all the aspects of education or only relate to religious education. The Committee adopted the more restrictive approach, as proposed by the UK.[71] Finally, the UK proposed that the State should merely 'have regard to the liberty of the parents'. This, however, was not reflected in its proposed text which provided:

Everyone has the right to education. [No person shall be denied the right to education.] In the exercise of any functions which it may assume in relation to education and to teaching, the State must respect the liberty of parents to ensure the religious education of their children in conformity with their own convictions.[72]

The Committee of Ministers, at its seventh Session held in March, established a Committee of Jurists to examine the Report of the Committee of Experts and put the Draft Protocol 'in proper form'.[73] This Committee met on 18 and 19 April and amended the draft by adopting the negative formulation of the right and replacing the obligation to respect parental rights with the requirement that the State 'shall have regard' to them. In consequence, the text adopted was identical to that which had been proposed by the UK to the Committee of Experts.[74]

The Committee of Ministers once again passed the draft back to the Committee of Experts which, at its meetings on 5 and 6 June, amended the text by substituting 'creeds' for 'convictions'.[75] This was not a cosmetic alteration and was intended to ensure that the text would only concern the religious convictions of parents. This meant that parents who had no religious convictions (including atheists and agnostics) could not prevent their children being instructed in, or educated in accordance with, the tenets of a religion.[76] In addition, because there was no

[70] The negative formulation, as proposed by the UK, had been advanced in order to confirm that there was no obligation upon a State to provide an education. Most, but not all, of the States which preferred the positive formulation did not dispute this. But *cf.* the Swedish view that the positive formulation obliged a State to provide an education for those children who were not being privately educated. Report of the Committee of Experts (Doc. CM/WP I(51) 40 of 24 February 1951), *ibid.*, pp. 208–210.

[71] *Ibid.*.   [72] *Ibid.*.   [73] *Ibid.*, pp. 214–220.

[74] Report of the Committee of Ministers, 19 April 1951 (Doc. CM (51) 33 Final: A 4421 with corrigendum A 4475), *CETP*, vol. VII, p. 252. Both Denmark and Turkey had submitted further amendments but the Committee was unclear as to whether these fell within its remit and so referred them back to the Committee of Ministers. These were ultimately rejected by the Committee of Experts to which they were referred.

[75] This had first been suggested by the Swedish delegation at the April Committee (*ibid.*, p. 252).

[76] See the Commentary to the Draft Protocol (Doc. AS/JA (3) 13; A 5904, 18 September 1951), *CETP*, vol. VIII, pp. 10–12.

reference to philosophical convictions of a non-religious nature, there could be no question of a parent insisting that a child be educated in accordance with communist principles.[77]

The Committee also added a final sentence which referred to 'the right of parents to send their children to schools, other than those established by the State, which conform to the standards laid down by law'.[78] This was intended to confirm the right of individuals to establish private schools. When this text was circulated to governments, it attracted two further amendments. Turkey sought to have the Committee's amendment deleted,[79] whilst the UK proposed that it be reworded so as to read 'where schools have been established by the State, to send their children to any other school of their choice, provided that such schools conform to the requirements of law'.[80]

The purpose of this amendment was, once again, to remove any suggestion that the State was under an obligation to provide education. Nevertheless, the threat of renewed controversy prompted the deletion of this final sentence altogether[81] and the final text placed before the Committee of Ministers, and unanimously adopted in August 1951, provided that:

No person shall be denied the right to education. In the exercise of any functions which it may assume in relation to education and to teaching, the State shall have regard to the rights of parents to ensure the religious education of their children in conformity with their own creeds.[82]

This was the most restrictive of all the proposals yet adopted and when it was forwarded to the Assembly's Legal Committee it provoked a storm of protest. All the alterations were deplored, with the sole exception of the negative phraseology of the opening sentence, and it asked the Com-

---

[77] *Ibid.*, p. 12 and see also p. 192. Robertson, 'The ECHR: Recent Developments' p. 362, who noted it would 'force governments which might be fighting Communism abroad to permit the education of Young Communists at home'. However, as M. Teitgen pointed out, this difficulty was covered by Article 17 of the Convention which provided that: 'Nothing in this Convention may be interpreted as implying for any State, group or person any right to engage in any activity or perform any act aimed at the destruction of any of the rights and freedoms set forth herein or at their limitation to a greater extent than that provided for in the Convention' (*CETP*, vol. VIII, p. 92).

[78] Doc. CM/WP VI (51) 19 of 5 June 1951. *CETP*, vol. VII, p. 300.

[79] Doc. CM/Adj. (51) 36; A 5461, 16 July 1951. *CETP*, vol. VII, p. 314.

[80] Doc. CM/Adj. 51) 34; A 5444, 16 July 1951. *Ibid.*, p. 314.

[81] See Doc. CM (51) 64 revised; A 5578 of 1 August 1951. *CETP*, vol. VII, pp. 326–330.

[82] *CETP*, vol. VII, pp. 336, 338. This was acknowledged by Robertson to be the most restrictive of all the formulations adopted (*ibid.*, vol. VIII, p. 194).

mittee of Ministers to reverse the changes by adopting yet another formulation, which provided:

No person shall be denied the right to education. In the exercise of any functions which it assumes in relation to education and to teaching the State shall respect the right of parents to ensure such education and teaching in conformity with their own religious and philosophical convictions.[83]

This text was endorsed by the Assembly at the close of an impassioned debate. M. Teitgen castigated the requirement that States 'have regard' to parental rights, saying that the words had no meaning or legal significance: 'Totalitarian regimes which hang their adversaries "have regard" – at the end of the rope – to the latter's right to live.'[84] He also deplored the decision to restrict the article to religious, as opposed to philosophical, convictions: 'it is our desire to protect the right of parents and the respect for their convictions as regards the education and teaching of their children . . . whatever these may be, and it is not for the State to judge'.[85] He was supported in this by numerous speakers.

It was left to Mr Renton of the UK to sound a note of caution and scepticism. Whilst agreeing that the requirement to 'have regard' to parental rights was meaningless, he did not think that an obligation to 'respect' amounted to very much more. He also doubted the wisdom of accepting the paramountcy of the parents' philosophical convictions, arguing that 'we can exaggerate the prudence of parents. There are parents . . . who do not believe that their children should stay on an extra year at school, or after the age of 14. Should parents' views in that matter be respected?' and that 'when . . . the State is instructed to respect the philosophical rights of the parents, the State might even be asked to place limitations upon the education of the children, which would be quite unphilosophical'.[86] He concluded that, whilst the draft of the Committee of Ministers was meaningless, that of the Legal Committee was unworkable and he 'preferred the meaningless to the unworkable'[87] and urged that it be reconsidered yet again. Nevertheless, the bulk of the Assembly,

---

[83] *CETP*, vol. VIII, p. 36.

[84] *Ibid.*, p. 88. M. Teitgen had been asked to prepare a Report on the Committee of Ministers' draft (Doc. Consultative Assembly no. 93, 4 December 1959, *CETP*, vol. VIII, p. 66) and this formed the basis of the discussion in the Assembly on 7–8 December.

[85] *Ibid.*, p. 90.

[86] *Ibid.*, p. 108. Mr Renton gave the example of vegetarianism. This was ridiculed by M. Penot (France) on the grounds that he did not consider a choice of diet to be an outward expression of philosophical opinion (p. 134). This admirably illustrates the problems which Mr Renton faced.

[87] *Ibid.*, p. 110.

recalling their recent experiences of the dangers of unfettered State involvement in education,[88] adopted the Legal Committee's proposal by seventy-five votes, with twenty-three abstentions.[89]

Rather than continue to try to seek a consensus, the Minister's Advisors, meeting prior to the Tenth Session of the Committee of Ministers in March 1952, decided to present the text adopted by the Assembly to the Committee, it being understood that a number of States would make reservations when signing the Protocol.[90] The Protocol was duly adopted on 19 March 1952[91] and signed the following day. Greece,[92] Sweden,[93] Turkey[94] and the United Kingdom[95] all made reservations with respect to Article 2, whilst Ireland[96] and the Netherlands[97] made declarations

---

[88] E.g. Miss Weber (FRG), *ibid.*, pp. 112–114; Mme Rehling (FRG), *ibid.*, pp. 128–130.

[89] *Ibid.*, p. 168.   [90] *Ibid.*, pp. 198–202.

[91] Resolution (52)1, *ibid.*, p. 202.

[92] The Greek reservation, made at the time of signature on 20 March 1952, provided that: 'the application of the word "philosophical", which is the penultimate word of the second sentence of Article 2, will, in Greece, conform with the relevant provisions of internal legislation' (*CEPT*, vol. VIII, p. 218). The reservation was withdrawn with effect from 1 January 1984. See H/Inf (85) 1, p. 11.

[93] The Swedish reservation, made at the time of ratification on 22 June 1953, provided that: 'Sweden could not grant to parents the right to obtain, by reason of their philosophical convictions, dispensation for their children from the obligation of taking part in certain parts of the education in the public schools, and also to the effect that the dispensation from the obligation of taking part in the teaching of Christianity in these schools could only be granted for children of another faith than the Swedish Church in respect of whom a satisfactory religious instruction had been arranged. This reservation is based on the provisions of the new rule of 17 March 1953 for the establishment of secondary education within the Kingdom and also on the analogous provisions concerning other educational establishments.' This reservation was withdrawn as of 1 January 1995. See H/INF (95) 2, p. 3.

[94] The Turkish reservation, made at the time of ratification on 18 May 1954, provided that: 'Article 2 of the Protocol shall not affect the provisions of Law No. 430 of 3rd March 1924 relating to the unification of education.'

[95] The UK reservation, made at the time of signature on 3 November 1952, provided that: 'the principle affirmed in the second sentence of Article 2 is accepted by the United Kingdom only in so far as it is compatible with the provision of efficient instruction and training, and the avoidance of unreasonable public expenditure.' The UK entered a similar reservation with respect to Gibraltar and Guernsey (but not Jersey) and further reservations concerning the use of corporal punishment in Anguilla, British Virgin Islands, the Cayman Islands, Monserrat, St Helena and Dependencies and the Turk and Caicos Islands when extending the Protocol to these territories on 22 February 1988. See *YBECHR* 31 (1988), 6.

[96] The Irish Declaration provided: 'Article 2 of the Protocol is not sufficiently explicit in ensuring to parents the right to provide education for their children in their homes or in schools of the parents' own choice, whether or not such schools are private schools or are schools recognized or established by the State.' (See *CETP*, vol. VIII, pp. 204, 208.)

[97] The Netherlands' Declaration provided that: 'the State should not only respect the

recording their dissatisfaction with it. Portugal[98] and Malta[99] also made a reservation upon ratification, and declarations relating to Article 2 have recently been made by Bulgaria[100] and Romania.[101]

Although of comparatively narrow scope, Article 2 was much broader than had been thought desirable by the Committee of Ministers. It also left several important questions unanswered. In particular, there was no clear understanding of what amounted to a 'philosophical conviction'. As Robertson pointed out: 'the notion of 'philosophical convictions' remains a nebulous and even elastic concept. Does it include vegetarianism, or polygamy, or nudism or the tenets of the anti-vivisectionist? Where shall the line be drawn between philosophical convictions whose freedom should properly be respected and the convictions of cranks or faddists?'[102] As will be seen in the following chapters, the practice of the Court and Commission, with respect to Article 9 of the Convention as well as Article 2 of the First Protocol, has done little to help answer both this and other basic questions concerning the scope of the freedom of religion as set out in the ECHR.

rights of parents in the matter of education but, if need be, ensure the possibility of exercising those rights by appropriate financial measures.' (*CETP*, vol. VIII, pp. 204, 208).

[98] The Portuguese reservation, made upon ratification on 9 November 1978, accepted Article 2 subject to constitutional provisions 'which provide for the non-denominationality of public education, the supervision of private education by the State and the validity of legal provisions concerning the setting up of private educational establishments'. See *YBECHR* 21 (1978), 18. This was withdrawn on 11 May 1987. See *YBECHR* 21 (1987), 4.

[99] The Maltese reservation, made upon ratification on 12 December 1966, is identical to the UK reservation, but ends with the additional qualification, 'having regard to the fact that the population of Malta is overwhelmingly Roman Catholic'. See *YBECHR* 9 (1966), 26.

[100] The Bulgarian Declaration, made upon ratification on 7 September 1992, provides that: 'The second provision of Article 2 of the Protocol must not be interpreted as imposing on the State additional financial commitments relating to educational establishments with a specific philosophical or religious orientation other than the commitments of the Bulgarian State provided for in the Constitution and in legislation in force in the Country.' See H/INF (92) 3, p. 1.

[101] The Romanian Declaration, made upon ratification on 20 June 1994, provides that: 'Romania interprets Article 2 of the first Protocol to the Convention as not imposing any supplementary financial burdens connected with private educational institutions other than those established by domestic legislation.' See H/INF (95) 1, p. 4.

[102] Robertson, 'The ECHR: Recent Developments', p. 362. Presumably, the impact of education along these lines was not considered sufficient to trigger the prohibition of activities aimed at the destruction or limitation of any of the Convention rights and freedoms set out in Article 17 of the Convention.

11 The application of Article 9 of the European Convention on Human Rights

The European Commission and Court of Human Rights have both been called upon to consider the scope of Article 9.[1] Unfortunately, the resulting jurisprudence is not entirely satisfactory. There are a number of possible reasons for this, but two factors have been particularly important. The first is that there were no early cases in which the Court set out guiding principles. Compared to other articles of the Convention, the Court has had few opportunities to consider Article 9 and the most important of these, the *Kokkinakis* case,[2] was only decided in 1993. Moreover, that decision was soon followed by the *Otto-Preminger-Institut* case[3] which explored the degree to which the sensibilities of religious believers could justify restrictions upon the scope of the freedom of expression under Article 10(2). The tension between these cases, and between the Court and Commission, is currently being tested in the *Wingrove*,[4] *Ahmet*[5] and *Manoussakis*[6] cases.

---

[1] For general examinations see J. E. S. Fawcett, *The Application of the European Convention on Human Rights*, 2nd edn (Oxford: Clarendon Press, 1987), pp. 235–250; P. Van Dijk and G. J. H. Van Hoof, *Theory and Practice of the European Convention on Human Rights*, 2nd edn (Daventer: Kluwer, 1990), pp. 397–407; D. J. Harris, M. O'Boyle and C. Warbrick, *Law of the European Convention on Human Rights* (London: Butterworths, 1995), pp. 356–371; R. Goy, 'La Garantie Européenne de la Liberté de Religion', *RDP* 107 (1991), 5; C. Skakkabaek, 'Article 9 of the European Convention on Human Rights' (Council of Europe, H(92)16, 1992).

[2] *Kokkinakis v. Greece*, Ser. A, no. 260-A (1993).

[3] *Otto-Preminger-Institut v. Austria*, Ser. A, no. 295-A (1994).

[4] *Wingrove v. UK*, No. 17419/90, Rep. 1995. Referred to the Court in March 1995. The hearings took place in March 1996 (see below, p. 340).

[5] *Ahmet v. Greece*, No. 18877/91, Rep. 1995. Referred to the Court in June 1995.

[6] *Manoussakis v. Greece*, No. 18748/91, Rep. 1995. Referred to the Court in July 1995. The hearings took place in May 1996 and the Judgment is still awaited at the time of writing. See also the substantially similar case of *Pentidis, Katharios and Stagopoulos v. Greece* No. 23238/94, Rep. 1996, referred to the Court in April 1996.

The second general factor is that many of the applications considered by the Commission in its early years fell into a number of distinct categories, such as cases concerning conscientious objectors or prisoners' rights. Although the principles established within these groups of cases had a certain internal consistency, there were some contradictions between the categories. This encouraged subsequent cases to be considered within whichever category seemed most appropriate, rather than in the light of Article 9 as a whole.[7] In consequence, not only have all the various elements of Article 9 not been thoroughly analysed, but where such analysis has been attempted it has been overly influenced by the background provided by the general category into which the case has fallen.

In its recent judgments the Court has indicated a preference for a more holistic approach than that hitherto adopted by the Commission. However, its judgments lack precision and, for this reason alone, are unlikely to prompt any major revision of previous practice, although they may well affect the nature of the reasoning. Nevertheless, the Court's views concerning Article 9 also provide a touchstone by which the application of the rather complicated – and convoluted – distinctions drawn by the Commission can be appraised.

The following sections will examine the work of the Court and Commission in relation to the various elements of Article 9, rather than by the category into which the case falls. Although it is neither possible nor desirable to disentangle the cases from their contexts, this method of presentation will help focus attention upon the substantive content of freedom of religion rather than upon the situation in which it is being exercised.

The general principles

The *Kokkinakis* case provided the Court with its first real opportunity to set out its approach to Article 9. Mr Kokkinakis was a Jehovah's Witness. He had been arrested for proselytism, a criminal offence in Greece, more than sixty times over a period of fifty years and had been interned and imprisoned on several occasions. In 1986 he was arrested whilst visiting and talking with the wife of the Cantor of the local Orthodox Church and

---

[7] For example, Goy, 'La Garantie Européenne de la Liberté de Religion', who considers whether the Convention guarantee extends to certain classes of person (pp. 23–30) and examines the freedom to manifest a religion or belief enjoyed by various categories (pp. 34–42).

was subsequently convicted. His application to the Commission alleged breaches of Articles 7, 9 and 10 of the Convention.[8] The Greek Government accepted that it had breached the rights of the Applicant under Article 9(1) and the Commission's decision, therefore, turned on the question of whether this breach was justified by reference to Article 9(2).[9] The Commission did, however, confirm that 'the measure in question constituted interference with the exercise of the applicant's right under Article 9(1) of the Convention to manifest his religion'.

The Court agreed with the Commission that this case revealed a breach of Article 9. For both the Court and Commission, this was because the method of reasoning used by the Greek court to justify the conviction was inadequate,[10] not because the restrictions placed upon proselytism amounted to a violation. Indeed, the Court said:

The fundamental nature of the rights guaranteed in Article 9(1) is . . . reflected in the wording of the paragraph providing for its limitation . . . [I]t recognises that in democratic societies, in which several religions coexist within one and the same population, it may be necessary to place restrictions on this freedom in order to reconcile the interests of the various groups and ensure that everyone's beliefs are respected.[11]

In consequence, the Court had little of substance to say concerning the interpretation of Article 9(1). It did, however, state that:

As enshrined in Article 9, freedom of thought, conscience and religion is one of the foundations of a 'democratic society' within the meaning of the Convention. It is, in its religious dimension, one of the most vital elements that go to make up the identity of believers and their conception of life, but it is also a precious asset for atheists, agnostics, sceptics and the unconcerned. The pluralism indissociable from a democratic society, which has been dearly won over the centuries, depends on it.[12]

Stirring though this may be, it does not shed much light on how Article 9 is to be applied in practice. It does, however, encapsulate the problem that had to be addressed: how can the fundamental right of one individual to the freedom of thought, conscience and religion be reconciled with the fundamental right of another to the same freedom, when the very

---

[8] Claims relating to Articles 5(1) and 6(1) and (2) were also submitted but were declared inadmissible.
[9] *Kokkinakis v. Greece*, No. 14307/88, Rep. 1991, para. 56.
[10] *Ibid.*, paras. 72–74; Ser. A, no. 260–A (1993), para. 49. The lack of proportion between the criminal penalty and the conduct in question was also said to be a 'decisive factor' for the Commission (*ibid.*, para. 74).
[11] *Kokkinakis v. Greece*, Ser. A, no. 260–A (1993), para. 33.
[12] *Ibid.*, para. 31. See also *Valsamis v. Greece*, No. 21787/93, Rep. 1995, para. 47.

possession of those beliefs might require a believer to present his views to others?[13] This problem does not lie comfortably within the scheme of protection provided by the Convention, which was built upon the assumption that the individual's freedom of religion needed to be protected from doctrinally inspired encroachment by the State.

The scheme of protection

At first sight, the language of Article 9 is deceptively simple. It is, however, necessary to distinguish between several closely related aspects of the enjoyment of the rights conferred.

First, a general distinction must be drawn between the freedom of thought, conscience and religion, which is 'passive' in nature, and the 'active' right to manifest a religion or belief. A source of particular confusion is that the expression of the 'active' right might take the form of an individual asserting a right not to be required to act in a particular fashion. This is still an aspect of the 'expression' or 'manifestation' of religion or belief, even though the individual concerned is seeking not to participate in, for example, the armed forces or a compulsory scheme. Although well understood,[14] this tends to blunt the sharpness of the distinction.

The passive enjoyment of the right to freedom of thought, conscience and religion is absolute in the sense that the restrictions set out in Article 9(2) only relate to the manifestation of a religion or belief. However, a person does not have a right to enjoy their freedom of thought, conscience and religion untroubled by actions which challenge or offend against such convictions. The 'passive' enjoyment of the freedom of thought, conscience and religion must be balanced against the 'active' right of manifestation when the two come into conflict.

Secondly, it should be remembered that the second sentence of Article 9 only relates to the manifestation of a religion or belief and not to the manifestation of patterns of thought or conscience, which are covered by the general right to freedom of expression found in Article 10 of the

---

[13] The dilemma is elegantly phrased by Judge Martens in his Partly Dissenting Opinion in the *Kokkinakis* case as 'a possible conflict between two subjects of the right to freedom of religion: [which] sets the rights of those whose religious faith encourages or requires such activity against the rights of those targeted to maintain their beliefs' (*ibid.*, p. 37, para. 15).

[14] E.g. Fawcett, *The Application of the ECHR*, p. 238 and Van Dijk and Van Hoof, *Theory and Practice of the ECHR*, p. 398.

Convention. Of course, expressions of religion or belief are themselves within the scope of Article 10[15] but, as the Commission made clear in the *Kokkinakis* case: 'When the exercise of the right to freedom of expression consists in the freedom to manifest one's religion or belief in worship, teaching, practice or observance, it is primarily the right guaranteed by Article 9 of the Convention which is applicable.'[16] This distinction seems clear enough. Everyone has the right to freedom of thought, conscience and religion under Article 9. Article 9 also protects manifestations of religion or belief. Expressions of thought and conscience are protected by Article 10, as would be any form of expression of a religion or belief which was not a 'manifestation' for the purposes of Article 9. In the interests of clarity, it is best to reserve the term 'manifestation' to describe a particular form of expression which is only relevant to 'religion or belief'. This means that whereas a religion or belief can be both expressed or manifested, a pattern of 'thought' or 'conscience' can only be 'expressed'. Therefore, there can be no question of manifesting or 'actualizing' thought or conscience under Article 9. Expressions of thought or conscience are the exclusive preserve of Article 10.

One consequence of this is that conflicts between the 'passive' right to freedom of thought, conscience and religion and the 'active' freedom of expression can fall for consideration under either Article 9 or Article 10, depending on the nature of the belief and the manner in which it is presented. For example, the applicant in the *Kokkinakis* case sought to challenge the beliefs of the Cantor's wife by placing his own religious beliefs before her. The restriction placed by Greek law upon this manifestation of Mr Kokkinakis's religious belief therefore raised issues under Article 9(2). This is to be contrasted with the *Otto-Preminger-Institut* case in which the applicants challenged the seizure and forfeiture of a film allegedly 'disparaging' or 'insulting' to Roman Catholic belief. Since the film was not itself an expression or manifestation of a religious

---

[15] A particular problem can arise out of the relationship between Article 10 and Article 11, the right to freedom of assembly. The Commission takes the view that when expression takes the form of a march or demonstration, it is Article 11 which is primarily involved. E.g., *Rassemblement Jurassein and Unité Jurassein v. Switzerland*, No. 8191/78, 17 DR 93 (Dec. 1979), 118; *Christians against Racism and Fascism v. UK*, No. 8440/78, 21 DR 138 (Dec. 1980), 147–148; *Plattform 'Ärzte für das Leben' v. Austria*, No. 10126/82, 44 DR 65 (Dec. 1985). A manifestation of a religion by way of religious procession would seem to fall within Article 9, but other forms of collective manifestation might raise issues under Article 11 rather than Article 9, as would collective acts of expression not amounting to a manifestation. See *Çiraklar v. Turkey*, No. 19601/92, 80 DR 46 (Dec. 1995), 52.

[16] *Kokkinakis v. Greece*, No. 14307/88, Rep. 1991, para. 79.

belief, Article 9 – the *lex specialis* – was not in question and the validity of the State's action was examined in relation to Article 10(2) of the Convention.[17]

However, difficulties have arisen for a number of reasons. The first concerns the scope of the terms 'belief' and 'manifestation'. It has been clear from the outset that 'belief' embraced philosophical convictions akin to religions and which occupied a similarly central place in the lives of believers. As will be seen below, it has also come to include beliefs which are held as an adjunct to, or as a corollary of, religious beliefs. At the same time, the concept of a 'manifestation' has also been accorded a meaning beyond the mere practice of rites associated with worship. The difficulty is that the manifestation of a philosophical belief can look very much like an expression of an individual's conscience. Nevertheless, the distinction is there. Article 9 does not protect the manifestation of every aspect of a person's conscience. It embraces only those manifestations which are based upon the range of beliefs that are held to be akin to religious convictions.

The second difficulty arises from the claim that the 'passive' right to freedom of thought, conscience and religion found in the first sentence of Article 9(1) carries with it an implied right of expression or manifestation. This claim blurs the distinction between the two distinct elements of Article 9 and between Articles 9 and 10. Since the terms 'expression' and 'manifestation' have a particular place in the scheme of the Convention, the term 'actualize' will be used to describe this claim when it is considered below.

Who has rights under Article 9?

The rights contained in Article 9 belong to 'everyone'. The rights of individuals are clearly included but the ability of an organization, such as a church, to claim to be a victim of a violation in its own right was initially a matter of some controversy.[18] In *Church of X v. United Kingdom* the Commission decided that 'a corporation, being a legal and not a

---

[17] *Otto-Preminger-Institut v. Austria*, Ser. A, no. 295–A (1994), para. 43. See also *X Ltd and Y v. UK* (the *Gay News* case), No. 8710/79, 28 DR 77 (Dec. 1982).

[18] Under Article 25, the Commission may receive petitions 'from any person, non-governmental organization or group of individuals claiming to be the victim of a violation by one of the High Contracting Parties of the rights set forth in this Convention . . .'. Thus a petition submitted by an organization or association could be declared admissible only if it is deemed to have rights under Article 9.

natural person, is incapable of having or exercising the rights mentioned in Article 9, paragraph (1) of the Convention'.[19] The Commission subsequently justified this view on the basis that the rights of a church as an organization were adequately protected by the rights granted to its members.[20] Nevertheless, in X and the Church of Scientology v. Sweden it reversed its opinion, saying: 'When a church body lodges an application under the Convention it does so, in reality, on behalf of its members. It should, therefore, be accepted that a church body is capable of possessing and exercising the rights contained in Article 9(1) in its own capacity as a representative of its members.'[21] This has been criticized on the grounds that it merely allowed the church to 'stand in the shoes' of its members and failed to acknowledge the right of a church to manifest its religion in its own right.[22] Subsequent decisions, however, have confirmed that churches and other forms of legal person are, in principle, beneficiaries of the rights set out in Article 9 and can lodge applications in their own name.[23]

However, not every legal person is able to claim rights under Article 9. The Commission has made it clear that only organizations akin to a church may do so. This includes 'associations with religious and philosophical objects'[24] but does not include profit-making corporate bodies. In Company X v. Switzerland[25] a printing company unsuccessfully challenged the obligation imposed upon it by the Canton of Zürich to pay ecclesiastical taxes in favour of the Roman Catholic and Protestant Churches. This appears to have been an attempt to lessen the tax liability of a commercial company that had no connection with any religious or philosophical

---

[19] Church of X v. UK, No. 3798/68, 29 CD 70 (Dec. 1968).
[20] X v. Denmark, No. 7374/76, 5 DR 156 (Dec. 1976).
[21] X and the Church of Scientology v. Sweden, No. 7805/77, 16 DR 68 (Dec. 1979), 70. See also Omkarananda and the Divine Light Zentrum v. Switzerland, No. 8118/77, 25 DR 105 (Dec. 1981), 117.
[22] Van Dijk and Van Hoof, Theory and Practice of the ECHR, p. 405. It is, however, doubtful whether a church as an organization has a capacity to manifest its beliefs independently of the actions of its members and so this would seem to be enough.
[23] See Kontackt-Information-Therapie and Hagen v. Austria, No. 11921/86, 57 DR 81 (Dec. 1988), 88; A. R. M. Chappell v. UK, No. 12587/86, 53 DR 241 (Dec. 1987), 246; Iglesia Bautisti 'El Salvador' and Ortega Moratilla v. Spain, No. 17522/90, 72 DR 256 (Dec. 1992). Given that in Autronic AG v. Switzerland, Ser. A, no. 178 (1990) the Court confirmed that legal entities enjoy freedom of expression under Article 10, there is no reason to suppose that it would take a different view.
[24] See Omkarananda and the Divine Light Zentrum v. Switzerland, No. 8118/77, 25 DR 105 (Dec. 1981), 117 in which the Commission confirmed the standing of the second applicant (a religious and philosophical institution).
[25] Company X v. Switzerland, No. 7865/77, 16 DR 85 (Dec. 1979), 86–87.

association. If a profit-making corporate body does have a sufficient connection with such an association – for example, a trading company wholly owned by a religious association – it might be thought to be more difficult to justify a claim that its profit-making nature automatically prevents it from having rights under Article 9. Nevertheless in *Kustannus oy Vapaa Ajattelija AB, Vappa-Ajattelijain Liitto-Fritänkaras Förbund r.y. and Sundström v. Finland* the Commission decided that the first applicant, a limited liability company principally owned by the second applicant (an association of 'freethinkers' working for the separation of church and State), was required to pay taxes, including church taxes in the same way as any other limited liability company 'regardless of the underlying purpose of its activities.[26]

The Commission has also decided that even a non-profit-making association is unable to exercise all of the rights contained in Article 9. In *Kontakt-Information-Therapie and Hagen v. Austria* the Commission decided that an association could enjoy the freedom of religion but not of conscience. The first applicant, a private non-profit-making organization, ran a rehabilitation centre for drug abusers. The second applicant was a therapist employed by the organization. The therapist was required to give evidence in criminal proceedings against a former client, thus breaching his promise of confidentiality, a promise upon which relationships with clients depended. Rather than dismiss the first applicant's petition, in so far as it related to Article 9, on the ground that the organization was not a victim of the alleged violation (indeed, the organization did not even claim to be a victim), the Commission chose to stress that whereas the freedom of religion could be exercised by a legal person, the freedom of conscience could not.[27]

This seems to have been based upon the premise that a legal person has no 'conscience'. Since the freedom of religion or belief includes the right of manifestation and a church, as an organization, is neither more nor less capable of having a religion or belief than any other legal person is of having a conscience, it is difficult to see the reason for this. The Commission should have examined whether the drug rehabilitation centre qualified as a religious or philosophical organization for the purposes of Article 9 rather than dismiss it on the basis of its inability to enjoy the right of freedom of conscience. This might be compared with the decision

---

[26] *Kustannus oy Vapaa Ajattelija AB, Vapaa-Ajattelija Liitto-Fritänkarnas Förbund r.y. and Sundström v. Finland*, No. 20471/92 (unreported). For the question of whether Article 9 embraces tax liabilities generally, see below, p. 310.

[27] *Kontakt-Information-Therapie and Hagen v. Austria*, No. 11921/86, 57 DR 81 (Dec. 1988), 89.

in *Plattform 'Ärzte für das Leben' v. Austria*, where the Commission seems to have assumed that a doctors' association, opposed to legalized abortion, was capable of having rights under Article 9.[28] If these organizations were not religious or philosophical in nature, they should not have been entitled to express or manifest their 'beliefs' under Article 9 at all. They would, of course, have been able to claim a violation of their freedom of expression under Article 10. However, there might be activities which would be classified as a 'manifestation' for the purposes of Article 9 which do not fall within the scope of Article 10. Moreover, the application of Article 9(2) as opposed to Article 10(2) might also lead to different results.[29]

What is a 'religion or belief'?

Distinguishing between those legal persons which have rights under Article 9 and those which do not turns upon the question of whether the organization in question is deemed to be religious or philosophical in character. This is just one aspect of the more general question of distinguishing between patterns of 'thought and conscience' on the one hand and of 'religion or belief' on the other.[30] This distinction is central to the scheme of the article since it is the key to distinguishing between the forms of belief which give rise to the freedom of manifestation and those which do not.

This was considered by the Commission in *Arrowsmith v. UK*. The applicant, a pacifist, had been distributing leaflets to members of the armed forces urging them not to serve in Northern Ireland. This raised two questions under Article 9: was 'pacifism' a 'belief' and, if so, was the act of distributing leaflets of this nature a 'manifestation' of that belief?

---

[28] *Plattform 'Ärzte für das Leben' v. Austria*, No. 10126/82, 44 DR 65 (Dec. 1985), 71. The complaint under Article 9 was deemed inadmissible on other grounds.

[29] Article 9(2) is examined in chapter 12.

[30] It is preferable not to seek to distinguish between religions and beliefs, since nothing turns on the distinction in the current context and an attempt to categorize certain beliefs as either being, or not amounting to, a religion is likely to provoke unnecessary disagreement. Equally, there seems little reason to seek to distinguish between 'thought' and 'conscience'. It might, however, be wondered whether these are in themselves terms of art and, in consequence, whether there are forms of thinking which fall outside the scope of Article 9 altogether. Van Dijk and Van Hoof, *Theory and Practice of the ECHR*, p. 397 and n. 1031 take the view that it embraces any idea or view. The danger with this approach is that if taken in marginal cases it might justify a lowering of the high threshold of protection accorded to the right to hold (but not act upon) such thoughts.

The Commission accepted that the right to manifest beliefs extended to beliefs of a non-religious nature and did embrace pacifism.[31] However, it also made it clear that not all ideas or views were to be equated with a 'belief' for the purposes of the second sentence of Article 9.[32] Similarly, in the case of *Campbell and Cosans v. UK* the Court, in the context of Article 2 of the First Protocol, equated the word 'conviction' with 'belief' and said that a belief was 'not synonymous with the words "opinions" or "ideas"'.[33] Therefore, it is necessary to consider what is needed to elevate an 'opinion' which may be held under Article 9, and expressed under Article 10, into a 'belief' which may be both held and manifested under Article 9.

Unfortunately, there is little guidance. In *Campbell and Cosans* the Court said that 'the term "beliefs" . . . denotes views that attain a certain level of cogency, seriousness, cohesion and importance'.[34] What might be called the 'mainstream' religious traditions are clearly embraced, as is demonstrated by numerous applications concerning Christianity, Judaism,[35] Islam,[36] Hinduism,[37] Sikhism[38] and Buddhism[39]. The relevance of Article 9 to Jehovah's Witnesses,[40] the Church of Scientology[41] and the Moon Sect[42] has also been acknowledged.

There is a considerable advantage in being able to place one's belief within the bounds of an accepted form of religious belief since this

---

[31] *Arrowsmith v. UK*, No. 7050/75, Rep. 1978, para. 69, 19 DR 5, 19.

[32] This confirmed the view of the UK Government that Article 9 was more restrictive in scope than Article 10, which applied to 'opinions' and 'ideas' (*ibid.*, para. 42). This underlines the degree to which Article 9 is *lex specialis* in relation to Article 10.

[33] *Campbell and Cosans v. UK*, Ser. A, no. 48 (1982), para. 36.

[34] *Ibid.* Again, this was in relation to analogous issues under Article 2 of the First Protocol. See below, p. 348.

[35] E.g. *D v. France*, No. 10180/82, 35 DR 199 (Dec. 1983).

[36] E.g. *X v. UK*, No. 8160/78, 22 DR 27 (Dec. 1981); *Khan v. UK*, No. 11579/85, 48 DR 253 (Dec. 1986); *Yanasik v. Turkey*, No. 14524/89, 74 DR 14 (Dec. 1993); *Karaduman v. Turkey*, No. 16278/90, 74 DR 93 (Dec. 1993).

[37] *Chauhan v. UK*, No. 11518/85, 65 DR 41 (Rep. 1990); *ISKCON and others v. UK*, No. 20490/92, 76-A DR 90 (Dec. 1994).

[38] E.g. *X v. UK*, No. 8160/78, 22 DR 27 (Dec. 1981).

[39] E.g. *X v. UK*, No. 6886/75, 5 DR 100 (Dec. 1976).

[40] E.g. *N v. Sweden*, No. 10410/83, 40 DR 203 (Dec. 1984); *Hoffman v. Austria*, Ser. A, no. 255-C (1993); *Kokkinakis v. Greece*, Ser. A, no. 260-A (1993); *Manoussakis v. Greece*, No. 18748/91, Rep. 1995; *Valsamis v. Greece* No. 21787/93, Rep. 1995; *Efstratiou v. Greece*, No. 24095/94, Rep. 1996; *X v. Bulgaria*, No. 28626/95 (Inf. note 131, p. 6) (1996).

[41] E.g. *X and the Church of Scientology v. Sweden*, No. 7805/77, 16 DR 68 (1979); *Church of Scientology v. Sweden and 128 of its Members*, No. 8282/78, 21 DR 109 (Dec. 1980).

[42] *X v. Austria*, No. 8652/79, 26 DR 89 (1981).

ensures that it will cross the threshold of 'seriousness'.[43] If there is any doubt surrounding the status of any alleged 'religion', the applicant must demonstrate its existence. In one case the applicant, a prisoner, claimed to be an adherent of the 'Wicca' religion. The Commission noted that 'the applicant has not mentioned any facts making it possible to establish the existence of the Wicca religion'.[44] This would seem to suggest that whilst the burden of proof lies with the applicant it is not set very highly. This, however, probably reflects the hopelessness of that application as a whole. In *Chappell v. UK* the Commission avoided deciding whether Druidism was a religion for the purposes of Article 9(1) but 'assumed, for the purpose of this application, that it is a religion or belief as it finds the complaint anyway manifestly ill-founded'.[45] This suggests the existence of a very real issue to which there is no easy answer. It is likely that the Commission will use the availability of alternative grounds as a means of solving this problem whenever possible.

Where an applicant relies upon a belief of a non-religious nature then, once again, it is more likely to be accepted as falling within the scope of Article 9 if it relates to a well-established school of thought. Thus atheism[46] and pacifism[47] are accounted beliefs for this purpose whilst in *Hazar, Hazar and Acik v. Turkey* the Commission was prepared to accept, for the purposes of admissibility, that communism fell within its terms.[48] Other opinions, which, at first sight, are not so obviously encompassed within the definition given by the Court in *Campbell and Cosans* seem to be

---

[43] K. Rimanque, 'Freedom of Conscience and Minority Groups', in *Freedom of Conscience*, Leiden Seminar Proceedings (Strasbourg: Council of Europe, 1993) p. 144 at pp. 155–157 points to the difficulty that this might cause members of minority groups whose religious beliefs and practices may not be well understood.

[44] *X v. UK*, No. 7291/75, 11 DR 55 (Dec. 1977).

[45] A. R. M. *Chappell v. UK*, No. 12587/86, 53 DR 241 (Dec. 1987) at 246. The Druids had been barred from performing ceremonies at Stonehenge at the time of the summer solstice. The Commission accepted the argument that these restrictions were justified under Article 9(2). It should be noted that in his judgment Mr Justice McNeil had accepted that Druidism was a religion for the purposes of Article 9 of the Convention.

[46] *Angeleni v. Sweden*, No. 10491/83, 40 DR 41 (Dec. 1986).

[47] *Arrowsmith v. UK*, No. 7050/75, Rep. 1978, para. 69, 19 DR 5, 19; *C v. UK*, No. 10358/83, 37 DR 142 (Dec. 1983); *Le Cour Grandmaison and Fritz v. France*, Nos. 11567/85 and 11568/85, 53 DR 150 (Dec. 1987).

[48] *Hazar, Hazar and Acik v. Turkey*, Nos. 16311/90, 16312/90 and 16313/90 (joined), 72 DR 200 (Dec. 1991). See also *United Communist Party of Turkey and others v. Turkey*, No. 21237/93 (Dec. 1994), Inf. note 123, p. 2 and *Yazar and others, for the Peoples' Work Party v. Turkey*, Nos. 22723/93, 22724/93 and 22725/93 (Dec. 1995), Inf. note 125, p. 2. This is rather ironic, given that the original purpose of the instrument was to aid the struggle against further communist incursions into the States of Western Europe.

acceptable if they have achieved a certain level of formality, such as the formation of an association.[49] Whether this also embraces political parties is unclear.

Even here, however, some fine lines exist. In *Plattform 'Ärzte für das Leben' v. Austria*[50] an association of doctors espousing anti-abortionist views was considered to be within the scope of Article 9. The association was neither a religious community nor a society concerned with the advancement of a general understanding of being. It was, rather, a single issue pressure group. Nevertheless, the aims of the association were directly related to a matter of belief that itself was derived from religious conviction. This might be compared with *Vereniging Rechtswinkels Utrecht v. the Netherlands*[51] in which an association giving free legal advice to prisoners could not rely on Article 9 in order to gain access to a prison since its aims, though 'idealistic', did not amount to a 'belief' for the purposes of Article 9.

Where an individual relies upon his own private beliefs, and which are not derived from membership of or adherence to a particular religion, generally accepted stance or an association of some kind, then the claim is likely to fall outside the scope of Article 9. In *McFeeley et al. v. UK* the applicants, who claimed to be political prisoners, argued that it was contrary to their beliefs and conscience to wear prison uniforms and engage in prison work.[52] The UK Government argued that 'the term "belief" . . . relates to the holding of spiritual or philosophical convictions which have an identifiable formal content. It does not extend to mere "opinions" or deeply held feelings about certain matters.'[53] Whilst not addressing this directly, the Commission did conclude that 'the right to . . . a preferential status for a certain category of prisoner is not amongst the rights guaranteed by . . . Article 9'.[54] The subsequent case of *X v. UK*[55] was equally equivocal. The Commission was again faced with an applicant who claimed to be a political prisoner and, in consequence, refused to wear prison clothes. Recalling *McFeeley*, the Commission observed that 'even assuming that the applicant had shown that he were a "political prisoner" he has failed to show that his political views were such as to

---

[49] Although this best seems to explain elements of practice, it is somewhat paradoxical that the right of these associations to bring applications has been a matter of doubt.

[50] *Plattform 'Ärzte für das Leben' v. Austria*, No. 10126/82, 44 DR 65 (Dec. 1985). In the same way, claims relating to the freedom of expression may be subsumed within Article 11, concerning the freedom of assembly.

[51] *Vereniging Rechtswinkels Utrecht v. the Netherlands*, No. 11308/84, 46 DR 200 (Dec. 1986).

[52] *McFeeley et al. v. UK*, No. 8317/78, 20 DR 44 (Dec. 1980) at 76.

[53] *Ibid.*, p. 77.   [54] *Ibid.*

[55] *X v. UK*, No. 8231/78, 28 DR 5 (Dec. 1982).

require . . . not wearing prison clothes'.[56] This seems to suggest that it was the absence of this connection, rather than the nature of the belief, that was of prime importance.[57]

However, the decision in X v. *Federal Republic of Germany* adopted a stricter approach which placed private opinions beyond the reach of Article 9. The Commission decided that the applicant's wish to have his ashes scattered in his garden fell outside of its scope. It said: 'The desired action has certainly a strong personal motivation. However, the Commission does not find that it is a manifestation of any belief in the sense that some coherent view on fundamental problems can be seen as being expressed thereby.'[58] It would seem that the Article 9 right does not grant an individual the right to manifest a purely personal point of view and the matter is, perhaps, best summed up in the words used by the Government in *Arrowsmith v. UK* that 'the word "belief" connotes and requires the holding and expression of spiritual or philosophical convictions which, while not necessarily organized in the same sense of a religion, nevertheless have an identifiable formal content'.[59]

Does the freedom of thought, conscience and religion include the right of actualization?

Article 9 protects the manifestation of religion or belief, not manifestations of thought or conscience. Determining whether a form of behaviour is a 'manifestation' for the purposes of Article 9 raises a whole host of problems which will be considered in the next section. This section will examine an issue which straddles this divide and concerns the claim that the very fact of being entitled to hold certain views by virtue of the first sentence of Article 9(1) carries with it the right to behave in a particular fashion, even though it might relate to 'thought or conscience' rather than 'religion', or, if related to religion or belief, not amount to a manifestation for the purposes of the second sentence of Article 9(1): in other words, that the 'passive' right has an 'active' dimension. This claim is significant because any such behaviour legitimated on this basis would

---

[56] *Ibid.*, p. 27. For the related claim in relation to his beliefs as a Sikh see below, pp. 324, 326.
[57] See also *Revert and Legallais v. France*, Nos. 14331/88 and 14332/88 (joined), 62 DR 309 (Dec. 1989) which suggests that the applicants' disapproval of the stance taken by the professional body which they were required to join did violate Article 9 because they remained free to express their ideas in other ways, rather than because they were simply too general to qualify as beliefs.
[58] No. 8741/79, 24 DR 137 (Dec. 1981), 138.
[59] *Arrowsmith v. UK*, No. 7050/75, Rep. 1978, para. 42.

not be subject to the restrictions set out in Article 9(2) or, in so far as they were forms of expression, to those of Article 10(2).[60]

The bounds of Article 9: the *forum internum*

In what has become a standard recital,[61] the Commission has said that: 'Article 9 primarily protects the sphere of personal beliefs and religious creeds, i.e. the area which is sometimes called the *forum internum*.'[62] If this was all that the first sentence of Article 9 protected, there would be little difficulty in its application both because of its simplicity and the rarity of its being breached, since an applicant would have to show that external pressure sufficient to induce a forcible change in inner belief had been applied. In fact, the approach adopted is somewhat broader and focuses upon the danger of indoctrination inherent in being obliged to act by the State in a way that runs counter to one's inner beliefs. This follows from the comments made by the Court in the *Danish Sex Education* case that: 'The State is forbidden to pursue an aim of indoctrination that might be considered as not respecting parents' religious and philosophical convictions. This is the limit that must not be exceeded.'[63] Although this was said in the context of Article 2 of the First Protocol, the Court felt this was 'consistent . . . with Articles 8 to 10 of the Convention'.[64] The right to private thought does, then, protect a person from being subjected to actions intended to induce a change of mind. However, conduct reaching this threshold would almost inevitably amount to a breach of other Convention articles and in particular Article 3, prohibiting torture or

---

[60] These issues are addressed by B. Vermeulen, 'Scope and Limits of Conscientious Objections', in *Freedom of Conscience*, Leiden Seminar Proceedings (Strasbourg: Council of Europe, 1993), p. 74 at pp. 81–85 who not only concludes that 'external' freedom of conscience is not guaranteed by the Convention, but that it is incompatible with the very concept of a legal system.

[61] See, e.g., *C v. UK*, No. 10358/83, 37 DR 142 (Dec. 1983), 147; *V v. the Netherlands*, No. 10678/83, 39 DR 267 (Dec. 1983), 268; *Vereniging Rechtswinkels Utrecht v. the Netherlands*, No. 11308/84, 46 DR 200 (Dec. 1984), 202; *Van Den Dungen v. the Netherlands*, No. 22838/93, 80 DR 147 (Dec. 1995), 150; *Valsamis v. Greece*, No. 21787/93, Rep. 1995, para. 48; *Efstratiou v. Greece*, No. 24095/94, Rep. 1996, para. 48.

[62] It is this 'inner self' which is meant when reference is made to the 'private' sphere in the following sections. This usage should be distinguished from that which identifies the claim that the ECHR as an instrument is applicable to the relations between individuals as opposed to those between the individual and the State and which are the subject of A. Clapham, *Human Rights in the Private Sphere* (Oxford: Clarendon Press, 1993).

[63] *Kjeldsen, Busk Madsen and Pedersen v. Denmark* (*Danish Sex Education* case), Ser. A, no. 48 (1982), para. 53

[64] *Ibid.*

inhuman or degrading treatment or punishment.[65] Since the right to freedom of thought, conscience and religion is absolute, it might otherwise be argued that advertising, or any other means of changing peoples' opinions, might be covered.

Similarly, although Article 9(1) does not provide the right to be free from criticism, if such criticism threatens an individual's freedom of conscience then there will be a violation.[66] In the *Kokkinakis* case the State was entitled to protect its subjects from 'improper proselytism'.[67] Nevertheless, the individual derives only minimal protection from this 'safety net'.

The freedom from State-imposed compulsion

The negative aspect of the claim concerns the question of whether the bare statement of the right to 'thought, conscience and religion' carries with it a right to claim exemption from participation in schemes imposed by the State. This must be considered because not all such claims will fall within the limited scope of the freedom of manifestation.

The Commission has rejected applications submitted by individuals who have been required to participate in State-run pension schemes,[68] to vote in elections[69] or to submit to formalities of which they disapprove.[70] Provided that the individuals are able to continue in their beliefs, the *forum internum* remains untouched and there will be no breach of Article 9(1).[71] In *Bernard v. Luxembourg*, for example, the Commission rejected the

---

[65] For example, in *Hazar, Hazar and Acik v. Turkey*, Nos. 16311/90, 16312/90 and 16313/90 (joined), 72 DR 200 (Dec. 1991) the Commission declared admissible a complaint in which the applicants alleged, *inter alia*, that they had been convicted under a law which made it an offence simply to belong to the Communist Party. The matter, which raised many other questions, including points under Article 3, was subsequently resolved by friendly settlement. See 73 DR 111 (Rep. 1992).

[66] *Church of Scientology and 128 of its Members v. Sweden*, No. 8282/78, 21 DR 109 (Dec. 1980).

[67] *Kokkinakis v. Greece*, Ser. A, no. 260–A (1993), para. 48.

[68] E.g. *Reformed Church of X v. the Netherlands*, No. 1497/62, 5 YBECHR 286 (Dec. 1962); *X v. the Netherlands*, No. 2065/63, 8 YBECHR 266 (Dec. 1965).

[69] *X v. Austria*, No. 1718/62, 8 YBECHR 168 (Dec. 1965); *X v. Austria*, No. 4982/71, 15 YBECHR 468 (Dec. 1972).

[70] A considerable number of Applications of this nature have been declared inadmissible by the Commission. See, e.g., *X v. Federal Republic of Germany*, No. 6167/73, 1 DR 64 (Dec. 1974) concerning marriage formalities; *E & GR v. Austria*, No. 9781/82, 37 DR 42 (Dec. 1984) and *J and B Gottesmann v. Switzerland*, No. 10616/83, 40 DR 284 (Dec. 1984) concerning formalities for changing or relinquishing a religion; and *Fryske Nasjonale Partij and others v. the Netherlands*, No. 11100/84, 45 DR 240 (Dec. 1985) concerning formalities for electoral registration.

[71] The early decision of the Commission in the case of *X. v. the Netherlands*, No. 1068/61, 5 YBECHR 278 (Dec. 1962) considered that the imposition of formalities, in this case the

argument that in requiring children to attend lessons in society and morality, the State was interfering with the freedom of thought, conscience and religion, it being accepted that participation in such lessons did not amount to a form of indoctrination.[72]

In the *Darby* case, however, the Commission extended the range of protection afforded by the simple expedient of taking a more expansive view of what the *forum internum* comprised. The *Darby* case concerned a Finnish citizen who worked, but was not domiciled, in Sweden. In common with other non-residents who derived income from working in Sweden, he was taxed in the 'Common District'. His tax liabilities included payment of church tax to the Swedish Lutheran Church, of which the applicant was not a member. Swedish residents who were not members of the Church could claim exemption from the proportion of the church tax which supported the general work of the church, but this did not apply to non-residents taxed in the Common District.

The Commission expressed the view that 'the ... general right of freedom of religion under the first limb of Article 9(1) ... protects everyone from being compelled to be involved directly in religious activities against his will without being a member of the religious community carrying out those activities.'[73] It therefore required that 'a State respects the religious convictions of those who do not belong to the church, for instance by making it possible for them to be exempted from the obligation to make contributions to the church *for its religious activities*'.[74]

This did not amount to protecting an individual against compulsory involvement in activities taking place in the public sphere, since the support of a religious organization in its performance of public tasks entrusted to it by the State fell within the 'public' rather than 'private' sphere. Therefore, the State could demand that an individual, regardless of religion or belief, should support a church in its performance of

compulsory membership of a health service, was justified under Article 9(2). This implied that the requirement was a prima facie breach of Article 9(1). This is difficult to sustain in the light of the subsequent decisions, and in *Revert and Legallais v. France*, Nos. 14331/88 and 14332/88 (joined), 62 DR 309 (Dec. 1989) the Commission declared inadmissible an application relating to compulsory membership of a professional organization on the ground that such membership had no connection with personal beliefs at all.

[72] *Bernard v. Luxembourg*, No. 17187/90, 75 DR 57 (Dec. 1993). This decision is considered below, p. 353, in the context of Article 2 of the First Protocol.

[73] *Darby v. Sweden*, No. 11581/85, Rep. 1989, paras. 50–51.

[74] *Ibid.*, para. 58 (emphasis added).

functions such as the registration of births and marriages and maintaining burial grounds. On the other hand, the Commission felt that the *forum internum* was affected if an individual was required to support the purely religious activities of the church.

This represents a considerable enlargement of the *forum internum* and, whilst by no means an untenable distinction, it would be a very difficult line to draw. Two members of the Commission dissented from its finding on Article 9 because they believed that 'the fact that the applicant had to pay a tax . . . does not . . . infringe a right conferred on him by Article 9. He continued to have freedom to practise a religion, to manifest a religion, or to refrain from practising a religion.'[75] Moreover, when the case was heard by the Court, it was dealt with on the basis of the violation of Article 14 in conjunction with Article 1 of the First Protocol, concerning property rights, and no opinion was expressed concerning the possible violation of Article 9. The wider impact of the Commission's view is, therefore, uncertain.

The Commission itself proceeded with caution in *Valsamis v. Greece*. This application was presented by a twelve-year-old school girl and her parents, all of whom were Jehovah's Witnesses. The girl refused to participate in a march associated with the national holiday marking 28 October, arguing that this was a commemoration of war and conflicted with her pacifist beliefs. The Commission was of the opinion that the school was entitled to take disciplinary measures against her since, in its view, the procession was not of a military character and compulsory participation did not amount to an act of indoctrination, even though she was being required to act in a manner which, in her opinion, ran counter to her beliefs.[76]

It would seem, then, that apart from situations in which the imposition is so severe that it poses a potential threat to the *forum internum*, whatever protection is offered to this negative aspect is likely to be derived from the protection granted by the second sentence of Article 9(1) to the manifestation of a religion or belief. As will be seen, this has been interpreted restrictively and the net result is that Article 9 gives little protection against the demands placed upon individuals that they act in the public sphere in ways which are contrary to their beliefs. As the *Darby* case demonstrates, however, the *forum internum* can be interpreted in a

---

[75] Dissenting Opinion of Mr Schermers and Sir Basil Hall, *ibid.*, p. 15.

[76] *Valsamis v. Greece*, No. 21787/93, Rep. 1995, paras. 40, 50. See also the substantially similar case of *Efstratiou and others v. Greece*, No. 24095/94, Rep. 1996, paras. 40, 50. Her parents also argued that their rights under Article 2 of the First Protocol had been violated. This is considered below, p. 357, n. 67.

number of ways. The more restrictive views taken by the Commission in most of the cases considered above might be ripe for reconsideration in the light of its more relaxed attitude in the *Darby* case, although the hesitancy of the Court to adopt a similar line of reasoning, and the reluctance of the Commission to build on it, suggests that caution is needed.

The freedom to act

In its positive form, this claim concerns the right to engage in activities which flow from patterns of thought, conscience or religion. Such claims must be treated with extreme caution. In the *Kokkinakis* case, the Court observed that: 'While religious freedom is primarily a matter of individual conscience, it also implies, *inter alia*, freedom to "manifest [one]'s religion"'. Bearing witness in words and deeds is bound up with the existence of religious convictions.'[77] This suggests that this need is met by the freedom of manifestation, which represents the limits of what might be enjoyed by virtue of Article 9 above and beyond the general right to freedom of expression in Article 10. This was confirmed, albeit by implication, in the *Kokkinakis* case when the Court observed that:

> The fundamental nature of the rights guaranteed in Article 9(1) is also reflected in the wording of the paragraph providing for the limitations on them . . . which . . . refers only to 'freedom to manifest one's religion or belief'. In so doing, it recognizes that in democratic societies, in which several religions coexist within one and the same population, it may be necessary to place restrictions on this freedom in order to reconcile the interests of the various groups and ensure that everyone's beliefs are respected.[78]

Although it may appear odd to demonstrate the fundamental nature of a right by pointing to the restrictions which can be placed upon its enjoyment, it seems clear that if the Court felt it necessary to ensure that actions taken in accordance with religious beliefs should not be allowed to impact unduly upon the equally fundamental rights, it would not be prepared to accept the argument that the bare statement of the freedom of thought, conscience and religion could carry with it a right to 'actualize' in a fashion that evaded the restrictions upon manifestation and expression found within the Convention.[79]

---

[77] *Kokkinakis v. Greece*, Ser. A no. 260–A (1993), para. 31.

[78] *Ibid.*, para. 33.

[79] But *cf.* the Partly Dissenting Opinion of Judge Martens (*ibid.*, p. 37, para. 14). He accepted that the freedoms of thought, conscience and religion enshrined in Article 9(1) were absolute and left no room for State interference. From this, however, he

Another danger – though some might think it an attraction – of accepting this claim is that it could be used to create rights not expressly provided for in the Convention. The case of *Johnston v. Ireland* provides a good illustration of how this might come about. The applicant claimed that his inability to obtain a divorce under Irish law, which would have enabled him to be free to marry the woman with whom he was then living and by whom he had had a child, violated his freedom of conscience. The respondent Government argued that Article 9 protected 'only the right not to be coerced into living in a manner contrary to one's religious beliefs'.[80]

The Commission ultimately rejected the complaint under Article 9. If a person freely chooses to marry, knowing that a divorce will not be available, it is not possible to question its unavailability simply because a divorce is subsequently wanted. The Convention did not contain a right to divorce and Article 9 could not be used to create it.[81] The Commission has, for similar reasons, refused to accept that the first sentence of Article 9 implies such rights as the right to hold public office,[82] the right not to be deported[83] or the right of an association to be accepted as a political party.[84]

What is meant by 'freedom'?

The protection offered by the first sentence of Article 9 is, then, narrowly circumscribed. It cannot be used to extend the scope of the freedom to hold a pattern of thought, conscience or religion beyond the *forum internum* – the 'private sphere'. In particular, it cannot be used to justify claims to exercise rights in the public sphere since they are unnecessary to private belief. It may be irksome to discover that a church or its

---

concluded that since this absolute freedom included the right to change one's religion, it was of no concern to the State if somebody attempted to induce another to change his religion. This cannot be correct, since it would mean that there was an inherent right to manifest a religious belief in teaching that was not subject to State regulation in order to secure the rights of others, as is expressly provided for by the remainder of the article.

[80] *Johnston v. Ireland*, No. 9672/82, 34 DR 131 (Dec. 1983), 141.

[81] *Johnston v. Ireland*, Ser. A, no. 112 (1986) and see Van Dijk and Van Hoof, *Theory and Practice of the ECHR*, pp. 444–445. If Article 9 could be used to create a right to divorce, it might also be invoked by a spouse who did not wish to be divorced in situations where this was possible without consent, particularly in the absence of fault.

[82] *Demeester v. Belgium*, No. 8493/79, 25 DR 210 (Dec. 1981).

[83] *Omkarananda and the Divine Light Zentrum v. Switzerland*, No. 8118/77, 25 DR 105 (Dec. 1981).

[84] *Association X, Y and Z v. Federal Republic of Germany*, No. 6850/74, 5 DR 90 (Dec. 1974), 93.

members cannot bring civil or criminal proceedings against those who criticize it but this does not prevent it from enjoying the right conferred by Article 9(1).[85]

This reflects the more general consideration that having the right to freedom of thought, conscience and religion does not mean that its enjoyment need be without cost. Exercising this freedom can result in disabilities and disadvantage, but there would only be a breach of the Convention if this involved discrimination within the meaning of Article 14. Thus, for example, when a clergyman complained that the State Church of Denmark had forbidden his imposing a requirement that parents attend five religious lessons as a condition for christening their children the Commission decided that 'in a State church system its servants are employed for the purpose of applying and teaching a specific religion. Their individual freedom of thought, conscience and religion is exercised at the moment they accept or refuse employment as clergymen, and their right to leave the church guarantees their freedom of religion in case they oppose its teachings.'[86]

Another example of this is provided by the decision in *E & GR v. Austria*.[87] Under Austrian law churches could levy contributions from

---

[85] See *Church of Scientology and 128 of its Members v. Sweden*, No. 8282/78, 21 DR 109 (Dec. 1980) at 111. See also *Choudhury v. UK*, No. 17439/90 in which a complaint concerning the failure of the blasphemy laws in the UK to extend protection to Islam was declared inadmissible. Since the Convention does not grant a right to bring a civil action or criminal charges against those who blaspheme, there can be no question of these laws being discriminatory under Article 14. But *cf*. Clapham, *Human Rights in the Private Sphere*, p. 319 who argued – in advance of the application – that if the Convention confers rights upon individuals in their mutual dealings, then the admittedly discriminatory nature of the laws relating to blasphemy would violate Article 14. The decision of the Commission in this case is open to re-evaluation in the light of the judgment of the Court in *Otto-Preminger-Institut v. Austria* (see Harris, O'Boyle and Warbrick, *Law of the ECHR*, p. 360 and below, p. 335.

[86] *X v. Denmark*, No. 7374/76, 5 DR 157 (Dec. 1976) at 158. See also *Prussner v. Germany*, No. 10901/84 (1987) 8 EHRR 79 concerning compulsory redundancy for the refusal of a clergyman to baptise infants; *Karlsson v. Sweden*, No. 12356/86, 57 DR 172 (Dec. 1988), 175 in which the applicant priest's views on the priesthood of women were incompatible with the view generally held by the Church, and which, in consequence, was not obliged to accept the applicant's candidacy for a post of vicar (senior priest) which might have required him to work with a female assistant priest; *Williamson v. UK*, No. 27008/95 (Dec. 1995), Inf. note 126, p. 4 concerning the complaint of a Church of England priest concerning the decision to ordain women; *X v. Sweden*, No. 24019/94 (Dec. 1996), Inf. note 133, p. 4 concerning the decision of the Swedish Church to use a new Finnish translation of its liturgy and to prohibit its Finnish-speaking parish in Stockholm from using the Finnish Church's liturgy.

[87] *E & GR v. Austria*, No. 9781/82, 37 DR 42 (Dec. 1984). See also *J and B Gottesmann v. Switzerland*, No. 10616/83, 40 DR 284 (Dec. 1984).

their members in accordance with State-approved regulations and the resulting duty to pay contributions could be enforced by means of a civil action. The applicants complained that this meant they either had to pay the contributions or leave the church. The Commission took the view that the applicants were free to practise or not practise their religion as they pleased since the obligation to pay was a consequence of their decision to remain in membership. Their freedom of religion was protected by their ability to leave the church.[88] As with the cases concerning the employment of clergy, the regulations were, ultimately, a matter of internal church order.[89]

This approach has also been followed in a number of other situations. In *X v. UK* the Commission noted that the applicant, a Muslim, was free to resign from his employment as a school teacher 'if and when he found that his teaching obligations conflicted with his religious duties'.[90] In fact, the applicant renegotiated his contract so that he was employed for four and a half days per week. It was irrelevant that this resulted in a loss of pay and affected his pension rights, chances of promotion and job security since his freedom to practice his religion was not lessened by any of these factors.

Exercising the freedom of religion or belief may, then, require personal sacrifice.[91] It may also result in criticism or even hostility and 'agitation' from other members of society. The Commission has accepted that a State could be held responsible if it tolerated a level of criticism and agitation that threatened the freedom of religion but there is no right to be free from criticism itself.[92] On the other hand, the State remains free to take action in the face of expressions of hostility if it wishes without incurring liability.[93]

Even governments themselves are not obliged to refrain from making

---

[88] *Ibid.*, 45.

[89] Had the State legislation obliged, as opposed to permitted, the Church to levy financial contributions from its members and enforce their payment through the courts, then the situation would have been different.

[90] *X v. UK*, No. 8160/78, 22 DR 27 (1981), 36.

[91] See also *X v. Sweden*, No. 20402/92 (Dec. 1994), Inf. note 122, p. 5 concerning the revocation of the right of Pentecostal ministers to celebrate marriages, and *X v. Austria*, No. 20996/92 (Dec. 1994), Inf. note 123, p. 4 concerning the appointment of a curator to perform the secular functions of a church following a schism.

[92] *Church of Scientology and 128 of its Members v. Sweden*, No. 8282/78, 21 DR 109 (Dec. 1980), 111.

[93] In *X v. Germany*, No. 19459/92 (Dec. 1993), Inf. note 111, p. 4 the Commission declared inadmissible a complaint from a naval captain that he had been dismissed for making anti-Semitic remarks at a private party.

things difficult for adherents of particular religions or beliefs. In *Church of X v. UK* the Government had placed a variety of restrictions upon foreign nationals who were members of the applicant Church and who were either seeking to come to, or were already in, the country for the purposes of either teaching or study at a college operated by the Church. The Commission thought that measures of this nature did not amount to a violation of Article 9 since they did not prevent members of the Church already in the country from attending the college, their churches or otherwise manifesting their religion or belief.[94] This might be true but it overlooked the accepted fact that the very purpose of the regulations was to make things as difficult as possible for the Church which the Government had decided was potentially harmful to its adherents.[95] If nothing else, the decision demonstrates just how minimal protection can be when the Convention is read strictly.

The question of conscientious objection to military service provides an example of the general approach adopted. The Commission has consistently taken the view that the Convention does not grant the right of conscientious objection.[96] In the *Grandrath* case the applicant, a Jehovah's Witness, had been imprisoned for refusing to perform both military or substitute civilian service. He had argued that freedom of conscience implied that, unless there was any interference with the fundamental rights of others, any decision taken by a person in accordance with the dictates of conscience should be respected.[97] The respondent Government argued that Article 9 did not grant the right of conscientious objection at all. The Commission took the view that, since Article 4(3)(b) of the Convention expressly recognized that 'civilian service may be imposed on

---

[94] *Church of X v. UK*, No. 3798/68, 29 CD 70 (Dec. 1968), 77.

[95] *Ibid.*, p. 71. This should have been considered in connection with Article 9(2). See F. Jacobs, *The European Convention on Human Rights* (Oxford: Clarendon Press, 1975), p. 148.

[96] *Cf.* Committee of Ministers of the Council of Europe, Recommendation No. R (87) 8 Regarding Conscientious Objection to Compulsory Military Service. This set out as a basic principle the proposition that: 'Anyone liable to conscription for military service who, for compelling reasons of conscience, refuses to be involved in the use of arms shall have the right to be released from the obligation to perform such service, on the conditions set out hereafter. Such persons may be liable to perform alternative service.' See also S. Rodota, 'Conscientious Objection to Military Service', in *Freedom of Conscience* (Strasbourg: Council of Europe, 1993), pp. 94–106.

[97] *Grandrath v. Federal Republic of Germany*, No. 2299/64, Rep. 1967, para. 9, 10 YBECHR 626, 632–636. This was accepted by one member of the Commission, Mr Ermacora. He felt, however, that military service was permitted under Article 9(2) as a limitation necessary for the protection of public order and that States had a discretion as to whether to allow exemptions for conscientious objectors (*ibid.*, para. 34, 10 YBECHR 626, 676).

conscientious objectors as a substitute for military service, it must be concluded that *objections of conscience do not, under the Convention, entitle a person to exemption from such service*.[98]

Although it has been subjected to much criticism, this decision has been applied on many subsequent occasions.[99] The principal criticism is that although Article 4(3)(b) recognizes that an individual might be liable for compulsory military, or substitute civilian, service, this is not incompatible with the view that Article 9 only permits the imposition of such service upon conscientious objectors if it can be justified under the terms of Article 9(2).[100] This, however, misses the point. Although the Commission did not examine the meaning of the term 'freedom of conscience or religion' because it thought that Article 4(3)(b) rendered this unnecessary,[101] there can be little doubt that had the Commission done so, it would not have found a violation since it was of the opinion that compulsory service could not interfere with the *forum internum* and found as a matter of fact that the applicant would have been able to manifest his beliefs within the meaning of Article 9 whilst fulfilling his obligation to perform substitute service.[102]

The key to understanding what is meant by 'freedom' lies in the

---

[98] *Ibid.*, para. 33, 10 *YBECHR* 626, 674 (emphasis in original).

[99] See, e.g., *X v. Austria*, No. 5591/72, 43 CD 161 (Dec. 1973); *X v. Federal Republic of Germany*, No. 7705/76, 9 DR 196 (Dec. 1977); *Johansen v. Norway*, No. 10600/83, 44 DR 155 (Dec. 1985); *A v. Switzerland*, No. 10640/83, 38 DR 219 (Dec. 1984); *Autio v. Finland*, No. 17086/90, 72 DR 245 (Dec. 1991); *X v. Belgium*, No. 24631/94 (Dec. 1995), Inf. note 126, p. 4. In *Tsirlis and Kouloumpas v. Greece*, No. 19233/91 and 19234/91, Rep. 1996, para. 117, the Commission observed that 'the Convention does not guarantee per se a right for religious ministers to be exempted from military service'.

[100] See Van Dijk and Van Hoof, *Theory and Practice of the ECHR*, p. 399. This was the view taken by Mr Eusthadiades in his concurring opinion in the *Grandrath* case and recently endorsed by Mrs J. Liddy in her Partly Dissenting Opinion in *Tsirlis and Kouloumpas v. Greece*, *ibid.*

[101] *Grandrath v. Federal Republic of Germany*, No. 2299/64, Rep. 1967, para. 32, 10 *YBECHR* 626, 674.

[102] *Ibid.*, para. 31, 10 *YBECHR* 626, 672. Had the imposition of military, or substitute, service prevented the applicant from manifesting his beliefs, this would then have raised issues under Article 9(2). See the Opinion of Mr Ermacora, n. 97 above. The applicant also argued that the relevant German legislation was discriminatory since Roman Catholic and Protestant ministers were exempted from military or substitute service. The Commission decided that there were legitimate grounds for this differentiation and so there was no violation of Article 14. For criticism of this aspect of the decision see Jacobs, *The European Convention on Human Rights*, p. 147. See also *X v. the Netherlands*, No. 22739/93 (Dec. 1995), Inf. note 123, p. 4 in which an application concerning the refusal to exempt a philosophy student from alternative civil service, although those studying for ecclesiastical or religious/humanitarian offices were so entitled, was declared inadmissible.

distinction drawn by the Commission between the public and the private spheres. The freedom of thought, conscience and religion is exercised in the private sphere, the *forum internum*. Penalties, disabilities and criticism do not prevent a person holding a pattern of thought, conscience or religion. The Convention does not prevent society from extracting a degree of sacrifice from individuals who subscribe to certain forms of belief. How great a sacrifice is not to be answered with reference to Article 9 alone which, on its own terms, would not necessarily prevent the compulsory establishment of religious ghettos provided that the freedom to manifest religion or belief was preserved. Taken to its logical conclusion, this would suggest that it would not necessarily be in breach of Article 9 to impose a penalty for simply holding a belief. However, this does seem to lie beyond the limit of acceptability, and in *Kalaç v. Turkey* the Commission considered the enforced early retirement of a military judge who held Islamic fundamentalist views was in violation of Article 9(1).[103]

The manifestation of religion or belief

The second sentence of Article 9(1) confers the right to manifest a religion or belief in 'worship, teaching, practice and observance'. This sentence was subject to close scrutiny in *Arrowsmith v. UK* in which the applicant, a pacifist, had been convicted for distributing leaflets urging UK troops to refuse to serve in Northern Ireland. Her claim raised issues under both Article 9 and Article 10. With regard to Article 9 she argued that the 'heads' of manifestations listed in Article 9 were not exhaustive but, if they were, that the distribution of the leaflets was a manifestation of her beliefs 'in practice' and thus fell within its terms anyway.[104]

The UK Government argued that these four heads provided an exhaustive catalogue of the forms of manifestation that were protected under Article 9 and that they were to be restrictively interpreted. In particular, it was argued that 'general conduct or behaviour which is merely consistent

---

[103] *Kalaç v. Turkey*, No. 20704/92, Rep. 1996, paras. 31–36, referred to the Court in April 1996. See also *Hazar, Hazar and Acik v. Turkey*, Nos. 16311/90, 16312/90 and 16313/90 (joined), 72 DR 200 (Dec. 1991) and 73 DR 111 (Rep. 1992) and n. 65 above; *Hamarattürk v. Turkey*, No. 18673/91 (Dec. 1995) concerning the dismissal from the armed forces of an airforce officer on account of his Islamic fundamentalist views. (Inf. note 123, p. 10; subsequently struck off following the failure of the applicant to provide observations on the merits of the case (Inf. note 132, p. 8)).

[104] *Arrowsmith v. UK*, No. 7050/75, Rep. 1978, para. 31.

with a religion or belief, or which flows from the belief or which even might serve to further the religion or belief, is not within the protection of Article 9(1)'.[105]

The parties' disagreement, therefore, centred upon whether the term 'practice' was to be understood as simply applying to acts analogous to worship or whether it extended to acts consequential upon religion or belief. This debate is central to any examination of what is meant by the term 'manifestation' because if the 'practice' of religion is understood in a broad fashion and ranges beyond those acts analogous to worship it will inevitably embrace those acts which can also be described as manifestations in the form of worship, teaching and observance. On the face of it, the Commission has adopted a fairly expansive approach but, on closer examination, it turns out that this is not the case.

In the *Arrowsmith* case the Commission agreed with the UK Government that 'the term "practice" . . . does not cover each act which is motivated and influenced by a religion or belief.[106] This has now become a standard recital endorsed on many subsequent occasions.[107] However, the Commission did not consider it to be as narrow as the Government had suggested. The Commission observed that 'public declarations proclaiming generally the idea of pacifism and urging the acceptance of a commitment to non-violence may be considered as a normal and recognized manifestation of pacifist belief'[108] and thought that if the leaflets in question had expressed pacifist views, then their distribution would have amounted to a manifestation within the sense of Article 9(1).[109]

This means either that the 'practice' of a religion or belief is to be

---

[105] *Ibid.*, para. 43.   [106] *Ibid.*, para. 71, 19 DR 5, 19.

[107] E.g. *C v. UK*, No. 10358/83, 37 DR 142 (Dec. 1983); *Vereniging Rechtswinkels Utrecht v. the Netherlands*, No. 11308/84, 46 DR 200 (Dec. 1986); *Khan v. UK*, No. 11579/85, 48 DR 253 (Dec. 1986); *Yanasik v. Turkey*, No. 14524/89, 74 DR 14 (Dec. 1993); *Karaduman v. Turkey*, No. 16278/90, 74 DR 93 (Dec. 1993); *B v. Switzerland*, No. 19898/92, 75 DR 223 (Dec. 1993); *Van Den Dungen v. the Netherlands*, No. 22838/93, 80 DR 147 (Dec. 1995); *Valsamis v. Greece*, No. 21767/93, Rep. 1995, para. 49. *Efstratiou v. Greece*, No. 24095/94, Rep. 1996, para. 49.

[108] *Arrowsmith v. UK*, No. 7050/75, Rep. 1978, para. 71, 19 DR 5, 19.

[109] *Ibid.*, paras. 71–75, 19 DR 5, 19–20. This might be contrasted with *Valsamis v. Greece*, No. 21787/93, Rep. 1995, paras. 48–50 and *Efstratiou v. Greece*, No. 24095/94, Rep. 1996, paras. 48–50 which suggest that the Commission did not believe that refusing to take part in a procession which, in the opinion of the applicants, was a commemoration of war, was a legitimate manifestation of pacifist beliefs. Too much should not be made of this, however, since there was a clear disagreement between the Commission and the applicants over the nature of the procession, the Commission considering it to be primarily the 'manifestation of a national holiday' (*ibid.*, paras. 34, 39). See also p. 297 above.

understood in a loose way and as embracing a range of activities which flow from one's religion or belief, or, if it is to be narrowly construed, that other heads of manifestation must be possible. The Commission did not make it clear which approach it was adopting. The first leaves the exact range of activities embraced by the term indeterminate whilst the second means that other 'heads' of manifestation could be advanced on a case by case basis. Subsequent practice has, however, focused on the elasticity inherent in the concept of 'practice' and avoided raising other heads of manifestation or delving deeply into the parameters of worship, teaching and observance.

For example, in the *Kokkinakis* case the Greek Government accepted that by entering his neighbour's house in order to attempt to convert her to his beliefs, the applicant was exercising his right to manifest his religion.[110] The Court endorsed this without finding it necessary to consider whether this was a form of 'teaching' or simply a 'manifestation', observing that 'freedom to manifest one's religion . . . includes in principle the right to try to convince one's neighbour, *for example* through teaching . . .'.[111] This tends to confirm that the key to understanding what amounts to a manifestation for the purposes of Article 9 lies in determining the scope of a 'practice'.

Once again, the *Arrowsmith* case provides the point of departure. The Commission said that 'when the actions of individuals do not actually express the belief concerned they cannot be as such protected by Article 9(1), even when they are motivated or influenced by it'.[112]

There are, then, a range of actions which, although motivated by beliefs, do not amount to a manifestation for the purposes of Article 9. On the facts of the *Arrowsmith* case it is, however, difficult to see how the 'practice' of a religion can embrace the distribution of leaflets explaining pacifism whilst not embracing actions which give practical expression to those views. This equates practice with propagation, which could be considered as a form of teaching and not a 'practice' at all.

In other cases, the Commission has accepted that conveying messages proclaiming the dangers of pornography, fornication and alcohol by word

---

[110] *Kokkinakis v. Greece*, No. 14307/88, Rep. 1991, para. 56.

[111] *Kokkinakis v. Greece*, Ser. A, no. 260–A (1993), para. 31 (emphasis added). But *cf.* the Dissenting Opinion of Judge Valticos (*ibid.*, p. 30): 'the term "teaching" in Article 9 undoubtedly refers to religious teaching in school curricula or in religious institutions, and not to personal door-to-door canvassing as in the present case'.

[112] *Arrowsmith v. UK*, No. 7050/75, Rep. 1978, para. 71, 19 DR 5, 19.

of mouth or by placard amounts to a manifestation.[113] On the face of it, these appear to be actions motivated by one's beliefs, rather than manifestations of the belief itself,[114] and are as such indistinguishable from the distribution of leaflets in the *Arrowsmith* case. On the other hand, the Commission has decided that not wishing to be buried in a cemetery but to have one's ashes scattered over one's own land did not amount to a manifestation of a belief.[115] Surely this is a very real attempt by an individual to manifest a personal belief in direct action?[116]

The principal approach adopted by the Commission when determining what amounts to an 'actual expression' centres upon the degree to which the activity in question represents a *necessary* expression of a religion or belief. An alternative approach, discernable in a small number of decisions, considers whether the act *gives* expression to a religion or belief.[117] Given the manner in which the 'necessary expression' test has been developed, the 'giving expression' approach is, strangely, the broader of the two. Both, however, have the practical effect of placing further restrictions upon the range of actions which will qualify as a manifestation.

'Necessary expressions'

In a number of cases the Commission has asked itself whether the particular activity in question was necessary for the fulfilment of the obligations incumbent upon those holding a particular religion or

---

[113] *X v. Sweden*, No. 9820/82 (1984) 5 *EHRR* 297. The Commission also accepted that shouting messages 'like a trumpet' in obedience to Isaiah was also a legitimate manifestation but was subject to legitimate restriction under Article 9(2).

[114] It must be remembered that Article 9 offers no real protection to the manifestation of purely private opinions and whilst such sentiments may be derived from religious convictions, they are not tenets of religious belief in their own right. A placard reading 'Christ died to save sinners' would manifest a religious belief for the purposes of Article 9, whereas a placard declaring 'Do not commit adultery' would not.

[115] *X v. Federal Republic of Germany*, No. 8741/79, 24 DR 137 (Dec. 1981), 138.

[116] In fact, the Commission did not consider this belief to be sufficiently coherent so as to qualify for consideration under Article 9 at all. *Ibid.*

[117] Although it would be unwise to extrapolate too much from the nuances in the Commission's reports, particularly since the choice of approach is closely related to the surrounding factual circumstances of the case. Nevertheless, it might be observed that decisions which follow the 'necessary expression' approach tend towards supporting the view that the heads of manifestation in Article 9 are finite, but that 'practice' is to be construed in a liberal fashion, whereas those decisions which adopted the 'direct expression' approach suggest that other heads of manifestation are to be contemplated since it would be difficult to accept that these fall within the most liberal definition of 'practice' that could legitimately be adopted.

belief.[118] This approach has been used in situations where the applicant is attempting to manifest a religion or belief in a way which would otherwise be barred by virtue of legitimate restrictions which impinge upon the scope of the freedom to act. The classic situation relates to prisoners but it has also been extended to those in professional, contractual or other forms of consensual relationship.

In *X v. Austria* the applicant was a prisoner who became converted to Buddhism whilst serving a twenty-year sentence for murder. He claimed that the prison authorities had obstructed his freedom to manifest his religion by not allowing him to grow a chin beard, preventing him from doing yoga exercises, denying him a prayer chain, not allowing him to subscribe to the periodical *Weltmission* and by refusing him access to books 'necessary for a further development of his philosophy of life' by obtaining them for the prison library.[119] The Commission rejected the first three of these contentions on the grounds that the restrictions which were in fact imposed upon him were justified under Article 9(2), but it also doubted whether a prayer chain was 'an indispensable element in the proper exercise of the Buddhist religion'.[120]

In a subsequent case the Commission also dismissed an application by a Buddhist prisoner who had been prevented by the prison authorities from sending material to a Buddhist magazine for publication. The applicant had argued that the exchange of ideas between Buddhists was an element in the exercise of their religion. The Commission observed that, whilst he had 'produced statements to the effect that communication with other Buddhists was an important part of his religious practice . . . he has failed

---

[118] This approach presupposes that there is an identifiable religion or belief with a formal content that does indeed place demands upon adherents. Its application might be difficult, if not impossible, in the context of a highly individualistic philosophy, such as, for example, humanism.

[119] *X v. Austria*, No. 1753/63, 8 *YBECHR* 174 (Dec. 1965), 184.

[120] *Ibid.* This would imply that growing a chin beard and doing yoga exercises were a necessary expression of his religion. The claim that his subscription to the periodical in question represented a part of the charity to which he was 'morally obliged' floundered when it was discovered to be a Catholic publication. The Commission rejected the final claim on the ground that the Convention did not oblige States to place religious materials at the disposal of prisoners. This should be contrasted with *X v. UK*, No. 6886/75, 5 DR 100 (Dec. 1976), in which the Commission considered that preventing a Tao Buddhist prisoner from having access to a religious and philosophical book which he had ordered did violate Article 9(1) but was justified under subsection (2) because it contained an illustrated chapter on the martial arts.

to prove that it was a necessary part of this practice that he should publish articles in a religious magazine'.[121]

The 'necessary expression' approach to determining whether an activity qualifies as a 'practice' was applied by the Commission in *X v. UK* in the wholly different context of contractual relations. The applicant was a Muslim who was employed by the Inner London Education Authority (ILEA) as a school teacher. For six years he had worked a full five-day week without attending a mosque for worship on Friday afternoons but, when relocated at a different school that was situated near a mosque, he began to do so. His request for formal permission was refused.

The Commission thought the applicant had not convincingly shown that 'he was required by Islam to disregard his continuing contractual obligation . . . and to attend the mosque during school time'. However, rather than base itself upon this ground, the Commission assumed the existence of a conflict between the applicant's religious and contractual obligations. Drawing on its previous decisions,[122] it felt that the ILEA was 'in principle entitled to rely on its own contract with the applicant' but that Article 9 required that 'the ILEA had to give due consideration to [the applicant's] religious position'[123] and concluded that, 'in their treatment of the applicant on the basis of his contract', they had done so.[124]

The relevance of this approach in this context is questionable. The entire point of considering whether an act is a 'necessary expression' of a religion or belief is to determine whether it amounts to a manifestation. If it qualifies as such, then it must be protected unless subject to lawful limitation under Article 9(2). This decision seems to introduce needless complexity since, as has been seen, the Commission has consistently taken the view that it is not necessary to ensure that the freedom to manifest a religion or belief is enjoyed without cost.[125] Given that the applicant had freely entered into a form of restrictive arrangement his freedom to manifest his religion had been compromised by his own actions and, provided that a minimum threshold was secured, more general aspects of his freedom could be secured by renegotiating his

---

[121] *X v. UK*, No. 5442/72, 1 DR 41 (Dec. 1974), 42. Although raised by the respondent, the Commission found it unnecessary to rely on Article 9(2) in this case.

[122] Principally *X v. Denmark*, No. 7374/76, 5 DR 157 (Dec. 1976). This case concerned a disagreement between a minister and his Church over the question of infant baptism. There was no question of disputing that this practice amounted to a 'necessary expression' of belief.

[123] *X v. UK*, No. 8160/78, 22 DR 27 (Dec. 1981), 36.

[124] *Ibid.*, p. 38.   [125] See above, p. 299.

contract or terminating his relationship.[126] This was the cost of his freedom.

The prison context is very different. Prisoners do not voluntarily subject themselves to the restrictions of prison life and are not free to leave if they find themselves unable to manifest their beliefs. It is quite justifiable to ensure that those legitimately subject to involuntary regimes are entitled to enjoy those forms of manifestation which are absolutely necessary to their beliefs. Recognizing their right to enjoy a broader range of practices would, however, be unjustifiable since they would be able to assert their freedom without bearing the additional element of cost that is imposed upon those seeking to exercise a similar right in general society. Adopting this approach which further reduces the scope of the 'practice' of religion or belief outside the context of involuntary regimes seems both unnecessary and undesirable.

Subsequent decisions have taken this process even further. The case of *C v. UK* concerned a member of the Religious Society of Friends (the Quakers) who had sought a guarantee that her income tax payments would not be used for military expenditure but would be directed towards peaceful purposes. It was argued that:

the manifestation in practice of pacifism requires that an adherent should oppose recourse to force in the settlement of disputes and therefore should not support, directly or indirectly, . . . defence related expenditure . . . The present case is . . . to be distinguished from the *Arrowsmith* case . . . because the diversion of . . . the applicant's taxes to peaceful purposes is not merely *consistent* with her beliefs, but *necessary* for the manifestation of them.[127]

The Commission took a very restrictive view of what amounted to the practice of a religion or belief. It stressed that Article 9 was primarily concerned with protecting the private sphere of personal beliefs and religious creeds but that it also 'protects acts which are intimately linked to these attitudes, such as acts of worship or devotion which are aspects of the practice of a religion or a belief in a generally recognised form'.[128]

Rather than consider whether the applicant was in fact obliged to act in the way she did in order to manifest her belief, the Commission drew a

---

[126] *X v. UK*, No. 5442/72, 1 DR 41 (Dec. 1974).

[127] *C v. UK*, No. 10358/83, 37 DR 142 (Dec. 1983) at 144. For an examination of the broader issues raised in this case see N. Grief, 'British Quakers, the Peace Tax and International Law', in M. W. Janis (ed.), *The Influence of Religion on the Development of International Law* (Dordrecht: Martinus Nijhoff, 1991), pp. 243–255; B. Forbes, 'Conscientious Objection to Taxation', in *Freedom and Conscience* (Strasbourg: Council of Europe, 1993), pp. 123–128.

[128] *Ibid.* The cases cited above, p. 294 n. 61, also endorse this statement.

distinction between the private and the public sphere and quoted the *Arrowsmith* case in support of the proposition that Article 9 'does not always guarantee the right to behave in the public sphere in a way which is dictated by such a belief: for instance by refusing to pay certain taxes because part of the revenue so raised may be applied for military expenditure'.[129]

At first sight this might suggest that the Commission was going beyond *Arrowsmith* and rejecting not only the idea that Article 9 protected acts 'motivated' or 'influenced' by religion or belief but also those acts in the public sphere which were 'dictated' by it. If this were so, Article 9 would offer very little protection indeed. Closer examination, however, shows that this is not necessarily the case. The Commission felt that 'the obligation to pay taxes is a general one which has no specific conscientious implication in itself' and, more significantly, 'the power of taxation is expressly recognized by the Convention system and is ascribed to the State by Article 1, First Protocol'. It therefore concluded that: 'Article 9 does not confer on the applicant the right to refuse, on the basis of his convictions, to abide by legislation, the operation of which is provided for in the Convention, and which applies neutrally and generally in the public sphere, without impinging upon the freedoms guaranteed by Article 9.'[130] Admittedly, the final statement is tautologous since it was the scope of those guarantees that was at issue. Nevertheless, the gist of the Commission's reasoning is clear enough: since the Convention explicitly permits general taxation, that power cannot be limited by reference to general considerations flowing from other articles. It was this aspect of the matter which meant that Article 9 could not be used to protect an action which seems to have been accepted to be a 'necessary' manifestation of pacifist belief.

Be that as it may, the formula used in *C v. UK*, and which reduced the content of a practice as a 'necessary expression' to 'acts intimately linked' to personal belief, 'such as acts of worship or devotion which are aspects of the practice of a religion or belief in a generally recognized form', has been used in subsequent cases. In *Yanasik v. Turkey* the Commission decided that a trainee cadet in a military establishment could be required to 'refrain from participating in the Muslim fundamentalist movement, whose aim and programme is to ensure the pre-eminence of religious rules' since 'by enrolling . . . an officer cadet submits of his own accord to military rules [which] may make cadets' freedom to practise their religion

---

[129] *Ibid.*   [130] *Ibid.*

subject to limitations as to time and place, without however negating it completely'.[131] Interestingly, the Commission noted that cadets were able to perform their religious duties within the requirements of military life, such as being 'able to pray and perform their other religious duties'.[132]

Similarly, in *Karaduman v. Turkey* the Commission decided that the refusal of a university student to be photographed without wearing a headscarf was an act which, although motivated by religious belief, was not a manifestation of that belief since: 'The purpose of the photograph affixed to a degree certificate is to identify the person concerned. It cannot be used by that person to manifest his religious beliefs.'[133] Clearly, this indicates a very restrictive view of what counts as a 'practice' and is reminiscent of the original test put forward by the UK Government in the *Arrowsmith* case.

'Giving expression' to beliefs

An alternative approach to determining whether a particular act is an actual expression of a religion or belief is not to consider whether the act is genuinely motivated *by* the belief itself but to consider objectively[134] whether it was motivated *by the intention to give expression* to the belief. *Knudsen v. Norway* illustrates this approach. The applicant was a vicar in the State Church who refused to perform those elements of his duties which he considered to be required of him by virtue of the State's part of his office (e.g. conducting marriages and keeping the birth register) in protest at newly enacted amendments to an Abortion Act. He was ultimately dismissed from his office, although allowed to continue to perform religious functions but not as a State employee. The Commission rejected his submission that he had lost his official post because of his religious beliefs because 'his dismissal ... was due to his refusal to perform functions that were administrative duties of his office ... [T]his refusal did not actually express the applicant's belief or religious view and it cannot, therefore, be considered as such to be protected by Article 9(1), even when it was motivated by it.'[135]

There was no doubt that the applicant's actions were motivated by his

---

[131] *Yanasik v. Turkey*, No. 14524/89, 74 DR 14 (Dec. 1993), 26.
[132] *Ibid.*
[133] *Karaduman v. Turkey*, No. 16278/90, 74 DR 93 (Dec. 1993), 109.
[134] *Cf.* Mr Opsahl in *Arrowsmith v. UK*, where he said that: 'Her [Arrowsmith's] acts were not only consistent with her belief, but genuinely *and objectively* expressed it when seen in their context' (No. 7070/75, Rep. 1978, p. 42, 19 DR 5, 27, emphasis added).
[135] *Knudsen v. Norway*, No. 11045/84, 42 DR 247 (Dec. 1983), 258.

beliefs, but since *Arrowsmith* this would clearly not be sufficient in itself. Had his refusal to perform his duties been intended to express his beliefs then Article 9 might have been of relevance, but since this was done by way of protest it could not amount to a 'manifestation' of them for the purposes of Article 9. If this approach had been adopted in *Yanasik v. Turkey* and *Karaduman v. Turkey*, the decisions would have been very different.

Even where the act does manifest a belief, however, the intent to manifest it must provide the principal motivation for the act. This is demonstrated by the case of *X and the Church of Scientology v. Sweden*[136] in which an injunction had been awarded against the applicants prohibiting them from advertising the sale of an 'E-Meter'[137] which it described as being 'an invaluable aid to measuring man's mental state and changes in it'. The Commission said that the manifestation of a belief in practice 'does not confer protection on statements of purported religious beliefs which appear as selling "arguments" in advertisements of a purely commercial nature by a religious group'. Thus an advertisement that gave details of church services would be covered, but one which offered objects, including religious artifacts, for sale would not, since such advertisements would be 'more the manifestation of a desire to market goods for profit than the manifestation of a belief in practice'.[138]

Towards a solution

The real problem, and the real solution to it, lies less in the precise parameters of the definitions than in the nature of the religion or belief in question. Different beliefs require different 'practices' of their adherents. What is a pacifist to do if not protest against violence? Contemplative religions may call their followers to prayer, whilst others will call for social action. Such matters might, perhaps, be more relevant to the question of whether the views held qualify as a religion or belief for the purposes of Article 9. Similarly, certain 'beliefs' could be excluded from the protection offered by Article 9 on the ground that they did not qualify as a 'religion' or 'belief' for its purposes because of the forms of manifesta-

---

[136] *X and the Church of Scientology v. Sweden*, No. 7805/77, 16 DR 68 (Dec. 1980).

[137] This was described as: 'A religious artifact used to measure the state of electrical characteristics of the "static field" surrounding the body and believed to reflect or indicate whether or not the confessing person has been relieved of the spiritual impediment of his sins' (*ibid.*, p. 69).

[138] *Ibid.*, p. 72. This is a difficult distinction to draw. Which side of the line might an advertisement selling tickets for a concert of music by a church choir fall?

tion that they took.[139] The difficulty with this approach is that it would mean adopting some *a priori* understanding of the forms of practical manifestation that were to be deemed acceptable in a qualifying religion or belief.

Although difficult, this is not impossible. Rather than doing so, however, the Commission has focused on the range of acts which are to be considered as 'manifestations' or has fallen back on the limitations upon enjoyment sanctioned by Article 9(2).[140] This is the line of least resistance and may well be preferred to resorting to dubious distinctions in order to decide which practices qualify as 'manifestations': if the leaflet at the centre of the *Arrowsmith* case had across its top the words 'Practical Pacifism' then, on the arguments of the Commission, it would have qualified as a practice of a protected belief. It is difficult to accept that the applicability of Article 9 should turn on such quirks of phraseology. Perhaps the answer might lie in taking a more rigorous view of what was to count as a protected religion or belief in the first place.

---

[139] *Cf.* the manner in which organizations commonly considered as 'charitable', in the sense of their being motivated by an intent to improve the lot of others, are not capable of being registered as a charity because of the means by which they pursue those ends.

[140] E.g. *X v. Austria*, No. 1747/62, 6 YBECHR 424 (Dec. 1963). The applicant claimed that his conviction for allegedly attempting to re-introduce National Socialism to Austria violated Article 9. Rather than consider whether Article 9(1) embraced a right to manifest National Socialism, the Commission considered that measures restricting such a right were justified under Article 9(2).

The root of the problems discussed in the previous chapter lies in the individual having the right not only to hold a religion or belief but also to be able to act in accordance with them. This makes it necessary to distinguish thought and conscience from religion and belief. It also makes it necessary to distinguish between actions which are manifestations of such beliefs and those which are not. The Court and Commission have spun a web of tortuous, and often untenable, distinctions intended to differentiate between the interests at stake.

When the interests concerned are those of the individual and of the State, then the 'public/private' sphere distinction is of some help, as has been seen in the context of cases relating to participation in State-run schemes. This distinction is of little relevance when the right to manifest a belief in the public sphere is itself at issue and there comes a point beyond which it is futile to attempt to evade the central question. That point was reached in the *Kokkinakis* case, which concerned the clash of rights between the individual wishing to spread his belief and the right of another to be protected in the enjoyment of her own, and could not be avoided. This can only be resolved by having regard to the range of limitations which might be legitimately placed upon the enjoyment of the rights articulated in Article 9(1) and which will be examined in this chapter.

The relationship between Article 15 and Article 9(2)

Whilst Article 9(2) allows certain limitations to be placed upon the freedom to manifest a religion or belief, both the freedom of manifestation and the freedom of thought, conscience and religion can themselves be subject to restrictions imposed in accordance with Article 15 of the

Convention. Article 15 permits States to derogate from their obligations under certain articles of the Convention, including Article 9, 'In times of war or other public emergency threatening the life of the nation', but this may be done only 'to the extent strictly required by the exigencies of the situation'.

The Convention organs, however, retain the ability to examine the legitimacy of the restrictions imposed and have interpreted the expression 'public emergency' in a restrictive fashion. In the *Lawless* case the Court said that these words referred to 'an exceptional crisis or emergency which affects the whole population and constitutes a threat to the organized life of the community of which the State is composed'.[1] The State, however, enjoys a wide 'margin of appreciation' when it comes to determining whether the situation is sufficient to justify derogating from its obligations. The role of the Convention organs is to determine whether the circumstances relied upon by the State justify that determination.[2]

If this is in fact the case, they must then consider whether the restrictions imposed are strictly required. Once again, the State is accorded a wide 'margin of appreciation' in determining this[3] since the Court has recognized that: 'By reason of their direct and continuous contact with the pressing needs of the moment, the national authorities are in principle in a better position than the international judge to decide

---

[1] *Lawless v. Ireland*, Ser. A, no. 3 (1961), para. 28. See J. Oráa, *Human Rights in States of Emergencies* (Oxford: Clarendon Press, 1992), pp. 16–20, 32.

[2] The extent of the margin of appreciation left to the State in determining this question is not entirely clear. In the *Lawless* case, the Court had taken the view that its role was to determine whether the authorities had sufficient reasons to believe that a public emergency existed. In *Denmark, Norway, Sweden and the Netherlands v. Greece* (the *Greek* case), however, the Commission applied these principles in a more stringent fashion, leaving a much reduced margin of appreciation to the State. (See Oráa, *Human Rights in States of Emergencies*, p. 19. But *cf.* F. Jacobs, *The European Convention on Human Rights* (Oxford: Clarendon Press, 1975), pp. 206–207 who argues that the *Greek* case represented a looser form of control.) In *Brannigan and McBride v. UK* Ser. A, no. 258–B (1993) the Court seemed to suggest that the State had an all but unlimited power to determine whether the life of the nation was threatened by a 'public emergency' (para. 43) but then went on to confirm the existence of such circumstances 'making its own assessment in the light of all the material before it' (para. 47).

[3] E.g., *Ireland v. UK*, Ser. A, no. 25 (1978) para. 214. J. G. Merrills, *The Development of International Law by the European Court of Human Rights*, 2nd edn (Manchester University Press, 1993), p. 154 suggests that this shows that the Court will uphold the respondent's view 'wherever it was reasonable'. This is to be determined in the light of the information available to the respondent government at the time the restrictions were 'originally taken and subsequently applied' (*Ireland v. UK, ibid*). For criticism of this view, see P. Van Dijk and G. J. H. Van Hoof, *Theory and Practice of the European Convention on Human Rights*, 2nd edn (Daventer: Kluwer, 1990), p. 554.

both on the presence of such an emergency and on the nature and scope of the derogations necessary to avert it.'[4]

Since Article 9(2) only allows restrictions to be placed upon the manifestation of religion or belief, any limitation placed upon the freedom of thought, conscience and religion must be justified under Article 15. This is likely to be difficult. Since the first sentence of Article 9(1) is principally concerned with the *forum internum*, derogating from this narrow band of rights in only the most serious of situations may seem a satisfactory compromise between the demands of the individual and of the State. Given that these rights are, however, chiefly exercised in the private sphere, it is questionable whether there is a need for any limitation at all. Article 3, which prohibits the use of torture or inhuman or degrading treatment or punishment, cannot be derogated from at all.[5] If vital aspects of physical well-being are accorded absolute protection it is at least arguable that essential aspects of intellectual autonomy should be similarly protected.[6]

Interference with the enjoyment of the right to freedom of thought, conscience and religion found in the first sentence of Article 9(1) is likely to exceed the limits of State discretion sanctioned by the Strasbourg organs. It is difficult to see how a State could ever justify intrusion into the *forum internum* (strictly understood),[7] no matter how serious the public emergency threatening the life of the nation. Restrictions upon the right to manifest a religion or belief are more likely to fall within the State's

---

[4] *Brannigan and McBride v. UK*, Ser. A, no. 258–B (1993), para. 43; *Ireland v. UK*, Ser. A, no. 25, para. 207. See also R. Higgins, 'Derogations under Human Rights Treaties', *BYIL* 48 (1976–1977) 281.

[5] Article 15(2).

[6] Article 8(1) can be seen as providing a 'bridge' between Articles 3 and 9. It says that: 'Everyone has the right to respect for his private and family life, his home and his correspondence.' This right is subject to limitations under subsection (2) of that article. It can be argued that Article 8 provides for the general protection of the 'private' sphere of life but that Article 3 and the first element of Article 9(1) go further and identify particular aspects of human well-being – physical and spiritual – and grant them an elevated status which ought not to be subject to restriction. The use of Article 8(1) as a means of residual protection is illustrated by *Costello-Roberts v. UK*, Ser. A, no. 247–C (1993) in which the Commission took the view that the 'slippering' of a seven-year-old boy in a private school, whilst not amounting to inhuman and degrading treatment under Article 3 of the Convention, did nevertheless amount to a violation of Article 8. (The Court, by a one-vote majority, decided that this action was not in breach of Article 8.)

[7] A broader understanding of what was encapsulated within the *forum internum*, as foreshadowed by the views of the Commission in *Darby v. Sweden*, would, however, suggest a greater likelihood of derogations to Article 9(1) being justified under Article 15.

margin of appreciation under Article 15 but are in any case sanctioned by Article 9(2).[8]

The conditions for limitation

Article 9(2) provides that:

Freedom to manifest one's religion or beliefs shall be subject only to such limitations as are prescribed by law and are necessary in a democratic society in the interests of public safety, for the protection of public order, health or morals, or for the protection of the rights and freedoms of others.

Other Convention articles are couched in similar, but not identical, terms[9] and the meaning of key elements has been examined in cases relating to them rather than to Article 9(2) itself. If a limitation upon the right of manifestation is to be permitted under Article 9(2) it must fulfil two criteria. First, it must be 'prescribed by law'[10] and, secondly, it must be 'necessary in a democratic society'. Similar thresholds apply to the applicability of restrictions under Articles 8(2), 10(2) and 11(2) of the Convention, Article 2(3) and 2(4) of the Fourth Protocol and Article 1(2) of the Seventh Protocol. A considerable body of case-law has developed around these limitations. Although it is beyond the scope of this work to examine these criteria in detail, an outline of the meaning attached to them will be given.[11]

---

[8] See also Oráa, *Human Rights in States of Emergencies*, p. 100. A State is, however, likely to enjoy a wider margin of appreciation under Article 15 than under Article 9(2).

[9] Limitations are attached to Article 8 (right to respect for private and family life), Article 10 (freedom of expression) and Article 11 (freedom of assembly and association) of the Convention, Article 2 of the Fourth Protocol (right to liberty of movement and freedom of choice of residence) and Article 1 of the Seventh Protocol (freedom of aliens from arbitrary expulsion).

[10] Article 8(2) uses the expression 'in accordance with the law' whereas Articles 10(2) and 11(2) follow Article 9(2). The Protocols use other variations. The French texts in all instances use the phrase 'prévues par la loi'. These various versions are to be understood as conveying the same meaning. See *Sunday Times v. UK*, Ser. A, no. 30 (1979), para. 48; *Silver and others v. UK*, Ser. A, no. 61 (1983), para. 85.

[11] See generally Van Dijk and Van Hoof, *Theory and Practice of the ECHR*, pp. 573–606; D. J. Harris, M. O'Boyle and C. Warbrick, *Law of the ECHR* (London: Butterworths, 1995), pp. 285–301; A. H. Robertson and J. G. Merrills, *Human Rights in Europe*, 3rd edn (Manchester University Press, 1993), pp. 195–208; R. J. MacDonald, 'The Margin of Appreciation in the Jurisprudence of the European Convention on Human Rights', in *International Law at the Time of its Codification: Essays in Honour of Roberto Ago* (Milan: 1987), p. 187; T. H. Jones, 'The Devaluation of Human Rights Under the European Convention', PL [1995] 430; S. Greer, *Public Interests and Human Rights in the European Convention on Human Rights* (Strasbourg: Council of Europe, H(95)1 (1995)).

As will be seen, although it is possible to ascribe a substantive content to the first of these requirements, the second is much more malleable and, as currently used, can only be properly examined in the context of each particular case. Since only a relatively small number of cases have directly concerned Article 9(2) it is even more difficult to predict how it might be applied. Nevertheless, by looking at the approach taken by the Strasbourg organs to these limitations it is possible to get some general pointers.

'Prescribed by law'

An essential prerequisite for any restriction placed upon the enjoyment of a right under these articles is that it has been sanctioned by the domestic legal system.[12] The Court has also established criteria relating to the 'quality' of the law in question. In the *Sunday Times* case the Court said that, first, 'the law must be adequately accessible: the citizen must be able to have an indication that is adequate in the circumstances of the legal rules applicable to a given case'.[13] Secondly, 'a norm cannot be regarded as a "law" unless it is formulated with sufficient precision to enable the citizen to regulate his conduct: he must be able – if need be with appropriate advice – to foresee to a degree that is reasonable in the circumstances, the consequences which a given action may entail'.[14] Finally, there must be safeguards against the arbitrary use of powers which interfere with the enjoyment of the rights in question.[15] These

---

[12] This embraces unwritten law (e.g., the common law, see *Sunday Times v. UK*, Ser. A, no. 30 (1979), para. 47) as well as 'secondary' sources (e.g. *De Wilde, Ooms and Versyp v. Belgium*, Ser. A, no. 12 (1971) and *Barthold v. FRG*, Ser. A, no. 90 (1985), para. 46.

[13] *Sunday Times v. UK*, Ser. A, no. 30 (1979), para. 49. In *Silver and others v. UK*, Ser. A, no. 61 (1983), para. 87 unpublished instructions to prison governors were considered not to have fulfilled this requirement.

[14] *Sunday Times v. UK* and *Silver and others v. UK, ibid.* Nevertheless, in *Müller v. Switzerland*, Ser. A, no. 133 (1988), para. 29 the Court recognized 'the impossibility of attaining absolute precision in the framing of laws, particularly in fields in which the situation changes according to the prevailing views of society' and that therefore 'the need to keep pace with changing circumstances means that many laws are inevitably couched in terms which, to a greater or lesser extent, are vague. Criminal-law provisions of obscenity fall within this category.' See also *Barthold v. FRG*, Ser. A, no. 90 (1985), para. 47 and *Ezelin v. France*, Ser. A, no. 202 (1991), para. 45.

[15] *Silver and others v. UK*, Ser. A, no. 61 (1983), para. 90; *Malone v. UK*, Ser. A, no. 82 (1984), para. 67; and see *Kruslin v. France* and *Huvig v. France*, Ser. A, nos. 176–A and 176–B (1990), paras. 33–35 in which the system used for telephone tapping in France fell foul of this requirement, despite the Government having pointed to the presence of seventeen separate safeguards.

principles have been applied in numerous cases and provide a potent source of restraint upon abuse of power.[16]

'Necessary in a democratic society'

Even if a restriction has been 'prescribed by law' it must still be 'necessary in a democratic society'. It is possible to see this as setting out two components, each needing separate consideration. However, there has been no real attempt to conceptualize 'democratic society',[17] and although some attempt has been made to determine the threshold of 'necessity',[18] the entire phrase has come to be associated with the requirement that the restriction be justified by a 'pressing social need' and the doctrine of the margin of appreciation.[19]

After reviewing the *Handyside* case, the Commission concluded that:

> the 'necessity' test cannot be applied in absolute terms, but required [*sic*] the assessment of various factors. Such factors include the nature of the right involved, the degree of interference, i.e. whether it was proportionate to the legitimate aim pursued, the nature of the public interest and the degree to which it requires protection in the circumstances of the case.[20]

This helpful summary indicates that all these factors are elements within a complex factual matrix. They are not neat compartments which can be examined in isolation. Whilst it is for the national authorities to make the initial assessment of whether a restriction is necessary in a democratic society, this goes 'hand in hand with a European supervision' and the Convention organs remain empowered 'to give the final ruling on

---

[16] In addition to the cases cited in the preceding footnotes see also *Herczegfalvy v. Austria*, Ser. A, no. 244 (1992), para. 91 which concerned the lack of specification associated with discretionary powers relating to detention in psychiatric institutions. For an example in the context of Article 9 see *Kalaç v. Turkey*, no. 20704/92, Rep. 1996, paras. 41–50, where the Commission was of the opinion that the compulsory early retirement of a military judge on account of his religious views had not been 'presented by law' in accordance with Article 9(2).

[17] It is, for example, unclear whether the words refer to an abstract 'democratic society' or to the particular democratic society in question. See the Individual Opinion of Mr Eustathiades to the Report of the Commission in *Grandrath v. FRG*, No. 2299/64, 10 YBECHR 640 (Rep. 1967) at 692. See also Greer, *Public Interests and Human Rights in the ECHR*, pp. 8–9; Harris, O'Boyle and Warbrick, *Law of the ECHR* pp. 408–411 (examining the relationship between Article 10 and democratic society).

[18] For example, in *Handyside v. UK*, Ser. A, no. 24 (1976), para. 48 the Court noted that 'whilst the adjective "necessary" . . . is not synonymous with "indispensable" . . . neither has it the flexibility of such expressions as "admissible", "ordinary", "useful", "reasonable" or "desirable"'.

[19] *Handyside v. UK, ibid.*; *Sunday Times v. UK*, Ser. A, no. 30 (1978), para. 59.

[20] *X and the Church of Scientology v. Sweden*, No. 7805/77, 16 DR 68 (Dec. 1979) at 73.

whether a "restriction" . . . is reconcilable' with the right in question.[21] In effect, this enables them to review the exercise of discretion which the Convention grants to States, although this is complicated by it being unclear whether it is for the applicant to prove that the restriction was unreasonable or for the State to prove that it was reasonable.[22]

The Court has acknowledged that 'the scope of the margin of appreciation will vary according to the circumstances, the subject matter and its background'[23] and does not depend solely upon which article of the Convention[24] or particular head of restriction is at issue.[25] This underlines the conclusion that the scope of the margin of appreciation given to governments in determining whether a limitation is 'necessary in a democratic society' will depend upon the relationship between the particular head of restriction relevant to the case, the nature of the right at issue and the circumstances in which it is exercised.[26] The Court

---

[21] *Handyside v. UK*, Ser. A, no. 24 (1976) and *Sunday Times v. UK*, Ser. A, no. 30 (1978). This has become a standard recital, frequently recalled. See, e.g., *Lingens v. Austria*, Ser. A, no. 103 (1986), para. 39; *Sunday Times (No. 2) v. UK*, Ser. A, no. 217 (1992), para. 50(d); *Vogt v. Germany*, Ser. A, no. 323 (1995), para. 52.

[22] See Van Dijk and Van Hoof, *Theory and Practice of the ECHR*, pp. 589–592; Greer, *Public Interests and Human Rights in the ECHR*, p. 9.

[23] E.g. *Rasmussen v. Denmark*, Ser. A, no. 87, (1984), para. 40, and see Jones, 'The Devaluation of Human Rights Under the European Convention,' p. 438.

[24] In both *Handyside v. UK*, Ser. A, no. 24 (1976) and *Dudgeon v. UK*, Ser. A, no. 59 (1983) the Court was willing to concede a wide margin of appreciation to the respondent government because the heart of the matter concerned the State's capacity to supervise the moral welfare of its citizens. It made no difference that the *Handyside* case concerned Article 10, but the *Dudgeon* case Article 8. This was confirmed by the Court in *Norris v. Ireland*, Ser. A, no. 142 (1988), para. 44.

[25] In *Sunday Times v. UK*, Ser. A, no. 30 (1979), para. 59, the Court said that 'the scope of the domestic power of appreciation is not identical as regards each of the aims listed in Article 10(2)'. The *Handyside* case concerned the 'protection of morals'. The view taken by the Contracting States of the 'requirement' of morals, observed the Court, 'varies from time to time and from place to place, especially in our era. Precisely the same cannot be said of the far more objective notion of "authority" of the judiciary. The domestic law and practice of the Contracting States reveal a fairly substantial measure of common ground in this area . . . Accordingly, here a more extensive European supervision corresponds to a less discretionary power of appreciation . . .'

[26] This final factor is illustrated by a string of cases brought under Article 10 concerning convictions for defamation. In *Lingens v. Austria*, Ser. A, no. 103–B (1986), para. 42, the Court said 'the limits of acceptable criticism are . . . wider as regards a politician . . . than as regards a private individual'. See also *Oberschlink v. Austria*, Ser. A, no. 204 (1991), para. 59; *Castells v. Spain*, Ser. A, no. 236 (1992), para. 46; *Schwabe v. Austria*, Ser. A. no. 242–B (1992), paras. 28–29. The Court made the same point in the context of Article 8 in *X and Y v. the Netherlands*, Ser. A, no. 91 (1985) at para. 24, where it said 'there are different ways of ensuring "respect for private life" and the nature of the States' obligation will depend on the particular aspect of private life that is at issue'.

addresses these issues by posing two questions. The first is 'did the restriction have a legitimate aim?', which means 'does the restriction fall within one of the heads of restriction relevant to the right in question?'. The second question is whether the restriction imposed was proportionate to the legitimate aim pursued.[27] If the answer to this question is affirmative, then the Court concludes that the restriction was 'necessary in a democratic society'.

The answers to these questions ultimately turn upon the importance placed upon the right in question and it is difficult to contest the conclusion that 'it is . . . hazardous to try to foretell whether in a given case the national authorities will be allowed a narrower or a wider margin of appreciation'.[28] Because they are so interdependent, none of these aspects can be examined convincingly in isolation. Nor does any one element of the 'factual matrix' – the head of restriction, the nature of the right or the circumstances in which its enjoyment is sought – have sufficient prominence to justify its use as the primary framework for analysis. In what follows the 'heads of restriction' have been used as a framework within which aspects of these relationships can be explored. The reason for this choice is based solely on convenience.

The heads of restriction and Article 9

Article 9(2) sets out four heads under which the right to manifest a religion or belief may be restricted. These are (i) public safety (ii) the protection of public order (iii) health or morals and (iv) the protection of the rights and freedoms of others. In all these areas States have been accorded a wide margin of appreciation but the nature of the right, and the specific form of its alleged breach, has caused it to be narrowed – sometimes to the point of disappearance – in a number of specific instances. In what follows, the general approach to these heads of restriction will be outlined and their relevance to and application in the context of Article 9 considered.

The protection of health or morals

In the *Handyside* case the Court took the view that where moral issues were concerned the views of the State would be accorded a high priority

---

[27] This requirement is derived from *Lingens v. Austria*, Ser. A, no. 103–B (1986), para. 40.
[28] Van Dijk and Van Hoof, *Theory and Practice of the ECHR*, p. 589.

because of the lack of a uniform concept of morals.[29] This does not mean that the State's view will always prevail. In the *Dudgeon* case the Court ultimately decided that, despite the width of the margin of appreciation, the criminalization of homosexual conduct between consenting adults over the age of twenty-one was not necessary in a democratic society. A number of reasons were given, including the point that the authorities had not enforced the law for a considerable period of time, therefore undermining the contention that it was necessary.[30] A more general point, however, concerned the emergence of a more tolerant attitude elsewhere in Europe which was said to reflect a European standard which ought to be taken into account when determining the necessity of the provision.[31]

The emergence of a common standard can, then, reduce the scope of the margin of appreciation accorded to States in relation to their oversight of moral questions.[32] The problem centres on determining whether this is in fact happening.[33] Since the Court is not bound by its previous decisions, cases will continue to test out the scope of the margin of appreciation where there is evidence of significant social change, either in the same State or elsewhere in Europe.[34] Once such a process begins, it can only be a matter of time before the Court yields to the pressure.

---

[29] See also *Müller and others v. Switzerland*, Ser. A, no. 133 (1988), para. 35: 'Today, as at the time of the *Handyside* judgment, it is not possible to find in the legal and social orders of the Contracting States a uniform European conception of morals.'

[30] *Dudgeon v. UK*, Ser. A, no. 59 (1983), para. 60.

[31] *Ibid.* See T. A. O'Donnell, 'The Margin of Appreciation Doctrine: Standards in the Jurisprudence of the European Court of Human Rights', HRQ 4 (1982), 474–496. This line of approach was subsequently endorsed in the analogous cases of *Norris v. Ireland*, Ser. A, no. 142 (1988), paras. 45–47 and by the Commission in *Modinos v. Cyprus*, No. 15070/89 (Rep. 1991), paras. 39–46, and not challenged by Cyprus before the Court (Ser. A, no. 259 (1993), para. 25).

[32] For an alternative approach, see *Open Door and Dublin Well Woman v. Ireland*, Ser. A, no. 246 (1992), paras. 68–80. In this case the Court decided that Ireland had breached Article 10 in making out a permanent injunction restraining the applicants from providing pregnant women with information concerning abortion facilities abroad. Although the Court accepted that the State had a wide margin of appreciation, it considered that the measures taken were disproportionate to the legitimate aim pursued, and said that they might also have had a detrimental impact upon the health of women unable to access the alternative sources of information which were available.

[33] The Court did not present any evidence to support its claim concerning the emergence of a European normative standard in the *Dudgeon* case. See MacDonald, 'The Margin of Appreciation in the Jurisprudence of the European Court of Human Rights', pp. 200–201; Van Dijk and Van Hoof, *Theory and Practice of the ECHR*, pp. 602–603.

[34] For example, in *Rees v. UK*, Ser. A, no. 106 (1986) the Court rejected the claim made by a transsexual to have his birth certificate altered to reflect his change of sex. In *Cossey v. UK*, Ser. A, no. 184 (1990) it was argued that, since such a refusal meant that Miss

A key factor in the *Dudgeon* case was that the case concerned 'a most intimate aspect of private life' and so 'there must exist particularly serious reasons before interferences on the part of the public authorities can be legitimate'.[35] If transposed to the context of Article 9 this factor will rarely be present since the restrictions in Article 9(2) only apply to the right to manifest a religion or belief, and tend not to relate only to such intimate matters.

It is, then, likely that the State will continue to be accorded a fairly generous margin of appreciation when restrictions placed upon the enjoyment of the freedom to manifest a religion or belief are justified on the basis of the protection of health or morals,[36] unless some evidence emerges of a general European standard that would reduce this in particular circumstances.[37]

Public interest exceptions

The 'public safety' and 'protection of public order' heads can be grouped together as being particular examples of a general category of 'public interest exceptions'.[38] Although it may be possible to conclude that the margin of appreciation will vary according to the particular head of limitation in question, it is more realistic to consider this to be a single

---

Cossey could not marry a man, this violated Article 12 of the Convention. The Court took the view that although some States would regard such a marriage as valid, there had not been a general abandonment of the traditional concept of marriage. A further challenge was made in *B v. France*, Ser. A, No. 232–C (1992) which succeeded in part because of the differences in the relevant practices of England and France (paras. 49–63), although on the general question the Court concluded that 'there is as yet no sufficiently broad consensus between the member States . . . to persuade the Court to reach opposite conclusions to those in its *Rees* and *Cossey* judgments' (para. 48). However, in *X, Y and Z v. UK*, No. 21830/93 (Rep. 1995), Inf. note 127, p. 8 the Commission took the view that the failure to recognize the role of a transsexual as father to a child born to his cohabitee by artificial insemination was a violation of Article 8 (this case was referred to the Court in October 1995) and in *X v. UK*, No. 25680/94 (Dec. 1995), Inf. note 129, p. 6, the Commission referred an application concerning the legal recognition of a change of sex to the UK Government for its observations.

[35] *Dudgeon v. UK*, Ser. A, no. 59 (1983), para. 52.

[36] See, for example, *X v. UK*, No. 8231/78, 28 DR 5 (Dec. 1982) in which the Commission decided that a high caste Sikh could be required to clean his prison cell even though this was contrary to the traditional Sikh practice.

[37] For example, a State which prohibited the use of certain forms of hallucinatory drugs in religious rituals could find its restriction lifted if it was clear that most other European States adopted a more relaxed attitude.

[38] See Greer, *Public Interests and Human Rights in the ECHR*, pp. 11ff. This also embraces 'the prevention of crime and disorder' and 'interests of national security' which are found in analogous articles of the Convention.

category, the application of which will vary depending upon the circumstances. Once again, this is an area in which the Convention organs tend to grant States a wide margin of appreciation.[39] There are, moreover, a number of decisions that suggest that in the particular contexts of penal establishments and the armed forces States will be accorded a particularly generous margin of appreciation.

For example, and in the context of Article 9, the Commission has used the concept of 'public order'[40] to justify refusing an applicant, a prisoner who was also a practising Buddhist, permission to grow a beard and to obtain a prayer chain, the latter also being justified in order to maintain prison discipline.[41] Even assuming that prisoners form a 'specific social group', it is difficult to see just how the cultivation of a beard poses a challenge to internal prison order.[42] It is even less clear how this can affect order in society as a whole. Nevertheless, it is clear from other cases[43] that governments have an extremely wide margin of appreciation in determining how order is to be maintained within prison establishments.[44] The governing factor appears to be the prison context, rather than the particular head under which the restriction is justified.

This is not to say that any restriction can be justified in the prison context on the basis of public order, or the prevention of crime and disorder: indeed, some of the early 'landmark' judgments of the Court upheld the rights of prisoners with regard to the privacy of their

---

[39] For example, in *X v. UK*, No 7992/77, 14 DR 234 (Dec. 1978) the Commission decided that the requirement that a Sikh motorcyclist wear a crash helmet was a justified interference.

[40] 'Public order' was defined in *Engel v. the Netherlands*, Ser. A, no. 22 (1976), para. 98 as 'the order that must prevail within the confines of a specific social group [where] disorder in that group can have repercussions on order in society as a whole'. This case concerned the application of Article 10(2) in the context of military disciplinary proceedings.

[41] *X v. Austria*, No. 1753/63, 8 YBECHR 174 (Dec. 1965), 184.

[42] It was said that it would hinder identification. If the applicant were the only prisoner to have a beard one would have thought it an aid, rather than a hindrance.

[43] It has been successfully invoked under Article 8(2) – e.g. *X v. UK*, No. 8231/78, 28 DR 5 (Dec. 1982: compulsory wearing of prison clothes); Article 10(2) – e.g. *McFeeley v. UK*, No. 8317/78, 20 DR 44 (Dec. 1980: restriction on access to means of mass communication); *X v. UK*, No. 5442/72, 1 DR 41 (Dec. 1974: Buddhist prisoner prohibited from submitting an article to a Buddhist journal for publication).

[44] This question usually arises in connection with Article 8(2), which allows for restrictions which are necessary, *inter alia*, 'for the prevention of crime and disorder'. Such restrictions are also permitted under Article 10(2). This is a wider formulation than that found in Article 9(2) since it does not link the restriction to the necessity to protect *public* order.

correspondence.[45] In addition, a benchmark is provided by the Standard Minimum Rules for Prisoners adopted by the Council of Ministers.[46] However, it is difficult to avoid the impression that the Commission does not set much store by the right of prisoners to manifest their beliefs and considers many of the applications to be frivolous.[47] Although the *Golder* case rejected the concept of 'inherent limitations' – that is, that certain forms of restriction were an inherent feature of lawful imprisonment[48] – the idea lives on in the latitude given to States to restrict the enjoyment of the rights in the context of penal establishments[49] and, indeed, other places of lawful detention.[50]

Military matters provide another area in which the State traditionally has been accorded a wide margin of appreciation. In *Arrowsmith v. UK* the Commission decided that although the applicant had not been manifesting her beliefs for the purposes of Article 9, her right to freedom of

---

[45] *Golder v. UK*, Ser. A, no. 18 (1975); *Silver and others v. UK*, Ser. A, no. 61 (1983). See also *Campbell and Fell v. UK*, Ser. A, no. 80 (1984); *Fox, Campbell and Hartley v. UK*, Ser. A, no. 182 (1990); *Campbell v. UK*, Ser. A, no. 233 (1992).

[46] The Standard Minimum Rules were originally adopted by Resolution (73) 5 and reformulated in Recommendation No. R (87) 3. As amended (additions italicized and deletions put in square brackets) the rules provide:

46. So far as is practicable, every prisoner shall be allowed to satisfy the needs of his religious, spiritual and moral life by attending the services or meetings provided in the institution and having in his possession any necessary books *or literature*.

47. 1. If the institution contains a sufficient number of prisoners of the same religion, a qualified representative of that religion shall be appointed and approved. If the number of prisoners justifies it, and conditions permit, the arrangement should be on a full-time basis.

2. A qualified representative appointed or approved under paragraph 1 shall be allowed to hold regular services and activities and to pay pastoral visits in private to prisoners of his religion at proper times.

3. Access to a qualified representative of any religion shall not be refused to any prisoner. [On the other hand] If any prisoner should object to a visit of any religious representative, [his attitude shall be fully respected] *the prisoner shall be allowed to refuse it.*

(*Cf.* The UN Standard Minimum Rules 41–42 (ECOSOC Res. 663 C (XXIV) of 31 July 1957) which are similar, but not identical.)

[47] E.g., *X v. UK*, No. 8231/78, 28 DR 5 (Dec. 1982), Sikh cleaning his prison cell, see also n. 36 above; *X v. UK*, No. 5947/72, 5 DR 8 (Dec. 1976), respect for dietary requirements of a prisoner who was an Orthodox Jew.

[48] See Jacobs, *The European Convention on Human Rights*, pp. 139 and 198–201; Merrills, *The Development of International Law by the European Court of Human Rights*, pp. 89–90. For an application of the 'inherent limitation' approach in the context of Article 9 see *Huber v. Austria*, No. 4517/70, 14 YBECHR 548 (Dec. 1970).

[49] Van Dijk and Van Hoof, *Theory and Practice of the ECHR*, pp. 575–576.

[50] A similar approach was taken in relation to persons held on remand in *Schönenberger and Durmaz v. Switzerland*, Ser. A, no. 137 (1988), para. 25.

expression under Article 10(1) had been breached by her arrest and conviction. However, the interference was justified under Article 10(2) since the desertion of soldiers could create a threat to national security and weaken the legitimate role of an army in a democratic society.[51] Since Article 10(2), unlike Article 9(2), includes 'national security' and 'territorial integrity' as grounds of restriction, it cannot be automatically assumed that, had there been a violation of Article 9(1), that would have been legitimate under Article 9(2). Nevertheless, in *Grandrath v. FRG* those members of the Commission who considered Article 9 to be applicable made it clear that the 'public order' exception would have justified the imposition of compulsory military or alternative civilian service.[52]

This seems to suggest that the nature of the public interest will make it difficult to override the State's evaluation of the necessity of a restriction imposed upon the enjoyment of the right of manifestation of a religion or belief within the context of the armed forces. But difficult does not mean impossible. In *Vereinigung Demokratischer Soldaten Österreichs and Gubi v. Austria*, the Court decided that the refusal of the Austrian Federal Minister of Defence to allow the circulation of a satirical magazine – *der Igel*, which was aimed at soldiers and discussed military matters in a critical fashion – within army barracks was not justified by Article 10(2).[53] The essential point was that the magazine, though critical, did not call into question the duty of obedience or the purpose of service in the armed forces and therefore did not represent a serious threat to military discipline. Whilst this serves to distinguish the case from *Arrowsmith*, it does seem that the Court was willing to go further in challenging the State's determination of the seriousness of the threat. This suggests that the traditional reticence of the Convention organs to delve into questions concerning the armed forces is receding, thus enhancing the prospect for claims under Article 9. The Commission may have the opportunity to consider this question directly, having recently declared admissible three applications

---

[51] *Arrowsmith v. UK*, No. 7050/75, Rep. 1978, paras. 85, 94, 19 DR 5, 22, 24; also *Le Cour Grandmaison and Fritz v. France*, Nos. 11567/85 and 11568/85 (joined), 53 DR 150 (Dec. 1987). Other cases in which the Court has allowed the State a broad margin of appreciation when interpreting the scope of restrictions upon Article 10(1) in the military context on the basis of national security include *Engel v. the Netherlands*, Ser. A, no. 22 (1976), paras.100–101 and *Hadjianastassiou v. Greece*, Ser. A, no. 252 (1992), paras. 44–47.

[52] *Grandrath v. FRG*, No. 2299/64, Rep. 1967, 10 *YBECHR* 627, 675 (Mr Ermacora and Mr Balta); although more hesitant, Mr Eustathiades also inclined towards this view (*ibid.*, 690–692).

[53] *Vereinigung Demokratischer Soldaten Österreichs and Gubi v. Austria*, Ser. A, no. 302 (1994).

concerning the conviction of officers in the Greek Airforce, members of the Pentecostal Church, for proselytism.[54]

The rights and freedoms of others

The final head of restriction is the 'protection of the rights and freedoms of others'. It functions as something of a 'catchall' and is particularly relevant for the application of Article 9 because the right to manifest a religion or belief is primarily exercised in the public sphere and will impact upon others. It has, for example, been used to justify silencing those whose actions are likely to provoke public indignation[55] and denying a prisoner access to a philosophical book containing information on martial arts,[56] and is also found added to a list of reasons which justify an interference with the right.[57] The very nature of this head of restriction requires a balance to be struck between the conflicting rights in question. Because of this, the context in which that right is asserted is extremely important, more so, perhaps, than when other heads of restriction are being considered.

It is clear, for example, that freedom of expression is rated very highly by the Court. Thus when acting in the role of 'public watchdog', press freedom is particularly favoured when pitted against the interests of the State, even when matters of national security are, allegedly, involved.[58] When balancing an individual's right of expression against State action intended to protect the rights and freedoms of others, however, the Court is more willing to accept the necessity of the interference. The final determination will depend upon the context in which the right is being asserted and whether the action taken in response is proportionate. For example, Article 10(2) makes specific mention of 'maintaining the authority and impartiality of the judiciary'. This must be weighed against the right of the individual to criticize the judiciary or the judicial process

---

[54] *Larissis, Mandalaridis and Sarandis v. Greece*, Nos. 23372/94, 26377/95 and 26378/95 (Dec. 1995), Inf. note 130, p. 2.

[55] E.g., *X v. Sweden*, No. 9820/82 (1984) 5 *EHRR* 297 (restriction on the manner in which the applicant could convey his religious messages); see also *X Ltd and Y v. UK* (the *Gay News* case), No. 8710/79, 28 DR 77 (Dec. 1982). Although the Commission dealt with this case under Article 10(2) it considered its reasoning to be as applicable to any issue that might have existed under Article 9(2).

[56] *X v. UK*, No. 6886/75, 5 DR 100 (Dec. 1976).

[57] E.g. *X v. Austria*, No. 1747/62, 11 CD 31 (Dec. 1964); *Chappell v. UK*, No. 12587/86, 53 DR 241 (Dec. 1987).

[58] *Observer and Guardian v. UK*, Ser. A, no. 216 (1991), para. 59(b); *Sunday Times v. UK (No. 2)*, Ser. A, no. 217 (1991), para. 50(b); *Castells v. Spain*, Ser. A, no. 236 (1992), para. 43.

since this is itself a matter of public concern.[59] The crucial factor is the relative importance placed upon the rights and the context within which they are brought into conflict.[60]

This poses particular problems in the context of Article 9 which, as has been argued above, is treated as *lex specialis* as regards Article 10 in the sense that it is seen as a particular form of the freedom of expression. However, this does not mean that the freedom of thought, conscience and religion will be granted a greater weight than the freedom of expression. In *Vogt v. Germany* the Court set out the basic principles laid down in its judgments concerning Article 10 in the following terms:

Freedom of expression constitutes one of the essential foundations of a democratic society and one of the basic conditions for its progress and each individual's self-fulfilment. Subject to paragraph 2 of Article 10, it is applicable not only to 'information' and 'ideas' which are favourably received or regarded as inoffensive or as a matter of indifference, but also to those that offend, shock or disturb; such are the demands of the pluralism, tolerance and broadmindedness without which there is no 'democratic society'. Freedom of expression, as enshrined in Article 10, is subject to a number of exceptions which, however, must be narrowly interpreted and the necessity for any restrictions must be convincingly established.[61]

This should be compared with the view expressed in the *Kokkinakis* case that:

As enshrined in Article 9, freedom of thought, conscience and religion is one of the foundations of a 'democratic society' within the meaning of the Convention.

---

[59] See *Barfod v. Denmark*, Ser. A, no. 149 (1989) in which there was held to be no violation of Article 10 in convicting a journalist for defaming the characters of two lay judges by asserting that they had not acted independently in a case. See also *Prager and Oberschlick v. Austria*, Ser. A, no. 313 (1995). Cf. *Thorgeir Thorgierson v. Iceland*, Ser. A, no. 239 (1992), in which the applicant successfully argued that Iceland had breached Article 10 in convicting a writer who had published articles which had called upon the Government to set up an impartial investigation into allegations of police brutality.

[60] *Jersild v. Denmark*, Ser. A, no. 298 (1994) provides a particularly acute example. The applicant, a journalist, had been convicted of a criminal offence in compiling a television programme in which members of the 'Greenjackets' expressed offensive racial comments. Despite the opprobrium associated with racism, it was decided that his conviction violated Article 10.

[61] *Vogt v. Germany*, Ser. A, no. 323 (1995), para. 52(i). This case concerned the dismissal of a school teacher who was an active member of the Communist Party. Although there was no suggestion that she had attempted to pass her views on to her pupils, this was deemed incompatible with her constitutional duty of political loyalty. The Court, without passing on the compatibility of the loyalty requirement with the Convention, concluded that sacking the applicant had been disproportionate to the aim (democratic stability) pursued. Had she held a civil service post which carried with it security risks, however, the matter would have been very different (*ibid.*, paras. 59–61).

It is, in its religious dimension, one of the most vital elements that go to make up the identity of believers and their conception of life, but it is also a precious asset for atheists, agnostics, sceptics and the unconcerned. The pluralism indissociable from a democratic society, which has been dearly won over the centuries, depends on it.[62]

The problem of lending substance to these competing claims lies at the heart of the judgments in the *Kokkinakis* case itself, as well as in *Otto-Preminger-Institut v. Austria* and *Wingrove v. UK* which combine to illuminate the contemporary approach to both Article 9(1) and (2). Although the language used draws upon Articles 9(2) and 10(2), these cases seek to resolve this conflict by reference to the principle of 'respect'. This will be examined in the following section but it should be noted that this is in some ways merely the logical result of a process which has seen a blurring of the basic distinction between the right to manifest a religion or belief, which is subject to limitation under both Article 9(2) and derogation under Article 15, and the freedom of thought, conscience and religion, which can only be derogated from by virtue of Article 15. This blurring is the product of the confusion within the controlling concepts of 'religion and belief' and 'manifestation', exacerbated by the failure of the Court and Commission always to ensure that a breach has actually occurred before moving on to consider whether State action was justified.

Trends in the application of Article 9(2)

Forms of approach

Many decisions betray a less than scrupulous approach to the application of the above principles identified in the previous sections. For example, it has already been seen that not every point of view qualifies as a 'religion or belief' which can be 'manifested'.[63] It is, then, difficult to justify the approach taken by the Commission in *X and Y v. the Netherlands* in which it expressed the view that: 'Insofar as the Netherlands law and practice on the care of minors may have interfered with [the applicant's] own opinion, the interference is justified under Article 9(2).'[64] The manifestation of a purely personal point of view is not protected by the Convention and restrictions placed upon it need no justification. The decision in *Chappell v. UK* is, in this respect, potentially retrograde. Rather than

---

[62] *Kokkinakis v. Greece*, Ser. A, no. 260–A (1993), para. 31.
[63] See above, p. 289.
[64] *X and Y v. the Netherlands*, No. 6753/74, 2 DR 118 (Dec. 1974) at 120.

determine whether Druidism was a religion or belief for the purposes of Article 9(1), it left the question open and decided that if there was a violation, it was justified under Article 9(2).[65]

In some early cases the Commission also took a relaxed attitude towards the question of whether an act qualified as a manifestation when they were clear that the restriction placed upon it would be justified under Article 9(2). In *X v. the Netherlands*, for example, the applicant argued that the system of compulsory motor car insurance violated Article 9(1) because 'according to his religious convictions, prosperity and adversity are meted out to human beings by God and it is not permissible to attempt in advance to prevent or reduce the effects of possible disasters'.[66] The Commission acknowledged that 'the first question arises as to whether the facts alleged could be considered to concern . . . Article 9(1)' but, rather than address this point, immediately said that 'the Netherlands legislation . . . [is] justified under Article 9(2)'.[67] Other early cases were dealt with in a similar fashion.[68]

X v. UK provides an example of a more rigorous approach. The applicant, a Buddhist serving a prison sentence, claimed that the denial of the right to submit articles for publication in a journal amounted to a violation of Article 9. It would have been comparatively straightforward for the Commission to reject this under Article 9(2) but it preferred to take the line that this was not a legitimate manifestation of his beliefs.[69] However, the decision of the Court in the *Kokkinakis* case once again indicated a willingness to consider whether a 'breach' of the Convention was justified by reference to Article 9(2) without fully airing the relevant issues under Article 9(1). As has already been mentioned, the Court said that restrictions imposed on *improper* proselytism by the State were justified under Article 9(2). Both the Court and the Commission concluded that no evidence had been produced which could justify the conclusion that

---

[65] *Chappell v. UK*, No. 12587/86, 53 DR 241 (Dec. 1987), 246.

[66] *X v. the Netherlands*, No. 2899/66, 23 CD 137 (Dec. 1967).   [67] *Ibid.*, p. 139.

[68] E.g. *X v. the Netherlands*, No. 1068/61, 5 YBECHR 278 (Dec. 1962), 284; *X v. Austria*, No. 1747/52, 6 YBECHR 124 (Dec. 1963), 442 444; *X v. Austria*, No. 1753/63, 8 YBECHR 174 (Dec. 1965), 184.

[69] *X v. UK*, No. 5442/72, 1 DR 41 (Dec. 1974), 42. It should be observed, however, that the Commission adopted the more stringent 'necessary expression' approach for determining what amounted to a manifestation. See above, pp. 307–312. *Cf. X v. UK*, No. 6886/75, 5 DR 100 (Dec. 1976) in which the Commission found that Article 9(1) was violated by the prison authorities withholding a book on Tao Buddhism which contained a section on the martial arts but that this was justified under Article 9(2).

improper proselytism had in fact occurred,[70] but surely 'improper proselytism' – which might include brainwashing, blackmail and violence –
ought not to be equated with a legitimate manifestation at all.[71] Rather
than proceed down these avenues of thought, however, the Court
approached the matter from an entirely different perspective.

Balancing the interests – the principle of respect

The essence of the *Kokkinakis* case lay in balancing the right of the
applicant to practise his religion by seeking to bring others to share in his
beliefs against the right of the State to intervene to protect others from
unwanted exposure to his points of view. The following extracts from
opinions appended to the judgment of the Court point to the possible
extremes of response. Judge Martens would have given priority to the
right of the applicant. He argued that:

> it is not within the province of the State to interfere in this conflict between
> proselytiser and proselytised. Firstly, because – since respect for human dignity
> and human freedom implies that the State is bound to accept that in principle
> everybody is capable of determining his own fate in the way that he deems best
> – there is no justification for the State to use its power 'to protect' the
> proselytised ... Secondly, because even the 'public order' argument cannot
> justify the use of coercive State power in a field where tolerance demands that
> 'free argument and debate' should be decisive. And thirdly, because under the
> Convention all religions and beliefs should, as far as the State is concerned, be
> equal.[72]

This is tantamount to abandoning the rights of the 'proselytized' who
would be left to their own resources in the protection of their freedom,
and would seem to ignore the obligation placed on States by Article 1 of
the Convention to 'secure to everyone within their jurisdiction the rights
and freedoms' in the Convention.

Judge Valticos, however, would have given priority to the right of the

---

[70] *Kokkinakis v. Greece*, No. 14307/88, Rep. 1991, paras. 72–73; Ser. A no. 260–A (1993),
paras. 48–49.

[71] It might be objected that the particular ground upon which the application is rejected
is not particularly significant and that it is often easier to deal with a case in this
manner. However, such an appeal to pragmatism simply defers the decision on the
underlying question to another occasion and, although it may seem the easy option at
the time, is likely to create more problems than it solves. More significantly, it also has
the effect of shifting the burden from the applicant to the respondent. Rather than
require the applicant to demonstrate the existence and breach of a right contained in
the Convention, the respondent is required to justify the limitation placed upon the
individual. Of course, some might consider this positively advantageous.

[72] *Kokkinakis v. Greece*, Ser. A, no. 260–A (1993), p. 37, para. 15.

individual not to be the object of the applicant's attentions and presents an equally extreme view, justice to which can only be done by quotation in full. He maintained that:

> On the one hand, we have a militant Jehovah's witness, a hardbitten adept of proselytism, a specialist in conversion, a martyr of the criminal courts whose earlier convictions have served only to harden him in his militancy, and, on the other, the ideal victim, a naïve woman, the wife of a cantor in the Orthodox Church (if he manages to convert her, what a triumph!). He swoops on her, trumpets that he has good news for her (the play on words is obvious, but no doubt not to her), manages to get himself let in and, as an experienced commercial traveller and cunning purveyor of the faith he wants to spread, expounds to her his intellectual wares cunningly wrapped up in a mantle of universal peace and radiant happiness. Who, indeed, would not like peace and universal happiness? But is this the mere exposition of Mr Kokkinakis's beliefs or is it not rather an attempt to beguile the simple soul of the cantor's wife? Does the Convention afford its protection to such undertakings? Certainly not.[73]

Of course, the question was not so simple. Mr Kokkinakis had certainly set out to undermine the faith of this woman, but this is what his own faith had required of him. To forbid him the right to exercise his faith in this way would be to deny him his right under the Convention.

The Court, as might be expected, adopted a middle path which emphasized the need 'to place restrictions on this freedom in order to reconcile the interests of the various groups and to ensure that everyone's beliefs are respected'.[74] Emphasis was placed on the need to ensure 'respect' and the case therefore turned on whether the restriction placed by Greek law upon the freedom to manifest a religious belief by way of proselytism did respect the freedoms of all concerned. The Court, like the Commission, considered this as raising issues under Article 9(2); that is, whether the restriction upon the exercise of the right of manifestation was justified. The decision of the Court on this point is unsatisfactory.

Proselytism is criminalized in Greece by virtue of Section 4 of Law no. 1363/1938 (as amended) and is defined as meaning:

> in particular, any direct or indirect attempt to intrude on the religion or beliefs of a person of a different religious persuasion, with the aim of undermining those beliefs, either by any kind of inducement or promise of an inducement or moral support or material assistance, or by fraudulent means or by taking advantage of his inexperience, trust, need, low intellect or naïvety.

The Court drew a distinction between 'bearing Christian witness' and 'improper proselytism' and, deriving inspiration from a Report of the

---

[73] *Ibid.*, p. 31.   [74] *Ibid.*, para. 33.

World Council of Churches (1956), expressed the view that whilst the former was 'an essential mission and a responsibility of every Christian and every Church' the latter represented 'a corruption or defamation of it'.[75] The Court then concluded that Law no. 1363/1938 was compatible with respect for freedom of religion if it was intended to punish improper proselytism, rather than 'Christian witness'.

At this point, one might have expected the Court to define improper proselytism in order to determine whether the restrictions on witness contained in Greek law were of a sufficiently restricted scope to warrant acceptance. Unfortunately, the Court abruptly changed tack and laconically observed that 'in their reasoning the Greek courts established the applicant's liability by merely reproducing the wording of section 4 and did not sufficiently specify in what way the accused had attempted to convince his neighbour by improper means. None of the facts set out warrants that finding.'[76]

It was for this reason – the lack of specificity in the judgment of the court – that the Court concluded there to have been a violation of Article 9(2) in that the Greek court had not shown that the conviction was 'necessary in a democratic society'. A further consequence was, as the Court observed, that this rendered it unnecessary to define what was meant by 'improper proselytism' for the purposes of its decision. As a result, we can conclude that improper proselytism will be found when zeal in spreading one's beliefs fails to demonstrate respect for the beliefs of others, but there is no real guidance concerning what 'respect' entails.

It seems as if the Court, perhaps unwittingly, seriously watered down the right to freedom of thought, conscience and religion. Since it was prepared to assess the degree to which the applicant's behaviour had interfered with the right of the Cantor's wife under Article 9(2), this suggests that even *improper* proselytism is a form of manifestation protected by Article 9(1) since it is only if a right under the Convention is at issue that the legitimacy of its being restricted under Article 9(2) arises. An alternative, and possibly more attractive, way of proceeding would have been to ask whether the act of proselytism in question was a legitimate exercise of the right to manifest one's religion or belief. This, however, would have required the Court to define the difference between a legitimate and an illegitimate exercise of the right of manifestation and it was not prepared to do this.

Perhaps this does not matter. It may be that the Court's decision

---

[75] *Ibid.*, para. 48.   [76] *Ibid.*, para. 49.

represents a further stage in the retreat from a schematic approach to the interpretation and application of Article 9. If Article 9 requires the State not only to respect the freedom of thought, conscience and religion but also to ensure that this right is respected by others, then it has little option but to intervene to protect the competing interests at stake. The question which will arise is whether the intervention – or the lack of an intervention – evidenced respect for the various beliefs at issue. Whether this is conducted with reference to Article 9(1) or (2), or, indeed, Article 10, becomes secondary to this primary purpose. However, it should not be thought that this renders the distinctions and discussions in the fore-going sections otiose. On the contrary, it makes them all the more pertinent since they form the background against which the strength of the competing interests – and, therefore, the necessity of the intervention – should be assessed. Unfortunately, the next case in which the Court undertook this exercise indicates the danger in losing sight of the rights which the Convention bestows upon the respective parties.

Subsequent developments

The *Otto-Preminger-Institut* case concerned the seizure and forfeiture of a film found to be blasphemous under Austrian law. The applicant associa-tion ran a cinema which advertised the showing of a film entitled *Council in Heaven*, which depicted God as a senile man, prostrating himself to the devil, erotic tension between the devil and the Virgin Mary, and Christ as a low-grade mental defective.[77] The Commission considered the film to be predominantly satirical in nature and stated that 'a complete prohibition which excludes any chance to discuss the message of the film must be seen as a disproportionate measure, except where there are very stringent reasons for such an act'.[78] Consequently, it concluded that the forfeiture and seizure of the film violated Article 10.

The Court reached the opposite conclusion. It described its task as 'weighing up of the conflicting interests of the exercise of two funda-mental freedoms guaranteed under the Convention, namely, the right of the applicant association to impart to the public controversial views . . . and the right of other persons to proper respect for their freedom of thought, conscience and religion.'[79]

There are two problems with this approach. The first is that the Convention does not contain a right to have one's religion 'respected' at

---

[77] *Otto-Preminger-Institut v. Austria*, Ser. A, no. 295–A (1994), para. 22.
[78] *Otto-Preminger-Institut v. Austria*, No. 13470/87, Rep. 1993, paras. 73, 77.
[79] *Otto-Preminger-Institut v. Austria*, Ser. A, no. 295–A (1994), para. 54.

all. It contains an absolute right to the freedom of thought, conscience and religion and it contains a qualified right to manifest a religion or belief. The *Kokkinakis* case permits a State to prevent a believer from manifesting his belief if improper means are used. It is the use of improper means which justifies the conclusion that the applicant is not respecting the freedom of others to their thoughts, conscience or religion. In the *Otto-Preminger-Institut* case the Court went beyond this by allowing the State to prevent an applicant from expressing views which were simply unpalatable to others on the grounds that 'the respect for religious feelings of believers as guaranteed by Article 9 can legitimately be thought to have been violated by provocative portrayals of objects of religious veneration; and such portrayals can be regarded as malicious violation of the spirit of tolerance, which must also be a feature of democratic society'.[80]

In fact, there is nothing particularly new in this. In *X Ltd and Y v. UK* (the *Gay News* case) the Commission, rejecting the suggestion that the English laws of blasphemy violated Article 10 of the Convention, expressed the view that: 'If it is accepted that the religious feelings of the citizen may deserve protection against indecent attacks on matters held sacred by him, then it can also be considered as necessary in a democratic society to stipulate that such attacks, if they gain a certain level of severity, shall constitute a criminal offence.'[81] Once again, however, there is no explanation of where this right comes from and it seems to emerge spontaneously out of the interaction of competing claims.[82] Both the *Gay News* and the *Otto-Preminger-Institut* cases involved balancing the right to freedom of expression under Article 10 against the rights of individuals under Article 9, whereas the *Kokkinakis* case concerned a clash between individuals both seeking to rely on Article 9. Given that in the former cases the restrictions imposed in the interests of the sensibilities of believers were ultimately upheld whilst in the latter the Court declined to pass on the key issue, there is a suggestion that Article 9, being *lex specialis* in relation to Article 10, is to be accorded a higher normative status,[83] although this may sit

---

[80] *Ibid.*, para. 47

[81] *X Ltd and Y v. UK*, No. 8710/79, 28 DR 77 (Dec. 1982), para. 12. Surprisingly, no reference was made to this in the *Otto-Preminger-Institut* case.

[82] Taken one stage further, it is the existence of this clash which results in the claim that the ECHR operates in the sphere of relations between individuals, for which see A. Clapham, *Human Rights in the Private Sphere* (Oxford: Clarendon Press, 1993), chapters 4 and 7.

[83] Harris, O'Boyle and Warbrick, *Law of the ECHR*, p. 359.

uneasily with the general philosophy underlying the application of Article 10.

The second problem, and perhaps the most worrying aspect of the *Otto-Preminger-Institut* case, is that the Court did not really seek to fulfil the task it set itself at all. After having established the need for 'respect' between competing interests,[84] the Court accorded the State an extremely broad margin of appreciation to determine whether the applicant's conduct had in fact accorded with the principle of respect. The Court confirmed the need for there to be a margin of appreciation on the grounds that: 'As in the case of "morals" it is not possible to discern throughout Europe a uniform conception of the significance of religion in society; even within a single country such conceptions may vary.'

Although it reiterated the point that the necessity of limitations had to be strictly demonstrated, the Court granted the authorities a generous margin of appreciation, based upon its ability to best interpret the feelings of the overwhelmingly Roman Catholic population of the Austrian Tyrol.[85] In effect, the Court backed away from exercising its supervisory role in relation to the degree of respect accorded to the rights at issue, chiefly for the want of a broader pan-European consensus on which it could draw in order to make an assessment. This would suggest that unless or until such a consensus emerges, the Court will remain reluctant to intervene in such circumstances.

The first signs of the Commission forging a European consensus have emerged in *Manoussakis and others v. Greece*. The applicants were a group of Jehovah's Witnesses who had each been fined and sentenced to a three-month prison sentence for having rented a private room for religious worship and ceremonies without having been granted[86] prior permission from the authorities. The Commission accepted that such a requirement was not in itself incompatible with the Convention but felt that the criminalization of unauthorized use was disproportionate. In reaching

---

[84] At least the Court did establish that there were competing convention interests at stake. In *Putz v. Austria*, No. 18892/91, 76 DR 51 (Dec. 1993) the Commission declared inadmissible a claim that the imposition of fines and sentences of imprisonment for offences against order in court did not violate Article 9 on the basis that this 'did not show any lack of respect for [the applicant's] freedom of thought under Article 9'. It is difficult to see the relevance of Article 9 to this situation at all.

[85] *Otto-Preminger-Institut v. Austria*, Ser. A, no. 295-A (1994), para. 56.

[86] Permission had been requested in June 1983, but no decision had been taken at the time of their being charged in March 1986. Indeed a result was still awaited when the Commission adopted its Report in May 1995 and the Commission felt that it was the dilatoriness of the State which was 'the real cause' of the conviction. *Manoussakis and others v. Greece*, No. 18748/91, Rep. 1995, para. 47.

this conclusion the Commission observed that 'it is difficult to see how the conviction secured against the applicants, who are members of a movement whose religious rites and practices are widely known and authorized in many European countries, can be considered to have been merited merely because they set up and used a place of worship without obtaining prior authorization from the authorities'.[87]

This may be of some assistance where the conduct of a State in relation to a particular group is noticeably out of step with that accorded to that group in other European countries, but this will not always be the case. In such circumstances, the only way forward is to exercise a greater degree of 'European supervision' by adopting a more interventionist approach which reduces the scope of the margin of appreciation. The Commission has indicated its willingness to do this in a number of recent situations.

In *Ahmet v. Greece* the applicant had been convicted of disrupting the peace by distributing material during an election campaign which referred to the Muslim population of Western Thrace as 'Turks', considered to be inflammatory. The Commission accepted that 'in order to avoid rifts between the Christian and Moslem population of Western Thrace and to maintain their peaceful co-existence, moderation in political discussions may be desirable'. However, given the context of an election campaign, in which freedom of expression was to be accorded a high priority and result in criminal proceedings only if no other form of response was adequate,[88] the Commission was of the opinion that a prison sentence was disproportionate to the legitimate aim pursued.[89]

A key factor in the Commission's thinking was 'the absence of clear elements of incitement to violence'.[90] Thus the Commission was prepared to make its own assessment of the threat to public order flowing from the distribution of the material when deciding upon the proportionality of the response, a matter which fell within the margin of appreciation left to the State in the *Otto-Preminger-Institut* case.

It is, however, the case of *Wingrove v. UK* which focuses attention upon the central divergence of approach between the Commission and Court

---

[87] *Ibid.* A further difficulty was the involvement of the Greek Orthodox Church in the authorization process. Although it did not pass upon this directly, the Commission felt that this raised 'a delicate issue' under Article 9(2). *Ibid.*, para. 46. The Commission has since reached the same conclusions in the similar case of *Pentidis and others v. Greece*, No. 23238/94, Rep. 1996, paras. 34–39.

[88] See *Castells v. Spain*, Ser. A, no. 236 (1992), para. 42.

[89] *Ahmet v. Greece*, No. 18877/91 (Dec. 1995), paras. 53–54.

[90] *Ibid.*, para. 53. The Commission has since declared a similar application admissible. See *Sadik v. Greece*, No. 25759/94 (Dec. 1996), Inf. note 132, p. 2.

most clearly. The *Wingrove* case concerned the refusal of the British Board of Film Classification to award a certificate to an eighteen-minute video film entitled *Visions of Ecstasy* on the ground that it potentially infringed the criminal law of blasphemy. The applicant alleged that this violated Article 10 of the Convention. The Commission thought that a refusal on this ground had the legitimate aim of seeking to protect the rights of others: whilst religious believers could not expect to be exempt from all criticism and must tolerate the denial by others of their beliefs, the State has a responsibility to ensure the peaceful enjoyment of believers' rights under Article 9 and the English law on blasphemy was 'intended to suppress behaviour likely to cause justified indignation amongst believing Christians'. In consequence, 'It was intended to protect the right of citizens not to be insulted in their religious feelings.'[91]

The Commission expressed the view that the freedom of artistic expression was subject to 'an obligation to avoid as far as possible expressions that are gratuitously offensive to others and thus an infringement of their rights, and which therefore do not contribute to any form of public debate capable of furthering progress in human affairs'. Drawing on the judgment of the Court in the *Otto-Preminger-Institut* case, it accepted that the State enjoyed a margin of appreciation but applied that margin in a way that reflected its original opinion in that case, rather than that of the Court. It concluded that given the short nature of the video – eighteen minutes, as opposed to a full-length film – and given that the blasphemous elements were 'fleeting' and less prominent than the equivalent elements of the film *Council in Heaven*, the refusal to grant a certificate was disproportionate to the legitimate aim pursued.[92]

The Commission also sought to distinguish the cases on the grounds that a video would be less likely to be seen by those who might be offended than would a film in a cinema or, by way of contrast with its earlier decisions in *Müller v. Switzerland* and the *Gay News* case, a picture in an art gallery or a poem in a magazine.[93] None of these grounds of distinction are particularly strong and the Commission was, in effect, reasserting the position it adopted in the *Otto-Preminger-Institut* case. The heart of the matter lies in the Commission's belief that: 'The fact that certain Christians, who had heard of the existence of the video, might be outraged by the thought that such a film was on public sale and available to those who wished to see it cannot ... amount to a sufficiently

[91] *Wingrove v. UK*, No. 17419/90, Rep. 1995, paras. 52–53.
[92] *Ibid.*, para. 66.   [93] *Ibid.*, para. 67.

compelling reason to prohibit its lawful supply.'[94] In the *Otto-Preminger-Institut* case the Court felt that such considerations were overridden by the State's margin of appreciation in assessing the degree of offence – and possible reaction – in the overwhelmingly Roman Catholic Tyrol. It must be said that the *Otto-Preminger-Institut* case encourages a maximalist response by religious believers to the provocations offered by controversial portrayals of, or comment upon, their beliefs. Indeed, it follows from the Court's judgment that if there was a likelihood of a sufficiently violent response, then the State might be under a duty to prevent it by prohibiting the work in question.[95] It remains to be seen whether the Court will accept the invitation to re-think its approach and exercise a greater degree of supervision or whether it will continue to defer in large measure to the State when assessing how this critical balance is to be struck.

Postscript

On 25 November 1996 the Court gave judgment in *Wingrove v. UK*. The Court accepted that the aim of the restriction had been 'the protection of "the rights and freedoms of others" within the meaning of Article 10(2)',[96] this being the 'protection against seriously offensive attacks on matters regarded as sacred by Christians'.[97] As to whether this was 'necessary in a democratic society', the Court concluded that 'there is as yet not sufficient common ground in the legal and social orders of the Member States of the Council of Europe to conclude that a system whereby a State can impose restrictions on the propagation of material on the basis that it is blasphemous is, in itself, unnecessary in a democratic society'.[98] It then observed that 'Whereas there is little scope under Article 10(2) . . . for restrictions on political speech or on debate of questions of public interest . . . a wider margin of appreciation is generally available to the Contracting States when regulating freedom of expression in relation to matters liable to offend intimate personal convictions within the sphere of morals or, especially, religion.' Moreover there 'is no uniform concep-

---

[94] *Ibid.*, para. 68.
[95] A positive duty to act in such a fashion was affirmed by the Court in *X and Y v. the Netherlands*, Ser. A, no. 91 (1985), para. 23 and *Plattform 'Ärzte für das Leben' v. Austria*, Ser. A, no. 139 (Dec. 1988), para. 23. See Clapham, *Human Rights in the Private Sphere*, p. 89 and Harris, O'Boyle and Warbrick, *Law of the ECHR*, pp. 359, 363.
[96] Judgement, para. 48.
[97] *Ibid.*, para. 57.   [98] *Ibid.*

tion of the requirements of "the protection of the rights of others" in relation to attacks on their religious convictions'.[99] The Court then noted that the English law of blasphemy required a 'high degree of profanation' which in itself constituted 'a safeguard against arbitrariness'.[100] Bearing both these factors in mind, the Court concluded by a 7–2 majority that the refusal to grant a classification was justified under Article 10(2) of the Convention.

At first sight, the judgment seems to follow the path set by the Court in the *Otto-Preminger Institut* case by according the State a broad margin of appreciation and it is clear that the Court sees no sign of a pan-European consensus emerging on these issues which would intrude into this. However, it goes further in that the impact of the video was assessed against the 'outrage and insult' that might be felt by believing Christians in general, rather than against the particular dangers associated with its being made available in a particularly sensitive locality. The significance of this aspect of the *Otto-Preminger Institut* case is now lessened. The Court was also dismissive of the Commission's use of the length and video format of the film as grounds of distinction. Even more important is the Court's reiteration of its belief that the exercise of the freedom of expression carries with it duties and responsibilities amongst which, 'in the context of religious beliefs, may legitimately be included a duty to avoid as far as possible an expression that is, in regard to objects of veneration, gratuitously offensive to others and profanatory'.[101] The development of this approach could extend the scope of the protection given by the Convention to religious believers and belief well beyond that offered by Article 9 itself.

---

[99] *Ibid.*, para. 58.
[100] *Ibid.*, para. 60. Importantly, the Court noted that the English law of blasphemy 'does not prohibit the expression, in any form, of views hostile to the Christian religion. Nor can it be said that opinions which are hostile to Christians necessarily fall within its ambit.'
[101] *Ibid.*, para. 52. *Otto-Preminger Institut v. Austria*, Ser. A, no. 295–A, para. 49.

13 The application of Article 2 of the First Protocol

It is clear from the *travaux préparatoires* that religious education lay at the heart of Article 2 of the First Protocol and that this was broadened out to include other forms of philosophical beliefs in order to incorporate beliefs which, whilst not of a religious nature, did nevertheless occupy a similarly central place in the life of the individual. It is also clear that the article was only meant to apply to the religious or philosophical education of children and not to the general system or conditions under which education was delivered. As will be seen, these two aspects of Article 2 have been treated in a somewhat cavalier fashion and in consequence it now has a very different scope from that which was originally intended. This, however, merely reflects a much more significant shift in perspective: rather than being seen as a form of '*lex specialis*' in relation to Article 9 of the Convention, the second sentence of Article 2 of the First Protocol is now seen as ancillary to the primary right to education.[1]

In part, this might be explained by the contexts within which the article has been considered by the Court and the Commission. Although it has been examined on many occasions, the essence of the jurisprudence is currently derived from three landmark cases, these being the *Belgian Linguistics* case,[2] the *Danish Sex Education* case,[3] and the case of *Campbell and*

---

[1] This is the short heading to be added to the article by Protocol 11, Article 2(4) and Appendix and is the title under which all its aspects are usually examined. For general examinations of this article see P. Van Dijk and G. J. H. Van Dijk, *Theory and Practice of the European Convention on Human Rights* (Daventer: Kluwer, 1990), pp. 467–477; A. H. Robertson and J. G. Merrills, *Human Rights in Europe*, 3rd edn (Manchester University Press, 1993), pp. 218–224; D. J. Harris, M. O'Boyle and C. Warbrick, *Law of the European Convention on Human Rights* (London: Butterworths, 1995), pp. 540–549.

[2] *Case relating to certain aspects of the laws on the use of languages in education in Belgium*, Ser. A, no. 6 (1968) (hereinafter cited as *Belgian Linguistics* case).

[3] *Kjeldsen, Busk Madsen and Pedersen v. Denmark*, Ser. A, no. 23 (1976).

Cosans.[4] None of these cases was directly concerned with religious education, although the religious beliefs of the applicants provided the background to the *Danish Sex Education* case. Of course, this itself reflects the fact that the initial fears of the drafters – of totalitarianism and indoctrination – did not materialize and so it is not surprising that the opening sentence, which provides that 'No person shall be denied the right to education' became the focus of attention, rather than the second sentence.

However, in the *Danish Sex Education* case, the Court went much further and subordinated the second sentence to the first, saying that 'Article 2 constitutes a whole and is dominated by its first sentence,' thus making 'the right set out in the second sentence of Article 2 . . . an adjunct of this fundamental right'.[5]

The nature of the 'right to education'

This chapter does not seek to examine what is meant by the right to education under the Protocol. Nevertheless, the general contours of that right need to be traced since they provide the parameters within which the rights of the parents, set out in the second sentence, have been developed. In the *Belgian Linguistics* case, the Court said that Article 2 'guarantees . . . a right of access to educational institutions existing at a given time'.[6] It noted that, when the Protocol was signed, all Member States of the Council of Europe possessed, and still did possess, a general official education system and that 'there neither was, nor is . . . any question of requiring each State to establish such a system, but merely guaranteeing to persons subject to the jurisdiction of the Contracting Parties the right, in principle, to avail themselves of the means of instruction existing at a given time'.[7] This has been confirmed on many occasions by both the Commission and the Court.[8]

---

[4] *Campbell and Cosans v. UK,* Ser. A, no. 48 (1982).

[5] *Kjeldsen, Busk Madsen and Pedersen v. Denmark,* Ser. A, no. 23 (1976) para. 52; *Campbell and Cosans v. UK,* Ser. A, no. 48 (1982), para. 34. See also *W and KL v. Sweden,* No. 10476/83, 45 DR 143 (Dec. 1985) at 148 and *Jordebo Foundation of Christian Schools and Jordebo v. Sweden,* No. 11533/85, 51 DR 125 (Dec. 1987) at 128.

[6] *Belgian Linguistics Case* Ser. A, no. 6 (1968), p. 31, para. 4. Access may be subject to regulations which 'may vary in time and place according to the needs and resources of the community and of individuals' (*ibid.,* p. 32, para.5).

[7] *Ibid.,* para. 3. The Commission also felt that it was 'impossible to conclude from these facts that Article 2 of the Protocol places on states any positive obligations in this matter' (Report of Commission (1967), Ser. B, vol. 3, p. 278, para. 375).

[8] See, for example, the judgment of the Court in *Kjeldsen, Busk Madsen and Pedersen v.*

Nevertheless, it has been argued that 'the exercise of the right to education . . . requires by implication the existence and the maintenance of a minimum of education provided by the state, since otherwise it would be illusory, in particular for those who have insufficient means'.[9] Similar views were also expressed in the individual and dissenting opinions to the Report of the Commission in the *Belgian Linguistics* case[10] and the Court has said recently that 'the State has an obligation to secure to children their right to education under Article 2 of Protocol No. 1'.[11] Although this could be taken to mean that the State is obliged to ensure that children are able to take advantage of the right to avail themselves of whatever forms of education are currently available within the State, it is difficult to deny that there is pressure for a more liberal interpretation which would guarantee to all children the right to basic education.[12]

A further question concerns the level of education which is addressed by the article. The Commission has in the past said that Article 2 'is concerned primarily with elementary education and not necessarily advanced studies'.[13] Although this is neither stated in the text nor very

Denmark, Ser. A, no. 23 (1976), para.50 and the Decisions of the Commission in *X v. UK* No. 5962/72, 2 DR 50 (Dec. 1975); *X and Y v. UK*, No. 7527/76, 11 DR 147 (1977); *X v. UK*, No. 8844/80, 23 DR 228 (Dec. 1980); *W & DM and M & HI v. UK*, Nos. 10228/82 and 10229/82 (joined), 37 DR 96 (Dec. 1984); *Jordebo Foundation of Christian Schools and Jordebo v. Sweden*, No. 11533/85, 51 DR 125 (Dec. 1987); *Glazewska v. Sweden*, No. 11655/85, 45 DR 300 (Dec. 1985); *Simpson v. UK*, No. 14688/89, 64 DR 188 (Dec. 1989).

[9] Van Dijk and Van Hoof, *Theory and Practice of the ECHR*, p. 467, quoted with approval in Robertson and Merrills, *Human Rights in Europe*, p. 220.

[10] Mr Sperduti (Ser. B, vol. 3, p. 280, para. 377(ii)) and Mr Balta, Mrs Janssen-Pevtschin and Mr Ermacora (*ibid.*, pp. 283–287, paras. 381–384).

[11] *Costello-Roberts v. UK*, Ser. A. no. 247–C (1993), para. 27.

[12] This is reinforced by the provision of the United Nations Convention on the Rights of the Child (1989), Article 28, which provides that: '1. State Parties recognize the right of the child to education, and with a view to achieving this right progressively and on the basis of equal opportunity, they shall, in particular: (a) make primary education compulsory and available free to all; . . .' This is substantially similar to the International Covenant on Economic, Social and Cultural Rights (1966), Article 13(2) (a). Article 4(a) of the Convention Against Discrimination in Education (1960) also provides State Parties with a progressive obligation 'to make primary education free and compulsory'. Even if it were possible, on a strict reading of Article 2 of the First Protocol, for a State to cease to provide for primary education, it would, in all likelihood, be in breach of its obligations under other international instruments to which it was a party.

[13] *X v. UK*, No. 5962/72, 2 DR 50 (Dec. 1975); *15 Foreign Students v. UK*, No. 7671/76, and fourteen other applications, 9 DR 185 (Dec. 1977); *Yanasik v. Turkey*, No. 14524/89, 74 DR 14 (Dec. 1993) ('not necessarily specialist advanced studies'). See also *Association X v. Sweden*, No. 6094/73, 9 DR 5 (Dec. 1977) at 8 where the Commission considered that compulsory membership of a student organization did not violate Article 2 'even assuming [it] is applicable in cases of education at university level'.

obvious from the drafting history it does accord with the original purpose of the Article. If it was chiefly intended to ensure that the child be educated in accordance with parental religious and philosophical convictions, it would be quite sensible to limit this to a period in which the wishes of the parent should be accorded primacy over the wishes of the child. This might loosely be equated with the period of 'basic' education. However, now that the Court has turned Article 2 on its head and focuses upon the right to education *per se*, it is difficult to see why the fundamental right not to be denied access to such educational facilities that exist at a given time should be restricted to 'elementary' education,[14] particularly since there is no question of this obliging the State to allow unregulated access[15] or to increase its provision in order to meet demand.[16]

Parental rights in relation to a child's education

The second sentence of Article 2 provides that:

In the exercise of any functions which it assumes in relation to education and teaching, the State shall respect the right of parents to ensure such education and teaching in conformity with their own religious and philosophical convictions.

This raises a number of difficult questions of direct relevance to the protection of religious freedom, albeit in the specific context of parental rights with regard to State-regulated education. The key questions are, first, what types of parental convictions are to be respected? and, second, what is meant by obliging the State to 'respect' parental convictions? The answer to this second question is intimately connected with the question of the range of activities over which the rights of the parents extend. These questions will be considered after a preliminary point has been made concerning the extent to which the rights are those of the 'parent'.

It should be noted at the outset that the State is obliged to respect the rights of the parent with regard to the education of the child. Being a

---

[14] E.g., Van Dijk and Van Hoof, *Theory and Practice of the ECHR*, p. 473 believe that Article 2 embraces, in principle, secondary and higher education. *Cf.* Harris, O'Boyle and Warbrick, *Law of the ECHR*, p. 541, who take the view that it extends to all forms of education provided or permitted, but 'its focus is on primary education'.

[15] *X v. UK*, No. 8844/80, 23 DR 228 (Dec. 1980) at 229; *Glazewska v. Sweden*, No. 11655/85, 45 DR 300 (Dec. 1985) at 302.

[16] *W & DM and M & HI v. UK*, Nos. 10228/82 and 10229/82 (joined), 37 DR 96 (Dec. 1984) at 100 and see below, p. 359.

parental right, an educational institution cannot bring a claim in its own name relating to this aspect of Article 2.[17] Moreover, although the child clearly is a beneficiary of the right not to be denied access to education and can claim victim status, the child does not have an independent right to be educated in accordance with the religious or philosophical convictions of the parent and cannot claim to be the victim of a violation.[18] Nor is Article 2 concerned with the convictions that might be held by the child. Where, however, the convictions of the parent and child differ, the State could utilize the elasticity inherent in the nature of an obligation to respect parental wishes in order to justify paying greater heed to the wishes of the child if it wished to do so.[19]

Although Article 2 refers to 'parental' rights, this is to be understood as referring to the rights of those who are responsible in law for the education and upbringing of the child. If a child has been adopted, therefore, the natural parents lose their rights.[20] In *X. v. Sweden* the

---

[17] In *Jordebo Foundation of Christian Schools and Jordebo v. Sweden*, No. 11533/85, 51 DR 125 (Dec. 1987) at 128 the Commission adopted the view (taken in *Church of X v. UK*, No. 3798/68, 29 CD 70, 75 (Dec. 1968) in relation to both Article 9 of the Convention and Article 2 of the First Protocol and confirmed in the context of Article 2 in *Karnell and Hardt v. Sweden*, No. 4733/71, 39 CD 75, 79 (Dec. 1971)) that institutions could not claim victim status. However, the Commission had in the meantime changed its mind on the question of whether a legal person can have rights under Article 9 but this did not influence the decision in *Jordebo* (see above, p. 286). Given the wording of the second sentence of Article 2 this seems unexceptional and was approved of by K. Rimanque, 'Freedom of Conscience and Minority Groups', in *Freedom of Conscience* (Strasbourg: Council of Europe, 1993), p. 144 at p. 154. Institutions can, however, claim victim status as regards the right to education itself, in so far as the Commission is correct in its belief that it implies the right to establish and run private schools. See *Verein Gemeinsam Lernen v. Austria*, No. 23419/94, 82–A DR 41 (Dec. 1995) and see below, p. 360.

[18] This was confirmed by the Court in *Eriksson v. Sweden*, Ser. A, no. 156 (1989) para. 93. In *Simpson v. UK*, No. 14688/89, 64 DR 188 (Dec. 1989) the child applicant was able to claim victim status in relation to the first sentence of Article 2 but not with respect to the second.

[19] Cf. *X v. Denmark*, No. 6854/74, 7 DR 81 (Dec. 1976). Article 5(b) of the UNESCO Convention on Discrimination in Education (1960) suggests that where there is such a conflict the wishes of the child should take preference by providing that 'no person or group of persons should be compelled to receive religious instruction inconsistent with his or their convictions'. Cf. R. Goy, 'La Garantie Européenne de la Liberté de Religion' RDP 107 (1991), 5, 32–34 who argues that the right of the child yields to the interests of the parents and, taking this a stage further, suggests that this means that a child does not enjoy the freedom to change his religion, expressly provided for in Article 9.

[20] *X v. UK*, No. 7626/76, 11 DR 160 (1977). In this Decision the Commission held open the possibility that Article 2 imposed a duty on public authorities not to transfer parental authority to persons who did not share the convictions of the natural parents (*ibid.*,

Commission said that this right was an integral part of the right of custody and so it could not be exercised by a parent whose child had been taken into care by judicial order.[21] In the *Olsson* case, however, the Commission drew a distinction, subsequently accepted by the Court, between orders granting custody of a child to others and orders which placed a child under the care of a public authority. Although parents of children taken into care retained their rights under Article 2, the authorities were to 'have due regard' for them, thus offering a lesser degree of protection than is generally offered to parents.[22]

The interest of the parent crystallizes at the moment the child is taken into care. In the *Eriksson* case the Court and Commission both rejected the contention that an order prohibiting a mother from removing her daughter from a foster home infringed her right to have her child educated in accordance with the beliefs of the Pentecostalist movement, observing that the daughter had been taken into care before her mother's religious conversion had taken place.[23] Given that the authorities have assumed responsibility for the education of a child taken into care, this is not an unsatisfactory compromise between the conflicting interests. Following the Court's judgment in the *Olsson* case a friendly settlement was reached in a number of cases in which it had been claimed that the education of children taken into care had not accorded respect to the parents' wishes or religious beliefs.[24]

Finally, it must be remembered that Article 2 only relates to 'functions assumed by the State'. The nature of the functions embraced by the article is not clear. In the *Olsson* case the Court was faced with a situation in which the parents of a child placed in care were concerned that the foster parents would give the child a religious upbringing, contrary to their wishes. Although the Court dismissed this claim on the facts, the judgment did suggest that Article 2 extended to the 'general education' of

---

p. 168). See also the Report of the Commission (1986) reproduced in *Olsson v. Sweden*, Ser. A, no. 130 (1988) at pp. 63–64.

[21] *X. v. Sweden*, No. 7911/77, 12 DR 192 (Dec. 1977). This question had been left open in the earlier decision in *X v. the Netherlands*, No. 2648/65, 12 *YBECHR* 354 (Dec. 1968) at p. 364.

[22] *Olsson v. Sweden*, Ser. A, no. 130 (1988), paras. 92–96; Report of the Commission (1986), ibid., para. 183.

[23] *Eriksson v. Sweden*, Ser. A, no. 156 (1989), paras. 83–84. See also *X v. the Netherlands*, No. 2648/65, 12 *YBECHR* 354 (Dec. 1968) in which the father lost interest in religion after custody of his child had been taken from him.

[24] *Aminoff v. Sweden*, No. 10554/83, 43 DR 120 (Dec. 1985). This decision on admissibility was taken prior to the conclusion of *Olsson v. Sweden*, following which there was a friendly settlement. See 48 DR 82 (1986). See also the friendly settlement in *Ulla Widén v. Sweden*, No. 10723/83, 48 DR 93 (1986).

the children placed in care.[25] However, in the *Hoffman* case this was interpreted in a narrow fashion and it is difficult to reconcile this with the *Olsson* case.

In the *Hoffman* case the applicant claimed a violation of the Convention in that she had been denied custody of her children following her divorce. At the time of her marriage both she and her husband had been of the Catholic faith, into which the children had been baptised. The applicant had subsequently become a Jehovah's Witness and her ex-husband sought custody chiefly on the grounds that it would be detrimental to the children to be brought up as Jehovah's Witnesses. In addition, however, the Austrian Religious Education Act provided that children could only be brought up in a faith other than that originally held by both parents at the time of marriage if both consented.

Although the Commission and the Court found there to be a violation of Article 8 of the Convention in conjunction with Article 14 (in that there had been discrimination on the grounds of religion), the Commission did not see this as raising any issues under Article 2 of the First Protocol. The Commission seems to have accepted the Government's contention that 'this right concerns the education of children in public schools' since it was of the view that 'the functions which the State assumes in relation to education and teaching are not at issue in the present case. The Supreme Court applied the Religious Education Act only in relation to the religious education of the applicant's children at home.'[26] Thus the 'functions assumed' related to the provision within, and regulation of, establishments providing a formal system of education.[27] The fact that the Austrian law prevented the applicant from raising her children within the framework of her beliefs did not raise issues under this article.

Which parental convictions are to be respected?

The original purpose of Article 2 was to offer safeguards against children being subjected to forms of religious instruction that ran counter to the beliefs of their parents and the phrase 'philosophical convictions' was

---

[25] *Olsson v. Sweden*, Ser. A, no. 130 (1988) para. 95.

[26] *Hoffman v. Austria*, Report of the Commission (1992), paras. 113–114, reproduced in *Hoffman v. Austria*, Ser. A, no. 255–C (1993), p. 45. This was tacitly endorsed by the Court, which did not think it necessary to re-examine this issue, which had not been pursued before it (*ibid.*, para. 39).

[27] *Cf.* Van Dijk and Van Hoof, *Theory and Practice of the ECHR*, p. 474 who, following the *Olsson* case, concluded that 'the second sentence also applies to situations outside the framework of teaching institutions'.

added in order to include beliefs which, whilst not religious as such, were of a similar nature.[28] This view was confirmed in the *Belgian Linguistics* case, by both the Commission and the Court, the Court considering that: 'To interpret the terms "religious" and "philosophical" as covering linguistic preferences would amount to a distortion of their ordinary and usual meaning and to read into the Convention something which is not there.'[29] It would have been difficult to reach any other conclusion on this point, given that both the Commission and the Court noted that the *travaux préparatoires* revealed that proposals to include linguistic preferences had been explicitly rejected. This, however, meant that it was unnecessary for them to consider the true scope of these words and when they returned to this phrase in the *Campbell and Cosans* case a very different approach was adopted.

The applicants in *Campbell and Cosans* had argued that their views opposing the use of corporal punishment in schools qualified as a 'philosophical conviction'.[30] This was accepted by both the Commission[31] and the Court[32] and is no longer a matter of any doubt.[33] The Commission

---

[28] See above, pp. 276–280.

[29] *Belgian Linguistics* case, Ser. A, no. 6 (1968), p. 32, para. 6.

[30] The applicants did not suggest that their convictions on this matter were of a religious nature. See *Campbell and Cosans v. UK*, Report of the Commission (1980), Ser. B, no. 42, p. 35, para. 83.

[31] By a majority of nine votes to five. The dissenting Members of the Commission did not accept that views concerning disciplinary procedures qualified as 'philosophical convictions'. See *ibid.*, pp. 45–47.

[32] Judge Sir Vincent Evans dissented on this point, saying that 'the views of parents on such matters as the use of corporal punishment are as much outside the intended scope of the provisions as are their linguistic preferences' (*Campbell and Cosans v. UK*, Ser. A, no. 48 (1982), pp. 21–24 at p. 22).

[33] Following the Judgment of the Court in the *Campbell and Cosans* case, the UK Government reached a friendly settlement in a number of cases where the evidence of the parent's convictions concerning corporal punishment was well established. See, among others, *Townend Sr, and Jr, v. UK*, No. 9119/80, 50 DR 36 (Dec. 1987); *K. Durairaj, M. Baker (ex-Durairaj) and A. Durairaj v. UK*, No. 9114/80, 52 DR 13 (Dec. 1987); *B and D v. UK (s.n. J. V. and E. Brant v. UK)*, No. 9303/81, 52 DR 21 (Dec. 1987). This point was also conceded by the Government in other cases, such as *Jarman v. UK*, No. 11648/85, 56 DR 181 (Dec. 1988). In the case of *M. and K. Warwick v. UK*, No. 9471/81, 36 DR 49 (Dec. 1984) and 60 DR 5 (Rep. 1986) the Commission concluded that the refusal of the school authorities to give assurances to a parent that corporal punishment would not be inflicted on her child amounted to a failure to respect her philosophical convictions. The UK subsequently abolished corporal punishment in State schools by virtue of the Education Act 1986, ss. 47 and 48. See Committee of Ministers Resolution DH(89) 5 in 60 DR 22, and R. Churchill and R. Young, 'Compliance with the Judgments of the European Court of Human Rights and Decisions of the Committee of Ministers: the Experience of the United Kingdom 1975–1987', *BYIL* 62 (1991), 283, 287–291.

accepted that the *travaux préparatoires* showed that the reference to 'philosophical convictions' was intended to embrace agnosticism as an alternative to religious beliefs, but observed that 'notwithstanding the intention of the drafters . . . the term chosen by them for this purpose has undoubtedly a wider meaning'[34] and so 'it would be contrary to the ordinary and usual meaning of the expression . . . in its context and in the light of the purpose and object of Article 2 of the Protocol to interpret it to cover solely agnostic opinions'.[35]

The Commission proceeded to define philosophical convictions as being 'those ideas based on human knowledge and reasoning concerning the world, life, society, etc., which a person adopts and professes according to the dictates of his or her conscience. These ideas can more briefly be characterised as a person's outlook on life including, in particular, a concept of human behaviour in society.'[36] The Court likened the word 'conviction' to the term 'belief' found in Article 9 of the Convention and confirmed that this meant that the view put forward had to 'attain a certain level of cogency, seriousness, cohesion and importance'.[37]

This aspect of Article 9 has been considered above and it has been shown that it can be used as an effective filter for distinguishing between those sets of beliefs which are embraced within the article and those which are not. This is, however, a relatively objective control mechanism, since, although certainly capable of subjective interpretation,[38] its application ultimately depends upon what the believer actually thinks and does. No matter how idiosyncratic, if these criteria are met the belief will fall within the ambit of the article.

In *Campbell and Cosans*, however, both the Commission and the Court placed greater emphasis upon the philosophical nature of the belief than on the fact that the applicants held what might be called a 'qualifying belief'. The Court concluded that:

[34] *Campbell and Cosans v. UK*, Report of Commission (1980), Ser. B, no. 42, p. 36, para. 90. It supported this opinion by referring to the *Danish Sex Education* case. The cases are, however, distinguishable since the latter concerned an aspect of religious belief.

[35] *Ibid.*, para. 36. The cogency of this is questionable. The Commission claimed that, in using the word 'philosophical', the drafters had used a term that was wider than was necessary to fulfil their purpose. It makes little sense to then claim that this wider interpretation is now necessary in order to fulfil that purpose. Nevertheless, this view was not contested by the respondent government before the Court. See Memorial of UK, Ser. B, no. 42, p. 79, para. 3. 15.

[36] Report of Commission (1980), Ser. B, no. 42, p. 37, para. 92.

[37] *Campbell and Cosans v. UK*, Ser. A, no. 48 (1982), para. 36.

[38] This is particularly so of the criterion of 'importance'. This, however, refers to the importance of the belief *to the believer*, rather than to the observer.

The Commission pointed out that the word 'philosophy' bears numerous meanings: it is used to allude to a fully fledged system of thought or, rather loosely, to views on more or less trivial matters. The Court agrees with the Commission that neither of these two extremes can be adopted for the purposes of interpreting Article 2: the former would too narrowly restrict the scope of a right that is guaranteed to all parents and the latter might result in the inclusion of matters of insufficient weight or substance.[39]

Clearly, it is not necessary to demonstrate a perfect adherence to principles of stoicism or to socratic methodology; on the other hand, not every whim or passing fancy can be accorded the status of the philosophical belief. This is unexceptionable. However, rather than attempt to define the parameters of acceptable philosophical thought, the Court took the view that: '"Philosophical Convictions" in the present context denotes . . . such convictions as are worthy of respect in a "democratic society" and are not incompatible with human dignity'.[40]

The Court emphasized the nebulous nature of a 'philosophical' conviction in order to justify its abandonment of any attempt to establish some objective control mechanism. Instead, it adopted a far more subjective approach to the question of whether the views held by the applicant should be accorded respect. It determined the question not on the basis of whether the applicant had a philosophical belief which was not being respected but on the basis of whether it felt that the conviction in question was 'worthy' of respect. Hence the Court concluded that: 'The applicant's views relate to a weighty and substantial aspect of human life and behaviour, namely the integrity of the person, the propriety or otherwise of the infliction of corporal punishment and the exclusion of the distress which the risk of such punishment entails.'[41] This has more to do with the Court's assessment of the overall seriousness of the complaint than with the nature of the applicant's belief. The UK

---

[39] *Campbell and Cosans v. UK* Ser. A, no. 48 (1982), para. 36.
[40] *Ibid.*
[41] *Ibid.* The 'belief' must still meet the criteria of cogency, seriousness, cohesion and importance but, if it passes these tests, it must now be judged to be 'worthy of respect'. Its having fulfilled these criteria is not in itself sufficient. This is illustrated by *X, Y and Z v. UK*, No. 8566/79, 31 DR 50 (Dec. 1982) in which the applicants objected to their son's corporal punishment at school. Although such views are clearly accepted as philosophical convictions for the purposes of Article 2, the Commission declared the application inadmissible because they had not informed the school of their opposition and had, in fact, told their son not to accept corporal punishment 'if he thought it was unjustified'. This implied that they were not, in fact, opposed to it in principle and so they had not fulfilled the threshold criteria. See also *B and D v. UK*, No. 9303/81, 49 DR 44 (Dec. 1986) at pp. 49–50.

Government had argued that if the applicant's views were equated with 'philosophical convictions' in this fashion, there was no reason why the views of parents who objected to any disciplinary measures, such as extra homework, should not also qualify.[42] Although it did not meet this argument head on, the Court's answer would presumably have been that it did not set as much store on the rights of children to play at home in the evenings as it did upon their physical integrity. This might seem convincing but it does not explain why one set of values – no corporal punishment – is elevated into a 'philosophical conviction' whilst another – no punitive disciplinary sanction – is downgraded to an 'opinion' or 'idea' and, therefore, beyond its reach.[43] Nevertheless, the Commission has subsequently confirmed that 'it would not be contrary to Article 2 . . . for pupils to be suspended or expelled, provided that the national regulations did not prevent them from enrolling in another establishment in order to pursue their studies'.[44]

It is, then, evident that the second sentence of Article 2 is now taken to embrace not only religious beliefs but also any set of beliefs which are seriously held and which, in the opinion of the Strasbourg organs, are worthy of respect in the educational context.[45] This does not mean that 'anything' goes but that there is a twofold approach. First, the parent must demonstrate that the belief fulfils the fourfold test of 'cogency, seriousness, cohesion and importance' in order that it may qualify as a 'conviction'.[46] This is to be applied in an objective fashion.[47] The Court or Commission then considers whether it feels that, in the light of the Convention as a whole, account ought to be taken of it.

---

[42] See UK Memorial, Ser. B, no. 42, p. 82, para. 3. 26 and Public Hearing, *ibid.*, p. 150. This submission was based upon the views of the five dissenting members of the Commission (*ibid.*, p. 46 and see n. 31 above).

[43] *Cf. Campbell and Cosans v. UK*, Ser. A, no. 48 (1982), para. 36. Article 10 of the Convention guarantees the freedom to express 'opinions' and 'ideas' but it does not embrace the right to have a child educated in accordance with them. Naturally, the parents remain free to express such opinions and ideas that fall short of 'philosophical convictions' to their children.

[44] *Yanasik v. Turkey*, No. 14524/89, 74 DR 14 (Dec. 1993) at 27.

[45] *Cf.* Robertson and Merrills, *Human Rights in Europe*, pp. 221–222, who raise the question of whether the views of the parents concerning the linguistic education of their children would amount to a 'conviction' in the light of the decision in *Campbell and Cosans*.

[46] The burden of proof clearly rests on the applicant. In *Bernard and others v. Luxembourg*, No. 17187/90, 75 DR 57 (Dec. 1993) the Commission noted that 'the applicants have not described the nature of their philosophical convictions in any detail', when recalling the need to pass the threshold of the 'fourfold' test set out in *Campbell and Cosans*.

[47] See Van Dijk and Van Hoof, *Theory and Practice of the ECHR*, p. 472.

The subjectivity of the second stage does make it difficult to predict with certainty the likely outcome of novel applications. There appears to be a reluctance to declare that a given belief does not qualify for respect. In *X, Y and Z v. Federal Republic of Germany* the Commission considered the degree of respect due under Article 2 to beliefs concerning the content of a school's mathematics syllabus[48] and, in *X and Y v. UK* to the belief that 'children of similar academic ability should be taught together by university-qualified trained staff'.[49] It would have been interesting to have seen the reasoning that led the Commission to conclude that these convictions did indeed fulfil the relevant criteria.

It is, perhaps, significant that both of these applications were declared inadmissible on other grounds. Other applications declared inadmissible have also left open the question of whether the beliefs of a parent concerning the desirability of a disabled child attending a special school amounted to a 'deep-founded philosophical conviction' or was simply a point of disagreement between the parent and the authorities concerning the best way of providing the child with an education.[50] It may well be appropriate to avoid the appearance of belittling the significance of a person's belief when it is not necessary to do so.

Nevertheless, there are limits. For example, in *Campbell and Cosans* the Court took the view that, in order to be deemed worthy of respect, the philosophical convictions of the parents 'must not conflict with the fundamental right of the child to education'.[51] This approach is illustrated by the decision of the Commission in *Bernard v. Luxembourg*. The applicant complained of a violation of Article 14 of the Convention,[52] in that parents holding religious convictions could exempt children from

---

[48] *X, Y and Z v. Federal Republic of Germany*, No. 9411/81, 29 DR 224 (Dec. 1982).

[49] *X and Y v. UK*, No. 7527/76, 11 DR 147 (Dec. 1977) at 149.

[50] *Graeme v. UK*, No. 13887/88, 64 DR 158 (Dec. 1990); *PD and LD v. UK*, No. 14135/88, 62 DR 292 (Dec. 1989); *Klerks v. the Netherlands*, No. 25212/94, 82–A DR 129 (Dec. 1995). In these cases parents wished to have their children educated in a 'normal' school. *Cf. Simpson v. UK*, No. 14688/89, 64 DR 188 (Dec. 1989) in which the applicant, a disabled child, objected to being placed in a large comprehensive, rather than a special school. The nature of the applicant's belief did not arise in the latter case, since the Commission was concerned with the child-applicant's right to education, rather than with the question of whether a child was receiving an education in conformity with a parent-applicant's beliefs. Although his mother's 'philosophical convictions' were raised by the child, this was dismissed *ratione personae*, since 'it was not clear why the applicant's mother could not have lodged an application on her own behalf' (*ibid.*, at p. 194). Had the mother made such an application, however, the above decisions suggest that it would have had little prospect of success.

[51] *Campbell and Cosans v. UK*, Ser. A, no. 48 (1982), para. 36.

[52] See below, nn. 63 and 81.

classes in religion and morality if no teacher of their religion was available, whereas parents holding philosophical convictions of a non-religious nature could not withdraw their children from the alternative classes in morality and society. The Commission, declaring the application inadmissible, took the view that there was an objective and reasonable justification for this, although quite what this was is entirely unclear. However, the decision seems to have been driven by the belief that requiring children to attend classes in morality and society either could not offend against the philosophical convictions of parents[53] or, if it did, would be overridden by the consideration that 'parental convictions, for the purposes of Article 2 of Protocol No.1, are convictions which do not conflict with the child's fundamental right to education. Where, instead of supporting the child's right to education, the parents' rights come into conflict with it, the child's rights must prevail.'[54]

Clearly, not all parental convictions are deemed worthy of respect within the Convention framework and the 'philosophical' nature, or otherwise, of such beliefs is not necessarily the determining factor. The following section will continue exploring this theme by considering the nature of the 'respect' which those beliefs which qualify as religions or 'philosophical convictions' for the purposes of Article 2 receive.

'Respect' for parental convictions

Almost inevitably, when one element of a definition is relaxed another tends to be tightened so that the final position is often little different to that which was previously the case. As the range of 'beliefs' to which Article 2 applies has been broadened, the degree to which they are accorded 'respect' has suffered something of a diminution. The *travaux préparatoires* demonstrate that the word 'respect' was inserted into the text as a replacement for the phrase 'to have regard for', which was considered inadequate since it amounted to little more than a procedural requirement: a State could 'have regard' to the views of the parents yet still decide to ride roughshod over them.[55] Thus the obligation to 'respect'

---

[53] *Bernard v. Luxembourg*, No. 17187/90, 75 DR 57 (Dec. 1993) at 75. It should be recalled, however, that the Commission was not convinced that the parents possessed a 'philosophical conviction' that fell to be respected in the first place. See above, p. 296.

[54] *Ibid.*, p. 73. The authority quoted in support of this proposition (*Graeme v. UK*, No. 13887/88, 64 DR 158 (Dec. 1990)) was concerned with the application of Article 9(2) of the Convention, which has no direct counterpart in Article 2 of the Protocol. This may go some way towards explaining the almost impenetrable nature of the Decision.

[55] See above, pp. 277–278.

the rights of the parents was intended to convey a substantive right, albeit of a limited nature.

In essence, the second sentence of Article 2 was intended to address a very simple situation. The State would not be obliged to provide for religious instruction in schools but, if it did, the child of Roman Catholic parents, for example, should not be forced to attend classes in which religious instruction was given in accordance with a Protestant tradition. Much has changed, however, and it seems as if the rights of the parents have been weakened, rather than enhanced, by the broadening scope of the article. This can be demonstrated by looking at a number of particular questions that have arisen in connection with this right.

The scope of the right

The *Danish Sex Education* case concerned Danish legislation which provided for compulsory sex education in State schools. This took two forms, a 'general survey' given by special lectures (special sex education) and by integrating sex education with conventional school subjects in a natural and objective way (compulsory integrated sex education). Parents could exempt their children from the former but not the latter.[56] The applicants claimed that integrated sex education was contrary to their beliefs as Christians and therefore violated Article 2. The Danish Government argued that the second sentence of Article 2 'implies solely the right for parents to have their children exempted from classes offering "religious instructions of a denominational nature" '.[57] The Court rejected this, saying that: 'Article 2, which applies to each of the State's functions in relation to education and to teaching, does not permit a distinction to be drawn between religious instruction and other subjects. It enjoins the State to respect parents' convictions, be they religious or philosophical, throughout the entire State education programme.'[58]

At first sight, this might seem to be a significant advance, taking the scope of the right beyond the narrow confines of denominational religious teaching and spreading it across the entire educational field.[59] In reality,

---

[56] See Executive Order No. 313 of 15 June 1972: *Kjeldsen, Busk Madsen and Pedersen v. Denmark*, Scr. A, no. 23 (1976), para. 31 and Report of the Commission (1975), Ser. B, no. 21, p. 41, paras. 141–146.

[57] *Kjeldsen, Busk Madsen and Pedersen v. Denmark*, Ser. A, no. 23 (1976), para. 51.

[58] *Ibid.*, para. 52.

[59] It should be noted that in both the Convention on Discrimination in Education (1960) Article 5(1)(b), and the United Nations Covenant on Economic, Social and Cultural Rights (1966), Article 13(3), respect for parental liberty is restricted to 'the religious and moral education of the children in conformity with their own convictions'.

however, it represents a serious diminution of parental rights since the Court took the view that:

the second sentence of Article 2 of the Protocol does not prevent States from imparting through teaching or education information or knowledge of a directly or indirectly religious or philosophical kind. It does not even permit parents to object to the integration of such teaching or education in the school curriculum, for otherwise all institutional teaching would run the risk of proving impracticable. In fact, it seems very difficult for many of the subjects taught at school not to have, to a greater or lesser extent, some philosophical complexion or implications. The same is true of religious affinities if one remembers the existence of religions forming a very broad dogmatic and moral entity which has or may have answers to every question of a philosophical, cosmological or moral nature.[60]

This all but destroys the right which the Court was purporting to protect. It reduced the content of the right for 'respect' to its most basic form and concluded, in what has since become a standard recitation, that:

in fulfilling the functions assumed by it in regard to education and teaching [the State] must take care that information or knowledge included in the curriculum is conveyed in an objective, critical and pluralistic manner. The State is forbidden to pursue an aim of indoctrination that might be considered as not respecting the parents' religious and philosophical convictions. That is the limit of what must not be exceeded.[61]

It is clear that the Court considered that this standard applied to both direct and integrated teaching, although it was, strictly speaking, only concerned with the latter. This flowed from the Court's perception of the unified nature of the right set out in Article 2, seeing the primary obligation as being not to 'deny the right to education' and the right set out in the second sentence as 'an adjunct of this fundamental right'.[62]

The result of this is that parents can now only object to education in the tenets of religions or philosophies other than their own if the purpose of such education can be equated with indoctrination. A parent cannot seek to 'insulate' a child from instruction which critically examines the foundations of a parent's belief or which seeks to explain the basis of

---

[60] Ibid., para. 53.

[61] Ibid. See also 40 Mothers v. Sweden, No. 6853/74, 9 DR 27 (Dec. 1977); X and Y v. UK, No. 7527/76, 11 DR 147 (Dec. 1977); Seven Individuals v. Sweden, No. 8811/79, 29 DR 104 (Dec. 1982); X, Y and Z v. Federal Republic of Germany, No. 9411/81, 29 DR 224 (Dec. 1982); W & DM and M & HI v. UK, Nos. 10228/82 and 10229/82 (joined), 37 DR 96 (Dec. 1984); Graeme v. UK, No. 13887/88, 64 DR 158 (Dec. 1990); Valsamis v. Greece, No. 21787/93, Rep. 1995, para. 36.

[62] Kjeldsen, Busk Madsen and Pedersen v. Denmark, Ser. A, no. 23 (1976), para. 52.

other faiths or philosophies in a general or comparative fashion. Nor can a parent object to compulsory attendance at classes providing general education in moral and social issues.[63] The Commission has accepted that 'a particular school or staff member of a school may abuse the manner of applying given instructions as to education and teaching' and that the authorities would be responsible for any such abuse.[64] Although there is yet to be a case in which the Commission has found that the practice of a school amounted to indoctrination contrary to Article 2,[65] the Commission has accepted that the right of a parent to have their convictions respected could justify a school interfering with a teacher's freedom of expression under Article 10 of the Convention.[66] Although it might be possible for a parent to be successful in an application which concerned the failure of a school to ensure that its staff conformed to the regulatory framework, it is unlikely that a successful challenge could be mounted against the framework itself on the grounds that it either embodied principles or manifested a general educational philosophy opposed to that of the parent.[67]

[63] See X v. Belgium, No. 17568/90, Inf. note 107, p. 3 (Dec. 1992), in which the Commission declared a complaint concerning an obligation for children to attend either a course in religious or moral education inadmissible, and Bernard v. Luxembourg, No. 17187/90, 75 DR 57 (Dec. 1993) considered above, n. 53.

[64] 40 Mothers v. Sweden, No. 6853/74, 9 DR 27 (Dec. 1977) at 31.

[65] In Karnell and Hardt v. Sweden, No. 4733/71, 14 YBECHR 676 (1971), the Commission declared admissible (neither party contesting admissibility) a case concerning the refusal of the respondent government to exempt children of members of the Evangelical-Lutheran Church of Sweden from compulsory religious instruction. The applicants subsequently withdrew their application following an agreement that the children could be exempted from compulsory religious instruction and that such instruction would not be incorporated into lessons given to classes in which the exempted children were present. See F. Castberg, The European Convention on Human Rights (Leiden: Sijthoff, 1974), p. 180; F. Jacobs, The European Convention on Human Rights (Oxford: Clarendon Press, 1975), p. 175.

[66] X v. UK, No. 8010/77, 16 DR 101 (Dec. 1979). In this case a teacher of English and mathematics at a non-denominational school was dismissed after refusing to stop giving religious instruction during class time, holding 'evangelical clubs' on school premises and wearing stickers carrying religious and anti-abortion slogans. This was held to be justified as being necessary in a democratic society for the protection of the rights and freedoms of others within the meaning of Article 10(2) of the Convention.

[67] In Seven Individuals v. Sweden, No. 8811/79, 29 DR 104 (Dec. 1982) the Commission rejected the argument that prohibiting corporal punishment in schools amounted to an attempt to indoctrinate children of parents who, as members of a Protestant Free Church and basing themselves on various biblical texts and doctrinal works, believed in 'traditional' means of bringing up children, including physical punishment. See also Valsamis v. Greece, No. 21787/93, Rep. 1995, paras. 38–40 in which the Commission refused to accept that the rights of parents, who were Jehovah's Witnesses, under Article 2 had been violated when their daughter was subject to a disciplinary sanction

This might be considered a positive development, but it evidences a much lower threshold of 'respect' for the rights of the parent than was originally contemplated. This is graphically demonstrated by the decision of the Commission in *W & DM and M and HI v. UK* in which it declared that 'the essence of Article 2 . . . is the safeguarding of pluralism and tolerance in public education and the prohibition on indoctrination, parents' religious and philosophical convictions having to be respected, albeit not necessarily reflected, in the State school system.'[68]

This development has been facilitated by the willingness of the Strasbourg organs to accept very general ideas as legitimate 'philosophical convictions' for the purposes of Article 2. The decisions which demonstrate the least respect for the rights of parents often concern applications which challenge general organizational aspects of the State school system.[69] Such cases could be dismissed on other grounds but the Court has made it more difficult to do so by making the determination subjective. It is easier to water down the content of the right of 'respect' than to dismiss an application on the grounds that the applicant's belief either fails to qualify as a 'philosophical conviction' for the purposes of Article 2 or is not worthy of respect in a democratic society.

Article 2, then, ensures that children shall not be subjected to indoctrination against the wishes of their parents in any sphere of elementary education. This does not, however, prevent them from being educated under a system to which the parents have objections. Nor does it prevent them from receiving information on matters to which parents object. What is prevented is compulsory participation in acts of religious worship and classes which teach a religious or philosophical belief *as* a belief:[70] compulsory religious instruction is suspect, religious knowledge is not. General teaching in morals – conveyed through the medium of a religious (but not philosophical) belief if necessary – is beyond reproach. If the threshold of 'indoctrination' is not reached, the rights of the parents are

for refusing to participate in an obligatory parade on a national holiday which, they claimed, commemorated war. The Commission did, however, find a violation of Article 2 of the First Protocol in conjunction with Article 13 of the Convention (*ibid.*, paras. 67–69). The case was referred to the Court in September 1995. The Commission has subsequently reached a similar set of conclusions in the case of *Efstratiou and others v. Greece*, No. 24095/94, Rep. 1996, which was referred to the Court in May 1996.

[68] *W & DM and M & HI v. UK*, Nos. 10228/82 and 10229/82 (joined), 27 DR 92 (Dec. 1984) at 99–100.

[69] In *W & DM and M & HI v. UK*, the applicants claimed that they were philosophically opposed to comprehensive education (*ibid.*, 97–98).

[70] E.g. *Karnell and Hardt v. Sweden*, No. 4733/71, 14 YBECHR 664 and 767 (1971), for which see above, n. 65.

deemed to be adequately safeguarded by their being able to have their children educated elsewhere. If, however, there is a danger of 'indoctrination', the availability of alternative education, either within a given school or in the locality, remains a relevant consideration.

The nature of the belief, and its perceived significance, is likely to be a determining factor and it may well be that there are two rules operating under a common rubric. If parents hold a religious or philosophical belief and a school teaches, as a matter of belief, another, then there is a danger of 'indoctrination' and the availability of an alternative is an important element of determining whether the obligation has been breached. If the State religion is taught in all but one school, 500 miles from a child's place of residence, the merely theoretical possibility of an alternative style of education is not sufficient. If, on the other hand, the complaint concerns aspects of the general organization of the education system, it is more likely that the existence of hypothetical possibilities will suffice. In short, the closer the circumstances are to what might be called the 'core' meaning of the article, the greater will be the degree of 'respect' that must be accorded.

The provision of educational facilities

In the *Belgian Linguistics* case the Court confirmed what was already abundantly clear from the *travaux préparatoires* – that there was no obligation upon States to provide for any particular form of education. This remains the case, irrespective of whether or not article 2 now embraces an obligation concerning the provision of basic education.[71] In *Graeme v. UK* the Commission made it clear that 'Article 2 . . . for practical reasons, could not require that educational facilities provided by the State cater for all parental philosophical or religious convictions'.[72] If parents wish to have their children educated outside of the State system, either at a private school or at home, they must be free to do so.[73] This does not mean that they must be *able* to do so. Provided that it does not amount to indoctrinating children in a particular set of values, the State can organize the State schooling system in any way it chooses. The inability of parents to take advantage of other options cannot alter this. This remains

---

[71] See above, p. 343.

[72] *Graeme v. UK*, No. 13887/88, 64 DR 158 (Dec. 1990) at 166.

[73] The State retains the right to monitor the basic educational development of children taught at home and take appropriate action to ensure that appropriate standards are met. See *Family H v. UK*, No. 10233/83, 37 DR 105 (Dec. 1984) and *X v. Federal Republic of Germany*, No. 19844/92, Inf. note 106, p. 3 (July 1992).

unaffected by the unavailability of places in alternative schools within the State sector,[74] the availability of schooling in a particular place[75] or the inability of parents to afford school fees.[76]

Although it is not dealt with explicitly, the Commission has said that Article 2 'guarantees the right to start and run a private school', albeit 'subject to regulation by the State in order to ensure a proper educational system as a whole'.[77] It is quite clear, however, that the State is not under any obligation to provide any assistance, financial or otherwise, in order to establish or maintain schools which conform to the religious or philosophical convictions of parents.[78] There might, however, be a breach if funds are distributed to denominational schools in a discriminatory fashion.[79]

In *X v. UK* the applicant had sought to establish a non-denominational school in Northern Ireland, believing that existing state schools were under the influence of the Protestant faith and private schools under the influence of Roman Catholicism. Although the State would meet 100 per cent of the recurring costs and 85 per cent of the capital costs, it was claimed that the need to bear 15 per cent of the initial costs presented an insurmountable obstacle. Even if it were insurmountable, this would not have justified a finding that there had been a breach of Article 2. The

---

[74] *X and Y v. UK*, No. 7527/76, 11 DR 147 (Dec. 1977).

[75] In *Guzzardi v. Italy*, No. 7367/76, 8 DR 185 (Dec. 1977) the applicant was subject to a compulsory residence order which required that he reside on the island of Asinara for a three-year period. He complained, *inter alia*, that if his son were permitted to live with him, he could not exercise his right to have him educated since there was no school on the island. The Commission declared this aspect of his application inadmissible (*ibid.*, at 210).

[76] Although the Commission accepted the force of the argument that high fees rendered alternatives unrealistic in its Report in *Campbell and Cosans v. UK*, Ser. B, no. 42 (1980), pp. 38–39, it subsequently rejected such an argument in *W & DM and M & HI v. UK*, Nos. 10228/82 and 10229/82 (joined), 37 DR 96 (Dec. 1984) at 100.

[77] *Jordebo Foundation of Christian Schools and Jordebo v. Sweden*, No. 11533/85, 51 DR 125 (Dec. 1987); *Verein Gemeinsam Lernen v. Austria*, No. 23419/94, 82–A DR 41 (Dec. 1995). The first sentence of Article 2 refers only to education, not to teaching. However, in *Kjeldsen, Busk Madsen and Pedersen v. Denmark*, Ser. A, no. 48 (1982), para. 50 the Court suggested that, when read as a whole, Article 2 embraced the right to establish private schools. See Van Dijk and Van Hoof, *Theory and Practice of the ECHR*, p. 470 but *cf.* Harris, O'Boyle and Warbrick, *Law of the ECHR*, pp. 543–544 which adopts a more cautious approach.

[78] In addition to the material cited in nn. 72–77 above, see also *40 Mothers v. Sweden*, No. 6853/74, 9 DR 27 (Dec 1977); *X v. UK*, No. 7782/77, 14 DR 179 (Dec. 1978); *W and KL v. Sweden*, No. 10476/83, 45 DR 143 (Dec. 1985). In *ISKCON and others v. UK*, No. 20490/92, 76–A DR 90 (Dec. 1994) at 111 it was made clear that the religious nature of an educative foundation did not prevent the State from applying ordinary planning controls, even if this affected worship and the education of children.

[79] See generally Harris, O'Boyle and Warbrick, *Law of the ECHR*, pp. 547–549.

Commission did, however, proceed to examine, *ex officio*, whether the difference in the amount of the subsidy offered to State schools and voluntary schools breached Article 14 of the Convention in conjunction with Article 2 of the First Protocol and concluded that even if Article 2 did not give rise to an obligation to subsidize any particular type of education, 'Article 14 would require that the authorities do not discriminate in the provision of available financial subsidies'.[80]

Nevertheless, it is only those inequalities of treatment between those in analogous situations and for which no objective and reasonable justification can be found that fall foul of Article 14[81] and the Commission felt that, given that the ownership of the non-denominational school would be vested in trustees representing the body concerned, the stipulation that that body should find 15 per cent of the capital costs was neither unreasonable nor disproportionate.[82]

This does suggest that there might be some boundaries to the level of differentiation which the State might make when determining access to, and the level of, subsidies. There is, however, a tendency to allow the State considerable latitude when determining this question. In *W and KL v. Sweden*, for example, the applicants complained that their children, who were attending a private school, had been denied school social assistance, which was provided by the local authorities to children attending other schools, both State and private. The Commission not only rejected the

---

[80] *X v. UK*, No. 7782/77, 14 DR 179 (Dec. 1978) at 182. Article 14 has no autonomous existence and is only relevant in relation to a right contained within the Convention or protocols. Nevertheless, it is accepted that it is enough for the alleged right to be within the ambit of a provision of the Convention. Therefore, even though there is no right to a subsidy, since the Protocol does include the right to establish a school (above, n. 77) Article 14 can have relevance to the distribution of whatever subsidies the State chooses to make available to existing schools and to those seeking to establish new schools, assuming that such a right is recognized. See Van Dijk and Van Hoof, *Theory and Practice of the ECHR*, pp. 535–536.

On the other hand, the Commission did not adopt this approach in the earlier cases of *Church of X v. UK*, No. 3798/68, 12 YBECHR 306 (1969) and *Association X v. Sweden*, No. 6094/73, 9 DR 5 (Dec. 1977) at 9, nor in its subsequent decisions in *X v. Sweden*, No. 10201 and *Y v. Sweden*, No. 10202/82, unpublished decisions of 7 May 1984; and *W and KL v. Sweden*, No. 10476/83, 45 DR 143 (Dec. 1985).

[81] See generally Van Dijk and Van Hoof, *Theory and Practice of the ECHR*, pp. 532–548 (who conclude at p. 545 that Article 14 'has been deprived of much of its meaning'); Harris, O'Boyle and Warbrick, *Law of the ECHR*, pp. 462–488. For the application of Article 14 in relation to Article 2 of the First Protocol in another context see *Bernard v. Luxembourg*, No. 17187/90, 75 DR 57 (Dec. 1993), above, n. 53. In *Karnell and Hardt v. Sweden*, No. 4733/71, 39 CD 75 (Dec. 1971) the Commission raised the question of discrimination but a friendly settlement was reached. See above, n. 65.

[82] *X v. UK*, No. 7782/77, 14 DR 179 (Dec. 1978) at 182.

applicability of Article 14 to the differentiation between pupils attending State and private schools but felt that, as between the private schools, 'the local authorities are best placed to make decisions (including necessary budgetary decisions) relating to the education in their districts. The difference in treatment which may result from this independence has, in the Commission's opinion, an objective and reasonable basis.'[83]

Similarly, in *Verein Gemeinsam Lernen v. Austria* the Commission decided that it was not discriminatory to place hurdles before non-religious schools seeking State subsidies which were not placed before religious schools. The requirement in question was that the school be 'needed'. It was accepted that there was a 'need' for the school, in the sense that a number of parents wished to send their children to it, but that this did not amount to a 'need' for the purposes of granting a subsidy. This was to be judged in the light of whether the provision of the school was 'needed' in order to alleviate a burden which would otherwise fall upon the State. The Commission considered that this extra requirement did not amount to discrimination and was justified in terms of Article 14 because 'the church schools are so widespread that if the educational services which they provide fell to be met by the State, there would be a considerable burden on the State as it would have to make up the shortfall'.[84] In short, the need for them was so clear that it did not need to be demonstrated. The same could not be said for non-religious schools.

This would suggest that taking Article 14 in conjunction with Article 2 of the First Protocol is unlikely to improve significantly the position of those seeking access to funds in order to set up or maintain educational establishments that accord with their religious or philosophical convictions.[85]

---

[83] *W and KL v. Sweden*, No. 10476/83, 45 DR 143 (Dec. 1985) at 150.

[84] *Verein Gemeinsam Lernen v. Austria*, No. 23419/94, 82–A DR 41 (Dec. 1995) at 46.

[85] Another area in which the potential impact of Article 14 has been considered concerns the recognition of an educational institution. In *Church of X v. UK*, No. 3798/68, 12 YBECHR 306 (1969) the Commission decided that 'in deciding whether to recognize an institution as an educational establishment, [a State] is entitled to have regard to certain minimum educational standards . . . therefore, any Governmental measures which are taken to differentiate between institutions on such a basis do not constitute discrimination within the meaning of Article 14 of the Convention'. It would, then, seem that, provided that basic standards are met, a State could not either refuse to recognize, or cease to recognize, an establishment. Once again, however, it is likely that the discretion accorded to the State might reduce this protection to near vanishing point.

14   An interim conclusion

If this book were to have a subtitle, it might well be 'from Sumeria to Strasbourg'. This is not to suggest that the story of the inter-relationship of religion and international law has reached its fulfilment in the European Convention on Human Rights. The scope of this book has been limited to the principal instruments applicable in the European theatre and it has not looked at the development of similar norms and practice under them in other regional conventions, such as the Inter-American Convention on Human Rights (1969)[1] and the African Charter on Human and Peoples' Rights (1981).[2] Other international instruments which bear upon the protection of the religious freedoms of particular categories of

---

[1] 1144 *UNTS* 123. Article 12 provides:
1. Everyone has the right to freedom of conscience and of religion. This includes the freedom to maintain or to change one's religion or beliefs, and freedom to profess or disseminate one's religion or beliefs either individually or together with others, in public or in private.
2. No one shall be subject to restrictions that might impair his freedom to maintain or to change his religion or beliefs.
3. Freedom to manifest one's religion and beliefs may be subject only to the limitations prescribed by law that are necessary to protect public safety, order, health, or morals, or the rights or freedoms of others.
4. Parents or guardians, as the case may be, have the right to provide for the religious and moral education of their children or wards that is in accord with their own convictions.

The freedom of thought is linked with the freedom of expression under Article 13 of the Convention. Article 12 represents a considerable elaboration of Article III of the 1948 American Declaration of the Rights and Duties of Man, which provides that 'every person has the freedom to profess a religious faith, and to manifest and practice it both in public and in private'.

[2] Article 8 provides:
Freedom of conscience, the profession and free practice of religion shall be guaranteed. No one may, subject to law and order, be submitted to measures restricting the exercise of these freedoms.

people, such as the UN Conventions on the Elimination of All Forms of Racial Discrimination (1966),[3] on the Rights of the Child (1989)[4] and on Migrant Workers (1991),[5] and the ILO Conventions Nos. 111 (1958)[6] and 169 (1989),[7] have also fallen beyond the bounds of this study. This is not because they are unimportant. They all take their place within the complex web of protective norms and mechanisms. However, the instruments that have been examined form the central pillar around which other instruments have developed and against which they are to be assessed; the ambiguities and uncertainties surrounding their interpretation and application pervade the entire subject.

The purpose of this book has been to examine the manner in which religious freedom has been recognized in international law and the interpretation that is currently placed upon it. From an historical perspective, an important factor has been the desire of dominant powers to cast a protective mantle around the religious freedoms of groups with whom they feel a religious, racial or cultural affinity and which are thought to be threatened in the enjoyment of their beliefs by the territorial sovereign. This impulse provided the germ for the minority treaty system of the

---

[3] Article 5(d)(vii) obliges States Parties to prohibit and eliminate racial discrimination in the enjoyment of the right to freedom of thought, conscience and religion.

[4] Article 14 provides:
   1. States Parties shall respect the right of the child to freedom of thought, conscience and religion.
   2. States Parties shall respect the rights and duties of the parents and, where applicable, legal guardians, to provide direction to the child in the exercise of his or her right in a manner consistent with the evolving capacities of the child.
   3. Freedom to manifest one's religion or beliefs may be subject only to such limitations as are prescribed by law and are necessary to protect public safety, order, health or morals, or the fundamental rights and freedoms of others.
   This Convention is of particular importance because of its near universal application, having been ratified by 190 States (as at 31 December 1995).

[5] Text in ILM 30 (1991), 1517. Article 12 applies the wording of Article 18 of the ICCPR to the rights of migrant workers and members of their families.

[6] Discrimination (Employment and Occupation) Convention, 1958 (No. 111), 362 UNTS 31. By the end of January 1996 this had been ratified by 120 States and it obliges States to pursue policies to promote equality of opportunity and treatment in employment and occupation 'with a view to eliminating discrimination' on a number of grounds, including religion. See H. K. Nielsen, 'The Concept of Discrimination in ILO Convention No. 111', ICLQ 43 (1994) 827, 835–836.

[7] Convention Concerning Indigenous and Tribal Peoples in Independent Countries, 1989 (No. 169), Article 5 of which requires that in applying the Convention's provisions, 'the social, cultural, religious and spiritual values and practices' of the peoples concerned be recognized and protected, whilst Article 7 provides that: 'The peoples concerned shall have the right to decide their own priorities for the process of development as it affects their lives, beliefs, institutions and spiritual well-being . . .'

inter-war years, and the current textual statements, such as Articles 18 of the UDHR and the ICCPR and Article 9 of the ECHR, emerged out of the reaction to its failure.

Such impulses have, however, rarely been reflected in State practice unless they also accorded with broader policies. The dismemberment of the Ottoman Empire, for example, combined religious concerns with commercial and security matters. The 1878 Treaty of Berlin recognized the potential threat to international peace and security that could flow from the creation of States which did not recognize the religious rights of all, and the peace settlement following the First World War eventually gave primacy to this as its principal justification. The notion that international peace and security is dependent upon respect for human rights is now firmly embedded in the international consciousness.

However, unlike other elements of the 'human rights canon', such as the prohibition upon the use of torture, it has proven difficult to develop the freedom of religion as a human right in isolation from other concepts. The drafting of the 1981 Declaration is illuminating since it demonstrates how, having been 'liberated' from the concept of minority rights by the UDHR, the emphasis turned away from the articulation of the freedom of religion itself and became entwined with the concept of discrimination. Whilst the prohibition of discrimination in the enjoyment of the right is a further addition to the armoury of protection, it begs the underlying questions concerning the nature of the right itself. This lack of specificity has been most evident in the work of the Human Rights Committee and the Special Rapporteur. As might be expected, a greater degree of rigour has attended the application of Article 9 of the ECHR but, as recent cases have demonstrated, the Strasbourg organs have themselves blurred the freedom of religion into a general mélange of mutual respect not only between religions but between the freedom of religion and other human rights. This suggests that whilst international law might provide a degree of protection for religious liberty, it may not go as far as some religious believers consider necessary and this opens up the question of whether, and how, they might choose to go beyond the limits set by the international legal order.

It is against this background – the failure of the system of human rights protection under international law to address fully or convincingly the content and place of religious liberty in contemporary international society – that a number of parallel developments must be noted. In general terms, it is possible to see religious liberty as having been approached, first, through the concept of minority rights and, secondly, after a brief flourishing as an autonomous concept, from the perspective of non-discrimination. Whilst minority concerns clothed the (legitimate) security concerns of States in the inter-war years, discrimination clothed the (legitimate) concerns of the era of decolonization and the expansion of the international community. The collapse of communism in Central and Eastern Europe and the disintegration of Yugoslavia have accelerated the rehabilitation of minority rights both as a vehicle for the expression of concern and as a means of protection within Europe. However, as in the inter-war years, the real emphasis rests upon the security rather than the human rights dimension.

It is beyond the scope of this work to explore fully these themes, since they do not add to an understanding of the content of religious liberty as a human right. They must, however, be touched upon, albeit briefly and in the context of this general conclusion to the work as a whole, since they illustrate the path along which current thinking is developing and suggest that, despite the lavish use of grandiloquent phraseology, recent pronouncements have more of a symbolic than practical relevance for the protection of religious liberty as a human right under international law.

The OSCE

The Organization (formerly Conference, CSCE) for Security and Cooperation in Europe is now truer to its name than at the outset of the Helsinki Process which saw its birth: indeed, in retrospect it is possible to see in this political agreement the seeds that led to the collapse of Eastern European communism. Central to this was the acceptance by the Soviet Union of undertakings relating to human rights, particularly the freedom of religion. Indeed, Guiding Principle VII of the Helsinki Final Act of 1975 was entitled 'Respect of human rights and fundamental freedoms, including the freedom of thought, conscience, religion or belief' and provided that:

The participating States will respect human rights and fundamental freedoms, including the freedom of thought, conscience, religion or belief.
. . .
Within the framework the participating States will recognize and respect the freedom of the individual to profess and practice, alone or in community with others, religion or belief acting in accordance with the dictates of his own conscience.[8]

---

[8] Final Act of the Conference on Security and Cooperation in Europe (Helsinki Final Act),
1 August 1975, *ILM* 14 (1975), 1292, 1295.

This principle was reaffirmed[9] and expanded upon in the Vienna Concluding Document of 1989 which 'transformed the very general statement of principle relating to freedom of religion found in the Helsinki Final Act into very specific instructions addressed to the participating states'.[10] Principles 16 and 17 of the Vienna Concluding Document provide:

16. In order to ensure the freedom of the individual to profess and practise religion or belief the participating States will, *inter alia,*

(16.1) take effective measures to prevent and eliminate discrimination against individuals or communities, on the grounds of religion or belief in the recognition, exercise and enjoyment of human rights and fundamental freedoms in all fields of civil, political, economic, social and cultural life, and ensure the effective equality between believers and non-believers;

(16.2) foster a climate of mutual tolerance and respect between believers of different communities as well as between believers and non-believers;

(16.3) grant upon their request to communities of believers, practising or prepared to practise their faith within the constitutional framework of their States, recognition of the status provided for them in their respective countries;

(16.4) respect the right of these religious communities to
 – establish and maintain freely accessible places of worship or assembly,
 – organize themselves according to their own hierarchical and institutional structure,
 – select, appoint and replace their personnel in accordance with their respective requirements and standards as well as with any freely accepted arrangement between them and their State,
 – solicit and receive voluntary financial and other contributions;

(16.5) engage in consultations with religious faiths, institutions and organizations in order to achieve a better understanding of the requirements of religious freedom;

(16.6) respect the right of everyone to give and receive religious education in the language of his choice, individually or in association with others;

(16.7) in this context respect, *inter alia,* the liberty of parents to ensure the religious and moral education of their children in conformity with their own convictions;

(16.8) allow the training of religious personnel in appropriate institutions;

[9] They were also affirmed in the 1983 Madrid Concluding Document, Principle 10, *ILM* 22 (1983), 1395, 1399.

[10] T. Buergenthal, 'The CSCE and the Promotion of Racial and Religious Tolerance', *Is.YHR* 22 (1993), 31, 37.

(16.9)   respect the right of individual believers and communities of believers to acquire, possess, and use sacred books, religious publications in the language of their choice and other articles and materials related to the practice of religion or belief;

(16.10)   allow religious faiths, institutions and organizations to produce and import and disseminate religious publications and materials;

(16.11)   favourably consider the interest of religious communities to partici- pate in public dialogue, including through the mass media.

17.   The participating States recognize that the exercise of the above- mentioned rights relating to the freedom of religion or belief may be subject only to such limitations as are provided by law and consistent with their obligations under international law and with their inter- national commitments. They will ensure in their laws and regulations and in their application the full and effective implementation of the freedom of thought, conscience, religion or belief.[11]

Despite the length of this catalogue, it compares unfavourably with Article 9 of the ECHR since it embraces only a limited range of manifesta- tions of religious belief, notably those most closely associated with acts of worship. A further broadening of the OSCE commitments, bringing them closer to both the form and content of Article 9 of the ECHR, took place at the Copenhagen meeting of the Conference on the Human Dimension of the CSCE in 1990. This provides:

[The participating States reaffirm that] everyone will have the right to freedom of thought, conscience and religion. This right includes freedom to change one's religion or belief and freedom to manifest one's religion or belief, either alone or in community with others, in public or in private, through worship, teaching, practice and observance. The exercise of these rights may be subject only to such restrictions as are prescribed by law and are consistent with international standards.[12]

Of course, CSCE commitments were never intended to supplant the ECHR but originally provided a series of political commitments which would form a basis upon which to examine the human rights situation in European countries outside of the Council of Europe. As the Council of Europe grows to embrace most of the European OSCE countries, the OSCE Principles will facilitate dialogue and debate through an alternative institutional network.[13]

---

[11] Vienna Concluding Document, 19 January 1989, *ILM* 28 (1989), 527, 534.

[12] Document of the Copenhagen Meeting of the Conference on the Human Dimension of the CSCE (1990), Section II (9.4), *ILM* 29 (1990), 1305, 1311.

[13] This topic received its first formal consideration within the CSCE/OSCE framework at a seminar organized by the ODIHR in Warsaw from 16 to 19 April 1996. This focused upon the 'Constitutional, Legal and Administrative aspects of the Freedom of Religion'

The OSCE is, however, more than a human rights mechanism and the connection between human rights and security lies at the heart of its aims.[14] At the same time, the OSCE has become increasingly concerned with the security threat posed by national minorities and these trends have come together in the establishment of the OSCE High Commissioner for National Minorities whose function is to 'provide "early warning" and, as appropriate, "early action", at the earliest possible stage in regard to tensions involving national minority issues that have the potential to develop into a conflict within the CSCE area, affecting peace, stability, or relations between participating States.'[15]

These trends have been crystallized in the 1994 Budapest Summit Declaration which emphasizes that: 'Human rights and fundamental freedoms, the rule of law and democratic institutions are the foundations of peace and security, representing a crucial contribution to conflict prevention, within a comprehensive concept of security. The protection of human rights, including the rights of persons belonging to national minorities, is an essential foundation of democratic civil society.'[16]

At the same time, the Declaration seems to signal a changed attitude towards the freedom of religion. Rather than be considered in its own right, it is placed within the context of 'tolerance and non-discrimination' and is decidedly half-hearted in its endorsement of the principle: 'Reaffirming their commitment to ensure freedom of conscience and religion and to foster a climate of mutual tolerance and respect between believers of different communities as well as between believers and non-believers, they expressed their concern about the exploitation of religion for aggressive nationalist ends.'[17] This mirrors the way in which the freedom of religion has fared under international law since 1945. After having

and, in common with other ODIHR seminars, did not produce an official statement. The reports of the Rapporteurs of the working groups, however, all highlighted the tensions surrounding conditions of registration, sects, conscientious objection and, above all, proselytism, as critical areas for further study, and around which there was no common consensus.

[14] The Guiding Principles of the 1975 Helsinki Final Act comprise Section 1(a) under the heading 'Questions relating to Security in Europe'.

[15] Helsinki Concluding Document, 'The Challenges of Change', 10 July 1992, ILM 31 (1992), 1385, 1395. It was agreed in principle to appoint a High Commission in the Charter of Paris for a New Europe, 21 November 1990, ILM 30 (1991), 190, 199 and considered in detail by a Committee of Experts in July 1991. See ILM 30 (1991), 1692 and D. McGoldrick, 'The Development of the CSCE after the Helsinki 1992 Conference', ICLQ 42 (1993), 411, 424–427.

[16] Budapest Summit Declaration 'Towards a Genuine Partnership in a New Era', 6 December 1994, Decision VII(2), ILM 34 (1995), 764, 793.

[17] Decision VII(27), ibid., p. 799.

been accorded a central place within the scheme of human rights protection and political concern, changing circumstances have caused its role to be re-evaluated and downgraded: religious freedom becomes more of a security threat than a human right and the key to controlling that threat lies in the protection of national minorities.

Minority rights

The UN

Minority rights have regained much of the prominence they once held within the international scheme of human rights protection.[18] The first step in this process was the commissioning of the *Capotorti Report* of 1977 by the Sub-Commission on Prevention of Discrimination and Protection of Minorities.[19] This proposed that a declaration be drafted and, in 1992, the UN General Assembly adopted the Declaration on the Rights of Persons Belonging to National or Ethnic, Religious and Linguistic Minorities.[20] Although some informal proposals have been made, there was,[21] and is, however, no impetus for this to be followed up by a Convention. Indeed, in Res. 1995/24 the CHR: '*Appeals* to States which so wish to consider making bilateral and multilateral arrangements or agreements in order to protect the rights of persons belonging to national or ethnic, religious or linguistic minorities in their countries, in accordance with the Declaration.'[22] At the same time, the Resolution endorsed the proposal of the Sub-Commission[23] to establish a working group to promote the Declaration. The mandate of this working group is very limited and it has no 'complaints' function.[24] The relationship between minority rights protection and security was emphasized by the UN

---

[18] See also above, p. 180.

[19] Study on the Rights of Persons belonging to Ethnic, Religious and Linguistic Minorities, E/CN.4/Sub.2/384/Rev.1; published by the UN in 1991, Sales No. E.78.XIV.1.

[20] GA Res. 47/135 of 18 December 1992. Text reproduced in *ILM* 32 (1993) 911; *HRLJ* 14 (1993), 54.

[21] See S. J. Roth, 'Toward a Minority Convention: its Need and Content', *Is.YHR* 20 (1990), 93; reprinted in Y. Dinstein and M. Tabory (eds.), *The Protection of Minorities and Human Rights* (Dordrecht: Martinus Nijhoff, 1992), p. 83.

[22] CHR Res. 1995/24. See Report of the CHR, 51st Session, 1995, E/CN.4/1995/176, p. 92. See also ECOSOC Res. 1995/31 of 25 July 1995.

[23] See the working paper of the Special Rapporteur of the Sub-Commission, Mr Eide, E/CN.4/Sub.2/1994/36 and Sub-Commission Res. 1994/22 of 19 August 1994.

[24] The working group has stated that it sees itself as 'a forum for dialogue and the exchange of ideas, information and experiences leading to proposals for constructive group accommodation and further measures to promote and protect the rights of

Secretary General in his 1992 Report, *An Agenda for Peace*, in which he stated:

One requirement for solutions to [conflicts caused by ethnic, religious or linguistic groups claiming statehood] lies in commitment to human rights with a special sensitivity to those of minorities whether ethnic, religious, social or linguistic. The League of Nations provided a machinery for the international protection of minorities. The General Assembly will soon have before it a Declaration on the rights of minorities. That instrument, together with the increasingly efficient machinery of the United Nations dealing with human rights, should enhance the situations of minorities as well as the stability of States.[25]

The Council of Europe

Within the Council of Europe, minority issues have also gained a new prominence.[26] The European Commission for Democracy through Law (the Venice Commission) adopted a draft convention for the protection of minorities in 1991.[27] However, rather than adopt this approach, in 1992 the Parliamentary Assembly of the Council of Europe called upon the Committee of Ministers to draw up an additional protocol on the rights of minorities to the European Convention on Human Rights[28] and in Recommendation 1201 proposed a text in the hope that it would be adopted at the Council of Europe Summit Meeting at Vienna in 1993.[29] At the Summit, however, the decision was taken not to draft a protocol to the Convention but 'to draft with minimum delay a framework convention specifying the principles which contracting States commit

---

persons belonging to minorities'. Report of the Working Group on Minorities on its First Session, August 1995, E/CN.4/Sub.2/1996/2, para. 95.

[25] 'An Agenda For Peace: Preventive Diplomacy, Peacemaking and Peace-Keeping', A/47/277, 17 June 1992, para. 18. See also G. Alfredsson and A. de Zayas, 'Minority Rights: Protection by the UN', *HRLJ* 12 (1993), 1.

[26] For an examination of the existing protection afforded to minority groups by the ECHR and an overview of attempts to extend the range of protection, see generally G. Gilbert, 'The Legal Protection Accorded to Minority Groups in Europe', *NYIL* 23 (1992), 67 and C. Hillgruber and M. Jestaedt, *The European Convention on Human Rights and the Protection of National Minorities* (Cologne: Verlag Wissenschaft und Politik, 1994).

[27] Text in *HRLJ* 12 (1991), 269. This was originally intended for adoption by the CSCE. See Gilbert, 'The Legal Protection Accorded to Minority Groups in Europe', pp. 94–103.

[28] Recommendation 1177 and Order No. 474 on the Rights of Minorities of 5 February 1992.

[29] Recommendation 1201 and Order No. 484 of 1 February 1993. Text reproduced in *HRLJ* 14 (1993), 144 and commented upon by H. Klebes, 'Draft Protocol on Minority Rights to the ECHR', *HRLJ* 14 (1992), 140.

themselves to respect, in order to assure the protection of national minorities'.[30]

An *ad hoc* Committee for the Protection of National Minorities (CAHMIN) was established in November 1993 and the Framework Convention for the Protection of National Minorities was adopted in February 1995.[31] This Convention was not well received by the Parliamentary Assembly which, in Recommendation 1255, lamented the decision not to proceed with its original proposal for a protocol to the ECHR and again called upon the Committee to do so.[32] The CAHMIN reported to the Committee of Ministers upon its attempts to do so in November 1995. The Report highlighted the considerable obstacles of a 'legal, political and economic nature' and was divided over whether to recommend the adoption of the limited range of rights agreed upon, continue its work or suspend the work altogether.[33]

In the light of its meagre results and evident lack of enthusiasm for continuing the task, the Committee of Ministers decided in January 1996 to suspend the work of the CAHMIN in drafting an additional protocol. Predictably, the Parliamentary Assembly was 'profoundly disappointed' by this decision, but, rather than continue to press for the adoption of a protocol, in Recommendation 1285 it expressed an intention to use the draft contained in Recommendation 1201 'as a reference text' when considering the work of the Committee on minority issues.[34]

One of the many differences between the Framework Convention and the Draft Protocol endorsed by the Parliamentary Assembly is that whereas the proposed protocol would have linked the substantive rights to the implementation machinery of the ECHR, the Framework Convention leaves it to the Committee of Ministers to monitor the compliance of States,[35] assisted by an advisory committee of experts.[36] This suggests a

---

[30] Council of Europe, Vienna Declaration, 9 October 1993, Appendix II, *HRLJ* 14 (1993), 373, 375.

[31] Framework Convention for the Protection of National Minorities, (1995) ETS 157, *ILM* 34 (1995), 351.

[32] Recommendation 1255 and Order No. 501 of 31 January 1995. Text reproduced in *HRLJ* 16 (1995), 113.

[33] Activity Report, 10 November 1995, CAHMIN (95) 22 Addendum, pp. 6–7.

[34] Recommendation 1285 of 23 January 1996.

[35] Article 24. Article 25 requires contracting parties to inform the Council of Europe of measures taken to implement the principles within one year of its entry into force and periodically thereafter at the request of the Committee of Ministers.

[36] Article 26. It should be noted that the text does not require these to be 'independent' experts. In Order No. 501 the Parliamentary Assembly instructed its Committee on Legal Affairs and Human Rights 'to make sure that the advisory committee to be set up

continued reluctance to have minority issues considered outside of the political sphere and reinforces the view that, although couched in the language of human rights, States see minority rights as having wider ramifications.

Whether or not this is so, the Framework Convention does add a further element to the pattern of protection of religious freedom in that Article 7 obliges States to 'ensure respect for the right of every person belonging to a national minority to . . . freedom of thought, conscience and religion', whilst Article 8 provides that:

The parties undertake to recognize that every person belonging to a national minority has the right to manifest his or her religion or belief and to establish religious institutions, organizations and associations.

Moreover, parties also undertake to 'promote the conditions necessary' for members of national minorities to 'preserve essential elements of their identity, namely their religion . . .'[37] and are required, 'where appropriate', to take measures through education and research 'to foster knowledge of the culture, history, language and religion of their national minorities and of the majority'.[38]

This must be qualified by the need for the minority to respect the rights of the majority and of other national minorities[39] and, most importantly, that the Framework Convention is to be read in such a way as to conform to the provisions of the ECHR where there is a common subject matter.[40] The impact of this will depend upon what is seen as the 'subject matter'. Since the ECHR does not address minority rights *per se*, in one sense there is no commonality at all. If – as was probably intended – the subject matter refers to the substantive right, then the chief point of difference (albeit an important difference) would lie in the extent to which the Framework Convention implies a positive obligation upon the State to act. The extent of such obligations under the Framework Convention is not clear.

Above all else, however, the Framework Convention – unlike the

---

by the Committee of Ministers in accordance with Article 26 of the framework Convention may be as independent, effective and transparent as possible'. Work on this is currently progressing.

[37] Article 5.

[38] Article 12. See also Article 6, by which parties undertake to encourage 'a spirit of tolerance and intercultural dialogue' and 'undertake to take appropriate measures to protect persons who may be subject to threats or acts of discrimination, hostility or violence as a result of their ethnic, cultural, linguistic or religious identity'.

[39] Article 20.   [40] Article 23.

Parliamentary Assembly's Draft Protocol – does not contain any definition of a national minority and so the beneficiaries of the obligations assumed remain problematic. One point is, however, clear. Not all religious groups will qualify as national minorities for the purposes of the Convention even if they are themselves a minority religion: this is not a convention for the protection of religious minorities. It may prove a useful vehicle for addressing the problems faced by some religious minorities but not others. For example, the position of Jehovah's Witnesses, the subject of much attention under the ECHR, would fall outside the scope of national minority rights protection. National minority rights protection, however defined, fails to reach the most vulnerable of religious minority groups. The protection of the religious liberty of national minorities is merely a facet of the protection of broader aspects of cultural identity and, as has been reiterated throughout this work, it is potentially distorting to see it as an aspect of the freedom of religion at all.

The recognition of States

If the recent trend towards the protection of minority rights derives much of its current force from security concerns, then this itself flows, at least in part, from the consequences of the break-up of both the Soviet Union and the former Yugoslavia. In 1991 the European Community set out Guidelines on the Recognition of States in Eastern Europe and the Soviet Union. These stressed:

respect for the provisions of the Charter of the United Nations and the commitments subscribed to in the Final Act of Helsinki and in the Charter of Paris, especially with regard to the rule of law, democracy and human rights; guarantees for the rights of ethnic and national groups and minorities in accordance with the commitments subscribed to in the framework of the CSCE.[41]

These Guidelines were supplemented as regards the former Yugoslavia with a further Declaration which invited the former Republics of Yugoslavia to notify the EC if they wished to be recognized as independent States, such recognition being conditional upon their acceptance of the commitments set out in the Guidelines and acceptance of other commitments concerning human rights and rights of national or ethnic groups. These applications were considered by what became known as the

---

[41] EC Declaration on the Guidelines on Recognition of New States in Eastern Europe and the Soviet Union, 16 December 1991, *EJIL* 4 (1993), 72.

'Badinter Commission' which had been established to consider matters arising out of the break-up of Yugoslavia.[42]

The Opinions of the Commission include examinations of the human rights provisions of the Republics' constitutions.[43] It is, then, clear that the human rights record of the aspirant States was an important element – formally, at least – in the decision whether or not to recognize the Republics as States.[44] Moreover, in the General Framework Agreement for Peace in Bosnia and Herzegovina (December 1995), human rights commitments were extracted from all sides as a part of the settlement process, extending the operation of a formidable range of international human rights instruments to the territories and establishing a Human Rights Commission with wide-ranging powers.[45]

There is some irony in the international community using the occasion of recognition to insist upon the acceptance of human rights obligations by States in the Balkan region, since this is a direct echo of the practice of the Great Powers in the latter half of the last century, exemplified by the 1878 Treaty of Berlin. It was the failure of this as a means of protection that helped forge a consensus around the principles underlying the inter-war minority treaty system, the failures of which in turn ushered in the emphasis upon individual rights in the post-war era. This model is now increasingly considered inadequate to address fully the needs of communities and ensure that human rights abuses do not present threats to international peace and security. Moreover, none of them have proved particularly effective vehicles for the advancement of the freedom of religion as a general concept.

The importance – indeed, centrality – of the freedom of thought, conscience and religion is understood by the international community and firmly embedded within the system of human rights protection. The capacity of international human rights instruments and mechanisms to add definition to the concept and grant it a place commensurate with the

---

[42] EC Declaration on the Former Yugoslavia, 16 December 1991, *EJIL* 4 (1993), 73.

[43] Opinions No. 4 (Bosnia-Herzegovina), No. 5 (Croatia), No. 6 (Macedonia) and No. 7 (Slovenia), *ILR* 92 (1993), 173–194.

[44] The recommendations of the Badinter Commission were not strictly followed in the cases of Bosnia-Herzegovina and Croatia, where recognition did take place against its advice, and in the case of Macedonia where the dispute surrounding its name delayed according the recognition which the Commission had recommended. See C. Warbrick, 'Recognition of States Part 2', *ICLQ* 42 (1993), 433–438; R. Rich, 'Recognition of States: The Collapse of Yugoslavia and the Soviet Union', *EJIL* 4 (1993), 36, 47–53.

[45] General Framework Agreement, Annex 4, Article II and Annex VI (Human Rights). *ILM* 35 (1996), 75, 119, 130–136.

nature of the beliefs and the opinions of believers is, as has been seen, a matter of some doubt. The freedom of thought, conscience and religion may be protected as a human right: but this does not mean that the relationship between a secularist concept of human rights and religious perspectives of the rights and duties of the individual can, or should, be determined exclusively from and through its perspectives.

Bibliography

Alfredsson, G., de Zayas, A., 'Minority Rights: Protection by the UN', *HRLJ* 12 (1993), 1

Anand, R. P., 'Sovereign Equality of States in International Law', *HR* 197 (1986–II), 9

Ago, R., 'Pluralism and the Origins of the International Community', *IYIL* 3 (1978), 3

'The First International Communities in the Mediterranean World', *BYIL* 53 (1982), 213

Alston, P., *The United Nations and Human Rights: A Critical Appraisal*, Oxford: Clarendon Press, 1992

Ayala, B., *De Iure et Officiis Bellicis et Disciplina Militari Libri III*, J. Westlake (ed)., *The Classics of International Law, No. 2*, 2 vols., Washington DC: Carnegie Institution of Washington, 1912

de Azcárate, P., *League of Nations and National Minorities: An Experiment*, trans. E. E. Brooke, Washington: Carnegie Endowment of International Peace, 1945

Bainton, R. H., *Classical Attitudes to War and Peace*, London: Hodder & Stoughton, 1961

Beddard, R., *Human Rights and Europe*, 3rd edn, Cambridge: Grotius Publications, 1993

Benecke, G. (ed)., *Germany in the Thirty Years War*, London: Edwin Arnold, 1978

Bentwich, N., *The Religious Foundations of Internationalism*, 2nd edn, George Allen and Unwin, 1959

Bettenson, H. (ed.), *Documents of the Christian Church*, 2nd edn, Oxford University Press, 1963

Bossuyt, M. J., *Guide to the 'Travaux Préparatoires' of the International Covenant on Civil and Political Rights*, Dordrecht: Martinus Nijhoff, 1987

Brownlie, I., *International Law and the Use of Force by States*, Oxford: Clarendon Press, 1963

Buckel, G. E., *Life of Benjamin Disraeli, Earl of Beaconsfield*, vol. VI, London: John Murray, 1920

Buergenthal, T., 'The CSCE and the Promotion of Racial and Religious Tolerance', *Is.YHR* 22 (1993), 31

Bull, H., Kingsbury, B., Roberts, A. (eds.), *Hugo Grotius and International Relations*, Oxford, Clarendon Press, 1990

Burián von Rajecz, S. (Count), *Austria in Dissolution*, London: Ernest Benn, 1925

Cadoux, C. J., *The Early Christian Attitude to War*, London: Headly Bros, 1919

Cassese, A., *International Law in a Divided World*, Oxford: Clarendon Press, 1986

Castberg, F., *The European Convention on Human Rights*, Leiden: Sijthoff, 1974

Castellan, G., *History of the Balkans from Mohammed the Conqueror to Stalin*, Boulder: East European Monographs; distributed by Columbia University Press, New York, 1992

Chadwick, H., *The Early Church*, Harmondsworth: Penguin, 1967

Churchill, R., Young, R., 'Compliance with the Judgments of the European Court of Human Rights and Decisions of the Committee of Ministers: the Experience of the United Kingdom 1975–1987', *BYIL* 62 (1991), 283

Clapham, A., *Human Rights in the Private Sphere*, Oxford: Clarendon Press, 1993

Clark, R. S., 'The United Nations and Religious Freedom', *New York Univ. Journal of Int. Law and Pol.* 11 (1978), 197

Claydon, J., 'The Treaty Protection of Religious Rights: UN Draft Convention on the Elimination of All Forms of Intolerance and of Discrimination based on Religion or Belief', *Santa Clara Lawyer* 12 (1972), 403

Coggins, R. J., *The Cambridge Bible Commentary: The First and Second Book of Chronicles*, Cambridge University Press, 1976

Council of Europe, *Collected Edition of the 'Travaux Préparatoires' of the European Convention on Human Rights*, 8 vols., The Hague: Martinus Nijhoff, 1975–1985

Czernin, O. (Count), *In the World War*, London: Cassell, 1919

Davison R. H., 'Russian Skill and Turkish Imbecility', *Slavic Studies* 35(3) (1976), 463

    Essays in Ottoman and Turkish History 1774–1923: The Impact of the West, London: Saqi Books, 1990

De Lima, F. X., *Intervention in International Law*, The Hague: Uitgeverij Pax, 1971

Dickson, B., 'The UN and Freedom of Religion', *ICLQ* 44 (1995), 327

Dinstein, Y., 'Freedom of Religion and the Protection of Religious Minorities', *Is.YHR* 20 (1990), 155

Dinstein, Y., Tabory, M. (eds.), *The Protection of Minorities and Human Rights*, Dordrecht, Martinus Nijhoff, 1992

Djordjevic, D. (ed.), *The Creation of Yugoslavia 1914–1918*, Santa Barbara, CA: Clio Press, 1980

Eide, A. (ed.), *The Universal Declaration of Human Rights: A Commentary*, Oslo: Scandinavian University Press, 1992

Ermacora, F., 'The Protection of Minorities before the United Nations', *HR* 182 (1983), 250

Evans, I., 'The Protection of Minorities', *BYIL* 4 (1923–24), 95

Fawcett, J. E. S., *The Application of the European Convention on Human Rights*, 2nd edn, Oxford: Clarendon Press, 1987

Feinberg, N., *La Question des Minorites à la Conference de la Paix de 1919–1920 et l'action Juives en faveur de la Protection International des Minorities*, Paris: Rousseau et Cie, 1929

Feinburg, N., 'The International Protection of Human Rights and the Jewish Question (An Historical Survey)', *Is.LR* 3 (1968), 487

Fischer-Galati, S., *Ottoman Imperialism and German Protestantism: 1521–1555*, Cambridge, MA: Harvard University Press, 1959

Forbes, B., 'Conscientious Objection to Taxation', in *Freedom of Conscience*, Strasbourg: Council of Europe, 1993, p. 123

Fouques-Duparc, J., *La Protection des Minorités de Race, de Langue et de Religion*, Paris: Librairie Dalloz, 1922

Frazee, C. A., *Catholics and Sultans: The Church and the Ottoman Empire 1453–1923*, London: Cambridge University Press, 1983

Ganji, M., *The International Protection of Human Rights*, Geneva: Librairie E. Droz, 1962

Gentili, A., *De Jure Belli Libri Tres*, trans. J. C. Rolfe, 2 vols., *The Classics of International Law, No. 16*, Oxford: Clarendon Press, 1933 for the Carnegie Endowment for International Peace

Gibbon, E., *The Decline and Fall of the Roman Empire* (first published 1776), D. Womersley (ed.), London: Allen Lane, 1994

Gilbert, G., 'The Legal Protection Accorded to Minority Groups in Europe', *NYIL* 33 (1992), 67

Goodrich, L. M., Hambro, E., Simons, P. (eds.), *Charter of the United Nations*, 3rd and rev. edn, New York: Columbia University Press, 1969

Goy, R., 'La Garantie Européenne de la Liberté de Religion', *RDP* 107 (1991), 5

Gray, J., *Rebellions and Revolutions: China from the 1800s to the 1900s*, Oxford University Press, 1990

Greenwood, C., 'New World Order or Old? The Invasion of Kuwait and the Rule of Law', *MLR* 55 (1992), 153

Greer, S., *Public Interests and Human Rights in the European Convention on Human Rights*, Strasbourg: Council of Europe, H(95)1, 1995

Grewe, W. H. (ed.), *Fontes Historiae Iuris Gentium*, Berlin: Walter de Gruyter, 1988

Gross, L., 'The Peace of Westphalia', *AJIL* 42 (1948), 20

Grotius, H., *De Iure Belli ac Pacis Libri Tres*, trans. F. W. Kelsey, 2 vols., *The Classics of International Law, No. 3*, Oxford: Clarendon Press, 1925 for the Carnegie Endowment for International Peace

Harnack, A., *Militia Christi: the Christian Religion and the Military in the First Three Centuries*, trans. D. M. Gracie, Philadelphia: Fortress Press, 1981

Harris, D. J., O'Boyle, M., Warbrick, C., *Law of the European Convention on Human Rights*, London: Butterworths, 1995

Headlam-Morley, A., *Sir James Headlam-Morley: A Memoir of the Paris Peace Conference 1919*, London: Methuen, 1972

Headlam-Morley, J., *Studies in Diplomatic History*, London: Methuen, 1930

Helgeland, J., 'Christians and the Roman Army, AD 173–337', *Church History* 43 (1974), 149

Helgeland, J., Daly R. J., Burns, J. P., *Christians and the Military: the Early Experience*, Philadelphia: Fortress Press, 1985

Henkin, L. (ed.), *The International Bill of Rights: The Covenant on Civil and Political Rights*, New York: Columbia University Press, 1981

Herodotus, *The Histories*, trans. A. de Sélincourt, Harmondsworth: Penguin, 1954

Higgins, R., *The Development of International Law through the Political Organs of the United Nations*, Oxford University Press, 1963

  'Derogations under Human Rights Treaties', *BYIL* 48 (1976–1977), 281

Hillgruber, C., Jestaedt, M., *The European Convention on Human Rights and the Protection of National Minorities*, Cologne: Verlag Wissenschaft und Politik, 1994

Holland, T. E., *The Concert of Europe in the Eastern Question*, Oxford: Clarendon Press, 1885

Hooke, S. H., *Middle Eastern Mythology*, Harmondsworth: Penguin, 1963

House, E. M., Seymour, C. (eds.), *What Really Happened at Paris*, London: Hodder & Stoughton, 1921

Housley, N., *The Italian Crusades: the Papal–Angevin Alliance and the Crusades against Christian Lay-powers, 1254–1343*, Oxford: Clarendon Press, 1982

Humphrey, J. P., *Human Rights and the United Nations: A Great Adventure*, Dobbs Ferry, NY: Transnational Publishers, 1984

Jacobs, F., *The European Convention on Human Rights*, Oxford: Clarendon Press, 1975

Janis, M. W. (ed.), *The Influence of Religion on the Development of International Law*, Dordrecht: Martinus Nijhoff, 1991

Janowsky, O. I., *The Jews and Minority Rights (1898–1919)*, New York: Columbia University Press, 1933

Jelavich, B., *History of the Balkans: Eighteenth and Nineteenth Centuries*, vol. I, Cambridge University Press, 1983

  Russia's Balkan Entanglements, 1806–1914, Cambridge University Press, 1991

Johnson, J. T., *Ideology, Reason and the Limitation of War: Religious and Secular Concepts, 1200–1740*, Princeton, NJ: Princeton University Press, 1975

Jolowicz, H. F., Nicholas, B., *Historical Introduction to the Study of Roman Law*, 3rd edn, Cambridge University Press, 1972

Jones, G. J., *The United Nations and the Domestic Jurisdiction of States*, Cardiff: University of Wales Press and the Welsh Centre for International Affairs, 1979

Jones, M. G., 'National Minorities: A Case Study in International Protection', *Law and Contemporary Problems*, 4 (1949), 599

Jones, T. H., 'The Devaluation of Human Rights Under the European Convention, *PL* [1995], 430

Kaeckenbeeck, G., *The International Experiment of Upper Silesia: A Study in the Working of the Upper Silesian Settlement 1922–1937*, London: Oxford University Press, 1942

Kazantsakis, N., *The Fratricides*, trans. A. G. Dallas, London: Faber and Faber, 1974

Keen, M. H., *The Laws of War in the Late Middle Ages*, London: Routledge and Kegan Paul, 1965

Kelsay, J. K., Johnson, J. T. (eds.), *Just War and Jihad: Historical and Theoretical Perspectives on War and Peace in Western and Islamic Traditions*, Westport, CT: Greenwood Press, 1991

Kelsen, H., *The Law of the United Nations*, London: Stevens, 1950

Kertesz, S. D., 'Human Rights in the Peace Treaties', *Law and Contemporary Problems*,14 (1949), 627

Klebes, H., 'Draft Protocol on Minority Rights to the ECHR', *HRLJ* 14 (1992), 140

Kossmann, E. H., *The Low Countries: 1740–1940*, Oxford: Clarendon Press, 1978

Kramer, S. N., *Sumerian Mythology: a Study of Spiritual and Literary Achievement in the Third Millennium BC*, Philadelphia: American Philosophical Society, 1944

Ladas, S. P., *The Exchange of Minorities: Bulgaria, Greece and Turkey*, New York: Macmillan, 1932

Laligant, M., 'Le project de Convention des Nations Unies sur l'élimination de toutes les forms d'intolérance religieuse', *Revue Belge de Droit International* 5 (1969), 175

Lane Fox, R., *Alexander the Great*, London: Allen Lane, 1973

Lauterpacht, H., 'The Universal Declaration of Human Rights', *BYIL* 25 (1948), 354

International Law and Human Rights, London: Stevens, 1950

Lederer, I. J., *Yugoslavia at the Paris Peace Conference: A Study in Frontiermaking*, New Haven: Yale University Press, 1963

Legnano, G. de [John], *De Bello, de Repraesaliis et de duello*, T. E. Holland (ed)., *The Classics of International Law, No. 8*, Oxford: Clarendon Press, 1917 for the Carnegie Institution of Washington

Lerner, N., *The UN Convention on the Elimination of all Forms of Racial Discrimination*, 2nd edn, Alphen aan den Rijn, The Netherlands: Sijthoff & Noordhoff, 1980

'Toward a Draft Declaration against Religious Intolerance and Discrimination', *Is.YHR* 11 (1981), 82

'The Final Text of the UN Declaration against Intolerance and Discrimination based on Religion or Belief', *Is.YHR* 12 (1982), 185

Liang, Y.-L., 'Observance in Bulgaria, Hungary and Romania of Human Rights and Fundamental Freedoms: Request for an Advisory Opinion on Certain Questions', *AJIL* 44 (1950), 100

Link, A. S. (ed.), *The Papers of Woodrow Wilson*, Princeton NJ: Princeton University Press, 1986

Little, D., Kelsey, J., Sachedina, A. A. (eds.), *Human Rights and the Conflict of Cultures: Western and Islamic Perspectives on Religious Liberty*, Columbia: University of South Carolina Press, 1988

Lloyd George, D., *The Truth About the Peace Treaties*, London: Victor Gollancz, 1938

Luard, E. (ed.), *The International Protection of Human Rights*, London: Thames and Hudson, 1967

Lundgreen-Nielsen, K., *The Polish Problem at the Paris Peace Conference*, Odense University Press, 1979

Macartney, C. A., *National States and National Minorities*, London: Oxford University Press, 1934

MacDonald, R. J., 'The Margin of Appreciation in the Jurisprudence of the European Convention on Human Rights', in *International Law at the Time of its Codification: Essays in Honour of Roberto Ago*, Milan: 1987

Mair, L. P., *The Protection of Minorities*, London: Christophers, 1928

Mantoux, P., *Les Délibérations du Conseil des Quatres, 24 Mars – 28 Juin 1919*, Paris: Éditions du Centre National de la Recherche Scientifique, 1955

Marston, G., 'The United Kingdom's Part in the Preparation of the European Convention on Human Rights', *ICLQ* 42 (1993), 767

McDougal, M. S., Lasswell, H. D., Chen, L.-C., 'The Right to Religious Freedom and World Public Order: The Emerging Norm of Nondiscrimination', *Mich. L. Rev.* 74 (1976), 865

Human Rights and World Public Order, New Haven: Yale University Press, 1980

McGoldrick, D., *The Human Rights Committee: Its Role in the Development of the International Covenant on Civil and Political Rights*, Oxford: Clarendon Press, 1991

'The Development of the CSCE after the Helsinki 1992 Conference', *ICLQ* 42 (1993), 411

McKean, W., *Equality and Discrimination under International Law*, Oxford: Clarendon Press, 1983

Meron, T. (ed.), *Human Rights in International Law*, Oxford: Clarendon Press, 1984

Human Rights and Humanitarian Norms as Customary Law, Oxford: Clarendon Press, 1989

Merrills, J. G., *The Development of International Law by the European Court of Human Rights*, 2nd edn, Manchester University Press, 1993

Miller, D. H., *My Diary at the Peace Conference*, privately published

The Drafting of the Covenant, 2 vols., New York: G. P. Putnam's Sons, 1928

Muldoon, J., *Popes, Lawyers and Infidels: the Church and the non-Christian World 1250–1550*, Philadelphia: University of Pennsylvania Press, 1979

Namier, J., *Lewis Namier: A Biography*, London: Oxford University Press, 1971

Nicholson, H., *The Congress of Vienna: A Study in Allied Unity: 1812–1822*, London: Constable, 1946

Nielsen, H. K., 'The Concept of Discrimination in ILO Convention No. 111', *ICLQ* 43 (1994), 827

Noble, T. F. X., *The Republic of St Peter: The Birth of the Papal State 680–825*, Philadelphia: University of Pennsylvania Press, 1984

Nowak, M., *UN Covenant on Civil and Political Rights: CCPR Commentary*, Kehl am Rhein: N. P. Engel, 1993

'The Activities of the UN Human Rights Committee: Developments from 1 August 1992 through 31 July 1995', *HRLJ* 16 (1995), 377

Nussbaum, A., *A Concise History of the Law of Nations*, rev. edn, New York: Macmillan, 1954

O'Donnell, T. A., 'The Margin of Appreciation Doctrine: Standards in the Jurisprudence of the European Court of Human Rights', *HRQ* 4 (1982), 474

Oráa, J., *Human Rights in States of Emergencies*, Oxford: Clarendon Press, 1992

Pagès, G., *The Thirty Years War*, Paris; Payot, 1939. Trans. D. Maland and
    J. Hooper, London: A & C Black, 1970
Palmer, A., *The Decline and Fall of the Ottoman Empire*, London: John Murray, 1992
Phillimore, R. J., *Commentaries Upon International Law*, 3rd edn, London:
    Butterworths, 1879
Phillipson, C., *The International Law and Custom of Ancient Greece and Rome*, London:
    Macmillan, 1911
Pritchard, J. B. (ed.), *Ancient Near Eastern Texts relating to the Old Testament*,
    Princeton NJ: Princeton University Press, 1950
Psomiades, H. J., *The Eastern Question: The Last Phase*, Thessalonika: Institute for
    Balkan Studies, 1968
Reznikoff, C. (ed.), *Louis Marshall: Champion of Liberty*, Philadelphia: The Jewish
    Publication Society of America, 1957
Ribeiro, A. V. d'A., 'The Special Rapporteur for Religious Intolerance', *Bulletin of
    Human Rights*, 90/1 (1991), 1
Rich, R., 'Recognition of States: The Collapse of Yugoslavia and the Soviet
    Union', *EJIL* 4 (1993), 36
Rimanque, K., 'Freedom of Conscience and Minority Groups', in *Freedom of
    Conscience*, Strasbourg: Council of Europe, 1993, p. 144
Robertson, A. H., 'The European Convention of Human Rights', *BYIL* 27 (1950),
    143
    'The European Convention of Human Rights: Recent Developments', *BYIL* 28
    (1951), 359
Robertson, A. H., Merrills, J. G., *Human Rights in Europe*, 3rd edn, Manchester
    University Press, 1993
Robinson, J., *Were the Minority Treaties a Failure?*, New York: Institute of Jewish
    Affairs, 1943
    'International Protection of Minorities: A Global View', *Is.YHR* 1 (1971), 61
Rodota, S., 'Conscientious Objection to Military Service', in *Freedom of Conscience*,
    Strasbourg: Council of Europe, 1993, p. 94
Ronzitti, N., *Rescuing Nationals Abroad Through Military Coercion and Intervention on
    Grounds of Humanity*, Dordrecht: Martinus Nijhoff, 1985
Rosting, H., 'Protection of Minorities by the League of Nations', *AJIL* 17 (1923), 641
Roth, S. J., 'Toward a Minority Convention: Its Need and Content', *Is.YHR* 20
    (1990), 93
Rougier, A., 'La théorie de l'intervention d'humanité', *RGDIP* 17 (1910), 468
Russell, F. H., *The Just War in the Middle Ages*, Cambridge University Press, 1975
Russell, R. B., *A History of the United Nations Charter: The Role of the United States
    1940–1945*, Washington DC: The Brookings Institute, 1958
Ryan, E. A., 'The Rejection of Military Service by the Early Christians', *Theological
    Review*, XIII 1 (1952), 1
Sanders, N. K. (trans.), *Poems of Heaven and Hell from Ancient Mesopotamia*,
    Harmondsworth: Penguin, 1971
Schwleb, E., 'The International Convention on the Elimination of all Forms of
    Racial Discrimination', *ICLQ* 15 (1966), 996

Seton-Watson, H. and C., *The Making of a New Europe: R. W. Seton-Watson and the Last Years of Austria-Hungary*, London: Methuen, 1981

Seton-Watson, R. W., *Disraeli, Gladstone and the Eastern Question: a Study in Diplomacy and Party Politics*, London: Macmillan, 1935

Seymour, C., *The Intimate Papers of Colonel House*, 4 vols., London: Ernest Benn, 1926, 1928

Shannon, R. T., *Gladstone and the Bulgarian Agitation 1876*, London: Nelson, 1963

Shaw, S. J., *History of the Ottoman Empire and Modern Turkey*, vol. I, Cambridge University Press, 1976

Shaw, S. J. and E.K., *History of the Ottoman Empire and Modern Turkey*, vol. II, Cambridge University Press, 1977

Sheehan, J. J., *Oxford History of Modern Europe: German History 1770–1866*, Oxford: Clarendon Press, 1989

Simma B. (ed.), *The Charter of the United Nations: A Commentary*, Oxford: Clarendon Press, 1994

Skakkabaek, C., 'Article 9 of the European Convention on Human Rights', Council of Europe, H(92)16, 1992

Sloane, B., 'General Assembly Resolutions Revisited', *BYIL* 58 (1987), 41

Soggin, J. A., *A History of Israel: From the Beginning to the Bar Kochba Revolt, AD 135*, London: SCM Press Ltd, 1984

Sohn, L. B., 'How American International Lawyers Prepared for the San Francisco Bill of Rights', *AJIL* 89 (1995), 540

Spector, S. D., *Romania at the Paris Peace Conference*, New York: Bookman Associates, Inc., 1962

Stowell, E. C., *Intervention in International Law*, Washington DC: John Byrne and Co., 1921

Sullivan, D. J., 'Advancing the Freedom of Religion or Belief Through the UN Declaration on the Elimination of Religious Intolerance and Discrimination', *AJIL* 82 (1988), 487

Swindler, L. (ed.), *Religious Liberty and Human Rights in Nations and Religions*, Philadelphia: Ecumenical Press, Temple University/New York: Hippocrene Books, 1986

Temperley, H. W. V. (ed.), *A History of the Peace Conference of Paris*, 6 vols., London: Henry Frowde and Hodder and Stoughton, for the Institute of International Affairs, 1920–1924

Thornberry, P., *International Law and the Rights of Minorities*, Oxford: Clarendon Press, 1991

Thorpe, L., *Two Lives of Charlemagne*, Harmondsworth: Penguin, 1969

Tooke, J. D., *The Just War in Aquinas and Grotius*, London: SPCK, 1965

Toynbee, A., *Mankind and Mother Earth*, Oxford University Press, 1976

Trollope, A., *Nina Balakta* (first published 1867), London: Oxford University Press, 1946

Van Boven, T., 'Advances and Obstacles in Building Understanding and Respect between People of Diverse Religion or Beliefs', *HRQ* 13 (1991), 438

Van der Molen, G. H. J., *Alberico Gentili and the Development of International Law*, 2nd edn, Leyden: A. W. Sijthoff, 1968

Van Dijk, P., Van Hoof, G. J. H., *Theory and Practice of the European Convention on Human Rights*, Daventer: Kluwer, 1990

Vattel, *The Law of Nations or the Principles of Natural Law*, 2 vols., Trans. C. G. Fenwick, *The Classics of International Law, No. 4*, Washington DC: Carnegie Institution of Washington, 1916

Vellacott, P., *The Oresteian Trilogy*, Harmondsworth: Penguin, 1956

Vermeulen, B., 'Scope and Limits of Conscientious Objections', in *Freedom of Conscience*, Strasbourg: Council of Europe, 1993, p. 74

Victoria, F. de, *De Indis et De Iure Belli Relectiones*, being parts of *Relectiones theologicae XII*, 2 vols., E. Nys (ed.), *The Classics of International Law, No. 7*, Washington DC: Carnegie Institution of Washington, 1917

Von Elbe, J., 'The Evolution of the Concept of the Just War in International Law', *AJIL* 33 (1939), 665

Walters, F. P., *A History of the League of Nations*, 2 vols., London: Oxford University Press, 1952

Warbrick, C., 'Recognition of States Part 2', *ICLQ* 42 (1993), 433

Weissbrodt, D., 'The Three "Theme" Special Rapporteurs of the UN Commission on Human Rights', *AJIL* 80 (1986), 685

Wilson, H. A., *International Law and the Use of Force by National Liberation Movements*, Oxford: Clarendon Press, 1988

Wilson Harris, H., *The Peace in the Making*, London: Swarthmore Press Ltd, 1919

Windass, S., *Christianity Versus Violence: A Social and Historical Study of War and Christianity*, London: Steed and Ward, 1964

Woito, R. (ed.), *International Human Rights Kit*, Berkeley, CA: World Without War Council, 1977

Workman, H. B., *Persecution in the Early Church* (first published 1906), Oxford University Press, 1980

Zimmermann, M., 'La crise de l'organisation international à la fin du moyen âge', *HR* 44 (1933–II), 315

Zouche, R., *Iuris et Iudicii Fecialis sive Iuris inter Gentes, et Quaestionum de Eodem Explicatio*, 2 vols., trans. J. L. Brierly, *The Classics of International Law, No. 1*, Washington DC: Carnegie Institution of Washington, 1911

Zwart, T., *The Admissibility of Human Rights Petitions*, Dordrecht: Martinus Nijhoff, 1994.

Index

Books in the series